India's Nuclear Bomb

A

Philip E. Lilienthal

.   .   .

B O O K

The Philip E. Lilienthal imprint
honors special books
in commemoration of a man whose work
at the University of California Press from 1954 to 1979
was marked by dedication to young authors
and to high standards in the field of Asian Studies.
Friends, family, authors, and foundations have together
endowed the Lilienthal Fund, which enables the Press
to publish under this imprint selected books
in a way that reflects the taste and judgment
of a great and beloved editor.

India's Nuclear Bomb

The Impact on Global Proliferation

George Perkovich

UNIVERSITY OF CALIFORNIA PRESS

Berkeley   Los Angeles   London

The publisher gratefully acknowledges the generous contribution
to this book provided by the Philip E. Lilienthal Asian Studies
Endowment, which is supported by a major gift from Sally Lilienthal.

University of California Press
Berkeley and Los Angeles, California

University of California Press, Ltd.
London, England

First Paperback Printing 2001

Photographs courtesy of the *Hindu,* the *Indian Express,*
and the National Institute of Advanced Studies.
Map and table courtesy of the Carnegie Endowment
for International Peace.

Library of Congress Cataloging-in-Publication Data

Perkovich, George, 1958–
    India's nuclear bomb: the impact on global proliferation / George Perkovich.
        p.   cm.
    "Philip E. Lilienthal Asian studies imprint."
    Includes bibliographical references and index.
    ISBN 0-520-23210-0 (pbk. : alk. paper)
        1. Nuclear weapons—India.   2. India—Military policy.   3. World
    politics—1989–   I. Title.
    UA840.P47   2000
    355.02′ 17′ 0954—dc21

                                                         99-37464
                                                            CIP

Printed in the United States of America

08   07   06   05   04   03   02   01

10   9   8   7   6   5   4   3   2   1

The paper used in this publication meets the minimum requirements of
ANSI / NISO Z39.48-1992 (R 1997) (*Permanence of Paper*). ∞

To my mother, Florine, and the memory of my father, Judge George R. Perkovich Jr., who made this work possible, and to my wife, Bobbi Snow, and my son, Jake, who made it satisfying.

CONTENTS

ACKNOWLEDGMENTS

As with any large undertaking, this book and I have benefited enormously from the assistance, grace, insight, and goodwill of many people. Often authors thank their families last but not least, but my debt to my family is so enormous I must thank them first and foremost. My wife, Bobbi Snow, and my son, Jake, did more than bear my obsession with this project and the several years of distracted weekends and evenings—they actually encouraged me to keep going. Whatever guilt I feel over the time spent away from them is self-imposed; their generosity of spirit has been remarkable. I only hope the result warrants their gift.

This project would not have happened without the active encouragement, support, and indulgence of my employers at the W. Alton Jones Foundation. Writing books is not part of the job description, yet my boss and friend, Dr. Pete Myers, never once wavered in his support of me and this project, and I will always be indebted to him for this. Similarly, the board of the foundation has created a singular environment conducive to openness and creativity. Jamie Bennett, Jamie Cameron, Barney Curry, Pat Edgerton, Brad Edgerton, Bill Edgerton, Diane Edgerton Miller, Scott McVay, and all of their families have provided intellectual, spiritual, and material sustenance to my family and me in this project and everything else. All of my other colleagues at the foundation have helped more than they know, too, most particularly Kay Mason, Lisa Stewart, Bill Hoehn, Kristen Svokko, and in the realm of computers, Brian Wheeler and Judith Carlin.

Given the peculiarities of the Indian system and the absence of available written records, this book depends heavily on interviews with former and current high-ranking officials and others familiar with the ins and outs of Indian policymaking. Many interviewees are identified in the text and notes, and I thank them again here for their generosity and insights. Many others, however, are not identified. Nothing in this book compromises the national security of India, yet it is conceivable that sources of some of the information contained here could suffer reprisals if their identities were known. If this history provides useful information to the Indian people, then much of the debt will be owed to the dozens of Indian interviewees who informed it. My gratitude to all of them, named and unnamed.

So, too, thanks to current and former American officials who shared their experiences and perspectives with me. They have worked with great care and dedication, often thanklessly, on difficult problems in a region whose importance is often underappreciated.

Beyond the specific issues addressed in interviews, this project and I have benefited greatly from weeks of stimulating, sometimes mutually exasperating, conversations in India. Among those interlocutors I can list here are V. S. Arunachalam, Dipankar Banerjee, Kanti Bajpai, Praful Bidwai, P. R. Chari, Brahma Chellaney, Giri Deshingkar, Eric Gonsalves, Inder Malhotra, Amitabh Mattoo, Raja Mohan, K. C. Pant, Raja Ramanna, Varun Sahi, Arun Singh, Jasjit Singh, Jaswant Singh, Rakesh Sood, K. Subrahmanyam, and the late K. Sundarji. None of these fine people bear responsibility for any failings in this book. I also owe special thanks to Chris Smith for bringing me to India the first time, beginning a journey of infatuation, awe, respect, bewilderment, frustration, and, ultimately, friendships.

Chapters of this book also benefited enormously from critical review by many readers, nearly a dozen of whom in India and the United States are better left unnamed to spare them for any blame for the faults I have committed. Others can be thanked, a few for reading almost all of the chapters in various stages—Stephen P. Cohen, Marvin Miller, Joe and Frank Perkovich, and, with an emphasis on the theoretical sections, Scott Sagan. Many others read large chunks or particular chapters with keen critical eyes: David Albright, Harry Barnes, Joe Bradarich, Avner Cohen, Zachary Davis, Sumit Ganguly, Robert Goheen, Dick Graham, Thomas W. Graham, Rodney Jones, Alan Lightman, Robert Oakley, Mitchell Reiss, Ashley Tellis, and Frank Wisner.

This project began at the University of Virginia, where I was guided gently and insightfully by Melvyn Leffler, David Newsom, Michael Smith, and Kenneth Thompson. Instead of a painful ordeal, they facilitated a pleasant and enlightening experience. Similarly, my friend and frequent adviser Frank von Hippel encouraged me through this and other experiences with good humor.

The National Security Archive in Washington, D.C., provided plentiful raw material for this book, in the form of its extensive and well-organized collection of declassified U.S. government documents. Bill Burr and Joyce Battle there were enormously helpful. Leonard S. Spector, then at the Carnegie Endowment for International Peace, generously gave access to his extensive files. Michael Krepon and his associates at the Henry L. Stimson Center—Khurshid Khoja and Michael Newbill, particularly—provided encouragement, news clippings, and other friendly help. Special thanks are also due to Malini Parthasarathy, executive editor of the *Hindu,* and Shekhar Gupta and A. Hariharan of the *Indian Express* for providing the photographs used here.

Having heard publishing horror stories from other writers, I owe special gratitude to Jim Clark of the University of California Press for his alacrity, warm encouragement, and dedication to this project. He and his assistant Katherine Bell and their colleagues are special. Impressions staff and their editor, Tony Calli-han, provided excellent and friendly production coordination and copyediting. Thank you.

Lastly, for additional personal and intellectual sustenance, thanks to Steve Wagner (from the beginning), Karl and Jenny Ackerman, the Grahams, Kay and Davis Parker, the New Year's Eve group, the basketball guys at Olin's, Ethan Miller, Paul Perkovich, Katie Bradarich, all the Snow-Perkovich-Bradarich nieces and nephews, and the mother of the brood, Florine Perkovich.

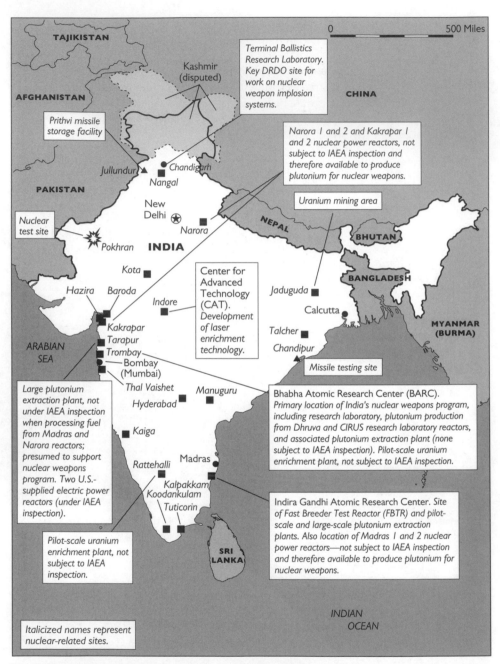

TAJIKISTAN

AFGHANISTAN

CHINA

Kashmir (disputed)

Terminal Ballistics Research Laboratory. Key DRDO site for work on nuclear weapon implosion systems.

Prithvi missile storage facility

Narora 1 and 2 and Kakrapar 1 and 2 nuclear power reactors, not subject to IAEA inspection and therefore available to produce plutonium for nuclear weapons.

PAKISTAN

Jullundur • Chandigarh
Nangal

New Delhi ✪

Nuclear test site

✸ Pokhran **INDIA**   Narora ■

NEPAL

BHUTAN

Uranium mining area

BANGLADESH

Kota ■

Hazira Baroda
Indore ■

Center for Advanced Technology (CAT). Development of laser enrichment technology.

Jaduguda ■

Calcutta

MYANMAR (BURMA)

Kakrapar
Tarapur
Trombay
Bombay (Mumbai)

ARABIAN SEA

Talcher ■
Chandipur

Missile testing site

Large plutonium extraction plant, not under IAEA inspection when processing fuel from Madras and Narora reactors; presumed to support nuclear weapons program. Two U.S.-supplied electric power reactors (under IAEA inspection).

Thal Vaishet
Hyderabad

Manuguru ■

Kaiga ■

Bhabha Atomic Research Center (BARC). Primary location of India's nuclear weapons program, including research laboratory, plutonium production from Dhruva and CIRUS research laboratory reactors, and associated plutonium extraction plant (none subject to IAEA inspection). Pilot-scale uranium enrichment plant, not subject to IAEA inspection.

Rattehalli

Madras ■

Kalpakkam
Koodankulam
Tuticorin

Indira Gandhi Atomic Research Center. Site of Fast Breeder Test Reactor (FBTR) and pilot-scale and large-scale plutonium extraction plants. Also location of Madras 1 and 2 nuclear power reactors—not subject to IAEA inspection and therefore available to produce plutonium for nuclear weapons.

Pilot-scale uranium enrichment plant, not subject to IAEA inspection.

SRI LANKA

Italicized names represent nuclear-related sites.

INDIAN OCEAN

Key Nuclear Weapon Infrastructure Sites. Adapted from Carnegie Endowment for International Peace, *Tracking Nuclear Proliferation 1998*. Used by permission.

Introduction

The impish, round-faced physicist wiped sweat from his brow in the 107-degree heat. Sixty-one, he was too old to be wearing army fatigues. They provided less heat relief than light white cotton. Yet, there he was, a South Indian Brahmin in the Rajasthani desert, the chairman of the Indian Atomic Energy Commission pretending to be an army major general. Dr. Rajagopala Chidambaram was about to make his mark on Indian, and perhaps world history.[1] At his side sat Dr. A. P. J. Abdul Kalam, a short sixty-six-year-old aeronautical engineer with long white hair, a Muslim with a self-professed fondness for Hindu culture who now bore the alias Major General Prithviraj. The code name betrayed the ironic wits of these men and their colleagues. Prithviraj was New Delhi's twelfth-century Hindu ruler, and Prithvi was the name of India's first nuclear-capable ballistic missile, which Kalam had helped bring into the world.

Chidambaram and Kalam were not playing soldier; they were sitting, disguised, in a small control room listening to a fateful countdown: five, four, three, two, one . . . They were leaders of the strategic weapons establishment, an enclave of scientists and engineers in India's defense research and atomic energy institutions who for five decades had been pushing India to join the exclusive club of nuclear weapon states.[2] Now, on May 11, 1998, they were on the verge of crossing the threshold unambiguously.

Almost exactly twenty-four years earlier, in May 1974, Chidambaram and a couple of dozen fellow scientists and engineers had encamped at this same desert site 150 kilometers from the Pakistani border, near the village of Pokhran. During the nights as they lay on cots in the hot air they looked to the skies and searched for the light of a passing American satellite, wondering whether they would be detected as they prepared to conduct India's first nuclear explosion. They went unnoticed, and on May 18, 1974, the team detonated what India's leader, Indira Gandhi, insisted was a "peaceful nuclear explosive." But the ambivalence of this peaceful nomenclature meant trouble for the strategic weaponeers. Indira Gandhi and successive prime ministers resisted the scientists' and engineers' desires to conduct additional tests and develop an overt nuclear weapon program. Moral doubt, political turmoil, and the censure of the United States and the international community put the brakes on their plans. For twenty-four years the scientists and engineers pushed against the Indian government's self-restraint.

Now, in the hot May of 1998, veterans like Chidambaram and newer additions to the enclave like Kalam and K. Santhanam were on the verge of manifesting decades of theoretical and experimental work. The team in Pokhran had learned lessons from previous frustrated testing attempts, most recently in 1995, when U.S. satellites had spotted them. Washington then exerted considerable pressure on India's prime minister to desist, which he did. This time, more than two years later, the scientists, engineers, and laborers employed elaborate camouflage—including the fatigues on their backs to make them look like army men, not bomb builders and testers. They worked in the open desert only when they knew spy satellites were not overhead. And this time they had the firm blessing of a new government led by the Bharatiya Janata Party (BJP), which unlike all previous ruling parties rejected India's normative aversion to nuclear weapons. The BJP wanted the bomb, and the strategic enclave wanted to give it to them. Together they were going to show themselves and the world that they had mastered the ultimate in human power over nature, the hydrogen bomb.

At 3:45 P.M. local time, the countdown ended and the desert rumbled. Three nuclear devices exploded simultaneously. The scientists, engineers, and army laborers cheered. It was possible that India, and perhaps the world, would never be the same. Whether for good or ill remained to be learned.

Prime Minister Atal Behari Vajpayee, a soft-spoken seventy-one-year-old bachelor who had built his Hindu revivalist party into a formidable political presence, declared that India was now a nuclear weapon power. Its exact capabilities—quantitatively and qualitatively—remained uncertain to the Indian public and the outside world. Yet India certainly possessed now-proven designs for compact fission weapons of destructive power akin to the bombs that destroyed Hiroshima and Nagasaki, and probably for more powerful boosted-fission weapons. With subsequent refinement, thermonuclear weapons, or H-bombs, were also now within India's grasp. In 1998, analysts believed India possessed roughly twenty-five ready-to-assemble fission weapons, with enough weapon-grade plutonium for perhaps an additional twenty-five, depending on assumptions regarding warhead designs.[3] India also operated a pilot plant for extracting tritium from heavy water, a key isotope for boosted-fission and thermonuclear weapons. Several means existed for delivering these weapons. Imported Jaguar and Mirage-2000 fighter-bomber aircraft conceivably were capable of performing this role, and some unknown number of these aircraft had been modified to conduct nuclear missions. India also possessed a few dozen Prithvi ballistic missiles with ranges from 150 to 250 kilometers. These conceivably could carry nuclear weapons to targets in Pakistan.[4] The longer-range Agni missile was still under development. A first-generation design of the Agni system had been tested three times, to ranges of approximately 1,000 kilometers, and in 1998 the Defence Research and Development Organisation was preparing to flight-test an improved version intended to range up to 2,500 kilometers. The Agni was now slated to be the nuclear weapon delivery system against China. Indian strategic analysts suggested that the state should advance its ballistic missile capabilities to the point where targets 5,000 kilometers away could be reached.

However, India still lacked a national security and defense strategy to determine the role of nuclear weapons. Since 1974, India had pursued a "nuclear option" strategy. This entailed the capability to assemble nuclear weapons quickly—within hours or a few days—paired with the expressed intention not to do so until a grave threat to its security arose. The nuclear option reflected India's normative aversion to nuclear weapons, its emphasis on global nuclear disarmament, and political leaders' preferences to concentrate resources and energy on economic development. Indian leaders and some strategic analysts believed that nuclear deterrence could be effected without prior deployment of nuclear weapons mated to their delivery systems. They categorically rejected the doctrines and arms racing of the cold war superpowers. They tended to view preparations for fighting a nuclear war as excessively dangerous, costly, and immoral. In South Asia, especially, the proximity of India and Pakistan to each other made the risks of radiation fallout great even if an aggressor could execute an early strike. Instead of building redundant nuclear arsenals on hair-trigger alert in the name of *certain* mutual destruction, the few Indians who attended to these issues believed that it was adequate to make an adversary *uncertain* that nuclear threats or attacks on India would *not* be met with nuclear reprisals. Nuclear weapons pose such horrifying threats, they argued, that this approach was adequate to deter a rational adversary. No greater capability would deter an irrational adversary.

Nonetheless, in the 1990s, Indian strategists and a few politicians began seriously to question the adequacy of the "option" strategy and nonweaponized deterrence. The Nuclear Non-Proliferation Treaty was extended indefinitely in 1995, perpetuating the possession of nuclear weapons by the United States, Russia, Britain, France, and China for the indefinite future while denying the rest of the world these weapons. This outraged Indian specialists and the attentive public, prompting rethinking of India's own nuclear policy. Some Indian military and nongovernmental strategists had long ago decided that the country should deploy nuclear weapons. For them, the developments in the mid-1990s offered another political opportunity to make their case. True believers in nuclear disarmament had been driven from effective power by 1998 or had been disillusioned by the failure of the major powers to pursue nuclear disarmament even after the cold war's end. Cynics who had used complaints about inadequate progress in nuclear disarmament to cover India's own ongoing nuclear weapons and ballistic missile programs wanted to lift the veil. The strategic enclave had run out of patience. After twenty-four years of self-restraint, the May 1998 nuclear tests reflected all of these changes.

Still, no new doctrine guided the tests, only vague imperatives to show national will and status. Nor did a consensus emerge after the tests on what India's nuclear doctrine should be. Several developments seemed likely. India might or might not decide to deploy nuclear weapons on aircraft or ballistic missiles in an overt, readily usable posture. Deployment or not, the state would develop formal command and control arrangements to demonstrate clearly that India could and would respond to nuclear threats against it. India would also maintain its traditional insistence that it would not use nuclear weapons first. That is, India would launch nuclear weapons only in retaliation to a nuclear attack. India also would eschew nuclear-war-fighting doctrines in hopes of limiting the number of nuclear weapons it would possess to a minimum necessary to cause politically unacceptable damage to an aggressor. However, it remained unclear whether partisan political pressures within India and Pakistan would thrust the two states into an arms race despite their professed desires to minimize their arsenals. Even settling on and implementing these basic doctrinal principles would require overcoming inertia, interservice rivalries, political fractiousness, and preoccupation with more pressing domestic issues.

OBJECTIVES, THEMES, AND SUMMARY FINDINGS

India's Nuclear Bomb is first and foremost an analytic history of how India's nuclear explosive program evolved from its inception in 1947 through the early aftermath of the May 1998 nuclear tests. Each chapter uncovers actions and decision-making processes generally unreported in the existing literature. The history is divided into three phases. Chapters 1 through 7 chronicle the period from 1947 through 1974, during which Indian scientists developed the technical means to produce nuclear weapons within a polity that had moral doubts and competing priorities. This first phase culminated in 1974 when the scientists finally persuaded the government to authorize the first nuclear explosive test. Chapters 8 through 12 chronicle the second phase, from 1975 through 1995, in which India surprised itself, the United States, and much of the world by not conducting follow-up nuclear tests and not building a nuclear arsenal. Indian scientists and engineers continued, often secretly, to develop nuclear weapon and ballistic missile capabilities during this period, but moral and political doubts, domestic turmoil, and competing national and international priorities caused India's leadership to refrain from evolving nuclear postures and policies like those of the United States, Russia, the United Kingdom, France, China, and Israel. India's policy of self-restraint began to give way in 1995 due to developments in the international nonproliferation regime and political changes within India. This marked the transition to the 1998 nuclear tests and the third phase of India's nuclear history, as recorded in chapters 13 through 15.

By shedding light on the past, the book seeks also to illuminate how India and other states may move in the future. Leading theories and expectations regarding nuclear "behavior" derive primarily from the U.S. and Soviet experiences as well as from modern European history. Yet, in the future, other states, particularly in Asia, seem likely to play equally important roles in international security. The Indian case can yield useful insights into the dynamics of this larger set of states in the post–cold war world. Thus, history, international relations theory, and nonproliferation policy meet or perhaps collide in this volume, particularly in the concluding chapter, which considers the meaning of India's nuclear policy for global nuclear theory and policy.

Three major questions are answered in this volume.

1) *Why did India develop its nuclear weapon capability when it did and the way it did?*

Conventional wisdom holds that India has sought and acquired nuclear weapon capability to redress threats to its security. China and Pakistan, separately or together, pose the threat. The U.S. Defense Department's 1996 publication *Proliferation: Threat and Response* reflected this typical assessment:

> The bitter rivalry between India and Pakistan which dates to the partitioning of the subcontinent in 1947, remains the impetus behind the proliferation of NBC [nuclear, biological, and chemical] weapons and missiles in the region. The security dynamics of the region are complicated further by India's perception of China as a threat. . . . India's pursuit of nuclear weapons was first spurred by a 1962 border clash with China and by Beijing's 1964 nuclear test.[5]

The official U.S. understanding of why India (and Pakistan) possesses nuclear weapon capability echoes the dominant scholarly conception of nuclear proliferation. Structural Realism, arguably the most influential theory in the international relations field, predicts or explains that states in an anarchic international environment will seek to maximize their power for self-preservation or, more neatly, their security.[6] If an adversary or adversaries possess nuclear weapons, or appear likely to in the future, a state would be expected to seek nuclear capability to balance that threat in the absence of alternative means.[7] Applying this theoretical model to India leads to the common conclusion that the "central cause of Indian nuclear proliferation is a realist one, it was to match the capabilities of China. . . . Only India's nuclear capabilities could elevate India to a position where it could not be subject to Chinese nuclear coercion."[8]

(Structural Realism is an outgrowth of the Realist school of thought in international relations. Each is based on assumptions and axioms about how states behave in the international system, along the lines summarized above. When referring to these schools of thought and their formal assumptions, this text capitalizes "Realism" and "Realist." This is to distinguish Realism as a conceptual and policymaking paradigm from the use of the term "realism" to connote an actor's awareness that the international milieu is a frequently rough place where leaders and states have mixed motives ranging from idealism to power lust, and where threats of violence often appear, requiring leaders to prepare for the worst. One may realistically comprehend international realities without subscribing to Realism or Structural Realism as schools of thought or "manuals" for policymaking.)

Assuming that states such as India make decisions according to Realist models and are driven primarily by national security imperatives, Western theorists and policymakers expect that India should build *and deploy* a nuclear arsenal of sufficient quantity and operational quality to ensure that it could withstand an adversary's first strike and retaliate with enough nuclear force to end a war on India's terms.[9] Indeed, according to these theories India should have built, deployed, and operationally fine-tuned such a survivable second-strike arsenal long ago.[10]

The following chapters demonstrate that the prevalent explanation of why and how India developed nuclear weapon capability, as just summarized, is based on a number of erroneous "facts" and assumptions. Moreover, the story told through this conventional explanation is woefully incomplete. Whereas most theorists and policymakers dealing with nuclear proliferation posit that security concerns singularly determine state nuclear policies, this study shows that India's development of nuclear weapon capability only vaguely responded to an ill-defined security threat. Furthermore, India's forbearance in proceeding further to deploy a nuclear arsenal—from 1964 to 1998, and perhaps beyond—also cannot be explained primarily by reference to external security considerations or the universal applicability of Western models of nuclear deterrence.

Domestic factors, including moral and political norms, have been more significant in determining India's nuclear policy, as this book details. Often, tensions between domestic interests have made this policy appear ambivalent and ambiguous. India has been torn between a moral antagonism toward the production of weapons of mass destruction, on one hand, and on the other hand, an ambition to be regarded as a major power in a world where the recognized great powers rely on nuclear weapons for security and prestige. India's domestic imperative to foster socioeconomic development has clashed with an interest in building up military strength. India's policymaking processes and institutions also have affected its nuclear history: Indian political leaders and the leading scientists have consciously excluded the military from nuclear decision making, again for internal reasons. Each of these material and ideological factors has been in some way affected by India's colonial past and postcolonial identity. Acquiring nuclear weapons proves that Indian scientists are as talented as those of the world's dominant powers; doing so in the face of the U.S.-led nonproliferation regime, which Indians consider a system of "nuclear apartheid," reasserts India's repudiation of colonialism. Yet, if India followed fully the nuclear paths of the United States, the United Kingdom, or China, it would violate its own quest to be morally superior to and more humane than these states. These and other related factors largely explain the twists and turns of India's nuclear history from 1947 through 1998.

2) *What are the factors that keep India from stopping or reversing its nuclear weapon program?*

Proliferation entails state decisions to acquire nuclear weapons. Nonproliferation involves decisions to verifiably abjure and, in some cases, "reverse" acquisition of nuclear weapons. The latter practice of eliminating capabilities actually amounts to *un*proliferation, or disarmament. Proliferation and unproliferation are distinct phenomena, even if they are often conceptualized as flip sides of the same coin. (As the cold war major powers shaped the lexicon and framework of global nuclear policy and the nonproliferation regime, they distinguished between their own accretions of nuclear weapons and the acquisition of nuclear weapons by other states. They called the latter "proliferation." Similarly, they distinguished arms control and disarmament from "nonproliferation," overlooking the essential similarity between disarmament and the hoped-for nonproliferation process of rolling back nascent nuclear weapon capabilities. This book maintains the traditional categorical and lexicographic distinction for convenience's sake and refers to the objective of reversing proliferation as "unproliferation" instead of disarmament, although the same processes are required to achieve either objective.)

Almost all of the existing literature assumes that to reverse proliferation it is necessary only to know and remove the causes that drove a state to acquire nuclear capability in the first place. Assuming that security concerns singularly determine state interests in acquiring nuclear weapons, the prevalent literature posits that if insecurities are removed, unproliferation should occur. However, India's nuclear program challenges these assumptions. India's nuclear weapon capabilities have assumed deeply rooted *domestic* importance independent of security considerations. The process of building nuclear weapon capabilities has created interests, bureaucratic actors, beliefs, perspectives, and expectations within the state and society. That is, proliferation qualitatively changes the state that engages in it, altering the array of interests that must be addressed before unproliferation can occur. The Indian case suggests that these changes and their effects are particularly important in democracies.

This is not to say that security considerations have been unimportant. India probably will not relinquish its nuclear weapon capabilities as long as Pakistan possesses similar capabilities and as long as the Sino-Indian border dispute remains unresolved and those two nations' strategic relationship unsettled.

Yet, as the narrative chapters of this volume detail and the conclusion analyzes, specific domestic factors greatly complicate the prospect of India's formally constraining or eliminating its nuclear weapon and ballistic missile capabilities. These factors include the perception that nuclear capabilities symbolize India's achievement of scientific-technical prowess and national sovereignty and establish India's membership in the aristocracy of nuclear states who set the standards of international rank. India also perceives the U.S.-led nonproliferation regime as a racist, colonial project to deny India the fruits of its own labor and the tools of its own security. These perceptions have become stronger as India's nuclear capabilities have grown, and they have become politically potent thanks to the exertions of the strategic enclave. As the conclusion of this volume suggests, democracy in India—and perhaps in other states—makes unproliferation even less likely. This has major implications in light of the fact that seven of the eight declared and undeclared nuclear weapon states today are democracies and the hope of stopping the further spread of nuclear weapons over time may depend on these states' willingness to pursue nuclear disarmament, or unproliferation.[11]

3) *What effects has the United States had on India's nuclear intentions and capabilities?*

The extant literature concludes that the United States generally has failed to develop coherent and effective policies toward South Asia.[12] Lacking major intrinsic interest in South Asia, the United States viewed India and Pakistan largely as pawns in the cold war. This instrumental approach exacerbated the inevitable difficulties posed by deep cultural differences and postcolonial antagonisms between the United States and the South Asian nations. Worse still, the intractability of Indo-Pak enmity and rivalry has made it extremely difficult for the United States to pursue solid relations with both states at the same time. However, even allowing for this inauspicious backdrop, in the specific realm of nuclear non-proliferation policy, Washington's interactions with India have been particularly ineffective in reducing India's motivations to acquire nuclear weapon capability. On the other hand, U.S. policy and the international nonproliferation regime have imposed costs and obstacles that have induced Indian leaders to constrain their capabilities.

U.S. reluctance to pursue nuclear disarmament seriously has imposed an additional political and strategic handicap on nonproliferation policy toward India. To be sure, U.S. officials and strategists argue plausibly that India has used inadequate disarmament progress as a pretext for its own weapons program. In this American view, the nuclear postures and policies of the United States and the other declared nuclear weapon states have no real security bearing on India's policies and are therefore irrelevant to the unproliferation problem. However, even if this were true, the argument misses the fundamental point: decisions to stop or roll back a nuclear weapon program are profoundly political, especially in a democracy. Even if the five declared nuclear weapon states pose no genuine security threats affecting India's nuclear policy—including China, whose nuclear posture is linked to those of Russia and America—strong political links connect the five to India. Political parties in democracies, especially ambitious postcolonial democracies like India, will insist that their governments seek equity in international relations. The equity imperative applied to nuclear policy has meant that India would not stop or abandon its nuclear weapon and missile programs without concomitant nuclear disarmament by the five "major" powers. American policymakers and analysts thinking and acting within a *security-first narrative* have failed to appreciate that India and other states have seen nuclear policies primarily through a *political narrative*. The Indian experience suggests that the United States and the other four nuclear "haves" cannot indefinitely keep other states from acquiring nuclear weapons unless the five reverse course and dedicate themselves to creating the conditions for the elimination of nuclear weapons. The contrary view constitutes one of the illusions that India has exploded, as discussed more fully in the concluding chapter.

INSTITUTIONAL FRAMEWORK OF
INDIAN NUCLEAR POLICYMAKING

India's governance of nuclear policy has been one of the most remarkable features of the history recorded here. Before proceeding to the livelier narrative, it is useful to set the stage by laying out the structure of Indian policymaking. Indian nuclear policymaking has been highly personalized and concentrated in a handful of political leaders and scientists. While many of the state's activities have been secret, the issue of whether to build, test, and deploy a nuclear arsenal has been debated more openly and longer than in any other nation. This debate has also featured unusual attention to moral and international political norms.

Constitutionally, the president of India, as Head of State, serves as "Supreme Commander" of the armed forces. However, the preponderance of power in India resides with the prime minister, who is elected by peers in the lower house of the Parliament, the Lok Sabha. The prime minister has, by tradition, always held the position of cabinet minister responsible for science and technology, which includes the Departments of Atomic Energy and Space (the latter was created in 1972). In the prime minister's capacity as minister of the Department of Atomic Energy, he or she has worked closely with the department's senior scientist/technologist, who serves as chairman of the Atomic Energy Commission. Successive chairmen have exerted extraordinary influence over India's nuclear activities and policies. Indeed, there are no means within India's institutional structure to provide independent scientifically expert checks and balances on the nuclear and defense establishments.

Within the government a Cabinet Committee on Political Affairs has formed the highest decision-making group, although in 1998 the government set out to create a National Security Council, which would assume an important role in this area. In addition to the prime minister, the Cabinet Committee traditionally consists of the ministers for external affairs, defense, home affairs, and finance, and, serving as secretary but not a member, the cabinet secretary. This body thus represents the most important bureaucracies involved in Indian nuclear policy. However, prime ministers have formulated policies without consulting the Cabinet Committee, as this study records in key instances.

The Ministry of External Affairs traditionally has not been involved in decisions regarding the development and testing of nuclear (and missile) technologies, but it has played a key role in formulating India's positions on arms control and nonproliferation matters. The Ministry of Defence also has commonly had little influence on major nuclear policy decisions. However, among other functions, it oversees the military services (army, navy, and air force) and the Defence Research and Development Organisation (DRDO). The director general of the DRDO has always been a scientist or engineer who serves as scientific adviser to the defense minister. Beginning in 1982, the DRDO head joined the Atomic Energy Commission chairman as a major shaper of nuclear weapon and ballistic missile policies and programs. The Finance Ministry manages the state budget and evaluates the affordability of programs proposed by the Atomic Energy Commission and the DRDO. Representatives of the Finance Ministry serve as secretaries to the Atomic Energy Commission and the Ministry of Defence.

The Parliament, or legislative branch of the Indian governmental system, has little formal power to affect nuclear policy beyond its roles in questioning government ministers and overseeing financial accounts.

The minimal role of the military in Indian nuclear policy deserves special notice. The founders of independent India, influenced by the British legacy, decided from the beginning to separate the military from national security decision making.[13] India's early leaders feared the potential of military coups, as have been common in developing countries. These leaders also sought to prevent military forces from demanding and receiving heavy budget allocations. Thus, the military played no role in the early nuclear program, neither advocating nor seeking to influence it, but instead honorably and completely subordinated itself to civil control.[14] As the eminent scholar Stephen P. Cohen concluded in his seminal 1971 study of the Indian Army, "India has no single department or institution adequately equipped, either intellectually or politically, to make decisions or even to study such an important issue as nuclear weapons procurement."[15] As India heads into the twenty-first century, the role of the military in nuclear policy stands as a major issue for the government to resolve.

THEORETICAL AND HISTORICAL LITERATURE

Few theories of nuclear proliferation have been formally elaborated. Whereas numerous theoretical treatments exist of U.S.-Soviet nuclear interactions and of nuclear doctrine generally, the separate questions of why, when, and how states will seek nuclear weapons have been left relatively unaddressed in theoretical terms.[16] More typically, writers and policymakers extrapolate from the general insights of Realist theory to answer these questions about nuclear policy "behavior."

If there are few theories of nuclear proliferation, there are numerous case studies of nuclear weapon programs. Many of these describe the development of nuclear weapons by the United States, the Soviet Union, the United Kingdom, France, and China prior to the formation of the nonproliferation regime.[17] Other studies describe the quest for nuclear weapon capability in Israel,[18] South Africa,[19] Pakistan,[20] Brazil, and Argentina.[21] Several volumes include collected studies of these and other nuclear proliferation cases.[22]

While a few significant studies have been conducted on the Indian nuclear program, the literature lacks a detailed enough picture to show confidently why and how India's nuclear policies and practices evolved the way they did. Two of the best volumes on the Indian nuclear program, Ashok Kapur's *India's Nuclear Option* and Shyam Bhatia's *India's Nuclear Bomb*, lack post-1974 data from interviews, declassified U.S. documents, and outside analysts that would have filled in important gaps and provided more insight into the major decision to conduct the test in 1974.[23] In 1993, the Indian scholar Brahma Chellaney produced an impressive volume on the Indian-American conflict over nuclear proliferation, but he concentrated on the period after the 1974 nuclear test and mistakenly accepted the inadequate extant versions of the program's early history.[24] In late 1998, Itty Abraham published a trenchant study of the early years of India's nuclear program that deserves notice.[25] Several other volumes and long articles have contributed importantly but not fully to the record.[26] The best among them have concentrated more on analyzing or defending the Indian program's motivations and achievements than on describing factually how it evolved.[27]

The absence of an adequately detailed narrative of the Indian nuclear program's evolution has consequences. It has impaired the Indian polity's capacity to debate with adequate knowledge what has been done in the nuclear field, by whom, for what reasons, and at what costs. It has contributed to the failure of American and other international policymakers and analysts to understand India's thinking and acting and to identify more positive methods for interacting with India. In terms of scholarship, the inadequate historical literature has allowed the emergence of distorted or excessively narrow international relations theories regarding state behavior in the nuclear field.

LIMITS AND METHODOLOGY

India is an extremely important case to examine. The nation's size, potential, standing in the international system, democratic system of governance, place in the Sino-Pakistani-Indian security triangle, moral traditions, and other features give it exceptional academic and practical import. Its experiences can illuminate nuclear policy dynamics in other states. At the same time, India is a unique case in the nuclear proliferation field. Thus, an understanding of the Indian case may be only partially transferable to other cases. This itself suggests an important theoretical and policy lesson: each case is different in vital ways. General theories of state behavior in an anarchic international system or of nuclear proliferation may ultimately confuse as much as they illuminate.

The singularity of the Indian case removes some of the burden of treating the Pakistani case in the same volume. Often the two nations and their nuclear programs are joined like Siamese twins in scholarly publications and governmental bureaus. This is natural given the history and the clear interactive effects each has on the other. To understand the Indian nuclear program and the polity's attachment to it, Pakistan must be taken into view. However, India's nuclear program began decades before any nuclear threat emerged from Pakistan. Moreover, in causative terms, the Indian case differs in important ways from Pakistan's. Unlike India, Pakistan's quest for nuclear weapon capability derives unambiguously from security concerns. Fear of Indian military power and consequent political pressure explains why Pakistan sought nuclear weapons capability. The same cannot be said for India: fear of China's, or later Pakistan's, military power does not fully explain India's nuclear program. So, too, the opportunities for and likely dynamics of inducing Pakistan to abandon its nuclear program differ from those involved with India. Thus, it is appropriate to treat the two cases separately.

Obtaining accurate, official data on the Indian nuclear program and decision making around it is difficult. India maintains a system of extreme secrecy over nuclear matters. A legacy of the British Official Secrets Act, Indian law bars official files from being declassified and imposes strict lifelong penalties on "leakers." The Atomic Energy Act entitles the Central Government of India to "declare as 'restricted information' " basically anything it wants having to do with atomic energy and related activities.[28] As a result, little but the most anodyne information on the nuclear establishment has been publicly released. Files simply are not declassified or otherwise made available for scholarly investigation. Even if files were accessible, Indian nuclear policy has tended to be made orally and rather informally. Decisions are recorded in official files, but the analysis, debate, and motivations behind them tend not to be included.[29] This forces analysts to rely on public sources such as the press, biographies, secondary treatments that may be informed by inside knowledge, and, importantly, interviews with relevant officials. Declassified U.S. government documents also can be very insightful. All of these sources inform the current study, which has also benefited enormously from the corrections, criticisms, and comments of knowledgeable Indian readers.

Another caveat concerns China. To the extent that security threats have motivated India's nuclear policy, China and Pakistan loom largest. While this study questions the degree to which security considerations actually have caused Indian nuclear decisions, China undoubtedly has constituted an important factor. (Pakistan became a more acute concern in the mid-1970s when it began to seek nuclear weapons to counter India's capability.) An exhaustive examination of the Indian nuclear program, therefore, ideally would provide a detailed description of China's political-military capabilities and intentions toward India. Such a thorough analysis of the Chinese factor would augment an evaluation of the objective, as opposed to subjective, validity of Indian assumptions about China. While it is beyond the scope of this study to include a detailed analysis of Chinese actions and policies toward India, the narrative does report important developments in Sino-Indian relations. Still, the focus remains on the arguments Indian actors made regarding the nature of the Chinese threat and India's means for redressing it.

ONE

Developing the Technological Base
for the Nuclear Option

1948–1963

"Nuclear power" is a manifold term. It can describe the production of electricity as well as a state possessing nuclear weapons. The ambiguity of "nuclear power" makes the term especially appropriate in relation to the Indian quest for nuclear capability begun by Prime Minister Jawaharlal Nehru and Atomic Energy Commission (AEC) Chairman Homi Bhabha. Even before India gained independence in 1947, these men sought to win for their country all the prestige, status, and economic benefits associated with being a nuclear power, including the option of building "the bomb" if necessary. The capacity to master the atom represented modernity, potential prosperity, transcendence of the colonial past, individual and national prowess, and international leverage.

Indian legend and commentary generally deny that the quest for nuclear power was ambiguous from the beginning. Typically it is said that Nehru intended for India to use nuclear technology and know-how exclusively for peaceful purposes. In the Indian scholar T. T. Poulose's words: "There was no guile in his nuclear policy as it originated from a mind imbued with high idealism, deep sense of history and a world view and always with a vision of a strong and modern India. Nehru's nuclear decisions were not the outcome of any national debate but deeply rooted in his scientific temper, abhorrence of nuclear weapons and nuclear allergy after the supreme tragedy at Hiroshima and Nagasaki."[1] Most of Nehru's speeches reflect this genuinely peaceful intention. For example, he told the lower house of Parliament, the Lok Sabha, in 1957, "[W]e have declared quite clearly that we are not interested in and we will not make these bombs, even if we have the capacity to do so."[2]

Perhaps Nehru's image as a world leader of singular moral stature, the heir to Mahatma Gandhi, would have been tarnished if he were shown to have embraced the military usefulness of nuclear power. Thus, according to conventional wisdom, it was Bhabha, the brilliant and ambitious physicist, not Nehru, who gave the dual military and civilian purpose to the Indian nuclear program.[3] And indeed, the record indicates that Bhabha drove India's nuclear policy. His plans in the early 1950s for acquiring plutonium before it could be put to any economic use, and his analysis of how a nation could produce nuclear weapons despite international safeguards, represented a conscious strategy for developing India's nuclear weapon option. By the late 1950s he would state privately his desire that India should build atomic bombs.

Closer scrutiny, however, reveals that Nehru also accepted, albeit reticently and ambivalently, the potential military deterrent and international power embodied in nuclear weapon capability. As he said in a 1946 speech in Bombay:

> As long as the world is constituted as it is, every country will have to devise and use the latest scientific devices for its protection. I have no doubt India will develop her scientific researches and I hope Indian scientists will use the atomic force for constructive purposes. But if India is threatened she will inevitably try to defend herself by all means at her disposal. I hope India in common with other countries will prevent the use of atomic bombs.[4]

As this chapter shows, Nehru's words and actions, and most important, his support of Bhabha's actions, indicate an essential duality and ambiguity that characterized India's nuclear program through 1997, and that may continue to obtain after the nuclear tests of 1998. The moralist visionary Nehru abhorred the wanton destructiveness of nuclear weapons and saw them as anathema to the unique spirit of India. He visualized a world wherein power is exercised peacefully by moral suasion and political acumen, a world of idealism in many ways. This Nehru disparaged massive military arsenals and classical Realpolitik.[5] At the same time, however, there was another Nehru, the ambitious, realist prime minister who recognized that nuclear weapon capability could enhance India's status and power in the Western-dominated world whose logic he understood well from his Cambridge education and his reading in science and European history. Indian leaders from Nehru on have preferred to avoid binary, black-or-white choices. As one longtime Indian defense official said regarding India's nuclear decision making: "[T]he Hindu mind does not accept the 'either/or', 'black or white', 'yes or no' template of the West. We prefer 'grays and browns' and 'yes and no.' "[6]

Nehru struggled to synthesize the power emanating from Western technical culture and the humanistic wisdom of India. Whereas Gandhi loathed the modern, technological world and celebrated the virtues of rusticity, Nehru believed that the well-being of India and its poor masses depended on the adoption of modern technology. With an impoverished, burgeoning population, the challenge of producing rapid economic growth while preserving democracy was daunting.

Nehru sought a "third way" to transform India's exceptionally complicated socio-economic order, an approach that "takes the best from all existing systems—the Russian, the American and others—and seeks to create something suited to one's own history and philosophy."[7] To effect this third way, Nehru would rely on science and technology, including the scientific spirit, as valuable tools. This led to state economic planning, heavy investment in large industrial enterprises including the nuclear establishment, and public sector control over large industry. Agriculture and small, decentralized development received shorter shrift as less modern priorities.

Atomic science and technology assumed a special place in the overall plans for the technological development and modernization of India. The need to increase availability of electrical power was a paramount objective, and Nehru saw atomic energy as the most dramatic means of achieving it. Thus, in 1948, the Indian government took direct responsibility for the atomic energy sector, one of three industrial sectors over which public monopoly was established.[8]

Yet, in the late 1940s the memory of the bombings of Hiroshima and Nagasaki also informed considerations of atomic energy. This was especially true in India, where Asian identity and Nehru's position on the global stage induced reflection on the meaning of nuclear weapons. Nuclear technology provides human beings with godlike power to exploit nature and enhance their well-being as well as to destroy. Nehru recognized and grappled with the duality of nuclear know-how and technology, and specifically the dilemmas presented by nuclear weapons.

> On the one hand [Nehru noted], the nuclear bomb and the destruction of Nagasaki and Hiroshima illustrates the horrendous revolution that has taken place in military technology and on the other, the application of nuclear energy to peaceful and constructive purposes has opened limitless possibilities for human development, prosperity and overabundance. This major challenge confronts our times with a choice between co-destruction and co-prosperity and makes it imperative for the world to outlaw war, particularly nuclear war.[9]

But what if war, particularly nuclear war, could not be outlawed? That prospect certainly occurred to a man as learned and worldly as Nehru. In that case, as Nehru said in the 1946 speech in Bombay and intimated at other times (as discussed later in this chapter), India must possess the option to wield the greatest of military technology.

This chapter describes the beginning of India's nuclear program and explains when and how the program acquired its potential military dimension. It explores the factors affecting the program's development—the roles of key individuals, the economic and technological dynamics driving it, the political and psychological importance of nuclear capability for India, and the influence of the external environment and foreign actors on it, particularly the United States. This chapter shows that Bhabha and Nehru took India to a unique position of restrained nuclear weapon capability with little regard for particular security concerns.

FORMATION OF THE NUCLEAR STATE-WITHIN-THE-STATE, 1948

India's nuclear program was born from the visionary mind and dynamic leadership of Homi Bhabha. Scion of a wealthy Parsi family, Bhabha combined Western tastes and attitudes with a nationalistic determination to raise India's rank in the world. He favored Western dress, enjoyed deep friendships with leading British and continental European scientists, and partook of Viennese opera whenever he could. At the same time he negotiated defiantly and confidently with Western representatives to overcome the legacy of colonialism and elevate Indian science onto the world stage. As a former protégé in the Atomic Energy Commission recalled, "Bhabha displayed none of the diffidence that many Indian scientists felt in front of White men. This was inspiring to many of us."[10]

Bhabha earned his Ph.D. in physics from Cambridge University in 1935, writing on cosmic ray physics. Before returning to India in 1939, Bhabha visited the institutes and laboratories of some of Europe's greatest physicists. There he met, among others, Niels Bohr, James Franck, and Enrico Fermi, who would play important roles in the U.S. Manhattan Project, roles that Bhabha apparently deduced as early as 1944.[11] They represented the elite community of world-class scientists to which Bhabha was drawn by virtue of his talent, education, tastes, and upbringing. If race and colonial roots kept Bhabha and other Indian scientists from being fully embraced by this community, creating a world-class atomic energy establishment could overcome the hurt.

Upon his return to India, Bhabha took a post as Reader in Theoretical Physics at the Indian Institute of Science in Bangalore.[12] He was promoted to Professor of Cosmic Ray Research in 1941, when he was also elected Fellow of the Royal Society at the remarkably young age of 31. In 1944, a year before the first nuclear explosion at Alamogordo, New Mexico, Bhabha wrote a grant-request letter to the Sir Dorab Tata Trust, a philanthropy named after the patriarch of the great Indian industrial family, to whom Bhabha was related through his paternal aunt.[13] Bhabha proposed that the Trust fund an institute of fundamental research that would enter India into the field of nuclear research. "When nuclear energy has been successfully applied for power production in, say, a couple of decades from now," Bhabha prophesied, "India will not have to look abroad for its experts but will find them ready at hand."[14] To strengthen his appeal, Bhabha reflected that he had previously been motivated to accept a position at a "good university in Europe or America" but now was inclined to stay in India "provided proper appreciation and financial support are forthcoming."[15] Subtly, Bhabha revealed his ambition to establish himself and India as sources of world-class science. His confident demand for autonomy and resources set the tone for the development of the Indian nuclear program under his direction. The Tata Trust funded Bhabha's proposal, and the Tata Institute of Fundamental Research (TIFR) opened in 1945 with Bhabha as director and a budget of Rs. 80,000.[16]

Bhabha would frequently refer to the institute as "the cradle of the Indian atomic energy programme."[17]

As the nuclear program grew from infancy at TIFR, it was singularly unfettered by bureaucratic interference from the central government and exceptionally endowed given the scarce financial resources available.[18] According to M. G. K. Menon, a later director of the institute, its budget "grew at the rate of about 30% per annum over the first ten years, and about 15% per annum over the second decade."[19] The institute, as well as the Atomic Energy Establishment at Trombay, benefited from Bhabha's refined tastes and his determination that the facilities under his control should be adorned with art and elaborate gardens, notwithstanding India's poor fiscal health.[20] The Atomic Energy Establishment became the home of offices, laboratories, and eventually nuclear reactors, plutonium reprocessing, and uranium enrichment plants.

In 1946 the Atomic Energy Research Committee was formed under the chairmanship of Bhabha. It aimed to promote education in nuclear physics in Indian colleges and universities. Through the Tata Institute and the Atomic Energy Research Committee, Bhabha sought to modernize India by cultivating the talent and knowledge required to master the most advanced field of science and technology at the time, atomic energy. He, like Nehru, whom he first met in 1937, accepted the looming view that mastery over the energy potential in the atomic nucleus represented the apogee of science.[21] The colonial British regime had purposely retarded Indian industrial development, but Nehru and Bhabha envisioned that Indian science would overcome this legacy and achieve the highest symbol of modernity.

In this period, no field of science and technology appeared more promising and prestigious than atomic energy.[22] Proponents of nuclear power believed that electricity from atomic reactors held the key to economic development. This belief stemmed from an axiom that economic development derives in direct proportion to energy consumption, and energy consumption depends on energy supply. Therefore, a major leap in energy supply should translate directly to a major leap in economic development. Many experts saw atomic energy as the best or only source for rapid increases in energy supply in countries not endowed with other sources of fuel.[23]

The euphoria over the economic potential of atomic energy in the late 1940s tended to blind observers to the great economic and technical uncertainties ahead. At this stage, "experts" could only guess at the costs of constructing, fueling, and operating nuclear plants.[24] In India, however, debate over the true costs and great technical difficulties of harnessing atomic power generally did not occur. Bhabha and Nehru were determined to move ahead on the supposition that nuclear power would provide the nation with cost-effective electricity, development, prestige, and, if needed, nuclear weapon capability.

In 1948 Nehru introduced before the Constituent Assembly an Atomic Energy Act to create an Atomic Energy Commission and the legal framework for its operation. The act was modeled on Britain's Atomic Energy Act but imposed even greater secrecy over research and development than did either the British or the American atomic energy legislation. The act called for research and development of atomic energy in complete secrecy and established state ownership of all relevant raw materials, particularly uranium and thorium. The AEC was created to train scientists and engineers for work in the relevant fields of physics, chemistry, and metallurgy and to manage the surveying and locating of atomic mineral deposits. (The Atomic Energy Act would be revised as India's nuclear program advanced and moved into reactor design, construction, and operation.)

In passing the Atomic Energy Act, the Constituent Assembly engaged in a brief but illuminating debate overlooked by many subsequent histories and commentaries. The debate revealed the essential ambiguity of the incipient nuclear program and provides useful evidence for evaluating the common claim that India's nuclear program began with no intention to develop nuclear weapon capabilities.

The debate centered on the stringent secrecy in which the AEC was to operate. A lone vocal critic argued that the secrecy provisions went beyond the legislation governing the U.S. and British Atomic Energy Commissions, despite the difference that the latter two nations possessed nuclear weapons and India's purpose was peaceful. Nehru, anticipating questions to come, introduced the bill with a defensively couched offensive. He noted that "[m]ost people probably think of atomic energy [as] something producing atomic bombs," which therefore casts a shroud of secrecy over the field. However, he argued that the case for secrecy in India derived from the need to protect Indian materials and prospective know-how from being exploited by the industrialized countries in a colonial manner, and also to assure secrecy-minded states like the United States and the United Kingdom that if they cooperated with India in this field their secrets would be protected.[25]

Nehru was followed by three parliamentarians who emphasized the importance of pursuing atomic energy only for peaceful purposes and who evinced concern about India's wherewithal to fund such research. Then Dr. B. Pattabhi Sitaramayya of Madras rose for a long and interesting speech bemoaning the tendency of the advanced technological states to use science secretively "to promote the war-spirit and preparation for war."[26] As the scholar Itty Abraham has noted, Dr. Sitaramayya, a chemist, feared that monopoly and secrecy would inevitably corrupt the enterprise in India, as elsewhere, and cause "the preparations of war, more than of peace."[27]

Thus the stage was set for the Atomic Energy Act's only forceful critic, S. V. Krishnamurthy Rao, who began by saying, "[T]he Central Government is taking very extraordinary powers and these powers will have very far-reaching effect on the nuclear research in India."[28] He asked why India should impose greater secrecy than the United States and the United Kingdom, which were, unlike India, also building nuclear weapons.[29] Rao continued by questioning whether India had "the wherewithal for all this secrecy and research" and positing that the

Indian bill did not allow for the oversight and checking and balancing mechanisms contained even in the U.S. Atomic Energy Act.

In response, Prime Minister Nehru singled out Rao for having "criticised every feature of the Bill," despite Rao's claim to support the act. Nehru addressed concerns about cost and the availability of requisite scientific and technical equipment. Then he dismissed as "undesirable" Rao's call for an advisory committee to oversee the nuclear scientists. Nehru ignored Rao's challenge over the secrecy issue. So Rao interrupted, "May I know if secrecy is insisted upon even for research for peaceful purposes?"

NEHRU: Not theoretical research. Secrecy comes in when you think in terms of the production or use of atomic energy. That is the central effort to produce atomic energy.

RAO: In the Bill passed in the United Kingdom secrecy is restricted only for defence purposes.

NEHRU: I do not know how you are to distinguish between the two.[30]

Here the debate stopped with Nehru acknowledging that rhetorical distinctions between military and peaceful atomic projects could not obscure the reality that development and application of atomic know-how and technology is essentially dual-purpose. The bill, with minor amendments, passed.

Then Professor Shibban Lal Saksena asked for the floor and, wearing the mantle of a hardened Realist, evocatively criticized the naïveté of the foregoing debate:

Science is power, both for good and for evil. . . . If we have not got the knowledge and the ability to use this power, there is no virtue in our saying that we shall not use it for destructive purposes and that other people should not so use it. . . . Besides, as a realist I must say that in today's world when the clouds of war hang all around us we cannot but prepare ourselves for our defence. It is also a fact that the respect that a nation enjoys is directly proportional to its armed might. We might not engage in war and we might do our best to stop war but the effective way of stopping war is only when we have got the means or power to have our might felt all over the world. Today although we are the second biggest nation in population we have not got a seat on the Security Council and we have the humiliating spectacle of our delegate withdrawing from the contest for a seat on it. I think if India which has been a slave country for the last two hundred years is to come unto her own she must very soon come inline with the great powers of the world; and for that we must develop our military potential. . . . We all know that atomic energy is today the most important scientific discovery. Unless we spend upon it lavishly and unless we use all our resources, both in men and in materials, for its development, we shall not be making the best use of our talents and materials. . . . *Until we have the capacity to use atomic energy for destructive warfare it will have no meaning for us to say that we shall not use atomic energy for destructive purposes.*[31]

Now, Nehru stepped forward for his peroration. Given his prior insistence on the peaceful essence of the nuclear project, Nehru might have been expected to rebuff or decisively recast Saksena's invocation of military nuclear power. Instead he did not challenge Saksena's portrayal but merely acknowledged that the nuclear project in India, as in the United States and Great Britain, was a potential source of military as well as economic power:

> There is just one aspect to which I should like again to draw the attention of the House. Somehow we cannot help associating atomic energy with war. That is the present context of our lives. Nevertheless, the important thing today is that atomic energy is a vast source of power that is coming to the world and it is something even more important than the coming in of wars and the like. . . . Consider the past few hundred years of history, the world developed a new source of power, that is steam—the steam engine and the like—and the industrial age came in. India with all her many virtues did not develop that source of power. It became a backward country in that sense; it became a slave country because of that. . . . Now we are facing the atomic age; we are on the verge of it. And this is obviously something infinitely more powerful than either steam or electricity. . . . The point I should like the House to consider is this, that if we are to remain abreast in the world as a nation which keeps ahead of things, we must develop this atomic energy quite apart from war—indeed I think we must develop it for the purpose of using it for peaceful purposes. It is in that hope that we should develop this. *Of course, if we are compelled as a nation to use it for other purposes, possibly no pious sentiments of any of us will stop the nation from using it that way.* But I do hope that our outlook in regard to this atomic energy is going to be a peaceful one for the development of human life and happiness and not one of war and hatred.[32]

The reactors, facilities, and experts that make up nuclear establishments are inherently dual-purpose. Therefore, it would be technically specious to insist that a nuclear program is inherently peaceful. Intentions are what determine usage. Here, at the level of intention, Nehru did not rule out military use. He recognized the military potential of the new project on which India was embarking under his and Bhabha's leadership. Contrary to most Indian and external historiography and conventional understanding, the founders of India's nuclear establishment recognized and welcomed from the beginning the options its military dimension gave to India, notwithstanding Nehru's genuine hope that India could retain a purely peaceful mission. They did this in 1948, before the Communist takeover of China, before any military threat from China was appreciated, and, indeed, before any major external military threat to India was posited.

The Indian AEC was established on August 10, 1948, pursuant to the Atomic Energy Act. A Department of Scientific Research was responsible for both the Atomic Energy Research Committee and the AEC. Joining Bhabha on the three-member AEC were Dr. S. S. Bhatnagar and Dr. K. S. Krishnan; all three had been named to the Scientific Advisory Committee to the Ministry of Defence, which had been created in July.[33]

The AEC fell formally under the direct personal oversight of the prime minister. In practical terms, however, Bhabha called the shots, conceptualizing and implementing the program. Indeed, India's evolving nuclear policies cannot be explained without recognizing the central role of this individual. Bhabha insisted that the AEC would operate with unusual freedom from governmental control.[34] He would take large shares of precious government funds available for scientific research and development, and he would manage them autonomously, sometimes lavishly. His autonomy grew after 1954 when the Department of Atomic Energy (DAE) was created with Bhabha as its secretary.[35] With a generally quiescent Parliament and a protective shield of secrecy, Bhabha's primary interaction with the Indian government came through his frequent private meetings with Nehru.[36] The two men shared similar backgrounds and enjoyed a good rapport: both were born to wealth and influence, Cambridge educated, connoisseurs of culture, and world-class in knowledge, ability, and outlook.[37] Bhabha, a lifelong bachelor, and Nehru, a widower, devoted their time and energies to achievement, with few distractions. In many ways, the Nehru-Bhabha relationship constituted the only potentially real mechanism to check and balance the nuclear program. Yet, rather than being watchful and balancing, the relationship appears to have been friendly and symbiotic.[38]

EARLY NUCLEAR FRICTION WITH
THE UNITED STATES, 1948 TO 1953

From the beginning, there was friction between India's nuclear program and the larger international effort to control nuclear technology and materials. In 1948, the United Nations grappled with the U.S.-inspired attempt to establish international control over fissile materials and the facilities that could mine, process, and utilize them, both for peaceful and military purposes. The Baruch Plan had been proposed in 1946 and had not yet been put to rest. That proposal to create an international Atomic Development Authority to own and operate all materials, technologies, and facilities with potential nuclear weapon applications caused significant consternation for newly independent India. Holding great stock in an atomic future, India feared that the Baruch Plan amounted to a colonial strategy by the United States. Thus, the Indian delegate to the UN discussions of the plan, Nehru's sister, Mrs. Vijayalakshmi Pandit, insisted that international ownership of fissile ores such as thorium would deprive the country of an important economic asset in the future.[39] India took a stance that would characterize its nuclear diplomacy for decades: it supported the principle of ensuring that nuclear materials and capabilities would be used only for peaceful purposes, but it resisted any measures that would allow some states to retain nuclear weapons while denying others the full freedom to exploit their resources as they saw fit. India was and would remain fiercely jealous of its sovereignty, resistant to any inequalities and inequities, wary of any semblance of colonialism, and righteous in its demands for disarmament.

By 1952, following the demise of the Baruch Plan and other efforts to impose international controls on national nuclear programs, India's plans for the application of nuclear energy began to take more programmatic form. India had signed a nuclear cooperation agreement with France in 1951, and in 1952 Nehru unveiled a four-year plan to begin developing India's nuclear capability, starting with surveying for atomic materials and processing monazite to obtain thorium.[40] Applications of atomic energy in medicine and biology were also announced. Bhabha began discreetly to seek technical information on reactor theory, design, and technology from the United States, and soon, from Canada and the United Kingdom, while negotiating with all three to sell or trade them raw materials such as monazite and beryl ore—the source of beryllium, which was vital for British and American nuclear weapons.[41] The thrust of these activities was to move beyond theoretical research to applications of technology, leading soon to the construction and operation of research reactors.

India's movement toward nuclear independence soon ran afoul of U.S. interests. In July 1953 an Indian government-owned company prepared to put two tons of thorium nitrate on a Polish ship in Bombay slated for eventual delivery to China.[42] Thorium nitrate is a material useful as a potential nuclear fuel. American law—the Mutual Defense Assistance Act of 1951—required that the United States deny any form of military, economic, or financial assistance to a country trading such material to the Soviet Union or its satellites, which included China. Thus, U.S. Ambassador to India George V. Allen informed Nehru that transfer of the thorium nitrate would compel the United States to cut off all aid programs in India. Nehru responded vehemently that India would never vitiate its sovereignty and allow the United States to dictate what India could trade with whom. Nor would India accept political strings attached to aid. The dispute brewed through the summer as Nehru remained intransigent and U.S. officials confronted an unbending legal mandate. Finally, Secretary of State John Foster Dulles offered a compromise whereby India agreed to state that the thorium nitrate was going to China only for commercial purposes, and that India had contracted with China without knowledge of the U.S. legislation's applicability.[43] India declared that although it did not accept the U.S. legislation as binding, there was no plan for further shipments of such commodities to destinations prohibited by the American law. The United States agreed to buy all of the thorium nitrate that India wished to export in the future at a mutually acceptable price.

The thorium nitrate episode exacerbated already-strained Indo-American relations and foreshadowed similar disputes between India's sovereign interests in nuclear independence and American laws and policies designed to prevent nuclear proliferation.

U.S. MILITARY AID TO PAKISTAN AND ITS EFFECT ON INDIA, 1954

Nineteen fifty-four saw an even more important precedent-setting interaction between the United States and the newly independent subcontinent. Since 1947, the United States had placed India and Pakistan on the lower rung of its strategic concerns. Europe, the Middle East, and East Asia were higher priorities. To the extent that Washington had a policy toward the subcontinent, its aim was to be evenhanded and not get drawn into the diplomatic imbroglio over Kashmir.[44] Still, in the late 1940s, American policymakers tended to see India as more important to U.S. interests than Pakistan. However, they refrained from solidifying the relationship by extending economic aid sought by India. Nehru's moralistic, independent streak and apparent contempt for the United States alienated key American leaders who in any case did not see regional interests compelling enough to divert resources from other areas.[45] Meanwhile, in the early 1950s, Pakistani leaders began courting the United States, hoping to win the military and economic assistance required to address Pakistan's weaknesses and shore it up against India's relative strength. Unlike Nehru, Pakistan's leaders did not hesitate to express respect for the United States and disdain for communism. They highlighted their nation's strategic location near the Persian Gulf to the south and near the Soviet Union and China to the north.[46]

The Pakistani seduction worked. The courtship began in earnest during Secretary of State John Foster Dulles's May 1953 trip to India and Pakistan. Determined to build a global network of relationships to contain communism, Dulles hoped to size up opportunities along the southern periphery of the Soviet Union and China. From Pakistan, Dulles cabled Washington that he had "encountered . . . genuine feeling of friendship. . . . Pakistan is one country that has moral courage to do its part resisting communism."[47] Dulles elaborated on this impression in a June 1 meeting of the U.S. National Security Council, where he expressed high regard for the "martial and religious qualities of the Pakistanis," and contrasted this impression with a view of Nehru as "an utterly impractical statesman."[48] Desperate to leverage the favorable American attitude into military aid, Pakistan's army chief, General Mohammad Ayub Khan, came to Washington in the fall of 1953 to press for an arms supply arrangement. Ayub cleverly leaked his proposal and Washington's sympathetic reception of it to the *New York Times* in early November. This prompted an outcry in India, where denunciations of the United States' perfidy only reaffirmed much of Washington's disdain for India's leadership.[49]

Nehru reacted to these press warnings privately at first. He conveyed to Pakistan's Prime Minister Mohammed Ali Bogra that "if vast armies are built up in Pakistan with the aid of American money . . . [a]ll of our problems will have to be seen in a new light."[50] Nehru amplified his concerns in a letter to his chief ministers in which he argued that U.S. aid would change the balance of power in the region and exacerbate threats against India "whether the U.S. wants that or not."[51] The effect, he wrote, would be to intensify India's nonalignment with and "resentment against the U.S."[52] Of course, Nehru as prime minister could make his prediction of India's reaction self-fulfilling. Yet his analysis of how U.S. military aid to Pakistan might be used was prophetic, even if he misperceived Washington's intentions, which were anticommunist, not anti-Indian.[53] The military aid issue, coming in tandem with the dispute over India's thorium nitrate shipment to China, made Nehru ill disposed to indulge Washington's geopolitical priorities.

U.S. military aid to Pakistan was officially reported to Nehru in late February 1954 in a letter from President Dwight Eisenhower emphasizing that the United States would strive to prevent Pakistan's use of U.S. military assistance against India and offering military aid to India itself.[54] Nehru calmly informed the American emissary, Ambassador George Allen, that the problem was not American motives but rather the effects of its action internationally and within India and Pakistan. Nehru's private calm belied what would soon be a public storm. The Indian press, public opinion, government leaders, and Nehru himself decried the American move as an export of militarism and the cold war to the subcontinent, threatening the peace and stability of the region.[55] Nehru rejected Eisenhower's offer of military aid to India (a rejection he would rescind during the 1962 war with China). Among other things, Nehru sought to cut back on people-to-people contact between the United States and India, particularly the sending of Indian students to the United States.[56] This gesture bespoke Indian weakness: the most India could "do" to the United States was withdraw from a program intended to benefit Indian students. However, the episode illuminated an important and lasting dynamic. India had neither the power nor the resources with which to hurt the United States, but it was willing to hurt itself in the process of defying Washington over principle. The act of "saying no" to the United States became a manifestation of Indian sovereignty and dignity.

U.S. military assistance to Pakistan upset India for years. Responding to the issue in a Lok Sabha debate on the defense budget in March 1956, Nehru urged the body to take the long view of how India should build up its strength and not preoccupy itself with the role of outside powers. In a world with major nuclear powers, he concluded, "The equation of defence is your defence forces plus your industrial and technological background, plus, thirdly, the economy of the country, and fourthly, the spirit of the people."[57] With this equation in mind, Nehru asserted that, "industrially considered," India was somewhat ahead of China."[58] In the field of atomic energy, he noted, "we are in the first half a dozen countries of the world or somewhere near that."[59] It was here, in industrial development, including atomic energy, that India should concentrate its attention in order to strengthen its national defense. In the meantime, Nehru declared, "The right approach to defence is to avoid having unfriendly relations with other countries."[60] This speech, including the subtle reference to atomic energy, reflected Nehru's general belief that Indian greatness required first and foremost industrial development that would strengthen the nation's overall well-being, political stability, and potential.

The military-aid-to-Pakistan episode set a lasting pattern that significantly inhibited the United States' ability to engage India on matters such as nuclear proliferation. The U.S. government clearly did not understand the psychology and politics of India and of Indo-Pak relations. Nor did Dulles, Vice President Nixon, and others understand Pakistan's intentions. Washington badly underestimated the possibility that Pakistani officials were playing on U.S. anticommunist policy to establish a security relationship aimed at rivaling India. When Indians saw how American military aid emboldened Pakistani leaders, they became highly mistrustful of and resistant to American diplomacy in the region.

INDIA'S EXPANDING NUCLEAR PLANS AND RESISTANCE TO INTERNATIONAL CONTROLS, 1953 TO 1957

During 1953 and 1954, the U.S.-Indian "dialogue" on international control of atomic energy and disarmament intensified. On December 8, 1953, President Eisenhower delivered his famous Atoms for Peace speech before the UN General Assembly. Highlighting the dangers of nuclear war and arms racing, he urged the world community instead to harvest the power of atomic fission and fusion for peaceful uses.[61] Eisenhower proposed an Atomic Energy Agency that would act as a "bank" to receive deposits of fissionable materials taken from American and Soviet weapon stockpiles. The agency would then manage the allocation of fissionable material to power-needy countries. The vision of a fissile material bank was much more modest than the Baruch Plan's Atomic Development Authority, which would have controlled all facets of the nuclear fuel cycle worldwide. Still, Eisenhower's plan would internationalize controls over some relevant activities. Moreover, it enabled the United States to capture the international political high ground by demonstrating its commitment to peace and arms control.

Nehru offered India's most thorough early reaction to Atoms for Peace in an important speech before the Lok Sabha on May 10, 1954. The initial verdict was negative. Nehru began by stating the imperative of controlling and eventually eliminating nuclear weapons. But he quickly acknowledged that "[t]hey cannot be controlled by a mere desire or demand for banning them."[62] Nor did Nehru believe that the United Nations offered a clear modality for controlling or banning nuclear weapons. Referring unmistakably, but indirectly, to China, Nehru said that the United Nations "cannot control any nation which is not in it, which it refuses to admit and with which it would not have anything to do."[63] Thus, to the extent that China posed a potential nuclear threat to India, Eisenhower's plans for the United Nations to establish an international nuclear agency were especially problematic.

Moreover, the specter of a wide-reaching international agency that would control the world's atomic industry raised alarms of colonialism. Stressing that electricity-starved countries like India needed atomic energy more than others, Nehru fretted that the least needy would control the international agency to the disadvantage of the most needy. This was unacceptable. Nehru doubted whether an international agency would escape domination by the major powers.[64] India advocated elimination of nuclear weapons or equitable controls over atomic energy but could not foresee how this could be done. Therefore, India should concentrate on developing its nuclear science and industry. Nehru dedicated the second half of his speech to exhorting the Lok Sabha to support plans to expand India's atomic energy activities.

As the debate over the proposed international agency proceeded in the United Nations, India's delegate followed Nehru's logic and adopted the stance of a constructive critic. India's acerbic UN representative, V. K. Krishna Menon, stated that countries such as India should have full say in the constitution and rule setting of an international atomic agency, and that the agency should not force developing countries into the disadvantageous role of raw material suppliers while it controlled reactor operations, reprocessing, and so forth.[65] In 1956, India combined these two principal concerns in a proposed amendment to the draft statute for the International Atomic Energy Agency (IAEA).[66] By this time India had been invited by the United States to join directly in the negotiations over the prospective agency.

Meanwhile, Homi Bhabha was developing and publicizing an ambitious plan to tap the power of the atom for India's economic development. In November 1954, Bhabha presented his vision to the Conference on the Development of Atomic Energy for Peaceful Purposes, held in New Delhi. The plan, which the Indian government would adopt formally in 1958, comprised three stages.[67] First, India would build natural uranium-fueled reactors (with Canadian assistance) to produce power and, as an important by-product, plutonium. Second, reactors would be built to run on fuel composed of plutonium recycled from the first-stage reactors and thorium, which India possessed in abundance. When fissioned in these second-phase reactors, the combined plutonium-thorium fuel would produce uranium-233 as a by-product. This U-233 would be the key element of the third stage, wherein India would construct breeder reactors whose fuel would be composed of U-233 and thorium. The "burning" of this fuel would produce more U-233 than would be consumed through fission, thereby "breeding" the U-233 fuel. Because India has an abundant supply of thorium, the breeding of the U-233 meant that an unlimited supply of mixed thorium–uranium-233 fuel would be created.

Bhabha's plan was quixotic. Commercial nuclear power stations had yet to begin operating anywhere on earth. In India, scientists outside Bhabha's orbit raised doubts about the wisdom of investing heavily in his program, and about its autonomy and location in Bombay. Led by the Bengali physicist Meghnad Saha, the critics highlighted the AEC's already-apparent failure to meet claimed targets, such as the construction of a nuclear reactor by 1954.[68] At a September 1954 meeting of leading politicians at Nehru's residence, Saha, who was also a member of Parliament, called for an advisory board of scientists and politicians to oversee the nuclear program and, in practice, clip Bhabha's wings.[69] "[S]ensing the mood," according to Raja Ramanna, Nehru asked Bhabha to organize a national conference to allow India's prominent scientists a chance to discuss these plans.[70] The

November 26–27, 1954, meeting was orchestrated to provide a semblance of "due process" and enable Bhabha to get on with his program. Saha criticized the program and, particularly, the rein and resources Bhabha would be given to run it from Bombay.[71] Among other things, Saha argued that outstanding scientific departments and facilities should be developed within India's universities rather than concentrated in one specialized agency. But Bhabha and his supporters carried the day, and their plans went forward.

Bhabha based his pitch for nuclear power on two broad premises and several more specific claims about cost. The first premise was that the correlation between a nation's per capita energy consumption and its levels of economic development is actually causative. That is, a rapid expansion of India's electricity output would translate directly into rapid economic development (as opposed, for example, to the other way around, with economic development leading to increased energy production and use). Second, "the resources of hydroelectric power and conventional fuels in India are insufficient to enable it to reach a standard of living equivalent to the present US level."[72] Therefore, Bhabha argued, "atomic energy offers the 'only chance' of raising the standard of living in India's and Pakistan's combined populations of 450,000,000."[73] Bhabha then claimed that atomic energy was affordable. In the near term, he asserted, India could have electricity from nuclear plants at costs competitive with conventional sources, particularly coal.[74] With no detailed analysis, he said that India could build the necessary plants at costs lower than those British nuclear proponents had projected for constructing reactors in the United Kingdom.[75]

Plutonium was central to Bhabha's plan. He saw it as a necessary alternative to uranium fuel, recognizing India's lack of extensive natural uranium resources. Plutonium would be produced in the first stage of the program and then utilized heavily as a fuel in the second stage, yielding the uranium-233 that would provide an unending fuel supply for the breeder reactors of the third stage. To get from "here" to "there" India first had to master nuclear reactor technology. This process began with the Apsara research reactor, whose construction began in 1955 based on British engineering drawings, and which went critical in 1956 with enriched uranium fuel supplied by the United Kingdom.[76] More important than Apsara was the Canadian-Indian Reactor, U.S. (or CIRUS), a forty-megawatt research reactor that Canada in 1955 offered to build as part of the Colombo Plan.[77] Canada offered to pay all the foreign exchange costs of building the $14 million reactor (which ultimately cost $24 million). Ottawa attached no strict safeguards on how the plutonium produced by the reactor would be used, other than obtaining a commitment by India in a secret annex to the treaty that the reactor and resultant fissile materials would be used only for peaceful purposes.[78] Indian technicians raced to produce indigenously the fuel rods for the reactor's first loading in 1960, in order to stake a better legal and political claim to India's using the resultant plutonium as it saw fit, including for explosives.[79] CIRUS's reliance on metal uranium fuel meant that the reactor had to be operated in such a way that fuel would be irradiated only a relatively short time before being removed. This low burn up resulted in the production of large amounts of weapon-grade plutonium, some of which was used ultimately in India's 1974 peaceful nuclear explosion.[80]

While the CIRUS reactor was being constructed, Bhabha decided in 1958 to build a plant at Trombay to extract plutonium from spent fuel.[81] Construction of that plant, named Phoenix, began in April 1961, based on the Purex (plutonium-uranium extraction) reprocessing technique developed by the United States and made known internationally through the Atoms for Peace program's declassification of such know-how. An American firm, Vitro International, was contracted to prepare blueprints for the Indian plant, although Indian engineers subsequently modified the plans in the actual construction of the plant.[82] The Phoenix plant, paired with CIRUS, provided India with its first weapon-grade plutonium in 1964.

India's ambitious nuclear plans collided with the U.S.-led international effort to establish tight safeguards on the acquisition and use of nuclear fuels and facilities. The safeguards initiative entailed a basic bargain and a series of detailed terms. The bargain required states that received technical assistance, materials, and other aid from the international agency (or from states party to the agency) to accept the agency's auditing of records and periodic inspection of facilities and materials. The agency could not impose safeguards: states would request them, knowing that assistance would not be supplied without safeguard provisions.

Homi Bhabha played the decisive role in India's successful effort to weaken the scope of safeguards. As envisioned in the September 10, 1956, draft statute, plutonium and other special fissionable materials were to be deposited with the proposed international agency, except for quantities that the agency would allow a state to retain for specified nonmilitary use under safeguards.[83] Bhabha fiercely rejected this broad grant of agency authority over plutonium reprocessing and possession of resultant plutonium. "We consider it to be the inalienable right of States to produce and hold the fissionable material required for the peaceful power programmes," he declared at the September 27, 1956, conference on the IAEA statute.[84] Bhabha won. The final statute required only that agency safeguards would apply to fissile materials and relevant reactors in order to ensure that they would not be diverted to military use.[85] States could separate and maintain possession of plutonium as they wish, under safeguards where they apply. The physical capability of India or another country to divert plutonium to weapons use was maintained, although such a diversion would violate safeguard agreements if they applied to the materials in question. As Bhabha put it, the revised statute ensured that fissionable material "produced in Agency-aided projects in a country should be at the disposal of that country, which should have the right to decide whether it wished to go ahead with a particular use of that fissionable material or not. . . . In this way we ensured that the Agency would not be given powers which would enable it to interfere in the economic development and the economic life of the States concerned."[86]

Bolstering Bhabha's critique of safeguards was the argument that the technologically advanced states, particularly those that had nuclear weapons, would not need aid and therefore would be free from the safeguards applied to the less technologically independent. "We will stand on the brink of a dangerous era sharply dividing the world into atomic 'haves' and 'have nots' dominated by the Agency," he argued. Such a division would in itself create dangerous tensions that would defeat the very purposes of the safeguards, that is, to build "a secure and peaceful world."[87] This morally and politically charged argument proved difficult to rebut and has remained central to India's nuclear diplomacy to this day. India was determined to repudiate all vestiges of colonialism in relations with the leading global powers. In these and subsequent negotiations, Bhabha's forceful personality affected his counterparts. "He was very self-assured," the former chairman of the U.S. Atomic Energy Commission, Glenn Seaborg, recalled. "He was not easy to argue with. Polite but very sure of himself, he was never at a loss for words, and was most articulate. He was a very imposing presence."[88]

Bhabha knew all along that the proposed safeguard system could not prevent nations from developing nuclear weapons. Thus, India could accept the ultimate IAEA statute and receive international assistance without sacrificing its option to produce nuclear weapons. Indeed, India would use international assistance to further its weapon and civilian applications of nuclear power. This awareness was evident in Bhabha's September 27, 1956, speech on safeguards: "[T]here are many States, technically advanced, which may undertake with Agency aid, fulfilling all the present safeguards, but in addition run their own parallel programmes independently of the Agency in which they could use the experience and know-how obtained in Agency-aided projects, without being subject in any way to the system of safeguards."[89] Such parallel programs could be initiated for military applications. This is what India did in building its nuclear weapon capability.

Bhabha personally determined India's approach to the safeguards issue. By this time he was chairman of the AEC, director of the Tata Institute of Fundamental Research, director of the Atomic Energy Establishment at Trombay (renamed the Bhabha Atomic Research Centre after his death in 1966), director of Rare Earths Limited, and secretary of the new Department of Atomic Energy that had been formed in August 1954 under the direct charge of the prime minister.[90] He had continually increased his authority over India's nuclear program.[91] The man with plans to create India's option to produce nuclear weapons, Bhabha was also the man who would determine India's strategy and diplomacy for protecting that option against international efforts to ensure that nuclear materials and technology were not diverted from peaceful to military purposes. There was no noticeable debate in India over his stance—no discussion in Parliament or elsewhere of the national interest of keeping India's military options open.

In the United States, however, there was intragovernmental debate. Officials questioned whether the purpose of the IAEA should be to prevent nuclear materials and equipment provided by the United States and other technologically advanced nations from being diverted from peaceful to military uses or, instead, to ambitiously try to prevent new countries from developing nuclear weapon capabilities altogether. The former approach entailed a narrower set of agreements and arrangements than the latter, which would have to address all the activities of a would-be nuclear power. Proponents of the narrower approach won, led by U.S. Atomic Energy Commission Chairman Lewis Strauss. The AEC argued that incipient nuclear powers like France would reject a more ambitious approach and that the kinds of strict controls essential to prevent any development of nuclear weapons would naturally provoke demands for reciprocal inspections in the United States.[92] The Pentagon concurred, arguing against a more stringent IAEA system.[93] For his part, Secretary of State Dulles evinced political wariness about a too ambitious nonproliferation effort: "It would be difficult for nations to forego permanently their right to make nuclear weapons while the U.S., USSR, and U.K. continued to make them."[94]

Favoring cooperation over strict nuclear nonproliferation, the United States (and others) contributed significantly to the development of India's talent, determination, and technology in the field of nuclear power. In 1955, the United States began training foreign nuclear scientists and engineers and declassifying thousands of papers and reports on matters as important as methods for plutonium reprocessing.[95] India availed itself thoroughly of both forms of technological assistance. Between 1955 and 1974, India sent 1,104 scientists and engineers to the Argonne Laboratory School of Nuclear Science and Engineering in Illinois and other facilities. Indian nuclear experts mined the newly public technical literature for guidance in the design and operation of nuclear facilities.[96]

In early 1955, members of the U.S. Joint Committee on Atomic Energy visited India to promote the expansion of peaceful applications of atomic energy (and American markets and influence). This meeting engendered mutual interest in supplying India with heavy water that could be used to moderate the planned CIRUS reactor, which was the source of the plutonium India used in its 1974 peaceful nuclear explosion.[97] Also in 1955 Prime Minister Nehru persuaded the leaders of the international community to make Homi Bhabha the president of the first UN Conference on the Peaceful Uses of Atomic Energy, held in Geneva in July and August. This conference facilitated the dissemination of newly declassified technical papers on atomic energy. In sum, major U.S., Canadian, and British assistance began flowing to the Indian nuclear establishment in the mid-1950s.

This background indicates how inconsequential nonproliferation concerns were for U.S. (and Canadian) policymakers in this period. They concentrated instead on expanding the global market for nuclear technology, preserving America's unfettered capacity to expand its own nuclear arsenal, and resisting pressures for nuclear disarmament. In this climate, India's (and France's) efforts to weaken prospective

IAEA controls met relatively little resistance in Washington. To be sure, a small group of officials took the risks of proliferation seriously and saw India as a likely candidate. The physicist Isador Rabi, serving as chairman of the U.S. Atomic Energy Commission's General Advisory Committee, conveyed concerns about India's intentions to the State Department's atomic energy adviser, Gerard Smith, in a 1955 discussion: "Rabi said that we must get these controls [safeguards] working before our reactors are constructed abroad. He believed that even a country like India, when it had some plutonium production, would go into the weapons business. . . . I pointed out that I believed that no thought had been given to this problem in the current design activities of American manufacturers."[98]

As often happens in history, technology was spreading more rapidly than the capacity to analyze and control its implications. In accord with this greater interest in diffusion over control, AEC Chairman Lewis Strauss wrote President Eisenhower on August 10, 1956, that Dr. Bhabha viewed U.S. safeguards requests "as more or less of an insult to India's peaceful intentions." Strauss implied that the United States should accede to weak safeguard provisions rather than risk losing its new role of supplier to India.[99] By the time the United States and others decided that preventing nuclear proliferation was a high priority, India already possessed nuclear explosive capability.

ANALYZING BHABHA'S GRAND PLANS

Bhabha grossly overstated the economic merits of nuclear power, including the near-term value of separating plutonium. One fundamental flaw in his economic projections was the notion that a large increase of electrical power would lead almost automatically to rapid economic development. Energy capacity alone cannot create development—not without suitable transportation infrastructure, investment capital, manufacturing capabilities, markets, and social infrastructure.[100] On the contrary, the opportunity costs of overinvestment in power plants can undermine the creation of the wide range of capacities needed more immediately for overall development. High levels of per capita energy consumption do not mean that energy consumption linearly causes national wealth. The most efficient and productive economies achieve *declines* in per capita energy consumption per unit of gross domestic product, reflecting greater efficiencies in the use of energy. In short, by channeling India's capital investment into nuclear power before the rest of the national infrastructure and skilled manpower base had developed, Bhabha and Nehru unintentionally imposed excessively high opportunity costs on the national economy. Ironically this undermined the nuclear establishment for decades to come.[101] In the 1950s, however, the enthusiasm over India's nuclear plans, and international bullishness on nuclear power, overwhelmed more cautious analysis.

The second major problem was Bhabha's claim that India could build nuclear plants more cheaply than the technologically advanced states with their higher labor costs. The British economist I. M. D. Little analyzed Bhabha's assertions in a November 1958 article in the *Economic and Political Weekly* of Bombay and concluded prophetically that nuclear plants would not be economically advantageous in India. Little argued that Bhabha slanted his analysis of cost comparisons between coal-fired and nuclear power plants and overstated the cost advantages of constructing nuclear plants in India compared to such construction in industrially advanced countries.[102] Thomas W. Graham summarized India's nuclear experience through the 1970s: "Initial hopes that lower construction costs in India would reduce costs for nuclear power plants and heavy-water production plants were not realized."[103]

The third flaw centered on the assumption that India could build and effectively operate large plants early in its program. Experience shows that to offset the huge capital costs of construction, nuclear power plants must have at least 500 to 600 megawatts capacity, and preferably more. Indian and Western experts appreciated the importance of scale in the late 1950s, but they underestimated how big was enough. The Indian nuclear establishment planned for and built plants in the 150- to 220-megawatt range, fearing the difficulties of building and operating bigger plants. This proved to be a major economic handicap to nuclear power.

The fourth flaw was basing cost estimates on the assumption that plants would be operated at 80 percent load factors as Bhabha claimed.[104] Unfortunately, Indian nuclear plants through the mid-1990s operated at around 40 percent load factors, the lowest levels of output in the world, below levels needed for economic efficiency, and well below levels where it can be argued that nuclear power is economically competitive with conventionally fueled plants or energy efficiency measures.[105]

The fifth flaw was the assumption that heavy-water reactor technology would be the most economical. In fact, capital costs of heavy-water natural uranium reactors are higher than those of light-water reactors using slightly enriched uranium fuel. This cost was in turn exacerbated by the unanticipated reliance on importing heavy water from the West, necessitated when India's indigenous heavy-water plants were slow to come on line and frequently malfunctioned. Instead of reducing precious hard currency expenses, the natural uranium reactors' reliance on heavy water increased costs.

The bottom line is that India's investment in nuclear power in the 1950s and beyond represented a major diversion of capital into a relatively unproductive area for economic development. This is no doubt clearer in the 1990s, as India scales back public investment in nuclear power, than it was in the 1950s.[106] Yet, as the foregoing discussion indicates, important and accurate doubts were being raised internationally and, briefly, in India as Bhabha pushed India onto the nuclear pathway in the 1950s. The doubters were overwhelmed by the wishful and vested proponents of nuclear power in the United States, the IAEA, and India. Within India, Bhabha had ensured that no mechanisms were established for independent technical experts to analyze and debate the Atomic Energy Commission's plans and claims, a structural weakness that continues to this day.

The weaknesses in the case for the near- and medium-term economic utility of nuclear power in India were multiplied when it came to plutonium. Whatever cost-effective uses might be found for plutonium in power reactors in the future, the prospects in the 1950s were remote for a developing country like India. As it happened, the money invested sat and compounded interest expenses while the technology became outdated before the necessary complementary elements of the program were in place.[107] No doubt Bhabha and his supporters, including Nehru, did not intend for this to happen. They were alarmed by India's lack of natural uranium resources and seduced by the theoretical lure of using plutonium-breeding reactors to transform India's abundant thorium reserves into an unending source of cheap electricity. Unfortunately, there was no serious analytic or economic basis for this hope, certainly not enough on which to bet scarce national resources. Of course, India again was abetted in its miscalculations by Western proponents of nuclear power who were touting breeder technology prematurely.

If plutonium in the 1950s had no economic utility for the foreseeable future, it had utility as an explosive from the moment it was separated. Without the capacity to separate plutonium from spent fuel, India would not have a nuclear weapon option. Of this, Bhabha was keenly aware. His plans from 1958 onward reflected his interest in acquiring this option. In Bhabha's and his supporters' views, the bomb option justified the uneconomical cost.

Perhaps the most telling feature of India's early nuclear policymaking is the absence of real debate after the brief Saha-led skirmish in 1954. Bhabha articulated and undertook his ambitious plans with no effective opposition.[108] Nehru echoed and supported him. Indeed, in a 1957 Lok Sabha discussion of the Department of Atomic Energy budget, Nehru pointed out that from 1954 through 1956, the budget for atomic energy work "increased twelve-fold." He informed the House that "nobody in the Government of India—neither the Finance Ministry nor any other Ministry—anxious as we are to have economy to save money, has ever refused any urgent demand of the department."[109] In 1958 and 1959, the Atomic Energy Commission received Rs. 77.6 million, or more than 27 percent of all governmental investment in research and development.[110] By 1959 the Atomic Energy Establishment at Trombay had a staff of over one thousand scientists and engineers.[111] India was creating one of the world's largest collections of scientists and engineers dedicated to the state-of-the-art challenge of mastering the atom.

The unquestioning support of Bhabha's mission, and its growing momentum, reflected a number of phenomena. Few Indian politicians or journalists had the independent expertise to criticize the charismatic, internationally recognized physicist. India's scientists for the most part lacked reasons or standing to critique Bhabha's plans or the powerful Department of Atomic Energy. The ambitiousness and seeming feasibility of the project to match the richest and most powerful nations on earth excited the imagination and pride of the newly independent nation. At the time, it could have been argued that a more prosaic and organic approach to energy development would be more beneficial, but this would have sounded patronizing and colonial. If the United States, Canada, the United Kingdom, France, and other countries believed in nuclear power and were eager to assist India's nuclear development, why should Indians be suspicious of the economic and technical feasibility of the project?

AMBIGUITY OF INDIA'S INTENTIONS, 1957 TO 1960

One explanation for the international community's generally unquestioning regard of Bhabha's plutonium quest is that Nehru fervently insisted that India's purposes were purely peaceful. Erudite and moralistic, Nehru tended to be taken at his word when he professed that India would not build atom bombs. This was not unreasonable insofar as Nehru genuinely abhorred nuclear weapons and the international dynamics that fueled the arms race. He truly hoped that India would not be driven to build nuclear weapons. And in the late 1950s, Nehru could speak for India, notwithstanding inevitable opposition carping. The Congress party had a practical monopoly over power, thanks in large part to "[t]he Indian people's adulation of Nehru."[112] Beyond charisma, Nehru held sway because the economic plight of the common man did not worsen in the 1950s. This was due in part to the fact that "Nehru's foreign policy . . . did not demand vast expenditure on Defence that has diverted the developmental effort in many an under-developed country."[113]

Thus, observers tended to accept Nehru's word as India's, as when he declared on January 20, 1957, that "whatever the circumstances, we shall never use this atomic energy for evil purposes. There is no condition attached."[114] Perhaps only a cynic would have noted that Nehru began this proclamation by saying, "No man can prophesy about the future."[115] Similarly, six months later when addressing the Lok Sabha regarding the Department of Atomic Energy's plans, Nehru reiterated "that we are not interested in making atom bombs, even if we have the capacity to do so, and that in no event will we use atomic energy for destructive purposes."[116] Again, perhaps it would have been cynical to parse differences between the less categorical disavowal of "making" atom bombs and the clear rejection of *using* them, or to note that Nehru closed this speech by adding that "[t]he fact remains that if one has these fissionable materials and if one has the resources, then one can make a bomb, unless the world will be wise enough to come to some decision to stop the production of such bombs."[117]

While Nehru's numerous statements could be taken as unequivocal commitments not to develop atomic weapon capability, he and Bhabha were following a more sophisticated strategy.[118] Bhabha and Nehru understood and rhetorically welcomed the military potential of the nuclear program, particularly the plutonium separation plant, before 1962. The nuclear program created multiple options regardless of the label put on it.

Indeed, from late 1955 through 1960, and then later, Bhabha and Nehru directly and indirectly invoked the capability and possible intention to make nuclear explosives. Their statements betrayed genuine ambivalence and vacillation but also a clear awareness of the value of a nuclear weapon option. In 1955, according to Bertrand Goldschmidt, Bhabha suggested to Nehru that India should publicly and unilaterally renounce "the bomb," but Nehru responded that "they should discuss it again on the day when India was ready to produce one."[119] On January 30, 1958, Nehru coyly added a warning to the "peaceful purposes only" label while explaining how India would deal with the stationing of nuclear weapons in Pakistan or any other Asian nation: "We have the technical know-how for manufacturing the atom bomb. We can do it in three or four years if we divert sufficient resources in that direction. But, we have given the world an assurance that we shall never do so. We shall never use our knowledge of nuclear science for purposes of war."[120] This technically exaggerated statement of nuclear weapon capability, which resembled past and future statements by Bhabha, can be interpreted as an early evocation of nuclear deterrence by India.[121]

In 1958 Bhabha told Lord Blackett, his English friend, that he hoped to develop nuclear weapons.[122] Sir John Cockcroft, another English physicist friend of Bhabha's, stated in 1967 that despite Bhabha's public espousal of India's peaceful-use-only policy, "In discussions at small closed meetings, . . . he appeared to be in favour of making bombs for a Plowshare programme."[123] In December 1959, when the first concerns emerged over China's nuclear weapon ambitions, Bhabha told the Parliamentary Consultative Committee on Atomic Energy that India's atomic energy development program had progressed to the point where it could make atomic weapons without external aid if called upon to do so.

Bhabha's interest in developing nuclear weapons would become clearer in 1964, but in the late 1950s it could be argued that he, and particularly Nehru, envisioned not bombs but rather peaceful nuclear explosives. In late 1957 the United States had established a formal program to conduct peaceful nuclear explosions (PNEs, for short).[124] In 1958, at the second UN Conference on Peaceful Nuclear Explosives, the United States extolled the economic benefits of PNEs to an international audience, including leaders of the Indian AEC. The United States envisioned using PNEs for massive excavation projects, such as digging canals and harbors, releasing subterranean natural resources such as natural gas, and conducting pure scientific research.[125] However, despite early American and Soviet enthusiasm for the potential uses of PNEs, Bhabha and others in India did not evince serious interest in them until late 1964, as discussed in chapters 2 and 3. Even then Bhabha's notion was primarily to acquire atomic weapon capability under the guise of a peaceful program. As the Tata Institute of Fundamental Research scientist N. Seshagiri recorded in his study of India's peaceful nuclear explosives program, "it was only from 1970 . . . that India seriously began thinking about NEE," or nuclear explosives engineering, the term the then chairman of the AEC, Vikram Sarabhai, preferred over peaceful nuclear explosives.[126] In the late 1950s and early 1960s, the interest was to acquire weapon capability.

If Bhabha's and Nehru's early public allusions to India's nuclear weapon capability were reticent and guarded, the two men expressed more candid ambivalence in a 1960 conversation with Major General (ret.) Kenneth D. Nichols. Nichols was an American military engineer who had been responsible for overseeing the design, construction, and operation of the plants used in the Manhattan Project to produce enriched uranium and plutonium. In the 1950s he had served as the top military official in the U.S. nuclear establishment, the senior army member of the Military Liaison Committee to the Atomic Energy Committee.[127] In 1960, Nichols visited India as a consultant to Westinghouse and chairman of the board of Westinghouse International Atomic Power Company in Geneva, Switzerland. At Bhabha's request, Nichols came to India to discuss plans for building India's first nuclear power reactor.[128] Nichols managed to persuade Bhabha and several of his staff that American light-water reactors were superior to British gas-cooled reactors. That done, Bhabha asked Nichols to join him in a meeting with Nehru to "explain the advantages of opening competition to the U.S. suppliers."[129] After listening to Nichols's forty-five-minute pitch, Nehru agreed and "told Bhabha to open up the competition to include U.S. reactors."[130] Then, in a revealing episode, Nichols recorded that Nehru turned to Bhabha and asked,

> "Can you develop an atomic bomb?" Bhabha assured him that he could and in reply to Nehru's next question about time, he estimated that he would need about a year to do it. I was really astounded to be hearing these questions from the one I thought to be one of the world's most peace-loving leaders. He then asked me if I agreed with Bhabha, and I replied that I knew of no reason why Bhabha could not do it. He had men who were as qualified or more qualified than our young scientists were fifteen years earlier. He concluded by saying to Bhabha, "Well, don't do it until I tell you to."[131]

This extraordinary conversation has not been noted in the Indian or American literature on India's nuclear program. Nehru had thought and spoken about an Indian atomic bomb before. However, it seems peculiar that he would discuss such a sensitive matter with an American. Assuming Nichols's account is accurate, it seems that Nehru might have been using the uniquely qualified American interlocutor to assess Bhabha's ability to deliver what he had previously assured Nehru he could deliver. To whom else could Nehru turn to check Bhabha's claims? Bhabha was *the* authoritative figure. So Nehru could have decided that it was worth risking indiscretion in order to assess Bhabha's claims. Nichols was a safe audience insofar as he had worked on nuclear weapons and could not object to them in principle, and he would not risk his hopes of doing business with India by publicly questioning Nehru's or Bhabha's peaceful motives.

Remarkably, however, Bhabha's claim that India could produce a bomb in "about a year" had no basis in fact. The plutonium separation plant would not begin construction until 1961 and would not be completed until 1964. Perhaps Bhabha and Nichols, by his assent, meant that Indian scientists could produce a weapon within a year after acquiring the requisite amount of plutonium. But even this would have been grossly optimistic. History shows that such optimism is normal for passionate advocates of nuclear technology like Bhabha and Nichols. The American was also trying to persuade the Indians to buy his company's reactor technology.[132] Nichols had no interest in making Bhabha look bad by questioning him. Lastly, Nehru's admonition to Bhabha not to "do it until I tell you to" revealed the nature of Indian nuclear decision making. Two men would be involved as principals: Nehru and Bhabha, the prime minister and the chairman of the AEC.

THE NUCLEAR PROGRAM'S MOMENTUM BUILDS, 1960 TO 1962

The dual peaceful/military theme of the Indian nuclear program, and the contribution of foreign capital and technology to it, continued from 1960 through 1962. In August 1960 Nehru announced in the Lok Sabha that India would build its first power-generating nuclear station at Tarapur and would move ahead to construct the previously proposed plutonium separation plant at Trombay. During this period India successfully approached the United States to finance and supply the Tarapur power station, as is discussed more fully later in the chapter. Bhabha also traveled to Canada to further Indo-Canadian nuclear cooperation. There, in November 1960, he announced that the Soviet Union had agreed to design natural uranium and fast breeder power plants for India. This "agreement" never bore fruit, but it heightened Washington's cold war motivation to serve India's nuclear appetite and keep the Soviet Union out of India's good graces. In Canada, Bhabha's diplomacy would soon pay off with an agreement by Canada in 1963 to build a natural uranium power reactor in Rajasthan, the Rajasthan Atomic Power Station, Unit 1, or RAPS-I.[133]

By 1961 Bhabha had prevailed upon the Planning Commission to plan for major growth in nuclear power generation capacity. Under pressure to deliver results, Bhabha announced in February the solicitation of foreign contracts to build power plants. He wanted generous economic and safeguard terms and quick construction in order to bolster the economic standing of his enterprise. To motivate Western suppliers of technology, he suggested that momentum was growing behind Indo-Soviet nuclear cooperation. A *Statesman* newspaper headline reflected Bhabha's strategy: "India May Seek Soviet Aid if West Does Not Help."[134] Bhabha noted that "Western nuclear Powers would be reluctant to help India unless she accepted the International Atomic Agency's system of inspection and safeguards" and pointed out that the Soviet Union would not insist on safeguards.[135] On the home front, Bhabha responded to growing concern over the economic viability of nuclear power by arguing that India must plan ahead "10 to 15 years" and invest resources now to be ready to capitalize on nuclear power in the future.[136] He claimed that natural uranium reactors would spare India ongoing foreign exchange expenditures because the fuel could be produced indigenously.[137] He also declared that India might be in a position to develop breeder reactors in five years. Later, in August, Bhabha's AEC projected that India would produce 3,000 megawatts of electricity through nuclear plants by 1976.[138] (Thirty-seven years later India had little more than half this nuclear power supply.)

Unlike before, Bhabha's ambitious calls for investment in nuclear power triggered counterarguments in the press. The *Hindustan Times* editorialized that "in the current stage of fuel science and technology, thermal power stations are a cheaper source of energy than nuclear power stations."[139] Citing British assessments that "atomic power stations are unlikely to become as economical as coal-burning stations before 1970," the newspaper concluded, "It is obvious that this is not the right time for this country to commit any large amounts of scarce capital or technical resources to the commercial exploitation of techniques which may become rapidly outmoded."[140] Then, in a telling critique, the paper argued that the nuclear program "has never had the benefit of objective study. It is a strictly departmental project whose scientific and financial implications have never been discussed and defended before a critical audience."[141] The *Times of India* editorialized similarly, writing that the AEC's case for nuclear power "is by no means supported by the economics of nuclear power. . . . [A]s experience elsewhere shows, . . . nuclear power is being left behind, giving way to conventional fuels primarily as a result of rapid technological achievement" in thermal power. The paper continued, "Apparently there is no limit to the irrational ambitions of the A.E.C. which is currently persuading New Delhi to sanction a second power house."[142]

However, Nehru and Bhabha once again carried the day without serious opposition in Parliament.[143] The plans and budgets for India's nuclear complex went forward. This time Nehru and Bhabha subtly and indirectly invoked the strategic deterrent potential of the nuclear program to rally support for it. On January 9, 1961, Nehru told the National Development Council, "We are approaching a stage when it is possible for us . . . to make atomic weapons."[144] Five days later Nehru announced that India's third research reactor had gone critical and declared that if India wished to it could make nuclear weapons "within the next two or three years," adding, "absolutely under no circumstances shall we do so."[145] On February 2, in response to a question about how long it would take for India "to make nuclear weapons," Bhaba reaffirmed the program's dual-use potential by saying, "about two years I suppose."[146] Obviously, such invocations of nuclear weapon capability, couched as demurrals, would not have been made if Bhabha and Nehru did not think they would buttress support of a nuclear program that had come under mild questioning.

The nuclear establishment's power and reach were strengthened in September 1962, when Parliament adopted a revised Atomic Energy Act, tightening the secrecy and central government control over all activities related to atomic energy. The act provided for "the development, control and use of atomic energy for the welfare of the people of India and for other peaceful purposes and for matters connected therewith."[147] The last phrase, "for matters connected therewith," was broad enough to encompass India's subsequent development of nuclear weapon capability. Indeed, as Itty Abraham recorded, India's traditional focus on "peaceful uses" was largely absent from the act and the debate over it. Instead, the importance of nuclear power for national security was tacitly being elevated.[148]

Still, Indian diplomats maintained the call for nuclear disarmament. The United States, the Soviet Union, and the United Kingdom had been observing a nuclear test moratorium since 1958, but the superpowers were failing to formalize arms control and disarmament agreements. Serious negotiations were impeded by mistrust, military and technical momentum, and the difficulties of verification. India continued to urge initiatives to break the impasse.[149] Often these calls for major disarmament initiatives rankled the United States because the Indians portrayed Washington as the primary obstacle to progress.[150] In September 1961 the Soviet Union broke the testing moratorium. The United States and the United Kingdom resumed testing in turn. Tension mounted between India's demands for nuclear disarmament and the American, Soviet, British, and French possession of nuclear weapons. China's and India's lurking potential to build nuclear weapons further complicated the dynamic. India genuinely desired to see the world rid of nuclear weapons and other armaments, but it also took satisfaction from righteously demanding moral action on the part of the major powers. If the major powers failed, India would find moral and political justification for its own acquisition of nuclear weapon capability.

DOMESTIC CONTEXT OF NUCLEAR
DECISION MAKING, 1948 TO 1963

From 1948 through 1963, nuclear policy barely figured in Indian politics. This chapter has noted some of the few occasions upon which nuclear issues were debated. Yet these debates, while illuminating, assumed little importance in the overall Indian polity. Parliament did not exert itself on nuclear policy issues. When faint signs of challenge to the Congress party appeared after the 1957 Lok Sabha elections—which Congress won decisively, notwithstanding surprising gains by the Communist Party of India (CPI)—the issues of concern were rising taxes, poverty, unemployment and corruption.[151] Only after India's late-1962 defeat at the hands of China, did Nehru come under broad attack, as discussed later in this chapter. The hard-line Jana Sangh Party, a nascent opposition political party, soon issued a call for an Indian nuclear bomb. But others did not echo this call and the consensus remained that India's nuclear program should be entirely peaceful. Nehru's major potential rival at that point, Finance Minister Morarji Desai, was a devout Gandhian who would later demonstrate at some political risk his abhorrence of nuclear weapons.

Prior to 1964, as Shyam Bhatia recorded, none of India's five major English-language daily newspapers surveyed "devoted any attention to the possibility of an Indian nuclear weapons programme."[152] Extremely few entries on atomic power, nuclear weapons, and so forth appear in the indexes of major Indian and foreign books on Indian politics published in this period. In practically none of them does Homi Bhabha's name appear. Even India's specialist community in international affairs paid practically no attention to nuclear issues. As Bhatia noted, the quarterly journal of the Indian School of International Studies "did not publish a single article on nuclear problems in the period 1959–64."[153] *Indian Quarterly,* the journal of the Indian Council of World Affairs, did not discuss nuclear issues in its pages until 1965, in response to the Chinese test. A major book on defense issues, *Problems of Indian Defence,* published in 1960, devoted two pages to the idea of an Indian nuclear weapon program and concluded against it because an attack on India " 'can only be with conventional weapons along her frontiers by land and sea and air.' "[154] Major biographies of Nehru offer additional evidence of the place of nuclear policy in the grand sweep of Indian affairs before 1964. Despite Nehru's close involvement with Homi Bhabha, less than ten references to nuclear policy and Bhabha appear in the thousands of pages in the biographies by M. J. Akbar, Michael Brecher, Sarvepalli Gopal, Frank Moraes, and Stanley Wolpert.[155]

In short, while Bhabha and his colleagues, with Nehru's backing, were steadily developing India's nuclear weapon potential, the polity knew practically nothing about it. If this program was in the national interest, that interest was being defined by Homi Bhabha and Jawaharlal Nehru with no systematic analysis or debate.

INTERNATIONAL CONTEXT:
INDIA'S FOREIGN RELATIONS THROUGH 1963

When Bhabha and Nehru alluded to the potential military applications of nuclear capability they did not identify any particular foreign threat. As a relatively weak developing state, India's primary external interests related to the two major powers—the United States and the Soviet Union—and to China. In order to protect against undue influence by the major powers, India pursued a strategy of nonalignment. The strategy was formalized with the creation of the Non-aligned Movement at Bandung, Indonesia, in 1955, under Nehru's leadership. As a somewhat coordinated movement, this large "bloc" of Asian and African states could exert greater influence in the international system—through the United Nations and other institutions—than could any one of them alone.

India's foreign policy flowed from domestic needs.[156] The greatest priority from independence to the present day has been to enhance economic development while preserving the order, integrity, and democratic government of an ethnically, religiously, and linguistically diverse nation. "Ultimately," Nehru explained in 1947, "foreign policy is the outcome of economic policy and till that time, when India has properly evolved her economic policy, her foreign policy will be rather vague, rather inchoate, and will rather grope about."[157] Nonalignment fit India's circumstance well. By aligning with neither the West nor the East, India could reasonably hope to receive economic assistance from both and remain free from cold war military conflicts.

To the limited extent that international relations influenced India's early nuclear policy, the major factors were bilateral relations with China and the United States and the diplomacy of U.S.-Soviet arms control and disarmament. The following pages treat separately Indian relations with these key states in the 1948–1963 period, in part because these international relations did not bear heavily on nuclear policy. Yet they still need to be surveyed to establish the external context for later decisions. In succeeding chapters, foreign developments are treated within the narrative of India's nuclear policy development rather than in separate sections, as here.

The Soviet Union.   India's relationship with the Soviet Union evolved slowly and coolly from independence in 1947. Stalin held little regard for India.[158] Little positive engagement occurred until the Korean War, when India's active role in the United Nations to seek a negotiated settlement won Stalin's appreciation and Washington's disapproval. Upon Stalin's death in March 1953, the Soviet Union evinced increasing interest in India. In December the two countries signed a long-term trade agreement allowing Indian payment for goods in rupees, as distinguished from similar agreements with the West that required hard currency payments.[159] The warming trend continued, and in June 1955 Nehru traveled to the Soviet Union, where he was greeted enthusiastically. A Joint Declaration signed in Moscow heralded a major breakthrough in the two states' relations. In late 1955, Soviet Premier Nikolay Bulganin and then-Communist Party First Secretary Nikita Khrushchev made a reciprocal visit to India. In Srinagar, Bulganin declared that Kashmir was "part of the Indian people . . . the people of Kashmir have themselves decided to become part of India."[160] This departure from Stalin's line impressed the Indians.

Yet, the warming from Moscow came at a price. The Soviets used the 1955 visit to blast the United States, the United Kingdom, Pakistan, and Portugal (over the Portuguese colony in Goa). The predictable backlash in those nations' capitals, especially Washington, discomfited India. The credibility of its nonalignment policy was questioned. Nehru sought to disarm these criticisms directly when he said, "People in many parts of the world seem to think that if you are friendly with one person, that means that you are hostile and inimical to the other—as if you can only be friendly with one to be hostile to another."[161] Nehru's reaffirmation of nonaligned goodwill held little sway in cold war Washington.

Nineteen fifty-six brought the Suez and Hungarian crises and another episode of seeming Indian inconsistency. India harshly challenged the English and French intervention in the Middle East and sided with fellow-nonaligned Egypt. But concerning Hungary, India was more or less neutral on an issue that called for choosing sides. When India abstained or voted against UN resolutions calling for withdrawal of Soviet troops, the impression mounted that it was siding with the Soviet

Union regardless of the morality of the Soviet action and India's professions of nonalignment. As payback perhaps, the United States and other powers reintroduced the Kashmir issue in the United Nations in early 1957, upsetting India.

Indo-Soviet relations continued to deepen throughout 1960 and 1961. Nehru traveled to the Soviet Union in September 1961 and, along with President Kwame Nkrumah of Ghana, delivered a letter to Khrushchev, appealing to the United States and the Soviet Union to resume arms control and disarmament negotiations. An identical version of the letter was addressed to President John Kennedy. Soviet intransigence on the nuclear testing issue did not impede India from signing an agreement with Moscow for cooperation in the peaceful uses of atomic energy on October 6, 1961.[162] As noted previously, Bhabha eight months earlier had alluded to a potential nuclear cooperation agreement with the Soviet Union in part to leverage more American and Canadian nuclear assistance and less stringent safeguards.

The Soviets regarded Bhabha's entreaties warily and presciently. V. S. Emelyanov, a metallurgist and sometime diplomatic emissary, confided to an American official in late 1960 that "Bhabha had been pressing him for an arrangement to supply a power plant to India" but that Emelyanov had taken the position "that it was premature for such type of plant." Emelyanov warned that "India might be interested in atomic weapons in the future. India could make weapons from the plutonium that would be produced in the natural uranium reactors Dr. Bhabha wished." He also suggested that Bhabha's plan to use such a plant to produce plutonium for recycling in breeders was premature.[163] Ironically, Emelyanov's conservative observations cast doubt on the economic and "nonproliferation" wisdom of American nuclear aid to India.

Soviet-Indian relations cooled dramatically in October 1962 when Moscow appeared to betray India in the war with China, a development that is discussed more fully in the next section. Yet, after 1962, the relationship recovered fully as Moscow moved closer to India and Beijing moved to embrace Pakistan. In sum, the Soviet Union played little role in affecting India's nuclear policy in this period.

China.   The framework of Sino-Indian relations in the 1948–1963 period was defined by China's occupation of Tibet, on India's northern border, in 1950. China's aggrandizement alarmed the Indian leadership in classic geostrategic terms: the large neighbor had extended its reach. Yet newly independent and poor India had few means with which to deal with the changed circumstance.[164] Thus, on April 29, 1954, India officially recognized the People's Republic of China, signing an Agreement on Trade and Intercourse between Tibet Region of China and India. The agreement expressed the five principles of the two nations' relationship, which in India would become known as *Panchsheel:* "1) Mutual respect for each other's territorial integrity and sovereignty; 2) Mutual non-aggression; 3) Mutual non-interference in each other's internal affairs; 4) Equality and mutual benefit; and 5) Peaceful co-existence."[165] Reflecting on the agreement and its strategy later, Nehru explained that India needed to buy time before it could be strong enough to challenge China.[166]

Nehru and Chinese Premier Chou En-lai exchanged visits later in 1954. Each received warm and enthusiastic welcomes. Indian crowds greeted Chou with chants of "Chini-Hindi bhai bhai" (Chinese and Indians are brothers).[167] The exchanges reflected an Indian strategy of cultivating friendship with China.[168] Yet, beneath the surface lay a lingering dispute over three regions totaling 50,000 square miles of territory that Chinese maps recorded as Chinese and Indian maps as Indian. The confusion and dispute owed to the legacy of British colonialism and China's desire to revisit the matter now that Britain had quit India. Here India's and China's visions of the past and future collided. India believed that traditional patterns of settlement should influence the determination of the border. China sought to assert its new revolutionary sovereignty by negotiating border adjustments anew.[169]

The territorial dispute became pronounced in January 1959 when Chou En-lai wrote Nehru to officially claim the disputed three regions for China. This occurred against the backdrop of the Tibetan rebellion against Chinese rule, which caused the Dalai Lama to flee to India, leading China to launch verbal assaults on India. The details of the territorial dispute are beyond the scope of this study. It is enough to say that India and China negotiated fruitlessly throughout 1959 and into 1960 to resolve the matter.[170] During 1960 and 1961, India adopted a "forward policy" of moving forces into the gaps up to the border recognized by India. Nehru and Defence Minister Krishna Menon directly oversaw the placement of particular brigades, companies, and platoons, despite their lack of military experience or expertise.[171]

China at this time was racing to build atomic weapons. Although the Chinese nuclear program did not affect the border dispute with India—or India's overall security policies until 1964—the chronology of the Chinese effort must be noted. In January 1955, the Central Secretariat of the Chinese Politburo had decided to proceed with a program to develop nuclear weapons.[172] From 1955 to 1957, the Soviet Union established and began implementing substantial cooperation in the nuclear field, culminating in an October 15, 1957, agreement whereby the Soviet Union pledged to supply a prototype atom bomb to China.[173] In May 1958, the Chinese foreign minister told German journalists that China was determined to produce nuclear weapons.

Chinese nuclear allusions registered, albeit faintly, in India. In an annual Lok Sabha debate on the Department of Atomic Energy on March 10, 1959, two members introduced motions to discuss the need to expand atomic research into "the field of defence."[174] Nehru responded by assuring the Parliament that India's nuclear research was "more advanced and more widespread" than that of all but the advanced powers. In other words, India was ahead of China.[175] In December 1959, the Parliamentary Consultative Committee on Atomic Energy met behind closed doors and reportedly inquired about the possibility of China's acquisition of a nuclear weapon. By this time, Moscow had rescinded its offer to provide China with technical details or a working model for atomic weapons and was preparing to abrogate all nuclear cooperation agreements. However, this was not known in India.[176] Bhabha reportedly replied that India's nuclear program had itself progressed to the point where it could produce nuclear weapons indigenously if necessary.[177]

In March 1960 an Indian Rajya Sabha member triggered a false alarm that China would explode an atomic bomb on March 28. Bhabha and others quickly refuted this wild speculation, but it prompted several editorials in the Indian press predicting China's imminent acquisition of the bomb.[178] Nehru once again stepped forward to reassure his people and warn outsiders that India was "determined not to go in for making atomic bombs and the like. But we are equally determined not to be left behind in this advance in the use of this new power."[179] In October 1961, Field Marshal Bernard Montgomery visited China and reported in the London *Sunday Times* that Chou En-lai had told him that China "had decided to proceed with plans for developing nuclear weapons for the armed forces," but that this was not a high Chinese priority given more urgent needs.[180] In 1961, U.S. intelligence agencies estimated that China could detonate a nuclear device by 1962.[181]

Despite these murmurs, China's and India's incipient nuclear programs did not figure prominently in their relationship as it moved toward the 1962 war. Rather, the focus remained on the disputed territory along the border. By mid-1962, India had established forty-three new outposts in Ladakh and had occupied 2,500 square miles of the contested territory.[182] China responded by building up defenses along its side of the British McMahon Line. Both sides were moving toward conflict. India, in the spring of 1962, proposed a "stand back" measure to reduce tension and allow time for negotiation, but China rejected it. In July, Chinese troops surrounded an Indian forward post. In September, Chinese forces crossed the McMahon Line in the northeast. The Indians tried to counter but were outnumbered and lacked adequate lines of communication. Lieutenant General B. M. Kaul, commander in chief of the Eastern Command, flew to the region to inspect the situation and concluded that India could not defend.[183] On October 20, China launched large-scale attacks in both the western and eastern sectors of the disputed border, overrunning India's poorly reinforced positions. In the midst of a Chinese rout, Nehru confided to Krishna Menon that "we have been found lacking and there is an impression that we have approached these things in a somewhat amateurish way."[184] Menon was soon sacrificed from his defense minister's post as a result of the debacle.

Faced with military crisis, India found itself in a diplomatic cross fire between the United States, the Soviet Union, and China. By remarkable coincidence, the Sino-Indian conflict was occurring at the same time as the Cuban missile crisis. The latter preoccupied Moscow and Washington and provided an opportunity for Beijing to boost its standing in its rivalry with the Soviet Union for leadership of the communist world. Since 1959 the Soviet Union had demurred from taking fraternal Communist China's side in the South Asian border dispute, a failure of "class" allegiance that rankled Mao Tse-tung.[185] At the same time, Moscow did not respond to numerous Indian requests for mediation. As the Sino-Indian conflict mounted from 1959 to 1962, Chinese officials persistently urged their Soviet counterparts to recognize that "Nehru is the central figure in the anti-Chinese campaign in India, that he does not in any case want to resolve the question of the Sino-Indian border, even in some fixed period."[186] In October 1962, China again urged Moscow to take a "class position" on the border dispute and side with China. Preoccupied with Cuban affairs, Soviet leaders at first paid little heed to the looming clash in South Asia. However, on October 22, following President Kennedy's public announcement of the missile crisis, Soviet leaders scrambled to build Chinese and other communist support for their harrowing position in the Caribbean. On October 25, *Pravda* published a front-page article approved by the Central Committee rejecting the previous Soviet position on the Sino-Indian dispute and now deeming the McMahon line a "notorious" result of British imperialism that could not be considered valid.[187] *Pravda* argued further that India was being incited by imperialists. This clear and unexpected reversal alarmed Nehru. Indian officials understood the game—that the Cuban missile crisis and threat of war had drawn the Soviets toward China—but this provided no reassurance.[188] As the Cuban crisis wound down the Soviets realized that their overture to China had failed. Beijing mercilessly chastised Moscow for trading in the "liberty and rights" of Cuba.[189] With the Sino-Soviet split and the cooling of the Sino-Indian military conflict, Soviet leaders in early November flip-flopped yet again and, through *Pravda*, argued that China's position on the border dispute was unjustified.[190] However, by then the damage was done. India's inability to rely on the Soviet Union was clearly demonstrated. (However, only nine years later India and the Soviet Union would sign a Treaty of Peace, Friendship and Co-Operation largely to buttress India against China and solidify the Soviet position in South Asia against the United States and China.)

India meanwhile had turned to the United States on October 26 to request urgent military aid. President Kennedy, notwithstanding his immersion in the Cuban missile crisis, responded immediately with an offer of assistance. Nehru accepted, detailing in letters seen by no other senior officials besides Foreign Secretary M. J. Desai a request for twelve squadrons of U.S. fighters, and two squadrons of B-47 bombers, and an airlift of infantry weapons and light equipment for troops, as well as other assistance.[191] He asked that the United States not require a military alliance as a quid pro quo. The policy of nonalignment had to be maintained regardless of facts on the ground. The war ended before Kennedy could decide on the military air support, but the United States did deploy the aircraft carrier *Enterprise* to the region. Ironically, this was the very ship that would be the subject of lingering Indian resentment when President Richard Nixon dispatched it to the Bay of Bengal to buttress Pakistan in the 1971 war.

The war ended almost as abruptly as it had begun. China, on November 21, declared a unilateral cease-fire and withdrawal from much of the ground it had taken in India.[192] China's objectives had been minimal. India's strategic and military planning and practices clearly had been woeful. As Nehru said, "[W]e were getting out of touch with reality in the modern world and we were living in an artificial atmosphere of our own creation."[193] Despite fanciful calls for defiance by Indian hawks, India ultimately lived by the terms of the Chinese cease-fire, even if no formal acceptance of these terms was offered.[194] The border has remained the disputed object of halting negotiations to the present day.

Making matters worse for India (and the United States), in February 1963, China and Pakistan moved significantly closer by signing a border agreement that signaled an increasing Pakistani turn toward China. Pakistan had been growing steadily dissatisfied with the level of military assistance it was receiving from the United States. Washington's offer of military aid to India in late 1962 intensified Pakistan's desire for additional friends.[195] For India, the hoped-for American military assistance proved exceedingly difficult to obtain, and it did not offset the long-term implications of Sino-Pak cooperation.

In the aftermath of the 1962 debacle, India significantly increased its military spending and preparations. The defense budget for 1963–1964 was doubled in February 1963, amounting to 28 percent of the national budget, compared with 15 to 17 percent in previous years.[196] It would keep rising at an unprecedented pace, leading to inflation and price increases from 1963 onward.

In December 1962, the Jana Sangh Party made the first formal demand in Parliament for India to reverse its declared policy and produce nuclear weapons.[197] Nehru faced a demoralized nation and a press that asked whether India would "for ever" eschew a nuclear deterrent. "To be quite practical," he said, "either you have a very powerful deterrent" or you achieve little practical value with nuclear weapons. "[I]t is no good having something showy. . . . It will not have the slightest effect on India as such, if they [the Chinese] have a test tomorrow. . . . We are not going to make bombs, not even thinking of making bombs, [although] we are in nuclear science more advanced than China."[198] On March 25, 1963, during the Lok Sabha discussion of the Department of Atomic Energy budget, Nehru again faced a plea for developing nuclear weapons from the Jana Sangh parliamentarian Ramachandra Bade: "Only those who wish to see Russians or Chinese ruling India will oppose the development of nuclear weapons. I beg the Prime Minister to make full use of our research in atomic energy."[199] Again Nehru demurred: "On the one hand, we are asking the nuclear powers to give up their tests. How can we, without showing the utter insincerity of what we have always said, go in for doing the very thing which we have repeatedly asked the other powers not to do?"[200] Indeed, during this period the official policy remained unchanged. The nuclear establishment stayed on its course, which *already* was tending toward nuclear weapon capability. The polity as a whole focused on strengthening the nation's conventional military strength and finding the resources to pay for it without undermining national development.

Many possible conclusions can be drawn from this account of Sino-Indian developments. Clearly India was unprepared to deal militarily with China and lacked a serious military strategy. Yet, apart from incompetence and perhaps naïveté, the ill-preparedness of India's military reflected the tension between socioeconomic development and defense spending in democratic India. Nehru's India would not be a fortress state and instead would use words, imagery, moralism, nonalignment, and strategic size to protect its international interests. If it had chosen instead to become militarily strong, India would have undermined and bankrupted—literally and morally—the essential democratic character that enabled it to win independence through nonviolence. Unlike China, democratic India could not afford to put its more advanced nuclear program on a steep and dedicated military trajectory in this period or even afterward. Bhabha's atomic energy establishment was already proceeding apace to provide India with a bomb option, largely for "identity" reasons. Although Indian claims of being ahead of China in the nuclear realm appeared increasingly dubious, and security concerns mounted, domestic considerations militated against a radical acceleration of the bomb acquisition effort.

Still, the blundering defeat at the hands of China profoundly affected India. Nehru lost much of his vigor. In the unsettled political situation following his death in 1964, Indian political elites fretted over the need to revive national pride and reassure themselves and the populace that India could protect its position in a world proved crueler by the Chinese invasion. As is discussed in the following chapters, this concern did not translate into a clear military strategy or a dedicated nuclear weapon program, but it did heighten the desire of a growing number of political leaders to strengthen India's nuclear capabilities in a more threatening world than Nehru's idealism admitted.

Pakistan.   Pakistan did not play an important role in India's nuclear policy-making in the years from 1948 to 1963. Pakistan posed no nuclear threat. More broadly, throughout much of this period its armed forces struggled to recover from the disarray of partition. Although U.S. military assistance alarmed India, Pakistan remained the weaker of the two states. This military assessment, however, was complicated by the fact that India had to calibrate its forces to defend against not only Pakistan but also China. Still, on balance, the dominant sources of contention between India and Pakistan in this period were the Kashmir dispute and the fundamental discord over the very fact of Pakistan's existence as a separate state.

Pakistan was born weak and unstable, and it has remained so for decades, struggling to develop a political economy that would solidify prospects for the future. The nation was torn by deep fissures between Bengali East Pakistan and

Punjabi-dominated West Pakistan, between Punjabis and Sindhis, between pro-Western modernizers and xenophobic mullahs, and between the needs of economic development and military buildup. To solidify power in this dangerous mix, any leader or clique would be tempted to use such inflammatory issues as the role of Islam and the struggle for Kashmir as unifying principles.

Indian and Pakistani leaders have tied their respective nation's identity to not relinquishing Kashmir to the other.[201] India's essence as a secular state has "required" the integration of Muslim-majority Jammu and Kashmir to prove that Muslims could fare well in India. Pakistan's identity as an Islamic state has "required" that all major conglomerations of Muslims in South Asia live within it, a contention India rejected from the beginning.

Various efforts at outside mediation of the Kashmir problem were undertaken in the 1950s and later, to no avail. The increasingly friendly relationship between Pakistan and the United States, including, most important, the American provision of substantial military assistance to Pakistan begun in 1954, hardened India's resolve against negotiations. India argued that Pakistan intended to take Kashmir by force or threat of force, and that this approach could not be rewarded.

In 1956, Pakistan established an Atomic Energy Commission. This reflected the general international enthusiasm for atomic energy and Pakistan's interest in capitalizing on the international cooperation offered through the Atoms for Peace initiative. With a small base of scientists, engineers, and technology, Pakistan's program was modest in practice. It aimed first to develop human resources and to apply know-how and technology for agricultural and medical purposes. In August 1960, the United States gave Pakistan $350,000 to prepare for a first research reactor. In 1962, the IAEA approved a Pakistani request for U.S. assistance in transferring a five-megawatt pool-type research reactor and fuel to be installed at the Pakistan Institute of Nuclear Science and Technology (PINSTECH) facility in Rawalpindi. Also in 1962, Pakistan signed an agreement on nuclear cooperation with France, which in the 1970s would seek to supply Pakistan with a plutonium production reactor and separation plant. Within the Pakistani government in this period, the chief proponent of the nuclear program was Zulfikar Ali Bhutto, then minister of mineral and natural resources, and soon to be foreign minister and eventually president of Pakistan. Bhutto, unlike other Pakistani leaders, recognized the priority of developing science and technology, and particularly nuclear capability. He would begin speaking of the need for Pakistani nuclear weapons in 1965 and would launch a program to acquire this capability in 1972.

Pakistani leaders saw the United States as a crutch as they struggled in the late 1950s to stabilize the polity, develop its economy, and build up its military. Although American military aid always fell short of Pakistani desires, it provided vital support to Pakistan's armed forces. But U.S. assistance could not overcome Pakistan's fundamental weaknesses. Martial law was declared in Pakistan in 1958. By 1959, Washington increasingly doubted the wisdom and levels of its military assistance. Military assistance did not seem to help overcome the nation's profound internal flaws, as evidenced by Ayub Khan's takeover. The Pakistani military was dwarfing the rest of the economy, making it impossible for the state to support the armed forces without ongoing high levels of U.S. aid. An unsustainable relationship between Pakistan's military and its political economy was being created.[202] Also, U.S. aid to Pakistan was further alienating India at a time when the United States was concluding that India was the key to a stable, noncommunist subcontinent. Finally, the disparity between Pakistani demands for aid and what the United States was prepared to provide was prompting Ayub's eye to wander toward China.

Tensions between Pakistan and the United States grew with the arrival of John Kennedy in the White House. As a senator, Kennedy had been a major supporter of India. He felt even more strongly than Eisenhower that India was a key factor in Asia and that the United States must do more to improve relations with it. Events soon dashed some of these hopes, as described in the following pages, but from Pakistan's perspective the prognosis appeared negative. Washington's offer of military assistance to India in the 1962 Sino-Indian war drove Pakistani leaders to conclude that the special relationship with the West was waning.[203] As a hedge, and to add balancing weight against India, Pakistan turned to China. In late December 1962, Pakistan and China announced an agreement provisionally demarcating their border. In February 1963, Foreign Minister Bhutto signed the agreement during a celebrated trip to Beijing.[204] Thereafter, the United States learned that Premier Chou En-lai planned to visit Pakistan in early 1964. Pakistan sought to calm Washington's reactions to these developments and to rebuff counterpressures, by arguing that China pursued a moderate, cautious foreign policy, despite its rhetoric.[205] Ironically, this view would be shared by Henry Kissinger and Richard Nixon eight years later as they enlisted Pakistan secretly to open the door between the United States and China. But in the early 1960s, Washington and New Delhi shared concerns over Chinese-Pakistani cooperation. Still, in this early period, Pakistan did not factor into India's nuclear policy.

The United States.   American policy in the late 1950s and early 1960s augmented India's capability to acquire nuclear weapons. Although American experts recognized India's capacity to divert its nuclear program into military applications, nonproliferation was a secondary consideration to winning nuclear industry "markets" and containing communist influence in South Asia. Indeed, as discussed later in this section, some in the U.S. executive branch believed that the United States should consider helping India develop nuclear explosives in order to dissipate the political and psychological gains China was expected to achieve with its anticipated detonation of an atomic bomb.

President Eisenhower had never been completely convinced of the wisdom of the U.S. military alliance with Pakistan and was concerned that it harmed relations with India. In 1957, he decided to revise policy toward South Asia. In a January National Security Council (NSC) meeting he said that the accord with Pakistan was "perhaps the worst kind of a plan and a decision we could have made. It was a terrible error, but we now seemed hopelessly involved in it."[206] Eisenhower had come to support India's nonalignment, recognizing, among other factors, that the United States could not afford to maintain India if it became an ally. The reappraisal of policy toward India was recorded in a policy document—NSC 5701—on January 10, 1957.[207] The new guidance recognized India as "very important in itself to United States policy."[208] This importance was magnified by the cold war contest with China and the Soviet Union. U.S. officials further recognized that India interpreted the American alliance with Pakistan "as a potential danger to India's security."[209] Thus NSC 5701 proposed that the United States should not increase military aid to Pakistan. Writing days after the adoption of NSC 5701, implementers of the new U.S. policy understood that there was "no easy 'out' " to the dilemma of seeking better relations with both India and Pakistan, "but with patience there may be a chance eventually to persuade India that its oft expressed fears of United States support of Pakistani aggression are unfounded and indeed harmful to India's aspirations for a reputation of objectivity."[210] This hopeful note would be echoed for decades.

The Eisenhower administration proposed several measures to win Indian approval. The United States should offer increased military assistance, building on India's purchase since 1951 of $38 million in military goods and services. Increased bilateral trade was recommended, along with cultural exchanges. Administration officials decided to "actively encourage India to [consider] U.S. offers for bilateral assistance in the atomic reactor field," emphasizing the U.S. decision "to declassify considerable information about power reactors."[211] Training programs for Indian atomic energy specialists should also be undertaken.[212] These proposals to augment the Indian nuclear program were practically simultaneous to the debate over the IAEA safeguards system that saw the United States accede to India's demands for weaker controls.

India's severe economic distress motivated the Eisenhower administration and some members of Congress, including Senator John Kennedy, to increase U.S. aid to India, bilaterally and through augmented World Bank contributions. The motions for increased aid, however, met congressional opposition due to distaste for India's nonalignment policy, which was seen as anti-American. Still, in 1957 the United States did increase aid to India by a total of $225 million, and in 1958 by an additional $350 million through the World Bank.[213] In May 1959 the Conference on India and the United States gathered in Washington, signifying an incipient "Indian lobby" in the United States. As a result of these initiatives, U.S. aid grew from about $400 million in 1957 to $822 million in 1960, making the United States by far the largest foreign contributor to India.[214]

In December 1959, President Eisenhower became the first American president to visit India. The reception was overwhelming. Millions of Indians lined the streets to greet the presidential motorcade, the largest crowds seen in India since independence.[215] Eisenhower and Nehru discussed the gamut of issues during the four-day visit. Nehru expressed his concern and dismay over growing Chinese belligerence on the border question. Eisenhower emphasized his frustration over the difficulties of pursuing solid relations simultaneously with Pakistan and India and tried to reassure Nehru of his good intentions. The president reaffirmed the U.S. commitment not to permit Pakistan to use American military equipment to attack India.[216] In a private discussion, Nehru stated his desire for a declaration by India and Pakistan that neither would resort to force to settle their disputes, offering that if Pakistan would make such a pledge, India would worry less about U.S. military aid to Pakistan.[217] Seizing the moment, Eisenhower ordered the U.S. ambassador to Pakistan to pursue the no-war pledge with President Ayub Khan. Ayub rejected the initiative baldly, saying that his people would accuse him of giving away Kashmir.[218]

Nineteen sixty brought an opportunity for the United States to demonstrate the elevated importance of India in U.S. policy. Indian Defence Minister Krishna Menon, the acerbic, generally pro-Soviet critic of American policy, approached the U.S. ambassador to India and requested a sale of twenty-nine Fairchild C-119 transport planes.[219] The United States agreed quickly, pleased by this westward gesture after a number of years of no military cooperation. Shortly thereafter, Menon upped the ante by requesting state-of-the-art Sidewinder missiles, which Washington also had promised recently to Pakistan. This put to the test the U.S. policy of elevating India and trying to improve relations simultaneously with India and Pakistan. The State Department declined to take the test. It rejected the Sidewinder sale to India out of ongoing favoritism to Pakistan and recognition of Pakistan's "military alignment with us against the Communist bloc."[220] Pakistan's recent agreement to allow key U.S. intelligence-gathering facilities—a U-2 base and electronic eavesdropping station—to be built and operated on Pakistani territory was simply too valuable to risk in a controversy over American military aid to India. This relatively minor event reaffirmed the Indian view since 1954 that the United States placed Pakistan ahead of India and therefore must be regarded warily.

In September 1960 Eisenhower and Nehru met for the final time at the fall UN General Assembly session. The meeting occurred shortly after Francis Gary Powers's U-2 spy plane based in Pakistan was shot down over Soviet territory, upsetting U.S.-Soviet relations and causing the cancellation of Eisenhower's planned trip to Moscow for a summit with Khrushchev. This in turn dashed hopes for progress in U.S.-Soviet disarmament talks. Thus, when Nehru met with Eisenhower and resumed India's traditional push for progress on disarmament, particularly a nuclear test ban, Eisenhower responded pessimistically, highlighting Soviet recalcitrance on the thorny issue of verifying arms control. Nehru then irked the Americans by joining other nonaligned leaders at the General Assembly in publicly proposing a U.S.-Soviet summit on disarmament. Nehru knew full well that Eisenhower believed that Soviet intransigence made such a summit pointless. India's airy disarmament rhetoric ran so counter to the tough reality of U.S.-Soviet negotiations that American officials found it hard to take the Indians seriously.

Despite tensions over issues such as nuclear arms control, India by early 1961 had announced its interest in obtaining foreign contracts for construction of its first nuclear power plants.[221] (Research reactors were already operating.) An American team visited India from February 29 to March 18, 1960, to assess the desirability and feasibility of supplying American technology for the Indian power program.[222] The team generally concurred with Bhabha's earlier claims that the *operating* costs of nuclear plants located far from India's coal fields would be comparable to conventional power plants at these sites.[223] However, as a November 1959 U.S. Atomic Energy Commission memorandum noted, "the costs of constructing nuclear plants were much higher than those for conventional plants."[224] To make up the difference in capital costs, Bhabha asked the United States for very favorable financing terms: an Export-Import Bank loan to cover the additional capital cost of a nuclear power plant versus a conventional power plant in India, and a deferred payment plan for the reactor fuel India would have to import from the United States. Bhabha requested that the deferred payment be accepted in rupees or Indian commodities, reflecting India's scarce hard currency holdings.[225] The Eisenhower administration viewed Bhabha's request positively and began developing a proposal to consummate the arrangement.

In moving toward what became in 1963 a contract for American construction of two light-water power reactors at Tarapur, American officials were aware in general that India's nuclear program could potentially yield atomic weapons.[226] The Trombay plutonium reprocessing plant, on which construction began in April 1961, represented the key facility required for an Indian bomb. Yet, again, nuclear proliferation was a secondary concern of American policy throughout the mid-1950s to early 1960s.

Dramatic evidence of American ambivalence regarding proliferation can be seen in a recently declassified September 13, 1961, top secret memorandum from State Department official George McGhee to Secretary of State Dean Rusk. Although it is imperative not to overestimate the importance of a single proposed initiative that was not implemented, the McGhee memo indicated that people throughout the State Department seriously contemplated helping India acquire a nuclear explosive. The memo began by citing intelligence estimates that China "could detonate a nuclear device as early as 1962."[227] Such a demonstration of Chinese nuclear power would "likely . . . contribute to feelings that communism is the wave of the future and that Communist China is, or soon will become, too powerful to resist." To avert such a Chinese gain, the memo, which had the qualified concurrence of officers in relevant State Department bureaus, proposed "that it would be desirable if a friendly Asian power beat Communist China to the punch" by detonating a nuclear device first.[228] There was "no likelier candidate than India."[229] The memo estimated that India could "not many months hence" possess "enough fissionable material to produce a nuclear explosion."[230] Without going into exactly how it could be done, the memo suggested that the United

States should explore whether American technical assistance could help induce India to conduct a nuclear explosion ahead of China.

The discussion of the proposal's feasibility and advisability illuminated U.S. assessments of Indian interests and the constraints facing both India and the United States. The memo quoted Nehru during an August 31, 1961, visit to Yugoslavia stating his opposition to nuclear tests "at any time in any place." Yet the memo noted that a spokesman in New Delhi the same day made a less categorical statement, opposing nuclear explosions "except for peaceful purposes under controlled conditions."[231] The latter statement left an opportunity for the United States to explore conditions under which India might wish to conduct an explosion. The memorandum gave low odds that Nehru would agree but cited arguments that could be made to the Indian leader: an Indian detonation could forestall Chinese nuclear blackmail against India; it could reduce Chinese ability to intimidate India's neighbors; and it could nullify the Communist Party of India's (Nehru's chief opposition) opportunity to cite a first Chinese test as "evidence that communism . . . is superior to India's mixed economy."[232]

However, State Department officials also identified seven problems with the proposal, revealing important factors in India's nuclear program and U.S. policy toward the region. First, "India might require considerable technical assistance in order to explode a nuclear device before Communist China does." Second, the United States or the United Kingdom, or both, could be legally blocked from providing such assistance to another country. Third, "We are not good at keeping such things covert." Fourth, there really were not practical uses for a peaceful nuclear explosion, and fallout from it would cause alarm and outcry. Fifth, conducting an explosion without fallout was probably infeasible. Sixth, Pakistan would react extremely negatively and would feel betrayed if the U.S. role came to be known. Seventh, an Indian detonation could be used by China to leverage the Soviet Union to increase assistance to Beijing's nuclear program.[233] The memo reported that U.S. Ambassador to New Delhi John Kenneth Galbraith "strongly opposed" the idea and thought the chances of Nehru's assent were "roughly only one out of fifty."[234] In case the bold proposal were rejected by the U.S. government, or later by the Indians, the memo concluded by recommending "a covertly-mounted informational program" to diminish any benefits of status China might claim as a result of a nuclear explosion.[235]

Rusk ultimately declined McGhee's proposal, noting that he was "not convinced we should depart from our stated policy that we are opposed to the further extension of national nuclear weapons capability."[236] While the speculative proposal had no bearing on U.S. policy, it illustrated how American officials perceived "nuclear politics" in Asia, and particularly in India. Washington's priority of containing Soviet and Chinese influence in South Asia and promoting nuclear technology meant that nonproliferation interests would not impede overall relations with India in this period. However, the United States did not wish for India to develop nuclear weapons even to balance Communist China.

In May 1961, as the Kennedy administration was preparing to greatly boost loans and aid to India, Vice President Lyndon Johnson traveled to India and Pakistan to further America's positive engagement in the region.[237] However, while Johnson's interaction with Nehru was positive, the vice president, like Dulles before him and other key American officials after him, preferred the Pakistani leadership. Johnson told Kennedy that the military dictator and president, Ayub Khan, was "the singularly most impressive and, in his way, responsible head of state encountered on the trip." Johnson further suggested that the United States help modernize Pakistan's military because Ayub "wants to resolve the Kashmir dispute to release Indian and Pakistani troops to deter the Chinese rather than each other."[238] Once again, Pakistani leaders played the cold war chess game expertly to enhance their position in a very different contest with India.

Not surprisingly, Kennedy and Nehru could not manage to improve the relationship significantly. Nehru made his last visit to the United States in November 1961. Tired, distant, and unusually taciturn, the prime minister did little to engage the sympathetic president. Arthur Schlesinger recalled that Kennedy considered Nehru's visit "the worst state visit I have had."[239] Matters did not improve a month later when Indian forces seized the Portuguese colony of Goa, on the western Indian coast, south of Bombay. The extirpation of colonialists from India was inevitable. Yet the manner in which India executed it in Goa aroused U.S. indignation. After the United States harshly criticized India in the United Nations, Nehru and Kennedy exchanged sharp letters, which illuminate the abrasive texture of the two nations' relationship. Kennedy wrote:

> My major concern was and continues to be the effect of the action on our joint tasks, especially in terms of its impact on American opinion. Unfortunately the hard, obvious fact for our people was the resort to force—and by India. This was a shock to the majority who have admired your country's ardent advocacy of peaceful methods, and a reinforcement to those who did not enjoy what they called "irresponsible lectures." It is not an accident that the men who are taking most advantage of the Goa matter here are the same men who are already attacking our aid programs and our support for the UN.[240]

The Goa incident passed quickly enough, but the U.S.-Indian interaction over it foreshadowed the tensions that would emerge over nuclear issues.

Critics in the U.S. Congress now moved to reduce American aid to India, outraged that the recipient of the largest share of American foreign aid was so uncooperative. Kennedy lobbied intensively to resist the congressional move but was once again set back by a development in India. In the summer of 1962, Nehru, under the advice of Menon, agreed to pursue purchase of Soviet MiG-21 fighters on very favorable terms. This alarmed Washington, which proposed a counteroffer on less favorable terms, in conjunction with the United Kingdom. As Ambassador Galbraith noted, "The Senators thought the MiG purchase was a reaction to the cut [in aid]. The Indians thought the cut was punishment for the MiG deal. Since the latter leaked out, no one could say which came first."[241] This affair, too, set a pattern for subsequent interactions between India and the United States, as, for example, when the Brown Amendment of 1995–1996 reopened channels of military assistance to Pakistan.

When China invaded India in November 1962, as recounted earlier, India once again, despite prior rhetoric and tension, turned quickly to the United States for help. In the aftermath of the conflict the United States perceived an opportunity to promote resolution of the Kashmir dispute and to draw India closer to the West. The United States recognized that supplying arms to India would upset Pakistan unless there was an acceptable settlement on Kashmir. A joint British-American mission headed by Averell Harriman traveled to India and Pakistan to seek agreement on a diplomatic process to address Kashmir and to arrange U.S. and British assistance in bolstering India's military. Once again, however, talks over Kashmir failed. As Galbraith recognized in an interview with Dennis Kux, the Indians perceived that the United States was exploiting Nehru's postwar weakness to push India to the table. This left Nehru with only one option to reaffirm India's pride and power: refuse to budge on Kashmir.

The Kennedy administration, in conjunction with the United Kingdom, agreed in December 1962 to provide $120 million of short-term military assistance to India. The size of the package seemed niggardly to the Indians, and Galbraith viewed it as a lost opportunity "to bring India into much closer working association with the West."[242] Kennedy and his advisers still wished to develop a more substantial military assistance package for India in order to help reduce Chinese and Soviet influence in the subcontinent.[243] However, it took more than a year for the U.S. government finally to make an official offer to India, a modest $50 million in military aid for 1965 with no commitment for subsequent years. Some of the delay owed to the slippage in policymaking in the wake of President Kennedy's assassination, but more was due to Pakistan's intense protestations.[244] Try as it might, Washington could not escape from the zero-sum game of Indo-Pak relations and India's determination to maintain the appearance of nonalignment.

Despite the various contretemps of late 1962 and early 1963, American and Indian officials were concluding negotiations begun in 1961 for American supply of India's first nuclear power reactors, to be located at Tarapur, near Bombay. This negotiation was compartmentalized in the sense that neither the Americans nor the Indians claimed that they sought to have the 200-megawatt reactors built for broader security and foreign policy reasons. Both sides explained the desirability of the Tarapur plant (with two reactors housed in one building) narrowly in terms of economic and technological development. The United States wanted to avoid burdening the negotiations with what-ifs regarding India's potential for building nuclear weapons.

Still, the major point of contention in the negotiations was safeguards. Bhabha insisted as always that safeguards infringed on India's sovereignty. American negotiators wanted to cement the deal but were compelled by America's commitment to the IAEA system to press for the first-ever agreement for IAEA safeguards in a state receiving nuclear technology assistance. The parties finally reached a compromise whereby India agreed to use only U.S.-supplied enriched uranium fuel for the plants and would allow the IAEA, for the first time anywhere, to verify that this fuel was used only for peaceful purposes. The agreement also required U.S. approval of any subsequent reprocessing of the spent fuel to separate plutonium, which would in any case remain under safeguards. The major American gain was Indian acceptance of IAEA safeguards. India won limitation of the safeguards solely to the Tarapur facility and only as a quid pro quo for the fuel supplied by the United States, not for supply of the reactor. This would allow India to do what it wished with non-U.S.-supplied spent fuel from the reactor. However, the distinction was cloudy given that the agreement stipulated that the reactor "shall be operated on no other special nuclear material than that made available by the United States." The agreement also specified that no "material, equipment or device transferred to the Government of India . . . will be used for atomic weapons or for research on or development of atomic weapons or for any other military purpose."[245]

The Tarapur agreement immediately engendered some controversy in India. (The agreement would be the subject of acrimonious disputes between the two governments from 1978 through 1982, and again more mildly in 1993.) The Indian debate in 1963 focused not only on the acceptance of safeguards but also on India's choice of an American-supplied enriched uranium reactor instead of a natural uranium reactor, which was the technology on which India's ambitious nuclear plans otherwise relied. The deal's critics feared that the American-supplied technology would weaken India's self-sufficiency, making India dependent on fuel that only the United States (or other states with uranium enrichment facilities) could supply. Whereas India could produce natural uranium fuel indigenously, it had no plans to build an expensive and technologically difficult indigenous uranium enrichment plant. The critics also supposed, erroneously, that India would not need to rely on imports of heavy water if it built only natural uranium reactors. They therefore argued that the Tarapur contract entailed large foreign exchange liabilities.

Critics of the Tarapur deal tended to undervalue the extremely favorable financial terms the United States offered with the Tarapur plant—an $80 million credit at 0.75 percent interest over forty years, ten years more than the contract itself.[246] By 1963, in India as elsewhere, doubts were emerging about the economic viability of nuclear power. The Indian Atomic Energy Commission felt pressed to show economically useful results. Setting aside pride in self-reliance, the AEC argued that only a proven technology would demonstrate the near-term viability of nuclear power in India and provide immediate experience in operating a nuclear power plant in the interstate electricity grid.[247] Subsequent Indian commentators suggested tendentiously that the AEC was obscuring its true motivation, the favorable financial package.[248] This seems to suggest that financing should not have been vital—as if India did not face severe capital constraints. It also neglects the major time delays and cost overruns in building India's subsequent natural uranium reactors. Nationalist critics preferred not to acknowledge the compulsions of India's economic circumstances, the dependence on foreign technological assistance, and the possibility that the nation's ambitious nuclear power plans had been misguided given these circumstances.

The generous support for Tarapur also engendered debate in the U.S. Congress, although much of it transpired after the contract was signed. Objections centered not on the extremely generous terms of credit or the potential proliferation ramifications of the Indian nuclear program, but rather on India's "ungrateful" treatment of the United States. "I wouldn't be so skeptical," Senator George Aiken, a Republican from Vermont cautioned, "if I didn't have something to do with the wheat deal for India. When they were having famine conditions we shipped them wheat and they wouldn't let us land the wheat we were giving them until we paid customs duties on it."[249] Similarly, a congressman complained that American military aid to India in response to the Chinese aggression was prevented from reaching frontline troops by customs officials.[250] Referring to sharp Indian attacks on the U.S. position regarding Kashmir, Joint Committee on Atomic Energy Chairman John O. Pastore offered, "The American taxpayer sometimes is willing to do these things in order to stabilize these governments or so that they will be our friends. . . . But what difference does it make? We are still spending money to be rebuked, and that is a hard thing to take."[251] Still, the desire to promote nuclear power overcame all doubts.

Notwithstanding nuclear boosterism, a growing number of American national security officials began to take the proliferation challenge seriously in 1963. These concerns did not particularly affect the Tarapur negotiations, which had begun earlier. Rather, the emerging debate was prospective, looking ahead as part of a general assessment of future threats and priorities for U.S. nuclear policy in light of a prospective Partial Test Ban Treaty. Pentagon officials in February 1963 estimated that eight additional countries, including India, would be able to acquire rudimentary nuclear weapon capability in the next ten years, and that the cost of producing "a few weapons would come to about 150–175 million dollars."[252] In their memo, the Pentagon analysts noted that "[m]any countries have reduced the lead time and cost of acquiring weapons by getting research reactors and starting nuclear power programs. . . . [A] decision to initiate a 'peaceful' program provides a lower cost option, later, to have a military program."[253] The authors averred that India could conduct a first nuclear test in "4–5 years," but that the motivation to do so was "[l]ow but depends on China."[254] Based on this analysis, the authors concluded that "[t]he continued diffusion of nuclear weapons is clearly not in the interest of the US."[255] Accordingly, the secretary of defense endorsed a *"compre-hensive* test ban" as a "necessary, but not a sufficient condition for keeping the number of nuclear countries small."[256] By comparison, a ban only on atmospheric testing "would have a much more limited effect on diffusion than a comprehensive ban."[257]

Due to Soviet resistance to a comprehensive test ban treaty, the United States, the Soviet Union, and the United Kingdom could manage no more than the Partial Test Ban Treaty. Nehru hailed the treaty as a "watershed" that would "take us towards disarmament and peace."[258] India quickly signed it. While later Indian commentators demeaned the treaty as a half measure, the failure to proscribe underground tests afforded India the opportunity legally to conduct its nuclear explosion in 1974. It would be interesting to know whether Bhabha or other Indian officials discussed this "opening," and whether if a comprehensive ban had been agreed to in 1963 India would have gone forward with its nuclear weapon option. Here, as in most other instances, records of Indian governmental deliberations remain unavailable.

This survey of U.S.-Indian relations through 1963 reveals American policymakers caught in an irreconcilable tension between global cold war imperatives and the local, India-Pakistan conflict. The United States concentrated on Chinese and Soviet moves, seeing India and Pakistan as pawns in this larger game. On occasions when South Asia appeared important in its own right, the United States found itself unable to manage the regional game. The tension between the cold war and regional contests allowed Pakistan, in particular, to manipulate Washington for local advantage. Meanwhile, the zero-sum nature of Indo-Pak relations meant that American efforts to improve ties with one of the subcontinental states alienated the other. Usually India felt itself the aggrieved party, heightening its resentment of the United States. This in turn disposed many Americans against India. However, India still sought and received large measures of American economic aid. And when matters became dire, as during the 1962 Sino-Indian conflict, Nehru turned to the United States for emergency military help. Americans might then have expected an increased measure of gratitude and compliance with American interests, but India instead maintained the independent line and rhetoric that rankled the United States.

Interestingly, American nuclear assistance to India tended to move steadily forward on an independent track. Cold war considerations and the desire to promote the American share in a growing nuclear industry overwhelmed reservations that surrounded other forms of aid. When, in the late 1970s and afterward, nonproliferation became an abiding American policy objective, commentators would disparage the earlier nuclear assistance to India that proved vital to the overall development of India's nuclear establishment. Yet, in the 1950s and early 1960s, U.S. nonproliferation policy remained unfocused. The intelligence community and others recognized the nuclear weapon potential being developed by

India but chose to hope for the best rather than take decisive actions to retard this potential.

Overall, India's foreign relations in the 1948-to-1963 period showed that although Bhabha was consciously developing nuclear weapon capabilities prior to the emergence of a Chinese nuclear threat, international security considerations played little role in shaping Indian nuclear policy. Rather, the main motivations for India's initial plans to acquire the means to produce nuclear explosives had more to do with Bhabha's and Nehru's beliefs that nuclear technology offered India a shortcut to modernity and major power status. By mastering nuclear science and technology—and in the process, acquiring the potential to make nuclear weapons—India could transcend its recent colonial past. Bhabha and his successors also felt that manifesting nuclear prowess could refute racially tinged stereotypes about the capacities of Third World scientists. Nuclear capacity—primarily in the civilian power domain, but if necessary in weapons applications, too—increased India's self-regard and international standing.

TWO

The First Compromise Shift toward a "Peaceful Nuclear Explosive"

1964

Nineteen sixty-four brought pivotal changes to India's nuclear policy. First, Nehru died in May and was replaced by a politician with no international experience, Lal Bahadur Shastri. Then, before Shastri could consolidate authority, China shocked the Indian psyche and altered the international balance of power by detonating its first nuclear explosive device on October 16. This forced the Indian political system to decide what it should do with its own nascent nuclear program. Bhabha clearly wanted to build nuclear explosives, and he quickly attracted strong and passionate allies among the political elite and the press. But the new prime minister and other leading Congress party officials, along with the unobtrusive military, doubted the moral, economic, political, and strategic wisdom of departing from India's declared policy of eschewing nuclear weapons. The illuminating debate proceeded for several months before culminating in a quiet compromise that established India's pattern of nuclear ambiguity. This chapter chronicles that debate in detail, examining the factors that shaped India's nuclear policy for years to come.

BHABHA OUTLINES THE COURSE OF THINGS TO COME, 1964

From January 27 to February 1, 1964, the Pugwash Conference on Science and World Affairs convened in Udaipur, India, to address "Current Problems of Disarmament and World Security." At this meeting Homi Bhabha presented a paper that subtly revealed the strategy and motivation behind the nuclear program he had designed for India beginning in the mid-1950s. Bhabha began by noting that

nuclear weapons coupled with an adequate delivery system can enable a State to acquire the capacity to destroy more or less totally the cities, industry and all important targets in another State. It is then largely irrelevant whether the State so attacked has greater destructive power at its command. With the help of nuclear weapons, therefore, a State can acquire what we may call a position of absolute deterrence even against another having a many times greater destructive power under its control.[1]

Bhabha's description of nuclear deterrence could have applied to any nation or set of nations, but he quickly and tellingly focused on China: "[A] country with a huge population, such as China, must always present a threat to its smaller neighbours, a threat they can only meet either by collective security or by recourse to nuclear weapons to redress the imbalance in size."[2] Given India's policy of nonalignment, Bhabha seemed to be establishing an argument for acquiring nuclear weapons. But instead he took another tack and put the onus of India's nuclear choices on the United States and the Soviet Union. Bhabha proposed that if "any State is to be asked to renounce a possible dependence on nuclear weapons to redress the balance of power against a larger and more powerful State not having nuclear weapons, such as China, its security must be guaranteed by both the major nuclear powers."[3] In other words, if Washington and Moscow did not want India to build nuclear weapons, they had to guarantee India's security.

Bhabha stated that "a number" of countries had the technical capacity and wherewithal to produce nuclear weapons "within the next 5 or 10 years."[4] The production of nuclear weapons would provide small countries with a deliverable nuclear force "against a country not possessing a modern air-force and ground-to-air missiles," such as China. Minimizing the difficulty of obtaining adequate delivery systems, Bhabha continued, "If two countries, one possessing nuclear weapons and the other without them were to be permitted to fight out a war by themselves without any intervention by third parties, the possession of nuclear weapons might perhaps be decisive."[5]

Once again, Bhabha seemed to be supporting the attractiveness of India's developing nuclear weapons to deter China. But here he changed direction and argued that an increase in the number of states with nuclear weapons would harm U.S. and Soviet interests by actually reducing international stability. Thus he suggested that the two superpowers should remove proliferation incentives to countries like India either by providing security guarantees or by leading the way to nuclear disarmament.[6] Indian diplomacy would follow this logic for decades to come.

Bhabha then returned to a theme from his 1956 critique of proposed International Atomic Energy Agency safeguards. He reminded his audience that "any knowledge of operating a reactor for peaceful purposes can be employed later for operating a reactor for military purposes."[7] Moreover,

> it is easy to see that in certain circumstances aid given by the Agency with its full safeguards system in operation could help in accelerating a military programme. Let us assume that the country receiving aid receives from the Agency heavy water or fissile material for a reactor for peaceful purposes. If the country concerned already has

heavy water or fissile material, the loan of the Agency's heavy water or fissile material to that extent liberates the country's own materials for use in military programmes.[8]

In fact, this is how India proceeded to produce the nuclear explosive it tested in 1974, receiving heavy water and other assistance from the United States and Canada, not the IAEA. Bhabha had envisioned this strategy in 1956 when he outlined how states such as India could use international aid under safeguards to augment an unsafeguarded parallel explosives program.[9] It is impossible to know whether Bhabha in early 1964 truly wanted to avert India's pursuit of nuclear weapons or believed that it could be avoided. His personal interest and "faith" in nuclear disarmament always seemed weaker than Nehru's.[10] In any case, he gave his Pugwash audience a clear survey of the problem.

Bhabha's paper contained perhaps the clearest exposition yet of the security considerations that could guide India's nuclear program. Interestingly, the audience at the conference included several individuals who would become major players in India's subsequent nuclear decision making: Vikram Sarabhai, named chairman of the Atomic Energy Commission following Bhabha's death in 1966; V. C. Trivedi, who would become India's principal negotiator in the nonproliferation treaty talks; and Indira Gandhi. Assuming they were paying attention, they gained new insight into the nuclear weapon potential Bhabha and his colleagues had created through the development of India's nuclear program and the weakening of the IAEA safeguard provisions in the 1950s.

NEHRU DIES AND INDIA READIES FOR CHINA'S FIRST NUCLEAR TEST

In early 1964 India announced a five-year defense plan. It called for a doubling of expenditures to $2 billion by 1969. This amounted to 5 percent of national income, a significant burden for a poor nation that had to this point eschewed heavy military expenditures.[11] The United States pledged $500 million in military aid to India over five years, divided between grants and low-interest credits.[12] In implementing this aid, however, a disagreement emerged. India sought three squadrons of high-performance F-104 fighter aircraft, the same type of planes the United States had already supplied Pakistan. American officials, particularly in the Pentagon, steadfastly refused to supply such weapons to India, arguing that they would be of little use against China and would greatly upset U.S. relations with Pakistan.[13] After a simmering bilateral debate, the U.S. military aid package was limited to helping equip six Indian mountain divisions; augmenting communications, transportation, and air defense capabilities; and assisting Indian defense industries.[14] In September 1964 India turned to the Soviet Union to obtain advanced aircraft: forty-five MiG-21s and an agreement to build a Soviet factory in India where another four hundred MiGs were slated to be built. The MiG would become the standard Indian air interceptor.

In April 1964, India and Canada concluded an agreement for Canadian financing of the heavy-water-moderated CANDU (Canadian deuterium-uranium) power reactor—RAPS-I—to be built in the western state of Rajasthan by Indian engineers using Canadian technology and design assistance provided by Atomic Energy of Canada, Ltd. The agreement evidenced India's dependence on Canadian know-how, technology, and capital at this stage of its nuclear program. Canada would supply half the uranium fuel elements for the initial load, and subsequent fuel as requested, in case India could not meet its goals for indigenous fuel production. The agreement also specified other information sharing and assistance from Canada, including blueprints. Canada would provide a loan of $37 million to cover foreign exchange expenses for Canadian technology and services.[15]

As with the Indian-American negotiations over safeguards for the Tarapur plant, Canada and India engaged in difficult negotiations over safeguards that would apply to the Rajasthan station. Yet in this case a quicker solution was found. Canada accepted reciprocal Indian rights to inspect its Douglas Point (Ottawa) power station. India deemed this arrangement equitable and agreed that the technology and fuel provided by Canada would be used only for "peaceful purposes." The failure to define this term precisely led to tense Indian-Canadian discussions in 1971 when India appeared to be preparing to conduct a nuclear explosion. In his book *India's Nuclear Option*, Ashok Kapur recorded that in 1964 when Nehru approved Bhabha's memo describing the deal reached with Canada, he wrote a note in the margin "somewhat as follows": "Apart from building power stations and developing electricity there is always a built-in advantage of defence use if the need should arise."[16]

On May 27 Nehru died, removing independent India's dominant actor from the stage. At home and abroad, Nehru set India's course and represented the nation's wider aspirations. Through him India assumed a larger global presence than the standard measures of power would have allowed. In the important but generally closed domain of nuclear policy, Nehru made it possible for Bhabha to create one of the world's largest and most ambitious nuclear programs. No successive prime minister could be expected to understand all this secretive program's dimensions or fully appreciate the purpose and potential behind it. Nehru's public pronouncements were always perceived as passionate disavowals of Indian interests in seeking nuclear weapons. Thus, his successor, Lal Bahadur Shastri, thought he was inheriting an unambiguously peaceful nuclear program.

Two leaders could hardly be less alike than Nehru and Shastri. Nehru stood large in India and on the world stage—a tall, cosmopolitan aristocrat, highly educated and charismatic. Shastri, barely five feet tall, possessed different attributes. He had quit school at seventeen to join the Indian noncooperation movement in his native Uttar Pradesh, and he had never traveled outside India prior to becoming prime minister. Born poor, he eschewed wealth while rising through Congress party and governmental ranks where others might have enriched themselves through corruption.[17] Shastri maintained deep integrity and modesty throughout his life, becoming known as a conciliator without enemies. This unthreatening decency made him an ideal candidate for prime minister in the minds of the state Congress party leaders who would determine Nehru's successor. Having lived through the accretion of centralized, prime ministerial power during the Nehru years, the state political leaders wanted a weaker center that would allow them greater sway in a more collective leadership. Thus they contrived, with Nehru's support in the months prior to his death, to block the progress of the most likely successor, Morarji Desai, and promoted instead the unassuming Shastri.[18]

On June 2, 1964, Shastri received the reins. Nuclear policy and foreign affairs seemed distant concerns. Shastri's complete lack of knowledge and experience in these areas assumed little importance.

As prime minister, Shastri also took the role of minister of atomic energy. Less than a month into his tenure, the nation's weapon potential rose significantly when the first spent fuel (from the CIRUS research reactor) entered the plutonium reprocessing plant at Trombay.[19] The weapon-grade plutonium contained in this (and subsequent) spent fuel gave India the vital material from which to manufacture a nuclear explosive.[20] Many additional technological steps remained to be taken, and decisions to be made, but the potential of which Bhabha had spoken since the mid-1950s was now in hand. As Bhabha proudly told an All-India Radio audience, the nuclear establishment at Trombay was "by far the largest scientific and technical institution in the country, with a staff of some 1,550 scientists and engineers, and a total staff of nearly 7,000."[21] Bhabha emphasized with some exaggeration the indigenous "design and construction" of the plutonium reprocessing plant.[22] In fact, India based its understanding and design of the plutonium reprocessing plant on declassified U.S. plans for Purex reprocessing. An American firm, Vitro International, designed elements of the Phoenix plant, and the plant relied heavily on imported components and materials, particularly stainless steel. Despite exaggerating India's self-sufficiency in the Phoenix plant's design, Bhabha's central message to the public was that India had joined the world's technological elite.

By the late summer of 1964 the imminence of a Chinese nuclear detonation began to stir an Indian debate. On August 24 the *Statesman* editorialized that Indians now took seriously "Early claims by Mr. Nehru, presumably on Dr. Bhabha's assurance," that India had the know-how to build atomic weapons.[23] The paper noted that some in India wanted a change from the "unequivocal pledges not to use atomic energy for military purposes," and "they may become more vocal after the explosion of the first Chinese bomb."[24] Yet, the paper cautioned, "It is also necessary to remember that in the absence of an adequate delivery system, the bomb would make little difference to India's military strength." Mindful that India faced a severe food crisis and huge development challenges, the editorial concluded that "both bomb-production and effective delivery could be secured if the price is paid for it in terms of economic deprivation. But no responsible person has suggested that the object is worth that price; it could only become so under circumstances of dire military peril which do not exist now."[25] This editorial captured the dilemma that imposed caution on Indian leaders for decades to come. Yet, the pressure for India to flex its nuclear muscle was mounting rapidly.

On September 29, American Secretary of State Dean Rusk sought to steal some of China's thunder by announcing that the United States expected China to conduct an atmospheric nuclear test in the near future.[26] Less than a week later, Bhabha began a public and behind-the-scenes effort to push Shastri and the rest of the government to authorize more work targeted directly to the military applications of nuclear energy. Visiting London on October 4, he declared that India could explode an atom bomb within eighteen months of a decision to do so but added, "I do not think such a decision will be taken."[27] Those who knew Bhabha must have recognized that he was not endorsing forbearance but rather was trying to arouse domestic pressure for a bomb to overcome the Gandhian inclinations of the prime minister.[28] Shastri was at the time attending a Conference of Non-aligned Nations in Cairo, where he urged leaders of other states to "persuade China to desist from developing nuclear weapons." He added that India's nuclear establishment was "under firm orders not to make a single experiment, not to perfect a single device which is not needed for peaceful uses of atomic energy."[29] Bhabha and Shastri were destined to clash.

On October 9 the rising journalistic star Inder Malhotra issued a commentary in the *Statesman* predicting that the government could not and should not maintain the Nehruvian nuclear policy in the aftermath of the anticipated Chinese explosion. He began by decrying the government's casual response to Rusk's announcement of the forthcoming Chinese test and noted portentously that even some in the Congress party disliked the government's line.[30] Citing expert estimates that China would require "at least 10 years to develop a nuclear armoury of any consequence," Malhotra suggested that the "first fruits of the Chinese nuclear explosion will be psychological and political rather than military."[31] One aspect of the psychological gain would be to "give the coloured peoples in the world a sense of pride that one of them has been able to break what has hitherto been a monopoly of the white nations."[32] This racial dimension of the nuclear issue would remain an important, if often unstated, feature of Indian nuclear policy and U.S.-Indian nuclear diplomacy for decades to come.

Malhotra then rehearsed the arguments against departing from Nehru's and Shastri's eschewal of bomb building. First, a switch in policy would "destroy the 'image' India has so assiduously built as a uniquely peaceful nation."[33] Second, China would not be able to use nuclear weapons against India because it would trigger "thermo-nuclear retaliation by the two super Powers—the USA and the USSR." Third, India could take the high road and rally the nonaligned movement and the major powers to criticize China, thus turning psychology and politics against Beijing.

Without refuting these arguments directly, Malhotra identified and challenged the most potent reason against India's producing nuclear weapons—economics.

He argued that the nuclear threat simply negated the "wisdom of the decision not to divert resources from economic development to the manufacture of atomic weapons."Any price must be paid for security. Malhotra correctly predicted that "[t]he pressure for rethinking on this policy is therefore bound to grow; it is likely to emanate from the Opposition and from within the Congress Party."[34]

SIX WEEKS OF DEBATE SHIFT INDIA'S NUCLEAR POLICY, OCTOBER 16 TO NOVEMBER 27, 1964

The Chinese blast came on October 16. Shastri declared it a shock and danger to world peace.[35] However, he and the Indian press were somewhat distracted by the announcement a day earlier of Khruschev's fall from Soviet power. Hence the initial tone of Indian reactions was muted. Defence Minister Y. B. Chavan asserted that the bomb would not significantly increase China's military strength, pointing out that the short-term threat remained Chinese conventional forces.[36] India at this time relied on American analysis of the technology used in the Chinese device. President Johnson had emphasized in his October 16 announcement of the Chinese test that it was "a crude device" and that China still was far from achieving an effective nuclear capability.[37] (The United States and India later learned that the device was not so crude. This reassessment elevated public mistrust of the Indian government's handling of the challenge.) On October 18, President Lyndon Johnson sought further to reassure India and others by giving a major speech. He declared that "the nations that do not seek nuclear weapons can be sure that if they need our strong support against some threat of nuclear blackmail, then they will have it."[38] This vague suggestion of U.S. backing became important in the coming deliberations over India's national nuclear policy.

Debate intensified with each succeeding day and week. Because the new prime minister faced a serious struggle to consolidate his power within the Congress party, it is important to sketch the debate in some chronological detail. In politics the trend and momentum of debates matter greatly. If a "storm" appears to be subsiding, politicians tend to conclude that existing policies or coalitions can be maintained. If the storm continues to mount, then change may be required for political survival.

Two days after the Chinese test, the leader of the Samyukta Socialist Party, Nath Pai, told a press conference that India should actively consider acquiring a nuclear deterrent of its own. According to the daily *Indian Express*, Nath Pai urged "corrective measures to enable the country [to] regain its lost prestige in the comity of nations."[39] Yet he saw the nuclear challenge in a broader domestic context, arguing that the government must concentrate on solving the food crisis by ensuring equitable distribution at fair prices.[40] Foreign policy was only a secondary, though important, concern. The opposition was seizing on the Chinese test to challenge the overall leadership of the Shastri government.[41]

At this early stage in the debate, the major newspapers editorialized in favor of the government line. The *Hindustan Times* on October 19, for example, averred that "China's bomb is a grave provocation to India. . . . [N]evertheless prudence demands that our response is sober and realistic. Nothing would suit Mao's book better than our being hustled into a nuclear race."[42] An American Embassy cable to the State Department reported that in an October 20 conversation, Joint Secretary of the Ministry of External Affairs V. C. Trivedi told an embassy official that India remained committed to restrict its nuclear program to peaceful uses only.[43] "On the other hand," Trivedi acknowledged, according to the cable, "no one could at present gauge the degree of pressure that might be mounted on the Government to alter its present policy."[44]

In terms of India's technical capability at this time, an American National Intelligence Estimate completed on October 21 concluded that "India, given the facilities it now has, could produce and test a first nuclear device in one to three years after a decision to do so."[45] The estimate noted that the capacity of the plutonium separation plant at Trombay appeared excessive compared with the needs of India's peaceful nuclear program and that the plant was producing weapon-usable plutonium that a growing number of metallurgical specialists presumably could fashion into bomb cores.[46] Like Bhabha, the CIA's analysis overestimated the pace and effectiveness with which the Indian nuclear establishment would proceed and underestimated the competing interests that would dampen the urgency of producing the bomb.

Eight days after the Chinese test, Bhabha weighed into the debate with a now legendary broadcast on All India Radio. Echoing his Pugwash presentation in January, Bhabha told his listeners that "atomic weapons give a State possessing them in adequate numbers a deterrent power against attack from a much stronger State."[47] Not only were nuclear weapons a uniquely effective deterrent, they were also remarkably cheap, according to Bhabha. Citing a paper by American nuclear experts, Bhabha reported that "A 10 kiloton explosion . . . would cost $350,000 or Rs. 17.5 lakhs . . . while a two megaton explosion, i.e. one equivalent to 2 million tons of TNT, would cost $600,000 or Rs. 30 lakhs. On the other hand, at current prices of TNT, 2 million tons of it would cost some Rs. 150 crores [$300 million]."[48] Bhabha acknowledged that these figures derived from a study on "the peaceful uses of atomic explosions" for civil engineering projects like canals, harbors, and tunnels.[49] This was one of the earliest prominent invocations of the utility of peaceful nuclear explosives. Bhabha recognized the technical similarity between peaceful nuclear explosives and nuclear weapons when he continued his broadcast by speaking in terms of the affordability of "atomic bombs," not peaceful nuclear explosives. Extrapolating from the American figures, he concluded that "a stockpile of some 50 atomic bombs would cost under Rs. 10 crores [$21 million] and a stockpile of 50 two-megaton hydrogen bombs something of the order of Rs. 15 crores [$31.5 million]."[50] These cost projections became central in the subsequent Indian debate. They were grossly misleading insofar as they neglected the major costs of the reactors and reprocessing facilities required to produce the explosive materials and the associated costs of other infrastructure to design and produce weapons. The U.S. government soon sought to correct this mistaken cost estimate, and other Indian scientists warned the leadership that Bhabha's numbers were highly unreliable. Still, as the debate went on, Indian bomb advocates seized on Bhabha's argument about the utility and affordability of these devices.

Bhabha ended his radio address by urging the United Nations and the "great powers" to pursue nuclear disarmament in order "to create a climate favourable to countries which have the capability of making atomic weapons, but have voluntarily refrained from doing so."[51] Implicit in this statement and what had preceded it was the suggestion that if the great powers and the United Nations failed to achieve nuclear and general disarmament soon, states like India would likely move to acquire their own deterrent arsenals.

Press accounts of Bhabha's broadcast focused on "the low cost of nuclear weapons" and repeated his call for exertions by the world powers to remove this new threat.[52] The address was not interpreted publicly as a call to nuclear arms. However, on October 25, the president of the Delhi Pradesh Congress Committee, Mushtaq Ahmed, became the first important Congress party official to split with government policy and urge that "the only course for India is to produce her own atom bomb to defend herself."[53] The Hindu-nationalist Jana Sangh Party escalated its push for nuclear weapons in the October 26 edition of its weekly magazine, *Organiser:* "The eunuch Government decided years ago in its *ahimsic* [non-violent] idiocy to spend crores on nuclear power but not to use the same crores on developing the nuclear bomb. We had the chance to do it before China did it and so we could tell that we meant business and that we were ahead of China. In our criminal folly we missed it."[54] The rudiments of political struggle were now appearing.

On October 27 an executive body of the Congress party met to draft policy resolutions to be adopted at a major All India Congress Committee (AICC) meeting scheduled for November 7. The draft resolution, prepared by Foreign Minister Swaran Singh, approved the government's policy not to manufacture atomic bombs. However, in New Delhi, an intense debate was brewing, including within the Congress party.[55]

On October 28 the *Indian Express* published "a quick survey" of public opinion leaders across India. It revealed that Indian elites now took "for granted" Bhabha's claim that India could manufacture nuclear weapons within eighteen months.[56] However, "after the first mental shock caused by the Chinese announcement, Indian public opinion has generally sobered down to consider other aspects of the question of manufacturing atomic weapons."[57] According to the survey, "[T]he consensus of responsible thinking is that India should not rush into a mad race for nuclear arms." Those urging caution believed "that India cannot afford to get into a programme of manufacturing and stockpiling atom bombs without serious repercussions on its economy." In addition, many respondents did not believe that possessing atom bombs would solve "any problem." Many respondents felt that if China were to use or threaten to use nuclear weapons against India, the major powers would get drawn into the matter—a prospect that would deter China. Yet little informed analysis occurred of Washington's or Moscow's willingness and ability to intervene on India's behalf. Some argued that India should seek formal treaty commitments from the United States and the United Kingdom, while others, particularly the Communist parties, refused to countenance abandonment of nonalignment. Some put stock in a major push for global nuclear disarmament, while others discounted the likely effectiveness of such efforts. Thus, at this early stage of the debate, opinion on the narrower question of India's building nuclear weapons was negative, while answers to the broader problem of India's overall security strategy remained diffuse.

Cables from American diplomats in New Delhi gave Washington insight into the Indian debate. An October 29 dispatch reported that

> there appears to be a considerable body of opinion both within and outside Congress Party which favors Indian construction of bomb regardless of cost and of prior GOI [Government of India] pledges to restrict itself to peaceful uses of nuclear power. Support for moving ahead on bomb construction doubtless given fillip when Bhabha made disingenuous statement to radio audience Oct 24 that "atom bomb explosion" on same dimensions as Hiroshima would only cost India about $350,000.[58]

The cable continued with an informed analysis of the political dynamic affecting Prime Minister Shastri:

> Primin may well find himself in difficult position if he persists in no-bomb policy. His opponents within Congress are likely to make effort to capitalize on issue, which is ready-made one for those who have alleged that Shastri (unlike Morarji [Desai]) would be "weak" primin.[59]

Opposition attacks on the government's no-bomb line were manageable. The serious threat was from within the Congress party itself. And here, according to the U.S. Embassy cable, members already had lost confidence in Shastri's leadership due to his inability to solve a major food shortage.[60]

Indeed, the food crisis and related political turmoil, not the Chinese nuclear test, preoccupied the Indian polity. Indian consumers confronted scarce supplies of basic foodstuffs and rising prices of commodities that were available. This growing crisis stemmed from complex factors; defense spending certainly contributed significantly to it.[61] The defense budget for 1964, the equivalent of $1.8 billion, amounted to 28 percent of total government spending.[62] Clearly this expenditure was sucking resources away from agricultural and other investments. By comparison, spending on nuclear activities in 1964—$63 million—amounted to 1 percent of the total national budget.[63] From 1954 through 1964, U.S. government analysts concluded that India had spent $220 million on the nuclear program through the Department of Atomic Energy.[64] Thus, although spending on the nuclear program was rising rapidly in the early 1960s and was a major share of all government investment in scientific research and development, the direct impact on the economic crisis was small compared to defense spending.

In any case, to remain in power Shastri had to redress the food crisis. This required changes in the central Plan, something that political leaders in the states favored over the objections of the central planners. Shastri now set about reorganizing the government policymaking system, trying to shift power from the central Planning Commission, which had enjoyed preeminence under Nehru, to the central ministries and the states themselves.[65] In July, Shastri accentuated the shift in power by forming his own prime minister's secretariat to strengthen his weak hand against rivals in the Congress party who held cabinet positions and Planning Commission posts.[66] Shastri and his representatives struggled ineffectively through much of 1964 to devise mechanisms and incentives for increasing food production and stimulating deliveries to markets, especially from states with surpluses to those with shortages.[67] The crisis mounted. In September, weeks before the Chinese nuclear test, the opposition had generated enough support to compel a no-confidence debate against the government in the Lok Sabha. Shastri survived, but was chastened. "Simultaneously," Francine Frankel recorded, "Congress ministries in the states were bombarded with a spate of no-confidence motions that charged them with 'abject failure to tackle the food situation.' "[68] Meanwhile, Communist party factions were preparing to mobilize violent campaigns against the government.[69] In this menacing climate, Shastri tentatively began to reverse course and strengthen the central government's powers to compel producers to bring food to market and the states to impose rationing. Either way he turned, the prospects looked dim.

With domestic challenges lurking in the background and foreground, the debate on India's nuclear policy continued to mount. A second U.S. Embassy cable on October 29 recorded that an Indian Ministry of External Affairs official had told embassy personnel that "pressures within GOI for India to develop its own bomb were building up."[70] According to this informed source, "Bhabha was leading advocate for this group and he was actively campaigning to go down nuclear road."[71] Indeed, a six-hour discussion of nuclear policy had just occurred in a cabinet meeting, with Minister of External Affairs Swaran Singh and Minister of Railways and Congress party heavyweight S. K. Patil joining Bhabha in advocating a nuclear weapon–building program.[72] According to U.S. intelligence sources, only two cabinet ministers—Defence Minister Y. B. Chavan and Food and Agriculture Minister C. Subramaniam—opposed. In the first hint of the incremental process that would lead to the 1974 nuclear test, the Ministry of External Affairs source cited previously said that "discussions had gone far enough for Shastri to authorize Bhabha to come up with estimate of what was involved in India's attempting an underground 'explosion.' "[73]

Assuming that this source was correct, Shastri's authorization represented a concession to Bhabha's pressure and an important move forward. It also raises historical questions: If Bhabha had not already estimated what it would take for

India to conduct an explosion, how could he reasonably have been claiming for years that India could produce a bomb within twelve to eighteen months of a decision to do so? Was his October 24 radio statement that a ten-kiloton blast would cost $350,000 based on anything more than a misleading figure offered by American scientists in reference to American experiences? To have been making these prognostications for at least five years, Bhabha should have had some detailed analysis of the feasibility, technical requirements, and costs of building a bomb in India. If such detailed analysis existed, a new estimate was not needed. If it did not exist, Bhabha's earlier claims amounted to propaganda or salesmanship. The latter seems to have been the case. In a 1996 interview, Raja Ramanna, the scientist who in January 1965 was asked to direct the nuclear explosive project, said, "I don't think it would have been possible to do what Bhabha said—build a device in 18 months. A crash program could have been done, I suppose, but it would have been very expensive."[74]

In the debate to this point and subsequently, little serious analysis of India's technical capabilities was heard. Despite Bhabha's bombs-in-eighteen-months claims, India would only *begin* to acquire separated weapon-usable plutonium in early 1965. Of India's three research reactors, the Canadian-designed and cooperatively built CIRUS provided the only source of plutonium. It was theoretically capable of producing enough plutonium annually for no more than two rudimentary, Nagasaki-type devices. The Phoenix plutonium separation plant at Trombay had the capacity to reprocess more spent fuel than India could produce with its current and prospective reactors or that India could conceivably use for experimental or economic purposes. By 1964 India also had a large number of specialists working on plutonium metallurgy.[75] Again, this was ostensibly to develop know-how for manufacturing plutonium-based fuel for breeder reactors, although no such reactors were in the immediate offing. These metallurgists would be invaluable for manufacturing the fissionable core of a nuclear explosive. However, to produce a nuclear explosive would require additional know-how and equipment that was simply assumed by Indians and U.S. intelligence analysts in 1964 to be nonproblematic. An explosive device would still need to be designed. The difficulty of designing, producing, and testing the conventional high explosives required to compress the plutonium cores for a high-yield fission explosion would still have to be overcome. Neutron sources to initiate the chain reaction would still have to be produced. Even if all the elements of a nuclear explosive could be acquired and mastered, adequate means to deliver these weapons would have to be bought or built. These and other technical challenges proved much more difficult to meet than the debaters in 1964 recognized. Indeed, the 1964 debate stands out for its technical naïveté, in part because Bhabha wielded such authority and information was so tightly controlled that scientists who might have provided checks and balances remained silently sidelined.

Leaving aside technical issues, two forceful press commentaries on October 30 and 31 illuminated the policy debate. In the first, Inder Malhotra sharpened his earlier call for a more robust nuclear policy. He began by reporting that the Chinese bomb was actually more sophisticated than had first been assumed—it was made not of plutonium but of harder-to-produce enriched uranium.[76] Worse, China was moving rapidly to acquire the ability to deliver its bombs by "rockets," not merely aircraft. Missiles could render "most North Indian towns and almost all our major industrial centres . . . highly vulnerable targets."[77] Malhotra's threat assessment greatly overestimated China's interest in targeting India and neglected the Chinese priority in deterring the United States, which had threatened China with nuclear weapons in the Taiwan Strait crisis of 1954–1955, and the Soviet Union, which had broken with China.[78] As if the military threat were not bad enough, Malhotra argued that the "political and psychological consequences" were worse than the Indian political elite predicted. Contrary to expectations, the world's major powers, including the Soviet Union, had not reacted potently to punish or constrain China. "Under these circumstances," Malhotra suggested, "it seems reasonably clear that the Congress Working Committee's verdict against the manufacture of a nuclear bomb in India will not be accepted by Parliament and the people as the final word on the subject."[79]

Malhotra then urged a more open and thorough national debate, indicating his own view that it would be impossible to live with a decision not to make "the bomb" if an acute security threat emerged. To clinch his argument, the journalist turned to Bhabha: "Dr. Homi J. Bhabha, who is more competent to speak on the subject than most pundits, has made two important contributions to the debate. He has dispelled the belief that the cost of nuclear weapons is totally prohibitive; and he has pointed out that the only deterrent to a nuclear bomb is another nuclear bomb. Nothing else."[80]

If the Malhotra article represented a classic Realist case for nuclear weapons, a divergent, singularly Indian argument was offered the next day by Romesh Thapar in the *Economic Weekly*. This article, too, is worth examining in detail as it elucidated the tensions that affected India's nuclear policy for decades to come. The article began by reminding readers that the nuclear debate was occurring against the backdrop of "a fast deteriorating economic situation" that was demanding the "time and energy" of Indian decision makers.[81] Thapar cataloged a range of domestic and international issues besetting the prime minister and asked whether the threat from China was actually a military one, and whether it required a nuclear device in response. "[I]s the demand for an Indian bomb dictated by political calculations? . . . Does India need a bomb, or has she to lead a campaign to create an international pool of nuclear weapons and materials under an UN agency which guarantees the security of non-nuclear nations?"[82]

Thapar recognized the argument that nuclear weapons were required to put India into "the core of a power system" led by nuclear weapon states, now including China. But he noted that Indian bomb advocates overlooked "the political and economic techniques" by which the Communist powers mobilized their people in "a forced march."[83] India was not a chauvinistic or totalitarian state—

this was its genius. Yet, "Rapidly, nuclear-inspired, we create an image of ourselves which inevitably must have heavy Hindu overtones. A tremendous force of public opinion is built to permit the existing elite to mobilise and commandeer the people, chaining them to the wheels of production."[84] The identity of India as a secular democracy could be imperiled by the nationalism or chauvinism that would likely attend a crash program to build nuclear weapons. Whereas Malhotra and others tended to let the international environment set India's priorities and national identity, Thapar argued that "possession of a nuclear weapon does not give us the key to the future. Or as Shastri told the chief ministers, 'Our strength even in relations to externals lies in what our real strength is within.' "[85]

Here Thapar turned on the potent figure of Bhabha. "Dr Bhabha tempts us with the idea that we can produce the bomb within eighteen months. He has even priced the bomb—just 17 lakhs of rupees, cheaper than one of those Boeings we take little notice of."[86] But "who is going to check these budgetings of the Atomic Energy Commission? Moreover, is it possible to prevent the escalation of costs once the programme is under way?"[87] This questioning of Bhabha and the autonomy of the AEC departed bravely from the norm and pinpointed a major liability of India's nuclear decision making at the time and subsequently. Thapar argued prophetically that

> the sooner policy-makers in the Capital purge themselves of the thought that the bomb (atom or hydrogen!) could divert us like the proverbial circus, or that its detonation on the eve of the next elections would ensure a smashing victory for the ruling party at the polls, the better for all concerned. A bomb held by a beggar does not make him king when many others have more bombs than he and the capacity to deliver them where they hurt most.[88]

Instead of the bomb, the nation's fate rested on solving the economic crisis and ordering the political system, Thapar concluded.

Indian leaders would struggle for decades to balance Thapar's domestic considerations with Malhotra's "great power" arguments for producing nuclear weapons. The emerging policy of the "nuclear option" would reflect the unique Indian attempt to resolve this tension and gain the international status and deterrent power provided by nuclear weapon capability while preserving the interests of economics and national identity that militated against producing a nuclear arsenal. However, rather than resolving the tension between the opposing themes set forth by Malhotra and Thapar, the nuclear option would only manage it.

As the polity moved closer to the important meeting of the All India Congress Committee from November 7 to 9, Shastri continued publicly to emphasize the priority of rallying the international community—particularly the United States and the Soviet Union—to address the danger of nuclear proliferation in ways that would relieve threats to India. He was buttressed in this by a plea from the Swatantra Party's general secretary for the government to seek a nuclear umbrella from the United States.[89] The two Communist parties also argued, for different reasons, against acquiring nuclear weapons.[90]

When the AICC gathered, the party's leaders were surprised to receive a petition signed by one hundred members urging a closed debate on the nuclear issue, wherein a large number of the petitioners would demand that India acquire "an independent nuclear deterrent to protect herself against any possible threat from China."[91] Indeed, at the meeting, "the majority of speakers came out strongly and frankly in favour of India manufacturing atom bombs," according to the *Economic Weekly*.[92] However, Shastri and other top Congress figures counterattacked successfully. The *Hindustan Times* called Shastri's move "nothing short of a miracle."[93] On November 8, the AICC unanimously passed a resolution declaring that, in the summary of the *Hindu*, "India would continue to utilise nuclear energy for peaceful purposes and that India would not enter into a nuclear arms race."[94] Shastri declared, "We cannot at present think in terms of making atomic bombs in India. We must try to eliminate the atomic bombs in the world rather than enter into a nuclear arms competition."[95]

Shastri believed in this singular Indian mission, as Mahatma Gandhi and Jawaharlal Nehru had. Yet, he offered no concrete strategy for compelling or persuading the nuclear weapon states, including China, to give up their nuclear arms. Recognizing the political inadequacy of his largely rhetorical nuclear policy, Shastri and other Congress leaders were compelled to gesture positively toward those who demanded a major change of policy. The final resolution proclaimed that "efforts should be redoubled for the development of peaceful uses of atomic energy for the prosperity and well-being of the Indian people."[96] This ambiguous statement intimated that the peaceful nuclear program could produce explosives and it foreshadowed a policy shift that soon followed.

Explaining his anti-bomb policy to doubting party colleagues, Shastri focused on the economic and moral-political costs. He argued that production of a single atom bomb would cost Rs. 400 to 500 million ($84–105 million)—not the Rs. 100 million Bhabha claimed would be required for *fifty* atomic bombs. Noting that the nation was already suffering badly from the conventional arms buildup, Shastri argued that bomb building would force the abandonment of economic development plans.[97] Lest the disputation with Bhabha be lost on the audience, Shastri added that "scientists should realise that it was the responsibility of the Government to defend the country and adopt appropriate measures."[98] This was a clear warning to Bhabha to butt out of policymaking. Beyond economics, Shastri argued, as reported in the *Hindu*, that "the possession of nuclear weapons would be directly opposed to the policy of peace and non-violence" taught by Gandhi and Nehru.[99] Finally, were India to build nuclear weapons, he worried that "she could not be content with one or two bombs. The spirit of competition was bound to capture her."[100]

Although Shastri, Krishna Menon, and other Congress leaders carried the day, they still did not offer a compelling strategy for defending India's sovereignty. The primacy of domestic considerations was indicated by the three-tiered headline the *Hindustan Times* devoted to the AICC meeting: "AICC Keeps Rationing Issue Still Open—Food Policy Endorsed—PM Beats Off Challenge of 'Bomb Men.' "[101] India's greatest challenge remained the feeding of its people; nuclear policy was the province of a few scientists and politicians. The *Times of India* suggested that the debate was not over and "a fairly substantial body of opinion [remains] in support of the view that the only answer to the Chinese bomb is an Indian bomb of comparable or greater power." However, the newspaper concluded that the central point was that "a nuclear bomb is not feasible and, even if it were, would be entirely inconsistent with the country's interests."[102]

Over the next twelve days leading to a major Lok Sabha debate on foreign policy, advocates of building the bomb continued their campaign. The Praja Socialist Party weekly, *Janata*, editorialized on November 15 that "[m]uch nonsense had been said about not incurring the expense and sin of manufacturing nuclear weapons. There is really no justification for not making them when we have busied ourselves in the last two years in acquiring other instruments of modern war and even entering into the production of jet aircraft."[103] The *Economic Weekly* noted critically that the chief alternative being proposed to India's production of atomic weapons was alliance with the "West" but that such a move would jettison "the basic principles of our foreign policy or our national interest," namely nonalignment.[104]

More interestingly, Homi Bhabha on November 17 sought to rectify the impression that he supported acquisition of nuclear weapons. According to the *Times of India* account, he told the press that he opposed "India being stampeded into developing [a] nuclear arsenal merely because China has detonated a nuclear device."[105] Somewhat chastened by Shastri's and Menon's indirect attacks on his October 24 radio broadcast, Bhabha restated that American scientists were the source of his figures on the cost of a peaceful nuclear explosion. However, he did not back down about the cost-effectiveness of nuclear explosive power. He added that India's Atomic Energy Establishment at Trombay had accomplished a great deal over the past decade and planned to do more. "The essential point then," according to the *Times of India* account, "is not that India is incapable of making nuclear weapons, or cannot afford these in a purely economic sense, or cannot deliver them, or has nowhere to test them but that it is determined not to produce these on larger political considerations."[106] The headline conveying Bhabha's statement, "Atomic Energy for Peaceful Purposes—Bhabha Favours Policy," suggested he was once again aligned with the nation's leadership, but his message still favored nuclear robustness. (The hawkish interpretation of Bhabha's remarks certainly registered in Pakistan. *Dawn* reported on November 21 that Pakistani officials believed Bhabha was leading India on a course to produce nuclear weapons. "The point is that if India does not intend to manufacture these weapon [sic], why should India carry on research in their manufacture. . . . It is certain that India is not wasting its money unnecessarily in a purposeless experimentation without any intention to manufacture the atomic arms.")[107]

The Lok Sabha met November 23 and 24 to debate India's foreign policy for the first time since Nehru's death. The Parliament had been "warmed up" for the scheduled debate by Shastri's mishandling earlier in the day of several questions during "Question Hour." A parliamentarian, Hem Barua, had tauntingly asked the prime minister if the government's policy of not producing nuclear weapons was based on expert deliberations or rather "pre-conceived notions of half-baked morality." Shastri deflected the barb—as Prime Minister Morarji Desai would deflect a similar charge in 1978—but was then asked what the government would do if China attacked India with nuclear weapons. He replied, "Our policy stands, but who can guarantee what will happen in the future?"[108] This less-than-reassuring performance whetted the appetites of Shastri's critics within and outside the Congress party.

Three alternative motions on nuclear policy were proffered in the Lok Sabha's foreign policy debate: one called for immediate production of an atom bomb; one called for embarking on "nuclear-based defence installations in the country"; a third called for a general reorienting of foreign policy in light of the Chinese bomb. The debate revealed the cost of Nehru's dominance of postindependence foreign policy. Having been largely superfluous in the past, the parliamentarians lacked the expertise and sophistication to conduct a systematic analysis and debate of the nuclear issue. Parliaments around the world frequently betray ignorance of the arcana of nuclear doctrine and strategy; they are elected primarily to deal with matters closer to the pocketbooks, stomachs, and values of their constituents. The Indian Parliament suffered more than others from the absence of expert staffing and contributions from independent analysts. The debate wandered over and through several contentious issues with no clear resolution.[109]

Most broadly, the debaters in the Lok Sabha wrestled with the future viability of the Gandhian-Nehruvian legacy of nonviolence and India's singular moral approach to international affairs. The 1962 defeat by China had already raised doubts about this legacy. Critics, including many in the Congress party, believed that the real world demanded a more hardheaded, militarily robust approach to national security. Now that Nehru had passed from the scene, these indelicate questions could be raised. Shastri had invited attack with his refusal to consider changing India's purely peaceful nuclear policy and his statement at the Guntur AICC meeting in early November that Gandhi's and Nehru's "message of peace, nonviolence and disarmament" must guide India's approach.[110] Nath Pai, the leader of the Praja Socialist Party faction in the newly merged Samyukta Socialist Party, fired the first shot in the Lok Sabha debate: "Instead of making a very dispassionate and calm assessment of the Chinese possession of this dangerous, deadly weapon, we have been indulging once again in sentimental platitudes, confusing the whole issue and unnecessarily dragging [into the debate] Mahatma Gandhi, Pandit Jawaharlal Nehru and, for good measure, Lord Buddha and Samrat Ashoka also."[111]

The majority of subsequent speakers joined Nath Pai in questioning the sufficiency of moral exhortation in redressing the threat now posed by China. However, two speakers prior to Shastri—Bakar Ali Mirza and Krishna Menon—invoked Nehru and India's moral singularity to argue against seeking nuclear weapons.[112] Their Gandhian-Nehruvian understanding of India's national identity clearly represented an important and widespread value.

Security or military strategy emerged as a major theme in the debate only in the broadest sense of the terms. Parliamentarians offered no systematic analysis of the conventional or nuclear threat posed by China or of the military and diplomatic strategies India might pursue to reduce or counter these threats. Speakers generally took it for granted that Bhabha was right and India could produce an atomic bomb within approximately eighteen months if the government decided to do so.[113] The parliamentarians did not analyze the technical requirements of a militarily meaningful nuclear deterrent.[114] Instead, they offered highly generalized political notions of the new strategic environment and how India might operate within it.

M. R. Masani, the general secretary of the Swatantra Party, argued that China's acquisition of the bomb posed not a military threat but rather a psychological and political one.[115] He asserted plausibly that Russian technological assistance lay behind the Chinese bomb and argued, erroneously, that Moscow and Beijing would draw closer in the future.[116] Thus, India's policy of nonalignment would become untenable and India should instead seek alliance with the West to counter the Soviet-Chinese combination. While Masani's approach amounted to an explicit abandonment of nonalignment, Defence Minister Y. B. Chavan had days earlier suggested implicitly that India could be protected by the balance-of-power dynamics among the nuclear weapon states: "If any country uses nuclear weapons, it would not remain a local conflict. It would mean escalation into a major war." Chavan continued, "If such a war were to break out, we have friends to support us."[117] In this view, India did not have to abandon nonalignment but could simply rely tacitly on the two nuclear superpowers to deter China. Yet, by the time of the Lok Sabha debate, this sanguine outlook apparently had faded. No parliamentarian argued that India could passively rest its security on the belief that the United States or the Soviet Union, or both, would intercede decisively if China threatened or actually used nuclear weapons against India.

For those in the Lok Sabha who considered the Chinese a direct threat, India had two choices: to seek a nuclear security guarantee from the West or to counter the Chinese threat alone. Bhagwat Jha Azad of the Congress party represented the latter school of thought. He argued that Chinese intimidation required India to be prepared to "go all out to use nuclear power for the defence of the country."[118] Nath Pai lambasted the notion of turning to the United States for security assistance. He pointedly reminded the House that the United States had recently refused to supply F-104 fighters to India. India should acquire nuclear weapons "not to bomb Peking, Shanghai or Lhasa but only to warn China that we are not so helpless as she may think us to be."[119] In a similarly passionate vein, Harish Chandra Mathur of the Congress party argued that India should do whatever was necessary to stand up to China: "There is no other morality; our moral duty is the security of this country, the dignity of this country, the honour of this country and the safety of this country. Everything else will have to be subjugated to that."[120]

An independent MP, Frank Anthony, made a rare attempt to specify the Chinese threat. He declared that China was developing short-range "rockets and missiles" to be targeted at India, not at "distant countries like America and Britain."[121] This overlooked the technical fact that short-range missiles were stepping stones to longer-range missiles and that China's purpose was in fact to deter the United States and the Soviet Union. Anthony continued by detailing China's holdings of Russian-supplied bombers and its deployment of a massive army. "Our major confrontation, our only confrontation, a confrontation which means life or death for this country, is China."[122] And yet, despite this threat, Anthony concluded that technical shortcomings, the absence of adequate delivery systems, and competing resource priorities rendered it "unwise" for India "to enter the race for producing an atom bomb or a hydrogen bomb."[123] Everything in Anthony's analysis pointed to the need for nuclear weapons, yet in the end he could not see the feasibility of a crash program to acquire them.

Others did not accept the claim that China targeted India. R. K. Khadilkar, a Congress party MP from Khed, proclaimed that "China with its conventional arms is not capable of invading this country. Let us take a realistic view of the situation. . . . [T]his bomb is not directed towards India. . . . It is directed at the world powers, the super-powers. . . . It is directed against the nuclear monopoly of the western powers and not towards India."[124] This plausible analysis elicited derisive interruptions from the floor. Khadilkar continued, "Let this House realise that our conflict with China is a very limited conflict. It is not going to lead to war. This is the assessment of western statesmen, who are more mature."[125] The latter statement triggered a revealing uproar. One member denounced the speaker for representing the Chinese government. Another added that Khadilkar was "speaking for the American lobby."[126] If the merits of Khadilkar's analysis could not be challenged, his loyalties could be questioned.

Still, Khadilkar's speech seemed to embolden several others. Congress's V. B. Gandhi noted that "China has been cautious" in handling the Quemoy and Matsu disputes. "Also, take our own experience of aggression against our borders. China has desisted from pressing its advantage. That only shows that China is not as rash as it is made to appear."[127] Similarly, Ali Mirza pointed out that historically nuclear weapons had provided little usable power: "What gain has any country in the world got from the atom bomb? Has it helped France in Viet-Nam or Algiers? Has it helped Great Britain in Suez or Cyprus? Has it helped the USA anywhere in this wide world? This is only a terror. China said that it is a paper tiger. Because China has exploded one atom bomb, we are making a paper tiger a real tiger. This is not the correct approach."[128]

The most forceful advocates of an Indian bomb did not bother to analyze China's intentions or the nuclear threat Beijing posed to India. Rather, they argued intuitively and mechanistically in Realist fashion. U. M. Trivedi represented this view: "In Asia there are two giants; one of them is India and the other is China. If one giant grows and the other remains a dwarf, certainly, the dwarf will be killed, and there will be no time for the dwarf to arm himself."[129] He reminded the House that "today the theory in the world is that 'each nation unto itself.' "[130] Trivedi mocked the pretensions of those who urged an abandonment of nonalignment in favor of alliance with the West and lampooned those who argued moralistically for a Gandhian rejection of weapons of mass destruction. At the same time, Trivedi and others did not consider that alliances are useful means by which nations "unto themselves" seek security. Some argued that nonalignment prevented such alliances, but this overlooked the fact that the nonaligned movement itself was a quasi-alliance of large Third World nations intended in part to balance the power of the Soviet and Western bloc.

Generally, a number of important assumptions remained unexamined in this debate. India's self-image as a singular aspiring major power heightened the feeling that it should not seek the kinds of alliances upon which smaller or less powerful states rely. In terms of feasibility, U. M. Trivedi insisted that "money is no consideration" in determining such fundamental policies.[131]

But money was a consideration. Unfortunately no detailed and independently analyzed cost data were available to the debaters. Instead they could rely on, or challenge, several figures that had been put on the table in previous weeks: Bhabha's claims that a single nuclear device could be produced for Rs. 17.5 lakhs ($350,000) and that a fifty-weapon arsenal of fission bombs could be had for less than Rs. 10 crores ($21 million); Shastri's claim that a single atom bomb would cost Rs. 40–50 crores ($84–105 million); American scientist Christopher Hohenhemser's claim that a militarily significant nuclear program would cost Rs. 25 crores ($52.5 million) with an additional annual operating expense of Rs. 10 crores ($21 million). None of these figures included costs of delivery systems, which, historically in the United States, for example, are roughly seven times greater than the costs of producing the explosive weapons themselves.[132]

With no capacity to evaluate these numbers, the ensuing cost debate simply reflected the speakers' predilections. Those who argued against a bomb program cited the higher cost figures; those who argued for a bomb program cited Bhabha. Indeed, Bhabha became an important subtext of the debate. A number of speakers, led by Krishna Menon, implicitly or explicitly questioned both his cost figures and the appropriateness of his seeming to advocate a bomb program. Others, led by Harish Chandra Mathur, defended Bhabha's honor and expertise.[133]

Whatever their views of Bhabha, cost-minded critics of a bomb program argued that the essential point was that democratic India, unlike totalitarian China, could not afford to divert the resources required to produce and deliver a nuclear arsenal. As Masani noted:

> Marshal Chen Yi boasted that the Chinese must have their atom bomb even if they had to go without pants. In the brutal, heartless dictatorship over the Chinese people such as he exercises, he might get away with it. But can any democratic government, whatever the party, hope to survive in a democracy if it asks the people to do

without food and clothing so that the wretched bomb may be made? . . . What would be the consequences? The controversy over heavy industries, agriculture and consumer goods would immediately come to an end, because we would have no money either for agriculture, or consumer goods or heavy industries.[134]

Indeed, China had taken a course democratic India would not conceive of. China's 1958 guidelines for developing nuclear weapons stated that "[a]ny other projects for our country's reconstruction will have to take second place to the development of nuclear weapons."[135] The ten-year effort leading to the 1964 nuclear weapon test cost China the equivalent of $4.1 billion (U.S.) at 1957 prices, or $28 billion at 1996 prices![136]

Indian advocates of a nuclear weapon program, following the security-first logic of Realism, rejected the notion that defense interests could be traded off for other concerns. Nath Pai rebutted Masani directly: "Shri [Mr.] Masani talks of the price. I want to be free; so, I must pay the price."[137] In any case, Pai argued, "It does not cost Rs. 16 crores or some astronomical figure of crores of rupees as this to build the weapons. Shri Bhabha tells us that it costs Rs. 17 lakhs to produce one million ton TNT."[138]

Frank Anthony aptly summarized the conflicted and unresolved arguments for and against an Indian bomb: "I am aware that the cost of producing an atom bomb or a hydrogen bomb may be very crippling, I do not know of the cost. . . . I am aware of the fact that with almost a thousand crores of defence expenditure, the economic back of the country is breaking; that it is this defence expenditure that has contributed largely to the run-away inflation to the astronomical rise in food prices; I am aware of all that."[139] Anthony went on to suggest that maybe the Chinese aimed to "stampede" India into excessive defense spending in order to prompt internal crisis.[140] This echoed other voices who argued that China's main objective was to stir uncertainty in India and other Asian and African nations in hopes of increasing China's influence over them. On the one hand, Anthony concluded that India "should not enter the race for producing the atomic or a hydrogen bomb because of the cost and also because of the inability to deliver it."[141] But, he asked, "[w]hat then is the alternative?" Here he could only conclude that "[t]he immediate need today in my humble thinking is that we must pursue from today, from tomorrow, the development of nuclear technology and know-how."[142]

In many ways, the dilemmas and difficult trade-offs adduced by Anthony defined the situation India's leaders faced. In the final analysis, they, like Anthony, chose a middle ground. They deferred a decision for or against nuclear weapons. Instead they moved to speed the development of technology and know-how that would enable them later to decide to make weapons. But this shift in policy would not occur for several more days.

Now it was Prime Minister Shastri's turn to close the two-day debate. Speaking for thirty minutes in Hindi, Shastri first sought to disabuse his critics of the notion that moral considerations alone determined the government's resistance to building nuclear weapons. He was not naive. Instead, practical and "realistic" factors dictated a cautious and restrained approach. Most important, he said the cost of a major nuclear weapon–building program would have a disastrous effect on the already reeling economy. It would take governmental investment away from agriculture, exacerbate inflation, and raise prices on basic commodities that were already out of reach for the average citizen.[143] Rather than harm itself by building nuclear weapons, India must lead the world toward nuclear disarmament.

Yet Shastri seemed aware that domestically derived inhibitions could not justify an absolute rejection of nuclear weapons. Politically, if also perhaps strategically, a more robust policy was required. Thus, Shastri declared that the nonweapon policy was subject to change: "I cannot say that the present policy is deep-rooted, that it cannot be set aside, that it can never be changed. . . . [A]n individual may have a certain static policy . . . but in the political field we cannot do so. Here situations alter, changes take place, and we have to mould our policies accordingly. If there is a need to amend what we have said today, then we will say—all right, let us go ahead and do so."[144]

The *Hindustan Times* headline reporting Shastri's speech revealed the political-economic considerations influencing the prime minister: "Atom Bomb Policy Not Inflexible, Says PM—Economy Main Consideration—MPs Told to Keep Issue above Party Interest."[145] Shastri and the government's nuclear policy were the rope in a tug-of-war. Political forces within and outside the Congress party had pulled the prime minister toward the bomb, but economic priorities and moral leanings tugged the other way.

The Congress party, where the decisive power rested, appeared split. A bare majority favored building an independent deterrent, although this group's arguments tended to be unfocused.[146] A small minority, including Shastri himself, rejected an open shift to producing nuclear weapons and sought to emphasize global nuclear disarmament as the way to remove the Chinese threat. A middle group within the Congress party wanted neither to undertake nor exclude a bomb program but instead to study the issue seriously and enhance technological preparedness.[147] The middle group's approach would prevail in the ensuing days.

Unfortunately for Shastri, the tentative policy shift announced on November 24 did not satisfy his critics in the Congress party or the opposition, principally the Jana Sangh and the left-wing Samyukta Socialist Party, representing the short-lived merger of the Praja Socialist Party and the Socialist Party. The issue and attendant political storm were not dying down. The Executive Committee of the Congress Parliamentary Party met on November 26 to debate the nuclear issue further. The committee, whose support Shastri needed to retain his leadership post over time, sought to pull the prime minister toward a nuclear weapon program. To this end, several party leaders suggested that the government should enhance the pace and scope of nuclear science in India. K. C. Pant, who knew Bhabha well and served with him on the Board of Governors of the Indian

Institute of Science in Bangalore, urged that the nuclear establishment should increase its capacity to manufacture the bomb quickly if the need arose.[148] S. N. Mishra, leader of the Congress Socialist Forum, suggested the formation of a high-powered committee to examine the implications of the Chinese test.[149] Interestingly, none of the speakers at this meeting or the previous Lok Sabha debate demanded that military leaders be brought into discussions of the desirability and feasibility of manufacturing an Indian atomic bomb.

Shastri came under more fire on November 27, a momentous day in the history of India's nuclear policy. The Jana Sangh introduced a motion in the Lok Sabha calling for the manufacture of nuclear weapons. Shastri managed to win a voice vote against the resolution. Acknowledging that in his last speech he had downplayed the moral aspects of his opposition to an Indian bomb, Shastri on this day said that morality, or India's moral purposefulness, must also be factored into policymaking: "We do not claim that we are the noblest nation in the world. But certainly we have some noble traditions, and India does represent to some extent the desire to save humanity from wars and annihilation. We cannot give up this stand."[150] India's singular idealism in international affairs, demonstrated powerfully by Gandhi and adapted by Nehru, remained a real factor in the definition of national interest. Whereas Nehru actually had been ambivalent about India's acquisition of nuclear weapons, Shastri more simplistically and thoroughly believed that the nation should eschew nuclear weapons and instead rely on moral example and exhortations to the rest of the world to eliminate such weapons. A handful of atomic bombs, Shastri told the Lok Sabha, would not provide militarily decisive power in a world where the United States and the Soviet Union could annihilate even nuclear-armed nations like France and China.[151] Intuitively, Shastri felt that poor and democratic India would not be able to match poor and totalitarian China in a nuclear weapon competition.[152]

Notwithstanding his general disavowal of nuclear weapons for India, Shastri's speech revealed a crucial, largely unnoticed, change in policy. After reminding the House that India could produce a nuclear bomb within "two or three years" if necessary, Shastri reaffirmed the commitment of India's nuclear establishment to peaceful work only. Then, for the first time, the prime minister mentioned that this work should entail preparations of peaceful nuclear explosives for purposes such as tunneling through mountains. Invoking Bhabha, Shastri said, "nuclear devices" can be used both for destructive and for peaceful purposes:

> Dr. Bhabha has made it quite clear to me that as far as we can progress and improve upon nuclear devices, we should do so, as far as development is possible, we should resort to it so that we can reap its peaceful benefits and we can use it for the development of our nation. . . . Just assume that we have to use big tunnels and we have to clear huge areas, we have to wipe out mountains for development parks, and in this context if it is required to use nuclear devices for the good of the country as well as for the good of the world, so then our Atomic Energy Commission is pursuing these same objectives.[153]

Remarkably, neither the press nor the parliamentarians seemed to understand that Shastri had opened the door to the bomb. Technically, there is little distinction between a rudimentary nuclear weapon and a peaceful nuclear explosive—it is a semantic matter. Yet this seemed lost on the major English-language papers and the Lok Sabha. None of the headlines reporting Shastri's speech referred to the first-ever prime ministerial endorsement of an Indian nuclear explosives program.[154] Indeed, they left the impression that Shastri refused any change in policy: the *Hindustan Times* reported, "PM Refuses to Budge on Bomb"; the *Times of India* wrote, "P.M. Rejects Bomb Demand"; and the *National Herald* announced, "P.M.: Bhabha against Making A-Bomb—Inconclusive Debate on Non-official Resolution."[155]

EXPLAINING THE SHIFT IN POLICY

Shastri's statement represented an important turn, but only a half-turn. India's nuclear policy had now been put where Bhabha had wanted it for years, on a course leading to explosives. This fell short of an explicit commitment to nuclear weapons, but the technology now being sanctioned was similar. Many additional decisions would have to be made, but the logic of building the nuclear option around "peaceful" nuclear explosives was set. The shift occurred as a result of Bhabha proposing directly to Shastri the notion of moving ahead to prepare for a peaceful nuclear explosion. This appears to have happened on the morning of November 27. In his speech that day to the Lok Sabha, Shastri mentioned that he had just come from a meeting with Bhabha. Indeed, according to the *Times of India*, they met twice that day.[156] Much of Shastri's speech referred to Bhabha. The prime minister explained that Bhabha had been misunderstood as advocating a nuclear bomb. Rather, he said, Bhabha favored work on nuclear explosives *for peaceful purposes* and had specifically told the prime minister so. Most important for political purposes, Shastri told the Lok Sabha that Bhabha had now moved fully behind the prime minister's policy. This no doubt surprised many in the House. Shastri and Krishna Menon earlier had attacked Bhabha—implicitly, for he was too popular to be criticized directly—for interfering in policymaking. Now, on the twenty-seventh, Shastri said that Bhabha had been misquoted or misunderstood. According to Shastri, Bhabha had told him that the cost figures he had quoted in his October 24 radio broadcast were based on U.S. experience and did not apply to India. According to a newspaper account, "Dr. Bhabha had told him that even a plant for making atom bomb would involve a tremendous cost."[157] Moreover, Bhabha was completely against the bomb, according to Shastri.[158] What Bhabha did favor, with Shastri's agreement, was the use of atomic energy for peaceful purposes, "such as blasting passages through mountains."[159]

Bhabha knew that there was no meaningful technical distinction between a peaceful and a military nuclear explosive. He also knew that preserving nuclear cooperation with Canada and the United States required India to claim that all of its nuclear activities were "peaceful." Even if India avoided violating agreements by using *un*safeguarded materials and facilities to build a bomb, the United States, Canada, and others would react punitively. The overtly pro-bomb factions in the Parliament had failed to understand that manufacturing a bomb would risk India's civil nuclear program. In practical terms, therefore, the overt bomb-building option was untenable. However, a vaguer move to develop peaceful nuclear explosives would not stimulate recriminations, especially since the United States had its own peaceful nuclear explosives programs.

Yet, a policy of preparing the technology for *peaceful* nuclear explosives was too subtle to have calmed pro-bomb passions if this issue were truly central to Indian politics. The government could not publicly "wink" and let the Parliament and the press understand that preparation of peaceful nuclear explosions was actually code for work on a bomb.[160] This would cause adverse reactions in Washington, Ottawa, and elsewhere. However, if the Congress party, the press, and the public actually did not understand or care passionately about nuclear policy in its own right and instead took their cues from Bhabha, then a prime ministerial policy that satisfied Bhabha sufficed. The political point was to convince Congress party officials that Shastri's nuclear policy was robust enough to calm criticism. By bringing Bhabha onto his side, Shastri could ward off criticism on the nuclear issue, which in any case was understood superficially and debated symbolically compared to more pressing and familiar domestic issues.

The question is whether Shastri understood what he had given Bhabha. The prime minister's biographers have offered no insight; they have not even discussed his nuclear decision making.[161] His nontechnical background made him ill-prepared to explore the nuances of the peaceful nuclear explosions stance. His Gandhian leanings made it impossible for him to embrace an overt policy of acquiring nuclear weapons. Yet as a politician, he clearly welcomed the opportunity on November 27 to put the authoritative Bhabha back into alignment with himself. Did Shastri understand that the peaceful nuclear explosives project amounted to a major step toward nuclear weapons? Did he think there were technical distinctions between peaceful nuclear explosives and weapons? Did he believe that intentions mattered most, and that as long as he was in charge he could keep India's program entirely peaceful? Did he prefer not to think this through but merely to get Bhabha on his side by agreeing to whatever nonmilitaristic nuclear policy Bhabha pushed on him?

Interviews with former chairmen of the Indian Atomic Energy Commission shed some light on Bhabha's role and his interaction with Shastri. Raja Ramanna, who would soon head the project to explore preparations for a peaceful nuclear explosion, said in an interview that "[it] was really Bhabha's crusade. He asked Shastri to permit us to make calculations for SNEPP [Study Nuclear Explosion for Peaceful Purposes]. Shastri was a Gandhian. He was not interested in these matters. Bhabha and Shastri did not hit it off."[162] When asked why he thought Shastri would have endorsed peaceful nuclear explosives in his November 27, 1964, speech, Ramanna said, "Such a statement must have come from Bhabha."[163] Another former high-ranking AEC official echoed Ramanna and said that the impetus came from Bhabha, adding that "Bhabha was able to obtain approval to do theoretical studies only."[164]

With this background, the best way to account for Shastri's policy shift from October to late November is to focus on politics within the Congress party. Shastri's hold on power had been tentative from the beginning. The severe food and price crises further undermined his colleagues' confidence that his leadership would help them retain their positions at the polls.[165] The 1962 rout at the hands of China had already cast an aura of incompetence and airiness around Congress's conduct of security policy. A similar passivity in the face of the Chinese test would have tarnished the party's image further. With so much else going wrong, Shastri and his colleagues could not afford to appear as weak defenders of India's national pride and strength. Thus, Shastri's no-bomb position could not rally a majority even within the party. To maintain his leadership he had to shift.[166] For reasons outlined previously, the most viable alternative was a policy to develop peaceful nuclear explosives. It avoided repudiating Shastri's own moral principles. It avoided the economic disaster of a crash bomb-building program. It avoided disruption of nuclear cooperation with the United States and Canada. And it won the support of Bhabha, whose authority could then protect Shastri against further attacks on this issue.[167] Only such an ambiguous policy could do this much and this little simultaneously. The fact that it was not informed by a systematic analysis of the military security challenge posed by China violated Western theoretical models of nuclear decision making, but in India domestic considerations mattered more.

THREE

The Search for Help Abroad and the Emergence of Nonproliferation

DECEMBER 1964–AUGUST 1965

Despite Lal Bahadur Shastri's new support of peaceful nuclear explosives, nuclear policy continued to be contested. This chapter describes how, to escape the nuclear box, Shastri launched in late 1964 and early 1965 a tentative, ill-conceived quest for security guarantees from the United States and the Soviet Union. At the same time, Homi Bhabha confronted the truth that his nuclear establishment could not produce a nuclear explosive in eighteen months as he had claimed. Thus he secretly sought help from the United States in early 1965. Unbeknownst to Bhabha, leading U.S. State and Defense Department officials at this time were secretly considering whether to make arrangements to provide India and other friendly Asian countries with U.S. nuclear weapons in the event of serious military threats against them from China. This tentative American policy option—unrecorded in previous literature—ultimately came to naught, as President Lyndon Johnson and other top officials unified around a policy of strict nonproliferation. Thus, Bhabha's entreaty for U.S. nuclear assistance was deflected and the Johnson administration joined other governments in serious negotiations of the Nuclear Non-Proliferation Treaty. As these negotiations got underway, India played a leading role, pursuing an outcome starkly different from that sought by the United States.

DEBATE OVER SECURITY GUARANTEES BEGINS

The intensity of the Indian nuclear policy debate slackened somewhat in late 1964 as Bhabha lined up behind the prime minister's policy and quiet explorations of a peaceful nuclear explosive initiative began. The focus shifted to the international milieu. Shastri, without benefit of bureaucratic analysis, launched a halfhearted, diffident, and ultimately futile search for security guarantees from the United States and the Soviet Union against possible nuclear threats from China.[1] The pursuit of security guarantees has been well documented and is reviewed only briefly here.[2]

The interest in a security guarantee against a Chinese nuclear threat was strengthened by President Lyndon Johnson's October 18, 1964, pledge that nations that did not seek nuclear weapons could count on "our strong support" if they were faced with "some threat of nuclear blackmail."[3] Although vague, Johnson's offer was intended to reassure India in response to the Chinese test. Shastri naturally picked it up. During a press conference in London on December 4, he suggested demurely that "it was for the nuclear powers to discuss some kind of guarantee which was needed not only by India but by all the non-nuclear countries."[4] Mindful of its nonalignment policy, India would not ask directly for such a guarantee but at the same time would welcome help. Days later Shastri explained that he could not put his idea "in more precise terms. I wanted to throw this idea out for the consideration of the big nuclear powers like the U.S.A. and the U.S.S.R." It was "for the nuclear powers to consider how to maintain peace in the world," he said.[5]

The press reported that Shastri had requested a "nuclear shield" for India, which seemed to imply abandonment of nonalignment. This triggered controversy. On December 6, Indian journalists asked for clarification. Shastri acknowledged raising the guarantee issue but denied using the term *shield*, saying he would prefer a different term.[6] Shastri recognized that a nuclear guarantee from the major powers could arouse objections by those against whom it was intended, namely China. More troubling to Indians who doubted the prime minister's fitness for foreign and security policy, Shastri admitted that he had not explored the matter with the United States or the Soviet Union.[7] He had merely floated the notion to British Prime Minister Harold Wilson, evidently assuming Wilson would then raise it with Moscow and Washington. For his part, Wilson said that Shastri had not actually requested protection against possible nuclear blackmail and that he, Wilson, had not made any commitment. In A. G. Noorani's words, "It soon became evident that Shastri had made the suggestion spontaneously without much prior deliberation and certainly without prior consultation with his Foreign Minister, Swaran Singh."[8] Singh was then in the United States, where, upon hearing of Shastri's overture, he expressed doubts that such guarantees were feasible.[9]

As the issue continued to be debated, Shastri emphasized that he did not seek protection specifically for India but rather for all nonnuclear nations. The central point, he reiterated, was the responsibility of the United States and the Soviet Union to prevent the spread and use of nuclear weapons, preferably by eliminating all nuclear arms.[10] However, in the ensuing months and years, neither the United States nor the Soviet Union would embrace this approach in any thoroughgoing way. Experts, journalists, and politicians would analyze the details of potential security guarantees: Would a general nuclear security guarantee be credible? Would the United States or Russia risk unleashing nuclear war against China on behalf of India? How would the guarantors decide when to act? What confidence could India have that the United States or the Soviet Union, or both, would not improve relations with China and withdraw the guarantee? For all the talk, these questions did not get answered. The potential guarantors in Washington and Moscow simply would not commit themselves to such a major undertaking; the prospective beneficiary, India, could not define specifically what it wanted.

India's determination to maintain the policy of nonalignment limited the potential for effective security assurances. While Swatantra Party leaders, particularly M. R. Masani, argued that nonalignment could be maintained even with explicit ties to the West, they tortured logic in doing so.[11] Masani himself believed nonalignment no longer served Indian interests, and he made a cogent case to this effect. He reminded his colleagues that Nehru had requested American military assistance in the desperate days of the Chinese attack in 1962 and that it would be irresponsible for leaders not to do whatever was necessary to protect their nation. Nonalignment should be a means to an end, not an end in itself: "I say today that no country can guarantee its sovereignty and independence unless it has the good sense to pool its security and independence in collective security with the other free countries of the world. We are living in a world where independence of the old type is outmoded and has no reality. It is a myth."[12]

Most of India's political elite refused to think as open-mindedly and logically as Masani, however. To the vast majority, nonalignment was an end in itself and could not be questioned. This meant that any acceptable nuclear guarantees must come from both the West and the Soviet Union or from the United Nations. Through 1965 and 1966, India concentrated on the UN route. But this approach was too amorphous and indirect to compel Washington, London, or Moscow to consider the nuclear security guarantee matter seriously. Even had they been pressed hard, it remains doubtful that the major powers would have been more forthcoming.[13]

BHABHA SECRETLY PROBES FOR U.S. TECHNICAL HELP; AMERICAN OFFICIALS SECRETLY CONSIDER SUPPLYING BOMBS TO "FRIENDLY" ASIAN STATES, 1965

As questions about India's entreaty for protection against China continued to be raised, the Congress party held its annual conference in early January 1965. The rancorous meeting concentrated on economic issues. The leadership continued to face the contradiction between demands for large governmental investments and economic regulation to reduce poverty, on one side, and the powerful interests of the landed and industrial classes who sought greater freedom for private enterprise and price incentives for agriculturalists on the other side.[14] The threat of orchestrated mass unrest loomed.

Still, nuclear policy was debated at the meeting. A large number of delegates urged the party to endorse India's acquisition of nuclear weapons. Others argued that if India chose not to build nuclear weapons itself, it should seek a nuclear umbrella from the major nuclear powers. Shastri and other top government officials insisted that India should maintain its no-bomb policy. The prime minister again argued that the nation's defense required first and foremost comprehensive economic development.

The nuclear debate was intense. According to the *Statesman*, "Most of the members who took part in the debate objected to the views expressed in the official resolution [not to acquire nuclear weapons] and pleaded for India's entry into the nuclear camp either through direct manufacture of the atom bomb or by accepting the nuclear umbrella."[15] Bomb advocates argued that Shastri had been unable to persuade any other Asian or African nations to support a mission to Beijing to press China not to produce nuclear weapons and that none of these nations had condemned China's test.[16] How then could India rely on international measures to blunt China's nuclear program or possible aggression against India? Bibhuti Mishra, the general secretary of the Congress Parliamentary Party, argued that India's prestige had suffered following the 1962 war and was now plummeting further in the aftermath of China's nuclear test. If Indian leaders saw fit to increase overall defense spending to deal with China, he saw no reason not to extend the logic and produce nuclear weapons.[17] Mishra added that the public wanted India not to lag behind China in nuclear capability and that if the government did not move accordingly, "the people will remove us from power."[18] K. C. Pant urged the formation of a committee to consider what India should do in light of the Chinese test.[19]

Shastri and those closest to him simply steamrollered their pro-bomb colleagues, powered by the authority of the highest office. According to the *New York Times*, "Each delegate who had proposed an amendment was asked publicly and individually to withdraw it. Most of those who were present did so. Those who failed to reply were regarded as having withdrawn."[20] As a result, Shastri managed to pass a resolution declaring that for "the present," India would restrict its nuclear program to peaceful purposes. "I do not know what may happen later, but our present policy is not to make an atom bomb and it is the right policy," he said.[21] The resolution emphasized that efforts should be "redoubled for the development of the peaceful use of atomic energy."[22] This formulation represented a compromise between those like Morarji Desai and Krishna Menon who categorically rejected India's acquisition of nuclear weapons and the outspoken delegates who urged a major shift toward manufacture of a deterrent. Though Desai's morally inspired stance did not reflect the majority of his party, he framed the issue in a way that highlighted the nation's predicament. According to the account in the *Statesman*, Desai said, "India . . . was now grappling with vital problems of providing food, clothing and shelter to her needy millions. 'How far is it sensible to divert the nation's already meagre resources to the fruitless pursuit of making nuclear devices?' he asked."[23] In a quintessentially Indian analysis, Desai added that he appreciated the logic of those arguing for Indian nuclear weapons, "But life is not logic and we are to consider the entire range of questions, both moral and practical."[24]

Lal Bahadur Shastri's new emphasis on speeding the development of nuclear energy for peaceful purposes gradually seemed to calm the opposition within the party and garner support in the press. The *Hindu* editorialized: "Nobody can seriously question the wisdom of the decision. We cannot, on moral and economic grounds, start making the atom bombs ourselves at this stage. And the prime minister was wise in leaving it at that and not committing the Government into abjuring the nuclear weapon for all time and under all circumstances."[25]

But as the *Hindu* and others noted, the "not for now" policy begged many questions. During a press conference on January 20, a journalist inquired whether anything should be made of the "ambiguity" in Shastri's statement. Shastri replied, "When I say for the present, the present is a very long period. It is not going to be a short one. . . . I cannot say anything as to what might happen in the distant future. So long as we are here, our policy is clear that we do not want that atom bombs should be manufactured in India."[26]

Behind the scenes, however, policy had changed. The Atomic Energy Establishment now had permission to begin theoretical preparations for a peaceful nuclear explosive. Homi Bhabha and his colleagues busied themselves to that end. Most intriguingly, the effort was not confined to Indian territory or technology, despite India's determination to develop nuclear capability in a self-sufficient manner. Incomplete evidence indicates that Bhabha may have sought an American nuclear explosive device or blueprints for one. Important American files covering U.S. interactions with the Indian Atomic Energy Commission in this period remain classified, but a handful of declassified documents, and the recollection of at least one American official serving at the time, suggest that Bhabha made entreaties to receive a Plowshare device (a peaceful nuclear explosive) or blueprints in late 1964 and early 1965. This evidence is presented here with the important caveat that additional documentation is required to confirm the matter.

By way of background it is important to record that the U.S. Atomic Energy Commission and officials in the State Department and the Pentagon at the behest of Secretary of State Dean Rusk were contemplating two independent, parallel alternatives to satisfy India's possible interest in acquiring nuclear capabilities to offset China's bomb. Existing evidence does not indicate that the officials involved in developing each of these alternatives knew about the other.

In 1964, the United States Atomic Energy Commission was stoking international enthusiasm for peaceful nuclear explosions (PNEs) for use on massive engineering projects such as canal excavations.[27] The U.S. nuclear establishment saw PNEs as a potentially useful spin-off from the nuclear weapon program. The AEC hoped that nuclear explosives could be used to excavate a second Panama Canal and won significant congressional funding for the PNE program with this in mind. Internationally, the leaders of the U.S. nuclear establishment, such as AEC Chairman Glenn Seaborg, proposed that the United States conduct explosions at low cost for non–nuclear weapon states. This would protect against the proliferation risks that would otherwise be posed by nations independently producing their own nuclear explosives. Seaborg and his colleagues hoped that the international market for U.S.-conducted PNEs would boost the popularity of nuclear technology and augment the AEC's standing and budgets in the United States.[28]

Desiring to help India offset the impact of China's nuclear test, the AEC in late November 1964 included Plowshare projects in their consideration of areas of potential cooperation with India. An AEC "discussion paper" noted that various U.S. agencies and the World Bank had expressed passive interest in "the role nuclear excavation projects might play in solving some of India's basic river problems."[29] The brainstorming paper suggested that the United States could undertake preliminary conversations with Bhabha on a joint U.S.-India evaluation of Plowshare applications, recognizing that any prospective cooperation would involve "U.S. devices, under sole U.S. control." In a paragraph revealing faulty intelligence, the AEC wrote:

> [T]here has been a great deal of speculation (due to remarks made by Dr. Bhahba) that India might elect [to] embark on Plowshare device development program as a "cover" and rationalization for a nuclear weapons program. This appears to be a highly remote possibility due to technical and economic considerations as well as the recent statements made by Mr. Shastri disavowing any intention on the part of the Indian Government to embark on a nuclear weapons program.[30]

Ironically, Shastri had announced his support for a PNE project in India (thereby enabling a "cover" for a bomb) the same week that the AEC discussion paper began circulating in Washington. The AEC paper concluded strangely that if the United States did conduct Plowshare detonations in India, "it could help deter India from embarking on an independent device development program of its own."[31]

While the U.S. Atomic Energy Commission was contemplating providing Plowshares services to India, advisers to Secretary of State Dean Rusk had requested Assistant Secretary of Defense for International Security Affairs John McNaughton and his staff to study "the possibilities of providing nuclear weapons under US custody" for use by "friendly Asian" military forces in the event that China threatened or attacked them.[32] McNaughton provided a preliminary version of the requested study to Deputy Under Secretary of State Llewellyn E. Thompson in the late fall of 1964, and Thompson forwarded it to Rusk on December 4. The study, which had not been cleared by Defense Secretary Robert McNamara, sought to give the United States means to counter the geopolitical and military gains China might otherwise win through its new nuclear weapon capability.

The basic idea was to make arrangements for friendly Asian countries to receive and militarily deliver low-yield tactical nuclear weapons that the United States would provide to them in the event of Chinese aggression.[33] The study contemplated making nuclear weapons available to Japan, India, Australia, New Zealand, the Philippines, the Republic of China (Taiwan), Pakistan, Thailand,

and the Republic of Korea (South Korea). The authors noted that American personnel would have to train military units in the recipient countries to handle and deliver the weapons.[34]

The study paid special attention to India. The authors estimated that India could produce and test a nuclear device "in one to three years after a decision to do so," and could produce "by 1970 about a dozen weapons in the 20 KT [kiloton] range."[35] While noting that the balance of political opinion in India still inclined against the bomb, the study averred that the "chances are better than even that India will decide to develop nuclear weapons within the next few years."[36] The authors believed that American security assurances in the face of Chinese nuclear threats would not be adequate to stem other Asian countries' demands for "some national capability."[37] Thus, "the primary objective of a U.S. nuclear assistance offer to India would be to preclude an independent national nuclear development program."[38]

The study recognized that providing nuclear weapons to India would complicate American relations with Pakistan. Thus the authors suggested that the offer to India "should be low key."[39] The United States would help India modify its fleet of Canberra bombers, train aircrews, provide dummy weapons for exercises, and supply "weapons effects data for planning and necessary target data to support the feasibility and desirability of weapon use."[40] Washington would provide the same basic assistance to Pakistan, too, in part to offset that country's reaction to the proposed U.S. arrangement with India. The United States would not store nuclear weapons in either country but instead would develop facilities in each to handle weapons if and when they were needed.[41]

Beyond reducing the proliferation incentives of China's neighbors, the Defense Department staff argued that the plan would give the "U.S. President . . . the option of allowing controlled use of nuclear weapons" against China, without running the more direct risks of escalation to a global conflict involving major U.S. forces. "It could assist in avoiding a direct confrontation between the U.S. and the USSR in a Far East regional conflict."[42] This suggested a possible way to satisfy the desire to "use" nuclear weapons to deter or prosecute war on foreign soil while avoiding escalation that could lead to attacks on the U.S. homeland. Nuclear deterrence ultimately rests on the threat of massive devastation being visited on combatants' homelands, but the United States sought to escape this pitfall of deterrence by finding ways to contain nuclear exchanges to the foreign battlefield or theater level. This possibility—as much as the aim of stemming proliferation in India and other states—motivated the Pentagon's approach to the problem.

However, the McNaughton staff study did not win higher approval over the subsequent months. Members of McNaughton's staff found the proposal highly problematic and prevailed upon their boss to bring the issue to Defense Secretary McNamara's concentrated attention, in hopes that McNamara would reject the proposal and prevail upon its initiator, Secretary of State Rusk, to abandon it.[43] The study also was contrary to the thrust of the Gilpatric Committee, which had been established by President Johnson at this time to determine what should be the United States' approach to the proliferation challenge. Indeed, Rusk's response to Llewellyn Thompson's cover memo conveying the Pentagon staff study indicated that the Secretary of State wanted the Gilpatric Committee to "consider possible exceptions to our policy of discouraging nuclear proliferation."[44] As discussed later in this chapter, the Gilpatric Committee report concluded that the United States should try its utmost to stop the spread of nuclear weapons, precluding provision of American weapons to other countries. This approach also precluded the U.S. Atomic Energy Commission's proposal to provide peaceful nuclear explosives to India or other states.

Of course, Bhabha did not know about the Defense Department's top-secret study or the U.S. AEC's internal deliberations on providing Plowshares assistance to India. However, he pursued the Plowshare issue himself on January 19, 1965, when former presidential science adviser Jerome Wiesner (then president of MIT) visited Trombay. A declassified cable from the State Department to the American embassies in New Delhi, Karachi, and London reported that Dr. Wiesner's "mission should focus on two of our major objectives in our effort [to] influence Indian nuclear policy. First of these is to help India demonstrate that its scientific and technological capabilities are at least equal to those of Chicoms."[45] The second objective was to reinforce Indian awareness of the "dangers and implications of proliferation" and evaluate the likelihood of India's "building and detonating a device to offset the Communist bomb."[46] The cable mentioned four types of cooperative projects: plutonium recycling, thorium recycling, training regarding peaceful uses of nuclear energy, and cooperation in space technology.[47] The cable stated further that "[w]e are interested in eliciting Indian ideas as to possible cooperative projects but wish to avoid reacting to them in manner which might suggest tentative acceptance." No mention was made of the possibility of cooperation in studying or developing peaceful nuclear explosives.

However, when Wiesner arrived in Bombay, Bhabha apparently broached the matter of American supply of a Plowshare device. On January 21 Wiesner, now back in New Delhi, left a report for John Palfrey, an AEC member who was arriving in India to attend the inauguration of the Trombay plutonium reprocessing plant. The report was also cabled to the secretary of state and the White House. In it, Wiesner recorded that "Bhabha is anxious to explore availability of Plowshare with you. He is interested in the possibility of making harbors and water reservoirs."[48]

Bhabha's apparent request, as relayed by Wiesner, elicited a quick cable back from the State Department to the AEC's John Palfrey in New Delhi. The department instructed Palfrey that "you may also, in your discretion, discuss generally Plowshare-type projects with Bhabha, bearing in mind limitations [in] this area with which you [are] fully familiar."[49]

Wiesner's report to Palfrey and the officials in Washington shed light on a number of other important issues. He concluded that the "main motivation to date" for those advocating an Indian bomb "is political, but there is also some desire for a deterrent against China and some vague feeling that if a nuclear mine field makes sense in Europe it could be useful on India-China border." The alternatives being considered in the "violent debate" going on in India "range from taking all necessary steps just short of building a bomb, to the actual construction of both a bomb and a delivery system."[50] Wiesner reported that Bhabha's October 24, 1964, statement about the low cost of a nuclear explosion had misled many in India, including the prime minister. This had prompted "many scientists" to complain to Shastri.[51] Wiesner believed that Bhabha still underestimated the cost: "He told me that he could make and test a crude nuclear device for approximately ten million dollars."[52] Thus, Wiesner recommended a U.S. effort to give the Indians a better cost estimate. He continued:

> Bhabha is still saying that it would be possible to make a nuclear explosion in 18 months. Many of the scientists object to this optimistic figure and at least two have written to the Primin stating that it was too optimistic. Bhabha apparently wants authority and resources to move forward without final decision regarding actual explosion. *No one has estimated what a real weapon system would cost or understands what will be done with it.*[53]

Wiesner's account of Bhabha's views and his critical evaluation of them illuminated the debate and decision-making process to come. According to former AEC Chairman Homi Sethna, there were only eight to ten scientists and engineers working around Bhabha on nuclear explosives questions, while hundreds of others worked on less controversial matters.[54] This led to tensions within the scientific community that Wiesner detected. Yet there was no system of checking and balancing Bhabha, no open means by which scientists could inform political decision makers of costs and benefits of particular policies. This lack of mechanisms for independently evaluating the AEC's claims and proposals would handicap India for decades.

The next available reference to Bhabha's quest for American nuclear assistance appears in a memorandum of a conversation between Bhabha and Under Secretary of State George Ball on February 22, 1965. Bhabha was visiting Washington for talks on nuclear cooperation and requested the meeting with Ball.[55] Bhabha steered the conversation to "the dilemma India faced regarding what to do to counteract the 'noise' of Communist China's nuclear explosion." According to the official notes, Bhabha "explained that India needed to make some dramatic 'peaceful' achievement to offset the prestige gained by Communist China among Africans and Asians."[56] Ball argued that the objective should be to persuade the major nonnuclear nations to forego nuclear weapons. Bhabha countered that to do this "a way must be found so that a nation will gain as much by not going for nuclear weapons as it might by developing them."[57] Bhabha then turned the conversation to the relative nuclear capabilities of various nations, including China and India. "Dr. Bhabha explained that the Chinese were greatly indebted to the

USSR for helping them on their weapons program." He emphasized that the Soviet Union must have "left the blueprints for a nuclear device with Communist China."[58]

Bhabha then dropped the bait in front of Ball. "Dr. Bhabha explained that if India went all out, it could produce a device in 18 months; *with a U.S. blueprint it could do the job in six months*."[59] To reinforce the logic of the tacit request, Bhabha reiterated how important the Soviet assistance had been in quickening China's capability. The logic of Bhabha's presentation, and the not-too-subtle mention of how an American blueprint would augment India's capacity, can fairly be interpreted as a backhanded request for an American blueprint or device. This interpretation is buttressed by Wiesner's earlier report that Bhabha asked about availability of a Plowshare device and by further evidence discussed below.

Bhabha closed the discussion by stating that India's plutonium separation plant was "quite large" and could in five years give India the capacity to "produce 100 nuclear bombs per year."[60] Nevertheless, Bhabha said, India retained its policy not to seek nuclear weapons. However, he added that "[i]f his government is to justify this policy, . . . ways must be found by which his country could gain at least as much by sticking to peaceful uses as it could by embarking on a weapons program."[61] In Bhabha's view, production of peaceful nuclear explosives could be distinguished politically or legally from a weapons program. Yet, technically, a peaceful nuclear device could "gain" India as much as a weapon could.

The Plowshare issue was also referenced in a long cable from the scientific attaché of the American Embassy in New Delhi reporting on a visit by several American officials, including the aforementioned John Palfrey, to Trombay for the January 22, 1965, formal inauguration of the plutonium reprocessing plant. This report revealed interesting details of the Indian Atomic Energy Establishment. For example, it noted that the maintenance of apparatuses throughout the establishment "is very difficult since cases were mentioned where it took over a year to get needed replacements and supplies from abroad."[62] The plutonium separation plant experienced surprises, according to the report. "While the plant was designed to handle 30 tons per year of rods, it is now felt it will handle at least five times this amount."[63] Less fortunately, the plant manager correctly told the American delegation, the plant "probably had experienced an explosion during operation but he did not realize it previously."[64] Overall, "[T]he operation is currently wholly dependent on the availability and utilization of fittings and supplies from USA or elsewhere. In fact the plant is now down for a month or two awaiting foreign parts and supplies. While it has been claimed by some that this is an all Indian design, an engineer pointed out that an American firm designed and provided the dissolving section among other things."[65] The report also mentioned that "[f]rom several sources Dr. Bhabha is said to favor the opportunity of proceeding to a point just short of the bomb. . . . Other influential scientists such as Dr. K. Chandrasekaran [a prominent mathematician at the Tata Institute] are very much against this proposal."[66]

With this general background, the embassy report concluded by referring to a prior discussion of an Indian request for a Plowshare nuclear device from the United States. Since the report was written almost two months after Wiesner's visit to Trombay, and after Bhabha's February visit to Washington, it appears to refer to discussions between January and March within the U.S. government regarding the possibility of providing India with a Plowshare device that India could then detonate as if it were indigenously made.

> The possibility of aiding India with something dramatic to give her status compara-ble with the Chinese bomb looks very difficult. Any country possessing something new would first use it themselves since everyone wants such status. By controlling newspaper releases the bulk of the population could be fooled by a Plowshare device, but all her neighbours would know and claim that India had not developed such a sophisticated device but obtained it elsewhere. . . . India's own capabilities for Plow-share and its applications are rather long term; furthermore India's scientific repu-tation would enjoy greater favor if some kind of non-nuclear work were exploited.[67]

Further hints of Bhabha's entreaty to the United States appeared in a letter that the chairman of the U.S. AEC, Glenn Seaborg, drafted to Bhabha summa-rizing their February 1965 discussions of potential nuclear cooperation between the two countries.[68] (This draft was not sent, as discussed below.) Seaborg noted that Bhabha had "indicated that it was conceivable that the US Plowshare Pro-gram might be able to make an important contribution, in time, to the solution of some of India's basic engineering problems."[69] In keeping with U.S. policy, Seaborg sought to limit the potential range of U.S. cooperation in this area to lec-tures and evaluation of how the technology could help India "solve some of its engineering problems."[70] He reminded Bhabha that the United States could not make a commitment to "proceed further on the matter" and stated that "political considerations" including "whatever implications the specific project involved had insofar as the Limited Test Ban Treaty is concerned" must be evaluated.[71] The tone of Seaborg's draft indicated that Bhabha had initiated the discussion and that the United States was mindful of the strict limitations that would be put on any U.S. provision of services or expertise in the area of nuclear explosives. Bhabha wanted a device or blueprints, or both, that could be used in India's own develop-ment of the technology, but American nuclear officials recognized the need to maintain strict U.S. controls on the technology.

By April 1965, the U.S. Atomic Energy Commission had become even more conservative regarding cooperation in the peaceful nuclear explosions field. Between Bhabha's February visit to Washington and April, nonproliferation became a greater priority of American policy, as is discussed in the following sec-tion. All of this was revealed in a letter Seaborg wrote to the chairman of the U.S. Congress Joint Committee on Atomic Energy on April 30, 1965. The letter listed seven potential cooperative ventures between the United States and the Indian Atomic Energy Commission. While this was the number of areas suggested in

Seaborg's unsent draft letter to Bhabha just discussed, all reference to cooperation regarding Plowshare devices was omitted in the April letter. Instead of Plowshare, Seaborg discussed, as Bhabha had inquired, "whether we would be prepared to make a moderate amount of plutonium available for research and development."[72] Bhabha's interest in receiving plutonium from the United States was curious, given the recent opening of the Indian plutonium separation plant at Trombay, but for the purposes of this discussion the omission of reference to Plowshare indicated Washington's sense that Bhabha's request had undesirable proliferation implications.

Recently declassified correspondence between then-U.S. Ambassador to India Chester Bowles and William J. Handley, the deputy assistant secretary of state for Near Eastern and South Asian Affairs, illuminates the matter further. Bowles wrote Handley on April 12 asking for more extensive updating from Washington, specifically regarding nuclear cooperation: "[R]ight now we haven't the slightest idea whatever happened to our proposals to deal with India's nuclear dilemma which was so much the subject of discussion late last fall. After getting Jerry Wiesner and Jack Palfrey to India and generating what we thought was a good deal of constructive effort, the problem has dropped from sight."[73]

The response to Bowles's query came nearly a month later. It began by lamenting that Bowles's job in New Delhi had been complicated by the postponement of a visit Prime Minister Shastri was scheduled to make to Washington in June 1965 and by the U.S. decision not to supply F-5 aircraft to India, due to the Rann of Kutch incident (discussed in chapter 4). Turning to the nuclear question, Handley stated that the department was finally able "to dislodge the Palfrey to Bhabha letter on scientific cooperation."[74] (This letter appears to have been based on Seaborg's earlier draft discussed above.) Handley wrote that the letter "had been stuck because of a major controversy in Washington over Ploughshare. As it came out, the Ploughshare portion of the letter was a casualty: this was the only way we could get the letter to move."[75] Clearly there had been a bureaucratic struggle over Plowshare, and even a rather minimal expert dialogue on the subject was ruled out. In any case, all of the cited documents suggest that Bhabha had in mind something more ambitious: supply of a nuclear explosive or blueprints for one.[76]

The Indian military apparently was thinking similarly to Bhabha regarding assistance from the West. In a secret December 1964 paper on "The Indian Nuclear Problem," an Arms Control and Disarmament Agency official, Henry S. Rowen, wrote that "[a]n Indian military study is reported to have concluded that India cannot afford a nuclear program, and that even if it had these weapons, they would be useless because of the lack of delivery means against China."[77] According to Rowen, the study concluded "that India should seek an arrangement with the West involving the commitment of Western nuclear support. This arrangement would involve concentrating on a delivery capability and 'know how' for the use of nuclear weapons."[78] Assuming that Rowen accurately reflected the Indian military view, several interesting conclusions can be drawn. First, the military backed Shastri and others who resisted political pressures to manufacture nuclear weapons, although relatively little was made of this in debate. Second, whether or not Bhabha was aware of the military's recommendation, his apparent entreaty for U.S. assistance in procuring a nuclear explosive device or blueprints was consistent with the military's preference for Western help, even if the military preferred more generic assistance than Bhabha had in mind. Third, the Indian military, unlike the powerful political class, cared less for nonalignment than for practical assistance in balancing China's power. In any case, the military did not enjoy significant influence in the policy-making process.

Bhabha's apparent effort to gain U.S. assistance in acquiring nuclear explosives had important implications. It reaffirmed the baselessness of his and Nehru's earlier claims that India could produce a nuclear weapon in "one year," or "18 months," or "two to three years." Bhabha and his colleagues appeared to lack the design knowledge and the technology required even to make an informed estimate of the cost and time required for India to produce a device. Despite the frequent claims of the nuclear program's self-sufficiency, it was highly dependent on information and technology from abroad. At the same time, neither Nehru, Shastri, nor others debating nuclear policy had the expertise required to question or scrutinize Bhabha's claims. The secrecy and autonomy of the nuclear establishment and the lack of qualified scientific expertise outside that establishment badly impaired the policy-making process. Yet, Bhabha found himself on the spot once Prime Minister Shastri approved the request to begin preparations for a peaceful nuclear explosive. To avoid having the entire nuclear program fall into disrepute for failing to deliver a nuclear explosive capability in a short time, Bhabha would have welcomed an important boost from the United States in the form of a Plowshare device or a design for one. One former colleague suggested in an interview that the Western-acculturated Bhabha may also have wanted to link India politically and strategically to the West.[79] Given Bhabha's autonomy and Shastri's own leanings, it can be speculated that Bhabha would not have informed Shastri or other political leaders of his approach to the United States. Indeed, U.S. officials in briefing Under Secretary of State Ball indicated that Shastri had excluded Bhabha "from certain high level GOI discussions of nuclear policy matters.[80]

Bhabha's quiet quest for U.S. help in nuclear explosive acquisition did not comport with India's overall policy line, much as the nuclear-weapon-sharing idea of Secretary of State Rusk and Defense Department officials did not fit the evolving U.S. policy. However, both approaches—now that they are visible—shed historical light on the boxes in which Indian and American officials operated. (Additional relevant documents remain to be declassified.)

Bhabha's maneuverability was limited by his desire to minimize awareness of the time required for his team to build an explosive device. More important, American assistance in such a sensitive area would have badly weakened the credibility and moral-political essence of India's nonalignment policy. Bhabha or others could have argued that this actually would have served India's national interest, but the issue was not open for real questioning. Even if Indian leaders had been willing to reconsider nonalignment, they then would have confronted the U.S. government's determination to maintain control over whatever nuclear explosive capability might be "shared" with developing countries.

Halfway around the world, the small number of American officials who contemplated providing nuclear weapons to India in extremis also were thinking creatively against the grain. However, they, too, did not adequately comprehend either the internal or the Indian resistance to their ideas. The Americans overestimated the priority Indian political leaders put on nuclear questions relative to more pressing domestic challenges. They badly underestimated the degree to which national pride and nonalignment would have made India's elected leaders reject prearrangements for the supply of American nuclear weapons. India's moral disdain for countries engaged in nuclear arms racing would have made it politically awkward to prepare in peacetime for provision of the same weapons that had been condemned. (In the event of war with China, the calculation would have changed, but then it likely would have been too late to prepare Indian forces to receive and effectively use American nuclear weapons.) While some American officials and Bhabha could think of ways to effect a wary nuclear embrace between the United States and India, broader considerations were driving the two states apart.

The United States provided India neither assistance in designing or producing a nuclear explosive device nor the promise of American nuclear weapons "on account." Although American officials, particularly in India, recognized the need for strengthening Shastri's position in order to reduce demand for the bomb, Washington would not offer decisive support. In sum, the United States rebuffed India's dual efforts—for guarantees or technical assistance—to seek international help in countering China's gains in prestige and potential political and military power. Instead, the United States launched a drive to draft and negotiate a nonproliferation treaty. India would be a primary target of this campaign, but it remained unclear how the effort to stop the further spread of nuclear weapons would solve the problem that China's nuclear weapons posed for India, militarily and politically.[81] India would be left to its own devices.

AMERICAN NONPROLIFERATION POLICY TAKES SHAPE

Beginning with an initiative by Ireland in 1958, elements in the international community had floated various proposals for a treaty to stop the spread of nuclear weapons. The United States, the Soviet Union, France, and others vacillated in their reactions to these proposals. In 1964 momentum had built to do something to ward off imminent proliferation. The United States confronted a dilemma: it could prevent proliferation by "sharing" nuclear control with key allies, thereby obviating their need for independent arsenals, or Washington could pursue a purer policy of promoting complete nuclear abstinence. The sharing concept was embodied in the Multilateral Force (MLF) proposal (first sketched in Washington in 1961) to establish an integrated NATO nuclear force based on surface ships armed with Polaris missiles with crews of mixed nationality. An executive body of representatives from the allies would collectively control the decision to launch the missiles, but under the U.S. proposal, Washington would retain the right to veto any launch decision. The aim was to encourage West German eschewal of nuclear weapons and to reassure NATO allies of U.S. commitments to them. The proposal elicited great controversy in Washington, in Europe, and between the Soviet Union and the United States. As Henry Kissinger noted, the MLF could not "at one and the same time satisfy demands for nuclear sharing and assuage concerns about nuclear proliferation."[82]

The tension between the MLF proposal and broader proliferation concerns was ultimately decided in favor of nonproliferation. This decision evolved between November 1964 and January 1965 when the presidentially appointed Gilpatric Committee presented its findings on U.S. nonproliferation objectives to President Lyndon Johnson. Much of the debate in Washington stemmed from the Chinese nuclear test and fear that it would stimulate nuclear proliferation elsewhere, particularly in India.[83] As the discussions of the Defense Department's nuclear-sharing idea and the AEC's Plowshare "rental" proposal indicated, U.S. officials were open to many ideas for countering the anticipated effects of the Chinese bomb. For its part, India prepared to introduce a resolution on nuclear nonproliferation to the UN General Assembly in November 1964.

Several declassified U.S. government papers illuminate Washington's thinking on the diplomatic dimensions of the proliferation challenge and India. On November 9, 1964, the Arms Control and Disarmament Agency produced a secret paper noting that India was proposing UN consideration of a resolution on "Non-Proliferation of Nuclear Weapons" that would prohibit the manufacture, acquisition, receipt, or transfer of nuclear weapons.[84] While the United States welcomed the gist of the Indian proposal, it feared that India, with Soviet encouragement, would define nonproliferation to exclude the possibility of putting nuclear weapons under a Multilateral Force in Europe. Thus, the ACDA paper recommended building on a previously introduced Irish nonproliferation resolution to create an acceptable draft that Ireland could then carry to the international community. Irish authorship would reduce the resistance that neutral nations would mount to an openly U.S.-authored initiative.[85]

Two additional papers prepared in early December analyzed the factors affecting India's potential nuclear weapon and nonproliferation policies. One, entitled "Value and Feasibility of a Nuclear Non-Proliferation Treaty," whose authorship is unclear, posited that India's interest in signing a nonproliferation treaty "may depend on their getting adequate assurance of aid in defense against China from the U.S. and perhaps also from the USSR."[86] The paper noted that the Indian government was resisting internal pressures to initiate a nuclear weapon program, in part because of the cost and difficulty of obtaining sophisticated long-range bombers or missiles to "mount a credible deterrent against China."[87] In addition, an Indian bomb program "would almost surely cause the Paks to try desperately to follow suit, perhaps with help from China."[88] The paper suggested that this latter possibility further disinclined Indian decision makers from mounting a weapon program, although this seems to overstate Indian attention to Pakistan at that time. Finally, the paper concluded that India probably would not "insist on keeping open a nuclear weapon option because of Chinese capability, especially if India is obtaining what it considers adequate military assistance in modern defense weapons."[89] This conclusion underestimated the nonmilitary factors behind India's nuclear policy as well as the willingness of the United States or others to supply adequate military assistance to offset demand for nuclear weapons.

A second State Department background paper covered similar terrain as the paper just discussed, but it pointed to a different conclusion. The paper began by listing the conditions that might convince the four countries of greatest concern—India, Israel, Sweden, and Japan—to sign a nonproliferation treaty. First, the Soviet Union and the United States must agree on a comprehensive test ban treaty and nonproliferation. Next, nations signing a nonproliferation treaty must be reassured that their rivals would also adhere to such a treaty. Third, international stability must be enhanced to give states confidence in resting their security on a treaty. Finally, substitutes must be found for the prestige attached to building nuclear weapons.[90] With this background, the paper raised doubts that India, over time, could be dissuaded from seeking nuclear weapons: "Under the aggressive leadership of Homi Bhabha, India's nuclear development program has . . . been moving steadily ahead. . . . Indeed, the operation and the characteristics of some parts of India's nuclear establishment suggest that Bhahba has at least been keeping open the option of manufacturing weapons. His recent public statements almost give the impression that Bhabha is actively lobbying for such a decision."[91] In addition, the paper concluded that China's ongoing nuclear program would steadily weaken Indian interest in signing a nonproliferation treaty.

This analysis proved prophetic, although not so much for the reasons stated. India would not sign the nonproliferation treaty, and the Indian nuclear program would proceed toward the 1974 nuclear test. But factors other than Chinese aggressiveness toward India would drive India's decision making. As the American Embassy in New Delhi reported, Indian officials were upset by the plaudits given by African and Asian nations to China's prowess. China was gaining *stature* as a result of its bomb. Worse still, it now appeared that China's nuclear technology was more advanced than had been anticipated, further demoralizing Indian elites regarding the two nations' relative achievements in this field that epitomized technical modernity and political power.[92]

The U.S. government's intense deliberation over a prospective nonproliferation treaty and tactics to win Indian accession to it continued into 1965. Most important, the Gilpatric Committee on Nuclear Proliferation was preparing its major report to President Johnson.[93] The secret, closely held report was finished on January 21. The committee began by asking whether American interests would be served better by blocking any further spread of nuclear weapons or instead by welcoming proliferation, especially in friendly countries such as Japan and India. The latter could then help balance the power of China and the Soviet Union, particularly in Asia. Some officials, such as Secretary of State Dean Rusk began the exercise inclined to welcome proliferation, at least on a discriminatory basis, as discussed earlier. However, as a result of the study, the committee concluded unanimously that "preventing the further spread of nuclear weapons is clearly in the national interest despite the difficult decisions that will be required."[94]

The Gilpatric Committee adduced several reasons for blocking proliferation. New nuclear capabilities, regardless of the friendliness of the nations possessing them, would "add complexity and instability to the deterrent balance between the United States and the Soviet Union" and would "aggravate suspicions and hostility among states neighboring new nuclear powers." This would "impede the vital task of controlling and reducing weapons around the world" and "eventually constitute direct military threats to the United States." Proliferation also would "place a wasteful burden on the aspirations of developing nations."[95] The committee posited that "[a]s additional nations obtained nuclear weapons, our diplomatic and military influence would wane, and strong pressures would arise to retreat to isolation to avoid the risk of involvement in nuclear war." This understanding of U.S. interests in nonproliferation remains operative today.

To combat proliferation, the committee argued that the United States and the Soviet Union would have to reduce their emphases on nuclear weapons and seek agreements on arms control measures.[96] The committee offered an ambitious list of nuclear arms control measures, including a comprehensive nuclear test ban treaty, a verified treaty to end production of fissile materials for weapons purposes, and a verified strategic delivery vehicle freeze coupled with significant agreed-upon reductions (e.g., 30 percent) in strategic force levels.[97] These steps would augment the prospects of a nuclear nonproliferation treaty, to which the committee assigned the highest priority.

The Gilpatric Committee and other American officials understood that India's willingness to abjure development of nuclear weapons depended in part on the availability of substitute means of security and prestige, as well as on disarmament by the nuclear powers. Indian leaders needed political cover and equity. Thus, the Gilpatric Committee suggested that the United States "should be prepared . . . to offer credible assurance of United States action in the event of a nuclear attack on India in exchange for an Indian commitment not to acquire nuclear weapons."[98] The committee also urged assisting India in "scientific programs designed to build the prestige she might otherwise attempt to obtain from the development of a nuclear device."[99] Yet in each case the Gilpatric Committee hedged its recommendations in deference to other U.S. interests: *formal* nuclear security guarantees should be avoided, and scientific cooperation should "not contribute significantly to future nuclear weapons capabilities."[100] As discussion of a prospective nonproliferation treaty mounted in 1965, the United States retreated from even the hedged position of the Gilpatric Committee.

INDIA PUTS DOWN ITS NONPROLIFERATION MARKER

On May 4, as nonproliferation rose on the international agenda, the Indian delegate to the 114-member UN Disarmament Commission, B. B. Chakravarty declared the five conditions that an effective nonproliferation treaty must meet to satisfy India.[101] First, the "nuclear powers" must undertake "not to transfer nuclear weapons or nuclear weapons technology to others." Second, those powers must agree "not to use nuclear weapons against countries which do not possess them." Third, the United Nations must "safeguard the security of countries which may be threatened by" nuclear weapon states or states near to possessing nuclear weapons. Fourth, India insisted on "tangible progress toward disarmament, including a comprehensive test ban treaty, a complete freeze on the production of nuclear weapons and means of delivery as well as substantial reduction in the existing stocks." Finally, India wanted a treaty committing "non-nuclear powers not to acquire or manufacture nuclear weapons." If the Gilpatric Committee's recommendations seemed ambitious to the U.S. government, the Indian agenda was still more demanding.

Assuming that such a treaty were to be completed soon with China's adherence, China would not be able to build and deploy a nuclear arsenal capable of threatening India militarily. Security guarantees would then reassure India against any residual Chinese nuclear capability or blackmail. If, on the other hand, China did not join the nonproliferation treaty, the recommended security guarantees would augment India's protection against blackmail or aggression by China. The security guarantees formulated in India's proposed treaty pointed to the United Nations, not to the United States and the Soviet Union, as the guarantors.

The United States envisioned a much more limited treaty. Mindful of the lingering Multilateral Force issue, Washington resisted language that would block any and all transfers of nuclear weapons to others. At the same time, the United States would not accept treaty requirements for specific measures of nuclear disarmament, with the exception of a comprehensive test ban treaty, which Washington did endorse. Nor was Washington or Moscow prepared to offer meaningful security guarantees to non–nuclear weapon states.

The American and Indian visions of an effective nonproliferation treaty formed the parameters of debate, with other nations in between. On June 15, 1965, the UN Disarmament Committee passed a U.S.-sponsored resolution to move the treaty negotiations to the Eighteen Nation Disarmament Committee (ENDC) in Geneva. The Soviet Union, after some resistance, agreed to this negotiating venue and mandate. Of the eighteen participating nations, five came from NATO, five from the Warsaw Pact, and eight from the nonaligned states.[102] The Geneva talks opened in late July 1965.

As the negotiations began, large gaps separated the negotiators' respective positions. Washington's wish to preserve the potential for sharing nuclear weapons with NATO allies generated intense debate among European nations, including the Soviet Union. Broader concerns regarding equity and disarmament animated the nonaligned countries.

The Indian representative in Geneva, V. C. Trivedi, launched a long and eloquent attack on the proposals offered by the United States and other nuclear weapon states. Trivedi was one of the few Indian officials with expertise in nuclear arms control and atomic energy matters. Although he was a civil servant, he appeared to have a major role in shaping, not merely representing, India's approach to the nonproliferation treaty negotiations. Trivedi shared Bhabha's belief that India should acquire nuclear explosives, although he did not say so publicly.[103] Trivedi argued that the treaty's focus on the non–nuclear weapon states was misplaced. Making an analogy to a drunkard emperor proscribing drinking in his empire, Trivedi argued that the nuclear weapon states should concentrate on eliminating their arsenals before dictating to others. He proposed a two-stage treaty whereby, first, the nuclear powers would agree not to transfer weapons or related technology to others and would also cease all production of nuclear weapons and delivery vehicles, followed by reductions in these capabilities. Only then, in the second stage, would the non–nuclear weapon states agree not to acquire or build nuclear weapons.[104] While emphasizing the requirement of disarming the nuclear "haves," Trivedi also cited the weakness of the security guarantees under discussion.

The relative emphasis of Trivedi's remarks indicated a subtle shift away from seeking security guarantees in favor of a tougher call for nuclear disarmament. This would more effectively alleviate India's concerns about China and, if negotiations failed, relieve pressures on India to constrain its nuclear program. India's determination to shift the burden of nonproliferation obligations onto the states that had already proliferated mounted as the negotiations continued through 1966 and 1967.

By late 1965, it was clear that the U.S. vision of a rather narrowly circumscribed nonproliferation treaty was unacceptable to many non–nuclear weapon states—not only India but also Japan, Sweden, and other formidable nations. Taking the initiative away from the superpowers, the eight nonaligned participants in the ENDC sponsored a resolution in the UN General Assembly (UNGA) framing the mandate for the nonproliferation treaty negotiations. This resolution— UNGA Resolution 2028 (XX)—passed by a vote of ninety-three to zero, with five abstentions, on November 23, 1965. The accepted negotiating mandate centered on five principles, three of which were most salient:

(a) The treaty should be void of any loop-holes which might permit nuclear or non-nuclear Powers to proliferate, directly or indirectly, nuclear weapons in any form;

(b) The treaty should embody an acceptable balance of mutual responsibilities and obligations of the nuclear and non-nuclear Powers;

(c) The treaty should be a step towards the achievement of general and complete disarmament and, more particularly, nuclear disarmament.[105]

Within this framework, the pillars of balanced and mutual obligations and of progress toward nuclear disarmament stood large and divisive. The negotiations would last three more years, as discussed in chapter 4.

At this point in late 1965, the internal deliberations of the U.S. government and the public demands of India revealed a fundamental divergence of interests. To produce a treaty that India could sign, the United States and the other nuclear weapon states would have to increase their willingness to satisfy India's interests in equity and security. Once again, some American officials, particularly those in India, recognized the need to do more. Ambassador Chester Bowles, for example, reminded his superiors in Washington that "India and those other non-nuclear powers which are now in position to make bomb cannot over period of time be diverted from producing nuclear weapons by moral exhortations and lectures from members of present nuclear club. Therefore certain amount of give as well as take is essential if we are to cope effectively with this critical situation."[106] Americans in Washington and New Delhi had identified factors that would reduce India's incentives to seek nuclear weapon capability, but the emerging nonproliferation policy failed to act on this analysis.

FOUR

War and Leadership Transitions at Home

AUGUST 1965–MAY 1966

Events soon drew Indian attention away from the quest for security guarantees and technical assistance from the United States. Military tensions between Pakistan and India mounted in the spring of 1965, leading to war. Before the implications of India's military victory in this conflict could be assimilated, the leadership of the nation and the nuclear establishment changed hands, following the sudden deaths of both Shastri and Bhabha in the space of two weeks. As this chapter describes, their successors, Indira Gandhi and Vikram Sarabhai, were thrust onto center stage in a period of domestic tribulation that motivated them not to make decisive moves in the nuclear field.

WAR WITH PAKISTAN

India and Pakistan fought a short but intense war in August and September 1965. The conflict was sparked by clashes in April in the marshy area near the Arabian Sea, southeast of Karachi, known as the Rann of Kutch. Pakistan had initiated a dispute in 1954 when it declared the Rann of Kutch a sea, not a marsh as India insisted it was. If the area were deemed a marsh, India would retain legal sovereignty over it, if a sea, the international boundary would run through its middle, giving Pakistan control over the northern half. The matter remained more or less quiescent for ten years. Then, in April 1965, as part of his policy of "leaning on India" to test Lal Bahadur Shastri's mettle, Pakistani President Ayub Khan began running military patrols in the area.[1] Indian forces moved to expel the Pakistanis. However, Pakistan's units outmaneuvered India's. Facing the rainy season and the risk of having its forces cut off by rising waters, India withdrew on April 27.

In mid-May Pakistan shifted the scene for the war's second act to Kashmir. Pakistani forces attacked a small Indian outpost in Kargil; Indian units counter-attacked successfully, moving into territory held by Pakistan since 1948.[2] The United Kingdom pressed both states successfully for a cease-fire, which was agreed to on June 27. Indian forces withdrew from recently captured outposts.[3] Shastri agreed further to submit the Rann of Kutch matter to legal arbitration, a position Nehru had rejected. This prompted a renewed domestic attack on the prime minister, already under scrutiny about his handling of nuclear issues and other foreign policy matters. Pakistan's Ayub had visited China in March 1965, raising the specter of Sino-Pakistani collaboration against India and leading Indian political actors to urge a tougher foreign policy.[4]

The June cease-fire turned out to be an intermission before the major act of the 1965 war. In this lull, Indian parliamentarians and the press condemned Shastri's apparent willingness to compromise on the Rann of Kutch and decried Pakistan's use of American-supplied arms. They noted bitterly that Washington had assured India that these arms would not be used against it.[5] Washington's postponement of the scheduled Shastri visit to the United States further angered the Indian polity. Indian animus toward the United States was exacerbated still more by President Lyndon Johnson's decision in June 1965 to halt routine approval of new aid commitments to India (and Pakistan). Johnson and some in Congress questioned whether India was making the tough decisions required to improve its economy.[6] The World Bank had recently concluded that India's economy would not grow without major reform to reduce governmental controls and licensing, to shift investment from industry to agriculture, and to devalue the rupee.[7] Johnson took it upon himself to pressure India to bear the political pain of instituting such major changes. As Dennis Kux described it, "Lyndon Johnson, in effect, became the US government's 'desk officer' for PL 480 food aid to India."[8] In the process he played the brand of hardball politics that made him legendary in America. The tactic worked: Indian advocates of agricultural reform used Johnson's leverage to push their own balky government to change policy. But the heavy-handed American intervention deepened India's suspicion of the United States.

Meanwhile, in the summer, Pakistan decided to undertake a much more serious military gambit to seize Kashmir, having contested India successfully in the Rann of Kutch. It is beyond the scope of this study to analyze the Pakistani motivations in detail, but Ayub Khan and his hawkish foreign minister, Zulfikar Ali Bhutto, appeared to believe that the balance of military power was more favorable to Pakistan than it would be in the future. U.S. weaponry had qualitatively improved Pakistan's forces. In March 1965, Ayub Khan and Bhutto had conducted positive meetings with Chinese Premier Chou En-lai in Beijing, boosting their confidence in China's support. On the other hand, India's post-1962 military buildup—bolstered by U.S. and British arms supplies—would likely erode Pakistan's relative position.[9] In late 1964 and early 1965 the central Indian government had tightened its grip on the state government of Kashmir as the ruling National Congress party of Kashmir merged with the Congress party.[10] Thus, the military and political equations affecting the balance of Indian and Pakistani power appeared unlikely to swing further to Pakistan's advantage and could worsen.

Finally, and more speculatively, some evidence suggests that India's nuclear program motivated Pakistani leaders to gamble on war in 1965. The Pakistani press, President Ayub Khan, and Foreign Minister Bhutto had concluded that India now was embarked on a nuclear weapon–building program. They noted that Homi Bhabha had claimed that India could build a nuclear weapon within twelve to eighteen months. A recently declassified U.S. government cable indicates that in November 1964, Ayub Khan "expressed his deep concern at prospect of rapidly developing Indian nuclear capability which could be readily converted from peaceful to war-like purposes."[11] Patrick Keatley of the (Manchester) *Guardian* reported on March 11, 1965, that the "spectre" of the nuclear bomb "haunted" Pakistan's leaders and "dominated" the discussions that Ayub and Bhutto had had the previous week with Chou En-lai in Beijing.[12] (Bhutto, in testimony during his 1977 trial for conspiring in the 1974 murder of a political opponent, as discussed in chapter 8, referred back to this meeting with Chou in ways that suggested that he at that time first sought Chinese assistance in helping Pakistan acquire nuclear weapon capability.) Interviewing Pakistani officials in 1965, Keatley was surprised by "the deep anxiety I had encountered in the key Ministries at Rawalpindi—particularly at Defence—over the possibility that 110 million Pakistanis will wake up one fine morning in the latter half of 1965 to learn from Radio Delhi that India has become the world's sixth nuclear Power."[13] Bhutto told Keatley that if India produced nuclear weapons "then we should have to eat grass and get one, or buy one, of our own."[14]

More research needs to be done to measure whether and how the prospective nuclear threat from India affected Pakistani leaders' decision to try to take Kashmir in 1965. Yet the depth of "nuclear" concern among Pakistani leaders at the time would have made it unnatural for them not to weigh this factor in their decision to go to war. Unaddressed in the existing literature, this would constitute the first case of nuclear proliferation in one country (India) prompting an adversary to undertake military action to "beat" the anticipated effects of nuclear deterrence.

The real 1965 war began on August 5 when Pakistan infiltrated several thousand guerrillas into Indian-held Kashmir, apparently hoping to spark an uprising by Muslims in the Kashmir valley.[15] On August 25, India sent several thousand troops to turn back the infiltrators and pursue them into Pakistani-held territory. The Indian forces succeeded and now held territory heretofore occupied by Pakistan.

Determined to reverse the tactical defeat, Ayub Khan launched a major attack on September 1. Pakistani armored forces moved into southern Kashmir, driving back Indian defenders. The Pakistanis continued eastward and approached the key road linking Srinagar, the capital of Jammu and Kashmir, with the body of

India.[16] Were Pakistan to take and hold this road, India's forces in Kashmir would have been cut off.

On September 6 the Indian Army counterattacked into West Pakistan.[17] Indian forces moved westward, south of Kashmir, toward Lahore. Smaller Indian units attacked southwest from the Ladakh region of Jammu and Kashmir. Both countries' air forces engaged in the fight. Facing a weak position in Kashmir, India sought to threaten the heart of Pakistan, raising the stakes immeasurably.

Between September 1 and 6 (and thereafter) the United States and the United Kingdom pressed for restraint—alone, together, and through the United Nations. President Johnson, however, preferred not to exert a dominant American role but rather to work through the United Nations, reflecting waning interest in the region.[18] The United States sought to dampen the conflict by embargoing military exports and suspending economic aid commitments to both India and Pakistan, while urging UN diplomacy. Similarly, Moscow supported UN efforts to end the war. UN Secretary General U. Thant traveled to the region between September 9 and 14 to seek a cease-fire agreement, but he met no success.

After ten days of fighting, Indian and Pakistani forces stalled. Indian units had stabilized a front fifteen miles inside the Pakistani border, near Lahore. Pakistani forces remained unable to take the road to Srinagar. Contrary to Pakistan's hopes and India's fears, the Indian forces fought effectively, winning some of the fiercest tank battles since World War II, despite the qualitative superiority of Pakistan's U.S.-supplied armor.

On September 17, as the militaries remained entrenched, China threatened to broaden the conflict by giving India an ultimatum to remove construction works in Tibet or face "grave consequences."[19] At the onset of the conflict, China had pledged its support to Pakistan, charging India with aggression. The Chinese ultimatum prompted stern warnings from Washington and Moscow. Shastri reacted calmly and strongly, denying most of China's charges and offering to investigate the others.[20] The combination of U.S.-Soviet pressure and Indian steadiness gave China pause. On September 19, Beijing prolonged its ultimatum, implicitly weakening it.[21] Again, contrary to Pakistani hopes and Indian fears, China was not prepared to take risks on a matter where its vital interests were not at stake.

Faced with UN demands for a cease-fire and recognizing that military supplies were running low and that the battlefield equation was unlikely to change significantly, India and Pakistan stopped fighting. India accepted the UN cease-fire call on September 20. Pakistan followed on September 22. According to Indian Defence Minister Y. B. Chavan, India suffered 2,226 military fatalities and 7,870 wounded.[22] Hari Ram Gupta cited a Pakistani source as declaring the number of Pakistani casualties at between 10,000 and 14,000.[23] Pakistan suffered major losses in armor and aircraft compared to India.[24]

The war provided a major lift to Shastri, the Indian military, and the polity at large, coming as it did less than three years after the ignominious defeat by China. Kashmir had been held, Chinese pressure rebuffed. For its part, Pakistan felt the loss of morale and martial confidence that had been so important to the new nation. Still, it had escaped a more serious defeat and held some leverage in Kashmir to negotiate, hopefully, an improved position in the dispute over the ultimate dispensation of the state.

With the war ended, India and Pakistan then had to resolve the peace. Outside intervention was required to manage the postwar settlement. Here the Soviet Union took the constructive lead. Soviet Premier Aleksei Kosygin earlier had offered his office as a mediator, and India and Pakistan accepted it in November. Following further preparatory negotiations, Shastri and Ayub traveled to Tashkent in Soviet Uzbekistan in January 1966 to settle the peace. Kosygin skillfully mediated an agreement formalized in the Tashkent Declaration of January 10. Among other things, the agreement called for both sides to withdraw their forces to positions held prior to August 5 and to repatriate prisoners of war.[25] Both states pledged "not to have recourse to force and to settle their disputes through peaceful means."[26] However, the Tashkent Declaration failed to resolve the fundamental problem of Kashmir, stating merely "that Jammu and Kashmir was discussed, and each of the sides set forth its respective position."[27]

The Tashkent Declaration received mixed reviews in India. The Congress party and the Communist parties celebrated it. Others denounced it.[28] At Tashkent, Shastri was under strong domestic pressure not to abandon the ground India had gained from Pakistani control in the mountainous passes of Kashmir.[29] When the Declaration yielded back this territory to Pakistan, it prompted an outcry, particularly from the non-Communist opposition.[30] Surrender of territory and the perceived eagerness to seek peace above all else demoralized those who wished for a more robust and powerful India. It appeared particularly pathetic coming at a time of apparent triumph. Furthermore, if morality were a special Indian value in foreign affairs, Shastri had failed even here by acceding to a Tashkent Declaration that did not name Pakistan as the aggressor.[31] These sentiments, and the experience of the war, rekindled the nuclear debate.

The 1965 war symbolized an American turning away from South Asia. The Johnson administration had decided not to take the lead in seeking a cease-fire but rather to work through the United Nations. The United States stood back as Kosygin assumed the role of peacemaker in South Asia—a remarkable development given the United States' prior and subsequent view of the region as a cold war battleground. Yet the war and the decade preceding it showed the intensity of the zero-sum contest between India and Pakistan. Washington had been unable to pursue close relations with both states simultaneously. Pakistan's use of American-supplied arms in the war against India, despite prior American assurances that this would not happen, heightened Indian mistrust. Washington's cutoff of military and economic aid to India and Pakistan during the war angered both nations—the Indians because it seemed unfair given Pakistan's instigation of the war; the Pakistanis because they thought the United States was an ally. Both India and Pakistan resisted intermittent U.S. attempts before and after the 1965 war to bring them to the table to address Kashmir. American economic aid to India had frustrated both the Indians—who resented their need of aid and the strings sometimes attached to it—and many in the United States, particularly the Congress. Thus, after the war, with little to show for the past decade's engagement, the United States virtually vacated the region.

NUCLEAR DEBATE INTENSIFIES

Paradoxically, the victory over Pakistan triggered renewed demands in India for nuclear weapons. The day before the cease-fire took effect, nearly one hundred members of Parliament from multiple parties, including Congress, issued a letter urging the prime minister to decide immediately to develop nuclear weapons.[32] Some of the erstwhile bomb advocates simply seized on whatever opportunity they could to stoke the debate, but for others the war had changed the equation. The problem was not Pakistan, but rather China and the United States. The ultimatum China issued to India was perceived to portend increased bullying from Beijing and growing collusion between it and Pakistan. This had to be contested. Even more outrageous to the petitioners was the United States' and other nations' cessation of aid to India (and Pakistan) during the conflict. Participants in the recent nuclear debate had speculated that the Western powers and the Soviet Union would assist India if it were threatened by China. The fate of aid during the war dashed this hope. India was clearly on its own. As the petitioning MPs wrote, "in the face of the collusion between China and Pakistan, [this] casts a clear and imperative duty on the Government to take an immediate decision to develop our nuclear weapons."[33]

During the ensuing weeks, politicians throughout India pressed the case for building the bomb.[34] Yet, Shastri held firm. In early November he responded to a written query in the Lok Sabha by declaring that "[d]espite the continued threat of aggression from China . . . [the] Government [has] continued to adhere to the decision not to go in for nuclear weapons but to work for their elimination instead."[35] Shastri added that the conflict with Pakistan provided no basis for altering this policy.

In an article based on an interview with Bhabha, the *New York Times* journalist Anthony Lukas reported rumors that "Prime Minister Shastri may have given the [nuclear] agency permission to work up to a point about three months short of exploding a device, after which it would have to halt and await a political decision before completing the rest of the work."[36] Lukas added that "any decision to go ahead and explode a device would be motivated by political and psychological considerations rather than military requirements." In the interview, however, Bhabha denied that the Atomic Energy Commission was preparing to explode a device: "We are still 18 months away from exploding either a bomb or a device for peaceful purposes and we are doing nothing to reduce that period."[37] Bhabha added that he had received no new instructions following the war with Pakistan. "The emergency changed nothing. Why should it?"[38]

There are many ways to interpret Bhabha's comments. The interpretation most consistent with the historical evidence is that Bhabha had in fact been authorized to begin preparatory work on a peaceful nuclear explosive in late 1964, and therefore no need existed to change policy *after the war with Pakistan.* Bhabha's apparent denial focused on being "18 months away from exploding a bomb or a device." Yet, this was a red herring. Despite his earlier claims of being this near to conducting an explosion, Bhabha knew that more time actually was required to stockpile the necessary plutonium, design a device, build and test the necessary nonnuclear components, and prepare a test site. If, by November 1965, progress had not yet been made to reduce the time required to ready an explosive, this was not due to policy but rather to unmet technological requirements. Given Bhabha's known preference for producing nuclear explosives, he would have used the renewed debate to press his case if he had not already been authorized to work in this direction. That he refrained from doing so, unlike in October and November 1964, suggested that he already had the authority he needed. As would be the case over the ensuing decades, the heated political debate over nuclear policy suffered from ignorance of what the nuclear establishment was already doing.

SHASTRI AND BHABHA DIE— INDIRA GANDHI AND VIKRAM SARABHAI TAKE OVER, 1966

Throughout 1966, the debate over India's nuclear policy continued. However, it occurred in the context of more important political-economic challenges. Lal Bahadur Shastri died suddenly of a heart attack within hours after signing the January 10 Tashkent Declaration. He would be spared further debate over the bomb, a subject anathema to his spirit. Instead, this issue would be left to Nehru's daughter, Indira Gandhi, who succeeded him as prime minister. She inherited a country beset by domestic troubles. Practically all sectors of the Indian economy were failing. Prices for consumer goods continued to rise, as did unemployment. Forty-one percent of India's government spending came from foreign aid and deficit financing.[39] India depended heavily on American food aid.

In early 1966, the U.S. Congress announced a suspension of American aid. The aid was only partially restored in February following an appeal by Mrs. Gandhi to President Johnson. Intense discussion of Indian agricultural policy and U.S. aid continued, while the United States, the International Monetary Fund (IMF), and the World Bank also pressed India for broader economic reforms. The donors emphasized the imperative of devaluing the rupee. After months of pressure, Mrs. Gandhi in June 1966 devalued the rupee by 36.5 percent. This was deemed necessary not only to win increased IMF and American aid but also to stimulate domestic production and exports while reducing the role of costly foreign-exchange imports. However, the devaluation exacerbated the economic hardship of the average Indian and outraged powerful industrial interests. Mrs. Gandhi had failed to prepare her Congress colleagues and the polity at large, betraying her relative ignorance of economics and her autocratic governing style. The rupee devaluation was portrayed as a neocolonial diktat by the United States. As the former Indian ambassador to the United States, B. K. Nehru told Dennis Kux, "It was as if devaluation had castrated India."[40] Two years later the episode would affect India's view of the nonproliferation treaty.

The debate over nuclear policy did not die down. Indeed, as if to symbolize the troubled political-economic context, more than ten workers at the then-under-construction Tarapur atomic power plant were killed in strike-related violence.[41] As the sovereign over the nuclear realm, Indira Gandhi found herself in a situation for which she had little expertise. She, like her father and Shastri, had to rely on the leaders of the Atomic Energy Commission to inform and advise her in this arcane area while she attended to the politics of decisions.

Less than two weeks into Indira Gandhi's reign—on January 24, 1966—Homi Bhabha died when the plane carrying him to Europe crashed into Mont Blanc. Bhabha's death at age fifty-six left a huge void in India's nuclear policymaking. While Indians and the international scientific establishment mourned the loss of India's scientific leader, Indira Gandhi was charged with both selecting his successor and defending a policy. It is impossible to know what the new prime minister believed the actual nuclear policy was. Shastri as prime minister and Bhabha as AEC chairman had shaped it, but there is no evidence regarding who else knew the whole agenda. The debates and rationale informing major decisions tended not to be recorded in files.[42] Leading scientists at the Atomic Energy Establishment in Trombay such as Raja Ramanna and Homi Sethna by early 1965 knew that preparatory work on a peaceful nuclear explosive had been authorized, as they were to lead the effort.[43] But the Indian public debate did not reflect awareness of the project. It is also possible that Indira Gandhi was not informed initially that work toward a peaceful nuclear explosive capability had been authorized by Shastri.[44] Bhabha would have been the one to brief the new prime minister on the project, but he died on the day she was sworn in as prime minister.[45]

The appointment of Bhabha's successor as chair of the Atomic Energy Commission entailed some controversy. Immediately upon Bhabha's death, Dharma Vira, the cabinet secretary and also a member of the AEC, became provisional AEC chairman. Homi Sethna, a chemical engineer who managed the building of the plutonium separation plant at Trombay, was named director of the Atomic Energy Establishment there, one of the many titles Bhabha had held.[46] However, more than three months lapsed before the new chairman of the Atomic Energy Commission was installed.[47] The most detailed account of this matter—only one paragraph—appeared in Raja Ramanna's autobiography. Ramanna wrote that Vira, "true to his bureaucratic training," appointed a committee to select the next chairman.[48] However, according to Ramanna, who was then director of physics at the Atomic Energy Establishment, the majority of AEC members rejected the committee approach, intimating that it would be somehow biased. Ramanna wrote that after "considerable discussion, we finally approached Mrs. Indira Gandhi . . . and requested her to make the final selection."[49] The first choice was Professor S. Chandrasekhar, a brilliant physicist at the University of Chicago; however, Chandrasekhar declined. Yet another round of discussions ensued.[50] Clearly there was significant jockeying within the AEC. Mrs. Gandhi must have been pushed from various sides, reflecting competing personal, programmatic, and political interests that cannot be specified from the existing record. The stakes were obviously high, given the great power Bhabha had established for the chairman's position and the absence of institutional checks and balances on the nuclear establishment.

Ultimately, the prime minister chose Vikram Sarabhai, a Cambridge-trained physicist and AEC member, who was then head of the Indian National Committee for Space Research, which operated under the Department of Atomic Energy. Ashok Kapur has suggested that Gandhi favored Sarabhai in part because he was from a fabulously wealthy Gujarati family and could help the prime minister ward off challenges from her main rival for power, Morarji Desai, who also hailed from Gujarat.[51]

Sarabhai was not the first choice of the scientists then working on the nuclear explosives project.[52] Ramanna has suggested that he had doubts that Sarabhai, given his concentration on space-related work, "would be able to get a grip on atomic energy developments . . . and give it [this work] any special orientation."[53] Indeed, Sarabhai questioned the morality and utility of nuclear weapons for India and would soon take steps to reverse the peaceful nuclear explosives project. While this may have harmonized with the wishes of some of the Indian scientific community, others who had been close to Bhabha found Sarabhai a less-than-ideal candidate. As one pro-explosive former high-ranking AEC official put it: "There was tension between some of us and Sarabhai. He was a peculiar fellow. He was a Gandhian, believed in peace at all costs. But, you know, he was so rich, his life was so different. He never went to school as a boy, but was educated at home. He never rubbed shoulders with common people; he was so sheltered."[54] In this man's view, Sarabhai lacked a sense of how tough the world could be and that India might need nuclear weapon capability. This buttresses the notion that Mrs. Gandhi selected Sarabhai more for political reasons than to reflect the preferences of the leaders of the nuclear establishment.

By the time Sarabhai was installed, the Indian representative to the nonproliferation treaty negotiations in Geneva, V. C. Trivedi, had sharpened India's position on the treaty. On February 15, 1966, Trivedi needled the United States and, to a lesser extent, the Soviet Union for trying to negotiate over the heads of India and the other nonaligned states. Insisting on equitable, mutual obligations between the haves and the have-nots, Trivedi clarified that this did not necessarily mean immediate and complete nuclear disarmament, as some dismissively portrayed the non-aligned to be arguing. Rather, as a first step the treaty should obligate nuclear and non–nuclear weapon states to "forgo further production of nuclear weapons and delivery vehicles designed to carry those weapons."[55] This formulation, applying equally to all states, seemed relatively practical and eminently fair. If enacted, it would have had the added advantage of blocking China from developing an arsenal threatening India, as China had not yet developed delivery vehicles for nuclear weapons. More broadly, Trivedi's speech established that security guarantees from the haves to the have-nots would not satisfy India, contrary to past impressions. The nuclear threat itself had to be addressed and eliminated.[56]

Trivedi's cogent attack caught the United States off guard. In testimony before the Senate in February, Secretary of State Dean Rusk admitted that "the interest on the part of the non-nuclear states as registered in the last few months is, surprisingly, not so much aimed at the question of assurances and guarantees as it is aimed at a clear demonstration that those who have nuclear weapons are proceeding on a path of disarmament."[57] Secretary of Defense Robert McNamara was one of the few American officials to accept the logic and conclusions of the Indians and their supporters, but his was a minority view within the U.S. government and it did not prevail.[58]

However, Washington was not ignoring the Indian nuclear problem. For much of 1965 and into early 1966, the State Department, along with the Defense Department, had been analyzing alternatives for heading off Indian acquisition of nuclear weapons. This included, once again, the possibility of sharing nuclear weapons with India. On March 16, 1966, officials presented Secretary of State Rusk a top secret memorandum and study of the subject.[59] The document responded to a 1965 request by the secretaries of state and defense and the national security adviser and was prepared to brief President Johnson prior to a pending meeting with Prime Minister Gandhi.

The memorandum to the president began by reporting a U.S. intelligence estimate that "on balance" India probably would embark on a nuclear weapon program "within the next few years."[60] Recognizing the U.S. interest in nonproliferation, the memorandum suggested that the United States "might in time have to be more responsive to Indian security needs, preferably in some way that will minimize our own commitment."[61] To explore the form that such response might take, a State Department–led study was attached for the president. It, too, began with an intelligence assessment indicating that India could test a first nuclear device within a year of a decision to do so but that leading Indian politicians currently did not favor such an effort, in part because of "US pressures against proliferation, particularly at a time when India is so dependent on the US to help alleviate India's critical food situation."[62] Nevertheless, the assessment opined that factors of prestige, "China's growing nuclear strength and the specter of Pakistani-Chinese cooperation against India" would lead India "within the next few years" to "detonate a nuclear device and proceed to produce weapons."[63]

"Assuming that the United States does not want to assist India to get its own nuclear weapons," the study proffered seven alternatives the United States could pursue "to keep India from deciding to produce" such weapons."[64] First, the United States could strive to complete a nonproliferation treaty and a comprehensive test ban treaty, although now the Joint Chiefs opposed the latter, in a reversal of their 1963 position. Second, Washington could cut off economic assistance and other aid if India decided to develop nuclear weapons. However, the study noted that this could weaken U.S. influence if pursued too rigorously. Third, the United States could offer a "formal military alliance" with India. The study deemed this unfeasible from the U.S. standpoint, unwelcome in India, and counterproductive vis-à-vis Pakistan and China. The study then posed three possible variations of security guarantees that the United States alone or with the Soviet Union could offer nonnuclear states or India alone. Each was dismissed. Finally, the authors suggested that the United States could offer to provide India with nuclear warheads to be delivered by Indian forces to "deter or retaliate to a Chinese nuclear attack."[65]

This last alternative revived the nuclear-sharing proposal drafted by Defense Department staff in late 1964, and the study's authors devoted several pages to its consideration. As before, the basic idea was to guarantee that the United States would assist India in acquiring "nuclear delivery capability" and then "provision of compatible nuclear warheads for the Indian delivery system."[66] The warheads would remain "under US custody (probably not on Indian soil) until such time as the Chinese used nuclear weapons against India, when they would be released by the US to India for Indian delivery on Chinese targets."[67] In return, India would forego its own production of nuclear weapons. Entrusting the actual delivery to India would, the authors hoped, reduce the likelihood of Soviet or Chinese retaliation against the United States.[68] The authors suggested that a parallel arrangement could be offered to Pakistan.

The nuclear sharing idea was serious enough, according to the study, that British officials had been briefed and had "indicated that they would wish to participate." The study described possible aircraft that could be used under such a plan, Indian air defense improvements and command and control systems that would be needed (provided with U.S. assistance), and targeting options in China. It was noted that eventually intermediate-range missiles would be required. Much of this, including any agreement to turn nuclear weapons over to India would require "new Congressional enabling legislation."[69]

At the end of the detailed discussion, Rusk joined with the secretary of defense, the Joint Chiefs of Staff, and the director of the Arms Control and Disarmament Agency in opposing "discussion of nuclear sharing arrangements with India at this time."[70] The primary explanation was that the "Secretary of Defense and the Joint Chiefs of Staff do not believe a nuclear sharing arrangement would do more than delay an Indian pro-nuclear decision."[71] Officials acknowledged difficulties stemming from India's desire to remain nonaligned, the risk of giving India too much of a nuclear role, and the impact on others, including "Pakistan, Japan and other US Asian allies, and the UK role East of Suez."[72] Yet, the authors still were not prepared to dismiss this two-year-old option once they confronted all the alternatives.

The study concluded that "[i]t is probable that, *without* a dramatic alternative, in a few years India will decide to become a nuclear power."[73] This would impair India's "economic (and political) viability, undermine India's conventional military power, drive Pakistan to the US, USSR, or Communist China for aid, and increase the likelihood of further proliferation."[74] These realizations drove the authors back to the nuclear sharing idea: "It is by no means clear that offer of a tangible nuclear sharing or support arrangement to India would head off an Indian decision to make its own nuclear weapons. It is, however, very unlikely that any other US action would have this result, and the importance of heading off such a decision warrants serious consideration of this approach."[75]

The memorandum finally recommended weakly that President Johnson should offer to Mrs. Gandhi that "[n]uclear powers should try to work out some arrangement to safeguard the security interests of non-nuclear powers." The president should say further that "if a growing Chinese Communist nuclear capability should ever pose a serious threat to India, [the president hoped] she would frankly discuss the question with us."[76] Once again, and not for the last time, the United States was unprepared to risk bold steps to motivate India to forego nuclear weapon capability.

American officials did attempt to influence the internal Indian debate by providing "sensitive" data on the costs of building even a small nuclear arsenal. Washington knew that a U.S. "hard sell" campaign on the high costs of the bomb would backfire, especially because in the "wake of devaluation [of the rupee] Indian sensitivity to real or imagined US pressure has only increased," according to a recently declassified State Department cable.[77] Yet the cost arguments were compelling enough that Washington wanted them made quietly to Indian officials and indirectly through foreign media contacts. The premise was that "India cannot just detonate one or two devices and stop, . . . as Atomic Energy Establishment head Sethna himself has pointed out."[78] India would need a much larger, deliverable arsenal to deter China—150 bombs, according to Sethna as cited by U.S. sources. This arsenal could not rely on bombers because they would be "highly vulnerable to Chinese air defenses."[79] Sophisticated delivery systems would be "far more" expensive than nuclear bombs themselves. American analysts estimated that "a simple" intermediate-range ballistic missile would cost an industrialized country about $800 million to develop, plus about $1 million per missile to produce and maintain a deterrent force over a five-year period.[80] The Americans acknowledged that the "pro-bomb group" in India had a "good argument that costs involved in testing first device ($30–40 million) [were] well within India's financial capabilities," and that a small program of "1–2 weapons 20 KT [kiloton] range per year at annual cost of $20–30 million" would be affordable.[81] However, the point was that this low-cost approach would not buy a viable deterrent force (according to U.S. doctrine) and that a viable force would "inevitably involve India in an increasingly expensive nuclear arms spiral."[82] As subsequent pages and chapters show, such cost considerations did weigh heavily on Indian decision makers.

Meanwhile, in New Delhi, Parliament was questioning Trivedi's February statement in Geneva minimizing the importance of security guarantees. On March 1, Lok Sabha members asked if the government would seek security guarantees or pacts with other powers as an alternative to building the bomb. Prime Minister Gandhi said no, but for curious reasons: China's explosion of nuclear weapons did not give "sufficient reason for us to change our policy in this matter."[83] The prime minister added that India did not want to "do anything which will precipitate the crisis and lead to the development of nuclear weapons in many more countries."[84] Once again, those arguing for restraint emphasized the importance of promoting nonproliferation and the hope that nuclear disarmament would help avoid a decision to break with the Gandhian-Nehruvian line against building nuclear weapons. And once again, neither the hawks nor the doves presented careful analyses of China's overall military capabilities and intentions toward India. Moreover, Mrs. Gandhi averred that if India manufactured a nuclear weapon Pakistan would follow suit, which was to be avoided.[85]

In May 1966 the new prime minister was compelled to engage more fully in the nuclear debate, despite more pressing political and economic concerns. At a Congress Parliamentary Party meeting, General Secretary K. C. Pant urged a position he had been pushing intermittently since early 1965: India should not rush into manufacturing nuclear weapons, but it should prepare the necessary technological capabilities to do so quickly if the need arose. This corresponded to the Shastri-Bhabha policy, but Pant arrived at this conclusion from his own analysis of the situation, which was helped by his scientific training (a master's degree in physical chemistry) and his general belief in Bhabha and the nuclear program.[86]

Concerns escalated after May 9, when China conducted its third nuclear weapon test, this time reportedly a thermonuclear device. Days later the U.S. government announced that the Chinese explosion was not from a thermonuclear weapon, although the device did contain an element, lithium-6, that could be instrumental in achieving the fusion entailed in thermonuclear bombs.[87]

On May 10, the Indian Parliament erupted into debate over nuclear policy. Minister of External Affairs Swaran Singh began by trying to reassure the body that the Chinese test had not come as a surprise and that India's policy reflected "a careful assessment" by the government in consultation with the "Service Chiefs and Atomic Energy experts."[88] He argued that the latest test "does not vitiate the earlier conclusion," although the "policy is kept under constant review."[89] This was patently inadequate to calm the emotions of the New Delhi elite. H. V. Kamath, a leader of the Praja Socialist Party denounced the government for adhering "pig-headedly or stubbornly to the hackneyed declaration of its policy, which can be summed up briefly as 'we can make the bomb, but we would not do it.' "[90] Kamath asked whether the government would at least follow up on Shastri's earlier exploration of obtaining nuclear security guarantees from the United States, the United Kingdom, or the Soviet Union. Swaran Singh answered lamely that the government had not specifically discussed this problem recently with the major powers.[91] This did not end the dismay in the Parliament, where decorum was barely maintained and the government found itself practically bereft of support.[92]

Then Prime Minister Gandhi entered the debate. Putting a robust face on the government's policy, she said, "We are building up our atomic power. Of course, we are using it for peaceful purposes; but in the mean time we are increasing our know-how and other competence."[93] She continued by questioning how "one bomb or two bombs will help us" but was interrupted by Nath Pai, who declared that "[i]t is only when you produce one that you can produce many."[94] Unable to rebut this, Mrs. Gandhi closed by saying vaguely that it was a mistake to think that China could "attack any country with nuclear weapons with impunity."[95]

These few prime ministerial utterances prompted extensive press commentary and interpretation. By saying that India was "building up" atomic power "for peaceful purposes, but *in the mean time* we are increasing our know-how and other competence," Mrs. Gandhi seemed to qualify the traditional formulation and imply a potential military application. Or so the press interpreted. The *Statesman* reported: "Most MPs irrespective of party distinction said this evening (May 10) that they detected in the Prime Minister's elucidation of her replies a subtle change in emphasis from her past pronouncements. This change, according to numerous MPs . . . is, in fact, a continuation of the late Shastri's statement that India's self-abnegation in relation to nuclear weapons could not be considered a commitment for all times."[96] Other outlets reported in a similar vein.

But did the prime minister choose her words knowingly? Did she mean to suggest a departure from the previously understood peaceful-uses-only policy? Was she in fact simply restating what Shastri had said in November, 1964, but which the press and Parliament had failed to comprehend earlier? Was the point not merely that the no-weapons policy could be changed but rather that the focus would be on developing a nuclear explosives capability under the cover of peaceful purposes?

Existing data do not allow definite answers to these questions. Having stirred press speculation, Mrs. Gandhi was asked days later whether she had in fact shifted policy. "I do not think so," she replied.[97] The reporter probed further, asking whether policy now included "acquisition of the know-how to manufacture the atom bomb?" Mrs. Gandhi answered truthfully but enigmatically, "I am not an expert in these matters."[98] Taken at face value, Mrs. Gandhi's answers seemed to indicate confusion over the exact meaning of her recent statements. Clearly, her answers were "evasive," as a then leader of the nuclear establishment recalled in 1997.[99] She had been briefed by Sarabhai who was the AEC chairman-designate. But given Sarabhai's soon-to-be-apparent antipathy to nuclear weapons, it was impossible to tell how he described the nuclear policy to Mrs. Gandhi. Was the prime minister evading acknowledgment that work on nuclear explosives was underway, or was she instead trying not to admit that there was no established policy?

A *Washington Post* story on May 12 shed some light on these questions. The reporter, Warren Unna, wrote that Bhabha had "reportedly told the government in 1964 that he was proceeding with technological exploration of military uses of the atom, and that the government could have two years to give him the final go-ahead on actual application. ... India's Department of Atomic Energy is said now to have informed Prime Minister Indira Gandhi that an up-or-down decision should be made in the next five months."[100] The apparently well-sourced report continued by quoting a "highly placed Indian official" who argued, "We don't want a bomb; we just want an explosion. In the diplomatic field, the lack of a demonstration of our nuclear capacity has been a drawback—and one that this government thinks it will not be able to withstand much longer. Every time there is a bang from China, the pressure goes up. This government, with troubles at home and a general election next year, is in no position to withstand pressures."[101] The government was in fact positioned to withstand pressure, in part because of the ascension of a chairman of the Atomic Energy Commission who opposed nuclear weapons. But an admixture of domestic political considerations and concerns about India's standing internationally did incline Mrs. Gandhi to signal a more robust policy.

Meanwhile, in the nonproliferation treaty negotiations in Geneva, the stage was being set to debate the question of peaceful nuclear explosives. On May 10, the day of Prime Minister Gandhi's important Lok Sabha statement, V. C. Trivedi framed India's negotiating position. After reemphasizing the agreed-upon mandate for balanced, mutual obligations among the nuclear haves and have-nots, Trivedi turned to "the question of control on the peaceful nuclear activities of nations."[102] He reiterated that India had always insisted that controls on the nuclear programs of non–nuclear weapon states could only be accepted with simultaneous agreements on disarmament by the nuclear weapon states, and, furthermore, that any such controls must be "mutual and balanced." This general principle preserved the legal "space" for India to conduct peaceful nuclear explosions, which Trivedi personally favored.

The PNE issue was extremely delicate for India. As the leading demander of nuclear disarmament, India's position would have been badly undermined by evidence that it was embarked on building its own nuclear weapon capability. At the same time, however, Indian diplomats sought to block efforts to proscribe national development of peaceful nuclear explosives. Thus, India's position in the debate over the nonproliferation treaty was bounded on one side by the traditional policy of abjuring nuclear weapons and, on the other side, by the desire to keep the nuclear option open by preserving the right to develop and conduct peaceful nuclear explosions.

Such was the scene Sarabhai entered in late May when he formally became chairman of the AEC and secretary of the Department of Atomic Energy.[103] Rather than clarify matters, he confused them further. Interviews and the public record indicate that Sarabhai moved rather quickly to stop the peaceful nuclear explosives project to which Shastri and Bhabha had agreed. In his first press conference after taking charge of the nuclear establishment, Sarabhai sought to devalue the putative benefits of nuclear weapons for India. His statement is worth quoting at length, as it aptly portrays the priority domestic considerations and technical limitations assumed in determining India's nuclear policy:

> I would like to emphasise that security can be endangered not only from outside but also from within. If you do not maintain the rate of progress of the economic development of the nation, I would suggest that you would face a most serious crisis, something that might disintegrate India as we know it. I would like to suggest then that when we set ourselves the goal of looking after the security of the nation, we should think of both internal as well as external threat, and this immediately brings about a very special nature of the problem [of building atomic bombs]. How do you produce a balance of internal development as well as maintain an adequate state of preparedness to resist aggression from outside? Do you have to do this all by yourself? To what extent would you use assistance from outside, whether it is for national development or for defence? These are the million dollar questions before us. So the real problem in this whole question relates to the utilisation of national resources for productive and social welfare against the burden of defence expenditure which a country can bear at any particular time.[104]

To this point, Sarabhai had indicated that threats to national security exist not only in the international environment but also in the domestic situation. He had tacitly questioned the national security rationale of nonalignment, addressing the problem of alternative strategies for balancing power. Then he turned specifically to whether nuclear weapons provided useful means for India's security:

> I think those who have studied military strategy would also agree that paper tigers do not provide security, that is you cannot bluff in regard to your military strength. If you want to rely on the atom bomb for safeguarding your security in the sense that say the USA or the USSR have got, a series of balanced deterrents; this is not achieved by exploding a bomb. It means a total defence system, a means of delivery in this case. You have to think in terms of long range missiles; it means radars, a high state of electronics, a high state of metallurgical and industrial base. How do you develop such a system? It is not only for the scientist to produce one prototype, and you then have a defence system. It requires a total commitment of national resources of a most stupendous magnitude, and so the cost of an atom bomb is really not very relevant to this issue of whether you go in for it or not. It is tied up with much wider issues. . . . I think India should view this whole question in relation to the sacrifice it is willing to make, viewing it in its totality. I fully agree with the Prime Minister . . . when she says that an atomic bomb explosion is not going to help our security. I fully share this feeling.[105]

The tone, gist, and details of Sarabhai's statement directly contradicted the position Bhabha had staked out since the late 1950s, and most vividly in his October 24, 1964, radio broadcast. Sarabhai also echoed the U.S. government analyses of the economic and technical hurdles India would have to overcome in "going nuclear." Whereas Bhabha had asserted that India could readily build a nuclear explosive at a cost of $350,000, Sarabhai said such a step would be worthless in security terms. Sarabhai ignored the political and psychological boosts such a demonstration would give to the nation (and its scientists) and the possibility that nuclear weapon capability could serve as an important national symbol both to Indians and to the rest of the world. Instead, he poured cold water over the impassioned debate. Having led the nascent Indian space program, Sarabhai knew the technical demands and costs entailed in delivery systems better than Bhabha and others working on nuclear explosives problems. As subsequent events would show, his caution was realistic, even if it ran counter to the preferences of leading colleagues in the nuclear establishment.

The Indian press did not miss the story, although it neglected the technical reasoning behind Sarabhai's reservations. Two headlines exemplified the coverage: "A-bomb alone not enough for security: Sarabhai," reported the *Hindustan Times;* "Stress on Development of Electronics Industry," headlined the *Financial Express.*[106]

Shortly before or after the June 1 speech, Sarabhai apparently ordered a stop to the nuclear explosive project. Several accounts, including prominently Ashok Kapur's, have suggested that Sarabhai acted on his own initiative.[107] Interviews with Raja Ramanna and Homi Sethna confirm this. According to Ramanna, "[I]mmediately when Sarabhai took over, he said that SNEPP was closed, we should not work on this. He said nothing should be done in the military sphere."[108] Sethna, in a separate interview, echoed this point: "Sarabhai ordered the papers taken away."[109] This raises several questions: Why did Sarabhai order the project to stop? What did it mean to stop it? Did the prime minister know of or make the decision?

Raja Ramanna has suggested that Sarabhai stopped formal work on the nuclear explosives project due at least in part to "his fundamental distaste towards nuclear weapons."[110] Ashok Kapur wrote that Sarabhai *and* Ramanna and Homi Sethna "were against SNEP on the ground that they could not carry it out."[111] However, this explanation seems dubious in terms of Ramanna's and Sethna's motivations. Ramanna was actually charged with overseeing the project and has never expressed doubt about its worthiness or his team's capacity to do it. Indeed, in a 1996 interview, Sethna called Kapur's explanation "utter nonsense!"[112] Sethna and Ramanna disagreed with Sarabhai's move to switch off the development of an explosive. It is reasonable to conclude, then, that Sarabhai acted for the reasons stated in his June 1 press conference and out of his general aversion to nuclear weapons, and that other leading figures like Ramanna and Sethna disagreed with him.

In any case, the impact was relatively slight. Ramanna acknowledged that "Sarabhai could not keep scientists from doing their work. He couldn't look over our shoulders."[113] The major practical impact was that "You couldn't go to him for money for various purposes. You could keep doing what you could if it was on resources you already had, but you couldn't go to him for help on anything new involving explosives."[114] Insofar as the earlier authorization of the nuclear explosives project had not included fabrication of components but had been confined primarily to calculations and design development, Sarabhai's decision was more important as a statement of purpose than as a limitation on practice. And even here, as Ramanna wrote in his autobiography, Sarabhai "was aware that existing political and popular opinion viewed the use of nuclear devices very positively and therefore wisely refrained from committing either for or against the nuclear programme in the country."[115] This vague formulation seems to hint that regardless of Sarabhai's personal preference and formal directive, he did little to root out the nascent peaceful nuclear explosive project.

Finally, it appears doubtful that Sarabhai acted with the prime minister's approval or knowledge. Homi Sethna, in an interview, said, "I don't think Mrs. Gandhi was aware that Sarabhai had shut down the PNE project."[116] Ramanna responded more elliptically but in a similar vein when asked if Mrs. Gandhi knew of Sarabhai's action: "When Mrs. Gandhi came to BARC (the Atomic Energy Establishment) she saw things, we showed her around, but she may not have understood what was going on."[117] However, another experienced Indian official insisted, in a 1997 interview, that the scientists who disagreed with Sarabhai's decision would have found a way to inform the prime minister.[118] Whether and how she would have acted on such information remains unclear. In any case, as the next two chapters show, from the time she became prime minister to the 1974 blast, Indira Gandhi never publicly disavowed India's interest in conducting peaceful nuclear explosions.

CONCLUSION

Between October 1964 and mid-1966—the period covered in this and the preceding two chapters—India's nuclear policy underwent important, halting shifts that reflected conflicting domestic and international pressures and interests. The ambitions and personal outlooks of a handful of key people also determined these shifts. Two scientists—Bhabha and Sarabhai—and two prime ministers—Shastri and Gandhi—played the leading roles, but their preferences were filtered through the screen of Congress party politics. As in the period from 1948 to 1963, little rigorous analysis was made of the strategic threats facing India or of alternate strategies for meeting those threats. The military was largely left out of the decision-making process. This left the initiative to the scientists. However, Bhabha did not think rigorously about nuclear weapons as military instruments. For him, the value of nuclear explosive capability was political and psychological—both in the personal and national sense. The basic capability to explode a device would enter him and India into the elite club that mattered most to him, the league of atomic scientists who symbolized the apogee of modernity. This club was not responsible for military strategy and requirements. They were scientists seeking the greatest power humankind had yet extracted from nature.

Sarabhai saw matters differently. Rather than asking what it would mean to his standing to lead India into the nuclear explosive club, he asked what material good it would do for India. His opposition to nuclear weapons in principle was magnified by his practical doubts both that India would achieve militarily significant security gains by building nuclear weapons and that India should take this course given its other priorities. The positions of Bhabha and Sarabhai represented a conflict expressed in the Indian debate since 1964. It was left to prime ministers to resolve the issue. Both Shastri and Gandhi looked to split differences and avoid the liabilities of either embracing nuclear weapons or rejecting this option completely.

The net result was a doubly ambiguous nuclear policy. The tentative, compromise authorization of work on peaceful nuclear explosives represented movement toward a dual peaceful/military capability, while India retained its declared intentions to use nuclear know-how only for peaceful purposes. On a second level, with Sarabhai's arrival, the PNE strategy itself became more ambiguous. Sarabhai's apparent, yet incomplete, cessation of the peaceful nuclear explosive project left it unclear whether India actually was preparing this capability. India's calculus for and against building nuclear weapons was influenced further by the tensions inherent in the nonproliferation treaty negotiations. For political and security reasons, India pressed hard for an equitable agreement that would stop the further acquisition of nuclear weapons and delivery systems by the nuclear weapon and non–nuclear weapon states alike. India's prominent opposition to nuclear weapons in these negotiations would have been badly compromised by signs that India was itself seeking to produce nuclear explosives.

The nuclear policy was therefore underdeveloped, as was the decision-making process itself. If explosive capability entailed a nuclear "option," the policy in 1966 appeared to be an option on the option.

FIVE

The Nuclear Non-Proliferation Treaty and Secretly Renewed Work on a Nuclear Explosive

1966–1968

Vikram Sarabhai's ascent to the chairmanship of the Atomic Energy Commission briefly curtailed *authorized* development of a nuclear explosive device. However, the nuclear establishment continued producing and separating weapon-grade plutonium and developing the expertise required to fabricate plutonium metal into explosive cores. In late 1967 or early 1968, Raja Ramanna quietly tasked the physicist R. Chidambaram to develop the equation of state for plutonium necessary to design a nuclear explosive (these calculations are described more fully later in the chapter). Scientists and engineers were recruited from other departments to begin related work on an implosion package. Publicly, India continued to insist that it would utilize nuclear know-how only for peaceful purposes.

In the period covered in this chapter and the next—roughly 1966 through 1970—domestic issues preoccupied India and Indira Gandhi, relegating nuclear issues to the background. To the extent that nuclear policy was debated, the Nuclear Non-Proliferation Treaty (NPT) became the central subject.[1] When the NPT was finished in June 1968, India withheld its signature.

DEBATE SHIFTS TO THE NUCLEAR NON-PROLIFERATION TREATY, 1966 TO 1967

In the summer of 1966, opponents of nuclear weapons rallied against the hawks, who had heretofore held the offensive. Perhaps emboldened by Vikram Sarabhai's arguments, 253 members of Parliament signed a memorandum supporting the government's policy of using nuclear know-how only for peaceful purposes.[2] All political parties except the Jana Sangh were represented in the memorandum. In addition, Indira Gandhi's principal rival for Congress party leadership, Morarji

Desai, reaffirmed his deep moral opposition to India's manufacture of nuclear weapons.[3]

The positions of the two competitors, Desai and Indira Gandhi, indicated the unusual character of Indian political culture and of the nuclear issue within it. Desai maintained a strict moral stance shared by only a minority of the political elite at a time when he could have been expected to press every advantage to unseat the prime minister. Perhaps he reckoned that the nuclear issue simply was not important enough in the scheme of India's political economy to hurt him decisively; in any case, he demonstrated a clear commitment to principle. For her part, Mrs. Gandhi did not choose to accentuate the contrast between herself and Desai on the issue. Perhaps she, too, calculated that nuclear policy would not decisively affect her or his political fortunes and that the issue was better left as low key as possible. In addition, Desai's position against nuclear weapons corresponded closely to the perceived moral views of Indira's father, Jawaharlal Nehru. This, too, could have kept her from publicly favoring development of military nuclear capabilities. The forbearance displayed by both competitors in not exploiting the "bomb" for political gain was remarkable and reflected the determination to maintain India's moral posture.

In October, China announced that it had test-launched a missile mounted with a nuclear warhead. This re-alarmed Indian elites and triggered renewed debate. However, a subtle shift in emotions and calculations could be detected. In an All India Radio debate on nuclear policy, the general secretary of the Congress Parliamentary Party, K. C. Pant, declared that discourse on the nuclear issue had become too strident and overwrought. Pant himself had pressed intermittently for a more robust nuclear policy since 1964, but now he reemphasized a research-and-development strategy that he had been recommending for the past year:

> We should not, I feel, take the political decision to go in for nuclear weapons today, above all because efforts are going on to bring about a treaty for nonproliferation of nuclear weapons. However, I do feel that we cannot afford to lag behind in the growth of acquisition of technological knowledge in the nuclear field and while we do not take the political decision we should keep the option open and reduce the time from the moment of decision to the moment of implementation to the very minimum.[4]

This was essentially the logic behind the Bhabha-Shastri compromise of November 1964 and the elliptical statement of Prime Minister Gandhi in the Lok Sabha on May 10, 1966. It amounted to a "nuclear option" strategy. Yet the policy had been so understated since 1964 that the political elite and the press had failed to give it adequate attention. The loud debate over whether India should manufacture a nuclear bomb floated like hot air over the material reality that the nuclear establishment at Trombay was slowly developing the technical capability for producing nuclear explosives. In spite of Sarabhai's private order to halt active preparations for nuclear explosives, the concept of developing India's overall explosive capability had begun to take hold as a viable strategy. Describing this work as "peaceful" would not, it was hoped, alarm foreign providers of the nuclear assistance that India badly needed. This approach also was ambiguous enough to spare India an expensive crash program and to protect the nation's position in the NPT negotiations. Thus, India actually had a viable policy to develop a nuclear weapon option, and Pant thought that the ongoing debate was both unnecessary and counterproductive. Looking back on it in 1997, Pant said that the dual purpose of the nuclear program did not need to be stated and that focusing on peaceful nuclear explosives was more sensible than an explicit bomb program that would have been very costly.[5]

Pant's statement to a domestic audience paralleled an argument Trivedi was making before the First Committee of the United Nations. By this time, the Indian government had formed a Secretaries' Committee in New Delhi to coordinate policy and communicate back and forth with Trivedi in Geneva.[6] Trivedi now explicitly opposed a U.S.-led effort to prohibit non–nuclear weapon states from conducting peaceful nuclear explosions. Trivedi defined the matter as one of principle, rather than of practice. India and other developing countries, he said, were "nowhere near" the point of conducting nuclear "explosions for building dams or canals or harbours."[7] Yet the theoretical possibility that India and other nations might someday be able and willing to conduct such explosions required that the issue be addressed. Principle demanded that these states retain the same "peaceful explosion" rights as the nuclear weapon states would have. To proscribe these rights, as the United States was proposing, smacked of colonialism, Trivedi argued—an unacceptable denial of "the benefit of science and technology to the developing nations of the world."[8] Besides, he added, India was devoting its "nuclear technology exclusively for peaceful purposes."[9]

The more the nonproliferation treaty negotiators met, the more apparent became the differences between India and the nuclear powers. India may have had logic, principle, and the 1965 negotiating mandate on its side, but the United States and the other nuclear weapon states had power on their side. On the four major issues of concern for India—ending further production of nuclear weapons and delivery systems; securing commitments to pursue nuclear disarmament; obtaining security guarantees; and retaining the right to conduct peaceful nuclear explosions—the nuclear weapon states offered little give. They concentrated their exertions on three narrower objectives: precluding the transfer of nuclear weapons and sensitive materials and know-how to other states; prohibiting receipt or production of nuclear weapons or explosive devices by heretofore non–nuclear weapon states; and ensuring that non–nuclear weapon states accept safeguards on their activities to verify that no diversion for weapons purposes would occur.[10] In other words, the United States and the Soviet Union were designing a treaty to stop the spread of nuclear weapons to other countries, while India was seeking a treaty that would, as part of the bargain, freeze and ultimately roll back the production of nuclear weapons that had already occurred. As Glenn Seaborg recounted, "both superpowers" regarded the demands for assurances and compensation by the non–nuclear weapon states "as something of an irritant."[11]

A SECURITY CALCULUS AGAINST NUCLEAR WEAPONS, 1966

By late 1966, the public debate over whether India should move decisively to build nuclear weapons had calmed. Whether from fatigue, diversion to more pressing issues, uncertainty over the nonproliferation treaty negotiations, or the persuasiveness of arguments like Pant's, the polity became more accepting of the government's policy. Thus, when China conducted its fifth nuclear test on December 28 the press reacted almost nonchalantly. According to G. G. Mirchandani, only one of the five English-language dailies in New Delhi editorialized on the Chinese test, and no prominent Indian leader commented on it publicly.[12]

The calm in the debate over nuclear policy paralleled an assessment of India's options by an important strategic analyst of the time. In an unusually informed and careful treatment of India's circumstance, the newly selected first director of the Institute for Defence Studies and Analyses, Major General Som Dutt, explained why India would not benefit from an attempt to manufacture nuclear weapons at this time. Som Dutt, who had retired in 1965 as commandant of the Defence Services Staff College, made his argument in a November 1966 Adelphi Paper for the Institute for Strategic Studies in London. Today, in the aftermath of India's May 1998 tests, Dutt's analysis appears even more astute.

Dutt began by declaring that India had "no wish to become a nuclear power" but that it did possess a "nuclear option."[13] After repeating the long-standing false claim that India could explode a nuclear device within "no more than a year," he indicated that the strengthening bonds between Pakistan and China were intensifying India's security concerns.[14] The threat from China was primarily "psychopolitical," a capacity to stimulate crises in Nepal, Bhutan, or the disputed regions of the northeast that India could be blackmailed from countering.[15] Regarding Pakistan, Dutt argued presciently that the threat was more long term and would entail a drive by Pakistan to develop nuclear weapons.

Against these potential security challenges, India was tempted to develop nuclear weapons. Dutt recognized that this would trigger a countervailing Pakistani quest for nuclear armaments, but he argued that this could not be discounted in any case. Another alternative for India was to seek security guarantees. Such guarantees by the superpowers to use nuclear weapons, or threathen to use them, against China in the event of a Chinese nuclear threat or attack would be dubious, however. Furthermore, the United States would insist on India's agreeing permanently to eschew acquisition of nuclear weapons in return for a guarantee, and India would find this unacceptable.[16] Dutt noted that the apparent absence of alternatives therefore brought many Indians back to the need for a national nuclear weapon capability as the only viable deterrent against blackmail or aggression. However, the problem remained to define what level of capability would be an adequate deterrent. Some argued that a rudimentary capability would bring "prestige" and "club membership" that would provide "political and diplomatic advantages" even if a militarily useful arsenal was out of reach.[17] Dutt lambasted this argument. The move toward a rudimentary nuclear weapon stockpile would undermine India's "moral stature" and risk antagonizing the superpowers, consequences not worth the candle.[18]

Dutt then questioned whether nuclear weapons would in fact meet the security challenges facing India and, if so, whether India could afford the quantity and quality of deliverable nuclear forces required to deter China. In reality, Dutt argued, China possessed a dubious military capability to wage a major conventional military campaign into India. China lacked the strategic mobility and logistics to conduct sustained land operations out of Tibet across the Himalayas and into Indian territory. Nor could China afford to divert forces from their internal missions, including in Tibet, and along the northern and western borders and the eastern seaboard.[19] China's growing nuclear capability did little to increase the likelihood of aggression against India. China remained vulnerable to U.S. nuclear capability and worried over its relationship with the Soviet Union. Threatening nuclear aggression against India would entail unacceptably grave risks vis-à-vis the superpowers. Dutt did not discount the possibility that China could still undertake "low-level conventional military aggression under cover of nuclear threats against her neighbours," but he argued that India's attainable nuclear weapon capability would do little to alter this possibility.[20]

Emphasizing that a viable deterrent must be survivable, Dutt, like Sarabhai, inventoried the requisite elements: warheads, delivery systems (including missiles), command and control systems, hardened and invulnerable missile sites, and effective air defenses.[21] To provide more than "a feeling of satisfaction," India would need "something approaching parity with China."[22] India must be able to deliver its nuclear weapons a great distance "to reach targets in China of sufficient importance to affect her power of political decision."[23] Yet, even if India could manage the production and deployment of the necessary forces, "she would be able to deter only certain forms of threat."[24] Dutt pointed out that American nuclear weapons had not prevented China from assisting the Viet Cong. He doubted that Indian nuclear weapons could alter China's ambitions in Asia. Nor would a nuclear arsenal alleviate the need for increased spending on conventional forces required to defend the borders with Pakistan and China.[25] Beijing's totalitarian leaders would find it much easier to compel their people to make the sacrifices required for military competition than would India's democratically elected leaders. "As far as Pakistan is concerned, to embark on an Indian nuclear programme would kill any remaining chances of arriving at an understanding with her."[26] Indeed, Dutt correctly predicted that an Indian nuclear weapon quest would force Pakistan "into China's arms, thus increasing India's predicament."[27] He argued that India should concentrate instead on trying to settle relations with Pakistan.

Finally, Dutt argued that anything more than a politically symbolic nuclear capability would be prohibitively expensive for India. Following Leonard Beaton's recent estimate, Dutt concluded that the annual budget for a survivable nuclear arsenal to threaten valued Chinese targets would cost on the order of $220 million per year over ten years.[28] This would entail a 20 percent increase in India's defense budget, which was already consuming roughly 30 percent of India's government spending.

On balance, Dutt concluded that the costs of going nuclear outweighed the putative benefits. These costs included direct expenses, "loss of moral stature," "the possibility of becoming a target for the nuclear powers," the invitation to China "to embark on a preventive war," "loss of the superpowers' support," and, "not least, the adverse effects that such a decision would have on India's non-nuclear neighbours."[29] The threats from China and Pakistan were not direct and dire enough, nor adequately redressable by nuclear weapons, to warrant production of a nuclear arsenal. Instead, Dutt argued, India should consider the "brave step" of abandoning the "rigid concept of non-alignment" and seek to develop "a working partnership among the free Asian powers" to balance China's power.[30] In the meantime, the "nuclear option" would suffice.

Few public analyses before or since have been so realistic and dispassionate in their assessments of threats and their exploration of strategic alternatives to non-alignment. Dutt was one of a small number to ask how China would react if India sought to build a nuclear arsenal. Bhabha and other proponents of manufacturing nuclear weapons tended not to analyze the effect on China. They seemed most intent on demonstrating nuclear capability *to themselves*.[31] In Lok Sabha debates and elsewhere, they acknowledged that the threat from China was political and psychological. They feared that throughout Asia, but particularly within India, China would be perceived as getting ahead and becoming stronger. The *self-regard* of the Indian elite was being undermined. Thus, to prove the prowess and mettle of postcolonial India to Indians themselves the leading scientists in the nuclear establishment and a larger number of politicians wanted to conduct a nuclear blast.[32] Had they analyzed the problem in strategic terms, they would have found it difficult to quarrel with Som Dutt's conclusions.

Interestingly, Dutt's analysis must have been compatible with the dominant view in the Ministry of Defence (MOD). This was the body that paid his salary as director of the MOD-created Institute for Defence Studies and Analyses. Indeed, in another late-1966 publication, the recently retired chief of the Indian Army staff, General J. N. Chaudhuri, reached conclusions similar to Dutt's: "As an effective weapon [the nuclear device] is a long way away. Faced with this position, the increased study of nuclear tactics in every branch of military affairs seems desirable but without cutting into the need to improve conventional strategy and tactics."[33] At this time there was no indication that the military favored diverting resources to building nuclear weapons. In any case, the military's impact on Indian nuclear policy was limited by strict civilian control of national security matters. In all of the press and parliamentary debate, virtually no one asked for the military's view or suggested a significant role for the military in shaping nuclear policy.

Meanwhile, the development of India's overall nuclear program continued apace, benefiting substantially from American and Canadian assistance. In December 1966, the United States, India, and the International Atomic Energy Agency signed a tripartite agreement for the supply of a small amount of U.S. plutonium to India for research purposes. On December 16, India and Canada signed an agreement to extend Canadian assistance through the design and construction of a second power reactor in Rajasthan, RAPS-II.[34] The safeguards agreement on this second plant were tougher than had been accepted for RAPS-I: now IAEA inspectors, instead of Canadian inspectors, would be allowed to ensure safeguards, and the safeguards would apply to the reactor fuel in perpetuity.[35] The tougher safeguards reflected in part the difference between Bhabha, who had negotiated the first agreement, and Sarabhai, who presided over the second. This agreement also evidenced growing Canadian interest in nonproliferation at a time when the nonproliferation treaty was being negotiated. Two days later, India announced plans to build a second plutonium separation plant and a second heavy-water production plant.[36] On January 12, 1967, Indira Gandhi formally renamed the Atomic Energy Establishment at Trombay the Bhabha Atomic Research Centre (BARC).[37] Bhabha's grandeur was being enshrined, and India's capacity to utilize atomic know-how increased.

NATIONAL ELECTIONS, 1967

Nuclear policy was among the least of Indira Gandhi's worries as her government careened toward the general elections of April 1967. The roadbed of the Indian political economy had fractured, eroded, and washed out. Pitfalls lay on all sides. Food became scarcer for average citizens, prices rose, disparities between the rich and the masses of poor sharpened, labor unrest spread, sectarian politics intensified, the specter of violence loomed. With agricultural and industrial production in crisis and foreign debt rising, the Indian government could not generate increased revenue. Public spending was falling. The Reserve Bank of India reported that 35 percent of the population was going undernourished.[38] The Nehruvian vision of a progressive, socialist Indian state lifting the fortunes of the people had been sundered by the failure of economic planning. The great father having passed, the daughter appeared uncertain and beleaguered.

The Congress party lacked the economic expertise and the political will to make the hard restructuring choices required for long-term growth. Well-developed skills of politicking, compromising, and patronage would not save the day. Prime Minister Gandhi had heeded foreign experts in devaluing the rupee, but she had underestimated the political preparations required to make it palatable. In the backlash, she abandoned the logic of economic reform that would have built upon the devaluation. Competing parties and interests made countless and irreconcilable demands on the government. Caught in this crossfire and trying to move along an unnavigable road, Indira Gandhi mouthed platitudes about advancing socialism and preserving democracy. She played to the masses by reiterating the Congress pledge that the state should dominate the "commanding heights of the economy," ensure against excessive disparity in incomes, and gain control over the banks.[39] But she offered no details and exuded no confidence that she would achieve these broad objectives or that they would redeem the troubled situation.

Against this backdrop, nuclear policy stood small in the election campaign. Nor were partisan splits on nuclear policy dramatic. The Swatantra Party's manifesto did not mention a nuclear threat from China and did not pronounce what steps India should take in the nuclear arena. Noting that Communist China was the "principal menace to freedom in Asia," the Swatantra urged formation of a regional security system to counter it.[40] The Communist Party of India (CPI) also did not mention Chinese nuclear capability or India's nuclear program but urged the strengthening of India's defenses with Indian-made weapons. In an interview, the party's chairman argued that it was beyond India's capability and economic wherewithal to manufacture nuclear arms.[41] The Communist Party of India (Marxist-CPI[M]), which had formed in 1964, also did not refer to China's nuclear weapons and called for a foreign policy opposed to imperialism and nuclear war.[42] The Praja Socialist Party (PSP) broke this pattern by recommending "harnessing the atom both for peaceful development as well as for the manufacture of nuclear weapons as a deterrent."[43] The PSP offshoot, the Samyukta Socialist Party, did not refer to the nuclear issue in its manifesto.[44] The only loud call for building nuclear weapons came from the Jana Sangh.[45]

The Congress party manifesto did not mention China's nuclear weapon capability or any plans by India to counter it. The left and right wings of the party, represented respectively by Krishna Menon and Morarji Desai, emphatically opposed building nuclear weapons. Local leaders and younger party figures wanted at least to keep the bomb option open. This array of intraparty interests militated against open debate of the issue. Nuclear issues were an elite affair, concentrated around New Delhi; election required appealing to the interests of India's far-flung, regionally oriented masses who cared about other things.

In the election, the Congress party suffered major losses—77 seats from its Lok Sabha standing in the 1962 election, falling from 361 to 284.[46] In the popular vote, Congress dropped from 44.7 percent in 1962 to 40.9 percent in 1967. The largest gainer in Lok Sabha seats was the (antinuclear) Swatantra Party, which went from 18 to 42. However, the greatest growth in electoral support went to the (pronuclear) Jana Sangh, which polled 9.3 percent of the vote, up from 6.4 percent in 1962. Jana Sangh's representation in the Lok Sabha rose from 14 to 35 seats. The two Communist parties combined totaled 42 seats, split 23 to 19. Congress fared even worse in state elections, where it lost majorities in Uttar Pradesh, Bihar, West Bengal, Orissa, Tamil Nadu, Kerala, Rajasthan, and Punjab.

Disastrous for the Congress party, the 1967 election represented a serious challenge and a potential opportunity for Indira Gandhi. The defeat in the states was considered most important, for it suggested an end to the one-party domination of the Indian polity. Congress might continue to enjoy a working majority at the center, but power would now be pulled toward the states under India's federal system. Forecasters predicted the emergence of coalition governments in the states and then, over time, at the center.[47] The election revealed ideological chaos. The center was not holding, but rather votes were moving toward mutually exclusive poles in terms of economic policies and political visions. Not surprisingly, major rifts now appeared within the Congress leadership. Morarji Desai increased his determination to unseat Indira Gandhi, while the powerful Syndicate, which had heretofore shaped internal Congress politics, was weakened and divided. A group of upstart Congress politicians, the "Young Turks," further fragmented the party by urging an accommodation with the two Communist parties and the Left as a means of recouping the lost support revealed by the elections.[48]

This fractious situation could have been disastrous for Indira Gandhi, as Desai and the old guard had the long knives out for her.[49] Yet the internal divisions also provided an opportunity to vanquish her opposition and consolidate power. Nothing focuses the attention of a politician more than a close electoral call. Gandhi spent the next four years building strength for her next referendum. Political considerations informed everything she did. Nuclear policy had not been a factor in the 1967 election; she tried to ensure that this subject would not hurt her in the future. And when the opportunity arose, she sought to play nuclear policy to her advantage.

NPT DEBATE COMES TO A HEAD, 1967 TO 1968

By 1967, the superpowers were concentrating their nonproliferation diplomacy on Articles I, II, and III of the draft treaty, while consigning the issues of disarmament, security guarantees, and the promotion of peaceful uses of atomic energy, including peaceful nuclear explosives, to the background. However, this prompted a large chorus of states to voice outrage. West Germany—though not party to the Eighteen Nation Disarmament Committee negotiations—noted that the proposed treaty failed to provide the "more comprehensive solutions" required to deal with the nuclear weapon menace.[50] Sweden, represented by Alva Myrdal, frequently inveighed against the treaty's unbalanced obligations and its failure to require nuclear disarmament.[51] Italy, a NATO member, agreed with this criticism, noting that the treaty concentrated only on the limited problem of future proliferation but failed to deal with "the extremely serious and urgent problem of those who have exploded nuclear devices."[52] Japan, too, expressed strong reservations, demanding that the treaty not impede the non–nuclear weapon states' development of nuclear industry, and that it must provide for security guarantees and significant progress toward nuclear disarmament.[53] The French defense minister characterized the treaty as an effort "to castrate the impotent."[54]

No critical voices were louder and more eloquent than India's. Bolstered by the agreed principles that were to guide the negotiations (UNGA Resolution 2028 [XX]), Trivedi continued to demand mutuality, balance, and serious provisions for halting the further acquisition of nuclear weapons and delivery vehicles by the nuclear powers. Yet, as the negotiations continued to draw greater international attention, a bifurcation was emerging in India's focus and interests.

The Indian nuclear policy debate was now divided into two almost distinct narratives. One centered on the national-technical policy of whether or not to manufacture nuclear weapons or explosive devices. Since 1964 this issue had preoccupied the few Indians involved in nuclear policy. However, by 1966 the perceived urgency for building a bomb had diminished somewhat, as previously discussed. In January 1967, Sarabhai categorically told visiting U.S. AEC Chairman Glenn Seaborg that India had no program to develop peaceful nuclear explosives "in progress or contemplated."[55] Although Sarabhai's formal subordinates would soon belie this statement and begin concrete design work, he expressed the official declared policy. More than nuclear weapons, India needed economic development and political stability. More than a divisive fight that would have raised questions about resource priorities and would have alarmed international aid donors, Prime Minister Gandhi needed to solidify her control of the Congress party.

The second narrative centered on the nonproliferation treaty. This was becoming the most compelling drama. The negotiations involved diplomacy, morality, and equity, and India was playing a leading role in them. In 1967 and 1968, the question shifted from whether India should *actually* produce nuclear weapons to whether India should sign a treaty relinquishing *the right* to produce weapons. The focus was less on what India should do technologically and militarily than on what the rest of the world should do morally and equitably. India's leaders, including Trivedi, did not mean to downplay the security stakes in the negotiations. The treaty they wanted would have achieved security by eliminating nuclear weapons. Short of that, they demanded treaty language that would freeze further acquisition of nuclear weapons by other states. This would have prevented China from developing a militarily useful nuclear arsenal and would have blocked Pakistan from developing nuclear weapon capabilities. India also still hoped that the major powers would address its security concerns with guarantees against nuclear blackmail and/or attack, equitably balancing obligations of nuclear forbearance with provisions of security protection.

But as the negotiations proceeded, the prospects of such a treaty dimmed. By the end of 1967, it was clear that no meaningful security guarantees would be proffered. Thus India wanted to keep its nuclear option open, which meant rejecting the treaty. But India was so central to the negotiations, and had become so deeply engaged in the debate over principles, that it could not leave the stage. What emerged was a morality play that further diminished the security focus of

Indian policy. The one important exception was India's fight to preserve the right to conduct peaceful nuclear explosions.

In February 1967, President Lyndon Johnson sought to augment negotiations with a message to the ENDC. In it, he downplayed the question of nuclear disarmament and emphasized the pressing need to stop the spread of nuclear weapons.[56] Then he turned to an issue increasingly dear to India and argued that there was no practical distinction between nuclear weapons and peaceful nuclear explosives. Meaningful nonproliferation required stopping the spread of both. Yet, the United States recognized the interest other nations might have in utilizing peaceful nuclear explosives for development purposes. Therefore, Johnson proposed that the nuclear weapon states, particularly the United States, should be prepared to provide peaceful nuclear explosive services, under due controls, to other nations at low cost.[57]

Johnson's speech reaffirmed the sense that the nonproliferation treaty negotiations were running counter to India's interests. He offered nothing in the way of disarmament but instead sought to prohibit the technical option dearest to India. His attempt to salve the hurt with a proposal to share nuclear explosive services only salted the wounds of colonialism. To Indians, the proposal suggested the logic that once-colonial nations like India could not be allowed to engage in value-added technological development, but rather they should buy value-added technologies from the developed powers.

On March 1, a diverse group of eminent Indians issued a statement urging the government not to sign the treaty as it was being shaped by the United States and the Soviet Union. "We have already abridged our sovereignty by agreeing to foreign inspection of our nuclear establishments. . . . By signing this treaty India will severely limit the number of her options without any counter-vailing credible security whatsoever."[58] This statement represented a broad tent under which people with diverse views could stand. It covered the sizable minority who favored building nuclear weapons, as well as a larger number who wanted to keep the option open even if they did not advocate building nuclear weapons at this time. This formulation also covered those who did not favor nuclear weapons but also opposed an inequitable treaty.

On March 27, the Lok Sabha convened a debate on nuclear policy. Explaining the context through which the government would evaluate the prospective treaty, Minister of External Affairs M. C. Chagla (who had replaced Swaran Singh) emphasized that as a nonaligned state, India was "not under anybody's political or any other umbrella. Therefore, there is no military pact under which we can be protected, if we are attacked by any nuclear power."[59] At the same time, Chagla reminded the House that India "has got a great nuclear capability."[60] India would not accept a treaty that impeded the further development and peaceful use of nuclear energy. At this point, a parliamentarian interjected with a demand that India must "remain free to develop its own nuclear capabilities and nuclear weapons" to counter China.[61] Chagla responded equivocally, acknowledging the threat from China but reaffirming that India's "present policy is we will not explode the bomb."[62] He added merely that the government would make security the highest priority in its final consideration of the treaty. According to then-Foreign Secretary C. S. Jha, Chagla and the prime minister both opposed India's signing of the treaty as it was then drafted.[63] However, the Secretaries' Committee had not given up hope that the treaty could be improved. In particular, India should seek clarification of how the major powers would protect non–nuclear weapon states' security and national development of nuclear energy for peaceful purposes.[64] This focus reflected the absence of even a sizable minority within the Secretaries' Committee who favored Indian acquisition of nuclear weapons.

In late April 1967, the Emergency Committee of the Indian cabinet dispatched the prime minister's secretary, L. K. Jha to Moscow, Paris, Washington, and London to explore these issues. As Jha was preparing to leave New Delhi, India received the latest working drafts of a treaty text from Moscow and Washington. The two nearly identical drafts were intended to impress upon India the common purpose of the two superpowers. Predictably, L. K. Jha found little reward on his tour of the nuclear powers' capitals. Whereas India sought firm and effective guarantees, the most Washington or Moscow would undertake was a general pledge of support along the lines offered by President Johnson following China's first nuclear test in October 1964.

In several of his key meetings in Washington, L. K. Jha was joined by Sarabhai (and Indian Ambassador to the United States B. K. Nehru). Two meetings revealed India's desire to escape from the hard choices inherent in the NPT. According to U.S. AEC Chairman Glenn Seaborg, Sarabhai and Nehru on April 14, 1967, proposed that a "U.S.-USSR guarantee against nuclear attack on non-nuclear countries was *all* that was needed—it could be a *substitute* for a nonproliferation treaty."[65] Although this approach would have begged vital issues—the need to stop the spread of nuclear weapons and the questions of disarmament, safeguards, and enforceability—it would have provided domestic and international political relief for India by removing the nonproliferation treaty from the table. India's dispute with the nuclear powers would have been made moot by the absence of the treaty itself. Presumably, the matter of peaceful nuclear explosions would have been left unaddressed, freeing India to do as it wished. Seaborg communicated the inadequacy of the idea to Sarabhai and Nehru.

In an April 18 meeting with Defense Secretary Robert McNamara, L. K. Jha cited two obstacles to signing the NPT. "One is the security problem vis-à-vis China," according to the U.S. memorandum of conversation. The other was "the fact that India has developed nuclear technology which contributes to Indian confidence and prestige, but which appears threatened by serious curtailment if India adheres to the NPT."[66] Sarabhai added that if the United States and the Soviet Union were not prepared to make nuclear disarmament "the next step," and if China would not sign the NPT, "then India is reluctant to give up the option of building the bomb." Sarabhai said that the present NPT is " 'not salable' " in

India, but "he hoped that Indian recalcitrance would not be seen as hiding a secret desire to build a bomb." He concluded by suggesting, in the note taker's paraphrase, that "the developing international nuclear situation possesses the characteristics of a Greek tragedy in which the actors are drawn inexorably to fates which they are seeking to avoid."[67]

While L. K. Jha, Sarabhai, and others were in Washington and London, Foreign Secretary C. S. Jha traveled to Cairo, Geneva, Rome, and Belgrade to press India's view on the treaty. He found general support for the argument that the treaty was one-sided. However, the more telling message was that even an imperfect NPT was an essential first step toward disarmament.[68] It now seemed evident that the nuclear powers had successfully limited the terms of the treaty. The negotiations henceforth concentrated on finding agreement between the superpowers and addressing the reservations of NATO members such as Germany.

Meanwhile, consternation mounted in India over the government's seemingly uncertain approach to the nonproliferation treaty. Opposition parties demanded rejection of the treaty as it now stood.[69] In late April, the *Indian Express* accused the government of abandoning its initial emphasis on retaining the right to produce nuclear weapons and instead "diverting public attention" to the "irrelevant" issue of a "nuclear guarantee."[70] The question of security guarantees had bedeviled Indians since Shastri first vaguely floated the idea in 1964. Now, in addressing the nonproliferation treaty, Indian representatives further confused the matter. At times they seemed to suggest that the absence of effective guarantees was the main objection to the treaty. Yet, at other times, Indian officials focused on other important reservations toward the treaty: the need for disarmament, or at least a freeze in nuclear weapon development; allowance of national peaceful nuclear explosive programs; assurance of Chinese participation in the treaty. But the issue of security guarantees always attracted greater attention, in part because it had profound implications for India's nonaligned identity.

Indian leaders found themselves in a daunting position from which it was natural to seek escape. Nonalignment had allowed India to play the two superpowers against each other while preserving Indian autonomy. Now, the United States and the Soviet Union presented a common front against India on a treaty that could severely limit the symbolically and materially vital nuclear program. India still required large amounts of economic aid from the United States and military supplies from the Soviet Union. American and Canadian assistance was still vital for India's nuclear power program. To defy an emerging international consensus on the nonproliferation treaty could risk these broader relationships. To oppose what was portrayed as a major step toward nonproliferation and disarmament—longstanding Indian objectives—could risk a loss of international credibility. At the same time, India's cogent objections to the treaty remained valid. To relent would be embarrassing as well as contrary to the declared interests behind those objections.

What bothered government critics most was the prospect that weak India ultimately would cave in to foreign pressure. Yet they need not have been so alarmed. Whether or not India would have been better off acceding to the treaty, the government decided in May 1967 that it would not do so without major accommodations to India's demands. C. S. Jha reported in his memoir that he, as foreign secretary, submitted a note to the cabinet reviewing the results of the visits to the nuclear power capitals. The note conveyed the failure to receive meaningful security guarantees and added, again, the criticisms of the unequal terms of the treaty and the prohibition of peaceful nuclear explosives. On "the basis of that note," according to Jha, "it was decided that India should not be a party to the draft treaty."[71] At the same time, the government decided to declare unilaterally that India had no intention to manufacture nuclear weapons.[72] Politically, this decision came only a month after the general elections when Indira Gandhi was struggling to solidify her control of the polity. Given that her chief rival, Morarji Desai, staunchly opposed signing the treaty, it would have been politically self-defeating for the prime minister to do otherwise and "give" Desai a popular issue. Thus, domestic political interests and the perceived demerits of the treaty coincided.

If C. S. Jha's account of this decision was correct, then India refrained from announcing it for a number of months.[73] The negotiations in Geneva were not complete, and India continued to participate actively and contribute to modest changes in the treaty text designed to accommodate some demands of the non–nuclear weapon states.

On May 23, 1967, Trivedi made two new, interesting points on the important matter of peaceful nuclear explosives.[74] One was perceptual and became fundamental in Indian nuclear diplomacy for decades to come, particularly during the test ban treaty negotiations in 1996. He said, "The civil nuclear Powers can tolerate a nuclear weapons apartheid, but not an atomic apartheid in their economic and peaceful development."[75] This invocation of the racial matter of apartheid revealed an important moral and "identity" dimension of the debate. Nuclear weapons were the manifestation and symbol of the world's dominant white nations; the nonproliferation treaty represented an effort to keep this power from the developing, mostly dark-skinned world.

More practically, Trivedi acknowledged "that the technology involved in the production of a nuclear weapon is the same as the technology which produces a peaceful nuclear explosive device."[76] This was the basis of American claims that a nonproliferation treaty would be meaningless if it allowed non–nuclear weapon states to produce nuclear explosive devices. These states could produce peaceful nuclear explosives and then withdraw from safeguard agreements and do what they would with their de facto bombs. Trivedi now conceded the American point, but he argued that the central issue was not the technology but the intention of its possessor: India's intentions were peaceful. India accepted that "such explosions must be adequately safeguarded" but demanded that "safeguards must apply equally to all nations."[77] The focus on intentions over capabilities remained characteristic of India's nuclear policy for the next thirty years.

On August 24, 1967, the United States and the Soviet Union submitted a joint draft nonproliferation treaty to the ENDC. The superpower agreement foreshadowed that a final treaty would emerge soon. Importantly, for India and other non–nuclear weapon states, the joint draft proffered no security guarantees and no commitment to pursue nuclear disarmament.[78] The closest it came to accommodating calls for disarmament and an end to further acquisition of nuclear weapons and delivery systems was preambular language regarding the "intention to achieve at the earliest possible date the cessation of the nuclear arms race."[79] The draft also proscribed production and/or detonation of peaceful nuclear explosives by non–nuclear weapon states.

Predictably, India deemed the draft inadequate, as Trivedi recorded in a September 28 statement to the ENDC.[80] The negotiations continued for months, focusing on terms of safeguards that would satisfy the European nuclear industrialists and Japan.[81] Subsequent drafts incorporated earlier preambular language into the treaty's text, as in Article VI, which called for "negotiations in good faith on effective measures relating to cessation of the nuclear arms race at an early date and to nuclear disarmament." A vague security guarantee to be provided by the United States, the Soviet Union, and the United Kingdom was added through a UN Security Council resolution voted on a week after the General Assembly approved the treaty on June 12, 1968.[82] Article IV was strengthened in succeeding drafts, until the final version obligated the more advanced states to "facilitate," not merely recognize, the right of all states to participate in "the fullest possible exchange of equipment, materials and scientific and technological information for the peaceful uses of nuclear energy."[83]

However, even with these changes and the parallel security assurance, the NPT failed to come close to meeting India's long-held demands. On October 6, 1967, Defence Minister Swaran Singh announced to the UN General Assembly that India would not sign such a treaty for reasons now well known. He added pointedly, but inaccurately, that "[c]ertain non-nuclear countries could have produced nuclear weapons several years ago, had they so desired, but have refrained from doing so."[84] Then, turning to the portentous issue of peaceful nuclear explosives, Singh marked the path India would continue to follow: "While the Government of India continues to be in favour of the non-proliferation of nuclear weapons, it is equally strongly in favour of the proliferation of nuclear technology for peaceful purposes, as an essential means by which the developing countries can benefit from the best advances of science and technology in this field."[85]

THE SCIENTISTS SECRETLY BEGIN
INTENSE DESIGN WORK, EARLY 1968

While Prime Minister Gandhi concentrated on politics and diplomats wrangled over the NPT, a small team of scientists at the Bhabha Atomic Research Centre initiated the most concerted effort yet to develop nuclear explosives. India's nuclear scientists to that point had not been organized to work on high-pressure physics and other specific problems associated with designing nuclear explosives. After Bhabha and Shastri's agreement in late 1964 to begin preparations for a peaceful nuclear explosive, Raja Ramanna had been asked in 1965 to lead the work, but relatively little progress had been made to date, thanks in part to technical difficulties and Sarabhai's opposition to "nuclear explosions of any kind."[86] Despite Bhabha's many boasts about his program's preparedness to make nuclear explosives, the necessary know-how had not yet been developed. Now, however, Ramanna, backed by the director of BARC, Homi Sethna, moved his team ahead.

In late 1967 or early 1968, Ramanna, then leader of the physics group at BARC, tapped Rajagopala Chidambaram to derive the equation of state of plutonium, a study necessary to design a nuclear explosive with a plutonium core.[87] Born in 1925, Ramanna, was (is) a proud and blunt English-trained physicist with a wry sense of humor and a wide-ranging intellect. A highly skilled and passionate pianist, his later thinking about nuclear weapons ranged from somber determination to display Indian prowess and power in a tough world to lofty aversion to nuclear arms racing. At bottom, though, as a leader of the nuclear establishment, Ramanna believed India should achieve its place in the international system by demonstrating nuclear explosive capability and resisting the colonial impositions of the prospective nonproliferation regime. Chidambaram, then thirty-two, had received his Ph.D. in physics from Madras University, where he was regarded as an outstanding student. Like Ramanna, a South Indian Brahmin, Chidambaram had begun work at BARC (then the Atomic Energy Establishment) in 1962. He would become an internationally regarded crystallographer, but now his energies were also diverted to leading the nuclear establishment's work in high-pressure physics in order to pave the way for the bomb.

The equation of state calculation that Chidambaram began working to "discover" describes the relation between the pressure, density, and temperature of a substance. In an implosion weapon, an initially subcritical spherical mass of plutonium (or uranium) metal is compressed symmetrically by a shock wave initiated by the detonation of high explosives surrounding the plutonium. After the compressed mass becomes critical, the fission chain reaction is initiated by injecting neutrons into it. At this time, the plutonium is dense enough that the injected neutrons collide with and preferentially split plutonium atoms rather than escape through the spherical surface. This leads to a chain reaction in which growing numbers of neutrons split plutonium atoms at an exponentially increasing rate. Substantial amounts of energy are thereby released in less than a microsecond before the fission process is terminated by the thermal expansion of the plutonium that has been transformed into a gaseous plasma. The expansion essentially disperses the plutonium and thereby deprives neutrons of sufficient "targets" to split. All of this occurs in a few millionths of a second.

In order to describe the compression and subsequent expansion of the plutonium core and the release of fission energy as a function of time, it is necessary to have an accurate equation of state that is valid over the very large ranges of pressure and temperature experienced in a fission explosive—millions of degrees and atmospheres. This equation can be derived from theory supplemented by experiments with shock waves. Without it, it is not possible to determine how much high explosive is necessary to compress plutonium to a desired density, and to determine the explosive yield of a device. In a sophisticated device, where the neutron initiator is not activated simply by the compression of the plutonium core itself, the equation of state also enables designers to determine the optimal time to trigger the neutron initiator to maximize the explosive yield.[88]

This major theoretical and applied project is what Chidambaram now undertook. "In 1968, when the design of the device used in the Pokhran explosion was initiated," he wrote in a rare public reference to this work, "very little was known in open literature about the compression behaviour of materials at ultra-high pressures and this information was not at all available for nuclear materials."[89] Chidambaram's first task was to analyze "scarce data on related elements in the literature" to derive constants to calculate the equation of state for plutonium.

From 1968 onward, Chidambaram began recruiting and coordinating individuals in other departments at BARC and in Defence Research and Development Organisation laboratories to design components for the chemical high-explosive mechanism that would be required to implode the fissile core of a device. Chidambaram would go on to become chairman of the AEC and preside over India's May 1998 nuclear explosive tests.

With Ramanna providing inspiration and bureaucratic leadership, key individuals were added to the explosives team. Ramanna, Chidambaram, and P. K. Iyengar—a top experimental physicist at BARC—identified necessary contributors and coordinated their work, in cooperation with Dr. B. D. Nag Chaudhuri, scientific adviser to the minister of defense and director of the Defence Research and Development Organisation. Ultimately, as detailed in chapter 7, they engaged between fifty and seventy-five scientists and engineers directly in the project.

The invigorated effort begun by early 1968 to develop a nuclear explosive raises important questions about political authorization. Sarabhai opposed work on nuclear explosives at this time, yet as chairman of the AEC he was nominally responsible. From interviews and published accounts, it appears that he eventually informed himself of the advancing theoretical and design work through informal discussions with Chidambaram, if not with others. In principle, Sethna, as director of BARC and Ramanna's superior, should have acted only on orders from Sarabhai, and at least should have informed his superior. Yet Sethna and Sarabhai deeply disliked each other, and the advocates of the nuclear explosive program at BARC did not accept Sarabhai's antagonism toward the effort.[90] Thus they proceeded on their own. And when Sarabhai became aware of the revived project he did not stop it. "If Sarabhai really had wanted to stop it, he could have," a knowledgeable former official suggested in a 1997 interview. "He was a gentleman, though, and he did not want to fight this fight."[91]

But what about the prime minister? The record does not indicate that Gandhi was aware in 1968 of the scientists' systematic move ahead. "She must have known some experiments were going on, but she probably did not have the full picture," according to the former official quoted above. The physicists apparently felt under no obligation to have formal prime ministerial approval. Because they did not require additional funds and were not proposing at that time actually to fabricate and detonate a nuclear device, they deemed specific political authorization unnecessary. As chapters 6 and 7 show, once the preparations got to the point when the scientists were ready to build and, they hoped, test the device, they then sought prime ministerial authorization.

The scientists acted without benefit of a national security strategy or requirement. During 1966 and 1967, Chinese armed forces intruded into the disputed northern border areas and the two countries' diplomatic relations grew nastier. Much of this owed to China's general belligerence during the cultural revolution and Beijing's desire to undermine India's position with other Third World countries by portraying it as a hapless beggar for American and Soviet assistance.[92] In the nuclear sphere, China in June 1967 tested its first thermonuclear weapon.[93] Still, neither the uniformed military nor the civilian heads of relevant ministries at this time analyzed India's security situation and concluded that nuclear explosives were required. The scientists involved in the nuclear explosive project have not cited specific Chinese threats or an articulated strategic rationale for nuclear weapons to explain their initiative. To the extent that they were motivated by anything more than the desire to demonstrate their prowess and India's general strength, it was a gut feeling that after 1962 India needed to have greater military capabilities to deal with potential aggression—and the scientists could provide it at little cost.[94]

NPT COMPLETED AND INDIA DOES NOT SIGN, 1968

Nothing in the nonproliferation treaty redrafts of January and March 1968 significantly addressed India's concerns. China had already denounced the treaty and stated its refusal to be bound by it in any way. Yet, if India was determined to vote against an inequitable treaty that foreclosed its nuclear options, the government also wanted to ameliorate international outcry and dampen domestic ardor for nuclear weapons. Thus, in an April 24, 1968, statement before the Lok Sabha, Prime Minister Gandhi forcefully articulated the case against India's acquisition of nuclear weapons.

> [T]he events of the last twenty years clearly show that the possession of nuclear weapons have not given any military advantage in situation[s] of bitter armed conflict which have sometimes taken place between nations possessing nuclear weapons and those who do not possess them. . . . We think that nuclear weapons are no substitute for military preparedness, involving conventional weapons. The choice before us involves not only the question of making a few atom bombs, but of engaging in

an arms race with sophisticated nuclear warheads and an effective missile delivery system. Such a course, I do not think would strengthen national security. On the other hand, it may well endanger our internal security by imposing a very heavy economic burden which would be in addition to the present expenditure on defence. Nothing will better serve the interests of those who are hostile to us than for us to lose our sense of perspective and to undertake measures which would undermine the basic progress of the country.[95]

This statement clearly echoed the views Sarabhai expressed in his first press conference as chairman of the AEC. Nothing in the intervening two years had diminished the technical and economic burden of building a workable nuclear arsenal. At the same time, however, the international community had done almost nothing to make it politically or substantively palatable for India to sign the NPT. India was not making a security case for its acquisition of nuclear weapons but rather a political and moral case against those states that had nuclear weapons and refused to disarm.

When a final cabinet meeting convened to confirm India's position, the benefits and drawbacks of signing the treaty were thoroughly analyzed by prepared papers from all relevant departments.[96] No official strongly advocated signing the treaty. Home Affairs Minister Y. B. Chavan argued sharply against it, citing the need to retain the nuclear weapons option to deal with China. Minister of Defence Swaran Singh responded that the military needed not nuclear weapons but greater conventional capabilities. Finance Minister Morarji Desai passionately opposed India's acquisition of nuclear weapons on moral grounds, but he just as stoutly rejected the NPT as a discriminatory device. According to Rodney Jones, Indira Gandhi summed up the situation accordingly: "Parliament and the public do not seem to be ready for India to sign the treaty, no one seems to want it."[97] With that, the meeting adjourned. When the Nuclear Non-Proliferation Treaty was put to a vote on June 12, India voiced its "nay."[98]

In forming its position on the treaty, unlike in other past and future deliberations on nuclear policy, the Indian government did engage in rather systematic evaluation of costs and benefits. The atomic energy establishment leadership did not appear to play a dominant role, in part because the personality, viewpoints, and leverage of Sarabhai differed significantly from Bhabha.[99] The general process was more orderly than the decisions in the 1950s to develop the technical basis for building nuclear weapons, the 1964–1966 debate on whether to do so, and the subsequent decisions from 1971 to 1974 to detonate a peaceful nuclear explosive. Furthermore, in addition to the able and informed diplomat in Geneva, V. C. Trivedi, India deployed a number of high-ranking emissaries around the world to explore ways out of the dilemma the nonproliferation treaty posed to the nation.

Yet, despite the relatively orderly decision-making process, the government was subjected to criticisms for appearing uncertain and inchoate. This stemmed in part from the endemic secrecy of the process. As the then-Foreign Secretary C. S.

Jha explained: "[T]he subject was dealt with at a high level and in secrecy. There were no papers to filter down to the lower echelons of the Minister of External Affairs and much of the consideration of this question was through oral discussion among the secretaries of the ministries concerned and in the Cabinet and at the capitals of some foreign countries."[100] Such a process naturally created an environment for rumor and speculation.

Still, nuclear policy was not a pressing concern among the public, and it would prove irrelevant in the 1971 election, as in the 1967 election before it. Roughly half of India's population lived rural lives removed from the arcana of nuclear policy and could not be expected to have strong, informed opinions on the relevant trade-offs. The policy debate was confined to a very small segment of the educated, urban population, particularly in New Delhi. But regardless of how the "public" is defined, the low salience of nuclear policy did not mean that the public did not care about the subject. Rather, Prime Minister Gandhi ensured that nuclear policy stayed within parameters that would not arouse public disapproval. The public passionately insisted that India not sign away the right to develop nuclear weapons as long as others had them, but it did not place a priority on India building a nuclear arsenal. Given the anticipated costs of an arsenal, developing the technical capacity to produce nuclear weapons was sufficient. Rejection of the NPT and preservation of the nuclear option were the policies of least political risk and greatest strategic maneuverability.[101]

International considerations also worked against signing the treaty. The greatest pressure on behalf of the treaty came from the greatest capitalist power, the United States, and from India's former colonial master, the United Kingdom. Although they had much more power than India, it worked against them. They had helped devise a treaty that India characterized as inequitable and colonial, a form of nuclear apartheid. As Raja Ramanna put it, "These nations chose to ignore the fact that by enforcing non-proliferation, they, along with other advanced nations, were asking us to give up a part of our national sovereignty, something which we had won after years of sustained struggle."[102]

Once nuclear policy and nonproliferation were cast as part of this neocolonial narrative, India's role was clear. The recent food and rupee devaluation wrangles with the United States only deepened India's resistance. As Homi Sethna explained in a 1996 interview:

> There were pressures on India to sign the NPT around 1967. There were two schools of thought. One said, "forget it," we should give up and sign the treaty. This school tried to put pressure on the other school which wanted to develop the nuclear option, but it did not succeed. You see, something else had happened recently. We were told [in 1966] to devalue the rupee, which we did. We were told that money would flow once we devalued, and it would be all milk and honey. But money did not flow in. So that was when we became extremely suspicious of U.S. advice about what was in our interest.[103]

Another former high-ranking defense scientist recalled in an interview, "Mrs. Gandhi never got over President Johnson's coercive management of each shipment of food aid in the 1966 food crisis."[104] India's national narrative simply disallowed major concessions to the evolving international nuclear nonproliferation regime.

Despite the hopeful belief by some American officials that India would finally accede to the treaty, the U.S. government as a whole was unwilling to undertake the kinds of initiatives that would induce India to do so, a pattern that would be repeated in 1996 over the Comprehensive Test Ban Treaty.[105] Nonproliferation was becoming a great American priority, but it still did not outweigh the determination to retain unfettered options for increasing and diversifying the United States' own nuclear arsenal. In this, the United States was joined by the Soviet Union, the United Kingdom, France, and China in a global bifurcation of nuclear capabilities and status that India could not abide.

SIX

Political Tumult and Inattention
to the Nuclear Program

1969–1971

It is natural to try to specify the moment at which Indira Gandhi decided to build and detonate India's first nuclear explosive device. However, in reality, the nuclear scientists and their colleagues in Defence Research and Development Organisation labs did much of the preparatory work without explicit political authorization as the prime minister was preoccupied by an intense political struggle and a split in the Congress party. They had begun doing serious design studies by 1968, and in 1970 the Bhabha Atomic Research Centre group sought to solve a weapon design problem by beginning construction of the Purnima reactor. Debate over nuclear policy reignited in 1970, and by the summer of 1971 the peaceful nuclear explosive initiative had strong momentum, a fact that Sarabhai and Gandhi articulated to international audiences. Explicit authorization to take the final steps and assemble a device did not come until 1972, as discussed in chapter 7. Thus, building the "bomb" did not entail a specific decision in time but rather a continuous accretion of scientific and technical capability and political momentum, stymied occasionally by countervailing political, moral, and economic considerations.

THE CONGRESS PARTY SPLITS

Domestic challenges beset Indira Gandhi during and after the NPT negotiations. Forty to 50 percent of the rural population lived below official poverty levels, a minimum of 220 million people.[1] Industrial investment continued to lag despite more liberal economic policies undertaken at the behest of the United States and international financial institutions. Economic inequalities grew. The political fragmentation that had manifested itself in the 1967 general elections continued.

Gandhi's and the Congress party's authority grew weaker. Within the party itself, the old guard plotted to unseat the prime minister.[2]

Ideological and generational fault lines ran through the Congress party. The Syndicate, including Morarji Desai as the chief rival to Indira Gandhi, emphasized private investment and entrepreneurship as the vehicles for economic growth. On the other side, Mrs. Gandhi and other eminent Congress leaders were moving leftward, in the direction of regional parties and the Communists, who called for greater state regulation and control of the economy. Generationally, the Syndicate represented Nehru's cohort, while his daughter was joining with the Young Turks, as they were known—younger activists within the Congress party who wanted to take it over and redirect it to reform society along more radical socialist principles.

The tectonic grinding along these lines became severe in the late spring and summer of 1969. Gandhi outmaneuvered the party old guard in a series of political skirmishes outside the scope of this study. The party president, S. Nijalingappa, counterattacked on November 12 by expelling her from the party. Then Congress party parliamentarians voted for a new leader and repudiated the party president and the Syndicate by electing Mrs. Gandhi. On November 22 and 23, the All India Congress Committee met to vote on its leadership and direction. A significant majority sided with Mrs. Gandhi. The party then split. Indira Gandhi's faction became known as Congress (R), for Requisition, while the Syndicate's faction became known as Congress (O), for Organisation.[3]

The split did nothing to solidify the Indian political economy. Tremors and aftershocks continued as Mrs. Gandhi acted to uphold her populist rhetoric. She nationalized the banks and abolished the "privy purses," a system of large pensions from the state to the old princely families.[4] These popular measures redounded to the prime minister's political benefit, but the political struggle continued through 1970.

On December 27, 1970, Indira Gandhi dissolved the Lok Sabha and called for national elections, a year ahead of the expiration of her five-year term. Coming after nearly three years of political struggle, the move reflected Mrs. Gandhi's confidence that her populist campaign and alliance with the Left would carry her to victory. She controlled the government and the largest faction of what had been the unified Congress party, but she still lacked an absolute majority in the Parliament. With the early election she sought not only to vanquish the old guard but also to shed her dependence on the former Communist factions with which she had aligned conveniently in the recent political struggle. She pursued this strategy by campaigning for radical economic reform—"Remove Poverty"—but insisting on parliamentary methods to facilitate reform. The latter provision distinguished her from the Communist parties.

She succeeded dramatically. The March 1971 elections gave Gandhi's Congress (R) 350 seats in the 518-member Lok Sabha.[5] The main traditional opposition parties suffered significantly: Swatantra's popular vote fell from 8 percent in 1967 to

3 percent; the Jana Sangh lost 11 of its 33 Lok Sabha seats. The Samyukta Social-ist Party (SSP) was practically wiped out, losing 14 of its previous 17 seats.[6] These results confirmed the low electoral salience of nuclear policy. (The Jana Sangh and SSP were the most vocal pro-bomb parties, while the Swatantra was the clear-est anti-bomb party.) The two Communist parties gained nothing in the election. Mrs. Gandhi captured the leftist sentiment for herself.[7] Indeed, her victory repre-sented a historic shift in Indian politics. Whereas in the past voters tended to coa-lesce in groups based on caste, religion, and local and regional identity, in this elec-tion the masses did not follow their local leaders, but instead voted directly for Mrs. Gandhi's Congress (R).[8]

However, with great victories come great expectations. Indira Gandhi had promised to end poverty and to improve the lives of the average Indian, but the means for achieving such grand ambitions were still lacking. Indeed, not only means but also coherent designs for economic development were absent. The Indian polity still contained plenty of actors ready to exploit failure at home or on the world stage. In such a situation, a political leader would be highly reluctant to divert personal energy and time to undertake a costly, technologically uncertain, and internationally risky nuclear weapon program. As a former close political ally of the prime minister put it, Mrs. Gandhi simply "did not have the time to con-centrate on the nuclear program or something as major as conducting a nuclear explosion."[9] Personal and national politics dwarfed international security consid-erations in India.

NUCLEAR PROGRAM EVOLVES
COVERTLY AND OVERTLY, 1970 TO 1971

Upon taking over the Atomic Energy Commission, Vikram Sarabhai had signaled the difficulties impeding the achievement of Homi Bhabha's grandiose plans for nuclear power. In contrast with Bhabha's overblown claims, Sarabhai recom-mended a cautious appraisal of costs and benefits. Indeed, Sarabhai took the unprecedented step of establishing a mechanism within the Department of Atomic Energy to evaluate programs and rationalize the personality-centered organization Bhabha had created. In July 1970, Sarabhai formally established an interdisciplinary Programme Analysis Group to help check and balance the DAE's far-flung projects. However, for real quality control and oversight a more independent and robust mechanism would have been needed.[10]

Sarabhai's antipathy toward nuclear weapons and even peaceful nuclear explo-sives has already been noted. In the 1966-to-1970 period *he* did little to expand the nuclear agenda. Instead, prior to unveiling his ten-year plan for the nuclear pro-gram in May 1970, Sarabhai managed the implementation of earlier projects and adopted a reserved position as India struggled through the NPT negotiations. However, his personal resistance to nuclear weapons may have slackened. Accord-ing to K. Subrahmanyam, the AEC chairman became more "hawkish" on the bomb as he saw how leading scientists and security specialists from the great powers professed reliance on nuclear deterrence.[11] This may explain Sarabhai's acquiescence as his subordinates secretly accelerated work on a nuclear explosive design, including construction of the small experimental Purnima reactor.

Construction of the Purnima research reactor apparently began in 1970, and it first operated in May 1972.[12] Despite its small size and cost, it provided data vital to the design of India's nuclear explosive device. The reactor continued the nuclear explosive preparations begun by the BARC team in late 1967 to early 1968. On the twentieth anniversary of the 1974 Pokhran explosion, Purnima's designer, P. K. Iyengar, reflected on the reactor's critical role:

> Purnima was a novel device, built with about 20 kg of plutonium, a variable geometry of reflectors, and a unique control system. This gave considerable experience and helped to benchmark calculations regarding the behaviour of a chain-reacting system made out of plutonium. The kinetic behaviour of the system just above critical could be well studied. Very clever physicists could then calculate the time behaviour of the core of a bomb on isotropic compression. What the critical parameters would be, how to achieve optimum explosive power, and its dependence on the first self-sustaining neutron trigger, were all investigated.[13]

Implicit in this statement was the admission that Indian scientists in the early 1970s still lacked important data required to confidently design an explosive device. The properties of plutonium-239—particularly its fast fission cross-section—must be known in order to predict a yield. (The fast fission cross-section records the probability that a nucleus of a given atom—PU-239 in this case—will be fissioned by an approaching neutron.) The United States and other nuclear weapon states had published relevant fast fission cross-section data to augment development of power reactors, but Indian scientists feared that these data could have been misinformation.[14] They wanted to construct this small, pulsed fast reactor to derive the data experimentally themselves to be sure.[15] Indeed, a rudimentary nuclear fission weapon is based on the same principles as a pulsed fast reactor, with the difference being that in a bomb the pulse is very big.

The decision making surrounding the Purnima reactor remains somewhat obscure. Purnima was justified after the fact as part of the fast breeder reactor program that the Department of Atomic Energy proposed in 1967.[16] The fast breeder program was destined to be housed at a new complex at Kalpakkam, near Madras in the eastern coastal state of Tamil Nadu.[17] Plans called for beginning construction there in July 1971 on an experimental fast breeder reactor, designed with French assistance.[18] Within the broader Kalpakkam complex, a zero-energy fast reactor and a pulsed fast reactor were also to be built.[19] Yet Purnima was built at Trombay, on the western coast, where the work on nuclear explosives was headquartered.[20] No pulsed fast reactor was built at Kalpakkam.

Purnima's real purpose was to facilitate design of nuclear explosives. Iyengar noted that "the physicists" had "persuaded" Sarabhai to adopt the overall fast reactor program and that the pulsed fast reactor was imbedded in it.[21] Iyengar recalled that the decision to build Purnima was made by the AEC leadership in 1969, following a visit by Iyengar to a similar Soviet reactor at Dubna. The decision did not require the prime minister's approval.[22] Iyengar hinted that Sarabhai had resisted the Purnima reactor, worrying that it could not be operated safely given India's technical expertise at the time and that it could lead to work on explosives.[23] In any case, Purnima was "built on a shoestring budget."[24] Indeed, according to the then director of the Bhabha Atomic Research Centre, "it was a string, without even a shoe."[25] Homi Sethna explained that there was no budget for Purnima and that the small project did not appear in the AEC's plans or books.[26] Rather, Sethna "taxed" each of the other divisions at BARC to collect material needed for Purnima: "somebody would give a window, someone a door—we patched it together taking a bit from here and there."[27] This may have been necessary because Sarabhai was dubious about the necessity of the reactor for civil purposes and did not share its proponents' enthusiasm for augmenting their capacity to design nuclear explosives.[28] Once again, as in the beginning of serious nuclear explosive design work in 1968, the Sethna-Ramanna-Iyengar-Chidambaram team was maneuvering around Sarabhai. Iyengar wryly noted that the United States, Canada, and the United Kingdom suspected that Purnima was to serve more than a basic research function, but that he managed to allay concerns when foreign visitors came on fact-finding missions.[29]

While the spotlight in 1970 shone on domestic political struggles and Prime Minister Gandhi's quest to consolidate power after the Congress party split, nuclear policy was reemerging as an important subject on the backstage. The Indian nuclear establishment and concerned elites began to press for more active development of nuclear capabilities now that the NPT struggle was over. On March 31, the Consultative Committee on Foreign Affairs and Atomic Energy persuaded the government to study, or restudy, the costs of developing nuclear weapons.[30] The parliamentarians hoped the new study would show that the costs of nuclear weapons would not be prohibitive. Around this time, April 1970, Sarabhai enlisted N. Seshagiri of the Tata Institute of Fundamental Research to conduct a cost-benefit analysis of a nuclear weapon program. According to Seshagiri, Sarabhai "anticipated that the result might show that the cost of a viable nuclear arsenal would be prohibitively heavy for India. He was certain that a nuclear arsenal could not be justified even if [peaceful nuclear explosives] were included."[31] From the available record it is impossible to tell whether Sarabhai intended Seshagiri's study to balance, or be part of, the review requested by the Consultative Committee.[32] Regardless, Seshagiri's account indicates that Sarabhai was still skeptical of building nuclear weapons.

As part of the assessments now under way, a secretary of the Atomic Energy Commission, N. Vellodi, visited the Stockholm International Peace Research Institute (SIPRI) on May 14, 1970, and queried analysts there about the utility of tactical nuclear weapons. According to a SIPRI analyst of the period, Milton Leitenberg, Vellodi said that the Indian government was conducting an internal review of the option to produce nuclear warheads, and that the "army was arguing in support of such a decision by claiming that tactical nuclear weapons in particular would be of use" to close Himalayan passes against a potential Chinese incursion.[33] Leitenberg, on the instructions of SIPRI Director Robert Neild, prepared a notebook of articles and analyses on tactical nuclear weapons and discussed the materials with Vellodi, expressing skepticism about the use of such weapons. K. Subrahmanyam recalled that in this period American strategists spoke of the utility of nuclear munitions in scenarios like the one that India faced in the Himalayas but that he, Vellodi, and others found the ideas nonsensical.[34]

Sarabhai's own doubts about the merits of a nuclear arsenal for India dampened an important potential source of pro-bomb pressure in the review process. However, he now believed that peaceful nuclear explosives could be valuable, extending the pathway begun by the Shastri-Bhabha compromise of November 1964. Sarabhai thus asked Seshagiri to conduct a cost-benefit analysis of peaceful nuclear explosives independent of a nuclear weapons program.[35] A year later, in July 1971, Seshagiri completed an analysis that confirmed Sarabhai's view that a nuclear arsenal would be exceedingly burdensome. But Seshagiri also concluded that producing and using nuclear explosives for engineering purposes was highly viable economically.[36]

The reinvigorated debate over India's nuclear policy gained intensity in April 1970 when China for the first time launched a long-range rocket carrying a satellite into orbit. This raised the specter of a significant Chinese ballistic missile capability to launch nuclear warheads at distant targets. The Chinese breakthrough did not divert the Indian polity from its internal focus, but it did elicit alarm. In the words of the Indian Institute of Public Opinion: "Reactions in certain circles bordered on the panicky. The Chinese space feat, it appeared, tended to warp our perspective: we felt humbled for having lost a race we never chose to enter. Patriotic voices were raised to undo the damage done to the nation's security, to its morale and—this was not said in so many words—to our national pride."[37] An August poll of literates in four major cities revealed that 69 percent of respondents would "like India to go nuclear."[38] Fifty-three percent of respondents felt that the Chinese satellite portended "greater danger to the security" of India, while 19 percent disagreed and 27 percent had no opinion.[39] However, when asked whether India should "go nuclear" if it entailed a "drastic cut in developmental expenditure," 54 percent said no.[40] Summarizing these results, the Indian Institute of Public Opinion concluded that "[i]t seems a case of a nation too exercised by the threat posed by the Chinese nuclear capability but not very willing to pay the price to buy security."[41] Outside the capital, the public still did not place a high value on developing nuclear weapons relative to India's other needs. (Nor did Indian leaders seek to redress any perceived nuclear threat directly through diplomacy with China.)

Elements within the Indian elite sought to exploit the Chinese satellite launch to influence the nuclear debate. On May 9 and 10, the Indian Parliamentary and

Scientific Committee organized a meeting of eminent scientists, academics, and politicians in Delhi and urged the government to revise its policy and produce nuclear weapons immediately.[42] The most intense advocates came from the Jana Sangh and the left wing of the Congress party. They and others argued that India's prestige and national security depended on nuclear weapons and that the quest to develop them would provide important economic spin-offs by accelerating industrial development. One group of "experts" asserted that a weapons program would create "50,000 jobs for engineers, scientists and technicians."[43] The nuclear scientists and Planning Commission representatives at the meeting claimed that India could produce nuclear weapons almost immediately, but they warned that developing delivery systems would take much longer and entail great expense. A number of options short of a crash program were discussed, including development and detonation of nuclear explosive devices for "peaceful" purposes. The meeting did not settle on a particular option but simply espoused the urgency of decisive movement toward "the bomb."

However, not all relevant sectors of the Indian system favored building nuclear weapons. Days after the May 10 confabulations, the former commander in chief of the Indian Army, General K. M. Cariappa, said, "It will be suicidal on our part to go nuclear as such a move will shatter our economy and jeopardize our development plans."[44] A similar view was expressed by former Ministry of Defence Secretary P. V. R. Rao.[45] This was consistent with an earlier pattern: many politicians, security intellectuals, and nuclear scientists fervently favored building nuclear weapons, while top military leaders evinced doubts or decorously stayed out of the debate. As before, neither the government nor the security intellectuals in New Delhi gave the military a significant say-so in their deliberations.

Yet the pattern was altered in at least one important way in 1970. Unlike in the Bhabha days, now India's nuclear establishment was headed by a bomb agnostic, if not a skeptic. On May 25 Sarabhai announced what became known as the Sarabhai Profile, a ten-year plan for the development of atomic energy and space research in India.[46] The Sarabhai Profile reflected a number of immediate and historical factors impinging on India's nuclear program. Sarabhai and his political superiors felt the need to dissipate the pro-bomb pressure that was building as a result of the reenergized debate. On May 17 Sarabhai had declared that India would not seek nuclear weapons but that it would retain the option for conducting underground nuclear explosions for peaceful purposes.[47]

Perhaps a greater impetus for Sarabhai's plan was the State Planning Commission's recent recommendation that Parliament should cut significantly the Department of Atomic Energy's funding.[48] The DAE had requested Rs. 3,981 million ($531 million) through March 1975, while the Planning Commission envisioned allocating only Rs. 2,689.3 million ($359 million).[49] This reflected the greater political-economic priority of other sectors of the economy and national budget. It also signaled disappointment over the failure of the nuclear establishment to live up to previous ambitious plans for utilizing atomic energy for development purposes. In 1954 and again in 1965, plans had called for the Atomic Energy Commission to have 600 megawatts of power on line by 1970–1971. Yet in 1970 only the two U.S.-supplied Tarapur reactors were operating, and their combined output was 420 megawatts.[50] Other projects lagged further behind. Bomb advocates blamed these failures on a lack of leadership since Bhabha's days, as if the plans had been feasible and had gone unfulfilled only because of inadequate willpower.[51] Sarabhai offered a more realistic and systematic assessment of the past, in order to build support for a somewhat more feasible, yet still demanding, agenda for the future.

The published version of Sarabhai's plans for 1970 to 1980 began by looking at the problem of developing atomic energy and space capabilities within the broader context of Indian industrial, management, and organizational resources. Sarabhai argued that the shortcomings of the Atomic Energy Commission stemmed from the inadequacies of the surrounding political economy on which it depended for manufacturing and human resources.[52] He also invoked the importance of atomic energy and space research for national defense and security, not merely for development.[53] This signified the increasingly apparent effort to justify the Atomic Energy Commission's mission and budget in national security terms, as the AEC steadily failed to realize its early promises to fuel national economic development.[54]

Admitting that "[t]he programme has slipped badly in relation to targets that were contemplated in the early 1960s," Sarabhai announced that projections for the future would be scaled back even further.[55] Whereas the AEC in 1954 had envisioned that nuclear plants would provide 8,000 megawatts of electricity in 1980–1981, the new plan called for 2,700 megawatts installed capacity by 1980–1981.[56] The 2,700-megawatt figure related directly to the ongoing plan to rely ultimately on plutonium/thorium breeder reactors. Natural-uranium fueled reactors producing roughly 2,700 megawatts of power would yield, according to AEC calculations, 900 kilograms of plutonium per year, which in turn would be sufficient to fuel one additional 400- to 500-megawatt fast breeder reactor "every other year during the 1980s."[57] Thus, India's atomic energy program was still guided by Bhabha's premature and unachievable vision of a speedy transition to the plutonium-then-thorium fuel cycle. While the military utility of plutonium was clearly recognized within the AEC, the new profile did not declare this added advantage.

The Sarabhai Profile elaborated the manifold industrial, infrastructural, and human resources required to achieve the still optimistic targets.[58] An additional three thousand trained engineers and scientists would be required, as well as "about twice that number of technicians and . . . other supporting staff."[59] Existing road and rail systems could not handle the heavy equipment and components that must be shipped to nuclear plant sites and therefore would have to be upgraded. The steel and electronics industries of India also would have to be significantly improved in quality and scale to provide components for planned nuclear plants and related facilities.[60] Without major investments in supporting industries and infrastructure, projects would continue to take excessively long to complete, exacerbating the interest payments and overall capital costs of the nuclear program. The need to drastically improve Indian industry and infrastructure pointed to the profound flaw in Bhabha's initial plan: it failed to recognize the nuclear program's organic dependence on the broader national economy. Greater development was a *precondition* for a major nuclear power program, not the other way around.

The costs of fulfilling the new, scaled-back plan would be great. Even excluding, as the Atomic Energy Commission did, the tremendous industrial and infrastructure investments required to support the nuclear program, the ten-year plan called for expenditures of Rs. 12,500 million, or approximately $1.67 billion at the exchange rate of the time.[61] This was slightly more than the annual defense budget at that time, which was itself slightly more than 20 percent of central government spending and 2.87 percent of GNP.[62] Averaged over the ten-year period, the requested funds would have amounted to a roughly 30 percent increase in annual DAE funding.[63] Of course, it was argued that if these costs were borne, the benefits would be great: "[F]ully 915 crores [$1.22 billion] are for projects of direct economic significance contributing to national development."[64] The projects and figures included in the profile did not include any activities that could be explicitly tied to developing and producing nuclear weapons. Additional activities and expenditures would have been necessary for a significant military program.

The Department of Atomic Energy's 1970 profile also presented the first major plans for space research. The space program had begun only in 1961, at Sarabhai's instigation, and had been placed in the DAE. Sarabhai's own work had concentrated on the nascent space program until he became chairman of the Atomic Energy Commission. The first task had been to develop a cadre of scientists and engineers to develop space research in India. Much of the early technological work was done through foreign cooperation, primarily with France, the United Kingdom, the Soviet Union, and the United States. With this international help and financing, a space launch facility was established near Trivandrum in southern India. The first launch from this facility was of a U.S.-provided Nike-Apache sounding rocket, on November 21, 1963.[65] Throughout the 1960s the program grew slowly. In 1969 a separate organization—the Indian Space Research Organisation (ISRO)—was created within the DAE. (This arrangement lasted until 1972 when a new Department of Space was created. Homi Sethna, upon assuming the chairmanship of the Atomic Energy Commission in 1972, moved to split off the space program in part because he wanted to avoid the controversy that would have arisen if the AEC were developing nuclear explosive capabilities *and* rockets, which would have given the impression that India was moving to become a full-fledged nuclear weapon power despite its claims to the contrary.)[66]

Sarabhai's 1970 profile emphasized three objectives for space research: to develop and deploy satellites for communications, particularly television broadcasting; to develop and utilize meteorological satellites to predict weather, particularly monsoons; and to apply remote sensing technology to detect crop and forest disease, measure snow coverage in the Himalayas to anticipate drought and flood conditions, and so forth.[67] The 1970 plan called on India to launch its first indigenously produced satellite in 1974 with a multistage rocket, the SLV-3.[68]

Sarabhai's profile did not point to potential missile applications. While some of the personnel from ISRO would assume leadership positions in the dedicated missile program created in 1983, Sarabhai clearly intended for the space organization to be a vehicle for India's economic and technological development.[69] He also decried the tendency to pursue state-of-the-art technological programs for their prestige, saying India should not embark "on grandiose schemes, whose primary impact is for show rather than for progress measured in hard economic and social terms."[70] And indeed, the proposed budget for the ten-year space plan was Rs. 1,650 million, roughly 13 percent of the spending proposed for atomic energy. However, even this nearly doubled what the government had planned to spend on space research in the 1969-to-1974 period.[71]

Unfortunately, as a contemporaneous U.S. government assessment noted, "Sarabhai's ambitious program is far too expensive, given India's other pressing needs, for the GOI to accept it in its entirety."[72] In the 1970–1971 fiscal year, the government deficit was higher than planned. Reflecting Prime Minister Gandhi's leftward tack, the government sought to stimulate employment through increased spending in politically sensitive sectors, particularly rural development. The Department of Atomic Energy's activities simply did not provide enough direct benefit to the citizenry or the economy to warrant a major, sustained budget increase.[73] True, a nuclear explosive project could serve as a symbolic coat of arms to gain entry to the international aristocracy. And an ambitious reactor program could symbolize an advanced scientific and engineering degree within the international nuclear establishment. Yet neither satisfied what ailed India.

Interestingly, the Sarabhai Profile did not mention peaceful nuclear explosives. This was remarkable given the frequency of contemporaneous references to conducting peaceful nuclear explosions, the strong Indian role in the NPT debate over peaceful nuclear explosives, and the fact that leading scientists and engineers in the nuclear establishment were assiduously developing this capability.[74] The record does not indicate whether the omission stemmed from Sarabhai's or the government's ambivalence, a desire not to stimulate controversy over the development of nuclear power in India, or international considerations. In any case, in July 1970, Sarabhai asserted that India was capable of conducting underground nuclear explosions and was internationally entitled to do so as a nonparty to the NPT.[75] On August 31, the prime minister informed the Parliament that the government was studying the economic and technical issues surrounding peaceful nuclear explosives.[76] Momentum was building to develop nuclear explosive capability.

MOMENTUM BUILDS TOWARD A "PEACEFUL"EXPLOSION, 1970 TO 1971

Throughout the summer of 1970, the nuclear debate intensified in the press, among foreign policy experts, and in the Parliament. Three camps emerged. One argued against nuclear weapons. A second argued for a crash program to build a small nuclear arsenal to be delivered first by aircraft and, in time, by crude, liquid-fueled ballistic missiles. A third argued for a steadier, less provocative long-term course to develop the capacity to deploy a small but sophisticated missile-based arsenal with attendant command, control, and warning infrastructure.

The director of the Terminal Ballistics Research Laboratory in Chandigarh, Sampooran Singh, provided the most sophisticated case for a crash nuclear weapon program in *India and the Nuclear Bomb.* Singh's laboratory housed what would become increasingly important work to develop conventional high-explosive systems for imploding the plutonium cores of India's nuclear devices in 1974 and 1998. Singh argued that "the Government's opposition to the nuclear weapons programme has in recent years been largely, if not solely, on economic grounds. There has been very little discussion of the political and strategic role of nuclear weapons in the country."[77] Singh wrote that "China's entry of the nuclear club has enhanced its national prestige and influence on the international scene. Its nuclear forces are now a symbol of national greatness, political power and importance."[78] This led Singh to conclude that India must follow suit: "So long as nuclear power and political power are correlated elements in world politics it is necessary that India take a close hard look at its defence posture on a long term basis, and view nuclear power as an integral part of its defence and deterrence system."[79]

The strategist K. Subrahmanyam took a more sophisticated line that clashed with Singh's and in the process provided the most incisive summary and analysis of the brewing debate. A thin, intensely intelligent Brahmin and a highly informed civil servant, Subrahmanyam had succeeded Major General Som Dutt as director of the Institute for Defence Studies and Analyses and argued as force-fully for nuclear weapons as Dutt had argued against them. In a compendium of four articles in the July 1970 issue of the institute's journal, Subrahmanyam framed the discussion. He argued that India suffered from "the total absence of an integrated view about the long-term technological and security requirements of the country" and complained that "the present type of generalist civil service administration" could not "tackle such issues."[80] Contrary to the government's position, he insisted that China posed a threat that must be countered through a systematic strategy of developing a survivable nuclear deterrent.[81] However, Subrahmanyam noted approvingly that "[e]ven the most ardent advocate of an Indian weapon programme does not visualise . . . the Chinese threat in terms of China using ballistic missiles to destroy Indian cities."[82] Rather, the threat was more general. As the *Hindu* editorialized on June 2, 1970, few "informed people in India perceive a real Chinese nuclear threat but the very proximity and enormity of Chinese power leaves no alternative for India except to go in for an adequate nuclear deterrent of its own."[83] A nuclear-armed China could exert its political will on India, engage in blackmail, and possibly probe with impunity the disputed Himalayan border. These were the sorts of threats that required a nuclear counter. If India would deploy a nuclear counter, Subrahmanyam argued, it would "stabilise the confrontation and ensure peace."[84] In his view, the government had offered no "logical and comprehensive explanation in regard to the strategy proposed to be employed by India in case of a nuclear threat."[85] (Ironically, around this time China was signaling to India a desire to normalize relations.)[86]

Subrahmanyam decried that India was guided by a sentimental policy instead of Realism: "The present set of decision makers, still from the generation which was closely associated with Nehru, feel that it would amount to betraying a cause and that India will lose whatever moral stature she still may have by taking such a decision" to acquire nuclear weapons.[87] Subrahmanyam argued, to the contrary, that nuclear weapons would serve India's moral purpose by ensuring peace through deterrence. "Once the obsession about the terrible damage caused by the use of nuclear weapons is shed and the weapons are looked at in terms of political power and the capability to deter, the arguments will fall into appropriate perspective."[88] Against the government's intuitive worry over the risks and costs inherent in nuclear arms racing, this leading bomb advocate posed an equally speculative faith that deploying nuclear weapons entailed little risk.

Yet, when Subrahmanyam surveyed India's technological and institutional capabilities to build and operate a sophisticated arsenal, he unintentionally highlighted some of the burdens that political leaders feared. First, he posited that India lacked adequate stocks of weapon-grade plutonium and would have to construct new, unsafeguarded reactors to remedy the situation. Moreover, to produce weapon-grade plutonium, as opposed to reactor-grade plutonium, the fuel elements in reactors would have to be changed with uneconomic rapidity, thereby raising the marginal costs of the nuclear program.[89] Alternatively, India could divert plutonium from the Canadian-supplied CIRUS and RAPS-I reactors. Yet, Subrahmanyam doubted the wisdom of breaking the peaceful-purposes-only agreements with Canada governing use of these reactors and their fuels.[90] To build and operate the requisite plutonium production reactors, India would also have to increase significantly its capacity to produce heavy water. This, too, would entail large expense and the overcoming of technological hurdles that, as it turned out, India would find exceedingly difficult to do. Subrahmanyam did not address the technological challenge of producing delivery systems.

Though he advocated acquiring nuclear weapons, Subrahmanyam inveighed against the proponents of a crash bomb-making program. Instead, he supported Sarabhai's ten-year plan and urged that India wait until the 1980s to go nuclear, when greater resources would be in hand and India would be more able to withstand international backlash. He acknowledged as Sarabhai had that India must radically improve and expand its electronics, computer, materials, and aerospace industries in order to create the foundation for an effective nuclear arsenal.[91] Still, to build a long-term weapons program would be vastly more expensive than the already fiscally ambitious Sarabhai Profile suggested. While Subrahmanyam did not attempt to put a figure on the kind of program he advocated, he indicated it would be closer in cost to what France was spending for its arsenal or to the amount that a recent United Nations commission had estimated for any new state seeking nuclear weapons.[92] The latter figure was $5.6 billion for a small, high-quality missile-based nuclear arsenal. This would have amounted to roughly five times India's 1970–1971 defense budget, or almost its entire annual central government expenditure, a tremendous cost even if spread over ten years. Subrahmanyam attacked his countrymen who asserted that India could build a similar arsenal at lower costs or could take a short cut by relying on delivery by aircraft or liquid-fueled missiles.[93]

But even if India, with all its economic and political difficulties and competing priorities, could afford to increase Department of Atomic Energy funding by a factor of five, other daunting challenges would remain. "[D]elivery vehicles and the warheads alone do not make a nuclear weapon system. The command and control is an essential part of it," Subrahmanyam noted.[94] It requires an elaborate technical infrastructure and institutional command system to ensure that nuclear weapons are not launched inadvertently or without authorization but also can be launched quickly under authority. And to detect emerging nuclear threats and incoming attacks, sophisticated surveillance and warning systems must be deployed. In 1970, relatively little was known in the "open" world about these systems and their costs. (Recent research indicates that the United States has spent roughly $831 billion in 1996 dollars on such targeting and control capabilities between 1940 and 1996, compared with $409 billion in developing, testing, and producing nuclear warheads themselves.)[95] He noted that in the debate over the costs of nuclear weapons "the significant investments in these areas are apt to be overlooked."[96]

Subrahmanyam wanted his analysis to move Indian nuclear policy toward the dedicated, long-term nuclear weapon program he advocated. However, the requirements he detailed had a cautionary effect. The institutional, moral, and economic factors that had kept India from embarking on a bomb-building program in the 1960s still obtained. Som Dutt's late-1966 analysis of India's strategic options remained more in tune with the nation's political and economic circumstances than Subrahmanyam's 1970 recommendations, even if the latter were more consistent with images of great military power. In 1970, Indian leaders were preoccupied with political struggles and an ongoing economic crisis. They could be excused from wondering if the bomb advocates had lost touch with the realities that confronted the nation. Rather than a clear, major nuclear weapon program, the most the political economy would bear was modest movement toward peaceful nuclear explosives. An Indian Institute of Public Opinion poll reported in August-September 1971 that 63 percent of those surveyed believed that India "should go nuclear," but that support dropped markedly, even compared to a similar poll a year earlier, when respondents were asked if they favored going nuclear even if it meant a "drastic cut in development expenditure."[97] In that case, only 38 percent wanted the bomb, and this number was distorted upward by the disproportionately hawkish views of those in Delhi (76 percent), compared with respondents in Calcutta (24 percent), Bombay (19 percent), and Madras (33 percent).[98]

In November 1970, the renewed Indian debate and official statements showing interest in peaceful nuclear explosions rang alarms in the U.S. government. On November 16, the United States sent India an aide-mémoire declaring that Washington would view an Indian nuclear explosion using plutonium derived from the CIRUS reactor, which was moderated by U.S.-supplied heavy water, as a violation of the U.S.-India nuclear cooperation agreement.[99] The United States argued that no distinction could be made between a peaceful nuclear explosive and a weapon. India responded by rejecting the U.S. interpretation and asserting its right to pursue any peaceful applications of nuclear energy, including peaceful nuclear explosives.[100] This exchange indicated U.S. awareness of Indian movement toward a nuclear test and foreshadowed the dispute that would embroil the two states following India's 1974 nuclear test.

Western newspapers reported in the summer of 1971 that India had begun work on nuclear explosives.[101] However, Prime Minister Gandhi was taking pains to distinguish between peaceful nuclear explosives and a full-fledged weapon program. On June 6, 1971, while visiting the island of Mauritius, she said, "[W]e have discussed this question deeply and rejected the idea of making the bomb. . . . Once we launch into making it, we would have to incur heavy expenses to keep abreast of nuclear weaponry and at the same time maintain conventional equipment."[102] Confronted with the portrait painted by those like K. Subrahmanyam, India's political leaders turned away in dismay. Even as a crisis was brewing on India's border with East Pakistan, the prime minister was explicitly abjuring nuclear weapons. However, if a full-fledged bomb program was out, a peaceful nuclear explosive was looking more likely. In September 1971, Sarabhai told an audience at the Fourth International Conference on the Peaceful Uses of Atomic Energy in Geneva that his scientists were developing nuclear explosive engineering (i.e., peaceful nuclear explosives) as a top priority.[103]

Prompted by Sarabhai's statement and goaded by an alarmed U.S. bureaucracy, Canadian Prime Minister Pierre Trudeau wrote to Indira Gandhi on October 1, 1971, declaring that "use of Canadian supplied material, equipment and facilities . . . for the development of a nuclear explosive device would inevitably call on our part for a reassessment of our nuclear cooperation arrangements with India."[104] Mrs. Gandhi replied by trying to finesse the potential costly dispute. She rejected Canada's right to interpret the cooperation agreement unilaterally, but she then downplayed the matter by suggesting that the problem of a nuclear explosion was "a hypothetical contingency" that need not be sorted out now.[105] It

is evident now, as it was then, that India was warily approaching a decision to prepare and detonate a nuclear explosive.

It is interesting to speculate whether and how India would have endeavored to
conduct a nuclear explosion under Sarabhai's leadership after 1971. The scientists
involved in the eventual nuclear test of 1974 hinted that Sarabhai had been an
impediment to their desire to build and detonate nuclear explosive devices.[106]
Reflecting the tensions among the Atomic Energy Commission's top leadership in
1971, Homi Sethna recalled in a later interview that he "almost quit" over disagreements with Sarabhai over research and development priorities and the general direction of the program but was persuaded by Indira Gandhi and her principal secretary, P. N. Haksar, to remain.[107]

When Sarabhai died suddenly of a heart attack on December 30, 1971, at the
age of fifty-two, the question of his vision for India's nuclear policy became moot.
The reins of the Atomic Energy Commission passed to the chemical engineer
Homi Sethna who had played a leading role in developing India's plutonium-
reprocessing and metallurgical capacities. Unlike Sarabhai, Sethna was a blunt,
plainspoken organizational leader not given to philosophical contemplation over
his work. He evinced no extraordinary moral aversion to nuclear weapons. Nor
did he share his predecessor's attachment to analyzing space and nuclear projects
in cost-benefit terms within the context of India's overall development needs.
Whatever Sarabhai might have done, Sethna was among the team that wanted
fervently to demonstrate Indian prowess and power with a dramatic act like detonating a nuclear explosive. Thus, as Raja Ramanna has recounted, "After Vikram
Sarabhai's death in 1971, India began to seriously consider conducting a Peaceful
Nuclear Explosion."[108] Ramanna and his colleagues had imparted technological
momentum to the project and Prime Minister Gandhi was emerging strongly
from the political challenges that had preoccupied her since 1967.

SEVEN

India Explodes a "Peaceful" Nuclear Device

1971–1974

By the end of 1971, the Atomic Energy Commission and the government were inclining publicly toward conducting a peaceful nuclear explosion. Advocates of the explosives program now controlled the Atomic Energy Commission. In 1972, Indira Gandhi, fresh from smashing electoral and military victories, assented to their request to authorize building a nuclear explosive device which could then be tested.

In the latter half of 1971, international developments assumed growing importance for India. Between July and December, the United States pursued a breakthrough in relations with China, using Pakistan as an intermediary; India and the Soviet Union signed a Treaty of Friendship and Cooperation; and India and Pakistan went to war. Yet, as this chapter shows, these important developments had less direct bearing on nuclear policy than is often assumed.

Instead, the decisive factors that led to the detonation of a nuclear device in 1974 were the Atomic Energy Commission's determination to prove its mettle and Indira Gandhi's sense that India would gain confidence in itself as a nation and her as a leader. The final decision to conduct the test was the result of an ad hoc, intuitive process that lacked rigorous security analysis.

FOREIGN POLICY DEVELOPMENTS, 1971

When Indira Gandhi called early for India's fifth general elections in December 1970, Pakistan was holding its first democratic election. The East Pakistan–based Awami League won a majority of seats. However, this victory came solely from votes in East Pakistan. The Awami League won no seats in West Pakistan. This reflected a fundamental split in the Pakistani state. The largest share of the population resided in the east, while the bureaucratic, military, and economic elite of the state lived in the west. The 1970 election amounted to a referendum for autonomy on the part of East Pakistanis. For their part, the Punjabi and Sindhi elites in the west would neither abide being led by Bengalis from the east nor grant them autonomy. The Pakistan Peoples Party, headed by Zulfikar Ali Bhutto, won the majority of West Pakistani seats. Determined to assume the prime ministership and end military rule, Bhutto and Pakistani President Yahya Khan entered negotiations with Bengali leader Mujibur Rahman to find a modus vivendi that would grant East Pakistan greater autonomy while satisfying the West Pakistani rulers, including the army. These negotiations failed, however, and on March 25, 1971, the western-controlled military cracked down in East Pakistan. Violent conflict ensued. Many East Pakistani political leaders escaped to India to form a government in exile, while nearly 10 million refugees from East Pakistan also flowed into India.[1] The repression and refugee exodus continued for months until a major war broke out in December between India and Pakistan, as is discussed in the next section.

The crisis in Pakistan occurred at the same time as major developments in Sino-American and Indo-Soviet relations. Each of these dramatically evolving relationships in turn influenced the other.

By 1971, India and the Soviet Union had begun an intense courtship. India had become increasingly reliant on Soviet military supplies, while Moscow viewed India as a growing regional power. In 1969, the two states had negotiated, but not signed, a treaty of friendship and cooperation.[2] Thus, as the Pakistani crisis unfolded, the Soviet Union moved closer to India's side. Still, Moscow had little interest in being implicated in a major confrontation that could detract from the strategic arms negotiations then underway with Washington.[3] On June 6–8, Indian Minister of External Affairs Swaran Singh traveled to Moscow to discuss events in East Pakistan and prepare the ground for signing and unveiling the friendship treaty.[4] Singh sought Soviet support for India's stance vis-à-vis Pakistan. India insisted that the unrest in East Pakistan could not and should not be resolved through military repression, that the flow of refugees into India must stop, that conditions must be created in East Pakistan to allow refugees to return, and that a political solution acceptable to East Pakistan must be negotiated.[5] India made it clear that failure to achieve these conditions threatened the peace and security of the region.

While India and the Soviet Union were tightening their embrace, U.S. National Security Adviser Henry Kissinger and President Richard Nixon were moving secretly to open relations with China in a strategy to pinch the Soviet Union in a triangular balance of power. Pakistan served as the discreet facilitator. On April 27, with the crackdown in East Pakistan entering its fifth week, the Pakistani ambassador to the United States informed the White House that Chou En-lai would welcome an American emissary to China.[6]

The priority of the daring breakthrough with China decisively influenced Washington's participation in the brewing Indo-Pak crisis and war. It also colored

India's perception of the emerging international environment. Distrust of the United States grew, along with attraction to the Soviet Union. Indo-American relations already had been exacerbated by antipathy between Nixon and Kissinger and Indira Gandhi, and by American disgruntlement over her leftward movement during and after the 1969 Congress party split. The situation worsened when Washington agreed in October 1970 to resume export of lethal military equipment to Pakistan.[7] At the same time, however, India rankled the United States by continuing to harangue over the war in Vietnam.[8]

Since the 1962 war with China, India had assumed (or hoped) that the U.S. could be relied upon to defend India diplomatically and even militarily against Chinese pressure or aggression. This comforting assumption evaporated when the Sino-American breakthrough was announced on July 15, 1971. Henry Kissinger telephoned India's ambassador to Washington on July 17 and notified him that "[w]e would be unable to help you against China" in the event of Chinese involvement in a war between India and Pakistan.[9] Shortly thereafter, on August 5, Pakistani President Yahya Khan threatened to go to war if an effort was made to "take away" East Pakistani territory.[10] Washington's deference and the Sino-American rapprochement had emboldened the Pakistani leadership.

But India already was preparing to announce its own breakthrough, long in the works. On August 9, India and the Soviet Union signed a Treaty of Peace, Friendship and Co-operation. While maintaining the veneer of Indian nonalignment, the treaty's Article IX declared that "In the event of either Party being subjected to an attack or a threat thereof, the . . . Parties shall immediately enter into mutual consultations in order to remove such threat and to take appropriate effective measures to ensure peace and the security of their countries."[11] The timing of the treaty's signing, if not its negotiation, was clearly motivated by India's desire for backing in case China tried to intervene politically or militarily in the looming conflict with Pakistan.[12] India assured Washington that the treaty was not aimed at the United States, but the context affected the White House's perception of South Asia. Whereas the State Department continued to see India's moves and the Indo-Pak conflict for what they were—manifestations of an intrastate and regional crisis—Nixon and Kissinger saw them as ominous turns in the cold war.[13]

When Indira Gandhi traveled to Washington in early November on a three-week tour of Western capitals to rally support for India in the Pakistani crisis, the discussions with Nixon and Kissinger proceeded disastrously. Kissinger called the Gandhi-Nixon sessions "the two most unfortunate meetings Nixon had with any foreign leader."[14] Beyond their personal enmity, the two leaders simply saw no merit in each other's perceptions of the Indo-Pak crisis and approaches to resolving it. Mrs. Gandhi felt that the crisis had been created wholly by Pakistan and must therefore be resolved by Pakistani actions to end repression, free Mujibur Rahman, and allow East Pakistan's autonomy so that refugees could return from India. Nixon believed that Mrs. Gandhi was exploiting the crisis out of a desire (shared by Moscow) to attack and dismember Pakistan, if not also to destroy West

Pakistan.[15] With these perceptions, American and Indian leaders were adding an Indo-American element to the Indo-Pak conflict.

WAR WITH PAKISTAN, NOVEMBER TO DECEMBER 1971

The Indo-Pak War was a defining moment for India, Pakistan, and now Bangladesh. Yet for the purposes of understanding India's nuclear policy, the war can be treated summarily. More important for nuclear policy was the conduct of the United States and the related concern that India was now being drawn uncomfortably into the dynamic between Washington, Moscow, and Beijing. This raised discomfiting questions about India's nonalignment.

In November 1971, events in East Pakistan spiralled out of control. Among the millions of refugees that had streamed into India, Bangladeshi "freedom fighters" used sanctuaries in India to attack Pakistani forces in the east under artillery cover from India. In late November, Prime Minister Gandhi authorized Indian forces to cross the border to "pursue" Pakistani forces. Kissinger took this as reaffirmation that India was the aggressor determined to escalate the conflict in a strategy to disintegrate West Pakistan.[16] On December 3, Pakistan assaulted air bases in western India. Pakistan declared war on December 4. India counterattacked decisively in East Pakistan, with concomitant probing attacks in the west.

Meanwhile, the United States on December 2 announced a suspension of military sales to India and days later froze economic assistance. Kissinger, against State Department advice, ordered U.S. spokesmen to declare that India was primarily responsible for the war.[17] Kissinger and Nixon insisted that the United States should "tilt" toward Pakistan. On December 10, as fighting between India and Pakistan intensified, the White House took the step that would embitter India to this day. It ordered the aircraft carrier USS *Enterprise* and nine supporting warships to the Bay of Bengal. This order was issued without consultation within the executive branch. Indeed, according to Raymond Garthoff, citing Admiral Elmo Zumwalt Jr., the order to the navy did not specify the force's mission.[18] In his memoirs, Kissinger explained that the carrier group was deployed "ostensibly for the evacuation of Americans, but in reality to give emphasis to our warnings against an attack on West Pakistan."[19] In "deeper" reality, Kissinger revealed parenthetically that "we also wanted to have forces in place in case the Soviet Union pressured China."[20]

Before the *Enterprise* could arrive in the Bay of Bengal—indeed on the same day its deployment was ordered—the Pakistani commander in East Pakistan offered a cease-fire. However, President Yahya Khan, under strong advice from the White House, over-rode the commander and insisted on a cease-fire in both East and West Pakistan, thereby continuing the war futilely in the east.[21] On December 11 and 12, the White House intensified the "big power" dynamic. Kissinger presented the Soviet Union an ultimatum to press India not to annex parts of West Pakistan. The Soviets replied that India had no aggressive intentions in the west.[22]

Indeed, on December 12 Prime Minister Gandhi declared this publicly. However, these statements did not calm the White House. Fearing without evidence that China was preparing to assist Pakistan militarily and that the Soviet Union might respond with threats in kind, the White House ordered the *Enterprise* battle group to proceed into the Bay of Bengal.[23] Later that day, December 12, the Chinese disabused Kissinger of his vision of Chinese military involvement. The Chinese ambassador told him that China favored a standstill cease-fire between India and Pakistan and had no interest in intervening.[24] Throughout the conflict China had rhetorically condemned India and the Soviet Union and had backed Pakistan. But China offered no significant deeds to match its words. Chinese leaders, unlike Kissinger and Nixon, recognized the conflict for what it was: an Indo-Pak affair that did not affect the interests of China or the Soviet Union directly enough to warrant major involvement.

To India, the arrival of the U.S. naval force was enigmatic, but nonetheless offensive. The United States declared that its purpose was to evacuate Americans from East Pakistan and did not specify that it was meant to deter India from dismembering West Pakistan, notwithstanding Kissinger's own view of this purpose. India chose not to deal directly with the American force, but instead it undertook air strikes on harbored Pakistani ships to cut off a possible evacuation of Pakistani armed forces via American boats.[25] The Soviet Union had assured India on December 13 that the United States would not intervene militarily and that Moscow would back up this reassurance by deploying its own naval force to the region.[26] China criticized both the Soviet Union and the United States for deploying military forces.[27]

On December 16, Pakistani forces in East Pakistan surrendered. Fighting continued for a day along the borders of Jammu and Kashmir, and Punjab and Sindh in the west. On December 17, India proposed an unconditional cease-fire in the west, which Pakistan accepted. The war was over.[28] Bangladesh was born from the dismemberment of Pakistan.

In terms of Indian nuclear policy, the war suggests several conclusions. India proved it could defeat Pakistan in battle. This contributed to Pakistan's determination to acquire nuclear weapons, an aim that was expressed in a secret January 1972 meeting convened by Zulfikar Ali Bhutto to launch the Pakistani nuclear weapon program. But the incipient Pakistani nuclear threat would not be cited by Indian leaders in explaining India's ensuing nuclear test in 1974. The war also indicated that China did not seek militarily to threaten India's security or challenge its preeminence in the subcontinent.[29] The newly formalized Indian-Soviet relationship buttressed India's security. Thus, as discussed more fully later in this chapter, the 1971 war did not create a security imperative to develop nuclear weapons.

The most ominous international development of the war was the United States' attempt to pressure India through gunboat diplomacy. Indian polemicists, down to the present day, cite the *Enterprise* deployment as an example of why India should deploy a nuclear arsenal of its own.[30] This obscures the fact that the American deployment did not reflect a true military security threat to India. It had been a misguided effort to signal constancy to China and forcefulness to the Soviet Union. India was merely a pawn in the Kissinger-Nixon game. However, had India seen the American military deployment in this light, the result still would have been negative. It raised the hugely important problem of esteem. The United States did not take India seriously, did not consider it important. How could India sustain its self-image as a great civilization and nation worthy of a leading place in the international system if the United States treated it as inconsequential? This question may not have diminished the national euphoria following the 1971 war, but it lurked in the minds of India's leaders and elites as time wore on.

AFTERMATH OF WAR AT HOME AND ABROAD, 1972 TO 1973

Nineteen seventy-two arrived with Indira Gandhi in an unassailable position. In Tariq Ali's words, "She was the 'liberator of Bangladesh'; she had destroyed the Pakistani military machine and brought down Yahya Khan. Even the most determined opposition leaders felt that they were destined to spend a long time in the wilderness."[31]

In the aftermath of Nixon and Kissinger's heavy-handed role in the 1971 Indo-Pak war, the U.S. government sought to make amends. This process began in 1973, following a rough period in 1972 when the United States drastically scaled back its Agency for International Development mission in India and the two governments remained antagonistic over U.S. policy in Vietnam.[32] The United States formally recognized Bangladesh in March 1973. Both American and Indian officials increasingly spoke of the desire to heal relations. However, each step forward seemed to be followed by an American-led stumble backward. For example, in mid-March 1973 when the United States announced release of a suspended $87.6 million development loan to India, Washington also declared it would provide Pakistan with new military equipment, albeit nonlethal weapons and spare parts.[33] This hit a tender and well-known Indian nerve and typified U.S.-Indian relations. Similarly, U.S. moves to expand the military facility at Diego Garcia, in the aftermath of the October 1973 Arab-Israeli war, prompted an Indian backlash. The base, on an Indian Ocean atoll one thousand miles off the coast of southern India, was increasingly important to support the U.S. military role in the Persian Gulf, but India saw it as an encroachment into its sphere of influence. The Soviet Union exploited the tension by rhetorically joining India's call to make the Indian Ocean a zone of peace. This issue would become more inflamed in the late 1970s and 1980s.[34]

In a further effort to improve relations, President Nixon expressed greater American regard for India in his annual Report to Congress in May 1973. "India emerged from the 1971 crisis with new confidence, power and responsibilities," the report stated. "The United States respects India as a major country. We are prepared to treat India in accordance with its new stature and responsibilities, on the basis of reciprocity."[35] Nixon added, "The United States will not join in any groupings or pursue any policies directed against India," specifying that Washington's normalization of relations with China was "not directed against India or inconsistent with our desire to enjoy good relations with India."[36] The United States at this time contributed to major increases in World Bank soft loans to India and settled a problem stemming from the accumulation of $3 billion worth of rupees in American accounts, by in effect writing off $2 billion and using the balance to cover American embassy expenses and other in-country expenditures.[37]

Despite the overt American appeal to Indian sensitivities, the Gandhi government remained bitter toward the United States. Whatever President Nixon might say, Mrs. Gandhi felt, in the words of the Indian author V. P. Dutt, that the United States

> had ignored India's basic interests, tried to create parity of strength between India and Pakistan, pumped large-scale armament into Islamabad and fanned the embers of an arms race in this region. It had given considerable economic assistance to India but had always attempted to trade it off for political leverage. Mrs. Gandhi said in a special interview to [Dutt] . . . that Washington did not look kindly upon strong, independent countries in Asia, did not apparently wish to see the emergence of a strong India.[38]

Mrs. Gandhi also perceived Nixon and Kissinger's pursuit of détente with the Soviet Union warily. "Detente should not become an occasion to build new balances of power and to redraw spheres of influence or to reinforce the opinion of certain Big Powers that they alone can be responsible for the shaping of the destinies of small nations," she declared in February 1973.[39]

India's wariness was not directed at the United States alone. Despite the 1971 Indo-Soviet treaty, India looked skeptically at Soviet offers of embrace in the 1972–1973 period. Soviet Communist Party General Secretary Leonid Brezhnev made a major visit to India in November 1973 to promote a plan for collective security in Asia. Moscow's effort to deepen its involvement in the region and, with an eye to balancing China, draw India closer to the Soviet Union, triggered Indian reservations. Treasuring its independence, India responded cautiously to the Soviet overture. Minister of External Affairs Swaran Singh assured Parliament that India would never endorse a militarily based system of collective security and would resist "any system of grouping of countries directed against any other country or group of countries."[40] While American officials and observers often doubted India's nonalignment, and could cite as evidence the 1971 Indo-Soviet treaty, Indian officials continued to insist that their policies were consistent with nonalignment.

To the north, Sino-Indian political relations had been harmed in the 1971 war when China sided with Pakistan and denounced India. However, Beijing did not enter the fray militarily on the side of Pakistan, despite Islamabad's wishes. In the aftermath of the war, China initially maintained a campaign of invective against India.[41] Soon, however, broader geopolitical imperatives compelled both India and China to improve relations. China resumed subtle steps begun in 1970 to put relations on a track toward normalization.[42] By 1976, relations had improved to the point that India decided to send an ambassador to China for the first time since 1961.

On the subcontinent, by 1973 India's political position was eroding slightly from its peak in the immediate aftermath of the 1971 war. Prime Minister Gandhi was criticized for not adequately pressing India's will in negotiations with Pakistan to implement normalization measures called for in the 1972 Simla Agreement following the 1971 war. Pakistan had won American and Chinese support in these negotiations. India had been unable to translate the battlefield rout into a solution to the endemic conflict with Pakistan, centered on Kashmir. Unbeknownst to India, Pakistan had now started its own nuclear weapon program. In Bangladesh, public opinion was becoming hostile toward India.[43]

Overall, then, in the pre-1974 period, India strove to maintain strategic autonomy in the midst of a complicated dynamic among the United States, the Soviet Union, and China. Yet, there was no acute challenge to India's security or foreign policy in this period. Indeed, in March 1973, the *Times of India* quoted Field Marshal Manekshaw's view that Indian security did not require nuclear weapons: "We cannot use them. Nuclear Weapons can be produced if our scientists apply their mind to it and if crores of rupees could be spent. But, in the meantime, millions of people have to wait for bare necessities of life like food, cloth and shelter."[44] However, Indian elites were frustrated by the United States' and the international community's failure to regard India as a major power. More than any other *international* consideration, the desire for major power status affected India's eagerness to demonstrate its nuclear capability.

The situation at home was not so sanguine. Nineteen seventy-two brought another severe drought, affecting 180 million citizens, exacerbating shortages of food, and fueling inflation.[45] In the period from 1972 to 1973, prices rose by 22 percent. Between 1973 and 1974 inflation rose to nearly 30 percent.[46] More than 40 percent of the population now lived below official poverty levels.[47] Unemployment rates were mounting, and not only among unskilled laborers. According to Kuldip Nayar, more than 75 percent of new college graduates in this period could not find work.[48] In 1972 and 1973 there were 12,089 strikes and sit-ins in Bombay alone.[49] There were strikes, protest marches, and clashes with the police in most parts of the country.[50]

The government lacked a strategy and means to redress these downward trends. The economic imperative of stimulating economic growth through greater incentives to private investment clashed with the political imperative of redressing inequities and caring for the poor. Fiscal resources fell utterly short. By late 1973, the draft Fifth Five-Year Plan called for more than twice the level of government investment and spending than spent during the Fourth Five-Year Plan, but there was no way to finance it.[51] All of this sharpened the disillusion over Indira Gandhi's promises in the 1971 campaign to "remove poverty."

Amidst this dreary economy, new corruption scandals emerged in 1972 that further lowered the populace's trust in the political class.[52] Still, in the 1972 elections to the state legislative assemblies Congress politicians won more than 70 percent of overall seats, and the party's vote share rose to 47 percent from the previous level of 42 percent in the 1967 elections.[53] Much of this success owed to the afterglow of the military victory months earlier, which Mrs. Gandhi and her Congress allies exploited fully.[54] Congress and Indira Gandhi also benefited from the diminished vigor and organizational capacity of the opposition—left and right.[55]

However, beneath the surface, Congress itself was falling into further disorder. The 1969–1970 co-optation of former Communists was now engendering a backlash from more traditional Nehruvian Congress members who feared an erosion of commitment to democracy within the party and the polity at large.[56] Fissures widened within the party on ideological, organizational, and generational lines. Factional infighting and political defections undermined Congress party rule in several states. Political disorder blighted Andhra Pradesh, Orissa, Uttar Pradesh, Bihar, Gujarat, Mysore and West Bengal in 1973.[57] Francine Frankel offered this summary of the political situation: "The prime minister, whose credibility had become identified with the implementation of peaceful and democratic socialist revolution, appeared helpless against the organizational decay in her own party, but was unable to admit these internal limitations without exposing the hollowness of her promises."[58]

Nuclear policy resurfaced in the Indian polity in 1972. In the Lok Sabha on March 17, the government was asked in writing whether the war with Pakistan "brought out the necessity for India to have more modern weapons" and, if so, "whether Government propose to embark upon the manufacture of nuclear bombs." The minister of defense, Jagjivan Ram, answered that army modernization was an ongoing process and that the "Government's policy with regard to production of nuclear weapons . . . is to use nuclear energy for peaceful purposes only. Government believe that the defence of our borders can be best ensured by adequate military preparedness based on conventional weapons. In their view the possession of nuclear weapons is no substitute for such military preparedness."[59]

Pressure continued to build within the Parliament for a more robust nuclear posture than Jagjivan Ram had offered in March. In two days of debate over the Ministry of Defence's budget in May, speakers from all parties except the two Communist parties called for developing nuclear weapons, or at least greater preparation of relevant elements of nuclear explosives.[60] Madhu Dandwate, a liberal socialist MP, dismissed arguments that building nuclear weapons would be too costly, arguing that much of the necessary expense was already being incurred in the production of atomic energy.[61] In a switch from the Swatantra Party's earlier opposition to nuclear weapons, its spokesman H. M. Patel argued that the bomb would deter enemies from undertaking misadventures against India.[62] Faced with this pressure, Defence Minister Ram emphasized unlike before that the "Atomic Energy Commission is studying the technology for conducting underground explosions for peaceful purposes."[63]

Interestingly, the newsmagazine *Link* followed its report of this parliamentary debate with a long, technically informed article on May 21 debunking the technical utility, economic effectiveness, and environmental safety of peaceful nuclear explosions. "Whatever the case for India to develop nuclear weapons—after the recent war with Pakistan, the case is stronger—it does not have any valid reason for wasting its resources on investigating the uses of peaceful explosions."[64] The magazine recognized that development of peaceful nuclear explosives provided "a convenient cover to an eventual weapons development programme," but it argued that if the government "has any plan to manufacture nuclear weapons inspite of [its] oft-repeated denials couched in ambiguous terms" it should go ahead and do so.[65] The magazine implied that in the future this could help avoid "the kind of blackmail" India faced from the United States in the December 1971 war.

The Parliament expressed interest in developing India's nuclear strength again in November 1972. A pointed query was made in the Lok Sabha regarding "progress . . . in feasibility study and other preparations for the experimental nuclear explosion for peaceful purposes." Indira Gandhi responded, in writing, in her capacity as Minister of Atomic Energy, that "[t]he Atomic Energy Commission is constantly reviewing the progress in the technology of underground nuclear explosions both from the theoretical and experimental angles and also taking into account their potential economic benefits and possible environmental hazards."[66] This coy statement indicated support in principle for conducting peaceful nuclear explosions and suggested simply that more time was needed before a final decision would be required. In this period, the Department of Atomic Energy was budgeted to receive Rs. 105 crores ($141 million) for 1971–1972, and Rs. 126 crores ($163 million) for 1972–1973. This was a significant increase, which if sustained, would have met the ten-year target of the 1970 Sarabhai Profile.[67]

THE PEACEFUL NUCLEAR EXPLOSION, 1974

No authoritative public chronology exists of Indian decision-making regarding the 1974 explosion. Indeed, according to two of the few officials who participated in the decision-making process, written records of policy deliberations were not kept. "There was not a single scrap of paper on it," then-Chairman of the Atomic Energy Commission Homi Sethna explained in an interview.[68] Furthermore, the final decision to detonate the nuclear device—which Mrs. Gandhi committed to paper the day *after* the test—was the culmination of many prior, incremental decisions to take essential technical and other preparatory steps to facilitate an explosion.[69] Among the key steps in this process were the following:

- Acquisition of fissile material—plutonium
- Completion of equation of state calculations for plutonium
- Design of an explosive device
- Effort to translate design into actual nonnuclear component hardware
- Fabrication of a plutonium core
- Identification of a test site
- Physical preparation of a test site
- Testing of a high-explosive system for the implosion device
- Fabrication and assembly of the device's components
- Completion of a neutron initiator
- Final assembly and emplacement in a test shaft
- Design, fabrication, and emplacement of postexplosion diagnostic instruments

As has been noted, small amounts of weapon-grade plutonium were separated in 1964 and continued to be accumulated thereafter. Design of a nuclear explosive device began in early 1965, then ostensibly was suspended by Vikram Sarabhai in late 1966. In late 1967 or early 1968, R. Chidambaram began work on the equation of state for plutonium, and with BARC colleagues and Defence Research and Development Organisation (DRDO) personnel undertook the preliminary theoretical and practical work necessary to design a nuclear explosive device. By the end of 1971 a basic design had been developed.[70] This design was enhanced and finalized after the Purnima reactor went on line in 1972. Explorations for possible test sites began in late 1972.[71]

Each of these preparatory steps could have been, and apparently was, undertaken without a final decision about whether or when to conduct an explosion. Each step, formally authorized by the prime minister or not, indicated momentum toward a major decision to authorize fabrication and detonation of a device. Indeed, Indian references to "the decision" to conduct the experiment generally refer to the time when the preparation of a device and test site was authorized. A further decision was required to sanction the test.

Existing public sources appear muddled regarding when authorization came for the direct preparations for the test, including fabrication of the device. Defence Minister Jagjivan Ram said in May 1974 that the "decision" had been made "three years ago," placing it sometime in 1971.[72] N. Seshagiri's account, and Sarabhai's own statement in September 1971 before the Fourth Atoms for Peace Conference, indicated that a decision to authorize preparation of a nuclear explosive device was made in the late summer of 1971. This was *prior* to the war with Pakistan and the U.S. deployment of the *Enterprise*, events which are often portrayed as prompting the decision. However, Homi Sethna told the Indian press that work on the device began in May 1972, emphasizing that it was he, not Sarabhai, who "gave the green signal to Dr. Ramanna and his colleagues to go ahead with this project."[73] In an interview with the author, Sethna said that Mrs. Gandhi authorized fabrication of a device for a peaceful nuclear explosion on September 7,

1972, the day of the tenth convocation of the Indian Institute of Technology, Powai (Bombay).[74] From these various sources, it may be conjectured that support in principle for developing a nuclear explosive device was solidified by late 1971, that concentrated work on building the vital components began in spring 1972, and that formal prime ministerial approval to make final preparations for a PNE occurred in September 1972.

Once the green light was given in 1972, work intensified simultaneously on all elements of the experiment: the electrical system within the device, the neutron initiator, the shape charges to implode the plutonium, the diagnostic equipment and instruments, and so on. Raja Ramanna, the director of the Bhabha Atomic Research Centre, oversaw and inspired the effort in cooperation with Dr. B. D. Nag Chaudhuri, scientific adviser to the minister of defense and director of the Defence Research and Development Organisation. P. K. Iyengar and R. Chidambaram both played leading scientific and management roles as they had from the late 1960s. Satinder Kumar Sikka worked closely with Chidambaram in designing the nuclear device, while Drs. Pranab Rebatiranjan Dastidar and Sekharipuram Narayana Aiyer Seshadri led the design and production of the explosive's electronic system.[75] Drs. Iya and Murthy, informed by their earlier work on polonium in French laboratories, developed the neutron initiator. N. S. Venkatesan directed the Terminal Ballistics Research Laboratory in Chandigarh, which was responsible for producing the conventional high-explosive system that was to implode the plutonium core. In 1975, Chaudhuri, Sethna, and Ramanna would receive India's second-highest civilian award, the Padma Vibhushan, for their contributions to the project. Iyengar, Venkatesan, Dastidar, Chidambaram, and Seshadri would receive the third-highest award, the Padma Shri.[76]

Great effort was made to minimize the number of people who knew of the project. Division heads were informed only when necessary to free key individuals under them from other work. In total, between 1967 and 1974, no more than seventy-five scientists and engineers participated directly in the production and ultimate detonation of the nuclear explosive.[77] (By comparison, "several thousand" scientists and engineers working in three shifts seven days a week were mobilized in China's initial atomic bomb project.)[78] Of course, thousands of Indians under the auspices of the civil nuclear program had built both the infrastructure necessary to acquire plutonium for the device and the institutions to train and support the BARC establishment.

In March 1973, the nonnuclear explosives system reportedly was tested by the Defence Research and Development Organisation in Andhra Pradesh.[79] This entailed detonating chemical explosives engineered to implode the plutonium core of a device with enough symmetry to produce a major fission explosion.

P. K. Iyengar recalled that "[t]he decision to make a hole in Pokhran . . . was taken in 1973."[80] Another informed source has indicated that physical preparation of the test site in Rajasthan began in September 1973.[81] This involved army personnel and therefore required written orders.[82]

According to Raja Ramanna, "all material problems had been tackled" by 1973.[83] However, this was somewhat misleading. Ramanna himself acknowledged in his autobiography that the nuclear establishment confronted difficulties and delays in producing the neutron initiator, code-named Flower.[84] Polonium was the troublesome ingredient in this initiator.[85] It was produced by irradiating bismuth in a nuclear reactor. To succeed, the bismuth had to be made 99.999 percent pure before it entered the reactor. Then the polonium had to be extracted and arrayed in a small device within the plutonium core that would allow the polonium to be mixed with beryllium at precisely the right time during the implosion to provide neutrons to initiate or "trigger" a chain reaction in the now supercritical mass of plutonium. The triggering neutrons are produced through the reaction of beryllium and polonium. If this reaction occurs too early or too late in the implosion process, the yield of the nuclear explosion suffers. The initiator designed by the Indian team was one and one-half centimeters long, placed in the center of the plutonium core, with a barrier separating the polonium and the beryllium. The beryllium component was formed as a shape charge so that upon compression it emitted a jet of beryllium into the polonium. The mixing of the two elements then produced the neutrons while the plutonium was supercritical.[86]

In producing the neutron initiator, the scientists and engineers ran into trouble, according to a former high-ranking Atomic Energy Commission official. "Everything we used to array the polonoium got chewed up—stainless steel, gold—it all got chewed up. Finally we made it work."[87] Once the polonium had been produced and extracted, the pressure was on to conduct the test quickly because polonium has a half-life of only 138 days.[88] If delay occurred, additional bismuth would have to be irradiated and the resulting polonium reinserted into the trigger to be irradiated and the resulting polonium reinserted into the trigger device.

On November 15, 1973, Prime Minister Indira Gandhi was asked in writing during a Rajya Sabha debate "whether any final decision has been taken to conduct experiments to develop nuclear blast technology for utilisation for peaceful purpose; and . . . if not, whether any time schedule has been set for the purpose." This question came a year to the day after a similar question was asked in the Lok Sabha. As in 1972, Mrs. Gandhi denied that a final decision had been made and a schedule set for a blast. However, her 1973 answer added a sentence: it is "only after satisfactory answers to all these problems are available [theoretical and experimental questions; economic questions; environmental and ecological effects] that the question of actual underground tests for peaceful purpose can be undertaken."[89] While vague, this statement indicated major momentum toward conducting a nuclear explosive test. Indeed, the scientists were working energetically to prepare the device and test site. The only decision that remained was the final one to schedule and conduct the detonation.

The Decision and the Process.   The time for final decisions came in early 1974. For these events, too, no exact chronology exists in public sources or in the stated recollections of participants. Raja Ramanna's autobiography offers what detail is available. He recounted "a round" of specific but undated meetings where the decision to test was in fact made. "Only a few, select people" participated in these meetings: P. N. Haksar, the former principal secretary to the prime minister; D. P. Dhar, the incumbent principal secretary; Dr. B. D. Nag Chaudhuri, scientific adviser to the defense minister; Homi Sethna, then chairman of the Atomic Energy Commission; and Ramanna. Mrs. Gandhi did not consult or inform the cabinet. According to Ashok Kapur, the defense minister, Jagjivan Ram, "the second most powerful member of the cabinet, was informed about the test on May 8, but he was not consulted about the decision." The minister of external affairs, Swaran Singh, was informed only forty-eight hours before the impending detonation.[90]

The first of a series of final decisive meetings probably was conducted in February.[91] In this round the discussion centered on "the economic repercussions and possible political fallout of the experiment," according to Ramanna.[92] Canada and the United States had earlier warned India that a nuclear test would violate their understanding of the bilateral nuclear cooperation agreements. However, neither specified the consequences that would ensue. Thus, Indian decision makers were not clear what fallout would blow from the United States and Canada. Indeed, in a 1996 interview, Homi Sethna stated that while India expected backlash, "we thought the U.S. would stick to its agreements. We thought the fuel supply relationship was a treaty which the U.S. could not break."[93] The Indian scientists were also destined to be surprised by Canada's sharp reaction.[94] Mrs. Gandhi's political advisers, Haksar and Dhar, had warned against such international repercussions but had been outweighed by the scientists.

In terms of possible domestic fallout, the political climate was worsening in 1974, despite a surprising yet narrow Congress party win in the Uttar Pradesh state elections in February 1974. Reporting in April on a tour of the country, the journalist Kuldip Nayar wrote that "the present system of parliamentary democracy cannot deliver the goods. People openly talk in terms of military dictatorship or communist revolution. Mismanagement at every step has led even the most conservative to talk about revolution because the whole system is held to be rotten to the core."[95] In January, Gujarat, the home state of Indira Gandhi's Congress party rival, Morarji Desai, erupted in rioting. Turmoil continued there for months. On March 11, Desai announced he would "fast unto death" to compel the prime minister to dissolve the state legislative assembly, which had become estranged from the populace. On March 15, Mrs. Gandhi gave in and dissolved the body.[96] This was a watershed in relations between the central government and the state opposition groups.[97] Mrs. Gandhi grew increasingly fearful (some would say paranoid) that she and her government were the targets of an internal conspiracy colluding with foreign elements, including possibly the U.S. CIA.[98]

In the state of Bihar, a seventy-two-year-old charismatic Gandhian firebrand, J. P. Narayan, was leading a large protest movement demanding "an allround revolution, political, economic, social, educational, moral and cultural."[99] Narayan and his "J. P. Movement" had paralyzed the Bihar state administration with strikes and agitations in March and April.[100] Meanwhile, political turmoil spread across the nation when railway workers called for a strike of 1.7 million workers to begin on May 8. Mrs. Gandhi received intelligence reports that Narayan was coordinating his activities with the railway strikers.[101] Prone to paranoia, she feared the potential of an uprising like Mohandas Gandhi had led in the 1942 Quit India movement against the British. The Right and the Left appeared to be attacking "all Government policies," in the words of a Congress party report.[102] Negotiations with the railway strikers quickly broke down and the strike commenced. The government responded harshly, arresting at least twenty thousand striking workers. The strike and the controversial government crackdown were still underway on May 18 when scientists detonated the nuclear device in Rajasthan.

Amidst a roiling domestic polity, a final meeting to green-light the nuclear experiment occurred "a few weeks before" May 18.[103] In Ramanna's view, "It was to be merely a formality as the preparations had advanced to such an extent that we could not have retraced our steps."[104] P. K. Iyengar, who was directly responsible for producing the device, concurred, saying, "Once the decision was taken to go ahead there was no vacillation." Nevertheless, as Ramanna recalled,

> Like all important decision-making processes, the final meeting on Pokhran was one which involved heated discussion. P. N. Dhar was vehemently opposed to the explosion as he felt it would damage our economy; Haksar took the view that the time was not ripe and gave his reasons; my own view was that it was now impossible to postpone the date given the expense, time and the critical stage the experiment had reached. Fortunately for my team Mrs. Gandhi decreed that the experiment should be carried out on schedule for the simple reason that India required such a demonstration.[105]

Ramanna's written account comports with what little other data exist. "The PNE was simply done when we were ready," Mrs. Gandhi told the American writer Rodney Jones. "We did it to show ourselves that we could do it. We couldn't be sure until we had tried it. We couldn't know how to use it for peaceful purpose until doing it. . . . We did it when the scientists were ready."[106]

Much speculation has been cast regarding Indira Gandhi's motivations for sanctioning the PNE in 1974. It was clearly her decision to make: in Indian nuclear policy before and after 1974, the prime minister has been sovereign.

Many Indian and foreign analysts have suggested that political considerations moved Mrs. Gandhi to authorize the detonation in early 1974. Indisputably the prime minister was thoroughly beleaguered. It would have been unnatural for any politician not to concentrate on her political standing when considering whether to authorize an act as dramatic as a PNE. By emphasizing the peaceful nature and intent of the test, she maintained the popular moral and political spirit of India's traditional nuclear policy. The test was cheap and did not divert precious resources from development. It boosted the morale of the nuclear establishment and thrilled the nation with a sense of prowess. In short, the PNE was a domestic political winner. It offered the least risky accommodation of the conflicting interests militating for and against nuclear weapons in India, even if it did not provide or reflect a rigorous military security strategy.

Yet Mrs. Gandhi never divulged such thoughts publicly.[107] Momentum had been building for the nuclear test well before the acute 1974 political crisis. The few men who interacted with her in the decision-making process and are willing to talk about it remain unsure of what motivated her. Did she participate in the argumentation during the few meetings where the decision was made? Did she ask questions and draw out speakers, revealing particular concerns or doubts? According to Ramanna, the answer is no. "She didn't speak in the meetings. She listened and then decided—that's all. . . . Mrs. Gandhi was a somewhat impenetrable mind. It's possible she thought she would gain political benefits, but it's difficult to say what was on her mind. She said, 'Let's have it.' "[108]

Whatever Mrs. Gandhi's calculus, the fact remained that conducting the PNE was not her idea. She disposed what others proposed: it was Ramanna, Sethna, Iyengar, Chidambaram, and, before them, Bhabha who made the PNE possible. It was the weaponeers who went to the prime minister seeking sanction. In doing so, they represented a nuclear establishment that had failed to deliver on promises of cheap civilian power and was now facing severe budget cuts. The Department of Atomic Energy budget for 1974–1975 was slated to drop 13 percent from the previous year, and the 1970 Sarabhai ten-year profile was already being revised downward.[109] Notwithstanding its poor performance and budgetary travails, the nuclear establishment was able to exert great influence on the prime minister, in part because Ramanna enjoyed an unusually close relationship with Mrs. Gandhi.[110] She simply trusted him and went with his advice.

Public arguments for "the bomb"—as distinct from the scientists' counsel—centered on a general belief that it would enhance India's regional and international status and power. The eminent scholar Bhabhani Sen Gupta summarized this view in his 1983 volume, *Nuclear Weapons?*:

> [T]he Chinese bomb ceased to be the main argument for the Indian bomb, perhaps because of the Chinese inability to help Pakistan in the 1971 war and also because of the initiatives taken by India to normalise relations with China. The arguments for the bomb now were: that without it India could not expect to be admitted to the corridors of global power, nor enjoy the status of the dominant regional power; that the bomb might quicken the process of normalising relations with China; that it would proclaim India's independence of the Soviet Union and compel the United States to change its attitude of hostility or benign neglect.[111]

This is an apt summary of the arguments of the pro-bomb segment of the Indian elite, and it indicates the nonspecific, nonmilitary gist of their sentiment. It also indicates the superficiality of the underlying analysis of how an Indian nuclear weapon effort would affect China and the United States.

However, the evidence does not suggest that foreign policy and security considerations played a decisive role in Mrs. Gandhi's decision or its timing. Planning and preparation for a peaceful nuclear explosion had been explicitly discussed and undertaken from late 1964 through 1974. It can be argued that these preparations reflected, in a delayed manner, a post-1964 calculation that India's security required nuclear weapons. However, this does not withstand scrutiny, nor does it explain India's insistence before and after 1974 that it abjured nuclear weapons. India's security environment between 1965 and 1970 had not worsened. If anything, the Nuclear Non-Proliferation Treaty's entry into force in 1970 created an international incentive not to test, insofar as India would risk recriminations for defying the norm of the new nonproliferation regime. From 1971 to 1974 India gained strength through the defeat of Pakistan and the treaty with the Soviet Union. If, for the sake of argument, the U.S. rapprochement with China and the deployment of the USS *Enterprise* to the Bay of Bengal significantly worsened India's security situation, then a decision to conduct a peaceful nuclear explosion whose preparations began *prior to* these developments hardly represented a robust security-motivated response to them. The PNE program was too unlike a nuclear weapon program to signify a meaningful militarily strategic response to a changed international environment. Possibly Mrs. Gandhi wanted to dissuade the United States, China, and the Soviet Union from infringing on India's autonomy. She clearly felt the need to demonstrate India's strength and standing to each power. This would not have been a security strategy per se, but rather a broader "power politics" initiative. Yet the Pokhran blast had the opposite effect. It increased U.S. and international pressure on India to conform to the nonproliferation regime. It appeared to have no effect on China, and it had the negative impact of hardening Pakistan's resolve to develop nuclear weapons.

The process surrounding the decision to conduct the PNE was as noteworthy as the decision itself. There was no systematic analysis of costs and benefits. India's foreign affairs establishment was not asked to assess likely international reactions and repercussions. The military services were not consulted about how nuclear weapon capability would affect their strategic planning, doctrine, or long-term budgets. There was no attempt to incorporate the soon-to-be-demonstrated nuclear capability into military or national security policy. As former Indian Defence Secretary K. B. Lall told the American analyst Neil Joeck in a 1984 interview: " 'The test' arose not out of a defence program. . . . If it was a defence project, there should have been some discussion. . . . I know up to May 1973 that . . . the Chairman of the Chiefs of Staff, the Defence Secretary, the Defence Minister [were not] involved. . . . [I]t did not arise out of thinking from the Defence Ministry or on security counts. It arose out of the . . . scientific community."[112] Lieutenant General A. M. Vohra, former vice chief of army staff, similarly told Joeck that the military at the time of the PNE had no plans whatsoever for weapon applications of the nuclear capability.[113] Indeed, Mrs. Gandhi herself emphasized in her 1978 interview with Rodney Jones that military considerations had not affected her decision. "No," she told him, "we don't want nuclear weapons. They only bring danger where there was none before."[114] This reflected both the prime minister's and the nuclear establishment's desire to exclude the military from nuclear policy. As a former Atomic Energy Commission chairman put it, "One thing we learned is never to allow the military or the bureaucrats to have a role in the nuclear program. The Indian program never took the army into confidence. We didn't discuss details with them. It wasn't a military program."[115]

Thus, the decision seemed based on intuition, bureaucratic and technological momentum, and the personal, enigmatic calculations of the politically beleaguered prime minister under the influence of trusted nuclear scientists. It was to be a marker of standing and power for a nation with great aspirations suffering diminished respect. Whatever the utility of such a message in gaining international respect for India, the prime minister could easily calculate that Indian *self-respect* would grow. Indeed, one reason Indian leaders value gains in international prestige is that such gains enhance their standing at home. Thus, in terms of enhancing domestic and international *status*, as opposed to serving a concrete military security need, the decision to demonstrate a nuclear explosive capacity was plausibly rational, even if it proved ineffective.

The Explosion and Celebration. At 8:05 in the morning on May 18, 1974, the desert village of Lokhari, near Pokhran (also spelled Pokharan) in the western Indian state of Rajasthan shook with the detonation of a nuclear explosive device 107 meters below the ground.[116] The scientists and technicians at the site had spent nervous days and nights under the stars, worrying over technical problems and the possibility that satellites passing overhead would detect them and lead to international pressure to block the test. On the day of the blast, humidity was so high that the team feared electronic shorts would cause an accident. When the countdown ended, and the desert rose, the scientific and technical doubts gave way to jubilation.

Announcing the blast, without specifying where it had occurred, the Indian government declared it "a peaceful nuclear explosion experiment." The Atomic Energy Commission stated that India had "no intention of producing nuclear weapons." Indira Gandhi told a press conference that "[t]here's nothing to get excited about. This is our normal research and study. But we are firmly committed to only peaceful uses of atomic energy."[117] Subsequent statements by the prime minister and other officials hewed strictly to the nation's peaceful intention not to build nuclear weapons.[118] Striking popular chords of anticolonialism, Mrs. Gandhi emphasized that the new nuclear know-how and technology would contribute to India's development, even if the economically advanced nations would try to suggest otherwise.[119] She also demurred when asked whether the blast would enhance her or India's prestige: "You know, I am never bothered about prestige, in whatever field it is."[120]

The Indian press responded ecstatically for the most part. The *Times of India* headline boomed, "Thrilled Nation Lauds Feat." The *Sunday Standard,* with editions in seven cities, declared, "Monopoly of Big Five Broken." "India Goes Nuclear at Last," knifed the *Motherland,* a newspaper allied with the pro-bomb Jana Sangh Party.[121] Other headlines proclaimed, "Indian Genius Triumphs," "A Great Landmark," and "Nation Is Thrilled."[122] The *Hindu* editorialized that "[n]o more thrilling news could have come to lift the drooping (because of the prevailing economic difficulties) spirits of the people than the Atomic Energy Commission's announcement yesterday."[123] The *Indian Express* reported that "India's nuclear blast has catapulted her into the front rank of nations. No longer is she dismissed as a 'pitiful giant.' "[124] More ambivalently, the *Hindustan Times* headline suggested, "The Nation Is Thrilled?" The *Economic Times* recorded wryly and presciently that the Indian people now felt "inches taller." Overall, however, the press lavished praise in huge front-page columns and attendant articles, relegating the previously dominant story of the railway strike to back pages.

The PNE provided an immediate political lift to Indira Gandhi. The opposition commended the government: "It's one of the most heartening bits of news in recent years," stated L. K. Advani, president of the Jana Sangh.[125] The socialist weekly *Janata* evinced great pride at the achievement.[126] As a *Washington Post* correspondent in India reported on May 19, the PNE had

> apparently extracted Prime Minister Indira Gandhi from the worst crisis of public confidence in her eight years of rule. . . . It was almost impossible today to find an Indian who did not take enormous pride in the government's achievement. "You've got to hand it to her," one said. "It's most impressive—although I personally deplore the idea of us being another nuclear power." . . . "Now we're the same as America and Russia and China," said a young man delivering newspapers on his bicycle. "We have the atomic bomb."[127]

The Jana Sangh's Central Working Committee issued a resolution on June 2 declaring that May 18 was "a red letter day in Indian history." The party saluted the Indian scientists who had "placed India on the nuclear map of the world."[128]

Still, there were sour notes. Morarji Desai doubted the necessity or wisdom of the PNE. He fretted that it would fuel popular appetite for nuclear weapons and that this was not in India's interest. He also suggested that Mrs. Gandhi's claims for the purely peaceful intentions of India's nuclear program would be less credible now.[129] The *Statesman Weekly* called the nuclear test "indefensible" and "irresponsible."[130] The Socialist party leader George Fernandes lampooned the notion that "exploding the nuclear device and . . . consequent membership of the so-called 'Nuclear Club' would give India any special leverage in world affairs."[131] Crying from the wilderness of a jail cell in which he had been placed during the railway strike and largely unheard amid the general euphoria over the test, Fernandes continued:

[T]he advocates of the Bomb cannot be oblivious of the fact that the present establishment and the system it represents are not capable of building an economic infrastructure that can sustain a nuclear technology, not to speak of a nuclear arsenal,
delivery system and the capacity to survive a nuclear attack to be able to deliver a
second strike. . . . And should any government discuss such a proposition seriously
without first taking steps to provide all citizens of the country with food, clothes,
shelter, pure drinking water, education and a chance to live a life befitting human
beings, such a government can be called nothing but criminal.[132]

(Fernandes would play a different tune in May 1998 when he served as defense
minister in the Bharatiya Janata Party [BJP] government and trumpeted the five
nuclear tests it ordered.)

A survey conducted by the Indian Institute of Public Opinion shortly after the
PNE indicated a "marked improvement overall on [Mrs. Gandhi's] favourable
ranking." This poll of more than one thousand literates in Bombay, Calcutta,
Madras, and New Delhi showed a rise from the prime minister's "all-time 'low' "
favorability rating in March 1974 to an "above normal" rating, although even after
the test Mrs. Gandhi's rating was not high.[133]

The atomic scientists became the toast of the nation. Prime Minister Gandhi
publicly congratulated them in a May 18 news conference with Homi Sethna: "It
is a significant achievement for them and the whole country. . . . We are proud of
them. They worked hard and have done a good clean job."[134] The *Times of India*
reported that "[o]vernight the three important nuclear scientists produced by this
country—Dr. Bhabha, Dr. Vikram Sarabhai and Dr. [sic] Sethna—have become
popular heros [sic]."[135] In the days, weeks, and months following the PNE, the
atomic scientists were lionized. "Explosion in the Desert: Meet the Scientists,"
headlined a typical magazine celebration of Sethna, Ramanna, and Iyengar
(overlooking Chidambaram's role).[136] This article, like many other accounts, heralded the prestige that the test and its makers had won for the nation: "India has
made its presence felt with a bang in the Rajasthan desert. Our scientists succeeded in carrying out a 'contained' underground nuclear explosion."[137] A left-
wing magazine wistfully celebrated "that India has to a very great extent become
self-reliant in nuclear science and she can within the next few years bring her
nuclear technology to such refinement that it could safely be exploited for the
needs of the common man as well as the nation."[138]

It did not matter that virtually none of these proud suppositions was true: the
nuclear explosion was not contained, but vented radioactivity; there was no new
development of a "clean" nuclear device; India's nuclear program was far from
self-reliant; and over the next decades the program would do little to meet the
needs of the common man. Nevertheless, this was not a time for questioning.[139]
Relevant data would not have been forthcoming anyway.

Indeed, the feeling of national prowess was the singular feature of the celebration. "[T]his test proves more than anything else . . . that given clear policies, India
has the talent, the resources and the infrastructure that makes for high achieve-

ment capability," boasted the *Hindustan Times*.[140] Unlike a transistor radio, a ship, or a hospital, a nuclear explosive represented the harnessing of the greatest physical power known to humankind, a physical power that the greatest nations on earth had imbued with transcendent political power as well. The Indian nation—at least in urban centers—believed that its aspiration for global greatness had been achieved.

The greatest potential damper on enthusiasm over the PNE would have been provable allegations that the expense was exorbitant. Cost had always been the major cause of public doubt about acquiring nuclear weapon capability.[141] The Indian press reported that American commentators had claimed that the test had cost $200 million.[142] This would have been a huge expense in 1974, when Indian statistics indicated that roughly 175 million people, or 30 percent of the population, lived below the poverty line and more than 70 percent of the population were illiterate. From 1969 to 1974 the government had spent $200 million on housing.

Naturally, then, the scientists sought to prove that the cost of the PNE was negligible. "The figure is Rs 32 lakhs," Sethna reportedly "exploded" when told of the $200 million American estimate.[143] Over time, Indian scientists and journalists have stuck close to the Rs. 32 lakhs figure, roughly equivalent to $370,000 in 1974. A more accurate and complete assessment of costs was offered by N. Seshagiri, who put it at "Rs 1,760 million in R&D over the last five years," or $220 million at the 1975 conversion rate.[144] It is largely an issue of apples and oranges: the cost of actually preparing a test site and exploding a device versus the cost of building and operating the plants to produce and manufacture the plutonium. Full cost accounting of nuclear programs is extremely complicated: should the cost of educating, training, and paying the scientists and engineers count? Which scientists and engineers? Should the cost of facilities used both for power reactor development and operations and for producing explosive devices be included? On what basis? Should opportunity costs imposed in the aftermath of the test be counted? These issues are subject to legitimate debate and could have generated some controversy in India, but as it happened, national pride stemmed such debate. Prime Minister Gandhi insisted that "[n]o new budgetary provision was made for [the test], there is no foreign exchange expenditure."[145]

Questionable Yield. Another potential controversy that never arose concerns the explosive yield of the test. AEC Chairman Homi Sethna told journalists on the evening of the test that its yield was between ten and fifteen kilotons.[146] Since then, practically all descriptions and commentaries on the test describe the yield at twelve kilotons or between twelve and fifteen kilotons.[147] In an authoritative paper Ramanna and Chidambaram prepared for an IAEA meeting on peaceful nuclear explosions in January 1975, the Indian scientists "estimated" the yield at about twelve kilotons.[148] Coincidentally or not, the twelve-kiloton figure matches the yield of the American bomb dropped on Hiroshima.

Since 1974, Indian journalists have periodically reported that measurements of the yield were inflated. In June 1978, the *Hindu* cited sources claiming that the yield had been considerably less than had been predicted.[149] A detailed August 30, 1981, article in the *Sunday Observer* (Bombay) reported that "some sources at the BARC maintain that independent measurements by some scientists put the yield at Pokhran to be as low as 2,000 tons of TNT," or two kilotons.[150] Despite these journalists' claims of inside sources, their reports of a lower yield have never shaken the accepted truth of a twelve-kiloton yield.

The uncertainty stems in part from the inexactness of seismic monitoring capabilities and interpretations. Technically, the most accurate way to determine the yield of a nuclear explosion is to conduct radiochemical analysis of the radioactive debris at the test site. Knowing this, a member of the audience at Chidambaram and Ramanna's 1975 IAEA presentation on the PNE asked whether the Indians had analyzed molten materials to determine the yield.[151] Either Chidambaram or Ramanna (the transcript is unclear which one spoke) responded, "We are planning to do this." Indeed, the *Annual Report of the Department of Atomic Energy, 1974–75*, stated that radiochemistry and physico-chemical investigations were conducted on samples taken from the PNE site.[152] Yet the Indian nuclear establishment has never publicly revealed the results of those analyses.[153]

In interviews with the author, two former chairmen of the Atomic Energy Commission said that the radiochemical analysis showed a lower-than-advertised yield. "The yield was much lower than had been stated," Sethna acknowledged in 1996.[154] P. K. Iyengar reported that "[t]he yield was checked against the measurements we had taken. It checked out very well, between 8 and 12 kilotons." When asked why the results of the radiochemical analysis had never been published, Iyengar responded, "What does it matter if it was 8 or 12 kilotons?" In a subsequent interview, Iyengar put the yield between eight and ten kilotons.[155] He added that the design was predicted to yield ten kilotons. Until the actual test data are released it will remain impossible to conclude exactly how much lower than advertised the actual yield was.[156] (U.S. technical analysts think the yield was on the order of "4 to 6 kilotons.")[157]

The questions surrounding the yield of the 1974 PNE matter for several reasons. In the 1970s and 1980s, the Indian nuclear establishment used the aura of prowess emanating from the Pokhran test to increase its status, influence, and institutional prerogatives. The establishment used its national defense role to maintain its secrecy and to protect itself from scrutiny by politicians, journalists, and competing interests that could vie with it for funds. Had the widely heralded achievement of 1974 been diminished by widespread knowledge of the device's inefficiency, the nuclear establishment could have lost some of its luster and leverage. Similarly, India's collective pride in achieving nuclear status could have been weakened. This is not to deny the impressive accomplishment of the Indian scientists and people in having created a massive nuclear establishment with a broad range of technical capabilities.

A poor performance by India's first test device also could have affected the decision to conduct nuclear tests twenty-four years later. According to Iyengar, "We never wanted to design something specifically with the geometry to be put on a rocket. We only wanted to demonstrate that we could trigger a significant explosion. That was it."[158] This helps explain why no elaborate instrumentation was used to evaluate the device, beyond seismic and gamma ray measurements, according to Iyengar. However, the rudimentary character and large size of the device would have given its potential military users doubts about the utility of the scientists' product in war. If, on top of that, the single test revealed disappointing technical proficiency, it could have raised questions in the military regarding the reliability of much more technically demanding weapon designs. These doubts then could have heightened pressures to conduct explosive tests of new designs to erase doubts over the 1974 experiment, as occurred in 1998. (Another implication of a lower-than-claimed yield for the 1974 test would emerge in 1998, as discussed in chapter 15: the seismographic calculation that the 1974 yield was close to twelve kilotons became the benchmark for drawing seismographic conclusions about the 1998 test yields.)

On the other hand, inexact simultaneity and symmetry of the implosion was the most likely cause of the poor yield of the PNE. As subsequent chapters show, after 1974 the AEC and DRDO teams made major gains in improving the simultaneity and symmetry of the conventional high explosive implosion of weapon cores. Improved implosion systems could be tested fully without using fissile cores. Hence, for twenty-four years following the Pokhran PNE, India managed to maintain a rudimentary nuclear deterrent without further nuclear explosive tests. When tests were conducted in 1998, no one questioned the effectiveness of the single full-scale fission device tested. Thus, the simplest explanation for not publicly analyzing the Pokhran test results is that the scientists did not want to expose themselves to criticism over technology that they themselves would now try to improve.

International Reactions.   International reactions to the Indian PNE were mixed at first. As P. N. Haksar noted, "[T]he non-aligned world as a whole has applauded the competence of our scientists and technologists."[159] France, through its Atomic Energy Commission, sent a congratulatory message to the chairman of the Indian Atomic Energy Commission.

American reaction to the Indian test was conflicted. U.S. officials acknowledged being surprised by the test, but a State Department source said, "It was only a matter of Indian leaders making up their minds and devoting the necessary resources."[160] The bureaucracy prepared a sharp criticism of India for undermining international nonproliferation efforts and sent a draft to Secretary of State Henry Kissinger, who was then conducting shuttle diplomacy in the Middle East. Kissinger rejected the proposed harsh language and substituted a more neutral statement. According to Dennis Kux, who had drafted the initial response, Kissinger concluded that "public scolding would not undo the event, but only add to US-Indian bilateral problems and reduce the influence Washington might have on India's future nuclear policy."[161] Kissinger was perhaps mindful of how U.S. policy during the 1971 Indo-Pak war had enraged India and set back Washington's relationship with New Delhi. Kissinger also had been generally neglectful of non-proliferation issues and did not want to highlight proliferation dangers now.[162] In subsequent months, as described in chapter 8, Congress would strengthen U.S. nonproliferation policy, prompted in large part by the Indian test as well as the perceived neglect on Kissinger's part.[163]

Still, the PNE did not stop Western countries, led by the United States, from increasing aid to India. Less than a month after the detonation, the Western industrial nations boosted economic aid by roughly $200 million. Indeed, the United States agreed to reschedule Indian debts amounting to more than $29 million. More paradoxically, the United States in June 1974 proceeded to ship an installment of previously approved uranium fuel to India's Tarapur reactor. The administration concluded that the Indian test did not violate any agreement with the United States and Washington was therefore mandated by the 1963 nuclear cooperation agreement and the related 1966 contract to sell enriched uranium to India for Tarapur.[164] However, the U.S. and Indian Atomic Energy Commissions then engaged in a brief epistolary negotiation over safeguards and other assurances that would be required before additional fuel would be sent to India. The two sides came to a formal agreement in September.[165] Meanwhile, in August 1974, Congress amended the International Development Assistance Act to direct American representatives on the board of the World Bank to "vote against any loan for the benefit of any country which develops any nuclear explosive device unless that country is or becomes" a party to the Nuclear Non-Proliferation Treaty. However, the United States did not rigorously uphold the spirit of this sanction: it regularly voted against loans to India by the World Bank but not did not press other lenders to do the same.[166]

In October 1974, Secretary of State Kissinger traveled to India to try to bolster relations. This was an act of the head, not the heart. On board the plane to New Delhi, Kissinger reviewed recent Indian press clippings and found several biting criticisms of himself and U.S. policy toward India, obviously planted by the Indian government. Kissinger growled to his aides that he should order the plane to refuel and take off, sparing him the torment of India and its leader, whom he could not abide.[167] However, Kissinger deplaned and duly delivered an important speech to the Indian Council of World Affairs, declaring his hope that the United States and India could develop a "mature" relationship based on American recognition of India's preeminence in the region.[168] The secretary added that the relationship could not "survive constant criticism of one by the other."[169] Mrs. Gandhi signaled her response by abruptly leaving New Delhi after meeting with Kissinger on the first day of his three-day visit.

Despite the tense personal atmosphere, Kissinger did convey an important message regarding nuclear policy. Kissinger's staff had prepared two sets of specific proposals for him to give the Indians. The first emphasized the United States' vital interest, which it hoped India shared, in ensuring that India not export sensitive nuclear materials, technology, or know-how to other countries without the recipients applying IAEA safeguards to them.[170] The second concerned subsequent Indian nuclear explosions. State Department officials assumed India would conduct further tests but hoped Kissinger might persuade the leadership to hold off "until after the May 1975 NPT Review Conference."[171] In any case, they wanted India to consider allowing "external safeguards" on all its chemical reprocessing plants to "establish the amount of plutonium produced and account for the disposition of such plutonium."[172] The Americans emphasized that this "would not preclude the use of this material as necessary for designated explosives applications," a position that would have boiled the blood of nonproliferation activists in Washington.[173]

These proposals reflected the Kissinger team's insight that pressuring India not to conduct further tests could "strengthen public support for future tests." Conversely, if the international community was restrained in its approach, "assertions of nationalistic pride eventually may give way to greater concern about India's economic priorities and ultimate strategic intentions."[174] According to a former official who accompanied Kissinger on the visit, he followed this brief adeptly. In his private meeting with Mrs. Gandhi, the secretary of state reportedly said something to the effect of, "Congratulations. You did it, you showed you could build nuclear weapons. You have the bomb. Now what do we do to keep from blowing up the world?"[175] Kissinger then offered to send U.S. nuclear experts quietly to India to work with Indian scientists to ensure that nuclear materials and potential explosive devices would be managed with a premium on safety and international security. To this end, he proposed that the two states conduct a quiet dialogue on nuclear issues. As the next chapter shows, India did not pick up on the offer for dialogue, but it did adopt a restrained export policy. More dramatically, India confounded American expectations and did not conduct further nuclear explosions. For its part, the U.S. Congress began imposing a much tougher nonproliferation line than Kissinger's.

Pakistan reacted predictably to the Indian blast. On May 19, Prime Minister Zulfikar Ali Bhutto declared that it was a threatening, "fateful development." Pakistan was "determined not to be intimidated" and would never fall prey to "nuclear blackmail" by India, he added.[176] On May 22, Prime Minister Gandhi wrote the following in a letter to Bhutto: "We remain fully committed to our traditional policy of developing nuclear energy entirely for peaceful purposes. The recent underground nuclear experiment conducted by our scientists in no way alters this policy. . . . There are no political or foreign policy implications of this test. We remain committed to settle all our differences with Pakistan peacefully through bilateral negotiations in accordance with the Simla Agreement."[177] Bhutto responded in a June 6 letter, denying any distinction between a peaceful and a military nuclear detonation and declaring India's new military capability "a permanent factor to be reckoned with." Pakistan called on the nuclear weapon states to provide non–nuclear weapon states with protection against nuclear threats and then canceled talks with India on normalization of relations, which had been scheduled for June 10.[178]

In October 1974, Pakistan announced plans to add up to twenty-four reactors by the year 2000 and acquire proficiency in all facets of the nuclear fuel cycle. On October 18, Pakistan signed a previously negotiated agreement with a French firm to construct a plutonium-reprocessing plant at Chashma.[179] Contrary to later propaganda, Pakistan had begun its dedicated effort to acquire nuclear weapon capability in 1972; still, the Indian PNE hardened Islamabad's resolve. U.S. Ambassador to India Daniel Patrick Moynihan communicated the strategic reper- cussions of India's test directly to Mrs. Gandhi when he delivered the official American response in May 1974: "India has made a huge mistake. Here you were the No. 1 hegemonic power in South Asia. Nobody was No. 2 and call Pakistan No. 3. Now in a decade's time, some Pakistani general will call you up and say I have four nuclear weapons and I want Kashmir. If not, we will drop them on you and we will all meet in heaven. And then what will you do?"[180]

The Indian blast also strengthened Pakistan's case for receiving American aid to build up its conventional forces. In February 1975 Prime Minister Bhutto visited Washington and won a removal of the ten-year-old ban on American sales of mil- itary equipment to Pakistan and India. India's own act had triggered the delivery of American military supplies to Pakistan, which so annoyed Indians.

Although India's long-term security interests were harmed by the boost the PNE gave to Pakistan's nuclear ambitions and its military-supply relationship with the United States, India also benefited narrowly from the increased international emphasis on nonproliferation after 1974. The new determination by the United States and others to block transfers of nuclear technology to nonparties to the NPT affected Pakistan immediately. Pakistan had planned to use French nuclear cooperation to provide technological infrastructure and training that could then augment production and operation of unsafeguarded plutonium production and separation plants for weapons purposes. But these plans were blocked. Driven "underground," Pakistan's nuclear program focused for the near term on produc- ing highly enriched uranium for nuclear weapons instead of plutonium. Pakistan had to establish an elaborate, clandestine purchasing network to import sensitive equipment for uranium enrichment. Thus, the post-1974 nonproliferation regime retarded Pakistan's quest to match India's nuclear weapon capability and raised the costs of doing so.

Canada evinced the strongest international reaction to Pokhran, reflecting a sense of betrayal at India's use of the Canadian-supplied CIRUS reactor as the source of the plutonium used in the PNE. On May 22, Canada froze all assistance to India for the Rajasthan II reactor and the Kota heavy-water plant, which were then under construction. Canada then made further cooperation conditional on New Delhi's acceptance of IAEA safeguards for all its nuclear activities, not just the already safeguarded Rajasthan I reactor and the U.S.-supplied reactors at Tarapur.[181]

The other major powers responded diversely to the PNE. Japan reacted sharply with an official statement of "regret" over the Indian move, which undermined nonproliferation efforts highly valued by Tokyo. Sweden also expressed concern about the effect of the test on the horizontal proliferation of nuclear weapons but softened this criticism by noting that the superpowers shared in the blame by having failed to meet their obligations toward nuclear disarmament under Article VI of the NPT.[182] The Soviet Union was privately displeased, given Moscow's genuine interest in preventing proliferation. However, Moscow only issued a tepid public criticism in deference to Indo-Soviet friendship.[183]

China responded to the Indian PNE with conscious aloofness, reporting the event without comment.[184] Subsequently, Chinese officials suggested that the PNE had no military significance.[185] Indeed, on August 29, 1974, the Indian deputy defense minister told Parliament that India was watching China's nuclear development but did not fear a Chinese nuclear threat.[186] If the PNE had been intended to heighten China's security concerns and thereby draw Beijing into an enhanced normalization process with India, it did not seem to have this effect.

Beyond the immediate reactions of individual countries, India's nuclear test prompted an intensive tightening of the international nonproliferation regime. This became most dramatic in the late 1970s, as discussed in the next chapter. Yet, as soon as June 1974, the gears began to grind when the Zangger committee—a collection of twenty states committed to coordinating export restrictions on key technologies and materials useful in nuclear weapons—met to formulate an agreement to coordinate tougher supply conditions.[187] On August 22, ten members of the committee filed identical memoranda with the International Atomic Energy Agency to establish procedures to regulate exports of a "trigger list" of material and equipment crucial for making a nuclear weapon.[188] All Zangger committee members agreed not to export "trigger list" items if the receiving state did not accept IAEA safeguards on the facilities to which these items were destined.

While Indian advocates of the PNE defiantly anticipated international reprisals, they were unprepared for what came.[189] The lack of any systematic military, technical, or political strategy to guide subsequent Indian nuclear policy soon became evident.[190] Mrs. Gandhi assured the Lok Sabha in her first address to that body after the PNE that "India does not accept the principle of apartheid in any matter and technology is no exception."[191] However, beyond this expression of anticolonial defiance, the strategic purpose of the explosion remained unclear while the costs began to mount.

CONCLUSION

The Pokhran blast stemmed primarily from domestic dynamics, and so, too, its implications were primarily internal. Prime Minister Gandhi gained an immediate, but only short-lived political benefit. Public opinion polling done in May 1974 reflected a boost, but by September, her approval rating had fallen steeply to an all-time low.[192] Domestic political and economic difficulties caused the fall. It was apparent that the demonstration of nuclear prowess in May was a rapidly wasting political asset. Indeed, a subsequent analysis of the June 1974 polling data noted that "over half the enthusiastic nuclear supporters admitted that our development of nuclear weapons was directly in contradiction with the principles of Gandhian non-violence. . . . Even more important, the lower income and education groups were far less enthusiastic about India's nuclear capability."[193] It was the Indian masses, and concerns about quotidian conditions in the country, that drove Mrs. Gandhi's popularity sharply down within months of the PNE.

The effects of the PNE on India's national security, defined in military terms, were also more mixed than the immediate euphoria suggested. Having acquired and demonstrated a capability to produce nuclear weapons, Mrs. Gandhi and subsequent leaders faced the question of what to do next. What meaning should be attached to this capability? What national strategy should rationalize it?

The atomic scientists had assumed that other tests would follow.[194] They saw Pokhran as the first step toward a full-fledged nuclear weapon program, although they did little to map a national security strategy that would incorporate this capability. However, Indira Gandhi and her successors did not oblige, as is detailed in the following chapters. Moral doubts, competing domestic priorities, and international considerations combined to turn India's prime ministers away from a nuclear weapon program. The international backlash to the PNE and the failure of the nuclear program to provide a durable boost to Mrs. Gandhi's popularity cooled her relations with the nuclear scientists. "After 1974," a former high-ranking official submitted in an interview, "she didn't want to hear anything about nuclear at all."[195] She felt that she had been misled into the nuclear test and upon reflection her doubts about the morality and worth of nuclear weapons intensified. "People say her refusal to allow other tests was due to U.S. pressure and so on, but it wasn't," argued the official quoted above. "She genuinely felt horrified by the bomb."[196] Thus, she resisted subsequent requests from the nuclear establishment to conduct more tests.

If, in the view of the scientists involved, Pokhran represented the first step in a strategy, the government's refusal to follow through over succeeding years rendered it astrategic. This was an important consequence of the program's secrecy and the failure to engage other knowledgeable and relevant institutions in a systematic determination of nuclear policy *before Pokhran*. The scientists, many of them South Indian Brahmins, were determined to demonstrate their brilliance in the greatest of scientific fields but did not want to lose their autonomy and sully themselves in the nitty-gritty of military affairs. Thus, after Pokhran, India found itself with an ad hoc process for deciding upon a post hoc strategy, a phenomenon that would be repeated in 1998.

India after 1974 formalized what had been unofficial previously: the "nuclear option" strategy. India possessed the technological capacity to develop nuclear weapons if security interests required it, but it would refrain from exercising this military option. This ambiguous, ambivalent strategy stemmed largely from internal considerations. India would try to take additional advantage of this approach internationally by arguing that it reflected India's promotion of worldwide nuclear disarmament. The "option" strategy satisfied twin objectives of retaining a moral high ground on disarmament while providing enough military potential to give adversaries pause.[197]

Yet, the policy of acquiring the wherewithal to deploy nuclear weapons without actually deploying them was militarily awkward. As discussed in subsequent chapters, critics, some of whom reflect the logic of Western nuclear strategists, argued that India did not gain the putative military and strategic benefits of a robust, second-strike nuclear force. This view became increasingly prevalent after 1995 and helped inspire the Indian government to conduct more nuclear tests near Pokhran in 1998. At the same time, by detonating a nuclear device in 1974 (and 1998) India did incur the penalties of the international nonproliferation regime. India's action also spurred the development of its most immediate adversary's nuclear program. Therein lay the unresolved contradictions borne by the "option" strategy and the 1974 detonation. This was the legacy of the first phase of India's nuclear policy, from 1947 to 1974.

EIGHT

The Nuclear Program Stalls

1975–1980

The Pokhran explosion demonstrated India's capability to produce nuclear weapons. In three decades of slow-but-steady work, India's scientists had driven the bumpy road up the technological foothills leading to nuclear weapons. Remarkably, however, their effort was then slowed. India did not proceed to build and deploy a nuclear arsenal. Additional advances up the incline from the Pokhran plateau occurred gradually, particularly in missile development and designs of more sophisticated nuclear weapons. Yet, prior to the 1998 nuclear tests, successive prime ministers kept their feet on the brake pedal, even as the strategic enclave pressed the accelerator. Conflicting interests and considerations, many of them domestic, were responsible for the self-restraint described in this and the succeeding four chapters. These factors emerge as answers to the question of why India did not conduct additional nuclear tests in the twenty-four years immediately following Pokhran. This question defines phase two of the Indian nuclear program.

UNITED STATES TIGHTENS THE NONPROLIFERATION SQUEEZE ON INDIA, 1975

Before the Pokhran explosion, independent experts and a few congressional aides in the United States had begun to express alarm over growing threats of nuclear weapon proliferation.[1] India's blast amplified the alarms and prompted demand for corrective nonproliferation action by the United States and other nations. It now became clear that a handful of energetic members of Congress would soon force the United States to tighten the nonproliferation regime and correct what they perceived to be the dangers of the Atoms-for-Peace approach of promoting dissemination of nuclear power without adequate safeguards against military applications.

In early 1975 the United States began rallying other leading industrial states to build on the August 1974 agreement by the Zangger committee to establish a "trigger list" of items that would not be supplied to non–nuclear weapon states. Officials in the Gerald Ford administration, particularly in the Arms Control and Disarmament Agency, felt that the United States should lead the way by restricting nuclear exports. However, Secretary of State Kissinger and others argued that this unilateral approach would only harm the U.S. nuclear industry and enable Europeans to fill the supply void. According to then-ACDA Director Fred Iklé, Kissinger hit upon the idea of a multilateral control arrangement instead of the unilateral approach.[2] In April 1975, Kissinger convened a secret meeting in London of what became the Nuclear Suppliers Group. The United States sought additional agreements by nuclear technology suppliers to strengthen the safeguards they would require in importing states. A major aim was to plug loopholes such as those that had allowed India to produce its "peaceful" nuclear explosive. An extensive list of equipment necessary to produce fissile materials and other requisites of nuclear weapons became subject to controls.[3] The Nuclear Suppliers Group became a relatively effective nonproliferation cartel.

To India, the tightening of controls on technology exports to states not a party to the NPT reaffirmed the "intellectual colonialism" of the U.S.-led nonproliferation regime.[4] At this time India was still hoping to revive Canadian assistance to complete the Rajasthan II power reactor and still depended on U.S. fuel to supply the two power reactors at Tarapur. Meanwhile, India's weapon potential was constrained by a shutdown of the plutonium-reprocessing plant at Trombay in 1975.[5] India's nuclear establishment was now on the defensive.

EMERGENCY AND THE FADING OF NUCLEAR POLICY, 1975

Nuclear policy was far from being one of Indira Gandhi's main concerns in 1975. The domestic disorder reflected in the 1974 railway workers' strike and the burgeoning J. P. movement continued to worsen. Mrs. Gandhi's opponents nationalized their campaign against her. In November 1974, leaders from the Jana Sangh, the Socialist party, a rival wing of the Congress party, and others had formed the National Coordination Committee, endorsing Narayan's call for manifold "social, economic, political, cultural and educational changes leading ultimately to total revolution."[6] In January 1975, leaders of Mrs. Gandhi's own Congress party faction and cabinet began to split, with some of them urging negotiations with Narayan on means to redress unemployment and corruption.[7] Mrs. Gandhi's hold on power weakened.

On June 12, 1975, the Allahabad High Court ruled against Indira Gandhi on a case brought in 1971 claiming that her election to the Lok Sabha should be overturned due to corrupt campaign practices. The court found the prime minister not guilty of the most serious charges, but it judged her guilty of two lesser ones.[8] This conviction automatically invalidated her 1971 election to the Lok Sabha, thus debarring her from holding any elective office during the next six years. She could appeal to the Supreme Court, but if that failed she would have to resign the prime ministership.

On the evening of June 25, Indira Gandhi did the unthinkable for the child of Jawaharlal Nehru. She formally requested President Fakhruddin Ali Ahmed to proclaim a national emergency. In the early morning of June 26, Mrs. Gandhi and a few close associates authorized the arrests of opposition leaders and opponents within the Congress party, including especially Jayaprakash Narayan and Morarji Desai. At 7:00 A.M., President Ahmed announced the State of Emergency. An hour later Indira Gandhi addressed the nation over All India Radio to explain that she was acting in response to "the deep seated and widespread conspiracy which has been brewing ever since I began to introduce certain progressive measures of benefit to the common man and woman in India."[9]

The proclamation of Emergency gave the central government unlimited authority, suspending fundamental individual rights and the authority of state governments. As a result of this general decree (and subsequent amplifications), the government ultimately arrested more than one hundred thousand citizens.[10] The press was severely censored; twenty-six political organizations were banned. In effect, Mrs. Gandhi and her followers cut off the body of Indian democracy, leaving only a head. This head could proclaim new policies to revive the economy, improve agriculture, raise wages, lower prices, and so on, but it had lost the means to implement them.

The Emergency would remain in effect from June 1975 to March 1977. During the first year some economic gains accrued. All told, the economy in 1975 and 1976 enjoyed growth of more than 8 percent, the best rate in recent years.[11] Still, by the second year of the Emergency, it became clear that the key agricultural sector had not been systematically improved and that the overall economy still suffered major structural flaws leading to unemployment, rising poverty, and stagnation that the government, despite its authoritarian powers, could not correct.[12]

During this period of domestic preoccupation, few developments occurred in India's nuclear policy, despite growing signs of Pakistani progress in acquiring the means to produce nuclear weapons. The Department of Atomic Energy continued to hype plans to build nuclear power plants: the director of the power reactor division said in January 1976 that India would have roughly 20,000 megawatts of nuclear-generated power installed by the year 2000.[13] But Indira Gandhi evinced no interest in furthering India's nuclear weapon potential. As Raja Ramanna put it in a 1996 interview, "Once [Pokhran] was done, Mrs. Gandhi said, 'No more. That's it.' " Homi Sethna confirmed this: "We said to Mrs. Gandhi, 'Do you want another one?' She said, 'I'll let you know.' She never let us know, so we stopped."[14] The media devoted little coverage to nuclear issues, and these issues were not central to political debates. Indeed, the causes as well as the conduct of the Emergency revealed the low salience of nuclear weapons in the lives of the Indian people.

U.S. NONPROLIFERATION POLICY RECALIBRATED, 1975

In 1975 the U.S. State Department tried to continue the quiet nuclear dialogue begun during Kissinger's October 1974 discussions with Indira Gandhi. According to a secret State Department memorandum of August 19, 1975, Ambassador Moynihan and his successor William Saxbe had conveyed to the prime minister in 1974 and 1975 a list of steps India could take to ensure that its nuclear program did not exacerbate proliferation elsewhere: "no PNE assistance to other states, IAEA safeguards over nuclear supply, restraint in supply of sensitive materials and technology, and physical protection of nuclear materials and facilities."[15] According to the memo, the Indians had "informally indicated that at least they would not export nuclear explosive technology." But Indian officials had avoided engaging the American ambassadors on the thornier questions of applying safeguards to additional Indian facilities and coordinating nonproliferation policies with other nuclear technology suppliers. In July or early August, Atomic Energy Commission Chairman Homi Sethna had told the American Consul General in Bombay that "there may be a policy review in the next month." Kissinger's staff worried that India might decide to "engage in nuclear exports," a concern that apparently outweighed the threat of India's own development of nuclear weapons.[16]

The State Department believed that "a second Indian nuclear test remains inevitable."[17] This historically interesting prediction may have revealed the authors' biases about the favorable utility of nuclear weapons, for their own analysis suggested some reasons why India should have been averse to another test. American officials recognized that a second test would increase Bhutto's capacity to win conventional military supplies from the United States, give Pakistan an excuse to accelerate work on nuclear explosives, complicate Indo-Pak relations, and jeopardize the U.S. Congress's and Canada's willingness to maintain civil nuclear exports to India.[18] Still, the Americans asserted that Mrs. Gandhi would find a second test useful "to distract domestic attention from [her] repressive policies."[19] A more realistic understanding of Indian domestic politics during the Emergency would have suggested that the opposition would have criticized a nuclear test as an act of cynical manipulation by the prime minister.

To break through the Indian silence on nuclear policy, Kissinger was advised to take the matter up with Minister of External Affairs Y. B. Chavan, who was then scheduled to visit Washington in early October. Kissinger was to encourage the Indians not to export sensitive technology or material to other countries. More delicately, he was to address a possible second explosive test, keeping in mind "*our basic policy of not pressuring the GOI on their nuclear explosive program.*"[20] This statement reflected the Realpolitik view that proliferation was inevitable in major states like India and that the United States should then minimize the potentially harmful consequences by maintaining friendly relations with such states. The Americans did not want India to develop nuclear weapons but thought that they could do little to prevent it.

Kissinger's low-pressure approach to India belied contemporary and subsequent Indian claims that United States pressure caused Mrs. Gandhi to abandon plans for follow-up nuclear tests.[21] American pressure did not become great until 1977–1978, after Mrs. Gandhi had been unseated, as will be discussed later. Rather, the decision not to allow an "inevitable" second test in the 1975–1976 period owed to personal, domestic, and other international considerations. The PNE had done nothing to prevent the political woes afflicting Indira Gandhi. Throughout this period she and her advisers hoped to persuade Canada to resume the cooperation badly needed by the nuclear power program. This consideration only intensified her own sense that perhaps Pokhran had been a mistake—that the scientists had misguided her by failing to anticipate the international backlash, and that she had violated a moral norm set by her father with little attendant gain.

PAKISTAN'S NUCLEAR PROGRAM ACCELERATES, 1975 TO 1976

Pakistan in 1975 accelerated its drive to acquire nuclear weapon capability. This effort had been launched by Prime Minister Zulfikar Ali Bhutto in January 1972, and was being administered by Atomic Energy Commission Chairman Munir Ahmad Khan. Khan, an American-educated nuclear engineer with extensive experience working in Vienna at the International Atomic Energy Agency, sought to build a large overall nuclear program that would provide much-needed electricity and medical and agricultural benefits to Pakistan, while at the same time providing training, technology, and political cover to allow for production of nuclear weapons. Pakistan sought French assistance to this end.

With Pakistan's nuclear program growing, Prime Minister Bhutto in early 1975 pressed the United States to lift the embargo on arms sales that had been imposed since the 1965 Indo-Pak war. As Bhutto prepared to come to Washington in February 1975, he initiated what would be a long-running, hard-to-manage tactic of using the veiled possibility of Pakistan's acquiring the bomb to prompt Washington to supply conventional arms as a more preferable alternative. He told the *Pakistan Times* that the nation's nuclear weapon policy was "under constant review" and depended on whether Washington would help it obtain sufficient conventional weapons to deter India, which would ostensibly obviate the need for nuclear arms.[22]

Upon arrival in Washington in late February, Bhutto found Secretary of State Kissinger receptive. The State Department announced on February 24 that Pakistan would now be eligible to buy up to $100 million in conventional arms. Kissinger felt this should not deeply upset India as it would not significantly erode its military predominance. However, State Department officials warned Kissinger that India's reaction would be "strongly adverse" and would "result in at least a temporary set-back to improving Indo-U.S. relations."[23] The United States would offer arms sales to India, too, although officials did not expect India to accept the offer.[24]

In explaining the recommended shift on arms supplies to President Gerald Ford, State Department officials argued that Ford should take the opportunity "to discuss nuclear issues with Bhutto, with a view toward gaining his agreement to forego or at least postpone development of a nuclear explosion option."[25] Toward this end, American officials extracted a secret, written note from the Pakistanis during Bhutto's February visit. The note stated that "[i]n developing its nuclear technology, Pakistan would not divert any of its urgently needed development resources to the expensive efforts required to produce a nuclear explosion provided its defence in the conventional field is assured."[26] When parsed in hindsight, this revealing note did not preclude efforts to produce nuclear explosives. Pakistani leaders maintained that the nuclear project was not prohibitively expensive. Therefore, if the cost would not impair economic development, Bhutto's disavowal would not obtain. Nor would outsiders be privy to the costs of a nuclear weapon program. In any case, the issue did not figure prominently in either the American or Pakistani diplomacy, which concentrated more on reassuring Pakistan of American friendship and supporting and strengthening Bhutto's position at home.

Still, India reacted with outrage to the American offer of military sales to Pakistan. Foreign Minister Y. B. Chavan canceled his planned visit to the United States, during which Kissinger was prepared to take up the nuclear export and testing issues. Mrs. Gandhi declared that the renewed arms sales policy amounted "to reopening of old wounds." India's ambassador in Washington, T. N. Kaul lambasted Kissinger's initiative, prompting Kissinger to cut the ambassador's access, thereby rendering his continued posting in Washington ineffectual.[27]

By the end of 1975, concern over Pakistan's nuclear ambitions mounted steeply, at least in the West. Washington pressed France for restraint in supplying Pakistan's nuclear program. When Prime Minister Bhutto visited Paris in late 1975 to keep the nuclear supply deal on track, he found the French much more demanding on safeguards.[28] The Pakistanis regretted France's new sensitivity regarding nonproliferation, but they did not want to jeopardize the advantages the Chashma reprocessing plant still would provide in training and designing civilian and weapon facilities. Pakistan and France agreed that the plant would be safeguarded, and submitted an application to the IAEA, which approved it in February 1976.[29]

The United States, France, and Pakistan continued their interactions over the reprocessing plant for nearly three years, until finally in 1978 France revoked the contract. Meanwhile, a most important development occurred in Pakistan in December 1975. At that time, Dr. A. Q. Khan, a metallurgist (and no relation to Munir Ahmad Khan), was visiting his native Pakistan on leave from his job at a large Dutch engineering firm, FDO. FDO was a major subcontractor on the European Uranium Enrichment Company—URENCO—project to build an advanced ultracentrifuge uranium enrichment plant that would provide enrichment services for European nuclear power programs. Earlier, in 1974, A. Q. Khan had written Prime Minister Bhutto offering his services to Pakistan's nuclear program, particularly in the area of uranium enrichment.[30] Bhutto, according to Zahid Malik's account, responded by asking Khan to contact him on his next visit to Pakistan, which occurred in December 1974. At that time, Khan disparaged the plans of Munir Ahmad Khan to acquire a plutonium-reprocessing plant and urged that he concentrate instead on building a centrifuge enrichment plant that could make bomb-grade uranium. Bhutto asked A. Q. Khan to consider returning to Pakistan to contribute to the nuclear program.[31] Now, a year later, with Khan back in Pakistan, Bhutto pressed harder. Khan assented, and agreed not to return to Holland but instead to take charge of the uranium enrichment effort. According to Malik, Bhutto excitedly "thumped his fist on the table and said, 'I will see the Hindu bastards now.' "[32]

Western media and intelligence reports and a Dutch court later concluded that A. Q. Khan brought with him stolen designs for the URENCO ultracentrifuge enrichment plant.[33] With these plans, Khan led a massive clandestine international procurement effort to acquire necessary components, material, and machinery to assemble the centrifuge enrichment plant at Kahuta, about an hour's drive east of Islamabad. Officially launched under A. Q. Khan's control in July 1976 and dubbed the Engineering Research Laboratories (Project 706), Kahuta became central to the Pakistani nuclear weapon program.[34]

Yet, acquisition of fissile material is not sufficient to make a bomb. Most important, designs and a neutron initiator are required to ensure that a weapon can be detonated with exact timing and predictable yield. Here, as in the case of uranium enrichment technology, it appears that Pakistan sought foreign assistance. This time, Pakistan approached China to provide the helping hand.

In late May 1976, Zulfikar Ali Bhutto traveled to China. Although the record is unclear, Bhutto's subsequent testimony and later American intelligence reports suggest that during this visit Bhutto persuaded China to provide important material help to the Pakistani bomb effort. In his late 1977 trial, following the military coup that displaced him from power, Bhutto testified that "my single most important achievement which I believe will dominate the portrait of my public life is an agreement which I arrived at after an assiduous and tenacious endeavor spanning over eleven years of negotiation. . . . [T]he agreement of mine, concluded in June 1976, will perhaps be my greatest achievement and contribution to the survival of our people and our nation."[35]

Bhutto's dating and his reference to contributing to the survival of Pakistan suggest that he was referring to an agreement whereby China would augment Pakistan's nuclear program. Moreover, his saying that he had been working on such an agreement for eleven years—since 1965—adds to the argument put forth in chapter 4 that Bhutto advocated the 1965 war with India at least in part to achieve military gains that Pakistani leaders feared would become out of reach when India acquired nuclear weapons. Bhutto thought this could happen in the eighteen-month span cited by Homi Bhabha in October 1964. Whether or not Bhutto began his quest for Chinese assistance as early as 1965, U.S. intelligence ultimately concluded that China assisted Pakistan in "the area of fissile material production and possibly also nuclear device design."[36]

There is no public evidence indicating that India was aware in 1976 of the uranium enrichment effort now underway or of China's pending role in the Pakistani bomb effort. In the period from 1975 to 1976, India and China took several steps toward normalizing relations. On April 15, 1975, India announced it would return an ambassador to China. China then reciprocated, restoring diplomatic relations that had been severed in 1962.[37] In 1977, the two countries resumed trade relations that also had been suspended since 1962.

Indo-Pak relations also improved in 1976 when Bhutto and Gandhi exchanged constructive letters in March and April aimed to rekindle the normalization of relations.[38] The exchange of letters led to a meeting of foreign secretaries in Islamabad in May, which resulted in an agreement to resume air overflights and the restoration of air traffic between the two countries, along with the reopening of rail links and commitments to explore modest trade.[39]

Thus, during this time of domestic preoccupation, India manifested little alarm over its external security situation. Having recently defeated Pakistan in war and now embroiled in internal struggles, the government had little interest in accelerating the nuclear program. India's defense budgets remained at their 1973 level of roughly 3 percent of GDP (falling in the 1975 budget to 2.8 percent).

UNITED STATES AND CANADA TIGHTEN
THE NONPROLIFERATION SQUEEZE, 1976

On May 18, 1976, exactly two years after the Pokhran explosion, Canada formally terminated its nuclear cooperation with India. The two states had negotiated fruitlessly in the aftermath of Pokhran to establish more stringent safeguards that would, among other things, preclude further nuclear explosions. The cutoff was a severe blow, given the major role that Canada's CANDU technology and related materials and training had played in the Indian nuclear power program. The nuclear establishment's pattern of time delays and cost overruns in completing nuclear reactors and heavy-water plants would be exacerbated without the Canadian assistance, thereby weakening the establishment's reputation and claim on national resources. It would have been natural for the leaders of the nuclear establishment to shift their public raison d'être toward a national defense mission. However, the potential for such a shift—at least a publicly acknowledged one—was severely limited by the political and economic costs that the strengthening nonproliferation regime could impose on India and by Mrs. Gandhi's post-1974 aversion to the nuclear weapon business. Thus, the nuclear establishment continued publicly to trumpet its projected contributions to national economic development.

Meanwhile, in Washington the U.S. Congress in June 1976 enacted the Symington Amendment to the Foreign Assistance Act, prohibiting U.S. economic or military assistance to any country importing enrichment or reprocessing technology unless that country accepted IAEA safeguards on all of its facilities.[40] The Symington Amendment aimed primarily to block France's sale of a reprocessing plant to Pakistan and to signal more broadly Congress's determination to stop U.S. assistance, and where possible, other states' assistance, to proliferation-sensitive countries.[41] Key senators already had begun in 1975 to attempt passage of still more demanding legislation to tighten U.S. export policies and punish states acquiring nuclear technology without fullscope safeguards—that is, safeguards on *all* nuclear facilities. These efforts continued through 1976, fueled in part by the executive branch's admission to the Senate in 1975 that U.S. heavy water had in fact been used in the CIRUS reactor that produced the plutonium for India's nuclear blast. This amounted technically to a violation of the U.S. understanding of the 1956 agreement by which the United States supplied heavy water to India.[42]

At this point, the nonproliferation debate in the United States was primarily a partisan struggle between the congressional and executive branches of government. Little analysis and care were given to determine actually how India's and Pakistan's nuclear programs could be influenced—that is, what motivated them to seek nuclear weapon capability and what could induce them to stop. The State Department continued to pursue "low-key" dialogue with the Indian Atomic Energy Commission regarding India's adherence to the London Nuclear Suppliers Group guidelines covering exports of sensitive materials. Yet, as of April 1976, India still had not responded to Kissinger's private 1974 proposal for serious dialogue on nuclear exports.[43] In any case, the generally tense bilateral relations and the friction over supplying fuel for the Tarapur reactor made the Indians chary of direct high-level talks on nuclear policy.

The prospects of serious analysis of Indian and Pakistani considerations dimmed further as nonproliferation policy became a major dividing issue between Jimmy Carter and the Ford administration in the mounting presidential campaign. Carter was a former nuclear engineer with a desire to end the nuclear arms race, and he made nonproliferation a central issue in his campaign.[44] Carter called for a critical review of plans to rely on plutonium as a commercial fuel in the United States. This meant also that the United States would reconsider nuclear cooperation with other nations, such as India, with a mind toward blocking their capacity to reprocess spent fuel originating from the United States. President Ford could not afford to cede the issue to Carter; his administration by now had recognized that policy must be changed.[45] On October 28, 1976, after politically rooted delays, Ford issued a major statement on nuclear policy.[46] Among other things, it called for halting reprocessing of spent fuel "unless there is sound reason to conclude that the world community can effectively overcome the associated risks of proliferation."[47] Internationally, the United States would pursue strengthening of export controls, safeguards, and other measures to minimize the risks of proliferation. No matter who won the election, then, U.S. nonproliferation policy would be tightened significantly, straining relations with India.

Ironically, however, Carter's interest in nonproliferation was matched by his determination to improve relations with India. Carter's mother, "Miss Lillian," had spent two years as a Peace Corps volunteer near Bombay in the late 1960s, giving the president a personal attachment to India. The new administration's foreign policy sought to downplay the cold war dimension of relations with countries in the Third World. The Carter team viewed India as an influential regional power that should be addressed on its own terms. Nonproliferation objectives would have to be integrated with the competing agenda of improving ties with India.

ELECTIONS—DESAI REPLACES GANDHI AND RULES OUT NUCLEAR TESTS, 1977

On January 18, 1977, Indira Gandhi went on national radio to announce that general elections would be held in March and that the rules of the Emergency would be relaxed to allow open electoral competition. Affirming her "unshakable faith in the power of the people," Mrs. Gandhi urged citizens to "uphold the fair name of India as a land committed to the path of reconciliation, peace and progress."[48]

The battle lines formed. Morarji Desai was released from jail the day elections were announced. The next day, January 19, the leaders of the four non-Communist opposition parties met at Desai's home to consider a combined campaign: the Hindu-nationalist Jana Sangh, the old Congress (O) party that had split with Indira Gandhi in 1969, the Socialist party, and the Bharatiya Lok Dal. On January 20, the four parties decided to contest the election under the common banner of the Janata Party.[49] In a portent of internecine conflict to come, the parties did not actually dissolve themselves into the new party, but rather united as independent units. The Janata group soon emerged as the leading contender against Mrs. Gandhi's Congress wing.[50]

The election was first and last about the Emergency, a referendum on Indira Gandhi. The competing parties all attacked the government's economic track record, particularly its failure to improve the plight of the poor and unemployed. Yet the political evils of the Emergency—the "trampling of democracy"—dominated the debate. The media and politicians practically ignored foreign and defense policy.

Nuclear policy did not figure in the campaign. The nation had celebrated the Pokhran blast only three years earlier. Politicians and pundits had debated nuclear policy since 1964 with varying degrees of intensity. Pakistan was clearly seeking nuclear weapon capability. The United States was targeting India in an international nonproliferation campaign. Yet, despite all of these stimuli, the political elite and the polity at large did not seek to clarify whether and how India should pursue nuclear weapons. Had Pokhran been a mistake? Did India's security require nuclear weapons? If so, how many of what kind under what doctrine? Did the military see a need for nuclear weapons? If nuclear weapons were not required, was India served by its present policy, which clearly impeded the further development of the civilian power program? These questions went unasked and unanswered. None of the competing parties mentioned nuclear policy in its election manifesto, save Jagjivan Ram's Congress for Democracy, which declared vaguely that "India shall continue to maintain its independence in respect of peaceful uses of nuclear energy. We shall always safeguard our national dignity and national honour—not in words but in deeds."[51]

India's attachment to democracy and the polity's concentration on its internal needs shone through the election. Indeed, the 1977 election reconfirmed the rule that Indians did not believe that nuclear weapons offered meaningful security. This helps explain India's nuclear restraint of the 1960s and suggests that the 1974 test was in many ways an aberration produced by the exertions of an isolated, prideful scientific establishment. Still, Pokhran had created new facts, and in its aftermath the leaders of India did little to adjust to them.

Polling began on March 16 and culminated on March 20. Mrs. Gandhi's Congress party was trounced. It had won 352 of 518 seats in the 1971 Lok Sabha elections; now it won only 153 of 540, with 35 percent of the popular vote.[52] The Janata won 270 seats on 43 percent of the vote—enough to form a government on its own. The Congress for Democracy, which had joined forces with the Janata, obtained 28 seats.[53]

For the first time, the Congress party would not lead independent India. At the age of eighty-one, Morarji Desai finally achieved his ambition and was named prime minister.[54] Unfortunately, the seeds of future conflict were sown in the new cabinet, which reflected the coalitional nature of the Janata. Leaders of the four main coalition parties received prominent posts, as did Jagjivan Ram of the Congress for Democracy.

Of particular interest from the standpoint of nuclear policy, Ram regained the defense minister's post that he had held in 1974 when he was excluded from decision making on the Pokhran test. Two top leaders of the pro-bomb Jana Sangh—L. K. Advani and Atal Behari Vajpayee—became, respectively, minister of information and broadcasting and minister of external affairs. Finance Minister H. M. Patel was also "very pro-bomb," according to a former chairman of the Atomic Energy Commission.[55] The placement of these men in such prominent cabinet posts could have indicated a major pro-bomb shift in India's nuclear policy, but the prime minister remained sovereign over the nuclear realm. Desai, like his predecessors, became minister of atomic energy.

Morarji Desai wasted little time before making his government's nuclear policy known. An ascetic, teetotaling Gandhian given to sometimes rambling discourse, Desai always had disparaged calls for India to acquire nuclear weapons, even as he insisted that India should not sign the discriminatory NPT. His Gandhian moral aversion to nuclear weapons was also informed by his belief as a former finance minister that the country could not afford a nuclear arms race. In his first press conference as prime minister, on March 24, he stated that the government did not believe in nuclear weapons and that he doubted the necessity of peaceful nuclear explosions.[56] In April, Desai told a West German interviewer, "I will give it to you in writing that we will not manufacture nuclear weapons. Even if the whole world arms itself with the bombs we will not do so."[57] He said that if internal pressure to build nuclear weapons became too strong, he would resign. On May 16, he declared that if a peaceful nuclear explosion were necessary, India would do it, but openly. "We will not do it in hide and seek manner. We will tell the people [what] we are doing and let them come and witness, and the use will also be open equally to others."[58] Desai added that "atomic weapons are no good for defence at all . . . they can't ever win a war."[59]

These early statements caused dismay among the small circle of strategic analysts and foreign policy experts most attentive to nuclear policy, and no doubt also among the leadership at BARC and the Atomic Energy Commission.[60] But other issues pressed more importantly on the polity.

Reflecting the practical isolation of the entire nuclear enterprise from the pressing developments within India, the Department of Atomic Energy had scrambled in the midst of the election campaign to recover from the suspension of Canadian assistance. Despite its claims of self-reliance, the Indian nuclear establishment found it exceedingly difficult to build and operate heavy-water plants, even with Canadian and French assistance. Now that the Canadians had pulled out, the problem grew more severe. In September 1976, the Indian government received a Soviet commitment to provide 200 tonnes of heavy water, 25 percent of which was immediately shipped without a formal safeguard agreement.[61] In early 1977 India sought the remaining tonnes so that it could start the second power reactor (RAPS-II) in Rajasthan. The Soviets at this point demanded that India accept safeguards on the reactor and, in perpetuity, on any plutonium produced within it, in whichever facilities this plutonium might be introduced. The aim was to ensure that heavy water would not be diverted to help in production of plutonium for explosive purposes.[62] Desperate for the assistance, the Desai government in the summer of 1977 assented to the safeguard demand. It is doubtful that Indira Gandhi or another leader would have done otherwise; the weakness of India's indigenous heavy-water production capacity did not allow an alternative. Meanwhile, in 1977 the Atomic Energy Commission began work on the 100-megawatt R-5 ("Dhruva") plutonium production reactor also at Trombay, to supplement the smaller and aging CIRUS reactor that had produced the plutonium used in the Pokhran blast.[63]

Desai became still more averse to an Indian bomb as he became familiar with the Atomic Energy Commission leaders and as he assessed the prospects of dealing with Jimmy Carter on nuclear issues. In early May President Carter had instructed the new U.S. ambassador to India, Robert Goheen, to tell Desai that "[i]f India would restrain from developing atomic weapons and agree to discuss nonproliferation, he would clear the pending Tarapur shipment."[64] (The U.S. Nuclear Regulatory Commission was holding up the transfer on nonproliferation grounds.) Goheen did this in his first call on Desai, and the prime minister responded, "I will never develop a bomb and, yes, we will engage in discussions."[65] Based on Desai's assurances, Carter issued an order in late April authorizing the shipment of reactor fuel to India, which went ahead when Congress declined to contest it.[66]

Desai's categorical statement to Carter was not made public. However, the quiet understanding between the two leaders set the stage for Desai to make his clearest repudiation yet of India's nuclear weapon development efforts. During question time in the Lok Sabha on July 13, 1977, Desai denied that India had accepted fullscope safeguards and a ban on the reprocessing of spent fuel from all reactors, not only the two at Tarapur, in return for resumption of U.S. fuel supplies. He was then asked whether India pledged not to undertake further peaceful nuclear explosions. His response signaled contempt for those who had undertaken the 1974 explosion and a determination not to do the same: "[T]he explosion that was made here for peaceful purposes—as it was claimed—has been misunderstood. And, therefore, it created all these difficulties. There is no question of any other explosion now for peaceful purposes. And this has been cleared out in our talks. Therefore, this is not going to arise now."[67]

Not only had Desai abandoned India's long-standing interest in peaceful nuclear explosions, he had pledged it to the Americans. Lest this seem like a capitulation, the prime minister insisted defiantly that India would not sign the NPT "as long as those who possess atomic weapons and go on doing the explosions do not give them up."[68] He also said that he would "never agree to any inspections by anybody, until they allow me to inspect their plants."[69]

The magnitude of Desai's statement on nuclear explosions registered on the parliamentarians. One asked how Desai's apparent disavowal of PNEs could be squared with the needs of the nuclear energy program. Desai again betrayed his disregard for the leadership of the Atomic Energy Commission and Indira Gandhi: "No such explosion is necessary, in my view. If the previous government had a different view, it is not my fault. They were wrong in saying so."[70] Y. B. Chavan, a powerful political player who had been defense minister under Shastri and external affairs minister in the just-defeated Congress government, asked pointedly, "Are we going by the personal views in this matter, or are we guided by certain scientific and technological views in this matter?"[71] Chavan's jab provoked a brief skirmish over which one of the two men had better scientific training, but the prime minister seemed to realize that Chavan's point was valid:

> I agree with him that I should not make a commitment for all future time. I cannot say that I know everything about the future or even now anything completely, but as

far as I have gone into the question, I have come to this conclusion that no explosion is necessary for a peaceful use, for use of atomic energy for peaceful purposes. That is the conclusion I have come to. That is why I said there was no question of an explosion. But, if anything is necessary, we can do it always in consultation with other people. Nobody will object to it if it is necessary, if they are convinced.[72]

This intense discussion reveals much about both the content and the process of Indian nuclear policymaking. Desai announced a new line and repudiated what had been a celebrated demonstration of national prowess only three years earlier—and he did it all on his own. Indeed, another parliamentarian, Subramaniam Swamy attacked Desai on just this point. Swamy asked whether Desai would "present a white paper or some document to this House so that this knowledge that is available to him, can also be made available to other Members of Parliament who could then at least revise their original stand that nuclear explosions are necessary for peaceful purpose?"[73]

"I do not propose to do any such thing," the prime minister defiantly barked.[74] Clearly, the prime minister and the leadership of the Atomic Energy Commission did not see eye to eye, unlike in the Nehru-Bhabha years.

Public reaction to Desai's new line was muted. A July 15 *Times of India* editorial noted that the Congress government had not conducted further tests since 1974, making Desai's statement less remarkable. It suggested that the question of further tests should be resolved by "a select group of scientists, economists and others familiar with the state of the art" and commented almost in passing that no such committee had been established.[75] In any case, the editorial concluded meekly, India's options on further tests were likely to be limited severely by dependence on American fuel for the Tarapur reactor and the leverage that provided to Washington. Other editorials appreciated Desai's intentions but respectfully urged that the government not foreclose options to develop nuclear technology.[76]

Desai continued throughout 1977 to reject further nuclear explosions.[77] The polity remained tolerant. When China carried out its twenty-second nuclear weapon test in late September, "there was not a ripple on the surface in India," according to G. G. Mirchandani.[78] Even the Jana Sangh took a detached view. The Jana Sangh officials in the new cabinet did not dissent from the prime minister's line. In one of the few articles devoted to nuclear issues in the party's newspaper in 1977, a retired air force wing commander, Maharaj K. Chopra, argued that Desai's views broke no "new ground."[79] The article noted that India's dependence on American nuclear assistance (and Canada's help before 1976) could not be escaped. The real problem was the nuclear establishment's failure to meet its promises. "It is sometimes amusing to contemplate the Congress charge that the Janata Government has clamped upon our nuclear advance. The fact is that during the Congress rule not even 40 per cent of the targets set by itself were achieved. Only one thing happened: a nuclear test."[80] Worse, following the "euphoria" over the test, "every incompetence and shortfall was swept beneath the carpet."[81] Congress's own traditional anti-bomb policy gave it no basis for putting the government on the defensive. Furthermore, the moralism of Desai's opposition to nuclear weapons resonated with India's national self-image. Indeed, the underlying tone of national discourse on nuclear policy was tired and resigned in 1977. The Pokhran blast had put India in a mirror-lined box; the reflection revealed the frailty of India's nuclear capacity, and the primacy of other issues.

COUP IN PAKISTAN, 1977

Pakistan experienced mounting political unrest in 1976 and early 1977, against a background of declining per capita income and rising foreign debt. In January 1977, Prime Minister Bhutto called for national and provincial assembly elections to be held in March. An alliance of varied political parties formed to contest Bhutto's Pakistan Peoples Party (PPP). In a country where politics frequently is a blood sport, the campaign and its aftermath were particularly nasty. The PPP won a landslide in the national poll, which immediately triggered claims of election fraud. The opposition group (the Pakistan National Alliance, or PNA) called for electoral reforms and a revote, threatening massive agitation if its demands were not met. A crisis ensued for several months.

In April, Bhutto and his advisers decided to impose martial law in Karachi, Lahore, and Hyderabad. The Lahore High Court ruled this order illegal on June 2, and it was rescinded on June 7. After negotiations, the government and the opposition agreed tentatively to hold new elections in October. However, the agreement was never formalized, and tensions continued to mount. Army General Zia-ul-Haq launched a military coup on July 5. Bhutto was arrested and martial law declared. Pakistan once again had descended into military dictatorship.

In the short term, the coup in Pakistan only marginally affected relations with India. India declared the coup "an internal affair of Pakistan." Foreign Minister Vajpayee, reiterated the government's desire to seek "good neighbourly" relations. Desai sent Zia a message reaffirming the desire for peace and friendship and offering Indian assistance to Pakistan in the field of peaceful nuclear research.[82] In February 1978, Vajpayee traveled to Pakistan and reached agreements to allow journalists from each country to be posted to the other and to undertake further trade negotiations. The tone of these and other interactions was markedly positive.

More ominously, however, martial rule in Pakistan meant that the military assumed control over the nuclear program. This was both ironic and portentous. Zulfikar Ali Bhutto had launched the nuclear weapon effort in part to give himself countervailing power vis-à-vis the army.[83] The army had always been the dominant institution in Pakistan, even when it did not rule directly. Bhutto had thought that if he could oversee the acquisition of nuclear weapons, he would gain political stature and control of the ultimate weapon, thereby diminishing the army's role. Now, however, General Zia and his subordinates moved quickly to assert sovereignty over the nuclear program.[84] Construction of the Kahuta uranium enrichment plant proceeded rapidly, while acquisition and development of technology necessary to trigger a nuclear device continued apace. The military's role meant that Pakistan's nuclear weapon capability would be ingrained in military planning much more deeply than India's had been or would be. It also meant that when democracy returned to Pakistan, elected civilian leaders would find it difficult to shape nuclear policy. Unlike in India, where prime ministers held sway over nuclear policy, Pakistan's civilian leaders would lack this scope. Pakistan's nuclear weapon capability became not only a symbolic and political asset but also a weapon whose potential use the military could do much to determine. The United States suspended military and economic assistance to Pakistan in September 1977 in part because it feared the militarization of Pakistan's nuclear weapon effort.

By the 1977–1978 period, Indian officials had detected Pakistan's clandestine procurement efforts in the United Kingdom and Germany and concluded that a bomb-making effort was well underway.[85] Although Indian nuclear scientists discounted Pakistan's ability to master the uranium enrichment process, other agencies informed the prime minister that the threat was real. Had Indian leaders thought about security and nuclear weapons as Western Realists assume they did, this should have prompted them to strengthen, if not militarize, the Indian nuclear program. Yet, the Indians did not.

THE U.S. CONGRESS FORCES THE
NONPROLIFERATION ISSUE, 1977 TO 1978

The nuclear programs of India and Pakistan posed a major challenge to the Carter administration's interest in nonproliferation. The president had ordered a review of U.S. nonproliferation policy upon entering office. On April 7, 1977, he revealed the administration's core objectives. Among other things, the United States would defer indefinitely its commercial reprocessing and recycling of plutonium, seek revision of international nuclear cooperation arrangements in order to reduce pressures for reprocessing, embargo export of equipment or technology useful for uranium enrichment and plutonium reprocessing, and strengthen international nonproliferation safeguards.[86]

At the same time, however, the election of Desai two months into Carter's presidency increased the president's optimistic desire to improve relations with India.[87] The Janata's pledge to pursue "genuine non-alignment," meaning a less pro-Soviet foreign policy, coincided favorably with Carter's geopolitical and bilateral hopes. Unfortunately, Carter's general interest in strengthening ties with India seemed destined to clash with his and Congress's toughening nonproliferation policies. Hoping to avoid this conflict, Carter began his interaction with Desai by communicating a desire to accommodate both states' interests. The administration sought to build goodwill in India throughout 1977. In July it sent Deputy Secretary of State Warren Christopher to New Delhi and, pointedly, not to Pakistan.

In December Carter rejected the Ford administration's earlier move to sell A-7 fighter-bombers to Pakistan.

However, Congress was moving to tie the administration's hands in dealing with India. On March 10, 1978, Congress passed the Nuclear Non-Proliferation Act (NNPA). The long and complicated legislation was the culmination of several years of intense intragovernmental debate informed by numerous official and non-governmental studies. Much of this had been prompted by India's 1974 nuclear explosion.

The NNPA mandated that the United States not export "source material, special nuclear material, production or utilization facilities, and any sensitive nuclear technology" to any country that does not maintain IAEA safeguards on "all peaceful nuclear activities" within its jurisdiction.[88] In other words, the United States would demand safeguards on *all* nuclear facilities in any state receiving significant U.S. nuclear exports. The law explicitly forbade the manufacture or detonation of "peaceful" nuclear explosive devices. The new legislation also forbade reprocessing U.S.-originated spent fuel without prior American approval.[89] Furthermore, the law proclaimed that no "nuclear materials and equipment or sensitive nuclear technology" shall be exported to any non–nuclear weapon state that has detonated a nuclear explosive device.[90] The United States would terminate nuclear cooperation with any state that violated this prohibition on detonating nuclear explosives or other specified U.S. requirements.[91]

The NNPA departed significantly from existing U.S. nuclear cooperation agreements, so Congress allowed an eighteen-month period to renegotiate such agreements with other states to satisfy the new requirements. If no new agreement was reached, a complete cutoff of assistance would occur in two years. This set the stage for intense negotiations between the United States and India, and between the executive branch and the Congress, over ongoing supply of fuel for the Tarapur reactors, pursuant to the 1963 U.S.-Indian nuclear cooperation agreement. (Anticipating this, the Carter administration had tried unsuccessfully to persuade Congress to exempt existing contracts from the NNPA's new fullscope safeguards requirement.)[92]

The NNPA reflected manifold interests, motivations, and assumptions. The champions of the legislation viewed it as an opportunity to correct the fundamental flaw of the Atoms for Peace program. Senator John Glenn, for example, offered that "in retrospect, with 20/20 hindsight, we should not have embarked upon an 'Atoms-for-Peace program' without having solved the radioactive waste disposal problem," and without having developed a "completely safeguardable" plutonium fuel cycle.[93] In particular, Glenn continued, "we should have tempered somewhat our exuberance in desiring to spread the benefits of nuclear power." This exuberance, he said, had led to the presentation of papers on plutonium separation at the first Atoms for Peace conference, which India had found useful in designing its first plutonium-reprocessing plant.[94] Other legislators and the nuclear industry did not share Glenn's critique, but the antiproliferation forces outweighed them.

Some in Congress also desired to correct prior executive branch inattention to nonproliferation. Republican Senator Charles Percy noted bitterly that for his first seven years in office, Henry Kissinger "had never spoken before Congress on nonproliferation."[95] Congress simply did not trust the executive branch to promote decisively the American and international interest in nonproliferation. Congress now intended "to tie the hands of the president and the international community," as the leading scholar of the NNPA concluded.[96]

The NNPA's proponents assumed that sanction-backed controls on U.S. exports could compel countries like India to abandon efforts to acquire nuclear explosives or in other cases rule out future efforts. As Senator Percy put it, India had been able to explode a nuclear device "without any concern that they would have any sanctions imposed against them. . . . But if we had just had a clear-cut policy from the outset that [an explosion] would be an action so contrary to our policy that we would sever our supply if technologies and materials were used for explosives, then I do not think they would have taken the action."[97] Percy's assumption had some merit: Indira Gandhi and her advisers, particularly the leaders of the nuclear establishment, did underestimate the punitive costs of the Pokhran blast. Yet, even if the ineluctable prospect of sanctions could deter a state from *beginning* to build and test nuclear explosives, it was not clear that such sanctions would compel elimination of nuclear weapon capabilities in countries like India that *already* had demonstrated them openly. The NNPA, as Percy assumed, could help block new cases of proliferation—a major accomplishment—but still not bring India into the nonproliferation fold.

This pointed to one of the flaws in the legislation: in the interest of universality, it precluded flexible tactics to deal with particular cases. This flaw bore specifically on the Indian challenge. In the thousands of pages of hearings and debate that had informed the NNPA, no systematic analysis of Indian motivations or decision-making appeared. As one of the key drafters of the legislation, Senate Governmental Affairs Committee aide Leonard Weiss, said in an interview, "Frankly, I'm not sure we cared all that much about India's motivations."[98] During this period, Weiss continued, "there was a lot of anti-Indian sentiment up here due to India's general foreign policy line." The Pokhran test had sundered the pro-India forces in Congress, mostly Democrats and liberal Republicans, and the Emergency had further alienated legislators. India therefore served as a useful example to help push the law through. "We really didn't think this would stop the Indians or other countries that really wanted to make a bomb, but we could raise their costs and time requirements," Weiss explained. Whatever the impact on India, the NNPA's drafters were determined to show the executive branch and the European nuclear technology suppliers that the United States was serious about nonproliferation. In Weiss's words, "We had to show purpose and put the State Department in a position to know that a cutoff was coming."

To be sure, some legislators and executive branch officials recognized some of India's motivations. Senator Glenn, for example, acknowledged that "[u]ntil the nuclear weapon states make some concrete progress toward nuclear disarmament, thereby channeling their own bases of national pride away from acquisition of nuclear weapons or weapons potential, we shall see little progress in reducing the perceived national security or prestige incentives toward acquiring fissile materials by nonweapon states."[99] Joseph Nye Jr., then deputy to the under secretary of state for security assistance, science, and technology, testified that

> we must be acutely sensitive to the political and security motivations that lead states to acquire nuclear explosive devices. This will necessitate insuring the credibility of existing security guarantees, making progress in achieving meaningful and verifiable arms control agreements that reduce nuclear weapon force levels and limit or prohibit nuclear testing, strengthening our alliances, and devaluing the prestige identified with a nuclear weapon capability.[100]

However, the United States and the Soviet Union proved unwilling in the 1970s, just as they had been in the 1960s, to provide robust nuclear security guarantees to countries like India, or to effect a nuclear test ban or major progress toward nuclear disarmament. Thus, the legislators ended up imposing severe "supply side" pressures against proliferation without providing necessary measures to reduce "demand" for nuclear capabilities in states like India.

The NNPA acknowledged that alternative energy policies should be encouraged to reduce developing countries' interests in proliferation-prone technology and materials. Title V of the legislation called for the United States to assist developing nations in "the development of non-nuclear energy resources." Ten million dollars was authorized to start such a program.[101] But this was only a gesture, and as time passed even the paltry initial funds designated for this purpose withered away.

The authors of the NNPA also recognized that countries such as India might be driven to reprocess spent fuel because they lacked alternative means for disposing of spent reactor fuel. Nuclear spent fuel and waste disposition was (and still is) problematic for all countries with nuclear plants. Nuclear power advocates dubiously had touted reprocessing as a partial solution to this problem. (Indeed, the United States and India assumed in 1963 that India would reprocess Tarapur spent fuel, albeit pending U.S. approval.) Hence, after much debate, the NNPA provided for the United States to accept foreign spent fuel for interim or permanent storage or disposition in order to reduce incentives to reprocess.[102] However, the inefficacy of this provision was foreshadowed prior to the NNPA's passage. In the summer of 1977, the Carter administration explored with India the possibility of purchasing excess spent fuel from Tarapur and returning it to the United States, which was allowed under the 1963 accord. However, logistical difficulties and opposition by U.S. environmentalists doomed this transaction. Washington also blanched at the prospect that under the terms of the 1963 agreement India could insist on the right to inspect the American facilities to which spent fuel would be transferred.[103] The United States wanted no such reciprocity.

The positive incentives envisioned in the NNPA still have not been delivered. With a few minor exceptions, the United States has not invited transfer of spent fuel back home. The U.S. government has proved unwilling or unable to provide security assurances, energy alternatives, or equitable devaluation of nuclear weapons to induce India to "trade in" perceived nuclear assets. Instead, the legislation amounted to a unilateral measure to coerce compliance with American nonproliferation policies.

To Indians, the NNPA smacked bitterly of colonialism. India deemed the American requirement to renegotiate the existing contract for supplies to the Tarapur reactor as a breach of international law, which, if effected, would free India from its obligations under the contract, including the safeguarding obligations at Tarapur and the prohibition on reprocessing without U.S. permission. U.S. Senator James McClure, the Republican nuclear industry advocate from Idaho, noted the political problems posed by the act: "We are requiring in this instance that we look at very, very sensitive matters within foreign countries, upon which foreign countries must, as a matter of their own security and their own pride, be able to run their own affairs, without direct interference by foreign countries, and they are going to resist to some degree dictation from a foreign country, even the United States."[104]

For the purposes of this narrative, the major result of the NNPA was to make Tarapur the central focus and problem of Indo-American relations for years to come. Scores of U.S. government meetings and hearings, thousands of pages of documents, and dozens of bilateral negotiations between India and the United States followed. The United States demanded by legislative fiat that India accept fullscope safeguards that in effect would eliminate its nuclear explosives capability. Otherwise, the United States would abrogate the agreement to provide fuel for the Tarapur nuclear reactors, on which much of Maharashtra state depended for electricity. India insisted that the United States could not unilaterally rewrite the contract. Otherwise, India would be free to increase its supply of nuclear explosive materials by ending safeguards on the Tarapur reactors or reprocessing the spent fuel they generated, or both. This alternative threatened U.S. nonproliferation interests. Overlaying the substantive dispute were questions of colonialism, national identity and sovereignty, and equity between the nuclear haves and have-nots—all of which have animated India's nuclear policy from the beginning.

CARTER AND DESAI EXCHANGE VISITS, 1978

With the passage of the NNPA looming on the horizon, President Jimmy Carter traveled to New Delhi for a two-day visit beginning January 1, 1978. Carter underscored the positive nature of the overture to India by not stopping in Pakistan. During the visit, Carter made several speeches in which he highlighted his commitment to human rights and America's respect for India's democracy. At the end, Carter and Desai issued the Delhi Declaration, which reaffirmed their commitments to democracy, national sovereignty, a more equitable international economic order, and the reduction and eventual elimination of nuclear weapons.[105]

However, the trip did not pass without controversy over nuclear policy. On the first morning of the visit, Carter emerged from a private meeting with Desai, during which the president had pledged to approve yet another pending fuel shipment to Tarapur in hope of receiving an accommodating Indian response. Desai did not reciprocate. Outside the meeting room, Carter turned to Secretary of State Cyrus Vance and spoke words that were unknowingly picked up by a press microphone: "I told him I would authorize the transfer of fuel now. . . . It didn't seem to make an impression on him. . . . When we get back, I think I should write him another letter, just cold and very blunt."[106] Given Indian sensitivities, the comment could have caused a great stir. However, Desai demonstrated his determination not to let nuclear policy detract from the overall relationship by saying that remarks "not intended to be heard, were not heard."[107] Some factions in India sought to play up the incident, but Desai's grace allowed it to pass diplomatically, although Indian elites remained perturbed.

The Indian public responded positively to Carter's engagement. Forty-six percent of respondents to an Indian Institute of Public Opinion survey reported that their opinion of Carter had "gone up" after the visit, while only 4 percent felt unfavorably.[108] According to the institute, "Even the traces of anti-Americanism—generated during the Nixon era—had vanished."[109] This sentiment arose despite the tensions over nonproliferation.[110] The urban residents polled saw Carter as a man of peace and goodwill.

Shortly after Carter's visit, the United States moved to increase American bilateral aid to India, which had been suspended due to the 1971 Indo-Pak war. The issue had not been addressed directly by Carter and Desai in New Delhi out of deference to Indian sensibilities.[111] A postsummit speech by Foreign Minister A. B. Vajpayee revealed the delicacy of the issue:

> It must also be said that Indo-American relations are now marked with a sense of equality that had eluded us before. For the first time in the history of our relations, a high-level dialogue was carried out without the inhibiting theme of aid or economic assistance featuring even once during the discussions. The traditional image of a donor-recipient relationship between the USA and India has been replaced by an equal partnership based on friendship and a common will to cooperate.[112]

In reality, Finance Minister H. M. Patel in earlier discussions with U.S. officials had abandoned the pretense that India did not need the help and had set the stage for the postsummit increase in American aid.[113] India's broad economy, like its nuclear power program, remained reliant on foreign assistance whether anyone liked it or not.

Throughout 1978 Desai maintained his rather bold stance against nuclear weapons and explosions in India. He did this despite growing political conflicts within the Janata Party and increasing pessimism among the populace about his

Figure 1. Prime Minister Jawaharlal Nehru unveiling the bronze tablet commemorating the formal inauguration of the Atomic Energy Establishment at Trombay, January 20, 1947. Dr. Homi Bhabha stands at Nehru's right. The establishment was renamed the Bhabha Atomic Research Centre after Bhabha's death in a 1966 plane crash.

Figure 2. The Bhabha Atomic Research Centre, Trombay, the heart of India's nuclear weapon program.

Figure 3. On the left, the Canada-India, or CIRUS, research reactor, supplied by Canada and formally inaugurated on January 16, 1961. This reactor produced the plutonium used in India's first nuclear explosive device. On the right, the Dhruva research reactor, which first went critical in 1985 and subsequently provided the major source of India's weapons plutonium. Neither reactor is under international safeguards.

Figure 4. Jawaharlal Nehru observing the grinding of a uranium fuel rod for the CIRUS reactor.

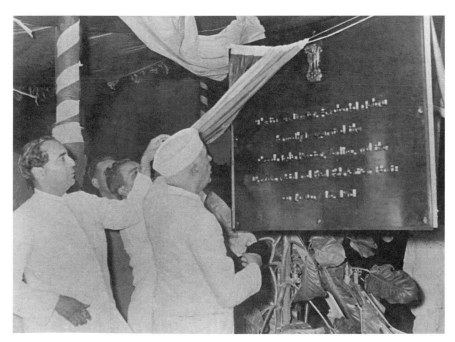

Figure 5. Jawaharlal Nehru, with Homi Bhabha, unveiling the plaque commemorating the formal inauguration of the CIRUS reactor, January 16, 1961.

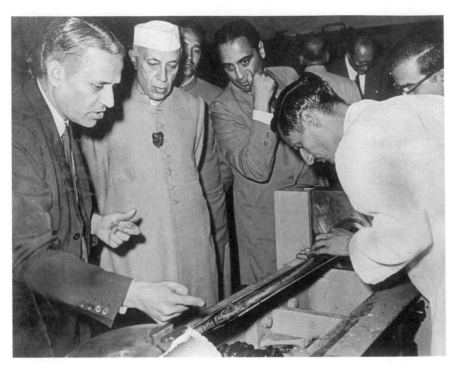

Figure 6. Jawaharlal Nehru, with Homi Bhabha on the right and Dr. Brahm Prakash, head of the Atomic Energy Establishment's metallurgy division, on the left, observing the canning of a uranium fuel rod in aluminum to be used in the CIRUS reactor.

Figure 7. The earth rises from the detonation of India's "peaceful nuclear explosive" near Pokhran, May 18, 1974.

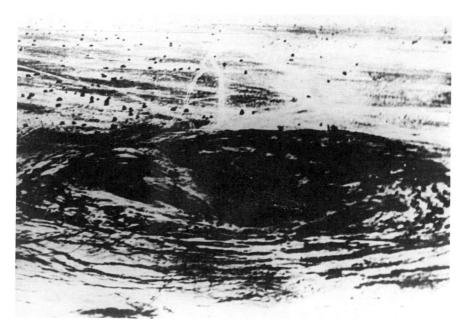

Figure 8. The crater left in the Thar Desert near Pokhran by the 1974 nuclear blast.

Figure 9. Prime Minister Indira Gandhi briefing the press on May 18, 1974, following the Pokhran nuclear experiment. On her right is Atomic Energy Commission Chairman Homi Sethna, and on her left, Minister for Information and Broadcasting Inder K. Gujral. Gujral later served as foreign minister, and from April 1997 to March 1998 as prime minister.

Figure 10. Prime Minister Indira Gandhi, on December 22, 1974, examining a piece of rock at the site of the May nuclear test. On her right is Congress party stalwart and future Defence Minister K. C. Pant. Pant left the Congress party in 1998 and became an adviser to the BJP government.

Figure 11. Dr. Raja Ramanna, who as director of the Bhabha Atomic Research Centre oversaw the production of India's first nuclear explosive and subsequently became chairman of the Atomic Energy Commission, minister of state for defence, and director general of the Defence Research and Development Organisation.

Figure 12. Then-Minister of External Affairs Atal Behari Vajpayee visiting the Forbidden City in Beijing on February 13, 1979. When Vajpayee authorized five nuclear weapon tests in 1998 he cited security threats from China and lingering tensions from the 1962 Sino-Indian war as reasons in a letter to President Bill Clinton.

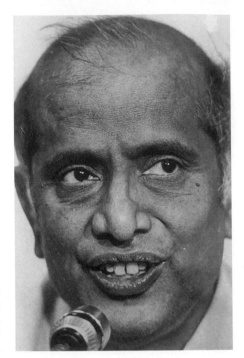

Figure 13. Dr. V. S. Arunachalam, director general of the Defence Research and Development Organisation and science adviser to the minister of defense from 1982 to 1992. Arunachalam initiated the Integrated Guided Missile Development Programme in 1983 and played a leading role in nuclear weapon development, coordinating work between the DRDO and the Atomic Energy Commission.

Figure 14. Dr. P. K. Iyengar, center, wearing suit. Iyengar played a major role in the 1974 Pokhran experiment and went on to serve as chairman of the Atomic Energy Commission from 1990 to 1993.

Figure 15. President Ronald Reagan and Prime Minister Rajiv Gandhi meeting in the White House, October 20, 1987. Reagan and Gandhi guided improvements in Indo-American relations between 1985 and 1988.

Figure 16. Dr. A. P. J. Abdul Kalam was brought into
the Defence Research and Development Organisation
to manage the Integrated Guided Missile Development
Programme in 1982, and in 1992 succeeded V. S.
Arunachalam as director general of the DRDO. Following the May 1998 tests, Kalam received credit as the
"father of the bomb."

Figure 17. Dr. Rajagopala Chidambaram. Appointed chairman of the Atomic Energy Commission in 1993, Chidambaram oversaw design of the five nuclear devices tested in May 1998. Beginning in 1968, he performed the vital calculations behind the 1974 nuclear test and continued to be a major scientific force behind India's bomb program.

Figure 18. Two mobile, 150-kilometer Prithvi missiles on Republic Day display in New Delhi. Heralded as "the pride of the nation," the Prithvi can carry nuclear warheads although the Indian government has insisted it is strictly a conventional weapon delivery system.

Figure 19. The medium-range Agni missile technology demonstrator rocketing into the sky on its first test flight, from a launching base in Orissa, May 22, 1989. In 1998, the Defence Research and Development Organisation was preparing to test an improved, follow-up Agni system, which would be the basis for a potential nuclear weapon delivery system to reach China.

Figure 20. Dr. Rajagopala Chidambaram (left), chairman of the Atomic Energy Commission and chief scientific steward of the nuclear bomb effort, and Dr. A. P. J. Abdul Kalam, director general of the Defence Research and Development Organisation, address the press following India's nuclear weapons tests in May 1998.

Figure 21. Celebrating the May 1998 tests during a visit to the Pokhran site, from left to right, Prime Minister Atal Behari Vajpayee, Defense Minister George Fernandes, Abdul Kalam, R. Chidambaram, Dr. Farooq Abdullah (in sunglasses), and Bhairon Singh Shekhawat.

government's capacity to overcome myriad political-economic difficulties. In state elections in February, Indira Gandhi's Congress party swept to decisive victories in Karnataka and Andhra Pradesh, heralding her potential to challenge the Janata government.[114] The Janata's 1978–1979 budget elicited widespread disapproval with its projection of a massive deficit that presaged price increases.[115] Neither foreign nor nuclear policy figured prominently in the February elections, as the polity concentrated on internal problems.

Desai traveled to the United States in June to attend a special session on disarmament of the UN General Assembly and to meet in Washington with President Carter. In his UN address, Desai reaffirmed his pledge "not to manufacture or acquire nuclear weapons even if the rest of the world did so." More boldly, he restated that India "abjured nuclear explosions even for peaceful purposes."[116] Desai subsequently told the American scholar Mitchell Reiss that he had read the text of his statement to the Indian cabinet, which had unanimously endorsed it.

During the June 13–14 trip to Washington, Desai met an American administration determined to sustain a cordial relationship with India and hoping to find a means of resolving the fullscope safeguards issue imposed by the NNPA. The United States recognized that Desai's domestic base was eroding due to factionalism and the apparent resurgence of Indira Gandhi.[117] Hence, Washington sought to avoid too much focus on nuclear issues and to address other concerns such as the April Communist coup in Afghanistan, American determination to forestall Pakistani acquisition of nuclear explosives, efforts to finalize the SALT II strategic nuclear arms control agreement and the Comprehensive Test Ban Treaty, and U.S. aid to India.[118] In a private meeting, Carter and Desai reaffirmed their positions on the nuclear export dispute, and Carter restated his ultimate goal of eliminating nuclear weapons.[119] In a meeting with other high-level officials from both sides, Desai evinced frustration over India's relations with China and modest hope that progress on the border dispute between the two countries could come.[120] If the Indians had wanted to make a security case for keeping open the nuclear weapon option, this would have been the time to do it, for U.S. officials like Zbigniew Brzezinski were sympathetic to such thinking. But Desai did not suggest that the ongoing border dispute with China affected India's nuclear policy.

Carter then inquired whether it would be "possible to have a nuclear weapons free zone in South Asia?" Desai demurred, arguing, "We have declared that we will not develop weapons. If the Pakistanis are concerned, let them declare that they will not have any weapons."[121] Desai continued by saying that Pakistan had nothing to fear from India. Alluding to past and perhaps future U.S. arms supplies to Pakistan, he said, "Pakistan is harming itself by armament. Even if you give arms to them and they make adventures they will regret it."[122]

The two leaders met again, along with their top foreign policy officials, on June 14. In addition to a largely reiterative discussion of Pakistan and the Afghan situation, Carter launched them on a consideration of nuclear arms control. Carter explained some of the detailed challenges remaining in the nuclear test ban negotiations, including the need to ensure that nuclear weapon stockpiles remain reliable until they are eliminated. Desai then revealed an outlook that no doubt bedeviled the Indian nuclear establishment. "Uncertainty on the reliability of stockpiles might be a good thing," he said.[123] This morally inspired and technologically disengaged view helps explain why Desai had renounced follow-up nuclear tests in India. In a meeting with congressional leaders on Capitol Hill, Desai intimated that if the nuclear weapon states stopped making nuclear weapons and undertook nuclear disarmament measures, India might change its mind and accept fullscope safeguards.[124]

Carter displayed his genuine respect for Desai and India by departing from the schedule and taking the prime minister for a personal tour of the Lincoln Memorial following the June 14 White House dinner. The warmth and thoughtfulness of the act touched Desai and the "audience" back in India. "This gesture," the *Statesman* reported, "unprecedented by any US President—speaks for itself when Indians back home ask how is the visit going."[125] In the lingering shadow of colonialism, respect from the president of the United States mattered greatly in India. Overall, the Desai trip added to the improving trend in Indo-American relations. The Indian press and populace generally viewed it as a success. For its part, the U.S. Congress responded in July by voting to sustain President Carter's order to export previously held-up fuel to Tarapur.

NUCLEAR PROGRAM WITHERS
TECHNOLOGICALLY AND POLITICALLY, 1978

Desai's largely successful foreign foray did not stop the domestic political turmoil in India. The Janata's left- and right-wing factions increasingly clashed on ideology and programs. Home Minister Charan Singh, a seventy-seven-year-old peasant leader, butted heads with Desai in an obvious drive to supplant him. This left the impression that politics had devolved into a contest of power-hungry old men.[126] "At times," the journalist Kuldip Nayar noted, the people "wonder if the leadership in the Janata has the capacity to retrieve them from the mire of hunger and want in which they have been stuck for years together. . . . It is not that the people want to go back to the Congress . . . but they do want the Janata to perform, to give them a sense of direction, to lead them."[127]

Indira Gandhi moved on June 17 to criticize the Janata's decision to abjure nuclear explosions even for peaceful purposes.[128] Mrs. Gandhi's statement was followed on June 19 with leaks to the eminent journalist G. K. Reddy, who reported in the *Hindu* that the Congress (I) party and the Communist Party of India (CPI) would soon "raise a big outcry" in Parliament "over what they consider to be a unilateral renunciation by the Prime Minister . . . without a proper mandate from Parliament."[129] Notwithstanding the irony that Mrs. Gandhi in 1974 had not consulted Parliament on the most momentous nuclear decision in India's history, her party now sought to criticize Desai over process. Reddy noted that the critics did not recommend "exercising the option to go in for a weapons programme." Rather, "they feel that by foreclosing the option [Desai] has unnecessarily denied himself the leverage he could legitimately exercise in compelling the nuclear weapon States to adopt a less discriminatory attitude" on nuclear issues. By not advocating further tests or the development of weapons, the Gandhi-led opposition revealed its own ambivalence about the nuclear program following Pokhran.

The Reddy article revealed still more about the tensions between the nuclear establishment at BARC and the political leadership. Reddy reported that the scientists were "apprehensive" over the "tendency to see and interpret India's nuclear policy largely in moral terms that have little relevance to the realities of life [and] might lead to a progressive down-grading of the priorities for research and development." To convey the scientists' sense of urgency, someone in the nuclear establishment had informed Reddy that the yield from the Pokhran blast "was considerably less than what should have been normally expected if everything had gone right." Moreover, Reddy claimed that the Pokhran test had been preceded by two failed attempts to detonate a nuclear device. Though this claim has never been proved, Reddy accurately revealed additional problems and frustrations. The Pokhran test did not provide enough data to enable the nuclear establishment publicly to discuss its findings or to develop effective uses for peaceful nuclear explosives. Thus, the scientists wanted to conduct a series of additional tests to master "the art of fission and fusion." According to Reddy, the "previous Government" had authorized such tests and the exploration of possible alternative sites in the Andaman and Nicobar islands. This potentially inflammatory claim about prior authorization was not true, however, according to interviews with former chairmen of the Atomic Energy Commission cited earlier in this chapter. By suggesting falsely that Mrs. Gandhi would have continued testing, the sources of Reddy's story sought to pressure Desai to revive the flagging nuclear program.

It did not work. Political machinations would not alter the reality that Reddy had recognized: "The Pokhran experiment, which should have proved to be a historic milestone in India's scientific advancement, has thus turned out to be the starting point for the subsequent slow-down of this ambitious programme." This turn of events was what now frustrated the BARC leadership. As of February 1978, BARC employed a staff of 3,172 scientists, 5,281 technicians, 1,198 administrators, and 2,342 maintenance and auxiliary personnel.[130] While the vast majority of these people did not work directly on explosives projects, the dramatic experiment at Pokhran had come to symbolize their handiwork. This stemmed largely from their failure to demonstrate prowess in the civilian application of nuclear energy. In December 1977, the heavy-water plant at Baroda had exploded just months after going on line. This jeopardized the nuclear establishment's reputation and its capacity to provide the moderator needed for reactors at Rajasthan and Madras, which now fell further behind schedule. India continued to suffer acute shortages of electricity, and the nuclear sector offered little hope of solving the problem.[131] In November 1978, *India Today* wrote that "India's nuclear authorities do not know whether they are coming or going."[132] "By all calculations," the article stated, "India's atomic power programme is more than a decade behind target." A revitalized explosives effort could have rekindled the nuclear establishment's morale and repute, but Desai dampened this flame.

The prime minister did little to hide his mistrust of the pro-explosives leadership at BARC. In June 1978, Ramanna was transferred from BARC to New Delhi, where he was named secretary of defense research, scientific adviser to the minister for defense, and director general of the Defence Research and Development Organisation. By then the relationship between Ramanna and AEC Chairman Homi Sethna had become badly strained, in part due to jealousies over credit for the Pokhran blast. Ramanna also complained to friends of ill health and general frustration.[133] His political benefactor, Indira Gandhi, was gone, and Desai's contempt of the explosives program rankled deeply. Ramanna welcomed the temporary escape from the Atomic Energy Commission but moved to New Delhi warily. An able, dynamic, and blunt administrator, he blanched at the Mughal ways of bureaucratic politics in New Delhi.[134] He knew that he could not wield effective power without the rank of government secretary or without the creation of a distinct department of defense research within the Defence Ministry. He won both, despite some bureaucratic opposition.[135] Ramanna managed to streamline programs and tighten the focus of defense research in his new posts. He enjoyed the respect of the armed services in part because, in his words, he had helped develop a "prototype weapon." This reference belied the official claim that the Pokhran device had been entirely peaceful.[136] Whatever his impact on defense research, Ramanna's move to New Delhi enabled Desai and his followers to keep an eye on him and reduce the potency of the nuclear establishment.[137]

In two late-July addresses to the Parliament, Desai rebuffed charges that his no-test position was halting nuclear research. However, in doing so he betrayed some technical confusion, arguing that "blasts" for "purposes of mining or water purposes or oil purposes" could be allowed but that "explosions" like the one at Pokhran were unnecessary and would not be sanctioned as long as he was prime minister.[138] It appeared that Desai had been put somewhat on the defensive by the charge that he was allowing his personal views to undermine the entire peaceful nuclear research program, in which Indian prowess and modernity had been symbolized. So he equivocated awkwardly by distinguishing between "blasts" and "explosions," and by saying that he could not rule out the former in the future.[139] Yet, in his harsh attack on the Pokhran test, Desai suggested that Indian scientists were split. Some wanted explosives for weapons and others did not. He indicated that some were providing him critical information on Pokhran, and this led to the following critique, which so frustrated Ramanna and others:

> It is Pokhran which created all this trouble, and without our gaining anything. If it had gained us something, I would have been very happy. That is why they [the U.S.]

are asking now for safeguards. They believe it is only for weapons and nothing else. . . . I do not believe that Mrs. Gandhi wanted to use it for any weapon purposes, even when she made the explosion. It was made for political purposes, if I may say so, and no other purpose. It did not advance any knowledge. I am getting all that material which is stored in cupboards, signed and sealed. I am trying to go through it and . . . find out what good it has done to us. Nobody knows yet, after all these years.[140]

Five days later, Desai returned to this controversy in a statement to the Rajya Sabha. He emphasized that Pokhran had caused the severe difficulties India now faced in maintaining international cooperation for nuclear research and development.[141] He also noted that "the main countries in which nuclear research is taking place are moving away from" peaceful nuclear explosions.[142] Desai urged the body to see nuclear policy "in the broader perspective of our traditions, our spiritual and moral values and our passion for" peace.[143] Whereas Nehru had seen the nuclear enterprise dualistically—as a vehicle of scientific-technological modernity and as a potential means of defense—Desai evinced a more Gandhian attitude toward technological modernism and nuclear weapons. Nehru had given the nuclear establishment great autonomy; Desai felt that this establishment had abused its autonomy and led India in a mistaken direction.

There is some reason to conclude that Desai was prepared to renounce India's nuclear weapon capabilities by accepting fullscope safeguards had the United States and the Soviet Union been prepared to oblige India's call for an end to the nuclear arms race. The scholar Paul Power reported that Desai told American officials during his June 1978 visit to Washington that he would accept fullscope safeguards when SALT II and a test ban treaty had been signed and military reactors were converted into civilian reactors and opened for inspection.[144] Then-Ambassador Robert Goheen stated in an interview that Desai had intimated similarly to the British high commissioner in New Delhi.[145] An Indian official from this period added in a 1998 interview that Foreign Minister Vajpayee, notwithstanding his leadership of the pro-bomb Jana Sangh, favored signing the NPT if the superpowers were prepared to end the nuclear arms race but that others in the foreign affairs establishment successfully blocked serious consideration of this option.[146] As it turned out, of course, the Soviet Union and the United States did not agree on a test ban treaty, SALT II was not ratified, and the nuclear weapon states still have not committed themselves not to build additional nuclear weapons. For his part, Vajpayee went on to become the prime minister who authorized India's five nuclear weapon tests in May 1998.

Desai's declarations against further nuclear tests neither helped nor hurt him in public opinion. The Indian Institute of Public Opinion aptly summarized public attitudes on nuclear policy at this time:

There is no overwhelming consensus on nuclear policy in Indian public opinion and there is more ambivalence towards nuclear development. The majority of the public categorically reject nuclear weapons but demand nuclear energy for peaceful purposes. They find nuclear explosions more acceptable than the Prime Minister's stand. But they are strongly on his side as far as health hazards and uses of nuclear fuel are concerned. . . . It is only the middle income and education groups who see some benefit in nuclear technology and even they reject the use of nuclear fuel under hazardous conditions in power plants . . . The current ambivalence is the end of nuclear development as an issue of national prestige in all cities except Delhi where it is still a priority. . . . The majority of people under the poverty line see no reason for nuclear development, even for peaceful purposes.[147]

Probing deeper, and with great plausibility, the institute explained the dichotomy between the views of the elite and the masses on the nuclear program: "The reason for this strong reaction by vocal elite groups is not hard to seek. *Ever since Pokharan, nuclear energy has become an issue of national prestige rather than on its merits of defence or efficiency. It has become a symbol of the technology and scientific advance we are seeking and which we believe are capable of achieving.*"[148]

Following the opening of power reactors and the Pokhran test, the nuclear establishment could no longer be judged by its claims and promises. It had to deliver. The deliverables could be measured in electricity output and, perhaps if India's moral self-identity allowed, in nuclear weapons. But here the trouble emerged. The program was patently failing to meet targets in power generation. On the weapon side, word was leaking that Pokhran had not been as great a technological feat as had been advertised, and it had invited international sanctions and discord that undermined the economic benefits of nuclear technology and India's relations with the major powers. A prime minister firmly rooted in the nation's singular moral tradition highlighted both the practical and normative costs of shifting the nuclear enterprise to an avowedly military purpose. These costs overrode the possible military-security arguments that could have been made in favor of building nuclear weapons to counter Pakistan and China. Once again, the ambiguity of the nuclear option best suited India's domestically centered national interest in a world where the major powers would not themselves abandon nuclear weapons.

DEVELOPMENTS IN PAKISTAN AND CHINA, 1978 TO 1979

Throughout 1978, the Janata government, under the guidance of Foreign Minister Vajpayee, continued its vigorous effort to improve relations with China and Pakistan. This effort remained largely disconnected from debate about India's nuclear policy, notwithstanding the growing signs of Pakistan's nuclear weapon ambitions.

Indian and Chinese officials exchanged warm words several times in early 1978, signaling a possible mutual interest in normalizing relations.[149] Neither side ignored the fundamental border dispute. The Indians also expressed concern about Chinese support for secessionist groups in Sikkim and about the two countries' divergent perspectives on Kashmir. Still, both accepted the premise that their differences should be addressed within the context of cooperative engagement, rather than as a precondition for it. Broader concerns also affected their relations: China and the United States were starting to formalize their relations in December 1978, in large part to counter the Soviet Union; Desai's policy of "genuine" nonalignment had signaled a greater balance in India's approach toward the United States and the Soviet Union; China could see the opportunity to attenuate India's ties to Moscow. In this fluid environment, India needed to protect its options to deal with all three more powerful states—the United States, the Soviet Union, and China—without alienating any one of them.

An October 1978 study by the Indian Institute of Public Opinion revealed that 77 percent of those surveyed favored normalization of relations with China.[150] For the first time since 1962, the institute reported, Indians had a favorable image of China. Still, the government could not ignore the border dispute even if the time for "rapprochement has never been more opportune or more propitious," in the words of the institute.[151]

With this background, Foreign Minister Vajpayee visited China in February 1979. Unfortunately, hopes for a breakthrough turned to embarrassed frustration when China invaded Vietnam during Vajpayee's visit. Vajpayee had not been forewarned either by his Chinese hosts or Indian intelligence, leaving him in an extremely awkward position. India had long criticized the U.S. intervention in Vietnam and could only view the Chinese aggression in a harsh light. Worse, as then-U.S. Ambassador Goheen recalled, a high-ranking Chinese official, in denying that his country was invading Vietnam, said it was only teaching the Vietnamese a lesson as it had taught India in 1962.[152] The Indians had seen Vajpayee's mission as a breakthrough foray into China; the Chinese revealed how ancillary India was to their interests. Clearly, India's hopes that China might want to address the border dispute had been illusory. Normalization would have to wait.

Still, the Desai government tried to maintain balance in India's foreign relations. When Soviet Prime Minister Alexei Kosygin visited New Delhi in March 1979 to pull India away from rapprochement with China, Desai rebuffed his pleas to dub China's intervention in Vietnam as an "aggression." Desai told Kosygin, "We stand for strong actions and not for strong words."[153] India did not want to foreclose its options toward China.

By 1979 Pakistan loomed as the most real threat to India. The Janata government continued to pursue progress in normalizing relations with Pakistan, but signs of an imminent Pakistani nuclear threat were unmistakable. In March, American intelligence notified Congress that Pakistan was commissioning the Kahuta centrifuge plant and was well on the road to producing bomb-grade uranium. On April 6, two days after the military regime hanged Zulfikar Ali Bhutto, Washington invoked the Symington Amendment and cut off military and economic aid to Pakistan on nonproliferation grounds. The implications registered loudly in India, where the press trumpeted the threat of the "Islamic Bomb."[154] If Pakistan's backer, the United States, could no longer ignore the nuclear danger to

India's west, Indian leaders must act. Facing estimates that Pakistan could explode a nuclear device by 1982, the Indian government was pressed to reinvigorate its own nuclear explosive program.[155] Soon, Morarji Desai would not be there to block it.

INDIA'S COALITION GOVERNMENT COLLAPSES, 1979

By early 1979, the Janata government had become fatally fractious. It had not met the population's post-Emergency expectations in terms of redressing unemployment and poverty and stimulating industrial growth. The Janata had satisfied the electorate's main political concern of 1977—restoration of democracy and domestic rights—but the transition from opposition to government had revealed major schisms. Acting from selfish motivations and competing ideologies, individuals and factions in the Janata group began to undermine each other. Meanwhile, social divisions widened. Rioting increased between Hindus and Muslims; high-caste Hindus attacked untouchables; labor became restless. The political elite in New Delhi was too busy jostling for advantage to lead the nation. Indira Gandhi, who had been expelled from the Parliament in December 1978, stood larger and larger offstage.

Foreign and defense policy remained ancillary issues. India was relying more and more on the Soviet Union for supplies of major conventional weapon systems that Indian forces required for modernization. Yet no systematic, strategic review occurred during the late 1970s. Parliament remained disengaged from defense policy, while the government allowed the military to seek largely symbolic weapons systems from abroad without the benefit of a coherent strategy.[156] Only the Tarapur dispute aroused much public passion in foreign policy. The nuclear establishment, the press, and swelling numbers of parliamentarians urged Desai to take a tougher line against American and other states' efforts to impose additional safeguards on India.

Against this background, Foreign Minister Vajpayee visited Washington in April 1979, holding a series of meetings with top-ranking American officials, including President Carter. (On March 23, the Nuclear Regulatory Commission had voted 3 to 2 to approve another license for Tarapur fuel, which had been held up since November 1977.) Vajpayee pressed the United States to do more to stop Pakistan's acquisition of nuclear weapon capability. He told Indian reporters that American officials estimated that Pakistan could produce a nuclear explosion in two to three years but that he believed that it could occur sooner.[157] Vajpayee contrasted Washington's unrelenting pressure on India regarding safeguards with what he perceived to be a relatively lax approach toward Pakistan.[158]

Time was running out for Jimmy Carter and Morarji Desai to lead the United States and India to an accommodation on nuclear policy. Both leaders were animated by moral principles and desired genuinely to rid the world of nuclear weapons. Both evinced willingness to exercise leadership within their countries to this end. Yet, as long as India insisted on major progress in nuclear disarmament to redress the discriminatory nature of the nonproliferation regime, both were hostage to the arms control negotiations between Washington and Moscow and the broader dynamic of the cold war nuclear arms race. American and Soviet negotiators were making progress in talks on the SALT II treaty to control strategic arms, but negotiations on a test ban treaty were deadlocked. Carter publicly lamented that his efforts in these negotiations had not "been adequate to encourage other countries like India," and he said that he found it "a little bit difficult" to press Desai when "we ourselves have not yet restrained the spread of nuclear weapons."[159]

In an attempt to bridge their nuclear differences, the two countries had agreed in December 1978 to establish an ad hoc Scientific Advisory Committee to examine alternative approaches to safeguards and determine whether IAEA safeguards impair the progress of nuclear energy programs.[160] This body was to comprise an Indian, an American, and two third-party scientists and was to be headed by the chairman of the IAEA. The initiative represented a quixotic hope that a more neutral expert body could solve a problem over which Washington and New Delhi were deadlocked. Within months it foundered over disagreements regarding the committee's writ to examine broader issues of proliferation and safeguards on nuclear weapon states that were anathema to the United States.[161]

In India, the dispute over safeguards symbolized resistance to American imperial power more than determination to manufacture nuclear weapons or test again. On the fifth anniversary of the Pokhran blast, *India Today* published a telling pictorial commemoration of the event. Adjacent to pictures of the blast crater, ruins of a village (Malka) evacuated before the test, and the village of Loharki, the magazine printed a caption including the following wry passage:

> [I]f the crater-like site of the atomic explosion offers an example of India's technological progress, just four kilometres away lies another, equally appropriate example of the other side of India. It is the village of Loharki, where, like in many of India's 500,000 villages, progress has only shown itself in the draft plans of the economic planners. . . . The village has no water system, neither does it have electricity. In the summer two wells . . . fail to provide sufficient water to the village's 1,500 population. Farming—primarily of maize—keeps the inhabitants occupied for just about four months in a year and for the rest of the time everyone is virtually unemployed.[162]

Irony is an easy journalistic mark in a poor country like India, but the dichotomy portrayed in the pictorial represented an important political-economic truth that could not be ignored. Nuclear explosives—peaceful or military—could not address the greatest challenges confronting India.

In late July, internecine political conflict finally drove eighty-three-year-old Morarji Desai from power. Leaders of numerous political factions now engaged in a free-for-all to supplant him. The ephemeral winner was Charan Singh, a bitter, seventy-seven-year-old Desai rival who headed a party centered on well-off peasants and who was backed cynically by Indira Gandhi. Singh offered little hope of putting India on a positive course. In the words of *India Today*, "Obstinancy, self-righteousness, dogmatism and ruthlessness have been the most prominent characteristics of his mental make-up."[163]

Singh had no experience or interest in foreign affairs or nuclear matters. The government he formed leaned leftward. In foreign policy this inclined it against the Desai-Vajpayee policy of improving India's relations with the West and China to balance ties with the Soviet Union. In security policy, the new government saw connections between domestic and foreign challenges. "[T]he concept of national defence must be much wider than the mere protection of the country's territorial integrity and sovereignty from perceptible military threats," Minister for Defence C. Subramaniam declared in October 1979. "What needs to be shielded equally is the whole spectrum of India's political, social, economic and technological progress from pressures arising out of the play of international forces."[164] This traditional inward-looking approach to security, when paired with Prime Minister Singh's bias against large-scale industrial enterprises, made Singh an unlikely champion of the modernization and international ambition represented by the nuclear establishment.

Still, given the ongoing signs of Pakistan's nuclear weapon effort, Singh was compelled to pronounce on India's nuclear policy. Within days of his ascension, a report emerged that he intended to "keep nuclear options open."[165] Although vague, the report suggested that the new government's overall repudiation of Desai's leadership might extend to his nuclear policies. The nuclear establishment and its political supporters doubtless sought to free the nuclear program from the constraints imposed by Desai. The prospect of such a change was suggested by Singh's Independence Day address on August 15, when he declared that India had not wanted to use nuclear energy for military purposes, "but we might have to reconsider our earlier decision if Pakistan goes ahead with the atom bomb."[166] The gist and tone of this statement differed from Desai's, but the meaning remained unclear. A day later, "government circles" sought to clarify it by saying, according to the *Statesman*, it was "not a deviation from India's stand." According to government sources, the prime minister "was speaking hypothetically and did not mean to doubt Pakistan's assurances that it would not make the bomb."[167]

As 1979 wound down, it became apparent that the Singh government could not last and elections would be called. On August 22, the president dissolved Parliament and elections were called for January 1980. Charan Singh continued as caretaker prime minister. Meanwhile, the clock ticked on the NNPA's requirement that nuclear cooperation be cut off by March 10, 1980, if fullscope safeguards were not agreed to. Singh's weak position precluded serious discussions with the United States on nuclear issues.[168] Looking toward the formation of a new government after January elections, Ambassador Goheen wrote a letter to key American senators reporting that "there has already been a distinct deterioration in the relationship between India and the United States over the past six months or so. It is only partially accounted for by Morarji's departure from the scene. Much of the cooling . . . springs from our protracted inability (unwillingness) to clear the pending licenses for Tarapur."[169] Goheen indicated that the Tarapur dispute animated pro-bomb circles in India to press for "the reestablishment of an explosives capability." The ambassador noted that the pro-bomb group "is still very much a minority. None of the major political leaders is advocating that India go for the bomb." Yet, he argued, cutting off nuclear cooperation would only strengthen Soviet influence in India when instability was mounting to India's west—in Afghanistan and Iran. The United States, he urged, should seek a stronger relationship with "this largest, most stable, and most genuinely secular of the region's states."

SOVIETS INVADE AFGHANISTAN AND THE NONPROLIFERATION DYNAMIC CHANGES, 1979

On December 25, 1979, Soviet forces entered Afghanistan, arriving in Kabul on December 27, where they anchored the Soviet occupation of the tormented country.[170] The invasion capped a brutal political struggle among communists and other factions that had roiled the country since April 1978. The ensuing war exacted an extremely heavy toll on Afghanistan, the Soviet Union, Pakistan, and, indirectly, the United States (in the form of terrorism, global weapons proliferation, and drug trafficking). The Soviet invasion also ended the superpower détente, which had been in effect since the 1970s, and with it the prospects of significant nuclear disarmament. All of this had major implications for India and for the U.S. role in dealing with nuclear proliferation in South Asia.

India's principal hope to stop the Pakistani nuclear program rested with Washington. The United States was Pakistan's major arms supplier and benefactor; leverage inhered in this relationship. Now, however, Washington's interest in pressuring Pakistan to stop its nuclear program would be compromised by the greater geopolitical determination to drive the Soviets from Afghanistan. Pakistan would be the base and conduit through which Washington would mobilize against the Soviets. Rather than alienating Pakistan by clamping down on its nuclear program, the United States appeared likely to strengthen Pakistan's conventional military strength.

The United States wasted no time in signaling its new priorities. On January 3, less than two months after a Pakistani mob had burned the U.S. Embassy in Islamabad, the Carter administration lifted the sanctions that had been imposed on Pakistan in 1979 pursuant to the Symington Amendment. For the next ten years the United States would refrain from exerting more than moderate diplomatic pressure on the Pakistani nuclear effort, eschewing the kinds of sanctions that India and nonproliferation activists in the United States favored. Instead, Washington sought to lure Pakistan away from nuclear weapons by supplying billions of dollars of conventional weaponry.

India's initial reaction to the Soviet invasion also followed a geopolitical logic. Indira Gandhi had swept back into power in the January 1980 elections (discussed later in the chapter), and she authorized only a tepid comment on the Soviet aggression. The Indian UN representative declared that Soviet forces had been invited by the Afghan government and that India had "no reason to doubt assurances . . . [by the Soviets] that they would withdraw when requested to do so by the Afghan Government."[171] Mrs. Gandhi, unlike Desai, favored a tilt toward the trustworthy Soviet Union as a means of balancing American and Chinese influence.[172] This infuriated American officials. In the face of American protests and disgruntlement among the nonaligned, Mrs. Gandhi soon realized that India must take a stronger stand. On January 18, following a meeting with British Foreign Secretary Lord Carrington, she declared that no country "is justified in entering another country."[173]

Clearly India was caught between a hard place and many rocks. The government did not want to alienate its major international backer—the Soviet Union—but it also could not afford to anger the United States. Nor did India want to jettison prospects of improving relations with Pakistan, or worse, allow Pakistan to use the Afghan crisis as a way of increasing threats toward India.[174] India feared that the United States or China, or both, would now be induced to dramatically step up the arming of Pakistan. And indeed, countering Soviet influence in Central and South Asia may have been an underappreciated reason for China's subsequent assistance to Pakistan's nuclear and missile programs. To head off the possibility of a Chinese-Pakistani-American axis, India would have to maintain as much goodwill as possible in Washington, while not allowing antagonism with China over its incursion into Vietnam to worsen. The challenge was daunting.

General Zia remained determined to acquire nuclear weapon capability. Indeed, in an interview with *India Today,* he revealed how this was proceeding: "We have no intentions of carrying out anything which can be controversial at present. We are only trying to acquire technology. It takes particularly long when you have to acquire this technology through backdoor, clandestine methods."[175] The developments in Pakistan made the self-restraint India subsequently showed in eschewing nuclear explosive testing and production more remarkable.

INDIRA GANDHI RETURNS TO POWER, 1980

A week after the Soviet Union invaded Afghanistan, the electoral polls opened in India. Indira Gandhi won a huge victory, with her Congress party taking 350 of 542 Lok Sabha seats. Her primary rivals—the Janata, now led by Jagjivan Ram, and the Lok Dal, headed by Charan Singh—fared miserably. The two Communist parties combined represented the most potent opposition.

Like the 1977 election, this one was essentially a referendum. Only now the object of public dissatisfaction was not Indira Gandhi but the Janata. As Gandhi put it to Tariq Ali: "They had their chance and what did they do? They made a big mess. The people voted us back into power with a big majority."[176] To the extent that the election revolved around issues, the primary concerns were law and order, "galloping inflation," and caste and communal conflict.[177]

Indira Gandhi had tried to make foreign policy a greater issue in this election than it ever had been. She attacked the Janata government for weakening India's traditional policy of nonalignment by drawing closer to the United States and for "appeasing" India's small neighbors.[178] However, Mrs. Gandhi's critique of Janata foreign policy appeared to have little impact on voters. "A majority of the people do not accept the view that there has, indeed, been a change after Indira Gandhi's return to power," concluded the Indian Institute of Public Opinion.[179]

Nuclear policy was not a salient issue. In the election manifestos, only three of the major parties took positions on whether India should build nuclear weapons. The Janata and Indira Gandhi's Congress party "strongly opposed" doing so, while Charan Singh's Lok Dal "totally supported" going for nuclear weapons. The other major Congress party—Congress (U)—and the two Communist parties took no positions on the nuclear issue.[180] The press and subsequent secondary treatments did not address nuclear policy in their analyses of the election.

However, the government still had to preside over the nuclear establishment, and the establishment was suffering. In the first postelection meeting of the Congress (I) Working Committee, the prime minister was asked, "If Pakistan can produce enriched uranium in two years starting from scratch, why can't our scientists do the same for Tarapur?" According to *India Today*, "Mrs. Gandhi merely smiled and scribbled a large question mark on her pad."[181] The Department of Atomic Energy—in its civilian and potential military work—appeared to be foundering. "[T]here is a great deal of resentment among scientists . . . and also among laymen, including politicians, about the lackadaisical manner in which it has been functioning for the last few years," *India Today* reported.[182] Heavy-water plants remained at least five years behind schedule, while construction of the Madras I and II reactors at Kalpakkam and the Narora I and II reactors in Uttar Pradesh also lagged badly.[183] On March 14, the Tarapur II reactor experienced a significant accident in which radioactive water gushed through a coolant line and flooded the reactor building.[184] The accident occurred just days after Homi Sethna had assured the public that the reactor was completely safe.

In terms of public perception and bureaucratic interests, prowess in one element of the nuclear program—be it reactors, heavy-water plants, or nuclear explosives—could reinvigorate the standing of the whole enterprise. However, since Pokhran, few such manifestations had occurred.[185] As *India Today* lamented, "The saddest part of the department's poor performance is that it has everything going for it in terms of political support and comparative economic advantages. The department is still the country's major showpiece and is able to obtain whatever funds it needs." However, the magazine continued, the department "is rather secretive about its activities and the umbrella under which it operates often hides more than it protects."[186]

The perceived deterioration of the nuclear complex, combined with the growing Pakistani nuclear threat, made it possible that Mrs. Gandhi would turn to nuclear explosives to demonstrate Indian robustness. On March 13, in the Rajya Sabha, she "ended the confusion about India's stand on peaceful nuclear tests, saying there would be no hesitation in conducting these in the national interest," according to the *Times of India*.[187] "We should not be caught napping," the prime minister insisted. In reopening the issue of nuclear explosions, Mrs. Gandhi derisively reviewed the policies of Morarji Desai.[188] She asserted, plausibly, that Desai had not consulted the nuclear establishment in deciding to preclude peaceful nuclear explosions. By implication she signaled that she would now ensure that the establishment's views and needs would be heeded.[189]

In revisiting the nuclear explosive option, Gandhi appeared to reverse Desai's position. In fact, she merely neutralized it. She did not say India *would* conduct nuclear explosions, only that it would not rule them out. This brought the policy back to its pre-Pokhran status. India possessed the capacity to produce and detonate nuclear explosives and would augment that capacity without declaring if and when it would exercise the option to deploy nuclear weapons. In declaratory terms, India continued to eschew nuclear weapons and urged the rest of the world to follow suit.

CONCLUSION

The central question of the period from 1975 to 1980 was whether India would follow the Pokhran explosion with other tests and the development of nuclear weapons. Remarkably, it did not. Several factors explain this self-restraint. From 1975 to 1977, Indira Gandhi concentrated on enormous political problems to which the nuclear program offered no solutions. Leaders of the nuclear establishment clearly wanted to proceed with follow-up tests, but the prime minister held decisive power. The scientists did not organize effective coalitions with the military or others to press the issue. In any case, it appeared that Mrs. Gandhi had second thoughts about the wisdom of the Pokhran experiment. She was discomfited by the departure from the morally inspired policy of rejecting nuclear weapons declared by her father and she was dismayed by the unexpected international pressures applied to India's political economy. In short, domestic considerations outweighed any putative international security benefits of nuclear weapons during the Emergency.

Morarji Desai intensified the principled aversion to nuclear weapons. Even though Desai was politically weak and presiding over a cabinet that included central figures of the pro-bomb Jana Sangh, the prime minister remained effectively unchallenged on nuclear policy. Desai's personal contempt for nuclear weapons was greater than that of the populace, but his Gandhian principles resonated with the political culture. Indian political culture was split—a moral desire to forego nuclear weapons was balanced by an openness to steps necessary to ensure the nation's security. It remained for the prime minister and his political colleagues and competitors to set the nation's course. If the leadership chose to pursue a more militarily robust line, the case could have been made. Once again, however, the balance of considerations determining India's national interest weighed more heavily against nuclear weapons.

More than any of his predecessors Desai doubted the nuclear establishment's designs. The establishment's failure to meet optimistic projections in building and operating nuclear facilities undermined its capacity to win political support. The traditional desire to keep the military from the center of national policymaking weakened the nuclear establishment's prospects, too. Civilian leaders recognized that the military necessarily would assume a major policymaking role if a nuclear arsenal were constructed and deployed. The exigencies of preparing for the conduct of nuclear war would demand the establishment of nuclear doctrines and command and control procedures that would follow operational requirements determined by military professionals. Desai, like his predecessors, wanted to avoid this. In this matter the prime minister was joined paradoxically by the nuclear scientists, who, despite their frustration over the government's reluctance to authorize further nuclear explosions, did not want to relinquish the paramount influence they had exercised over Indian policy. Even if the quiescent military could have been rallied to press for nuclear weapons, it is doubtful that Desai would have assented.

Lastly, American diplomacy in this period contributed significantly to India's self-restraint. Henry Kissinger's determination not to press India on further nuclear tests, but rather to offer a quiet dialogue on nuclear policy, gave Indira Gandhi room to wait. When the U.S. Congress stepped heavily onto the field in 1977 and 1978 with the passage of the proscriptive NNPA, it raised the potential costs of further weapon development at a time when India's nuclear power program could not afford to foreclose future assistance. Additional nuclear tests and development of weapons would have stymied the operation and expansion of the nuclear industry. While international pressure stimulated anticolonial impulses of defiance, this was mitigated by the arrival of Jimmy Carter. Carter's genuine care for India and aversion to nuclear weapons engendered goodwill, especially on the part of Morarji Desai. The Carter administration's effort to forestall a congressionally mandated rupture of nuclear cooperation gave India incentives not to take steps such as further nuclear tests, which would have ended all hope for this cooperation.

Still, by 1980, India's patience was wearing thin, and the likely provision of massive American military aid to Pakistan eroded the goodwill that remained. Pressures mounted on the new Indira Gandhi government to prepare countermeasures to Pakistan's growing nuclear threat.

NINE

More Robust Nuclear Policy Is Considered

1980–1984

From 1980 to 1984, India explored three principal alternatives to strengthen its security against the growing Pakistani nuclear threat. The first was to increase and demonstrate India's own nuclear strength. This included preparations to conduct another nuclear explosive test and, beginning in 1983, the development of missiles that could conceivably carry nuclear warheads. The second option was to attack key nuclear facilities in Pakistan. The third alternative was to use diplomacy to stabilize relations with Pakistan and improve India's ties with the United States. As this chapter describes, Indian decision makers contemplated and undertook steps consistent with each option without fully committing to any one of them. Most intriguing from the standpoint of nuclear policy, Indira Gandhi in late 1982 or early 1983 did tentatively authorize another nuclear explosion, but she changed her mind within twenty-four hours.

India's effort to deal with the emerging nuclear threat from Pakistan occurred against the backdrop of ongoing negotiations with the United States over fuel supplies for Tarapur. The Reagan administration came to office in January 1981 with a less activist approach to nonproliferation than the Carter administration. Ronald Reagan's determination to drive the Soviet Union from Afghanistan placed a premium on close ties with Pakistan, but the administration by 1982 had also recognized that geostrategic interests required a balanced approach to India. As Washington sought to improve ties with India and Pakistan, it tempered nonproliferation policy in the region, albeit in a way that ultimately exacerbated India's sense of threat from Pakistan.

By the time Indira Gandhi was assassinated in 1984, a temporary solution to the Tarapur dispute had been found and India had once again refrained from conducting another nuclear explosion. Instead of taking any decisive and risky measure to redress militarily the Pakistani threat, India pursued cautious diplomacy and concentrated on challenges to internal order, particularly in Punjab. This chapter chronicles how India decided to maintain its self-restraint in the face of external circumstances that according to Realist models should have led to militarization of the nuclear program.

DYNAMICS OF NUCLEAR POLICY CHANGE, 1980 TO 1981

In the beginning of her second tenure as Prime Minister, Indira Gandhi declared that she would not forswear further peaceful nuclear explosions.[1] Yet, as she kept the testing option open, Gandhi also invoked her father's and India's disavowal of nuclear weapons. In a published letter to a Hiroshima survivor, she recalled that on the day "the bomb was dropped over Hiroshima, my father, Jawaharlal Nehru, called it the 'death-dealer' and since then, we have stood for complete disarmament." She insisted that the 1974 PNE had been for peaceful purposes and that "India does not possess nuclear weapons and has no intention of developing or producing them."[2] This statement could have been pure propaganda, but Indira Gandhi's actions since 1974 suggested that it reflected her genuine desire.

Still, Mrs. Gandhi was the leader of a country now facing a clearly emerging nuclear threat from its erstwhile adversary. Pakistan's conventional military capability was also about to be augmented by the United States. So India in 1980 undertook plans to increase spending on and imports of advanced weapon systems in order to modernize forces that had gone without significant upgrading in the 1970s. In May 1980, Mrs. Gandhi completed a $1.63 billion arms supply deal with the Soviet Union, featuring the purchase of T-72 tanks and MiG-25 Foxbat aircraft.[3] In April 1981, reports emerged that the United States and Pakistan were preparing an agreement for the supply of $2.5 billion in military and economic aid to Pakistan over five years.[4] This amount was raised to $3.2 billion and the deal finalized in July. It included provision of forty F-16 fighters, the most advanced aircraft the United States had. The F-16s would constitute a major qualitative increase in Pakistan's capacity to threaten targets in India. India was not mollified when American officials argued that the supply of conventional weapons would reduce Pakistan's motivation to acquire nuclear arms.[5] In an August press conference, Indira Gandhi hinted at government plans to undertake a major defense spending program.[6]

India also moved in early 1981 to upgrade its nuclear weapon potential. According to U.S. intelligence sources, excavations began in February for a possible nuclear explosive test at the Pokhran site. These preparations became public in April when U.S. Senator Alan Cranston declared that executive branch sources had detected drilling for nuclear test shafts in both Pakistan and India.[7] Cranston reported that Pakistan was building a horizontal tunnel into a mountain in Baluchistan, forty miles from the Afghan border. The allegation of Indian preparations in the Rajasthan desert was confirmed plausibly by an Indian journalist who visited the area and filed a report in a May 1981 issue of the *Indian Express*.[8] When asked about these reports, Atomic Energy Commission Chairman Homi Sethna declined to comment. However, Sethna did say that a Pakistani nuclear explosion could come "any time from June onwards. Maybe this year or next year."[9] This overestimated Pakistan's preparations: the Pakistani nuclear establishment apparently had yet to complete the facilities that would be utilized to make the conventional high-explosive components of a nuclear bomb, and the Kahuta enrichment plant had yet to produce sufficient quantities of highly enriched uranium. This overestimation was strange coming from Sethna: in private he disparagingly dismissed Pakistan's capacity to develop nuclear weapons. The chairman seemed to be taking an opportunity to hint that India's Atomic Energy Commission must be prepared to respond in kind if Pakistan did test.

Evidently the nuclear establishment was being freed from the shackles in which Morarji Desai had placed it. In January 1981, a month before U.S. intelligence detected drilling activity at the Rajasthan test site, the government announced that Raja Ramanna would resume his post as director of the Bhabha Atomic Research Centre, with the additional power of being a secretary to the Department of Atomic Energy.[10] Ramanna was eager to return to Trombay to boost the nuclear program now that Mrs. Gandhi was back in power. The prime minister, according to Ramanna, saw his return as a means both to strengthen BARC and to remind a domestic audience that Desai had neglected the well-being of the nuclear establishment.[11]

Given Ramanna's role overseeing the 1974 PNE, it is reasonable to conclude that he wished to revive the nuclear explosive enterprise and that the prime minister anticipated this. Ramanna publicly stated that his priorities were to reinvigorate the nuclear energy program, complete the stalled Dhruva (R-5) research (and plutonium production) reactor at Trombay, and push forward the Fast Breeder Test Reactor at Kalpakkam.[12] In addition, he continued to support the efforts at BARC and the relevant Defence Research and Development Organisation laboratories to design a smaller, more efficient nuclear explosive device. Throughout 1981, Ramanna retained responsibilities as scientific adviser to the defense minister in New Delhi along with his resumed position at BARC. Ramanna's relationship with AEC Chairman Homi Sethna remained tense. After Ramanna had been called to New Delhi in 1978, Sethna tried to fill the BARC director's post with a permanent replacement, but Ramanna's allies blocked this move, ensuring that he could return to BARC.[13] Mrs. Gandhi's sending him back with the additional title of government secretary indicated that authority was shifting to Ramanna and that he would succeed Sethna.

In August 1981, further indication of a revived nuclear explosive program appeared when a respected Bombay journalist, Yogi Aggarwal, reported that "from the end of 1980 onwards, work on the development of components needed for another nuclear device was once again stepped up at the BARC."[14] Aggarwal's unusually detailed article reported that in March and April a team at BARC had prepared twelve kilograms of plutonium metal for machining into an explosive core.[15] Additional weapon-grade plutonium from CIRUS spent fuel had been reprocessed at the unsafeguarded Tarapur reprocessing plant, which began test operations in 1977, according to Aggarwal. This plutonium was slated for use in research reactors and apparently was incorporated into fuel for the then-under-construction Fast Breeder Test Reactor after France withdrew an earlier commitment to supply highly enriched uranium fuel. But the plutonium "could easily be diverted for weapons use as was done in March and April this year," said Aggarwal.[16] Aggarwal also reported that an "orchestrated campaign was being mounted through influential sections of the Indian press to go in for a nuclear weapons programme."[17]

India appeared to be following a two-track strategy. To strengthen its capabilities, it was preparing the test site in case Pakistan detonated a nuclear explosive, which India would then counter with a blast of its own. To show its moderate intentions, India's Ministry of External Affairs Secretary Eric Gonsalves in April 1981 privately told U.S. Assistant Secretary of State James Malone that India would not move "towards PNE activity" in the "current time-frame." However, he could not rule out a test over the longer term.[18]

India's test preparations paralleled growing elite and public concerns that the nation must counter Pakistan's looming nuclear capability. Indian commentators, like many in America, assumed that Pakistan would detonate a nuclear device once it was able to do so and that India would have to respond. In 1981, as in 1970, the most sophisticated proponent of India's "going nuclear" was K. Subrahmanyam, director of the Institute for Defence Studies and Analyses. Writing in the *Times of India* Sunday Supplement on April 26, Subrahmanyam lamented India's lack of a nuclear arsenal and, worse, the absence of serious planning for one. "There is no evidence of the Indian armed forces having a doctrine for the use of nuclear weapons," he warned.[19] Nor did India's largely civilian nuclear infrastructure provide enough weapon-desirable plutonium to enable India to stay ahead of Pakistan's dedicated nuclear weapon program. Positing that "a nuclear weapon can be deterred only by a nuclear weapon," Subrahmanyam argued that the only way "in which India can keep its options open" is "to exercise the nuclear option."[20] Building a nuclear arsenal also would force the United States to revise its "contemptuous" view of India "as a country with no will to power," and it "would enable us to deal with China on an equal basis."[21] Subrahmanyam recognized that he was making his political and strategic arguments in a political culture inspired by Mahatma Gandhi, so he devoted his closing paragraphs to interpretative quotations from Gandhi. He suggested that Gandhi advised that India must not be helpless but rather "conscious of her strength and power."[22] "No doubt Gandhiji expressed himself against the bomb," Subrahmanyam acknowledged, "but that was long before nuclear weapons became the legitimate international currency of power."[23] This remarkable essay wove the various strands of Indian insecurity, technological pride, anticolonialism, national ambition, and Gandhian morality into a tight argument for countering Pakistan in ways that India had not countered China after 1964.

Often a lone voice, Subrahmanyam now found a chorus of opinion shapers behind him. Major newspapers printed editorials and columns arguing that India had little choice but to end its renunciation of nuclear weapons.[24] Opposition leaders complained that the government was hyping the threat of war with Pakistan to divert public attention from domestic political strife, unemployment, and inflation, but these criticisms did not challenge the seriousness of the growing nuclear danger.[25] Most of the discussion in Parliament and the press remained superficial but leaned toward a more robust policy. Strangely, neither Parliament nor the press probed the earlier reports that the Atomic Energy Commission was preparing the Rajasthan test site.

In July, the Indian Institute of Public Opinion reported that nearly 70 percent of survey respondents wanted "India to manufacture a nuclear bomb," while only 19 percent opposed the proposition.[26] This represented the most support for manufacturing nuclear weapons since the institute began publishing surveys in the 1960s. "The Indian people in their preoccupation with national security . . . seem to be getting desperate," the institute reported. "The U.S. decision to rearm Pakistan with sophisticated weaponry seems to have convinced a large segment of the Indian people that exercising India's nuclear option alone would enable it to meet the challenge posed by the perceived change in the strategic balance," the institute concluded.[27] It remained to be seen whether the public's urge to find security in nuclear weaponry could or would be translated into political pressure on the government, but the avenue leading to the bomb was open once again if the government wanted to take it.

Army strategists were not immune to the growing interest in nuclear weapons. In early 1981, the commandant of the Army's College of Combat, Lieutenant General K. Sundarji, commissioned several dozen essays on the effects of nuclear weaponry on strategy and military operations in an environment where Pakistan and China possessed nuclear weapons.[28] Sundarji, a bright, cocksure character, would rise through the ranks to become chief of army staff in 1986. Now he emerged as an energetic champion of India's acquisition of nuclear forces. However, he and his colleagues couched the case for nuclear weapons carefully, mindful of official policy. In a largely academic presentation, they argued that an adversary possessing nuclear capabilities could threaten the concentration of conventional forces on which India's (and Pakistan's) military strategy traditionally rested. The countermeasure of dispersing forces with greater reliance on maneuverability would require greater resources than India could deploy in the near future. This implied that India would need nuclear weapons to deter attack on massed armored forces.[29]

For their part, Indian naval officers pointed to the U.S. naval presence in the Indian Ocean as cause for more robust policies. At a New Delhi symposium, the vice chief of naval staff, Vice Admiral M. R. Schunker, noted that the U.S. presence was geared primarily toward the Soviet Union, but he averred that "the memory of 'Exercise Enterprise, 1971' should alert us to the danger that super-power nuclear threats are not necessarily confined to mutual deterrent postures: that in certain situations, that threat can be directed against us also."[30] Still, Sundarji and his colleagues refrained from making a clear case for deploying nuclear weapons. They recognized that an open call for the bomb could engender controversy in a polity where the military was expected to defer to civilian leadership in the nuclear realm.

Despite the military's having expressed concern over the growing Pakistani nuclear threat, conventional force modernization received greater attention. From fiscal year 1981–1982 to 1986–1987 spending on Indian defense, excluding pensions, grew by 142 percent, 82 percent when accounting for inflation.[31] Yet this rapid increase went largely to major new weapons procurements that were not guided by a clear or efficient strategy. Purchases of a second aircraft carrier and forty exorbitantly expensive French Mirage 2000 fighters no doubt added to India's defense capability, but beyond their value as symbols of state-of-the-art weaponry, they did not represent a coherent, efficient defense strategy.[32] If the Indian government and military services were unable to develop a sound, integrated conventional military strategy, they were even less likely to collaborate in the creation of a nuclear weapon doctrine and program envisioned by the likes of Sundarji. From the military leadership's perspective, the problem stemmed from the absence of a national security policymaking apparatus that allowed the military a significant role in formulating strategy.[33]

Meanwhile, Indian diplomats continued to try to stabilize relations with Pakistan. In April 1980, Indira Gandhi had sent a special envoy to Pakistan to assess President Zia's intentions toward India and to convey her desire for improved relations. Then she herself met with Zia in what is now Harare, Zimbabwe. Zia responded in July by sending his top foreign affairs adviser, Agha Shahi, to India. This initial round of visits did little to transcend mutual acrimony, but by 1981 matters began to improve. In June, Indian Foreign Minister Narasimha Rao traveled to Pakistan. Rao downplayed concerns over nuclear issues and helped both sides produce a joint press statement reiterating "their policy of using nuclear energy only for peaceful purposes."[34] Other positive developments followed, including invitations for cultural figures to visit each other's country and a revival of competition between Indian and Pakistan cricket and field hockey teams.[35] In September, Pakistan announced its readiness to consult immediately with India "for the purposes of exchanging mutual guarantees of non-aggression and non-use of force."[36] India responded with warm caution, and following a series of diplomatic exchanges, Indira Gandhi proposed in February 1982 that the two countries sign a treaty of friendship and cooperation.[37] India and Pakistan then announced that their representatives would meet in Islamabad by the end of February to continue discussions on some form of agreement of nonaggression and friendship.

India also sought improved relations with China. In response to a Chinese missile test in June 1980, the Ministry of External Affairs declared that no "fresh threat" was posed to India.[38] The two nations held several meetings in 1981, culminating in a five-day December session in Beijing, where each side constructively probed the other's positions. Indian commentators noted calmly that neither side was eager to tackle the core territorial dispute and that India needed to proceed carefully so as not to alienate the Soviet Union or give impetus to China's relations with Pakistan.[39] China preferred to put off the border dispute while trying to advance relations on other fronts; India agreed to begin a process of discussions that would address simpler issues as a means to facilitate eventual progress on the seminal border dispute. Whatever their modest ambition and achievement, the constructive character of the talks with China signified progress.[40]

In September 1981, notwithstanding diplomatic progress, Indira Gandhi opened the door rhetorically to renewed nuclear testing. In an interview with an Australian journalist she said, "If you think just because Pakistan has done something (a nuclear explosion), we are going to rush into something; well, no. But we have said earlier that if we think it is in the interest of our science or development to have a peaceful nuclear explosion, we may have it."[41] The Desai policy of adamant aversion to nuclear explosives had been "corrected."[42] Even though Indira Gandhi continued to deny a desire to manufacture nuclear weapons and disavowed "belief in the deterrent theory," she had hedged her position on further nuclear explosions.[43]

THE REAGAN ADMINISTRATION, TARAPUR, AND NUCLEAR POWER, 1981 TO 1982

Washington's move to supply Pakistan with advanced weaponry heightened Indian concerns that the military-led Pakistani government could become more aggressive and that the United States would do little to stop Pakistan's nuclear program. Yet Indian advocates of acquiring nuclear weapons would have pressed their case regardless of U.S. policy. Aside from nuclear weapon issues, the most important questions raised by the inauguration of the Reagan administration in January 1981 concerned Washington's overall attitude toward India, the evolution of the cold war, conventional military aid to Pakistan, and the Tarapur dispute.

Ronald Reagan and his foreign policy team arrived in Washington with little interest in India, except as it related to the cold war contest with the Soviet Union.[44] The new administration at first saw India as a Soviet tool and was disinclined to care much for India's concerns over the arming of Pakistan. While the administration took a much less activist approach to nonproliferation than had the Carter administration, this offered little solace to India insofar as it meant Washington was less likely to pressure Pakistan to abandon its bomb program. Indeed, top Reagan administration officials were generally inclined not to hold aid to Pakistan hostage to nonproliferation considerations.[45] The Reagan administration's critical view of the World Bank and the International Monetary Fund also boded ill for India, which was increasingly dependent on these institutions.[46]

The Reagan administration's first interactions with India were acrimonious, beginning with the July agreement to provide Pakistan with $3.2 billion in arms and economic aid, including F-16s. When the U.S. ambassador to the United Nations, Jeane Kirkpatrick, visited New Delhi in August, Indira Gandhi publicly disagreed with Kirkpatrick's argument that the arms aid posed no threat to India.[47] Later in 1981, U.S. officials voiced disapproval of an Indian application for a $5.8 billion IMF loan. This upset the Indians, as National Security Adviser Robert "Bud" McFarlane discovered when he traveled to New Delhi and experienced the government's hostility over both the Pakistani arms supply and the treatment of the IMF application. McFarlane returned to Washington with little interest in dealing with India.[48]

Yet personal diplomacy soon put relations on a smoother track. In October 1981, Gandhi, Reagan, and other world leaders held a summit on global economic issues in Cancún, Mexico. The Indian and American governments could not have taken more different positions on questions of debt, aid, and trade policy, but in a private meeting Indira Gandhi and Ronald Reagan hit it off surprisingly well, at least as the Americans perceived it.[49] The Indian view was somewhat less sanguine, but still positive: Indira Gandhi's close adviser, Principal Secretary P. C. Alexander, recounted that she "was disillusioned about the whole meeting" because instead of addressing substantive issues at the highest level, "it ended up as a mere exercise in courtesy—a display of diplomatic politeness without a meeting of the minds." Mrs. Gandhi "was quite disappointed about" Reagan "and his lack of grasp of the issues."[50] Nevertheless, Indian officials recognized that the American side had been influenced positively by the meeting and decided to build on this good tone.

India's interest and the perceived warmth of the Gandhi-Reagan meeting coincided with the Reagan administration's view that the Tarapur dispute had to be resolved even at the cost of weakening American nonproliferation pressure on India. The Reagan team felt that the Carter administration's restrictive approach to nuclear exports had undermined the U.S. nuclear industry and relations with key allies without solving the proliferation problem or strengthening U.S. national security. The Reagan administration sought instead to relax export controls and the animus against plutonium reprocessing, especially in countries that could be friendly toward the United States in the global contest against the Soviet Union.[51] Rather than pursuing a rigid, unilateral effort to block proliferation everywhere, the Reagan administration would discriminate between countries that posed threats to the United States and those that did not. The administration would try to work cooperatively with less threatening countries to reduce proliferation incentives; with others it would take the approach of tightening international pressures. Pakistan and China fell into the category of states that should be engaged positively rather than punitively; India stood in a middle category.

In early 1981, administration officials picked up on earlier Indian "suggestions" that the 1963 Tarapur cooperation agreement should be suspended due to U.S. failure to fulfill its terms. However, in exploring an amicable divorce, the United States insisted that India should continue "at all times" the IAEA safeguards on the reactors and spent fuel and continue the commitment to use both for peaceful purposes only.[52] India rejected the proposal, despite an assurance by the chief U.S. negotiator, James Malone, that the United States would not press to retain the right of approving India's reprocessing of Tarapur spent fuel.[53] Around this time, Malone's Indian counterpart, Eric Gonsalves, informally floated the idea of finding a third-party fuel supplier to enable each side to get around the impasse. Malone responded positively.[54]

During a second round of talks in July in New Delhi, it was apparent that the United States sought to find a substitute supplier of fuel that, with Indian acceptance, would maintain the safeguard requirements. The Indian team, led by Homi Sethna and Eric Gonsalves, still argued that if the United States ended its supply relationship, India would not be obligated to maintain safeguards. Rather than embrace an alternate supplier, the Atomic Energy Commission would run the reactors on mixed oxide fuel (MOX), a blend of plutonium and uranium. This would allow the nuclear establishment to demonstrate its self-sufficiency and the wisdom of prior investments in plutonium reprocessing. However, behind the scenes Gonsalves was exploring the third-party supply alternative.

In December 1981, Indira Gandhi's broader foreign policy priorities and doubts about Indian technology led her to intervene. In a statement before a parliamentary consultative committee, she posed two conditions for resolving the dispute. First, the continued operation of the reactors must be assured. Second, India's decision would have to serve "the national interest and overall *bilateral relations with the U.S.*"[55] This was a significant, albeit understated, shift away from righteous nuclear defiance and toward pragmatic accommodation of the United States. One can speculate that having been persuaded by Sethna and Ramanna to undertake the Pokhran test in 1974, Mrs. Gandhi was not willing to follow uncritically the nuclear establishment's lead now and risk another break with the United States over nuclear policy. At this time she began doubting the long-term viability of relying on the Soviet Union to buttress India and wanted to become more independent and explore the possibility of purchasing high technology and military hardware from the United States.[56] Moreover, as Inder Malhotra found in an unpublished interview with Indira Gandhi, she did not have great confidence in Sethna's claims that MOX fuel would work in the plant. "Scientists can't always do what they say they can do," she said.[57] Indeed, according to Eric Gonsalves, Atomic Energy Commission scientists were divided over the feasibility of the MOX option. Some, led by Sethna, believed in theoretical calculations that India could separate adequate amounts of plutonium, fabricate MOX fuel, and run the reactors reliably on it. Others were less confident, mindful of past practical difficulties in turning theory into reality. Gonsalves saw the third-party option as a way to allow the scientists time to prove that they could run the reactors on MOX by 1993, when the Tarapur nuclear cooperation contract expired, while ensuring in the meantime that electricity supply needs were met.

Washington and New Delhi in early 1982 moved toward a settlement whereby the United States would abandon its demands that safeguards must be applied beyond the expiration of the supply contract in 1993 and France would replace the United States as the fuel supplier. After a few hitches, this agreement was completed in late 1982.

The poor condition of India's nuclear program contributed to this decision. Even had the nuclear establishment been able successfully to fabricate MOX fuel and run the Tarapur reactors on it, there was only enough plutonium to be reprocessed from Tarapur spent fuel for five or six years of operation.[58] This plutonium—or plutonium reprocessed from other reactors—was planned for use in the Fast Breeder Test Reactor. Sethna now acknowledged that using it in thermal reactors was inefficient.[59] More broadly, the nuclear program's performance in 1981 and 1982 inspired little confidence.[60] In October 1981, a serious leak of slightly radioactive water in the RAPS-I reactor at Kota, in Rajasthan, caused it to be closed for repair.[61]

Overall, the national nuclear program was budgeted for $505 million in fiscal year 1982–1983 and employed more than 32,000 people.[62] This amounted to 1.6 percent of total government spending (compared with 17 percent for defense expenditures).[63] Of the DAE's budget, 40 percent went for nuclear power projects, 15 percent for heavy-water plants, and 14 percent for BARC's activities. This expenditure accounted for a huge portion of the government's investment in science and technology, yet the payoff remained poor. The Tarapur and Rajasthan power stations operated at 54 percent capacity in 1981, making them economically less cost effective than thermal power stations.[64] The first unit at Rajasthan averaged one shutdown every thirteen days of its nine years in operation, and by early 1982 both units there were shut down indefinitely. The cost of RAPS-I had been originally estimated at Rs. 340 million but actually had been Rs. 733 million (roughly $100 million in 1972 exchange rates). RAPS-II came in 62 percent over budget.[65] India's heavy-water plants performed worse still, after being built far behind schedule and over budget. Among other things, this meant that the first power reactor at Madras could not begin operations until 1983, despite being completed in 1981, eight years behind original plans.[66] The forty-megawatt thermal Fast Breeder Test Reactor remained incomplete in 1982 and would not go critical until 1985, nine years behind schedule.

Many causes lay behind these failures. American refusal to meet contractual obligations for supplying Tarapur fuel lowered that power station's operation rate. Faulty designs and components supplied by Canada afflicted the RAPS-I unit. India's poor general infrastructure impaired the nuclear establishment. So, too, the weakness of India's power grid caused hundreds of nuclear plant shutdowns.[67] These flaws could not be blamed on the nuclear establishment, but many others could. The uncomfortable fact was that India's nuclear establishment had not achieved its frequently claimed self-reliance, and it therefore suffered enormously from the suspension of foreign technology and assistance following the Pokhran test. As *India Today* concluded, "almost none of this would have happened if it were not for the Pokharan blast, which in any case has not led to any new peaceful uses of nuclear energy."[68] The leaders of the AEC now suffered criticism for their establishment's poor performance, but they had in many ways brought it on themselves. It was they who had underestimated the international consequences of pushing Indira Gandhi to conduct the PNE. If they now hoped to test another nuclear device, they faced a more skeptical prime minister.

INDIRA'S DOMESTIC PREOCCUPATIONS, 1981 TO 1982

Reflecting the growing urgency of defense issues, Indira Gandhi had assumed the post of minister of defense upon returning to power in 1980. Yet domestic problems remained paramount to her government. Real threats to internal security emerged from the breadbasket state of Punjab, Kashmir, Tamil Nadu, Assam, and other northeastern states where militant groups engaged in armed struggle. The army was increasingly being called in to quell these conflicts, which were fueled by arms and other assistance that flowed from Pakistan and China to militant groups in the west and northeast. The greatest threat arose in Punjab, where Sikh nationalists organized under the Akali Dal had been pressing for decades for an independent Sikh state of Khalistan. By 1980, the Sikh political-religious movement had become splintered, and a radical faction emerged under the leadership of Sant Jarnail Singh Bhindranwale.[69] Bhindranwale and his followers began a campaign of violence in 1980, posing a grave threat to Indian order and national cohesion. Punjab is strategically vital because it is the key agricultural center of India and lies adjacent to Pakistan and Kashmir. This geography also makes Punjab a relatively easy avenue of entry for Pakistani efforts to subvert India through provision of arms and other support to Sikh separatists. Whatever the extent of Pakistan's actual involvement there, the threat compounded what was already a severe challenge to the state. As Inder Malhotra recorded, the Punjab upheaval became "Indira's principal preoccupation."[70]

Throughout 1981, Indira Gandhi sounded the alarm over these internal threats as well as Pakistan's mounting military capability. Opposition leaders naturally alleged that she was trying to distract the people from other domestic problems.[71] Mrs. Gandhi's Congress (I) party in late 1980 had questioned the effectiveness of India's parliamentary form of government and floated the notion that the state should switch to a presidential system. This heightened the opposition's distrust of Gandhi's ambition. Yet the opposition was now badly fragmented and incapable of mounting a cohesive national challenge to the government.[72] Polls showed generally strong support of the prime minister, even as two-thirds of respondents in a March 1981 survey of fourteen cities felt that "things are going badly" in the country.[73]

Economically, India suffered from rising prices and a parlous balance of payments position, necessitating the aforementioned request to the IMF for a $5 billion loan. This economic weakness compelled the government to avoid steps that would alienate the United States and other donors, such as ending safeguards on the Tarapur reactors or testing another nuclear explosive. In any case, more robust development of nuclear explosive capability would not redress the internal political turmoil.

In January 1982, Indira Gandhi shuffled her cabinet in a way that would have a subtle impact on nuclear policymaking for the next decade—during which India would have five prime ministers. She now wanted to transfer the defense ministership from herself to a highly trusted leader. She decided to move then-Finance Minister R. Venkataraman to defense. Normally she would not hesitate to move officials around, but she did hesitate in this case because she regarded Venkataraman so highly that she wanted to be sure that he did not feel slighted. But Venkataraman, a longtime politician from South India known for a judicious temperament and strong support of technology and industry, greeted news of the change enthusiastically. From 1982 to 1984 Venkataraman presided over important developments in India's nuclear and missile program, and in the process helped impose a bureaucratic buffer between the nuclear scientists and the prime minister. The prime minister and the leaders of the Defence Research and Development Organisation and BARC deeply respected him. His arrival as defense minister in January 1982 broadened the base of contributors to nuclear policymaking.

REAGAN-GANDHI SUMMIT IN WASHINGTON, 1982

In early 1982 the White House planned its yearly schedule of invitations to foreign heads of state and decided to include Indira Gandhi in it. The war in Afghanistan made it imperative to invite President Zia, which in turn suggested a similar bid to India, recognizing that Washington's overall policy in South Asia required an effort to build confidence in New Delhi.[74] The invitation was conveyed to Indira Gandhi on April 1 and she readily accepted.[75] Indian officials noted privately that she had been eager to come to the United States since her return to power.[76] Eleven years had passed since her last visit, an acrimonious affair on the eve of the 1971 Indo-Pak war, and she now wanted to improve ties between the countries.

Preceding the July state visit to the United States, reports emerged that India once again was preparing to conduct a nuclear explosion at the Rajasthan test site.[77] Indira Gandhi denied any intention to conduct such a test and suggested instead that the rumor was being spread by the Bharatiya Janata Party.[78] (The BJP had been formed in April 1980 to succeed and improve upon the Jana Sangh in the aftermath of the Janata government's 1979 collapse. The new party, led by Atal Behari Vajpayee, emphasized "Gandhian socialism" and, at first, a more mainstream approach to Hindu nationalism.)[79] Weeks before rumors of a test circulated in May, a number of foreign and security policy experts had met at a leading New Delhi think tank, the Centre for Policy Research, to explore India's security predicament. These intellectuals concluded that if Pakistan "went nuclear . . . no party and no government in India would be able to resist the demand that India must go nuclear too."[80] At the same time, however, the seminar participants acknowledged that the costs of a nuclear arms race would be "crippling by any reckoning" and would not allow "any saving in the expenditure on conventional weapons."[81]

The prospective costs of a nuclear arms contest and Indira Gandhi's pending trip to the United States made it unlikely that she would seriously consider authorizing a nuclear test at this time. Indeed, throughout 1982 she sought to downplay nuclear issues. Since December 1981, Indian officials studiously had avoided discussing even the Tarapur dispute, a measure of the government's desire to concentrate on other matters and avoid ill will with Washington.[82] In a January 1982 interview with a *U.S. News & World Report* correspondent, Indira Gandhi was asked whether India would follow suit if Pakistan developed a "nuclear military weapon." She replied, "I believe the threat is one of conventional arms and not of nuclear weapons. I'm very much against war of any kind, and nuclear war especially. But I don't think I can give a categorical answer and bind the Indian government to any position. As I say, I don't myself think, even if Pakistan does something like this, that we should do it. But it's not right for me to make any kind of categorical statement on it."[83]

Mrs. Gandhi's pending state visit elevated India to a higher plane in American policymaking. As then-Ambassador Harry Barnes recalled, "the whole tone of the relationship changed."[84] American officials appreciated the prime minister's recent efforts to downplay India's ties to the Soviet Union and her insistence that friendship with Moscow did not mean India could not try "to be friends with China or with the United States."[85] As the visit approached, Indian and American officials moved to resolve final details to end the Tarapur dispute.

Indira Gandhi arrived in Washington on July 30 and began a charm offensive that succeeded marvelously. Americans long tired by frequent Indian moralism and anti-Americanism were surprised by her engaging manner. The Indian delegation and press were equally buoyed by the eleven days of meetings, parties, and celebrations in Washington and other cities. As *India Today* reported, "she out-Reaganed Ronald Reagan at his own favourite game. She had clearly come to conquer and was determined to give it all she had which, as it turned out, was considerable."[86]

The chemistry and symbolism of the trip were most important, but the Indian and American delegations also made substantive gains. The two heads of state formalized an initiative for science and technology cooperation and designated

1985 as "the Year of India," calling for a major Indian art and cultural exhibition to tour the United States. And they finally put the rancorous Tarapur issue to rest by announcing that France would replace the United States as the supplier of reactor fuel and India would continue to safeguard the plant. The Reagan administration had managed to bypass the Nuclear Nonproliferation Act's requirement for safeguards on *all* of India's nuclear facilities, while India had relaxed its defiant position that the end of U.S. supply should mean the end of all Indian obligations. The two sides agreed to disagree on whether India must receive U.S. permission to reprocess spent fuel from Tarapur, tabling the problem for further discussion. The deal signified Indian pragmatism in the face of American congressional coercion. As Harry Barnes put it, "We had no arguments to refute Indian contentions that the United States had no legal basis for abrogating the agreement. We just pushed the question, Is abrogating the agreement going to get you anything?"[87] Higher Indian interests prevailed and enabled both sides diplomatically to get around the obstacle of single-issue (nonproliferation) congressional sanctions.

The Indian public—at least in major cities—believed that Indira Gandhi's visit helped improve relations with the United States.[88] However, slightly more than half of literate urban respondents to a public opinion poll had heard about the Tarapur agreement, and of those, opinions ranged widely on the benefits to India. Twelve percent thought it served the United States "only," while 8.2 percent thought it served India "only." Little more than five percent thought it served both countries, while the largest cohort (32.3 percent) thought it was "no final solution," and the second largest cohort (22.4 percent) could not say.[89] These figures indicated the low salience of the Tarapur issue when the context of a bitter nationalistic dispute with the United States was removed. Respondents felt that the most important problem between the United States and India was the U.S. supply of arms and F-16 aircraft to Pakistan.[90] The Pakistani threat—and the U.S. role in it—clearly loomed larger than the traditional Indian political demands for nuclear disarmament and resistance to IAEA safeguards.

DUBIOUS WARNINGS OF AN INDIAN ATTACK ON PAKISTAN'S NUCLEAR PLANTS, DECEMBER 1982

Seeking international favor, Indian and Pakistani leaders in early 1982 sought to demonstrate their desire for peace. Talks on respective proposals for a no-war pact or a treaty of friendship had stalled in February 1982 when the two sides exchanged recriminations over Kashmir. In June, Pakistan sought to revive the dialogue by submitting a revised draft agreement on nonaggression, renunciation of force, and promotion of good neighborly relations, and India responded by proposing a draft agreement for creating an Indo-Pak Joint Commission.[91] On August 11, Indian Foreign Secretary K. Rasgotra gave Pakistan a counterdraft of a treaty of peace, friendship, and cooperation. On November 1, Zia and Indira Gandhi held their first formal bilateral meeting, in New Delhi, which resulted in the creation of a joint commission to further relations and continue dialogue on each side's proposed treaties to renounce aggression and promote friendship.[92]

Intriguingly, however, in December 1982 U.S. intelligence sources leaked reports that India's military leaders had prepared a contingency plan for launching air strikes against Pakistan's uranium enrichment plant at Kahuta and the small reprocessing facility at PINSTECH in Rawalpindi. A front-page *Washington Post* story alleged that military advisers had proposed such a preemptive attack to Indira Gandhi "nine months ago"—March 1982—but that Mrs. Gandhi had rejected it.[93]

Indian officials called the report "absolute rubbish."[94] They countered that India and Pakistan were engaged in "a very serious exercise for bringing about a rapprochement between" the two countries, implying that this overrode any interest in a military strike.[95]

Situational logic suggested that the Indian military (or other agencies) at least would prepare contingency plans for destroying or weakening Pakistan's nuclear capability before it could be used to threaten India. Israel, too, fearing that Pakistan was colluding with more hard-line states such as Libya to develop an "Islamic Bomb," had an interest in removing the potential threat. Israel's attack on Iraq's Osiraq reactor in 1981 demonstrated its willingness to take this approach and prompted air force leaders to ask whether India could do the same to Pakistan. The Indian scholar W. P. S. Sidhu suggested indirect evidence that the Indian Air Force conducted a brief study in June 1981 on the feasibility of attacking Kahuta.[96] This was part of an air force review of strategy following the induction of British-procured Jaguar strike aircraft in 1980. Given the proximity of Pakistan, the air force argued that the Jaguar could be considered as a strategic weapon against Pakistan, if not China. A quick study was immediately conducted, and according to Sidhu's interview with the former Indian Air Force director of operations, it concluded that India could "attack and neutralise" Kahuta. Another Indian defense official recalled that the air force believed it could accomplish the mission but calculated that perhaps 50 percent of the attacking Jaguars would be lost, as they were slow-flying compared to the Pakistani F-16s that would defend the plant.[97] However, as the former director of operations reasoned, "The question was what will happen next? In my estimate, Pakistan would go to war. The international community would condemn us for doing something in peacetime, which the Israelis could get away with but India would not be able to get away with. In the end it will result in a war."[98]

Interviews with former Indian military, political, and nuclear officials corroborate this negative conclusion regarding the efficacy of an attack on Pakistan's nuclear infrastructure. These former officials acknowledged that India had photographs of the Kahuta facility and knew that it was defended against air attack by surface-to-air Crotale missiles and balloon barrages.[99] "If we attack Kahuta," a former air force leader explained, "the whole border would go up. It would be war."[100] He continued, "[T]he Israeli model [in attacking Iraq's Osiraq reactor] would not apply. A clean attack without escalation to a wider war could not be done in the Indo-Pak context." The notion of cooperating with Israel in such a strike raised even more problems. "We have 100 million Muslims in India," a former high-ranking defense official explained. "If we cooperated with the Israelis in attacking Pakistan it would be a huge political disaster and could cause severe internal problems."[101]

Finally, India had as much or more to lose than Pakistan in such an attack, insofar as Pakistan could then be expected to attack India's nuclear reactors and reprocessing plants with a grave risk of causing radioactive contamination in India. As a former high-ranking Atomic Energy Commission official put it, "[I]f we blew up Kahuta, uranium might be dispersed in Pakistan, but uranium is not nearly as toxic as plutonium, and our plants, which Pakistan could have counterattacked, have plutonium and are located closer to large populations."[102] Another former high-ranking official summed up the situation: "We knew we would have to live with Pakistan's nuclear capability, and there was no way around it."[103]

Still, Pakistani leaders were concerned over the reports of a potential preemptive attack. Sometime in 1983, probably after August, when Raja Ramanna was named to succeed Homi Sethna as chairman of the Atomic Energy Commission, Pakistan's AEC chairman, Munir Ahmad Khan, met with Ramanna at the Imperial Hotel in Vienna, where both were attending an IAEA meeting. Concerned by possible Indian-Israeli consideration of attacking Pakistan, Khan recounted to the author that he "pointed out that if such an attack took place against Kahuta or PINSTECH it would release very little radioactivity because we had only a small enrichment plant and a small research reactor at these places." However, he continued, "Pakistan would assume that [such an attack] came from India and would be forced to respond."[104] Khan, who emphasized that he was not negotiating on behalf of Pakistan but just making technical points, reminded Ramanna that a Pakistani counterattack on Trombay "would be huge and could release massive amounts of radiation to a large populated area causing a disaster." "Under the circumstances," he argued, "it would be better that India and Pakistan should not attack each other's facilities." Khan reported that Ramanna said he would discuss the matter with Mrs. Gandhi. Two years later, the two governments initiated an agreement not to attack each other's nuclear facilities. This "episode" revealed that a form of nuclear deterrence operated even when adversaries did not wield nuclear weapons but had nuclear facilities that could be blown up by conventional weapons causing radioactive contamination on one's own soil.

India did not undertake such an attack, having as much to lose as to gain. By early 1983, domestic political trouble was demanding Indira Gandhi's attention. January state assembly elections in the southern Indian states of Andhra Pradesh and Karnataka resulted in a major defeat for her Congress party.[105] In eight state assembly elections since 1980, her party had been able to win only 312 of the 1,150 seats it contested.[106] While a military gambit against Pakistan could have rallied political support temporarily to the government, such a move, even if successful, could not have offered lasting solace to the population.

MRS. GANDHI APPROVES A SECOND NUCLEAR BLAST, THEN CHANGES HER MIND, 1982 TO 1983

If destroying Pakistan's nuclear weapon capability was too risky, India's nuclear establishment naturally turned back to the option of strengthening India's nuclear deterrent. The top scientists at BARC and the DRDO knew that the Pokhran peaceful nuclear explosive was rudimentary and would have to be improved upon in order to provide the nation a deliverable, reliable counterstrike weapon. BARC director Ramanna and the man who succeeded him as director general of the DRDO, V. S. Arunachalam, pressed the government to allow another test. In late 1982 or early 1983, the two men led a series of meetings to prepare to make the case for another nuclear explosion to the prime minister.

Technically, the top scientists at BARC and the DRDO knew that subsystems of more advanced nuclear devices could be tested separately, without the international ramifications of a full-scale nuclear explosion. But like scientists and engineers in other nuclear weapon states, they felt that much greater confidence and knowledge would be gained by a full-yield test of an assembled device. The scientists since 1974 had worked quietly to produce more reliable neutron initiators, enhance the simultaneity of high explosive charges, miniaturize a device, and improve its yield-to-weight ratio. The team at BARC concentrated on improving the neutron initiator and other means to increase the yield of a nuclear device. Scientists and engineers in the DRDO—particularly at the Terminal Ballistics Research Laboratory in Chandigarh—strove to downsize the high explosive and electronic systems that would detonate that explosive to implode the plutonium core. By 1982, according to one of the officials involved, the team had produced a design for a device that would weigh between 170 and 200 kilograms, much lighter than the 1,000-kilogram 1974 device. The scientists now wanted to prove their work. (Hints emerged after the May 1998 tests that P. K. Iyengar and R. Chidambaram at BARC also had developed a boosted-fission design that they wanted to test in early 1983. Boosted-fission weapons are discussed more fully in the next chapter. They require tritium, which India was not publicly known to possess at the time, but which BARC could have been acquiring through irradiation of lithium in nuclear reactors.)

Sometime in late 1982 or more likely early 1983, Ramanna and Arunachalam made their case to the prime minister. She and her top advisers, Principal Secretary P. C. Alexander and Cabinet Secretary Krishnaswamy Rao Sahib, were at the Ministry of Defence for a meeting on another matter. At Defence Minister Venkataraman's behest they stayed after for an unannounced session to consider a prospective nuclear test. The location of the meetings and the roles of Venkataraman, Arunachalam, Alexander, and Rao Sahib indicated an important shift in Indian nuclear policymaking. Whereas in 1974 the defense minister had been excluded from deliberations and the Atomic Energy Commission leadership drove the process, now the top two relevant defense officials were intimately involved.

Also unlike the process leading up to the 1974 PNE, the prime minister did not participate in the scientists' deliberations until a recommendation was prepared for her. The prime minister retained the title and responsibility of minister of atomic energy, but she was represented on a more routine basis by Principal Secretary Alexander and Cabinet Secretary Rao Sahib, who both served on the six-member Atomic Energy Commission.[107]

Alexander had succeeded Rao Sahib as principal secretary in May 1981, with the latter moving over to become cabinet secretary. Both men, but particularly Alexander, now played important roles advising the prime minister on these matters. Alexander, a Christian from Kerala, had been selected to his post with a reputation for outstanding integrity and professionalism as a civil servant and an occasional UN official specializing in economic and trade issues. Rao Sahib had been a physics honor student in college and understood the virtues of science. He also appreciated the need to hold the leaders of scientific bureaucracies accountable within an overall framework of Indian interests.[108] Thus, the prime minister was now surrounded by independent-minded, professional advisers as she considered the scientists' request.

In the meeting, Ramanna and Arunachalam confined themselves to technical arguments for testing the new design. They did not portray their request as an explicit beginning of a nuclear weapon program, but rather as another experiment. "The whole point was should we or should we not—before Pakistan or after," one of the participants explained.[109] The scientists did not address the international or domestic ramifications of testing. However, they did add that the risk of pretest detection by the United States could be obviated by conducting the experiment at a site other than the Rajasthan desert. This option, alluded to only rarely in Indian commentaries, assumed problematically that U.S. satellites did not monitor other regions of India for signs of test preparations. It also indicated that the weaponeers were serious about going forward.[110] For his part, Venkataraman did not make a recommendation during this meeting. At its completion, Mrs. Gandhi tentatively approved the request for a nuclear test.[111]

However, within twenty-four hours, the prime minister changed her mind. She told Venkataraman to convey this reversal, and he notified Arunachalam, who in turn told Ramanna.[112] It is impossible to know exactly why Indira Gandhi reversed course. No public record exists of her deliberations, nor have Venkataraman or Alexander clarified the matter. Arunachalam and Ramanna were not told why. When this episode was first revealed publicly after the May 1998 tests, journalists and commentators suggested that the test plans had been leaked and foreign pressure forced Mrs. Gandhi to change her mind.[113] There is no evidence for this: her testing decision was unknown to American officials, as it was to all but a few Indian officials. Then-Ambassador to India Harry Barnes said that he was never asked to address the issue at the time, and it is unlikely that American pressure could have been exerted on India in this twenty-four-hour period.[114]

One can speculate that Mrs. Gandhi recalled the 1974 decision and its largely negative consequences, and her own often expressed abhorrence of nuclear weapons. In the absence of an actual Pakistani nuclear provocation in the form of an explosive test, she must have determined that India was better off holding its nuclear fire. It is also likely that after the meeting with the scientists, Alexander or Rao Sahib, or perhaps both, cautioned the prime minister about repercussions that the scientists had not addressed. Alexander's domestic and international expertise made him aware that a test would harm India's relations with other states at a time when the nation still depended heavily on foreign aid and loans, the World Bank, and the International Monetary Fund. He may have echoed the views of her earlier adviser, P. N. Haksar, who lamented to the author that "scientists are a very poor evaluator of a very complex phenomenon called politics."[115] Now, unlike in 1974, broader considerations and government advisers limited the influence of the strategic enclave. A nascent, informal, and impermanent process of checking and balancing the scientists had emerged. The press and Parliament demanded stronger government action to deal with the growing Pakistani threat, but they did not bear the responsibility of determining the costs and benefits of alternate courses. After this episode, Indira Gandhi "refused to entertain a meeting with us on that subject," according to a participant in the discussions.[116]

Notwithstanding the decision to forego another test, officials did not neglect Pakistan's increasing strength. In an April 19, 1983, speech to army commanders, Defence Minister Venkataraman expressed concern about increased foreign military assistance to Pakistan and acknowledged that Pakistan was continuing to acquire military nuclear capability.[117] He assured the commanders that their forces would be properly equipped, with an emphasis on indigenous defense production, but he also urged them to reduce overall expenditures. India would continue its policy of nuclear self-restraint.

INDIA LAUNCHES INTEGRATED GUIDED MISSILE PROGRAM, 1983

Nonetheless, the government in this period did move to augment India's long-term military strength. In 1983 India formally began a comprehensive effort to produce ballistic missiles by creating the Integrated Guided Missile Development Programme (IGMDP). Had Indian leaders been determined to build a nuclear weapon arsenal in the 1960s or 1970s, they would have initiated a dedicated missile program at that time. This was not done, and instead, as the following brief history describes, India dedicated its space program in the 1960s and 1970s to peaceful applications, relegating missile research and development to a largely ineffectual effort under the auspices of the Defence Research and Development Organisation. The shift to a dedicated missile program in 1983 resulted from accretion of technological capability, long-term need for advanced indigenous tactical and strategic weapon platforms, and desire to acquire weapons whose prestige and military role had been determined by the major powers whose stature India sought to share.

It is often suggested that India began the space program with military applications in mind. However, this overstates the case. As discussed in chapter 6, Vikram Sarabhai was the dominant figure in India's early space efforts and he evinced little interest in military applications. Rather, he saw the space program as a means for India to leapfrog into modernity by stimulating the growth of technology and industry in the fields of electronics, communications, cybernetics, and material engineering, all of which would enhance India's economic development.[118] If Sarabhai genuinely expressed reservations about military applications of nuclear energy, his determination to maintain a peaceful space program was even greater. The space effort, unlike the nuclear program, was his creation.

Sarabhai believed that India should collaborate with more technologically advanced countries. He sought engagement with space agencies in the United States, France, the United Kingdom, and the Soviet Union. From the late 1960s into the mid-1970s, Indian technologists indigenously developed and launched a number of sounding rockets based on French designs of a rocket propellant plant and on imported raw materials.[119] In this period work also began on India's first satellite launch vehicle, the SLV-3, which was formally approved as a project in 1973, a year after a Department of Space, directed by Satish Dhawan, had been spun off from the Department of Atomic Energy.[120] Unlike sounding rockets, launch vehicles are powerful enough to carry satellites (or warheads) into space. The SLV-3 project was based on the well-proven U.S. "Scout" rocket.[121] However, the SLV-3 was not a copy of Scout, in large part because it relied on indigenously produced component systems and fuel. Due to the bulk of the inertial guidance system and other subsystems produced in India, the Indian rocket ended up much heavier than Scout, reducing its payload capacity by more than 40 percent.[122] Two of the SLV-3's first three flights failed—in August 1979 and May 1981—while a success had occurred in July 1980.[123] A 1983 satellite deployment by the SLV-3 succeeded. With these remarkable achievements for a country with one of the lowest per capita incomes in the world, as Dhawan noted, India had gained the capacity to produce a medium-range ballistic missile.[124]

Still, the Indian Space Research Organisation at this time was reluctant to compromise its space programs and risk international sanctions by working on military missiles. For this and other reasons, the government now decided to create a separate program to develop guided missiles. This suited the Defence Research and Development Organisation's desire to take the Indian military into the space age. Since the early 1970s, the Defence Research and Development Laboratory (DRDL) at Hyderabad had been conducting R & D on missile systems. The director general of the Defence Research and Development Organisation, Dr. Nag Chaudhuri, had been an avid proponent of missiles and had encouraged the DRDL to develop a missile based on the Soviet liquid-fueled SAM-2, which India had bought. Work on this early Indian missile—"Project Devil"—had been conducted independently of ISRO's civilian space launch efforts and was abandoned in 1978 after a number of failures.[125] In the early 1980s, the DRDL had developed plans for a 150-kilometer surface-to-surface missile also to be based on the SAM-2. To manage this project and revitalize the DRDL, V. S. Arunachalam, the brilliant metallurgist now running the Defence Research and Development Organisation, tapped Dr. A. P. J. Abdul Kalam. One of the relatively few Muslims in the top echelon of Indian science and technology, Kalam had been transferred from the SLV-3 project after the rocket's first successful flight and named the leader of the space program's future projects group in Bangalore. Kalam had for some time been urging Ramanna—the DRDO director through 1981—and Arunachalam to put him in charge of the missile effort, and he got his wish in 1982.

More than a sign of connivance between the space and missile programs, Kalam's arrival stemmed from the fact that he was a highly regarded project manager.[126] The organizational culture at ISRO had allowed for greater creativity and accomplishment than had the more hierarchical culture of the Defence Research and Development Laboratory heretofore. Arunachalam had a can-do, entrepreneurial spirit buoyed by a lively sense of humor, and he wanted a manager of Kalam's capacity to help revitalize work on missiles. Kalam was a lifelong bachelor—like Homi Bhabha—known for tireless effort and good team leadership.

Kalam and Arunachalam had to struggle to revive the Defence Research and Development Laboratory and its funding. As Arunachalam put it, "the DRDL was like a bride all dressed up, but with no wedding to go to. They had a number of technologies on the boards, but no program to bring them to fruition."[127] In 1982, the laboratory, in conjunction with the military services, had begun planning for a series of missiles. The armed forces were most interested in the Nag antitank guided missile and two surface-to-air missiles, the Trishul and the Akash. Two more ambitious projects were also proposed, the Prithvi tactical surface-to-surface missile and the longer-range Agni missile, which was conceived to demonstrate the reentry technology required to give India the capability of carrying warheads— including nuclear—between 1,500 and 2,500 kilometers. This suite of missile programs could have seemed too ambitious to political leaders and fiscal planners, and Kalam and Arunachalam had sought to concentrate on the Prithvi, which grew out of the earlier Project Devil, or SSM-150 program.

A feasibility report on the missile program was prepared and presented at a meeting presided over by the defense minister in early 1983. This meeting was itself unusual in that it brought together for the first time the three service chiefs; the deputy minister for defense, Singh-Dev; the principal secretary, Dr. P. C. Alexander; the cabinet secretary, Krishnaswamy Rao Sahib; two Ministry of Finance officials; and other defense secretaries. They all listened to presentations given by Arunachalam, Kalam, and other scientists. Venkataraman believed that such meetings were necessary for programs needing large investments and that full participation from key government bodies would create the necessary political and bureaucratic will to undertake a major program in quick order. That evening, after the larger meeting, Venkataraman told Arunachalam and Kalam that instead of developing the five missiles seriatim, the DRDO should work on them all at once, as part of an Integrated Guided Missile Development Programme. This would allow the development of each missile to piggyback on the other technologically, and thereby reduce the time that would otherwise be required to produce one after the other.[128] Venkataraman urged them to budget fully at the outset for production and testing of the five missile systems.[129] As Kalam recalled, the scientists were "absolutely delighted" by the defense minister's encouragement and subsequent endorsement of their ambitious plan.

By the summer of 1983, with Venkataraman's backing and a financial analysis prepared by the Ministry of Defence, Arunachalam and Kalam presented their plans to the Cabinet Committee on Political Affairs, the government's highest decision-making body. In August 1983, this committee approved the proposal and the IGMDP was born, with a budget of Rs. 388 crores (about $370 million).[130] A month later, project leaders from the scores of defense and commercial laboratories and industrial enterprises that would be involved in the consortium gathered in Hyderabad to plot their collective research, development, testing, and production campaign.

Arunachalam and Kalam sought quick results. Beyond the obvious reasons, they recognized that the advanced technological countries might expand the nonproliferation regime to deny exports of missile-relevant technologies to countries like India. Hence, they sought to produce and acquire all key components and capabilities as quickly as possible, so if embargoes came the missile program would be able to proceed effectively. In addition, the scientists wanted to free India from dependence on the Soviet Union for missile technology. The drive for independence and quick results led to the innovative "consortium approach" to research, development, and production.

Time imperatives also dictated the choice of technologies, particularly for the Prithvi and Agni. The Prithvi's liquid-fueled engine derived from the SA-2, albeit in an improved form. According to Arunachalam, the liquid-fueled engines were selected—after debate with Kalam, who favored a solid-propellant system— because India had mastered production of this fuel and the capacity to control thrust directions with this type of missile to allow constant guidance to targets on an aerodynamic as opposed to a ballistic trajectory.[131] Moreover, the Prithvi is a mobile system to be deployed over India's bumpy roadways, and Arunachalam worried that solid propellant could be destabilized during transport, resulting in erratic performance. Concerns that the time-consuming and difficult in-field liquid-fueling process would render the Prithvi vulnerable and hard to use in war were rebutted by arguments that the Prithvi could be prefueled in sealed containers and thus safely used without fears of corrosion for a number of months. Moreover, India would have hundreds of presurveyed launch sites for the mobile missiles and Pakistan would not be able to detect launch points in real time. This would enable the missiles to be used without great risk of preemptive destruction.

In any case, reliance on the liquid-fueled system allowed relatively rapid production. India flight-tested the first Prithvi in February 1988, only five years after the IGMDP's inception.[132]

The Agni is less militarily usable than the Prithvi, but it was conceived originally not for production and deployment but rather to develop and prove India's capacity to deliver reentry vehicles (warheads) over a much longer distance. The first stage of the missile's first version was a SLV-3 solid-propellant rocket engine, while the second stage employed twin, liquid-fueled engines derived from the Prithvi.[133] The Agni was readied before the Missile Technology Control Regime formally went into effect in 1987, and it was first flight-tested in 1989.

If the Indian military had practically no role in shaping nuclear policy, its role in the missile program was somewhat greater. The scientific leaders of the DRDO created the impetus for the two systems theoretically capable of carrying nuclear warheads—the Prithvi and the Agni. However, the army and the air force were not ignored in the missile program, as they were in the nuclear program. In all military projects the services prepare a general staff quality requirement (GSQR) to specify the capabilities needed for the envisioned weapon's mission. This was done for the Prithvi, although the terms of the guidance were finalized only after the first flight test, in a form of reverse-justification engineering.[134] As chapters 10 and 11 record, the army has had difficulty assimilating the Prithvi.

The Agni program proceeded without a GSQR from the army, navy, or air force.[135] As Angathevar Baskaran learned in an interview with a former ISRO engineer, the Agni resulted not from strategic requirements but rather from "the motive to do something by utilising the available capability."[136] However, this underestimated the potential strategic attractiveness of a long-range, perhaps intercontinental, ballistic missile (ICBM) whose basic component systems, particularly for reentry, could be based on lessons learned in the Agni program, giving India a relatively low-cost option on a future full-fledged nuclear arsenal. Once the technology began to be demonstrated in the late 1980s, the air force worked to integrate its potential applications (and costs) into its planning and budgetary politicking.

Even as the government moved to create the technological option for a missile-based nuclear arsenal, it remained uncommitted to such an arsenal. The director of the DRDO, Arunachalam, did not conceive of the Prithvi as a nuclear weapon carrier. He argued that for security reasons it should not be deployed closer than fifty kilometers from Pakistan but that this would mean a nuclear weapon delivered by it would pose major risks of fallout blowing back into India. Moreover, Arunachalam recognized that advanced aircraft are a more cost-effective and reliable means of delivering nuclear weapons, with the added advantage that aircraft can be used for many missions.[137] The Agni was not intended for production or deployment. This meant that a truly dedicated nuclear delivery missile would have to await a follow-up to the first-generation Agni. To the extent that Indian decision makers envisioned the contingency of using nuclear weapons to retaliate against

Pakistan, aircraft, not the Prithvi or Agni, would be the delivery systems. Yet, as of 1983, India had not perfected or demonstrated the technology and procedures for delivering nuclear weapons by aircraft.[138] For her part, Indira Gandhi insisted that despite the missile program, India had "no intention of manufacturing" nuclear weapons. "We do not manufacture them and we will not utilise them," she told French journalists in March 1983.[139]

INDIA PROCURES HEAVY WATER, 1983

In late June 1983, as Secretary of State George Shultz traveled to New Delhi, residual problems arose with the U.S.-Indian agreement on Tarapur and Washington's lingering post-1981 concern over a possible second Indian nuclear test. India needed spare parts for the Tarapur reactors, which were suffering ongoing operational problems that degraded safety. However, according to the *Washington Post*, the White House was reluctant to approve export of spare parts "because it would require informing Congress of possible Indian preparations to conduct a second underground nuclear test."[140] Shultz exercised his rank in a June 30 meeting with Indian counterparts and pledged that the United States would go ahead with the export in order to remove an irritant in bilateral relations.[141] Shultz would be the last secretary of state to visit India until Madeleine Albright in 1997, and he took "more than a perfunctory interest in India," according to then-Ambassador Harry Barnes. The secretary was determined to work with New Delhi in a problem-solving manner. Although the promise of spare parts triggered congressional and media protests of "appeasement," Shultz's decision kept the issue from reigniting Indian animosity over U.S. nonproliferation policy.

In July 1983, India finally commissioned the Madras I nuclear plant in Tamil Nadu. This unsafeguarded plant could produce plutonium for explosive purposes as well as for the nascent breeder reactor program. However, in dedicating the plant, Indira Gandhi declared, according to *India News,* that "India had no intention of embarking on a nuclear weapons program" and wanted to concentrate on providing an "honorable life to the masses."[142] Before an audience of atomic energy officials and workers, she cited the new reactor and the overall nuclear program as an example of India's determination to be self-reliant. The press account of the event trumpeted that the Indian scientists had "mobilised all the available expertise in the country to make heavy water indigenously to meet the needs of the plant."[143]

Unfortunately, the reality was slightly less glorious. The Madras reactor originally had been slated for completion in 1973. It was finished finally in 1982 but unable to operate due to shortages of heavy water. By 1983, India possessed 547.6 tonnes of heavy water, 321 of which came from the Soviet Union between 1976 and 1982.[144] This was inadequate. To avoid having to put this reactor under international safeguards, India legally could not use heavy water imported from the United States, Canada, or the Soviet Union. Nor could India indigenously meet its existing unsafeguarded power and research reactors' needs for heavy water *and* start up the Madras reactor. Indigenous heavy-water production simply was too limited. Thus, when the Madras reactor began operating—and others did not shut down—it meant that the heavy water being used had to have come from "underground" sources. That is, India either could have diverted safeguarded heavy water from, say, the shut-down RAPS-I reactor, or could have secretly acquired additional heavy water outside of nonproliferation regime controls. RAPS-I did contain 150 tonnes of unsafeguarded heavy water that could have been transferred legally to the Madras reactor, but that would have left RAPS-I seriously depleted.[145] M. R. Srinivasan, then director of the power projects engineering division of the Department of Atomic Energy, insisted that "[t]here has been no diversion of heavy water from Rajasthan."[146]

Using detailed analysis and foreign government documents acquired later in the 1980s, the American researcher Gary Milhollin demonstrated that India met its need through clandestine purchases in 1982 and 1983 of 60 tonnes of Chinese-origin heavy water procured through a German middleman, Alfred Hempel. In 1983 Hempel also managed the diversion of 15 tonnes of Norwegian heavy water intended for Germany, which he combined with 4.7 tonnes of Soviet heavy water and sent to Bombay. This accounted in large part for a July 27, 1983, report by Praful Bidwai in the *Times of India* that 100 tonnes of reactor-grade heavy water from unknown sources had been shipped from Bombay to the Madras reactor site.[147] The diversion was confirmed indirectly by a 1988 Indian Comptroller and Auditor General report that concluded that between 1978 and 1986, India's indigenous heavy-water facilities had produced less than a third of the heavy water needed to start the Dhruva reactor (in 1985 as described in chapter 10) and the two Madras reactors.[148]

China was not a party to the Nuclear Non-Proliferation Treaty and could legally export unsafeguarded heavy water to India. Yet, had China knowingly done so, it would have suggested better-than-advertised Sino-Indian relations, as well as Chinese willingness to alienate both the United States and Pakistan. The German middleman probably made the issue moot for both the Indians and the Chinese, as well as the Russians—the sellers may not have known or cared where the material ended up, and the buyer whence it originated. By 1987, according to Leonard Spector, Chinese authorities "apparently realized the shipments were going to a potential adversary, India, and put an end to them."[149] However, Hempel's involvement did arguably violate German law to the extent that he misused German import licenses and on occasion may have transferred heavy water through German territory. In most cases he used a Swiss-based subsidiary to transfer shipments to India, sometimes with an additional routing through Dubai. From 1983 to 1987, Hempel frequently procured heavy water from the Soviet Union through his European licensee front for India, in quantities of less than 1,000 kilograms. This was the weight limit below which the IAEA did not require that NPT parties report such transfers.[150] U.S. intelligence, according to Milhollin, knew of Hempel's dubious nuclear supply activities early in 1981 and had alerted the German foreign office. German auditors did not examine Hempel's books until November 1983, at which point they discovered the shipment of sixty tonnes of Chinese heavy water to Bombay.[151]

Beyond illuminating holes in the nuclear nonproliferation regime, the episode highlighted India's ongoing dependence on foreign "assistance" in the nuclear program and the nuclear establishment's determination to obscure it.[152] Indeed, India would continue to buy heavy water clandestinely through 1987, as the Norwegian, West German, and Romanian governments eventually acknowledged.[153] Still, the government in New Delhi steadfastly denies that India received heavy water through clandestine trafficking. This denial may owe to national pride and the reluctance to be portrayed inaccurately as a violator of international legal commitments, but it also points to the occasional stealthiness of the Indian nuclear establishment—like the Israeli, Pakistani, and other nuclear establishments—in pursuing its objectives.

FOREIGN POLICY CONTEXT, LATE 1983

By the end of 1983, India's regional and international standing was mixed. Indira Gandhi served energetically at the beginning of her three-year term as chairperson of the Non-aligned Movement and hosted the "organization's" summit in Delhi in March 1983. Pakistan's President Zia attended the forum, and despite some contretemps over Kashmir, he and Mrs. Gandhi presided over the formal establishment of a joint commission between the two states on March 10. The joint commission met in Pakistan on June 4 and continued to discuss a possible treaty between the two countries. Yet ongoing concerns over alleged Pakistani support for insurgents in the Punjab and alleged Indian support of dissatisfied elements in Sindh prevented real progress.

More broadly, Indira Gandhi was determined to reassert Indian hegemony in South Asia as the United States continued to arm Pakistan, the Soviets remained in Afghanistan, and China buttressed Pakistan and perhaps insurgents in the northeast. In a July statement of what became known as the "Indira Doctrine," she proclaimed that "India will neither intervene in the domestic affairs of any states in the region, nor tolerate such intervention by an outside power. If external assistance is needed to meet an internal crisis, states should first look within the region for help."[154] India was where Mrs. Gandhi intended regional states to look, and this reassertion of regional primacy reflected the traditional Indian conception of the subcontinent as a cultural and geographic unity centered on India.

India's expression of its dominant role in South Asia prompted a backlash from Sri Lanka, Bangladesh, and Nepal.[155] India was caught betwixt and between, unable to achieve recognition as a global power and resented for its regional might. All of this contributed to a rise in the collective defense expenditures of South Asian states from around 3 percent of GNP in 1978 to about 4.5 percent in regional GNP in 1981.[156] Given the mass poverty and underdevelopment of the region, the trend was counterproductive even if security perceptions warranted the Indian defense buildup in the center of the region.

India's foreign policy in this period was Indira's foreign policy, as she was its dominant shaper and executor. On most of her foreign travels she did not bother to include Foreign Minister Narasimha Rao, even though she respected his acumen and relied on him as a trusted political adviser.[157] In evaluating her policy, the press tended to argue, as *India Today* did, that "domestic compulsions have outweighed other considerations. With a general election looming threateningly, a shrewd tactician like Mrs. Gandhi would hardly be likely to abandon any opportunity to take advantage of external situations to feather her domestic nest."[158] Yet, as the *Indian Express* noted, she lacked a strategy to stabilize relations with neighbors and provide India with a long-term base for exercising greater global sway.[159] Instead, "India seems to be seeking a global role in its foreign policy when all its day-to-day challenges are of a purely regional nature."[160] More robust nuclear and missile programs could have helped deter potential Pakistani aggression, but they could not solve the more immediate challenges issuing from Pakistan, from disaffected groups in India, or from India's other neighbors.

PAKISTAN'S BOMB LOOMS LARGER, 1984

By late 1983 and early 1984, India perceived a number of threats emanating from Pakistan. Beyond the ongoing signs of Pakistan's growing nuclear capability, the most immediate problem was fear that Pakistan supported or would support violent insurgency by Sikhs in Punjab. India reportedly had begun countering Pakistan by supporting dissident elements in the southern Pakistani state of Sindh.[161] New Delhi and Islamabad routinely denied the charges of subversion, but the traditions of both countries' intelligence services suggested that each was balancing the other's destabilizing acts. Both India and Pakistan positioned large numbers of army forces on their respective sides of the border, wanting to deter escalation. These military moves and the accompanying rhetoric stemmed primarily from domestic considerations—the interest of both governments to use the real and exaggerated threats of foreign intervention to impose internal order.[162] By February 1984 tensions abated.

However, February brought publication of an ominous interview with Pakistan's A. Q. Khan in the Urdu-language newspaper *Nawa-e-Waqt*. Celebrating Pakistan's capacity to enrich uranium in the face of anti-Islamic international obstacles, Khan boasted that "by the grace of God we have left India behind by many years in uranium enrichment . . . and [lifted] Pakistan to an eminent status at the international level in such a short time."[163] The capacity to enrich uranium meant that Pakistan could produce a bomb if "the President were to take this extreme step for the safety and security of the country."[164] Referring to the Pokhran blast, Khan noted that "[t]en years ago India has done this job, though other countries had helped it." Now, he said, "[w]e have the capability of doing it."[165]

Khan's bilious, boastful interview naturally affected the routinely scheduled March Indian debate over the defense budget and defense policy. The debate featured typical partisan wrangling over government policy, the nature of the overall Pakistani threat, and the trade-off between spending on defense and development. As usual, few parliamentarians attended the debate, whose outcome was a foregone conclusion. One critic aptly decried the government's failure to provide Parliament with the data and expertise needed "to understand in depth the problems of defence" on a level that Parliaments "in other democratic countries" do.[166] This same man wondered why, if India possessed a military advantage over Pakistan, the government was creating an "atmosphere" of imminent threat.[167] Others lamented the reliance on expensive weapons imports and the failure indigenously to produce modern tanks, aircraft, and other systems.[168] One noted that a recently retired high-ranking general had called for the creation of a National Security Council to rationalize planning and that this same general had said that India's greatest threat came "from within the country rather than from without."[169] The only mention of nuclear dangers came from a member who spoke generally about the risk that "if there is a nuclear conflagration anywhere in the world, the entire planet is going to be brought within its grip."[170]

Defence Minister Venkataraman calmly rebutted each criticism, knowing that the body was inclined to approve the requested budget. He deflected critics who demanded to know whether India in fact had a national security doctrine by explaining that "the definition of 'Doctrine' according to Oxford Dictionary is: 'religious, political, scientific, etc., belief, dogma or tenet.' We have no tenet. We have a pragmatic approach to the Defence problems."[171] On the nuclear question, he argued that "if there is one person who has consistently gone on with a campaign for nuclear disarmament, it is our Prime Minister."[172] He then added, "I do not know, and I cannot say, whether Pakistan has nuclear capability. How can anybody know?"[173] Venkataraman acknowledged reading reports that Pakistan had achieved uranium enrichment capability but said that other reports contradicted this. "But as far as Defence is concerned and as far as this Defence Minister is concerned, I will proceed on the footing that they have nuclear capability. But what we do on that is a different thing . . . ."[174]

Before he could complete the thought, a member intervened to ask whether Venkataraman had seen the recent disclosure by A. Q. Khan. He had, but suggested strangely that Khan may have had other motives such as "getting membership in the IAEA."[175] Another parliamentarian pressed on, asking what steps the government was taking based on Venkataraman's assumption that Pakistan did have nuclear capability. "I have already said . . . that you need not match the tank with the tank and this and that," the defense minister countered. "All that I am bound to do is to take note of such a situation and then make arrangements for meeting a contingency of that kind."[176] Here the sometimes frivolous, Harvard-educated member Dr. Subramaniam Swamy interjected, "No joint strike with the Israelis, I hope."[177] A quick exchange of barbs ensued, and then Venkataraman continued: "I want to make it clear that it is the definite, determined and express policy of this Government to use nuclear energy for peaceful purposes."[178] As Venkataraman knew, the prime minister had a year earlier flirted with another nuclear test and decided against it. All he could do was hedge.

However, the modest stir caused by A. Q. Khan's interview did not abate. A prominent journalist, K. C. Khanna, argued in the *Times of India* on March 28 that India should respond by declaring openly its nuclear weapons capabilities and matching Pakistan step-by-step.[179] On March 30, Minister of External Affairs Narasimha Rao addressed a parliamentary request that the government respond to reports of "nuclear collaboration between Pakistan and China." Rao referred to the Khan interview and to recent reports from the United States that China had transferred nuclear weapon design information to Pakistan.[180] This countered Khan's self-serving, incorrect claim of Pakistan's nuclear self-sufficiency. Rao continued that the government kept constant watch on all developments affecting India's security. When a member questioned whether India should "continue with [its] policy of using nuclear energy for peaceful purposes when Pakistan is preparing an atom bomb" with Chinese help, Rao ended by quoting a statement by the prime minister to the Lok Sabha on March 28: "Government is vigilant in the matter. Indian scientists are keeping abreast of all aspects of research and development connected with modern and relevant technologies."[181]

This mild statement belied the fact that the nuclear establishment had already prepared the Pokhran test site for another nuclear explosion and was eager to test a design advanced from the 1974 blast. However, mere word of Pakistan's nuclear capability was not enough to cause a change in the government's policy to refrain from further explosive tests or production of nuclear weapons. Without the internationally recognizable provocation of a Pakistani nuclear explosion, it would be difficult for the nuclear establishment to prevail on the prime minister to authorize an Indian detonation.

Yet India still faced the conundrum of how to respond to Pakistan's nuclear challenge. A preemptive attack to try to destroy Pakistan's capability remained unpromising, as did reliance on the United States to constrain the Pakistani nuclear program. Direct bilateral diplomacy could reduce the risk of conflict— and the risk of escalation to a nuclear arms race or the actual use of nuclear weapons—but no breakthroughs appeared likely. The Indian armed forces could increase their capacity to fight in a "nuclear environment" by developing weaponry and doctrine to advance quickly into Pakistan in the event of hostilities in hopes of blunting Pakistan's capability to deploy nuclear weapons. However, this would take time and offer no great reassurance. The least risky strategy was to bide time, avoid provocations, pursue diplomacy and keep the nuclear "powder" dry while downplaying either side's explicit interest in nuclear weaponry.

In accord with this approach, Indira Gandhi addressed an Air Force Commanders Conference in late April and acknowledged the increase in conventional security threats born of Pakistan's acquisition of advanced conventional weaponry. She did not mention nuclear weapons.[182] Still, despite the growing concerns over intentions and military threats, neither India nor Pakistan sought a conflict. In mid-May, Indian and Pakistani foreign secretaries met in Islamabad to resume discussions on the no-war and treaty of peace, friendship, and cooperation proposals.

Days later, Vice President George Bush traveled to India and Pakistan. In New Delhi, Bush tried to allay India's growing concern that beyond the personal niceties between Ronald Reagan and Indira Gandhi, U.S. policy was opposed to democratic India and favored the dictatorial regime of Pakistan.[183] Bush's visit itself symbolized high-level American interest in both India and Pakistan, and he used it to help remove bureaucratic obstacles to implementing the American-Indian Memorandum of Understanding on cooperation in high technology, which had been agreed to during the 1982 Washington summit.[184] The U.S. Departments of Defense and Energy and the Arms Control and Disarmament Agency had been reluctant to approve this cooperation for fear that India would not keep American equipment from the Soviet Union or from being used in the nuclear explosive program. In any case, progress on technology cooperation did little to diminish Indian concern about increased American military aid to Pakistan.

Nor did the American and Soviet failure to advance nuclear arms control satisfy India's long-standing calls for nuclear disarmament. Thus, in May 1984, Indira Gandhi joined with the leaders of Sweden, Mexico, Tanzania, Argentina, and Greece to issue a so-called "five continents" appeal for a freeze in the development and testing of nuclear weapons.[185] This initiative, organized by a New Zealand–based nongovernmental organization, expressed the international nuclear freeze movement's growing dissatisfaction with U.S.-Soviet nuclear weapon policies and provided a platform on which Rajiv Gandhi would later build a more detailed, phased plan for reversing the global nuclear arms race. India's role in this and subsequent international disarmament campaigns reinforced its normative position against nuclear weapons. This complicated any potential Indian consideration of conducting another nuclear explosive test.

THREAT AT HOME—THE GOLDEN TEMPLE CALAMITY, JUNE 1984

In June, after Bush's departure, India acted on what it perceived as its greatest security problem by deploying the army to take control in Punjab and roust the Sikh militants led by Sant Jarnail Singh Bhindranwale, who had been occupying the Golden Temple in Amritsar since the summer of 1982. Bhindranwale had instigated brutal acts of Sikh violence against Hindus in Punjab as part of an effort to drive them from the state and to prompt Sikhs living in other states to move to Punjab to avoid communal reprisals against them.[186] All of this was part of a strategy to create a separate Sikh state within the boundaries of Punjab. Bhindranwale had been arrested in September 1981 on murder conspiracy charges and then released on October 14 because the government—not a court—deemed the evidence insufficient to hold him. After his release he continued to inspire violent Sikh militancy. Having moved into the sacred Golden Temple compound in 1982, he animated his movement's insurgency with confidence that the government would be reluctant to risk Sikh outrage by entering the Golden Temple to detain him. The government pursued a variety of tactics over the next two years to calm the Sikh agitation by splitting factions, negotiating with alternative Sikh leaders, rallying Hindu counteragitation, and generally finding some compromise by which the Sikhs could be accommodated without creating a separate Sikh state. Meanwhile, Bhindranwale and his followers fortified the Golden Temple compound.

Finally, in June 1984, Mrs. Gandhi concluded that negotiations were fruitless and Bhindranwale and his followers could not be starved out of the sacred compound without risk of statewide uprisings.[187] A military assault became the only option in the prime minister's mind, and in that of the military leadership then headed on the scene by Lieutenant General K. Sundarji, the general officer commanding in chief, Western Command. On June 2, Mrs. Gandhi announced in a radio and television broadcast that the army was being called in to take control of security in the state. After taking positions around the Golden Temple, the army began firing on the night of June 3, a major Sikh holiday commemorating Guru Arjun Dev's martyrdom. The temple occupiers had called for a statewide uprising on this holy day, and the army feared that if it waited to begin the military operation, it would be surrounded by Sikhs marching into the Amritsar area. When the temple occupiers did not surrender, the army commenced a full-scale assault, Operation Blue Star, on June 5.

Army forces took unexpected casualties and encountered severe opposition, which led them to escalate the firepower directed at the Akal Takht, or Eternal Throne, one of the complex's most sacred buildings. In the end, on the morning of June 7, Bhindranwale and his closest associates were found dead in the basement of the Akal Takht. A subsequent government white paper stated that 493 people in the complex were killed and 86 injured. According to Tully and Jacob, the government's assessment left at least 1,600 people unaccounted for, although they do not suggest what fraction of these were killed or wounded.[188] The army, according to the government, suffered 83 deaths and 249 casualties, out of the roughly 1,000 men involved in the operation.[189] Although the army tried to spare the Golden Temple from damage, it was scarred, and other important buildings in the sacred complex were badly damaged.[190]

Recriminations over Operation Blue Star continue to this day. The narrow objective was accomplished, but at a terrible price in lives, sacred property, and Sikh-Hindu relations. Communal riots soon erupted in New Delhi and other cities, increasing the death toll and damage to the Indian state. Several Sikh army regiments mutinied in the aftermath, causing the most serious crisis of discipline in the Indian Army since independence.[191] The government compounded the communal problem first by laying blame for the debacle indiscriminately on the entire Sikh community, then by issuing a white paper that failed to distinguish between the separatist demands of Bhindranwale and his group and the more moderate demands of the Akali Dal party, which represented the majority of Sikhs. When the white paper failed to calm the polity, the government then resorted to blaming Pakistan and other "foreign hands" for the crisis.[192] According to Tully and Jacob's detailed investigation, Pakistan's role in the Punjab crisis was minimal, reflecting Zia's determination to avoid provoking a war that he believed Mrs. Gandhi might have welcomed as a distraction from her domestic problems.[193]

It would take years to stabilize Punjab, notwithstanding a formal settlement that was reached by Rajiv Gandhi and the Akali Dal in 1985. This settlement extended Punjab's sovereignty over the Sikh-majority city of Chandigarh, which had previously been administered by the central government and shared as the seat of state assemblies by both Punjab and Haryana. Chandigarh now became the capital of Punjab.

Operation Blue Star bore in several indirect ways on Indian nuclear policy. It led directly to Indira Gandhi's assassination by her Sikh bodyguards four months later. This opened the door for a potential change in nuclear policy if her successor, son Rajiv, had been so inclined. Second, the military operation itself intensified the political leadership's determination to keep the military out of policy-making.[194] This was unfair insofar as the army had not ordered itself into Amritsar but had been brought there by civilian leaders who had let the situation get out of control. Yet, tactical second-guessing over the conduct of the operation caused Rajiv Gandhi and his associates to react warily to General Sundarji's subsequent pressure to clarify nuclear policy and doctrine. This did not stop Sundarji's rise through the ranks to vice chief of the army and then, in 1986, to chief of army staff. But while politicians would increasingly rely on the army to restore domestic order, they, with few exceptions, resisted giving the services voice in policy formation. Third, the Golden Temple assault deepened the Indian polity's preoccupation with the challenge of internal order.

NUCLEAR TENSIONS ESCALATE— INDIRA GANDHI ASSASSINATED, OCTOBER 1984

As India struggled for calm after the unsettling events in Punjab, concerns over the U.S. role in Pakistan and its implications for India's nuclear security were reignited by several events and reports in early October. On October 5, Pakistan's *Nawa-e-Waqt* published an article from Washington alleging that President Reagan had written a letter to President Zia urging, among other things, that Pakistan undo work it may have undertaken to produce nuclear weapons. If Pakistan did so, and abandoned its nuclear weapon effort, the report alleged, "America is ready to provide the kind of atomic umbrella it provides to NATO member countries."[195] This report triggered alarms in India, prompting American officials to deny that the United States had offered to place Pakistan under its nuclear umbrella.[196] India's fears were compounded when, on October 10, U.S. Ambassador to Pakistan Deane Hinton told questioners following a speech in Lahore that the United States would be "responsive" if India attacked Pakistan.[197]

Hinton's comment referred indirectly to American press reports weeks earlier that U.S. intelligence officials had briefed Congress that Indian military advisers were once again urging Indira Gandhi to authorize an attack on Pakistan's nuclear facilities.[198] State Department officials had downplayed the reports as alarmist, but they acknowledged that some intelligence had been received about a possible Indian attack.[199] The intelligence focused on satellite photographs of the Ambala air base in Haryana (roughly three hundred miles from Kahuta), where two squadrons of Indian Jaguar fighter-bombers were based. Photographs taken in late summer appeared to show the Jaguars missing, triggering alarms that they had been redeployed for an attack on Kahuta.[200] In fact, according a former high-ranking Indian Air Force officer, the planes had been hidden in woods adjacent to the airfield as part of a passive air defense drill. "We had a tremendous laugh at the Americans," the officer recounted in an interview. "Satellites are good for intelligence, but they're not perfect."[201] Still, Pakistan reacted to the reports, prompting India to take precautionary measures in turn. Pakistan increased its air patrols over Kahuta, according to the Indian officer. "We said, 'fine, burn up your engines,' " he added chuckling. But India also alerted air defenses around the nuclear facilities at Trombay. The fact that both sides upped their defensive activities and became prepared for military action as a result of faulty intelligence kindled the situation for an unintended escalation if a spark had somehow been thrown into the mix. As the Indian officer acknowledged somberly, "If they think you're going to attack Kahuta, they may pre-empt you."[202]

The swirling rumors and reports apparently helped impel Mrs. Gandhi to tell a gathering of Indian Army commanders on October 11 that "Pakistan's nuclear program has brought about a qualitative change in our security environment."[203] She added that the United States continued to supply Pakistan with military equipment despite "evidence compiled by Americans themselves about Pakistan's nuclear program." The perception that Washington consciously ignored and did too little to stop Pakistan's nuclear program fueled India's feelings that it was being given short shrift. The perception intensified that Indian nuclear self-restraint was more than Washington or Pakistan deserved. Indeed, the imbroglio over a possible Indian attack on Pakistan and countervailing U.S. assurances to Islamabad occurred against the backdrop of a visit to Washington by Pakistan's Foreign Minister Sahibzada Yaqub Khan. Among other things, Yaqub Khan brought a new request for an American airborne early-warning system. Indian officials and commentators felt that the Pakistanis and the Americans were seeking pretexts for justifying ongoing military aid and strongly denied that India had any plans to attack Pakistan's nuclear facilities.[204] In a righteous sign of Indian pique over these developments, Indira Gandhi on October 16 sealed the Indo-Pak border.[205]

The episode only increased pressures to strengthen India's nuclear capabilities. In late 1984, *Foreign Report*, an "intelligence" newsletter published by the *Economist*, alleged that India was prepared to undertake a second nuclear explosion within two months and that Indian scientists were, perhaps, developing plans for a hydrogen bomb.[206] While highly speculative, the report reflected Western intelligence agencies' concerns that Indo-Pak nuclear competition was mounting.

Then, tragically, Indira Gandhi was assassinated on October 31. Her Sikh bodyguards, wreaking vengeance for the Golden Temple calamity, altered India's broad history and, perhaps, its nuclear trajectory. One can only speculate what might have happened had she remained alive in this period of escalating nuclear tension.

CONCLUSION

India faced dramatic, complicated strategic problems during the 1980-to-1984 period. U.S. aid to Pakistan in the Afghan war and Pakistan's advancing nuclear weapon program created the kind of external environment that, according to Realist theory, would call for robust countervailing developments of nuclear capability. Yet India again restrained itself. Despite pressures from the nuclear establishment and rising military voices urging acquisition of nuclear weapons, the prime minister refused to authorize another nuclear explosive test or other measures to weaponize India's nuclear capability. This reflected her post-1974 chariness toward the nuclear scientists and the military, as well as the increased role of professional, broad-gauged advisers in the prime minister's office who buffered the ambitions of the scientific community. The result chagrined advocates of nuclear weapons such as General Sundarji, who lamented after his retirement, "Between the mid-Seventies and the mid-Eighties, India's [nuclear] decision-making . . . appears to have enjoyed something between a drugged sleep and a deep postprandial siesta."[207] In this view, India suffered from the ongoing lack of institutional mechanisms to enable national security experts, including the military, to analyze security threats and prescribe short- or long-term security strategies. As Sundarji noted, "The really big secret is that India has no coherent nuclear weapon policy and worse still, she does not even have an institutionalised system for analysing and throwing up policy options in this regard."[208]

However, the government's position did not lack reason. Beyond Indira Gandhi's moral aversion to nuclear weapons, the alarms over possible conventional military attacks on nuclear facilities in Pakistan and India showed that even without nuclear bombs each state was already at risk. This may have created a rudimentary form of deterrence while raising fears that the region would become much less secure if an actual nuclear arms race broke out. Indira Gandhi and her closest political advisers had an intuitive sense that nuclear weapons would not provide usable solutions to India's external problems, and they recognized that India's well-being required other priorities. Internal disorder constituted the greatest threat to the state. Internal instability had mounted to the point where the army had been deployed for domestic purposes 82 times in fiscal 1982–1983, 96 times in 1983–1984, and 175 times in 1984–1985.[209]

At bottom, this period in India's history showed that a poor democracy cannot do everything that richer or less accountable governments can. Resource pressures and the needs of average voters forced Indian leaders to establish priorities. Their political antennae and intuitive sense that nuclear weapons are not usable, and are therefore something of a troublesome luxury, motivated them to buy time and keep their options open.

TEN

Nuclear Capabilities Grow and Policy Ambivalence Remains

NOVEMBER 1984–DECEMBER 1987

Indira Gandhi's tragic end deepened the people's attachment to the Nehru-Gandhi family, notwithstanding her many flaws. Son Rajiv quickly became heir to the democratic dynasty. From his swearing in on October 31, 1984, to his electoral defeat in November 1989, Rajiv largely determined India's nuclear policy, if not its capabilities.

Rajiv Gandhi emerged at a time when Pakistan was nearing the capacity to produce nuclear weapons. This increased pressures from within India's national security establishment to develop strategies and capabilities for maintaining political and military supremacy over Pakistan. This chapter describes several efforts by strategic advisers and military leaders to effect a clearer and more robust approach to nuclear policy, and Rajiv's reluctance to heed them. While the prime minister did not answer calls for building and deploying a nuclear arsenal, he also did not stop the strategic enclave from refining and experimentally proving fission weapons behind laboratory walls. Rajiv, more than his predecessors and successors, had a personal interest in technology and wanted to be kept informed of the program's development. No major steps like explosive testing could have been contemplated without Rajiv's involvement, but the scientists felt they had approval to continue to refine fission devices. They also felt it within their purview to develop designs for boosted-fission weapons and to explore the basic design and material inventory necessary to produce thermonuclear weapons.

Rajiv Gandhi and his key advisers recognized that defense modernization and overall technological development required improving ties with the United States, while maintaining good relations with the Soviet Union. These considerations reduced the political feasibility of assembling and deploying nuclear weapons. Instead, key advisers like Defence Research and Development Organisation

Director General Arunachalam pursued a strategy of developing capabilities without burnishing them provocatively.

THE NEW LEADER OF NUCLEAR POLICY: RAJIV GANDHI, DECEMBER 1984

Rajiv Gandhi was the unlikeliest of Indian prime ministers, were it not for his birth into the Nehru-Gandhi political dynasty. The deaths of his younger brother, Sanjay, in a flying accident in 1980 and then his mother in 1984 sealed his fate. Sanjay was the political son. For good and frequently ill he sought and wielded political influence under his mother's wing, and she clearly envisioned him as a future leader of India. Rajiv, on the other hand, lacked the temperament and desire for the rough and tumble of Indian politics. He preferred instead a more private life of upper-class, Western-oriented pleasure and the company of family and friends. His chosen career as a pilot for Indian Airlines suited his ambitions and temperament. He could be quietly in command, controlling an aircraft and his life without the constant mixing and struggling of politics. Yet, having been stripped of the dynastic cover provided by his brother, Rajiv was pulled into Indian politics in 1980 and then, in 1984, thrust onto its highest stage. While accounts of his interest in political power vary, most agree that he began political life reluctantly and never took to it naturally or adeptly.[1]

Rajiv took office less than nine hours after Indira Gandhi's death on October 31 and soon called for national elections. These were held in late December and resulted in Congress's winning 415 out of 542 seats, its greatest majority ever. Congress's 49 percent of the vote contrasted with the Bharatiya Janata Party's 7.7 percent and only 2 seats. The two Communist parties combined to win 28 seats. One issue dominated the campaign: the unity of India. The nation was haunted by the Punjab crisis, the postassassination violence of Hindus against Sikhs, and the ongoing insurgencies in Assam and elsewhere in the northeast. Rajiv promised to put the house in order, befitting the rise of a new generation of leaders who would end the corruption, back-scratching, and bickering of traditional Indian politics. The handsome forty-year-old prime minister adopted the mantle of "Mr. Clean."

From the beginning Rajiv was averse to the traditional ways of Indian bureaucracy and politics. His pilot's disposition and training, and his attraction to technology—particularly computers—inclined him toward a "cockpit mentality."[2] Orders should be given and then carried out with little need for politicking, compromising, or attending to competing interests and sensibilities. This affected his attitude toward the headstrong nuclear establishment. As a former high-ranking Atomic Energy Commission official put it: "Rajiv had this push-button attitude. He wanted to make a decision, push a button, and have things happen automatically, with little interest in hearing the views of others who may not agree with him."[3]

Foreign policy barely had been debated in the election, and nuclear policy even less so. In his earliest pronouncements on the nuclear threat from Pakistan, Rajiv struck a calming note. "At the moment," he declared in February 1985, "I don't see a situation arising when we would start . . . making the bomb. Just the fact that Pakistan made a bomb would not make us change our policy."[4]

This position reflected Rajiv's personal skepticism about the value of nuclear weapons for India and his desire to promote conciliation with Pakistan. In a broadcast to the nation two weeks after his mother's death, he declared that "[f]or nation-building, the first requisite is peace—peace with our neighbours and peace in the world. . . . We want to develop closer relations with each one of our immediate neighbours. . . . That is what we have offered to Pakistan."[5] Turning to nuclear weapons, the new prime minister said, "Indira Gandhi reminded us that the most important single challenge before the world today is the threat of nuclear war. We shall continue her relentless crusade against the arms race."[6] At this early stage, Rajiv "was totally against" nuclear weapons, recalled a former high-ranking defense official who worked closely with him on nuclear issues.[7] According to this official, Rajiv did not trust the leadership of the Atomic Energy Commission and felt that the scientists had mistakenly persuaded his mother to conduct the Pokhran test in 1974.

Raja Ramanna has acknowledged that his relations with Rajiv were strained. Rajiv, he wrote, adopted "swift changes in policy without much forethought—possible repercussions were ignored and experienced professionals were dismissed as 'fussy old men.' "[8] For his part, Rajiv resented the AEC old guard's tendency to treat him as the son of Indira Gandhi, not a formidable figure in his own right. Rajiv found patronizing and disrespectful the tendency of Ramanna or other scientists to refer to his mother's policies or statements in trying to persuade Rajiv of a point.[9] He also felt that the Department of Atomic Energy had not delivered the electrical power it was supposed to. The nuclear establishment's explanations for delays in power plant construction and operations exasperated him. His limited patience strained, Rajiv asked financial officials to evaluate other options for providing electricity, including the import of reactors from abroad. This in turn provoked resistance from Ramanna and the nuclear establishment.[10]

Rajiv was unlikely to step up overt work on nuclear weapons as he was more comfortable projecting India's image as a leader for nuclear disarmament. However, he did nothing to stop the scientists and engineers in the defense and atomic energy establishments from refining India's weapon options in case they should be needed. This seemingly contradictory or hypocritical approach may have reflected Rajiv's ambivalence. In any case, Indian officials reconciled it with the belief that intentions mattered greatly. They, unlike the declared nuclear powers, intended not to test and deploy a nuclear arsenal if they could avoid it.

DEVELOPMENTS IN PAKISTAN, MARCH TO APRIL 1985

Had Rajiv Gandhi been interested in building up India's nuclear weapon capability, Pakistan provided reasons for doing so. In early March 1985, American television broadcast an hour-long documentary on Pakistan's clandestine effort to procure bomb components, prompting additional Indian press commentary and debate on the Pakistani threat.[11] Also in March, a West German court convicted a German businessman of smuggling to Pakistan (between 1977 and 1980) an entire chemical plant for producing uranium hexafluoride—the gasified material used in uranium enrichment.[12] On March 14, A. Q. Khan gave another provocative interview, this time in a small-circulation Urdu weekly, *Hurmat*.[13] Khan insisted that Pakistan's nuclear program was entirely for peaceful purposes, yet he hinted that the nation could carry out "an atomic explosion in a very short time, if required, without conducting any test."[14]

To reaffirm Washington's determination to keep a lid on the Pakistani program, Under Secretary of State for Political Affairs Michael Armacost traveled to Islamabad in March. He sought reassurance that Pakistan would refrain from enriching uranium above 5 percent—as requested in Ronald Reagan's September 1984 letter to President Zia—and would not take other steps toward the manufacture of nuclear weapons.[15] But U.S. nonproliferation policy was subsidiary to working with Pakistan to help the Afghan mujahideen defeat the Soviets. Thus, Armacost packaged his nonproliferation imprecations with an offer of AIM-9L missiles for the F-16 aircraft the United States was supplying Pakistan. "We didn't want the Pakistanis to have nuclear weapons, but we were realistic on the need to provide incentives, not just sanctions," Armacost later explained.[16]

Indians felt that the United States could compel a weaker state like Pakistan to comply with its demands if it wanted to. The additional arms offer thus suggested that Washington was not seriously trying to stop Pakistan's nuclear program.[17] If Rajiv Gandhi was to avoid pressure to build up India's nuclear weapon effort, he needed to reassure his constituents that the United States would help constrain the Pakistani threat. The prime minister therefore planned to push the Reagan administration on these matters during his upcoming June visit to the United States.[18]

Rajiv also communicated his concerns to Pakistanis directly. In an April interview with Mushahid Hussain, editor of the *Muslim*, he categorically rejected the notion that nuclear weapons would stabilize Indo-Pak relations by creating a deterring "balance of terror." "I have never subscribed to the view that 'terror,' balanced or otherwise, would stabilise anything," he said. "A nuclear arms race in the subcontinent would only subject both our peoples to the worst possible fate on earth."[19]

However, Pakistan, as the weaker subcontinental state, did not share this antipathy toward nuclear deterrence. Hopes that the United States could induce Pakistani nuclear restraint foundered on a reality that American officials preferred to downplay and Indian officials chose to avoid: Pakistan would by hook or crook acquire nuclear weapons unless and until relations with India were normalized and Pakistani leaders felt no grave threat from India. Unlike the Indian nuclear program, which had complex roots and motives, Pakistan's quest derived simply from its fear and strategic inferiority vis-à-vis India. This meant that achieving nonproliferation in Pakistan required persuading India to accept formal constraints on its nuclear program. Yet, as a former high-ranking American arms control official of this period recalled, "If you ask me how much of my time was spent on the Indian proliferation problem, I'd say 'not much.'" He continued, "We were preoccupied with Pakistan, and even there the top political leadership at the State Department thought nonproliferation was a pain."[20] India received less attention in this former official's view because the administration saw it as a "reluctant proliferator" that was not very actively enhancing its nuclear weapon capabilities at this time.[21]

PRESSURE MOUNTS AGAIN IN INDIA, MAY 1985

By May 1985, the Indian press and Parliament demanded a more robust response to Pakistan's nuclear program. In a Lok Sabha debate, the former Janata government finance minister H. M. Patel urged that India must now go nuclear.[22] The BJP, too, resumed its traditional call for building the bomb. However, Rajiv Gandhi's enormous parliamentary majority meant that he could resist opposition calls. Yet, if his own party became agitated, as had happened to Shastri after the Chinese bomb test in 1964, the prime minister could be compelled to shift course. Perhaps sensing the growing concern within his ranks, Rajiv in early May sounded a harder line. In a major meeting of the All India Congress Committee (AICC) on May 4, he said, "We feel that they [Pakistan] are developing a nuclear weapon . . . [and] we are looking into various aspects of this question to see what action we should take."[23] "Unfortunately," he added, "[w]e are not convinced that all powers which can do so are trying to stop them," referring to the United States.

Some commentators interpreted Rajiv's statement to mean that India would now review and change its nuclear policy.[24] However, Defence Minister Narasimha Rao moved quickly at the AICC meeting to "clarify" the government's position. The interpretation that nuclear policy would be reviewed "is not warranted," Rao said, adding that he had "the support of the Prime Minister in this clarification." India did not want to be alarmist or at loggerheads with Pakistan. "We have to maintain [defence preparedness] whatever be our relations with Pakistan or whatever weapons it gets or not," Rao said.[25]

The government was conflicted. It felt that it should do something on the nuclear front and at the same time should avoid escalating nuclear competition. Meanwhile, other priorities remained greater. The AICC meeting concentrated on controlling prices and improving the lives of the poor, not on nuclear policy.[26] As before, the debate over nuclear policy went on primarily in the press and Parliament. The government sounded a tougher line largely for political effect. Any real decisions would be made by the prime minister in the context of competing political-economic priorities. Rajiv judged India's identity and interests not to lie in building, testing, or deploying nuclear weapons.

RAJIV VISITS THE UNITED STATES AND
TECHNOLOGY COOPERATION GROWS, JUNE 1985

Rajiv sought to continue his mother's foreign policy of nonalignment, mindful of India's special friendship and cooperation with the Soviet Union. His assumption of power predated Mikhail Gorbachev's rise in the Soviet Union by only a few months, and Rajiv quickly struck up a relationship with the new Soviet leader during a May 1985 visit to Moscow. Over the ensuing years the two would interact sympathetically, particularly over the issue of nuclear arms control and disarmament, which Gorbachev pursued creatively and cleverly on the world stage. The internal and global changes initiated by Gorbachev's restructuring of Soviet society profoundly altered India's constellation of interests, as is discussed later in the chapter.

India also sought ways to improve ties with the United States. The Reagan administration by now had determined that global and regional interests required more openness to India. Some conservatives saw India as a potential counter to Communist China in Asia, while others wanted to wean India away from the Soviet Union.[27] To be sure, lingering resentments in the American bureaucracy and Congress over India's alignment with the Soviet Union and its moralistic haughtiness toward the United States caused some to resist a shift in American policy. The Indian system, for its part, remained wary of America's imperialist intentions, practices, and power. Still, both sides now cautiously pursued closer ties.

India especially sought the cooperation of the United States in high-technology development, including defense systems. India's defense establishment recognized the superiority of American technology and wanted to reduce India's reliance on the Soviet Union. Washington and New Delhi finally completed negotiations of a Memorandum of Understanding (MOU) on technology transfer in December 1984. The challenge remained to design procedures to implement the MOU that would allay U.S. concerns that technology or know-how would be diverted from India to the Soviet Union or to non-agreed-to uses. In May 1985, a month before Rajiv Gandhi's scheduled visit to the United States, Ambassador Harry Barnes and Indian Foreign Secretary Romesh Bhandari signed the implementation agreement.[28] Also in May, Under Secretary of Defense for Policy Fred Iklé traveled to New Delhi to pursue increased Indo-American security cooperation. Iklé generally tried to remind India of its own interest in avoiding greater Soviet involvement in southern Asia—from Vietnam to Afghanistan. He held meetings with DRDO head Arunachalam and other officials regarding possible cooperation on the Light Combat Aircraft, which India sought to build indigenously as a long-term substitute for imported fighter aircraft and as a short-term means of gaining advanced technology and proficiency in aircraft engineering. The Iklé talks and subsequent meetings pointed to an agreement on the Light Combat Aircraft that would break a two-decade drought in defense cooperation between the two countries.[29]

High-technology cooperation bore importantly on India's nuclear policy. U.S. officials did not want to get burned by supplying technology to India that would help the Indian bomb and missile programs or wind up in other hands. This is precisely what congressional and nongovernmental nonproliferation activists argued would happen if the administration licensed exports of powerful computers and other technologies to India. For their part, Indian officials recognized that significant observable advances in the nuclear weapon program would interfere with the effort to establish high-technology links with the United States. Rajiv Gandhi and his advisers felt that developing India's high-technology base was more important to India's long-term interests than publicly proclaiming or exhibiting nuclear weapon capability. Neither side made the relationship between technology cooperation and nuclear restraint explicit. The Americans did not "preach" about constraining the Indian nuclear program: they knew that the Indians would then demand greater U.S. nonproliferation pressure on Pakistan, which the Americans did not think would work.[30] For their part, the Indians had no interest in making nonproliferation promises to the Americans, but they also knew from past experience that detectable new developments in the nuclear weapon area would cause problems.

Timing and personality made Rajiv Gandhi an ideal candidate to elevate relations with the United States. He came on the scene at a time when Soviet reform was relaxing some of the rigidity of the cold war framework, encouraging both Washington and New Delhi to explore new opportunities for interaction. Rajiv's interest in modern technology, his media appeal, and his more easygoing manner than his mother endeared him to American officials and audiences. As a leading American policymaker, Michael Armacost, put it, "[T]here was a serious attempt to engage the Indians and Rajiv personally. We were attempting to build a relationship with India as an increasingly important country."[31]

On June 5, Rajiv departed India for a tour that would take him to Egypt, France, Algeria, the United States, and Geneva. In pretrip interviews with American and other foreign correspondents he took a rather tough line, showing his Indian constituents and prospective American interlocutors that he would not be a pushover. He criticized the United States for doing too little to block nuclear proliferation in Pakistan and for supplying weaponry that forced India to divert its resources into an arms race "we didn't start."[32] Anticipating an American proposal for India and Pakistan to agree on mutual inspections of their nuclear establishments, he said that inspections would not be foolproof and therefore would not deter Pakistan from acquiring nuclear weapons.[33] On June 4, Rajiv gave a pretrip interview for the *Good Morning America* television program, in which he was asked if India had a nuclear weapon. "Absolutely categorically I can say we do not have a nuclear weapon," he responded. "We exploded an experimental device in 1974 and we have not carried on any more work on that line at all. We have not exploded any more devices. We have no stockpile. We do not have a nuclear weapon."[34] He also ruled out a preemptive military strike on Pakistan's nuclear facilities. When asked what India would do if Pakistan developed a nuclear weapon, Rajiv declared, "[T]hen we would have to really re-think all our policies."[35] Meanwhile, the weaponeers would develop the technological options to respond if necessary.

On June 5, the French newspaper *Le Monde* reported intriguingly that Gandhi had told reporters that if India decided to become a nuclear power it would take only a few weeks or months to do so.[36] Here the prime minister had let slip what the top scientists had told him when he asked why they were working so intently to refine nuclear explosive technology even though there was no program to build or deploy nuclear weapons: they said, "[I]f the government should ever want this capability, you shall have it."[37] The nuclear and defense scientific establishments continued refining their capabilities through laboratory and conventional high-explosive experiments, even if they were not allowed to conduct full-scale tests. Rajiv and the scientists reconciled laboratory work with the official denial that India possessed nuclear weapons or even a nuclear weapon program: in their view, intentions and actual weaponization mattered most. Know-how and preparedness gave them an option to transgress the political and moral taboos of possessing nuclear weapons, but as long as they did not actually and openly cross the line, they felt they could legitimately say that they did not seek nuclear weapons. Some, such as Roberta Wohlstetter, argued that this was nothing less than strategically motivated sophistry, and that India since at least the mid-1960s had been determined to build a nuclear arsenal.[38] Yet this view overlooked the ambivalence and hesitance of successive Indian prime ministers and the fact that they and the scientific establishment excluded the military from a role in nuclear policymaking. Key Indian actors genuinely did not see nuclear policy as a black-or-white, yes-or-no issue, although they were less "innocent" than their rhetoric frequently claimed. That is, they had decided not to decide one way or another to build a nuclear arsenal, but wanted to have the option to move either way.

Rajiv arrived in Washington on June 12 and was received with ceremonial splendor by President Reagan on the White House south lawn. Among other symbolically important activities, Rajiv was asked to address the U.S. Congress, something his mother was never invited to do in her three official visits to Washington but which his grandfather, Jawaharlal Nehru, had done in 1949.[39] From Washington, Rajiv traveled with Vice President George Bush to the NASA space center in Houston, reinforcing the new leader's image and appeal as a man of the high-technology future.

Manner and tone have always mattered in U.S.-Indian relations, frequently for the worst. Hence, the positive way in which the Indian and American leaders got along during this visit was important. Substantively, the summit accomplished relatively little because what India really wanted—beyond an American shutdown of the Pakistani nuclear program—was cooperation in high technology. This would take time to work out. The American side, particularly the Defense Department, was willing to sell weapons to India, but the Indians were less interested in buying complete systems than in joint development and production.[40] Thus, the two sides danced around the defense sales question. Reagan's team saw its own willingness to offer sales as a major sign of interest in India, but they did not want to seem too neglectful of nonproliferation and anti-Soviet concerns that would be raised in the bureaucracy and in Congress. India did not want to seem eager to buy, mindful of past difficulties and the potential controversy a new sensitive-technology agreement with the United States could elicit at home and in Moscow.[41]

India's highest priority was to win American participation in the Light Combat Aircraft project. Indian officials led by Arunachalam especially sought U.S. agreement to allow the transfer of General Electric 404 jet engines. The Indian Meteorological Department sought also to import a state-of-the art Cray supercomputer, model XMP-24. The working-level meetings between Indian and American officials concentrated on these issues within the rubric of implementing the technology cooperation MOU.

In the months following the June summit both sides sought to give practical meaning to their now-bolstered political relationship. In August 1985, Arunachalam traveled to the United States with a team of defense research officials that included his successor Abdul Kalam for two weeks of meetings with top American officials—Iklé, Secretary of Defense Caspar Weinberger, and National Security Adviser Robert McFarlane—and defense and electronics industry leaders.[42] The primary purpose was to explore possible partnerships in the design and production of components for the Light Combat Aircraft and to negotiate the purchase of jet engines from General Electric. Iklé found Arunachalam "extremely intelligent and extraordinarily informed." "We were astonished in the Defense Department," Iklé recalled, "with the detailed requests Arunachalam made for the latest pieces of aircraft technology. Our people were not aware of many of the items, so they had to call the manufacturers to find out about them. Invariably, it was the latest in technology, stuff that was not on the Pentagon's radar screen."[43] The Reagan-Gandhi summit and Iklé's solid credentials as a cold warrior helped break through Washington's anti-Soviet barriers to Indo-American technology cooperation.

However, the request for the Cray supercomputer raised more difficult problems for American officials. Despite Indian assurances that the computer would be used only for meteorological purposes—such as predicting monsoons to augment agricultural forecasting and civil preparedness for often deadly floods—both sides recognized that the machine's massive computational power could be used for designing nuclear warheads and ballistic missiles, deciphering cryptographic codes, and other security applications. The United States zealously sought to maintain its global advantage in this technology by limiting supercomputer exports only to close allies. The Indian request represented a watershed with major potential security implications. Reagan wanted to supply the computer, and said as much to Rajiv Gandhi when they met in October around the time of the UN General Assembly meeting in New York. However, the bureaucracy contested the matter into 1987, when a compromise was finally struck whereby the United States approved the sale of a less powerful Cray XMP-14 computer rather than the XMP-24.[44] This resolution of the supercomputer issue frustrated Indian officials, who had been encouraged by Reagan, but the United States saw it as a good faith effort to build on the successful June 1985 Gandhi-Reagan summit.

INDIA'S WEAPON POTENTIAL GROWS, AUGUST 1985

The shared Indian-American interest in intensifying high-technology cooperation motivated India to keep its nuclear weapon capabilities sub rosa. However, Pakistan continued to stimulate countervailing pressures. On July 11, 1985, ABC's *Good Morning America* reported that Pakistan successfully had tested the nonnuclear triggering package for a nuclear weapon.[45] This entailed the detonation of conventional high explosives arrayed around a dummy core of nonnuclear material simulated to replicate a core of highly enriched uranium. For an effective nuclear explosion to occur the conventional high explosives must be detonated in a way that directs a spherically symmetrical force on the weapon core, compressing it as one might an orange into the size of a grape, enabling the core to achieve supercriticality. Pakistan's achievement represented a major step toward nuclear weapons. At the same time, the Reagan administration wanted to avoid pressure to cut off Afghan war aid to Pakistan. Administration officials recruited Republican Senator Larry Pressler of South Dakota to sponsor a bill to allow aid to proceed as long as the president could certify that Pakistan did "not possess a nuclear explosive device."[46] The Pressler Amendment later became a controversial nonproliferation sanction against Pakistan, but it began as a means to facilitate aid over nonproliferation objections.

The Indian press reacted strongly to Pakistan's advance. The *Hindustan Times* editorialized, "[O]ur policy makers . . . should spell out appropriate countermeasures to meet the Pakistani threat. . . . Rajiv Gandhi may be right when he says that India does not want to have nuclear weapons, but what other options does he have to prevent Pakistan from using nuclear blackmail in the foreseeable future."[47] On July 21, the BJP national executive issued a resolution calling for "immediate steps" to develop "our own nuclear bomb."[48] The party declared that India could no longer afford a "policy of drift and escapism." All of the opposition parties except the Communists shared this criticism and the call for developing nuclear weapons.[49]

The government responded in two ways to this pressure. Rhetorically, Raja Ramanna told the Madras Press Club that India now had the capability to develop a nuclear delivery system and that "if anyone tries to twist our hand we could flex our muscles too."[50] Similarly, on August 7, the minister of state for external affairs told the Rajya Sabha that "we have kept our options open" and that if Pakistan goes nuclear, "we will reply . . . stone by stone."[51] The official added that India had the capacity to produce nuclear weapons but, in the words of the *Times of India,* "did not believe in flaunting its technical knowhow as its neighbour was doing."[52] If Pakistan believed that India lagged behind in nuclear technology, the minister of state said it had every right to "remain under this illusion." However, he continued, the Pakistanis will "come to their senses if they have an opportunity of knowing what we possess."[53] This tough language followed the government's traditional practice of issuing vague but robust-sounding statements to reassure the public that the nation's defenses were being maintained.

A more practical counter to the news from Pakistan came on August 8 when the Atomic Energy Commission announced that the 100-megawatt Dhruva research reactor had gone critical and would become operational by November. Dhruva, also known as R-5, was to supplement the CIRUS reactor and, according to the *Indian Express,* could produce enough weapon-grade plutonium for "fuelling up to 30 nuclear bombs per year."[54] This was a gross exaggeration. A more realistic calculation would have projected twenty to twenty-five kilograms of plutonium per year, or three to six fission bombs' worth of material.[55] Work had begun on Dhruva in 1973, and Raja Ramanna upon his return to BARC in 1981 had made its completion a top priority. Anil Kakodkar served as a key engineer on the Dhruva project and went on to become director of BARC in time to participate significantly in the 1998 nuclear tests. Ramanna and other Indian officials insisted that the nuclear program remained dedicated to peaceful applications. Yet they emphasized that Dhruva was free from safeguards, implying clearly that it significantly bolstered the country's nuclear weapon options.[56] The media did not miss the point. The *Indian Express* headline read: "Dhruva an N-bomb spinner."[57]

The BARC establishment was taking other measures as well to augment its nuclear weapon capabilities. According to reporters for *Nucleonics Week,* India in 1984 had imported nearly one hundred kilograms of pure beryllium from West Germany.[58] A layer of beryllium metal can be used around the plutonium core of a weapon to reflect neutrons and thereby greatly increase the weapon's yield, allowing reductions in the size and weight of the device. One hundred kilograms would be enough to "service" dozens of weapons. India also around this time commissioned a beryllium plant near Mumbai (Bombay).[59] The country possessed significant beryl ore reserves in Kerala and thus had the potential for indigenous production of beryllium metal, but it chose the import route in this period because it was simpler and quicker.

More speculatively, reports emerged from American and West German intelligence sources in late 1984 and spring 1985 that Indian scientists had begun work on thermonuclear weapons.[60] Among the evidence cited in these reports was the announcement by the Indian Department of Atomic Energy that it would develop an inertial confinement fusion process. Once in place, this capability would enable researchers to study high-energy density physics associated with a thermonuclear explosion and develop computer codes for nuclear weapon designs. India at this time, or shortly thereafter, was irradiating lithium in reactors to produce tritium, a hydrogen isotope vital in boosted-fission weapons, and was acquiring the capacity to chemically separate lithium-6, which could then be mixed with deuterium to produce lithium-6 deuteride, a material useful in the second stage of thermonuclear devices.[61] The West German report stated further that, based on unconfirmed intelligence, Prime Minister Gandhi had authorized development work on thermonuclear weapons.[62]

Interviews with defense and atomic energy scientists suggest a less clear-cut picture: the scientists' standard operating procedures would not have led them to seek formal permission merely to acquire data and material needed to design thermonuclear explosives. They may have begun such theoretical work at this time, but this did not mean the government now had authorized them to build thermonuclear weapons. Rather, design work concentrated primarily on fission weapons and secondarily on boosted-fission weapons. Thermonuclear weapons remained a more distant interest toward which basic studies now proceeded.

Boosted-fission weapons involve the placement of a small amount of a mixture of deuterium and tritium—as a gas or a solid pellet—in the interior of a bomb's fissile plutonium (or highly enriched uranium) core. In the more efficient type of fission weapons that the weaponeers were now designing, an air gap was effected between the plutonium core and the surrounding high explosive, a technique known as "levitation." This allows greater compression of the core, or "pit," from a given amount of high explosive, thereby increasing the weapon's yield-to-weight ratio. Boosting increases the weapon's yield—or allows for reduction of its size and weight—by using the tritium-deuterium combination to provide large numbers of neutrons to multiply the plutonium fission rate. The United States pioneered boosting in 1951.

Tritium and deuterium were also useful to the weaponeers' efforts to fabricate a more advanced neutron initiator for weapons. The existing initiator relied on a beryllium-polonium system, which had a major liability insofar as polonium's 138-day half-life required near-constant production of the material and limited options for dispersed deployment of ready-to-assemble weapons. The polonium-beryllium initiator would have to be replaced frequently, a process managed best in a laboratory environment, not at airbases or other potential deployment areas. A system based on deuterium and tritium would provide much greater handling and deployment flexibility. Designing and producing such an initiator became a priority over the next decade.

India still had not developed a military strategy or operational plans for nuclear weapons. The chiefs of staff, wrote the journalist G. K. Reddy, "[i]n their excessive preoccupation with the threat of conventional war by Pakistan, . . . have not been engaging in an in-depth strategic study of how India should deal with [Pakistan's] expected acquisition of nuclear capability."[63] According to this plausible account, "The defence establishment has been treating this as a matter of political and not military decision, while the atomic scientists have been awaiting a clear-cut directive from the top to step up their research and development."[64] Reddy continued, "[N]obody knows what the Government would do in the event of a successful nuclear test by Pakistan, although the general expectation is that it will be forced to go in for the bomb under pressure of public opinion."[65] Reddy called for the prime minister to take the advice of "experts who have spent years studying the complexities of the problem, not just bureaucrats who are content with thundering declarations reaffirming India's peaceful intentions."[66]

As the next section shows, some military leaders were keen to develop a nuclear strategy, and Rajiv Gandhi soon moved halfheartedly to give the services and the nuclear and defense scientists an opportunity to make their case. Meanwhile, the ominous nuclear developments in the subcontinent prompted U.S. officials to travel to the region in September to promote restraint. Michael Armacost and National Security Council official Donald Fortier visited Pakistan and India to urge Zia and Gandhi to undertake regional initiatives to slow, and hopefully freeze, their nuclear competition and, in Armacost's words, to "take the edge off their mutual suspicions."[67] However, Washington did not delude itself that this would be easy. As Armacost recalled:

> We were unlikely to make much progress in stopping the Pakistani program if we did not deal with their motivating regional factors, which meant India. But we encountered the old problem: the Indians said their concern was not only Pakistan, but also China. We would have to bring China into the process. But this would then lead to Russia's nuclear policies and on up to ours. So it was impossible to find a way to begin in the region.[68]

Whatever hopes the American diplomats had were dashed by the bitter Indian responses. Indian officials and the media pushed the burden back on the Americans to do more to curb the Pakistani nuclear program.

SECRET COMMITTEE FORMED TO EVALUATE NUCLEAR WEAPON OPTIONS AND NEEDS, SEPTEMBER 1985

In 1985 Rajiv Gandhi formed a small group, including Ramanna and K. Subrahmanyam, to consider India's defense planning needs.[69] At that time, Subrahmanyam reported, Rajiv "was anti-nuclear," but the planning group did discuss the nuclear issue in "successive meetings." In the group's last meeting, which Subrahmanyam recalled as occurring in November, Rajiv requested a small task force to assess the costs of a nuclear deterrent. Other participants interviewed were less clear about the exact timing, but the impetus for the task force was revealing. According to a knowledgeable participant, in the November meeting Rajiv had asked an economic adviser how a decisive move toward nuclear weapons would affect the economy.[70] This adviser said it would be disastrous. Rajiv then asked Navy Chief of Staff Admiral Tahliani for his view. Tahliani was the highest ranking military officer in the meeting, due to the absence of Army Chief of Staff General A. S. Vaidya. He said he would prefer to give a studied answer. The question was therefore left hanging. After the meeting Subrahmanyam and Ramanna met and decided to call Tahliani to urge him to set up a small, informal committee to answer the prime minister. Tahliani reportedly invited Ramanna and Subrahmanyam to his home, where they discussed the issue further, and Tahliani was persuaded in Vaidya's absence to task top staff officers to prepare a report for Rajiv. Tahliani then recruited Army Vice Chief of Staff K. Sundarji, Navy Vice Chief of Staff K. K. Nayyar and Deputy Chief of Air Staff John Greene to work with the AEC's R. Chidambaram and the DRDO's Abdul Kalam to sketch India's nuclear weapon requirements and the anticipated costs required to meet them.

The committee worked intensively and produced a report recommending that India build a minimal deterrent force, guided by a strict doctrine of no-first-use and dedicated only to retaliating against a nuclear attack on India. It was largely a theoretical exercise to answer what the nuclear deterrence policy and requirements should be. The committee did not consider, for example, whether and when India should conduct additional nuclear explosive tests. The report drew heavily on Sundarji's earlier writing, including his master's thesis completed for Madras University in 1983. The report was produced in three copies—one for the prime minister, one for the chiefs of staff committee, and one that Sundarji kept.[71]

Accounts vary on whether the committee geared itself to addressing the Pakistani threat, the Chinese threat, or both. One knowledgeable former official said in an interview that "we were worried about Pakistan and felt we should get the prime minister to take a decision one way or another" on the bomb.[72] Another official, who was aware of the report's contents but did not participate on the committee, said it was geared toward China and intended to "think through" the Agni missile project: "We're developing a missile, let's think through the requirements for a weapon to go with it, and determine what the doctrine should be." This view of the informal committee's purpose was confirmed by a third participant.[73] Sundarji's own writings tended to address overall deterrent requirements to deal with both Pakistan and China. Like the American theorist Kenneth Waltz, whom Sundarji often quoted, Sundarji believed nuclear deterrence was stabilizing and did not think India needed a nuclear "advantage" over Pakistan, merely a minimal deterrent. He did not mind Pakistan or China possessing nuclear weapons as long as India could hold hostage targets they valued dearly.[74] According to one participant, the report concluded that seventy to one hundred nuclear weapons would satisfy India's deterrent requirement.[75] However, Sundarji never convincingly addressed how programs and doctrines to deal with China could be prevented from causing unintended problems with Pakistan. The committee and those who knew about it were unanimous in their opinion that India should not consider first use of nuclear weapons. "It would go against everything we stand for. This would undermine not only our international position, but also our integrity," explained a former high-ranking Ministry of Defence official.[76]

According to K. Subrahmanyam, the task force concluded that India could have "a balanced minimum deterrent for Rs. 7,000 crores (at 1985 rupee value) in about 10 years," or $5.7 billion.[77] This force would contain warheads numbering "in low three digits," Subrahmanyam recalled.[78] It is impossible to evaluate this cost estimate without knowing the exact numbers and kinds of delivery systems and platforms the group envisioned—missiles, ballistic-missile submarines, advanced aircraft—or the warning, reconnaissance, and command and control infrastructure they thought necessary. India's total defense expenditure in fiscal year 1985–1986 was Rs. 7,987 crores, or $6.5 billion.

The committee's report was fated to be inconsequential. Rajiv Gandhi had no intention of moving toward a nuclear arsenal and requisite operational doctrine. This stemmed from his personal aversion to nuclear weapons, his sense that India had greater priorities, and his determination—like his predecessors'—to keep the military from taking a significant role in nuclear policymaking. Indeed, according to a knowledgeable adviser, Rajiv welcomed the committee's effort precisely to keep the vice chiefs busy and prevent them from agitating on nuclear issues from the outside. He felt that if he resisted their interests in addressing the nuclear challenge, they could complicate his management of policy. Thus, he readily accepted a study but had no intention of acting on it.[79]

Surprisingly, Rajiv's calculations dovetailed with those of the highest leadership of the Atomic Energy Commission. The AEC felt that it had developed a known nuclear explosive capability and could readily assemble air-deliverable nuclear weapons if the need arose. The civilian scientists did not want to lose their control over India's nuclear capability and policy formation and thus had always tried to limit the military services' input to prime ministers. "We still had a thing of not giving it to the army," a former Atomic Energy Commission leader explained retrospectively. "There were no command and control procedures, and we didn't want the army or any other service to have the bomb. They said, 'how can we retaliate if we don't have the weapons. We have to develop delivery systems,' " this man reported. "We told them that at the appropriate time we will get it to you."[80] He added that "the idea of militarizing the option was not appealing to Rajiv and his people. They were a little close to Gandhian ideals." Knowing this, the Atomic Energy Commission leadership privately advised the prime minister not to act on the committee's report, saying that the country was not ready economically to support the kind of arsenal envisioned. According to this source, the AEC leadership suggested instead that India wait until missiles had been developed and proved and then create a separate service to control the nuclear force.

Nuclear establishment leaders consistently doubted Pakistan's nuclear capabilities and the sometimes bombastic claims of A. Q. Khan. Referring to the 1985 news reports of Pakistan's growing capabilities, a former AEC chairman volunteered, "We did not take A. Q. Khan seriously. He was a metallurgist. They would not be capable of doing these things."[81] Other top nuclear officials of the 1970s and 1980s echoed this low regard for Pakistan's scientific and engineering prowess, which partially explains India's nonurgency in militarizing its nuclear option. The Brahminical contempt for the abilities of Pakistan's scientists and engineers also was intensified by the difficulties India's well-educated scientists had in trying to master large-scale uranium enrichment. (In November 1986, India announced that it, too, could enrich uranium to any required level, providing a political and psychological boost by matching Pakistan's technology and, potentially, providing highly enriched uranium for thermonuclear weapons.)[82] Cognitive dissonance may explain the Indian scientists' perspectives toward their Pakistani counterparts. The Indians recognized that Pakistan's enrichment program benefited enormously from designs stolen from Europe and assistance provided by China, but many still could not overcome their prejudices about Pakistani abilities. These doubts, paired with the atomic energy establishment's desire to keep control over the program, yielded the recommendation to the prime minister not to act on the vice chiefs' call for going forward.

Rajiv Gandhi expressed his position during a November trip to Japan when he told a television interviewer that "[w]e lived with Chinese weapon for long. But our relation with Pakistan is more turbulent." Still, he said, "[w]e have managed without" the bomb and "[w]e would like not to develop a weapon and we are not developing a weapon."[83] The prime minister acknowledged that India had increased its nuclear capability since the Pokhran test in 1974, but insisted that it is "entirely for peaceful purposes." Indeed, K. Subrahmanyam recalled that during this period Rajiv protested that Subrahmanyam's hawkish briefings on India's nuclear policy options never included the possibility of signing the NPT. After the late-1985 meetings discussed here, Subrahmanyam was not to meet with Rajiv again until 1991.[84]

RAJIV AND ZIA MEET, AGREE NOT TO ATTACK NUCLEAR FACILITIES, DECEMBER 1985

In the fall of 1985, the United States continued to press India and Pakistan to calm their nuclear competition and stabilize relations. Hoping to put international pressure on India, Pakistan's President Zia, at the United Nations General Assembly meeting in New York, called for India and Pakistan simultaneously to sign the NPT, accept mutual fullscope safeguards and inspections, and renounce the acquisition of nuclear weapons.[85] President Reagan duly endorsed the proposal, but, predictably, Rajiv Gandhi did not. The Indians did not think the Pakistanis were serious and in any case rejected a bilateral approach that excluded China in redressing what they viewed as a global nuclear problem.

Still, neither India nor Pakistan wanted war, and both sought to avoid the perception that their competition could lead to nuclear dangers. In December, Zia and Gandhi met in New Delhi and agreed on a process for normalizing relations, including confidence-building measures, the expansion of trade links, and resumption of talks on draft treaties on nonaggression and peace.[86] Importantly, the two leaders announced that they had made an agreement not to attack each other's nuclear facilities. The initiative came from Rajiv Gandhi and apparently stemmed from Indian wishes to end frequent speculation that India planned to attack Kahuta.[87] The Indians felt that the rumors of a pending attack were intended, perhaps by the Pakistanis, to raise tensions that could lead to crises. Hence, security would be enhanced by clarifying both sides' intentions. The agreement was not signed until December 31, 1988, and not ratified until 1991; it was implemented by exchanges of lists of each side's nuclear installations in 1992 and 1993. But in 1985, it signaled a very important awareness by both sides that conflict involving nuclear facilities, let alone nuclear weapons, should be avoided.[88]

The December meeting generated hope that Indo-Pak relations would accelerate toward normalization. According to *India Today*, Rajiv Gandhi had summoned key foreign affairs officials and told them that "he had decided to give Zia the benefit of the doubt. 'Let's take him at his word and put the ball in their court,' he said."[89] The Indians chose to downplay their concerns over Pakistan's nuclear ambitions and alleged support of ongoing Sikh extremism in Punjab in an attempt to improve the overall relationship.

MILITARY CRISIS: EXERCISE BRASSTACKS, JULY 1986 TO FEBRUARY 1987

Domestic developments and Indian concerns over the reinflamed crisis in Punjab soon diverted Indian and Pakistani leaders from their hopeful course. In India, Rajiv Gandhi's honeymoon with the polity was nearing its end. In a late-December speech to a Congress party centenary session in Bombay he rebuked operatives for failing to uphold the party's original promise as the trustee of India's great potential. He censured power brokers and government servants for lacking a "work ethic, . . . feeling for public cause, . . . [and] comprehension of national goals," and for having only "a grasping, mercenary outlook, devoid of competence, integrity and commitment."[90] This scathing assault prompted great bitterness among the old guard and created fissures within the party that soon widened. Meanwhile, the tentative 1985 resolution of the Sikh agitation in Punjab had unraveled, and strife and terrorism had resumed in the state, causing the problem to return to the top of the political agenda. This crisis in turn fueled communal tensions that Rajiv and his advisers now sought to exploit in a portentous departure from secular norms. These and other developments generated domestic political pressures that required increased attention and weakened the prime minister. Meanwhile, in Pakistan, domestic opposition to the Zia regime began to mount, too, diminishing the salience of improving ties with India.

In late January 1986, General K. Sundarji was named army chief of staff. Sundarji was the military's most vocal proponent of nuclear weapons. He knew that Rajiv Gandhi was unwilling to act on the just-completed committee report regarding India's nuclear deterrent. Still, without transgressing the boundaries of propriety, he continued to suggest that India would be better off with nuclear weapons to counter an adversary who possessed them. On March 4, Minister of State for Defence and close Rajiv Gandhi adviser Arun Singh appeared on a national television program and announced that the armed forces were undergoing an overhaul of strategy and technology and that the nuclear option was being reconsidered. However, there was less than met the eye in this statement: the vice chiefs' committee report on nuclear doctrine had already been cast aside by the prime minister. The Singh statement was for political effect.[91]

If nuclear policy was status quo, Rajiv Gandhi and Sundarji did set out in mid-1986 to demonstrate India's growing conventional military capabilities. They conceived the idea of holding the largest, most ambitious military exercise in the subcontinent's history to develop, test, and demonstrate India's capacity to conduct mobile armored warfare, with close air support, integrated by new communications and command and control systems. Dubbed "Exercise Brasstacks," the enterprise was to be conducted in four phases from May 1986 to March 1987, beginning with map and war game activities and building up in late 1986 and early 1987 into actual combined arm operations in the desert area of Rajasthan-Sindh along the Pakistan-India border. The exercise and the crisis it spawned were detailed in a major study, *Brasstacks and Beyond*, written by Kanti P. Bajpai, P. R. Chari, Pervaiz Iqbal Cheema, Stephen P. Cohen, and Sumit Ganguly and based on interviews with leading participants from India and Pakistan. For the purposes of this study, it is necessary only to describe the point at which the two sides approached a military crisis, the factors that led to that point, how the crisis was resolved, and whether there were nuclear dimensions to it.

In planning Exercise Brasstacks, Sundarji sought to assess, refine, and demonstrate the innovations he envisioned for modernizing India's armed forces. A man of bold thought and action, Sundarji wanted to go beyond rhetoric and paper studies to prove the military's mettle. Rajiv Gandhi was a novice in military affairs and was attracted to the grand scale of the planned exercise, without attaching a specific strategic purpose to it.[92] The exercise was predicated on a scenario wherein an insurgency in Kashmir had become unmanageable and Sikh militants in Indian Punjab were declaring an independent state of Khalistan. These developments were supposed to have encouraged Pakistan to intervene to detach both Kashmir and Khalistan from India. Pakistan's incursion was scripted to have dented Indian defenses to the point that India had to undertake a counteroffensive into Pakistan to draw Pakistani forces from their offensive in India.[93] In the latter operational phases of the exercise—December 1986 and January 1987—India had two armored divisions, one mechanized division, and six infantry divisions involved in an area roughly 100 miles by 150 miles in the Rajasthan desert adjacent to the northern segment of the Pakistani state of Sindh.

India did not inform Pakistan of the massive exercise's scope. Nor did Indian officials establish communication modalities to reassure Pakistan before and during the exercise that actual hostilities were not being undertaken.[94] All of this alarmed Pakistani leaders and led them to assume that India was at least warning Pakistan not to involve itself in the Punjab unrest and was testing Pakistan's will while manifesting India's greater might. The handful of Indian officials managing the exercise also failed to foresee that a crisis could emerge as Pakistan, in November and December, was conducting its own annual exercises on its side of the border in the same general region.

The events along the Indo-Pak border occurred largely out of the sight and minds of both governments until December and January. In the months preceding, key Indians and Pakistanis made important statements and revelations about nuclear policy with no apparent connection to the military exercises. For example, in September 1986, the *Times of India* reported that A. Q. Khan, in an interview published in the August 31 edition of the Lahore weekly *Chatan*, had claimed that Indira Gandhi had been deterred from attacking Pakistan's nuclear facilities in 1984 by Khan's earlier pronouncements that Pakistan "now is a nuclear power."[95] As Khan told *Chatan*, Mrs. Gandhi was "compelled to give up her idea."[96] A Bob Woodward article in the *Washington Post* on November 4 propelled the Pakistani threat further into the Indian psyche by claiming, among other things, that Pakistan had conducted additional explosive tests of the nonnuclear components of a bomb and could assemble a bomb in a week.[97] The Indian press then exaggerated the Woodward story in articles with headlines such as "Pak Has Tested Bomb: U.S. Report," "Nuclear Device Exploded by Pakistan," and "Pak Detonates Explosive Device."[98] The Indian government tried to correct and deflect the notion that Pakistan had tested a nuclear bomb, but the impression of threat remained.

Still, on November 27, 1986, as the Brasstacks exercise was about to begin its telling phase, Gandhi and Soviet Communist Party General Secretary Mikhail Gorbachev signed the Delhi Declaration, a lofty call for the restructuring of international relations, the replacement of "fear and suspicion" with "understanding and trust," and so on. The declaration specifically concentrated on steps to eliminate nuclear weapons, including a call to ban all tests.[99] Gorbachev also forwarded Soviet proposals for steps toward peace in Asia, which included suggestions that India and Pakistan engage in substantive talks on security. Indian officials dismayed Gorbachev by deflecting this appeal. The Soviets encountered India's predilection for moralistic, global rhetoric over hardheaded negotiations with direct adversaries. Earlier, in October, Rajiv stated during a visit to New Zealand that India had "deliberately rejected" the readily available option to develop nuclear weapons. "We are perhaps the only country in the world to do so."[100] Normative self-image, concerns about costs, and strategic risks all informed this position.

Thus, through the fall there was no hint that Exercise Brasstacks would devolve into a crisis. Yet this is what happened in December when Pakistan hedged against the provocative Indian deployment by shifting its Army Reserve North closer to the Indo-Pak border above Amritsar. Then, in the second week of January, Pakistan moved its Army Reserve South northward over the Sutlej river which positioned it to conduct a pincer movement with the northern group into Punjab or to advance into Jammu and Kashmir. The available record indicates that India did not detect the latter force's movement until up to two weeks after the fact. These developments occurred when Rajiv Gandhi was on vacation and were not conveyed immediately to him. When he returned and learned of the Pakistani deployment, he became highly alarmed and disaffected with those who had been managing the exercise, particularly Sundarji and Arun Singh. He almost offhandedly fired Foreign Secretary A. P. Venkateswaran in mid-January in a pique over the latter's performance at this time. The first public signs of a crisis emerged on January 18 when Sundarji gave an unusual press briefing to announce the dangerous moves of the Pakistan Army. Two days later, Rajiv Gandhi heightened the sense of urgency by giving only his second press conference since assuming office, in which he expressed grave concern over the concentration of Pakistani forces along the border.[101] Shortly thereafter, Rajiv Gandhi, now taking over decision making, ordered a massive airlift of troops into Punjab. Pakistan perceived these movements as an effort to block its forces as a precursor for Indian attacks into Pakistan.

Rajiv now considered the possibility that Pakistan might initiate war with India. In a meeting with a handful of senior bureaucrats and General Sundarji, he contemplated beating Pakistan to the draw by launching a preemptive attack on the Army Reserve South. This also would have included automatically an attack on Pakistan's nuclear facilities to remove the potential for a Pakistani nuclear riposte to India's attack. Relevant government agencies were not asked to contribute analyses or views to the discussion. Sundarji argued that India's cities could be protected from a Pakistani counterattack (perhaps a nuclear one), but, upon being probed, could not say how. One important adviser from the Ministry of Defence argued eloquently that "India and Pakistan have already fought their last war, and there is too much to lose in contemplating another one."[102] This view ultimately prevailed.

As the crisis mounted, both sides made conciliatory gestures to signal an interest in de-escalation. On January 23, Pakistan proposed urgent talks with India. The dormant telephone hotline between the two sides was finally activated. An Indian Foreign Ministry spokesman announced that India was ready to hold discussions with Pakistan.[103] On January 25, both sides agreed to talks while insisting that their military movements had been purely precautionary and defensive. Dialogue began on January 31 and resulted, on February 4, in an agreement for sector-by-sector withdrawals of troops from the border. The crisis then wound down.

Unbeknownst to the world, and apparently to Indian leaders who had already ruled out initiating war, Pakistan's A. Q. Khan had sought to inject a nuclear dimension into the crisis. Because Khan's "intervention" did not become known until March and did not necessarily reflect official Pakistani calculations it cannot be said to have influenced the Brasstacks crisis. (Indeed, as became apparent after Pakistan's nuclear tests in 1998, A. Q. Khan was not the decisive figure in the Pakistani nuclear weapon program.) However, as discussed below, Khan's statement affected subsequent perceptions of the role of nuclear weapons in Indo-Pak security relations. The episode began on January 28 when Dr. Khan received a visit from an eminent Pakistani journalist and friend, Mushahid Hussain, who had with him the Indian journalist Kuldip Nayar. Khan, Nayar, and Hussain subsequently disputed the nature and circumstances of the conversation or "interview," but it is accepted that Khan proclaimed that Pakistan had enriched uranium to weapon grade and could test an atomic bomb through laboratory simulations.[104] This meant, he added, that "[n]obody can undo Pakistan or take us for granted. We are here to stay and let it be clear that we shall use the bomb if our existence is threatened."[105] In fact, by this time Pakistan did have the necessary components to rapidly assemble a very small number of nuclear weapons for aircraft delivery against India, although these components were kept physically and bureaucratically separated under the overall control of Zia.

When Khan's words were published on March 1, the Indo-Pak crisis was over. It does not appear that Khan's message was conveyed to Indian officials during the crisis.[106] If Pakistani leaders intended to invoke the prospect of nuclear deterrence in this crisis, their signal was highly problematic and came too late. Khan had not taken into account the possibility that commercial interests would drive Nayar to shop his "hot story" around for a high bid, which took weeks. If the message had been received earlier, Indian officials would have been left to wonder whether it represented an official Pakistani threat or the rhetoric of a megalomaniacal scientist. Such vague signaling could have been extremely dangerous if India and Pakistan had deployed missile-based forces, especially insofar as neither side possessed real-time reconnaissance and warning systems to detect preparations or actual launches of these weapons. Future statements like Khan's could prompt Indian decision makers to assume the worst and undertake preemptive conventional or nuclear operations if both had nuclear weapons at the ready. Such promiscuous nuclear saber rattling could exacerbate crisis instability rather than achieve deterrence.

However, the principal lessons of the Brasstacks crisis went beyond nuclear weapons. As the Pakistani newspaper *Dawn* editorialized on January 27, the crisis was "the outcome of a series of missteps and miscalculations," requiring both sides to "recognize the need for prudence and circumspection in what they say or do."[107] In a great example of the "security dilemma," neither Indian nor Pakistani leaders intended to wage war against the other, yet India's exercise and Pakistan's defensive countermeasures signaled threats that heightened the other's insecurity and could have escalated to a war that neither wanted. To avert such crises, the two states would have to achieve some degree of transparency and agree to rules for military exercises. To their credit, India and Pakistan partially acted toward those ends in subsequent years by negotiating a series of confidence-building measures to improve military-to-military communications. In 1987, they established a hot line between their foreign secretaries.[108] However, many of these measures had not been implemented fully or constructively by the end of 1998.[109]

The Brasstacks crisis also revealed the danger in India of excessively centralized and personalized prime-ministerial decision making. Rajiv Gandhi had intensified the centralization of power begun by his mother. As the authors of *Brasstacks and Beyond* concluded, during the crisis he made "major decisions in a personal capacity, without the concerned bureaucracy properly examining the issues involved."[110] Once matters got dicey, Rajiv took over and largely excluded military, Ministry of Defence, and Ministry of External Affairs officials from his deliberations. This led to moves that exacerbated the danger. The liabilities of this type of decision making are greater in nuclear policy, where prime ministers and top scientists tend to exclude others from deliberations. This has generally led to cautious policies, but at the exceptional moments when major decisions were made, as in 1974 (and 1998 as is discussed in chapter 15), the lack of analysis and strategy led arguably to negative outcomes. Some defense scientists and experienced civil servants in the prime minister's office began to professionalize nuclear decision making after 1982, but India still lacked a durable system.

THE NUCLEAR DEBATE ESCALATES AND THE AEC EXPERIENCES PROBLEMS, 1986 TO 1987

In the aftermath of the Brasstacks crisis, Indian elites rose to the bait offered in A. Q. Khan's interview. Rajiv Gandhi and his government recognized that the core *external* security problem remained conventional and announced that defense spending would be increased by 43 percent for the year beginning April 1, 1987.[111] (The actual budget increase was 23 percent, which was then revised down to 19 percent as drought constrained spending.)[112] The announcement was intended to signify governmental resolve following the dramatic and largely inadvertent Brasstacks standoff.[113] Still, parliamentarians, the press, and strategic analysts fixed on the nuclear challenge. Even before A. Q. Khan's interview with Kuldip Nayar became public, the president of the BJP, L. K. Advani had said in late January that "India must produce the nuclear bomb as there is no alternative."[114] In the Rajya Sabha in late February, the opposition as well as Congress (I) party members had demanded a review of defense policy in light of Pakistan's nuclear program.[115] The clamor intensified as word of Khan's latest boast spread. Then-Cabinet Secretary B. G. Deshmukh recalled that General Sundarji around this time "spiritedly advocated going nuclear" in a briefing of the prime minister.[116]

However, as Deshmukh noted, "Rajiv Gandhi was very firm. . . . No doubt he did not want India to give up any option for going nuclear but he was very loathe to exercise this option except as a last resort."[117] Thus, the government tried to calm reactions by declaring that there was nothing new in Pakistan's claims or capabilities and that India had no intention of manufacturing nuclear weapons.[118] Indian leaders did not know for sure how far advanced Pakistan's nuclear capabilities were by this time. Still, as G. K. Reddy reported in the *Hindu* in early March, pressures were building to give India's nuclear scientists freer rein to develop nuclear capabilities to counter any Pakistani development and to make "a major policy decision on the exercise of the nuclear option."[119]

India Today in late March published a long article encapsulating the state of the debate. The magazine reported that Indian officials believed A. Q. Khan's interview was "a carefully calculated and specifically directed message with the covert blessings of Pakistan's military establishment" and that Pakistan intended both to deter India from militarily pressing Pakistan and to show the United States that Islamabad could not be compelled to give up the nuclear program.[120] According to a quick poll cited by *India Today*, 69 percent of those interviewed believed that Pakistan "had the bomb," and 68 percent "felt India should take a similar path."[121] The magazine reported that "knowledgeable circles" within India had confirmed that Israel had approached India about undertaking a military attack on Kahuta but that Indian officials had marshaled numerous reasons against doing so, along the lines discussed in chapter 9.[122] The other leading option before India would be to "go ahead and build the bomb."[123] But here the magazine pointed out that—barring "domestic political compulsions"—this alternative was unlikely to be pursued. *India Today* suggested that aside from K. Subrahmanyam and K. Sundarji, "the Indian Government appears to have no identifiable bomb lobby."[124]

The prime minister would have resisted a bomb lobby in any case because he had his own conception of how to deal with Pakistan. According to a former high-level adviser, Rajiv "took the Pakistani threat very seriously." However, "we didn't feel we had to best them. Even if they wiped part of us out, we could come back at them. They might even take some territory, but they could not keep it. We just needed to make sure they know, personally and privately, 'hey, man, if you nuke us, we will blow your country off the map.' "[125] In this former official's view, Rajiv felt that "we didn't need a launch-on-warning doctrine or system or all the wild stuff you Americans and the Soviets had. We would never go first, but we could wait and then hit them hard." Thus, Rajiv felt India could and should avoid the costly "hardened command and control systems, the bunkers, and other infrastructure" developed by the United States and the Soviet Union. "Such systems are provocative, they raise all sorts of difficult problems in civil-military relations, and you mostly need it if you are envisioning war-fighting, which we were not. We felt that as long as we could wipe them out, in a day or a week, that was enough."[126]

To be sure, atomic energy and defense scientists were prepared and perhaps eager to move ahead. By 1987 they believed India could assemble a deliverable nuclear weapon in weeks.[127] The top scientists shared this information with only a handful of others, including Rajiv, B. G. Deshmukh, and a few air force officers who would have been entrusted with preparing for air delivery. Air force officers at this time felt little confidence in this capability, as they had not acquired the means to modify aircraft for nuclear delivery and test the requisite systems.[128] Yet, as always, costs were a major inhibiting factor in building an actual arsenal. *India Today* cited estimates ranging from more than $5 billion over ten years for an arsenal of 150 or so warheads to $1.2 billion per year.[129] These figures were very close to the cost estimate produced by the 1985 task force, as recorded above. The accuracy of any such cost estimate was suspect, but the point was that the Indian democracy, with its competing priorities, could scarcely afford building a nuclear arsenal without major domestic sacrifices. *India Today*'s authors concluded from their interviews that India would probably move toward "covert nuclearisation," an option that could minimize expenses while reassuring the leadership that a counter was at hand in case Pakistan proved increasingly troublesome.[130] This is what the government did.

In the last days of March, Rajiv Gandhi sounded a more robust, albeit vague, line, saying, "We intend meeting President Zia's threat. We will give an adequate response."[131] Then, on March 30, Indian President Zail Singh made a rare foray into nuclear politics by declaring, in the words of the *Times of India*, that "India too could make a nuclear bomb if needed and that the neighbouring countries trying to destabilise this nation should take note of it."[132] Zail Singh, a Sikh who had been deeply pained by the Golden Temple debacle in 1984, not so subtly linked the nation's nuclear policy to Pakistan's alleged involvement in the ongoing crisis in Punjab. The debate continued throughout April as a growing number of parliamentarians urged the government to reconsider its nuclear policy. Finally, on April 27, Defence Minister K. C. Pant told the Lok Sabha that "the emerging nuclear threat to us from Pakistan is forcing us to review our options. . . . I assure the House that our response will be adequate to our perception of the threat."[133] This led observers to conclude that nuclear policy would be subject to serious reconsideration. The government and Rajiv Gandhi were being driven back from the clear late-1986 statements evincing the desire to avoid being drawn into nuclear weapon building.

Yet the status of India's nuclear establishment complicated any overt move toward nuclear weapons. The power program, despite some recent successes, was in bad shape. Raja Ramanna had recently announced a new Department of Atomic Energy fifteen-year plan to create 10,000 megawatts of nuclear power by the year 2000. In 1986, however, India nominally had 1,230 megawatts of installed nuclear power, and even this figure included the RAPS-I reactor, which had been shut down for several years, and neglected the recent "derating" of the two Tarapur reactors down from 210 megawatts each to 160. Thus, the new plan called for a wildly ambitious reactor construction and operation program.

The news from 1986 did not inspire confidence. Despite employing 21,500 scientists and engineers and almost 32,500 total staff—"at least a third, if not a good half" of all of India's manpower devoted to research and development, according to K. C. Khanna—the department's production of electricity had slipped to 2 percent of the national total.[134] The first of two reactors at the Madras Atomic Power Station (MAPS-I) had suffered major problems since it went on line in 1983. In one incident it leaked seven tonnes of precious heavy water. MAPS-II began commercial operation in March 1986 and also experienced several disruptions due to technical failures.[135] The beleaguered heavy-water production program was recovering from some of its most dramatic afflictions, but it was "still in a mess," according to Khanna.[136] Of greater significance for India's nuclear weapon potential, fuel vibrations caused the new plutonium production reactor, Dhruva, to be shut down shortly after it was commissioned in August 1985. Though the Department of Atomic Energy denied this for some time, it was admitted to the Lok Sabha in August 1986.[137] This meant that India lacked the additional twenty to twenty-five kilograms of unsafeguarded plutonium that Dhruva was slated to produce each year.[138]

To be sure, there were major achievements. India's first, experimental fifteen-megawatt-electric Fast Breeder Test Reactor (at Kalpakkam) went critical in October 1985. Reported by U.S. analysts to be about 80 percent indigenously built, the reactor made India the seventh country in the world to deploy breeder technology. Its production was a tribute to Raja Ramanna, who had made it a top priority upon his return to the Department of Atomic Energy in 1981. However, although the reactor went critical in 1985, construction on it was not finished until 1987, and the plant did not produce electric power until 1997. As of 1998, it did not operate above twelve megawatts-thermal, or one megawatt-electric, output.

In Ramanna's view, of course, inadequate financial resources were the major impediment to meeting planned targets. In 1986, plans called for the Department of Atomic Energy to receive only half its funding from the central government. As part of a general economic liberalization program in 1987, the government created the Nuclear Power Corporation of India as a commercial venture and set it up to float bonds and raise electricity tariffs in order to spare the government from continued heavy subsidies of the poorly performing nuclear power sector.[139] This effort to shift the funding burden to private markets would intensify over succeeding years and subject the nuclear establishment to market forces that would badly hamper it.

The reputation of the nuclear establishment suffered another blow in 1986 when the U.S. researcher Gary Milhollin published a report alleging in detail that India clandestinely had purchased large quantities of heavy water from international sources in order to provide the moderator necessary to operate the MAPS-I and other reactors.[140] (This issue is discussed in chapter 9.) When word of Milhollin's as yet unpublished study reached India, K. Subrahmanyam issued a counterattack in the *Times of India* on February 5. The well-informed Subrahmanyam did not deny that India had purchased heavy water from external sources. Indeed, he acknowledged that a respected Indian, Dr. G. Balachandran, had concluded in a November 23, 1985, article in the *Indian Express* that India must have imported at least seventy to ninety tonnes of heavy water in order to compensate for shortfalls in domestic production.[141] Instead, Subrahmanyam sought to put the issue in perspective by arguing correctly in his trenchant, aggressive style that "India would not have violated any international obligation even if the conclusion on imports is accepted since India is not a signatory to the NPT or any other international contractual obligation." Subrahmanyam then pointed out instances where other countries, including the United States, had either lost or diverted sensitive nuclear materials, including sales to Pakistan, without arousing outcry. In Subrahmanyam's view, India was being tarred with a brush that could just as well paint the United States, Israel, Pakistan, and other countries. The problem was the international system, not India's taking advantage of it.[142]

When Milhollin's *Foreign Policy* article appeared in September, it prompted further revealing discussion in India. Raja Ramanna raised the vital issue of race and colonialism in Indian perceptions of the nonproliferation regime. "We are all used to white people having a low opinion of us and I can see how jealous some of them become when we achieve total independence in our nuclear requirements," the AEC chairman reportedly commented.[143] Because India violated no legal commitment in importing heavy water, Milhollin's allegations seemed like missionary nonproliferation zealotry. Many Indians felt that the nonproliferation regime led by the United States and other Western countries appeared predicated on the assumption that dark-skinned people are somehow less capable of responsibly managing nuclear weapons than are Americans, Britains, the French, Russians, and Israelis, whose possession of nuclear weapons is accepted. The absence of any significant U.S. nonproliferation pressure on Israel, which is juridically in the same category as India and Pakistan and is believed to have assembled nuclear weapons, was proof for some Indians of the racial bias in U.S. policy.[144] (China's acceptance in the nuclear club is the racial exception that proves the rule, in this view.)

India's determination to repudiate any vestiges of colonialism, including within the Indian national psyche, is one reason why self-reliance has been such an important objective of the nuclear program. This made the heavy-water allegations doubly troubling: the white nonproliferation zealots were trying to tighten their grip on India, and India's lack of self-sufficiency in heavy-water production had made it dependent at least temporarily on foreign sources.

The issue of self-reliance exacerbated tensions within the overall nuclear establishment and, more clearly, between Ramanna and Rajiv Gandhi. If nuclear power was to supply up to 10 percent of the nation's electricity as called for in the DAE's fifteen-year plan, Rajiv and some of the scientists in the nuclear establishment felt India would need to import reactors. The Soviets had earlier offered to supply two 440-megawatt light-water enriched uranium reactors, and Gorbachev had recently repeated the offer to Gandhi.[145] Of course, India would have to apply safeguards to these or any other reactors supplied by parties to the NPT. Ramanna argued that turning to others for reactors "was totally unacceptable to the BARC establishment."[146] It would throw everything "to the winds—self-reliance, morale, protection from unilateral safeguards, freedom from dependence on fuel, spare parts and so on."[147]

Ramanna's proud position worsened his already strained relationship with Rajiv. This complicated prospects that Rajiv would accede to the nuclear scientists' interests in rising to meet the Pakistani nuclear threat. Both Rajiv and Ramanna compensated by placing greater stock in the advice of V. S. Arunachalam, who, as the chief defense scientist, was overseeing work related both to potential delivery systems and warhead implosion systems. Arunachalam enjoyed good relations with both Ramanna and Rajiv. Ramanna in 1982 had selected Arunachalam, then director of the Defence Metallurgical Research Laboratory in Hyderabad, to replace him as defense science adviser in New Delhi, enabling Ramanna to go back to Bombay. The two men respected each other's intellects and administrative talents. Unlike Ramanna, Arunachalam found Rajiv interested in the details of technology and open, at least with him, to give and take on important issues. Rajiv demonstrated his respect for the defense scientist by calling him "Arunji," an appellation of honor, and Arunachalam appealed to the prime minister's priorities by promoting civilian applications of science and technology.

Arunachalam believed that India must develop the means to retaliate against any nuclear attack, but he felt that the specifically nuclear elements of such a retaliatory capacity could be refined quietly in laboratories while the missile program progressed. The scientists were confident that India was able to deliver fission weapons against Pakistan by air. Rather than focus attention on controversial nuclear issues, Arunachalam sought to concentrate on strengthening India's overall technological capacity. More than Ramanna, he accepted that this would require international cooperation for some time. Arunachalam had the temperament to work with Rajiv and foreign officials to facilitate this cooperation. The Gandhi-Arunachalam relationship helped keep strategic programs quietly on track, integrating the work between the Atomic Energy Commission and the Defence Research and Development Organisation. This would set the stage for later progress in developing the technological and organizational modalities for a command and control system for nuclear retaliation.

However, the prime minister still doubted the nuclear establishment's performance and the general business of nuclear weapons. At times, according to a former high-ranking official, he would say, half in jest, "[Y]ou all are mad doctors. Our people need drinkable water and you spend your time on these bombs."[148] This attitude seems hard to reconcile with Rajiv's acquiescence in, if not encouragement of, the ongoing expansion of nuclear weapon capabilities. The most charitable explanation is that it reflected the traditional prime ministerial ambivalence about nuclear weapons in a nuclear-armed world.

The discord in the nuclear establishment became public in January 1987, when Ramanna's term as AEC chairman was due to expire. The government delayed naming a successor, prompting reports of schisms. According to the reports, the government intended to name Dr. M. R. Srinavasan, an engineer in charge of the nuclear power program, to succeed Ramanna. However, Ramanna and others involved in the nuclear explosive program favored the then director of the Bhabha Atomic Research Centre, Dr. P. K. Iyengar. According to a report by Inder Malhotra, Iyengar was prepared to resign if he did not get the top post.[149] Several issues underlay the discord. Iyengar was a key figure in the nuclear explosive program and specifically in the design of the Pokhran device. Ramanna and others feared that naming a man without experience in the bomb program would weaken it at a critical moment. The common worldwide tension between physicists and engineers also played a role here: to put it baldly, physicists generally regard themselves as superior to engineers. Bhabha and two of his three successors—Sarabhai and Ramanna—were physicists, and many felt that the only previous reign of an engineer—Homi Sethna—had been disappointing. Thus, the BARC team preferred that the physicist Iyengar get the job.

According to observers and some participants, Rajiv's naming of Srinavasan was intended to signal displeasure with Ramanna's and the BARC team's resistance to importing Soviet reactors and to downplay the military dimension of the nuclear program.[150] Moreover, Srinavasan had served longer in the Department of Atomic Energy than had Iyengar, so the decision could be rationalized on grounds of seniority. As events played out, the government delayed its final choice by asking Ramanna to stay on for a month. Finally, Srinavasan was formally appointed chairman while Rajiv privately promised Iyengar that he would succeed Srinavasan when his three-year tenure expired.[151] In any case, the center of gravity in the nuclear explosives domain had shifted to the Defence Research and Development Organisation.

This episode repeated a pattern of unsettling political and personnel decisions managed by Rajiv Gandhi. In the first thirty-nine months of his tenure, Rajiv reshuffled his cabinet twenty-three times, and changed twelve state chief ministers and sixteen All India Congress Committee general secretaries. The Defence Ministry portfolio changed hands five times and the minister of state for home affairs nine times.[152] Among other things, the constant shuffling of high-level officials reflected Rajiv Gandhi's unsteady position amid growing political turbulence. Nineteen eighty-seven brought a number of political setbacks. In June, the Congress (I) party was swept from power in state elections in Haryana, a traditional stronghold, marking the fifth party defeat in six state elections since Rajiv had become prime minister.[153] Most ominously, in April Swedish radio reported that the Bofors arms manufacturing conglomerate had made secret payments to Indian officials to win a $1.3 billion contract to supply 155-millimeter howitzers (and ammunition).[154] These charges set off governmental and press investigations that reverberated through the Indian polity for the rest of Rajiv's tenure. Charges of high-level corruption leading to the person of Rajiv Gandhi sapped his political strength and ultimately helped cause his defeat in 1989. In April 1987, Defence Minister V. P. Singh resigned and signaled interest in mounting a campaign against Gandhi, which he did, successfully, in 1989.[155] In this tumultuous atmosphere the prime minister showed little interest in devoting his energies to change India's nuclear policy.

DEVELOPMENTS ON THE SINO-INDIAN FRONT, 1986 TO 1987

India's relationship with China in the 1986–1987 period also affected nuclear policy, albeit in less direct ways than did the Indo-Pak crisis or internal politics. China made a positive overture toward India at the outset of Rajiv Gandhi's tenure, when the leading newspaper, the *People's Daily*, noted that the new prime minister had "made certain adjustments to [India's] foreign policy . . . and is making efforts to improve the situation in south Asia."[156] The government organ concluded that "the outlook is promising for a further development of relations between China and India." However, preoccupation with issues closer to home kept India from concentrating on China at this time.

In late 1986, tension mounted as India's Parliament amended the constitution to make the North East Frontier Agency—Arunachal Pradesh—a full-fledged state in the Indian union.[157] This state contained part of the territory whose sovereignty was disputed by India and China, so Beijing immediately issued a strong protest and a week later, on December 17, demanded territorial concessions in Arunachal Pradesh.[158] In the ensuing months, India and China built up their military presence in the region, with each reportedly deploying approximately 200,000 troops along its side of the border by May 1987. In March, the Indian press claimed that China was stockpiling nuclear weapons in Tibet, aimed at India, which China denied.[159] Stephen P. Cohen recalled later that local Indian Army commanders, as they mobilized against the Chinese, asked superiors whether the Chinese forces possessed nuclear weapons and how India would respond if China wielded them. Cohen reported that the commanders were told by their military superiors that civilian leaders had hedged on this matter, saying in effect, "[W]e will tell you when you need to know."[160] Charges and counter-charges followed between New Delhi and Beijing. However, both sides also took steps to signal their interest in preventing escalation. In an address to army commanders on April 27, Rajiv declared that India wanted to settle the boundary question with China through peaceful negotiations.[161] Chinese officials, too, conveyed privately and publicly that they had no hostile intentions.[162]

Unlike in 1962, India now enjoyed local military superiority over Chinese forces in the region, according to Western experts.[163] Also unlike in 1962, India's army was led by a talented, decisive general, K. Sundarji, who in the spring of 1987, shortly after Brasstacks, launched an exercise, "Chequerboard," in the Indian sector of the northeastern Himalyan region. The exercise may have alarmed China about India's intentions and also may have reflected India's military and civilian leaders' interest in testing whether the United States and the Soviet Union would back New Delhi if tensions mounted with China. Still, Sundarji simultaneously stated benignly that India recognized that the two countries had different perceptions of the border and that India's deployments gave China "the benefit of the doubt."[164] The rapid deployment of forces for the exercise boosted India's confidence that it could defend its side of the disputed border and increased China's receptivity to dealing with the problem diplomatically. By August, reports emerged that both India and China had begun pulling back troops from the border area.[165]

In the wake of this dispute, China and India agreed to schedule the eighth round of bilateral talks on the border issue, which Beijing recently had been reluctant to undertake.[166] The talks occurred in mid-November in New Delhi and, according to the official Indian media, took place "in an atmosphere free from tension." Despite the absence of a breakthrough, the talks "ended on a positive note."[167]

However, the near confrontation with China and, particularly, the allegations that China had deployed nuclear weapons in Tibet provided ammunition for India's nuclear hawks to reinsert the China argument in their calls for India to "go nuclear."[168] In the years since 1964, Pakistan had displaced China as the driving security and psychological threat animating India's interest in nuclear weapons, but strategists like K. Subrahmanyam and K. Sundarji always felt that China, not Pakistan, was the decisive nuclear adversary. China held the rising great power status India coveted, and India could not achieve this status if it was seen as strategically inferior to China. Yet the recent events in the northeast showed that India now had the conventional military strength to protect its territory against China and that China lacked an abiding interest in militarily prosecuting the dispute, much less threatening to use nuclear weapons to do so. Indeed, as a high-ranking Ministry of Defence official of that period recalled, "China actually has never made a nuclear threat against us."[169] Moreover, no Indian strategists had demonstrated how India could develop and deploy a survivable arsenal capable of meaningful military use against China without exacerbating India's overall security concerns.[170] The flare-up with China did little to change the government's nuclear policy. As Rajiv Gandhi put it in December 1987, "We have lived with the Chinese bomb for several years without feeling that we must produce our own."[171]

RAJIV AND REAGAN MEET AGAIN, OCTOBER 1987

In 1987, the United States again tried to persuade India and Pakistan to undertake mutual restraints. Pakistan, as it had before and would do later, proposed that the two nations agree to mutual inspections of each other's nuclear facilities. India predictably rejected this nonglobal approach in August, but this did not stop the Reagan administration from picking up the idea as part of its effort to persuade the U.S. Congress to hold off nonproliferation restrictions against Pakistan.[172] India again dismissed the idea in October when Rajiv Gandhi was preparing to come to Washington for his third meeting with President Reagan. A mutual inspection treaty, Rajiv argued, would not be enough to freeze the Pakistani program and would simply give the Reagan administration "an out . . . to turn a blind eye to what [the Pakistanis] are doing."[173]

Reagan and Gandhi met on October 20. They commended the progress since their 1985 meeting in expanding bilateral trade and overall cooperation in the fields of science, technology, and space, particularly the Light Combat Aircraft program. The prime minister confirmed that India had agreed to purchase the Cray XMP-14 supercomputer and expressed hope that the United States would work with India to upgrade its overall computing capability. Gandhi congratulated Reagan and Mikhail Gorbachev for completing the INF (intermediate-range nuclear forces)

Treaty to eliminate intermediate-range nuclear missiles from Europe and expressed his hope that this would be the beginning of the elimination of nuclear weapons altogether, an objective that Gandhi commended Reagan for advocating.[174]

In a press conference following the meeting, Gandhi opined that a cutoff of American aid to Pakistan would "definitely slow down, very much" the Pakistani nuclear program by reducing the indirect subsidies that enabled Islamabad to build nuclear weapons without diverting funds from other important priorities.[175] When asked whether Pakistan's acquisition of nuclear weapons would force India's hand, the prime minister said, "[W]e'll evaluate the situation when it comes." He explained, "We feel that the costs of going nuclear, not just the money cost, but all the other costs, are much too heavy and we would like to do anything to prevent ourselves going nuclear."[176]

Indian reaction to the visit was generally favorable. The press reported that Gandhi had managed to heighten American awareness of the need for greater pressure on the Pakistani nuclear program and that Washington's increased willingness to cooperate in the defense sector showed greater confidence in India.[177] Yet, a few weeks after his return, the prime minister took pains to explain in Parliament that India had not entered a "defense pact" with the United States and was not aiming for a defense treaty, but was merely furthering cooperation that would give India access to defense and other technology that it could not obtain elsewhere.[178] The traditional attachment to nonalignment and fear of losing sovereignty to the powerful grip of the United States required the government to mark the boundary of its relationship with Washington.

As 1987 ended, the polity focused on domestic problems, particularly the deepening charges of corruption against Rajiv Gandhi and those around him and the ongoing military conflict involving Indian forces in Sri Lanka. Indian troops had been deployed at the Sri Lankan government's request to help sort out the conflict between the Tamil minority and the Sinhalese majority in the north of the island but had taken major casualties. The Indian deployment spawned political recriminations in India and Sri Lanka with little to show for it. Still, concerns about Pakistan's nuclear program did not diminish. In December, the leader of the BJP, Atal Behari Vajpayee, called again on India to make nuclear weapons.[179] And, while on the surface, the government continued to avoid declarations or actions that would suggest that India was preparing to build nuclear weapons, the most informed analysts and policymakers felt that India should continue to advance its missile program, refine warhead designs and capabilities in the laboratories, and avoid taking any precipitate steps until the capabilities for a missile-based arsenal were at hand.

CONCLUSION

In many ways, India's nuclear policy during Rajiv Gandhi's leadership reflected his personal traits. Technology fascinated the prime minister and under his tenure the strategic enclave quietly advanced its technological capacity to build and deliver nuclear fission weapons, without pressing for nuclear explosive tests. Lofty visions also excited the dynamic young leader, who like many cohorts in this period of the cold war wished to see international relations transformed and nuclear weapons abolished. So Rajiv forwarded several plans to achieve nuclear disarmament.

Rajiv apparently managed to reconcile these lofty aims with India's ongoing development of nuclear weapon and missile capabilities. Pakistan posed a threat that could not be ignored. Just the same, India could show it wanted things to be different, and better, by disavowing nuclear weapons. And to avoid pressures to go nuclear, Rajiv, in league with the nuclear establishment, kept the military from intruding into nuclear policy. This admixture of realism and idealism fit a tradition started by his grandfather and continued by his mother. Yet Rajiv lacked Nehru's and Indira Gandhi's skills and presided over a decaying political system in a more complicated world. The growing undiscipline of the Indian and Pakistani political systems and challenges in the region increased the likelihood of nuclear weapon proliferation.

In this period, the Reagan administration, like American governments before, found it nearly impossible to reconcile the myriad interests at play in South Asia. Offers of high-technology cooperation with India, especially in the defense sector, did give the Indians reason to maintain self-restraint in their nuclear program and generally augmented regional and bilateral ties. But the United States could do little to redress the fundamental domestic weaknesses of both India and Pakistan or the essential conflict between them. These problems would reemerge in 1990 and afterward in ways that made nuclear nonproliferation a still more distant objective.

ELEVEN

The Nuclear Threat Grows Amid Political Uncertainty

1988–1990

From 1988 to 1990, India and Pakistan found themselves preoccupied with domestic turmoil and change. Major geopolitical shifts also occurred in the region as the Soviet Union began withdrawing forces from Afghanistan and the cold war came to an end. These shifts loosened the ties between Pakistan and the United States and between India and the Soviet Union. This in turn rendered Pakistan more susceptible to U.S. nonproliferation pressures and opened the way for China and India to improve their relationship free from the old constraints of the Russia-China-India triad.

Neither India nor Pakistan significantly changed its declared nuclear policies or rhetoric. However, India's ballistic missile program progressed to the point where it began flight-testing the Prithvi and Agni missiles in 1988 and 1989, respectively. The strategic enclave continued to enhance its nuclear weapon capabilities in laboratories and on missile test ranges. Between 1988 and 1990, according to one source, it readied at least two dozen nuclear weapons for quick assembly and potential dispersal to airbases for delivery by aircraft for retaliatory attacks against Pakistan.[1] India's policy remained not to cross the moral and political line into declared nuclear weapon status with a deployed arsenal. By now Pakistan, too, had acquired the capability to assemble nuclear weapons. In the spring of 1990, an insurrection in Kashmir turned into an Indo-Pak crisis that threatened to turn into a conflict, perhaps escalating to nuclear war as Pakistan moved to assemble a nuclear weapon. This prompted President George Bush to dispatch a team of U.S. officials to the region to help calm the situation. In the aftermath, a handful of Indian officials and strategists moved to rationalize the nation's nuclear policy and command and control procedures. Yet, notwithstanding the security threats around the state, India's leaders still chose not to assemble, test, or deploy a nuclear arsenal.

NUCLEAR AND MISSILE DEVELOPMENTS, 1988

In early 1988, negotiations advanced for the supply of two Soviet 1,000-megawatt pressurized-water reactors to India. These talks began in 1987 involving 440-megawatt reactors. Now India appeared ready to accept Soviet demands for international safeguards on the reactors and the return of spent fuel to the Soviet Union.[2] The Soviets were also prepared to provide generous financing terms and technical assistance for large nonnuclear power projects.[3] India needed foreign reactors even to begin meeting growth targets for nuclear power; this need overcame the nuclear establishment's desire for self-reliance.[4] Still, if foreign cooperation were necessary, leaders like Raja Ramanna and P. K. Iyengar preferred to deal with Western counterparts. As a then-high-ranking official said in an interview, "[O]ur guys didn't speak Russian, if they were trained abroad it was in English-speaking countries. The single guys didn't find it easy to deal with Russian women, the married guys' wives didn't like the idea of spending time in Russia. There was little pull to work with Russia."[5] However, with Prime Minister Gandhi's encouragement, the two sides signed an agreement in November 1988. The deal then languished for a decade due to reluctance in the Indian nuclear establishment, environmentalist opposition, and toughening Soviet payment terms.[6]

Meanwhile, scientists and engineers at BARC and in DRDO laboratories continued to refine nuclear weapon designs to reduce the size and weight of fission devices while increasing their explosive yield, and to develop boosted-fission weapon capability. Building on theoretical calculations, advances in engineering, and experimentation with components, teams overseen by Arunachalam and Iyengar and guided by Chidambaram, Abdul Kalam, K. Santhanam, Virender Singh Sethi, and others reduced the sizes and weights of nuclear fission devices. In doing this, the scientists and engineers continued to draw on literature obtained from public sources, including material on explosive lenses published by the Los Alamos and Lawrence Livermore National Laboratories.[7] The strategic enclave concentrated on improving the simultaneity of conventional high-explosive detonations to implode plutonium cores and on developing more advanced neutron initiators to optimize the explosive power of a given device. Theoretical work on thermonuclear weapons also continued.

These laboratory activities proceeded much as they had in the late 1960s when Ramanna, Chidambaram, Iyengar, and others had felt it within their authority to advance nuclear explosive capabilities as long as they did not actually assemble or test nuclear weapons. The prime minister approved major steps—the preparation of ready-to-assemble devices, the number of such devices, movement of weapon components within the country—giving the scientists proper authority for their actions. If all of this seemed like a surreptitious weapons program, the partici-pants saw it differently. "We were carrying out experiments without deadlines or any commitment that the technologies would be integrated into actual weapons or a full-fledged weapon program. There was no weapon program as such," explained a former official involved in these efforts.[8] Yet devices were made that could be turned into weapons if India was attacked.

At this point, whatever weapons India could assemble for retaliation against Pakistan were to be delivered by aircraft. French Mirage-2000, Soviet MiG-27, and British-French Jaguar fighter-bombers all possessed the capacity to carry nuclear weapons and the avionics desirable to conduct nuclear strike missions. It is probable that a handful of planes were being modified to be able to carry and release nuclear weapons.[9] Given the relatively short range of the Indian aircraft, those slated to deliver nuclear weapons would have to be launched from bases rel-atively close to designated targets, possibly Ambala (to strike in Punjab) and Jodh-pur (to strike in Sindh). American intelligence sources had noted that Indian aircraft had practiced "flip-toss" to "bomb-toss" maneuvers as would be required to release nuclear weapons.[10] Of course, as a former high-ranking Indian Air Force officer explained in an interview, "[A]ny air force learns and practices these maneuvers. In the late 1980s we had Jaguars, Mirages and MiG-27s that all prac-ticed toss-bombing. This happens to be a technique for delivering nuclear weapons, but it is also something you do for conventional bombs, too."[11] A former high-ranking U.S. Air Force nuclear weapon policy planner stated that American intelligence in the late 1980s and early 1990s "knew that aircraft were the Indians' delivery platforms." But this man added that "we had a lot of worries whether they could bolt it on right. It scared the beejesus out of me that they would have it fall on their own soil. Believe me, it's easier to have that happen than you think. We've done it, I know."[12] Indeed, between 1950 and 1968, eleven nuclear weapons fell out of or crashed with U.S. aircraft. India's air-delivery capability was more theoretical than test-proven.

Still, India's moral, economic, political, and strategic considerations militated against a crash program or open moves toward a deployable force. Instead, the missile program would be allowed to advance steadily to enhance India's options if the need arose to "go nuclear." And in that respect the first public breakthrough came on February 18, 1988, when the 150-kilometer Prithvi missile made its maiden flight test. The test demonstrated another major technological achieve-ment to the proud Indian leadership and population. "It signals our coming of age," a defense scientist told *India Today*.[14]

However, the Prithvi faced serious limitations as a militarily useful system. The Prithvi was to be transported to its operational area by an all-terrain, eight-wheeled Kolos Tatra truck, with each battery of four Prithvi carriers supported by a propellant tanker and a command post. To achieve accurate delivery to targets, precise coordinates of the launcher and the intended target are essential. Launch points can be surveyed beforehand, but obtaining exact coordinates of targets requires real-time, accurate pinpointing of the sort that can be provided by satellites or aerial reconnaissance drones. Into the late-1990s India did not possess these real-time target acquisition capabilities. Recognizing this limitation, the Indian Army at this time envisioned the weapon for use against concentrated enemy formations and other large fixed targets. Even then, concerns about the missile's accuracy imposed serious limitations. As retired army officer Lieutenant General Harwant Singh noted, "Prithvi's potential as a decisive weapon of war is not when it carries conventional munitions load, but when tipped with a nuclear device."[15] Yet Indian officials insisted publicly that it was not a nuclear delivery system.

The Prithvi test came at a moment when budgetary pressure exacerbated by a severe drought forced the government to cut back on defense spending. India also faced a foreign exchange crisis. Defense modernization had occurred largely through astrategic imports of expensive systems. When the 1988–1989 defense budget did not increase above the rate of inflation, it signaled a major downturn after seven years of a military "shopping binge."[16] As the former high-ranking air force officer mentioned above put it, "[T]he armed forces in the mid 1980s were not cost-conscious at all—were too lavish. We were like spoiled children. Then we realized that future budgets would not afford the large force structure we envisioned."[17]

In this new environment, the more innovative officers tried to look ahead to rationalize their military strategy and capabilities. They did this without guidance from political leaders. The former air force official lamented, "We don't have a National Security Council. No one knows anything. Ministers come and go, bureaucrats come and go. No one takes a long view toward strategy."[18] The one exception this man noted was during the brief tenure of Arun Singh as minister of state for defense—from 1986 to 1987—when an effort was made to involve military officers in developing a long-term strategy, but this initiative was aborted upon Singh's resignation in April 1987. (Singh was asked in 1990 to author a major strategic review, but the results were neither published nor implemented in any systematic way.) On their own, then, after 1988, a cadre of air force officers explored how they could best utilize existing aircraft and the potential Prithvi and Agni missiles. Led by Air Chief Marshal S. K. Mehra, these officers concluded that India should establish a Strategic Air Command that would develop doctrine and operational plans for managing advanced aircraft and prospective missile systems. The air force was reluctant to see "its" money invested in missiles over aircraft if the missiles such as the Prithvi were assumed to be carrying only conventional warheads. The service made this view known to the DRDO.[19] However, if the air force could plan on having missiles that would carry nuclear warheads, then it would back the missile program. Thus, for the purposes of strategic planning in the late 1980s, these officers developed notional plans for a Strategic Air Command based at the existing Central Command, relatively out of harm's way from surprise attack. However, there is little evidence that the effort resulted in changes in official nuclear policy. As an officer involved remarked, "[P]olitical guidance was not forthcoming."[20] The Indian government continued to insist that the Prithvi missile was a conventional weapon delivery system, not a nuclear one.

Military officers were not alone in lamenting the absence of a national security planning institution. Minister for Defence K. C. Pant was one who recognized the problem. In 1988, he tasked Additional Secretary P. R. Chari to draft a paper sketching how a national security council could be established and operated in India. When the draft was completed, Pant asked Chari to take soundings from the army chief of staff and others who would have to subscribe to it. These consultations revealed institutional and personal resistance to surrendering turf and authority to a new body. As the army chief, V. N. Sharma put it, "[A]ll decisions on defining the threat faced by my service will be made by me, not a national security council, and I will not abdicate my responsibility for decisionmaking in this regard."[21]

DRAMATIC CHANGES IN AND AROUND PAKISTAN, 1988

Unbeknownst to Indian planners in 1988, the cut in defense spending was made as the perceived threat from Pakistan was about to diminish. In February 1988, the Soviet Union announced its willingness to withdraw its forces from Afghanistan.[22] The Soviet withdrawal would greatly reduce Pakistan's rationale for building military capability and sap Washington's drive to arm it.

The Soviet move shocked the region's political and security systems. Then came the aftershock: on August 17, 1988, President Zia was killed when his plane crashed on return from a U.S. M1-Abrams tank demonstration. (Thirty others were killed, including U.S. Ambassador to Pakistan Arnold Raphel.) Zia's death—which many in Pakistan considered an unsolved assassination—transformed the Pakistani political scene just as the nation and region were beginning to assess the implications of the end of the Afghan war and, indeed, the cold war. Pakistan now moved toward long-awaited elections. In November 1988, Benazir Bhutto's Pakistan Peoples Party received a plurality of votes and she was tapped to form a minority government. The daughter of Zulfikar Ali Bhutto had returned to her native land in 1986 after years of exile in England and now sought to revive Pakistani democracy.

Benazir inherited a nuclear weapon program controlled by an army that was likely to resist any efforts to constrain it. She assumed tenuous power at the moment that the Reagan administration (in the interregnum before the Bush administration took over) was required, pursuant to the Pressler Amendment, to certify that Pakistan did not possess a nuclear explosive device. If certification could not be given, the United States would cut off military and economic assistance. The Reagan administration by now could not deflect intelligence that Pakistan's nuclear weapon capability had become highly advanced. Yet the administration did not want to handicap the new hopeful Bhutto government by cutting off much-needed aid over a nuclear program that she had not led. Thus, Reagan certified Pakistan's nonpossession of a nuclear explosive device with a carefully hedged letter to Congress suggesting that such certification would be more difficult in the future.[23] Bhutto had helped her case by declaring to American journalists that "[w]e want it clear beyond doubt that we're interested only in energy, not nuclear weapons."[24] Still, by this time, plausible reports had already emerged that Pakistan had accumulated enough highly enriched uranium for four to six nuclear weapons and that China had provided a design that enabled Pakistan to assemble weapons weighing only 400 pounds, a rather advanced capability.[25]

The end of the Afghan war and the tentative revival of democracy in Pakistan yielded some hope that Indo-Pak relations could be improved significantly, abating nuclear pressures. Rajiv and Benazir were new-generation leaders descended from luminous families, heirs to both power and tragedy. Perhaps they could find the chemistry, vision, and determination to set their nations on a course to normalize relations. In late December, Rajiv made his first visit to Pakistan to attend the fourth summit of the South Asian Association for Regional Cooperation (SAARC). In his remarks there he declared, "We rejoice in the prospect of friendship and co-operation between India and Pakistan." He joined with Benazir in endorsing confidence-building measures to reduce the military confrontation on the Siachen Glacier and, on Pakistan's part, to curtail support for Sikh separatists in Punjab.[26] The two leaders also finally signed the agreement negotiated in 1985 not to attack each other's nuclear facilities.

In May 1988, Rajiv presented to the UN General Assembly Special Session on Disarmament an "Action Plan" for a three-stage course to eliminate nuclear weapons by 2010.[27] Among the many actions urged in the plan, Gandhi called for the non–nuclear weapon states "not to cross the threshold into the acquisition of nuclear weapons." This clearly included India. The same year, Rajiv also proposed a scheme for eliminating nuclear weapons specifically from Asia, a departure from the traditional global approach. Under this plan, Asian states also would commit not to develop or acquire nuclear weapons, in return for guarantees that they would not be threatened with the use of such weapons.[28]

These proposals were too lofty to have a practical impact, particularly on the existing nuclear powers. Indeed, they almost certainly did not reflect even the views of the Ministry of External Affairs, the Ministry of Defence, or the nuclear establishment. Nuclear hawks in India went along because these initiatives had little chance of being effected and served to rally public opinion in much of the world against the nuclear weapon states. The initiatives did, however, indicate the prime minister's reluctance to authorize any departure from India's declared policy of rejecting nuclear weapons.[29]

RAJIV VISITS CHINA, DECEMBER 1988

In December 1988, Rajiv Gandhi became the first Indian prime minister since Nehru to travel to China. During this symbolically important visit, the two sides reaffirmed the principles of peaceful coexistence laid down by Nehru in the 1950s.

They agreed that "peace and tranquility" should be maintained as they worked to resolve the border dispute through consultations.[30] Rather than mire themselves in history, both governments sought to look toward a more positive future. They signed bilateral agreements to facilitate cooperation and exchanges in science and technology, prepare the way for resumed direct flights between the two countries, and conduct cultural exchanges. While Indian commentators generally bemoaned the failure to win Chinese concessions on the border dispute, the visit did impart momentum to the process of developing "good-neighbourly and friendly relations," in the words of a joint communiqué.[31]

The relaxation of Sino-Soviet tensions initiated by Gorbachev encouraged both India and China to attend to their relationship directly. India no longer risked alienating its Soviet friends, and China no longer needed to regard India through the Beijing-Moscow prism. Indian leaders had no illusions that India could afford to drop its guard against China, but the changing global situation and the businesslike tone of Sino-Indian relations diminished the "need" for expanding India's nuclear capability to deal with the Chinese threat. Indeed, as W. P. S. Sidhu noted, there was no indication that China's nuclear capability and its assistance to Pakistan's nuclear program were taken up directly with Beijing during Rajiv's tenure.[32]

POLITICS AND THE BEGINNING OF
THE INDO-PAK MISSILE RACE, 1989

Rajiv Gandhi left behind cascading political troubles when he traveled to China, and the trip did little to dam them. With elections on the horizon, the political tide at home promised to rise against the Congress party throughout 1989. For once, economics was not a major factor: in the second half of the 1980s economic growth averaged over 5 percent annually, inflation was moderate, and capital markets and corporate profits grew. Rather, corruption and the perceived lawlessness and selfishness of the political class turned the public against Rajiv.[33]

Rajiv spent 1989 warding off attacks for his role in the Bofors defense procurement kickback scandal and deflecting the mounting political campaign against him. The opposition was now led by V. P. Singh, the former Congress party finance and defense minister whom Rajiv had thrown out of the party in July 1987. In October 1988, Singh had helped build the Janata Dal party around non-BJP members of the 1977–1979 Janata coalition. Then, in November, the Janata Dal joined with a still larger collection of regional parties under the rubric of the National Front.[34] While the National Front coalition excluded the BJP, it did negotiate electoral strategies with the right-wing party to avoid splitting the anti-Congress vote in the elections due to be held by the end of 1989. No single opposition party could achieve an electoral majority to supplant the Congress, but together they looked strong enough to win enough votes to keep Congress from forming a government.

Domestic travails kept Rajiv from concentrating on foreign or nuclear policy in 1989.[35] However, this did not stop the momentum of either Pakistan's or India's nuclear and missile programs. On February 11, Pakistan conducted the first test launches of ballistic missiles: the HATF-1 and HATF-2 had ranges of 80 and 300 kilometers, respectively, and the reported capacity to carry payloads of up to 500 kilograms. ("Hatf" is the Arabic word for "deadly" and was the name of the sword used by the prophet Mohammad.)[36] Coming roughly a year after India's first launch of the Prithvi missile, the Pakistani tests manifested a determination not to be left behind in any strategic military competition with India. Pakistan's missile capabilities owed much to help from China and, through procurement, Western Europe.[37] The tests were announced over national television by Army Chief of Staff General Mirza Aslam Beg, not the civilian prime minister or president, revealing the balance of internal power in the Pakistani nuclear and missile programs.[38]

The Pakistani missile tests, and the Prithvi test before, reflected a new dimension in the Indo-Pak military competition at a time when the United States was leading an international effort to block missile proliferation. In April 1987, after years of discussions among the United States and other major Western technology-supplier countries, the Missile Technology Control Regime (MTCR) was formed to extend the international nonproliferation regime to missile delivery systems. (The suppliers had secretly implemented the control agreement beginning in 1985.)[39] The Soviet Union was not a formal member of the cartel, due to its exclusion from the original negotiations, but nonetheless a cooperating partner. Cartel members agreed not to export missiles capable of delivering 500-kilogram payloads more than 300 kilometers and other covered items, without case-by-case review.[40] If sales were approved, members agreed to negotiate strict end-use assurances.

The Indian and Pakistani systems tested thus far fell below the limit set by MTCR guidelines. Still, these missile programs reinforced the Bush administration's growing interest in curbing the spread of high technologies that could be used in developing missiles, including not only rocket and missile components and fabrication technologies but also computers and other assets instrumental in designing and testing missiles. Most of these technologies were dual use, meaning they could serve genuinely civilian as well as military purposes. This created tensions both within the advanced technological nations (potential suppliers) and between those advanced nations and countries such as India seeking to modernize their economies. American, European, and Russian vendors resisted efforts to constrict potential markets for their wares. India and other states viewed regimes that would control the supply of high technology as a reassertion of colonialism intended to keep them from advancing and eventually competing with more advanced economies.[41]

In the spring of 1989, India was preparing the first test launch of the medium-range Agni missile. The Indian missile program had consciously raced against impending nonproliferation controls, and the Defence Research and Development Organisation had largely succeeded, as the Agni test would show. With the missile ready, V. S. Arunachalam called to give U.S. Ambassador to India John Gunther Dean advance notification of the test. Dean urged that the test be canceled, but Arunachalam demurred. The missile was set for launch on April 20. However, technical problems caused the test to be aborted at the last instant on April 20 and again on May 1. American officials reportedly then made two additional approaches to the Ministry of External Affairs to press for cancellation in order to dampen the regional arms race.[42] In congressional testimony on May 18, CIA Director William Webster stated that there was growing concern over a regional arms race and intelligence indications that India was seeking "thermonuclear weapons capability."[43] On May 22 the Agni blasted off from the Chandipur Interim Test Range on the coast of the eastern state of Orissa.[44]

Indian officials and commentators lost no time in heralding the launch in terms reminiscent of the Pokhran celebration almost exactly fifteen years earlier. "Agni blossomed into a chariot of fire that propelled India into an exclusive club dominated by the world's technological and military giants," trumpeted *India Today*.[45] The missile scientists and engineers were lauded as avatars of Indian prowess and might. As in 1974, the test represented a vital theme in the national anticolonial narrative. In congratulating the scientists and the nation, Rajiv Gandhi, proclaimed: "We lost our Independence two centuries ago because we were disunited on the home front and not vigilant on the external front. We must remember that technological backwardness also leads to subjugation. Never again will we allow our freedom to be so compromised."[46] The Indian audience could not miss the prime minister's subtle effort to tie the test to his leadership in a time of disunity and intense political maneuvering against him.

The Agni was proclaimed as only a "technology demonstrator." Indian officials denied any intent to use the system to deliver nuclear weapons. Yet these qualifications were offered with a collective wink. In the words of the country's leading newsmagazine, "Armed with a nuclear warhead, Agni offers the potential to put India on par with China as far as military deterrence is concerned."[47] Even Rajiv Gandhi balanced his insistence that Agni "is not a weapons system" with the declaration that the program reflected "our commitment to the indigenous development of advanced technologies for the defence of the nation."[48] Agni's reputed range of 2,500 kilometers qualified it as the first weapon system that could hit targets deep inside China. However, foreign intelligence sources concluded that the Agni flew approximately only 800 kilometers, not far enough to menace China.[49]

No plan existed to chart how India could or should develop and integrate this technology into a nuclear arsenal with requisite command and control, reconnaissance, and warning systems that would provide a secure and reliable advantage in relation to China. Neither the government nor outside analysts detailed the cost and feasibility of catching up with China in this strategic realm. Indeed, as the former minister of state for defense, Arun Singh, noted in a 1996 paper,

"There is very little written or said at any level or in any forum about the specific requirements of or nature of a credible and adequate deterrent *vis-à-vis* China."[50] Even if parity in such strategic systems was not necessary to provide a robust deterrent, no one explained how security would be enhanced during the transition between 1989 and whenever India had a survivable minimal force. If China would not react adversely to India's development of a nuclear arsenal directed against it, then what was the threat warranting India's development of such an arsenal in the first place? If China would react by escalating security competition, how could India match China, starting as it did from far behind? Instead of addressing these questions, the Indian line of reasoning followed a simple logic: "India's need for ballistic missiles has been reinforced by several political and military factors. Among them are the perceived threat from Chinese nuclear missile deployments and the fact that IRBM [intermediate-range ballistic missile] and ICBM [intercontinental ballistic missile] capabilities have come to *symbolize political and military power in the world*."[51]

As with Pokhran, the U.S. Congress reacted strongly to the Agni test. Twenty-two senators wrote the president a letter immediately after the test decrying it as "a highly destabilizing development in the region" and demanding that the administration do more to stop the Indian missile program.[52] Indian and American officials were already scheduled to meet a week following the Agni test to discuss cooperation in space technology. Despite the senatorial concern, the Bush administration did not cancel the meeting. However, congressional pressure did compel the administration to reverse course and deny in June an export license for a $1.2 million rocket-testing device that simulated the heat and vibration of re-entry into the earth's atmosphere (Combined Acceleration Vibration Climatic Test System).[53] A California company, Ling Electronics Inc., had legally shipped a larger such device to India after April 1988, raising press and congressional charges that the Commerce Department had not adhered to MTCR guidelines.[54] American concerns over the missile proliferation threat also led to additional delays and conditions on a sale of a new supercomputer to India, the Cray XMP-22, which was twice as powerful as the previously sold XMP-14. The $50 million XMP-22 export was not approved until December 1990.[55] The Indian strategy of abjuring overt development of a nuclear arsenal in part to prevent international technology denial was now bumping up against reactions to the unmistakable strategic implications of the Agni program. Still, in July the Bush administration received India's Defence Minister K. C. Pant for high-level meetings in Washington, the first visit by an Indian defense minister since 1964.[56] During this visit, Pant gave a speech at MIT, declaring that "India does not subscribe to the doctrine of nuclear deterrence. However, India just cannot afford to overlook the fact that three major nuclear powers operate in its neighbourhood and Pakistan is engaged in a nuclear weapon programme. If we are to influence these major powers, then it becomes inescapably necessary for us to reckon with their nuclear deterrence belief concepts."[57] Pant's formulation vaguely signaled to

American and Indian audiences that the nation would not sit on its hands when faced with nuclear threats.

The Bush administration also wishfully tried cooperative tactics to persuade Pakistan to slow its nuclear program. In June 1989, Benazir Bhutto visited Washington, still insisting that Pakistan did not have or seek nuclear weapons. The United States knew differently but hoped that by maintaining a positive relationship with Benazir it could augment her capacity to control the nuclear program. To show the prime minister that Washington knew perhaps more than she did about the Pakistani program, CIA officials showed Benazir a mockup of a Pakistani nuclear bomb.[58] President Bush, according to Seymour Hersh, told Bhutto that the United States would not be able to certify *in 1990* that Pakistan did not possess a nuclear explosive device unless Pakistan could assure the United States that it would not enrich uranium above 5 percent and would not manufacture cores for nuclear bombs. Some U.S. officials believed Pakistan already had manufactured at least one core and a complementary implosion system; thus, the request to Bhutto amounted to a demand for a freeze, with hope that existing cores would be destroyed. Around this time, following Army Chief of Staff General Beg's trip to Washington for meetings with top U.S. officials, the Pakistanis agreed to "freeze" the nuclear program by not enriching uranium above the agreed level and not manufacturing cores.[59] However, the Pakistanis did continue design and laboratory work related to miniaturizing potential warheads and retained at least one unassembled weapon.[60]

Overall, in both Pakistan and India, mutual distrust, the creep of technology, and the undying ambitions of defense scientists and engineers were pushing up hard against the veneer of political disavowals regarding nuclear weapons. Washington was running out of ideas for stemming the underlying pressures.

ELECTIONS AND A NEW GOVERNMENT IN INDIA, NOVEMBER 1989

In India, domestic pressures against Rajiv Gandhi's government mounted. Hindu nationalism surged, fueled by a militant group within the Sangh Parivar family of organizations, the Vishwa Hindu Parishad (VHP). The VHP seized on a decades-old dispute over the alleged birthplace of Ram, the god-king of Ayodhya and hero of the *Ramayana* epic. Devout Hindus argued that Ram had been born at a site that was now occupied by a disused mosque built in the sixteenth century and, worse, that the mosque had been built from pillars of the Ram temple that Muslims had destroyed.[61] Militant Hindus led by the VHP, and aligned with the BJP, now sought to move the mosque and build a new Hindu temple on the site in an assertion of Hindu identity and politics. The BJP, which had only recently downplayed Hindu nationalism as a means to broaden its political base, now reversed course and presented itself as the vanguard of Hindus seeking to redress perceived excesses of affirmative action for Muslims and other traditional vote "banks" of the Congress party.

V. P. Singh, as leader of the Janata Dal, personally eschewed communal politics, but the National Front that he led needed the support of the BJP, as well as that of regional parties and the left-wing Communists. The dominant electoral issue was corruption and discontent with Rajiv Gandhi, but communalism frayed the social fabric to the point that any electoral victor would find it difficult to govern. Elections occurred on November 22 and 24, leaving the Congress party with 192 seats to the National Front's 144, led by the Janata Dal. The BJP won 86, a dramatic increase over its 1984 total of 2 Lok Sabha seats, and the Left won 52.[62] Rajiv knew he could not win cooperation from the BJP or the Left and thus declared that the Congress would not try to form a government, leaving the field to the National Front. In forming a government, V. P. Singh faced a daunting task of managing a coalition that included the opposing views and styles of the BJP and the Left Front. BJP members were not included in the new cabinet, but the party's support was necessary for the government to survive.

Nuclear policy did not figure significantly in the election.[63] Only the BJP called for the bomb, but the party was unlikely to bring down the new government over it. In an early statement on nuclear policy, V. P. Singh offered to conduct a dialogue on the issue with Pakistan, something Rajiv had rejected as pointless.[64]

Singh now brought Raja Ramanna back into a major position, naming him minister of state for defense. Singh held the minister for defense portfolio, making Ramanna's role all the more important. Ramanna's administrative talents and his reputation for presiding over the production of India's first nuclear explosive signaled that the new government would take strategic defense seriously. The signal was strengthened—unintentionally—in early 1990 when P. K. Iyengar was tapped to succeed M. R. Srinavasan, whose term had expired as chairman of the Atomic Energy Commission. Iyengar's role in the nuclear explosive program led some to read more into this appointment than was warranted: Rajiv had promised Iyengar the job in 1987. Still, two knowledgeable advocates of nuclear weapon capability now occupied important government posts, where they worked closely with Arunachalam and his team at the Defence Research and Development Organisation.

Just after Singh entered office, in December or early January, the prime minister noted with concern speculation in the press that Pakistan could detonate a nuclear device in the Sindh desert to deter India from acting against Pakistan in reaction to uprisings now underway in Punjab and Kashmir. V. P. Singh wanted to know more about this possible threat and what India could or should do to deal with it. He called a meeting of top advisers, including Arunachalam, Foreign Minister Inder K. Gujral, Principal Secretary B. G. Deshmukh, and Deputy Chairman of the Planning Commission Ramakrishna Hegde.[65] The prime minister also summoned the now "retired" Arun Singh to the meeting. The group was joined by a leading nuclear scientist from BARC. The prime minister did not believe Pakistan would actually use nuclear weapons against India, but he wanted his advisers to analyze all possible scenarios and how India should proceed. Arunachalam, representing the strategic enclave, told Singh that they were ready to conduct a nuclear test if he wanted them to and that if Pakistan waged a nuclear attack against India, the means existed to deliver a nuclear response.

No military officers attended this meeting, but in January or February Prime Minister Singh summoned Air Chief Marshal S. K. Mehra for a private discussion in which Singh asked whether Pakistan could launch a bolt-from-the-blue nuclear attack against India. Mehra reportedly answered that India could not prevent a treetop attack by Pakistani aircraft but that India could retaliate in kind.[66] This was the nature of nuclear deterrence, Mehra explained. Singh did not like the defenselessness and all-or-nothing character of this nuclear equation, but he accepted it. He instructed Mehra to increase the air force's preparations to carry out such missions. Mehra duly raised the air force's alert level according to the source of this story. The Air Chief Marshal then inquired vaguely of Army Chief of Staff General V. N. Sharma whether the prime minister had recently talked with him about nuclear issues and was told that he had not. Mehra then made the same inquiry to the chief of naval staff and received the same answer. This lack of coordination and formal policy deliberation concerned Mehra deeply, as it seriously undermined the military's capacity to fight effectively if a nuclear attack did occur. Mehra also was disturbed by the inadequate coordination between the air force and the scientific establishment in determining technical and operational requirements for nuclear weapon delivery.[67] However, the ad hoc, personalized approach by the prime minister continued a longstanding tradition, as did the exclusion of the collective military services from any formal nuclear policymaking role.

Singh elected not to conduct a nuclear test or take other "preemptive" steps in the nuclear realm. He had several reasons, as he recounted on the BBC's *Hard Talk* program in June 1998: "One was that with economic problems we did not think it wise at that time to invite sanctions. . . . [T]hat was the time when the country was thinking of going to the IMF or World Bank" for emergency funding.[68] "At the same time," Singh noted, "Punjab and Kashmir were in a delicate position" facing insurgencies. Singh wanted to be able to concentrate defense assets on the western border against Pakistan. Forces could be shifted from the north, thanks to improving relations with China, but "any explosion at that time would have changed the situation and we could not have achieved this relaxation of the Indo-Chinese border." Finally, Singh noted retrospectively and half-correctly, "Pakistan had not quite acquired the bomb," reducing any pressure he might have felt to conduct nuclear tests for political or strategic purposes. In fact, Pakistan possessed ready-to-assemble nuclear weapons.

Following these consultations, V. P. Singh requested Arun Singh to perform detailed modeling and analysis of the Indo-Pak nuclear relationship to anticipate possible circumstances under which Pakistan might use nuclear weapons and assess how India could or should prevent such use or respond to it. This helped prompt a secret commission, which Arunachalam established at the end of 1990, as discussed below. In the meantime, the prime minister backtracked on his initial call for nuclear dialogue with Pakistan and in February 1990 adopted the now standard stance that "India will have to review its peaceful nuclear policy if Pakistan manufactures nuclear weapons."[69]

In a bid to further strengthen policymaking, Singh proposed to create a National Security Council that would augment coordination among relevant ministries and the military services and increase the expertise and strategic clarity informing government policy. However, in forming the council, the government simply added one or two officials to the existing Cabinet Committee on Political Affairs, which consisted most importantly of the ministers for defense, home affairs, finance, and external affairs. This body was then to be assisted by a larger advisory board of experts, academics, scientists, journalists, former government officials, some chief ministers of states, and members of Parliament. In practice, the advisory board proved unwieldy and the National Security Council met only once before being abandoned.[70] The powerful ministries and ministers resisted ceding information or power to others and preferred operating under the Cabinet Committee on Political Affairs. If institutional reform was necessary to improve India's strategic security policy, it would have to wait.

THE FIRST NUCLEAR CRISIS?

In the spring of 1990 the violent discontent that had been brewing in Kashmir for the past couple of years escalated into a serious Indo-Pak confrontation. By some accounts, particularly Seymour Hersh's sensationalistic March 1993 article in the *New Yorker,* "On the Nuclear Edge," the two states verged on nuclear war.[71] Following Hersh's story a conventional wisdom developed that nuclear deterrence first began operating on the subcontinent in the 1990 crisis and helped avert war.[72] However, there are serious factual and interpretive flaws in this legend. While it is not necessary to recount the complexities of the Indo-Pak crisis in Kashmir, a brief recapitulation of the overall context helps set the scene for clarifying its nuclear dimensions and implications.

In 1987 the challenge to Indian governance in the Muslim-majority Kashmir valley grew acute in large part due to malfeasance in the conduct of April state elections. Rajiv Gandhi's Congress party was allied with the Jammu and Kashmir National Conference, a local party headed by Farooq Abdullah. Representatives of the allied parties engaged in systematic intimidation of voters, ballot box tampering, and harassment of electoral workers.[73] Having in effect rigged the elections, the Congress (I)–National Conference alliance won sixty out of seventy-six seats, based on just less than 50 percent of the popular vote. The illegitimacy of the election prompted Kashmiri opposition parties to conclude that standard politics would not satisfy their interests. Agitation and militancy now appeared as the most viable option for advocates of change. In 1988, violence mounted into a nascent insurgency demanding independence from India or Kashmir's alignment with Pakistan, or both.

Agitation grew through 1989. The Indian government responded with repressive measures and charges that the trouble was being fomented by Pakistan. After the Congress government's defeat in the November 1989 national elections, Kashmiri activists escalated their attack. In January 1990, the already-beleaguered New Delhi government appointed Jagmohan Malhotra as the governor of Jammu and Kashmir and sent him to the state with 150,000 paramilitary troops from border security forces to restore order.[74] Farooq Abdullah resigned as it became apparent that New Delhi was taking direct control of the state. Jagmohan then launched a campaign of repression to stem the insurgency. Meanwhile, on January 21, Pakistan's Foreign Minister Sahibzada Yakub Khan traveled to New Delhi, where he met Foreign Minister Inder K. Gujral and expressed serious concern about events in Kashmir. During the visit, he warned of "war clouds hovering over the subcontinent."[75] Gujral comprehended the nuclear connotations of Yakub's warning and reported immediately to Prime Minister Singh. Singh instructed Gujral to meet the Pakistani later that evening, which the foreign minister did, telling Yakub, "[D]o not mistake our kind words for weakness."[76] Gujral recalled that he made clear to Yakub "that we will be decisive and they should have no illusions about our resolve." According to Gujral, Yakub put up his hands as if to say that his bellicose threat earlier had been misinterpreted. The tone of the discussion then changed, according to Gujral.[77] Still, rhetoric and violence now entered an escalating cycle that threatened to widen the conflict into an interstate crisis.

On March 13, Benazir Bhutto traveled to the Pakistan-held portion of Kashmir and promised a "thousand-year war" to support the militants.[78] Bhutto's bellicosity reflected the influence of President Ghulam Ishaq Khan, Chief of Army Staff General Aslam Beg, and Pakistan's Inter-Services Intelligence Directorate (ISI), who were militantly anti-Indian and determined to up the ante in Kashmir by supporting what had been a spontaneous, indigenous uprising analogous to the Palestinian *intifada*. These two men and the ISI wielded enormous power in the Pakistani power structure and in many ways held the weak prime minister hostage. They welcomed the opportunity to flex Pakistan's muscles and, among other things, show the United States that Pakistan would free itself from undue American influence now that the war with Afghanistan was over. Beg was further emboldened by a trip he had taken to Tehran in February, where he claimed to have gained Iranian support that would enable Pakistan to win if war erupted over Kashmir.[79] In supporting Kashmiri irredentists, Pakistan sought deliberately to empower radical Islamic organizations, thereby combining the forces of religion and nationalism, a mixture that had been successful in Afghanistan against Soviet forces.

The aggressive attitude of Pakistan's key leaders put enormous pressure on the beleaguered Indian government, whose mishandling of the local situation in Kashmir had prompted the crisis. The BJP in early April passed a resolution demanding the government to "knock out the training camps and transit routes of the terrorists."[80] Rajiv Gandhi, now looking for opportunities to come back to power, urged "very strong steps on Kashmir." Stating that he knew "what is in the pipeline and what the capabilities are," he asked provocatively whether the government "has the guts to take strong steps."[81] The "pipeline" to which he referred could have meant nuclear weapons, unassembled models of which the Atomic Energy Commission and Defence Research and Development Organisation had now produced. Thus pressed, V. P. Singh on April 10 gave a speech calling on Indians to be "psychologically prepared" for war and warning Pakistan, "[Y]ou cannot get away with taking Kashmir without a war."[82] Mindful of Pakistan's decade-long advance in acquiring nuclear weapons capability and of Yakub Khan's ominous mention of "war clouds," Singh declared that if Pakistan deployed nuclear weapons, "India will have to take a second look at our policy. I think we will have no option but to match. Our scientists have the capability to match it."[83]

As the rhetoric heated, the chronic conventional arms firing across the Line of Control in Kashmir became more acute. India moved more troops into the region, deployed to prevent cross-border infiltration from Pakistan and to threaten hot pursuit or raids on training camps but not to launch concerted, major operations against Pakistan.[84] Meanwhile, south of Kashmir along the Indo-Pak border, both armies maintained and in some instances increased forces that had been deployed earlier for exercises. The Pakistanis were especially mindful of the Brasstacks experience in 1987 and wanted to ensure that India did not get a running start against them now. The Indian and Pakistani presses hyped the threats perceived in both countries. However, according to U.S. military attachés monitoring the situation from both Pakistan and India, neither side deployed its forces in ways suggesting imminent aggression.[85]

Neither India nor Pakistan seemed able or willing to defuse the situation.[86] They had talked themselves into corners from which domestic and interstate politics would not allow them to escape. Some positive steps had been taken: at the behest of U.S. Ambassador William Clark, India had authorized American military attachés to travel to the Line of Control in Kashmir and the conventional military staging areas in Rajasthan to see for themselves (and the Pakistanis) that no mobilization for invasion was occurring. Still, escalating rhetoric and earlier troop movements raised fears in the U.S. Embassies in New Delhi and Islamabad that the 1987 Brasstacks scenario might be repeated. Only now, the governments of both countries were too politically weak to back down if a major confrontation developed. American officials in Washington and Pakistan shared the alarm and sent messages to the governments of China, the Soviet Union, and European countries asking them to urge India and Pakistan to restrain themselves.[87]

In Washington the situation became urgent sometime in the late spring, when American intelligence detected that Pakistan was preparing to raise the stakes dramatically. While the exact details remain outside the public domain, it appears that the United States intercepted a message to the Pakistani Atomic Energy Commission (PAEC) ordering it to assemble at least one nuclear weapon.[88] As Paul Wolfowitz, then under secretary of defense told Mitchell Reiss, "We knew that Pakistan assembled a nuclear weapon."[89] Hersh and subsequent analysts have stated that the order went to Kahuta, the facility run by A. Q. Khan. But this seems an assumption influenced by A. Q. Khan's mythmaking and ignores the more important role of the Atomic Energy Commission scientists and engineers in the Pakistani nuclear program. As the chief AEC scientist on the Pakistani bomb team, Samar Mubarakmand, explained after the 1998 nuclear tests, "[T]here are at least 24 . . . links of the chain under PAEC carrying out important research in various fields connected with the country's nuclear program." A. Q. Khan's work was "one major link of the chain," but most of the effort beyond enriching uranium was done by the Pakistan Atomic Energy Commission, which for the 1998 blasts had "12 scientists involved in the entire exercise."[90] The PAEC also played the lead role in 1990 under the circumspect Munir Ahmad Khan; it was this establishment that was mobilized in 1990 to prepare at least one nuclear weapon. Knowledge of this mobilization set American officials in motion to defuse the crisis.[91]

Bush administration officials decided in the third week of May to send a high-level team to the region. National Security Council aide Richard Haass and Assistant Secretary of State for Near East and South Asian Affairs John Kelly left Washington with talking points and briefing materials that Deputy National Security Adviser Robert Gates would present to Pakistani and Indian leaders as head of the American delegation. The air force plane picked up Gates in Moscow, where he was doing advance work for the impending U.S.-Soviet summit, and headed for Pakistan. The central aim of the mission was to encourage both India and Pakistan to de-escalate the crisis. As Gates told Seymour Hersh, the main worry was that both governments were "too weak to stop a war. . . . There was the view that both sides were blundering toward a war."[92]

The American team arrived in Pakistan on May 20, and Gates and U.S. Ambassador to Pakistan Robert Oakley alone met with President Khan and General Beg. Prime Minister Bhutto was touring the Gulf states and unwilling to alter her schedule to meet with the Americans. By all accounts the meeting was rough. Gates told his counterparts that the United States had "war-gamed every conceivable scenario between you and the Indians. There isn't a single way you win. The only question is how much territory and how many military forces you will lose."[93] This was not what Beg wanted to hear or had been telling President Khan. According to Oakley, Ishaq Khan seemed startled by the presentation. The Americans also told the Pakistanis that their resumption of the nuclear weapon program had been detected and would force the United States to invoke the Pressler Amendment, cutting off economic and military aid to Pakistan. This and the general hard American line elicited protests from the two Pakistani hawks. They argued that the United States had overlooked India's bellicose behavior along the border and its threats to attack Pakistan.[94] In the end, the delegation won Khan's pledge that Pakistan would consider closing training camps for Kashmiri insurgents. In exchange, Gates promised to raise Pakistan's concerns with India. The

Pakistani pledge signaled a willingness to dissipate the crisis and would be conveyed to the Indian side to induce reciprocal measures. Gates gave the Pakistanis a list of confidence-building measures that could be undertaken with India, which he urged them to consider. He said he would give the same paper to the Indians.[95]

On May 21 Gates met in New Delhi with Prime Minister V. P. Singh, Principal Secretary B. G. Deshmukh, and Foreign Minister Gujral. Atypically, the tone of the meetings with the Indians was much more positive than with the Pakistanis. The Indians evinced no interest in going to war, but they expressed deep concern over the uprising in Kashmir and Pakistan's role in it. According to Haass, the message was that India was not deployed or intending to go to war but that the government could not tolerate Pakistani intervention in Kashmir forever. Fortunately, Gates could inform the Indians that Pakistan's president had pledged to close terrorist training camps. Although Pakistan later denied making such a pledge, and all the camps were not closed, Gates's message helped induce Indian restraint. The combination of Indian and Pakistani willingness to talk to each other even in a crisis atmosphere, and the diplomatic intervention of Moscow, Beijing, and the Gates mission, enabled the crisis to be dissipated. In a subsequent bilateral meeting in July, Pakistan and India agreed upon several of the confidence-building measures on Gates's list, with no reference to their derivation from the United States.[96] "For the first time," according to then-Indian High Commissioner to Pakistan J. N. Dixit, "India and Pakistan agreed to adopt to some extent a step-by-step approach in normalising relations through confidence-building measures."[97]

Importantly, the American team did not find the Indians worrying explicitly about a nuclear threat from Pakistan. The Indians did not know of the activity detected by American intelligence and Gates did not tell them about it.[98] Interviews with Indian officials who would have been alerted had New Delhi perceived this as a nuclear crisis corroborate the view that India perceived the situation in terms of domestic politics, instability in Kashmir, and Pakistani subversion, not a nuclear threat.[99] They worried about Pakistan's nuclear capability, but not as an acute threat at this moment. To be sure, Indian military officers had to plan for the worst. A high-ranking air force officer recalled asking the government at this time whether Pakistan had deliverable nuclear weapons. He was given no clear answer by the foreign intelligence service—the Research and Analysis Wing (RAW)—or other officials.[100] This officer thus assumed that Pakistan could wield a small number of nuclear weapons but would not initiate armed conflict with them and would probably target air bases if the nuclear firebreak were crossed.

In the retelling of the crisis following Hersh's account, the impression has been left that the imminence of *nuclear war* was what prompted the American mission. However, the reality was different. As Richard Haass explained, "[O]ne of the many areas where Hersh was wrong was that the nuclear dimension was the centerpiece of our visit. It wasn't. We wanted to be sure they would not stumble into war. We were concerned that they were on the brink of war, not nuclear war."[101]

The Americans worried that if war began it could escalate to nuclear exchanges, but as Haass noted, "[W]e didn't find them worrying about that." Indeed, the apparent insouciance in Pakistan and India regarding the risks of conflict escalation to the nuclear level is what made American officials react so strongly to the intelligence they had received.

The stakes went beyond war—even nuclear war—in South Asia. On the parochial level, Bush administration officials also worried that their nonproliferation policy was about to suffer an acute embarrassment, one that would certainly cause an uproar in Congress and elsewhere. Throughout the 1980s, the Republican administrations, joined by a bipartisan majority in Congress, had plied Pakistan with aid to drive the Soviets from Afghanistan, all the while asserting to nonproliferation critics that Pakistan would not cross the threshold and make nuclear weapons. Indeed, American military and economic assistance was justified in part as obviating Pakistan's need for nuclear weapons. Now the critics' charges were being proved true. Arms controllers in the administration already had concluded that time was running out on the president's capacity to certify in good faith that Pakistan did not possess a nuclear explosive device. They believed that a more fundamental approach to alleviate the causes of proliferation in South Asia was needed. But any alternative policy would be rendered more difficult to achieve if Pakistan brought nuclear weapons into the open now.

Historical analysis of the 1990 crisis has led many scholars and policymakers in the United States, India, and Pakistan to conclude that nuclear deterrence played an important role in preventing war. The most carefully constructed argument has been made by Devin Hagerty, who wrote in *International Security* that "[a] strong case can be made that India and Pakistan were deterred from war in 1990 by the existence of mutual nuclear weapon capabilities and the chance that, no matter what Indian and Pakistani decision-makers said or did, any military clash could escalate to the nuclear level."[102] However, Hagerty acknowledged a key empirical issue that undermines this case. For the role of nuclear deterrence to explain India's and Pakistan's restraint, he wrote, authoritative officials would have "to admit that they were planning to go to war, but were dissuaded from doing so by the possibility that conventional conflict might escalate to a nuclear exchange."[103] There is no evidence to date, especially on the Indian side, that leaders wanted anything but to avoid a war.[104] Rather than leaning forward toward conflict, both leaderships were being backed into it. Both sides recognized the now inherent possibility that war could escalate to the nuclear level, but this reality merely added to, and did not create, the mutual interest in turning away from conflict. The result would have been similar if neither possessed nuclear capabilities. (Although American officials probably would not have come to the region to mediate if they had not feared the possibility of its nuclearization.) Indian leaders told the Gates team they were prepared to join Pakistan in de-escalating the conflict without any reference to a nuclear shadow. Indeed, during this period, according to the then principal secretary to Prime Minister V. P. Singh, B. G. Deshmukh, "The defence establishment had . . . been directed to prepare plans for meeting any foreign threat or aggression on the basis of our not having any nuclear weapons."[105]

However, if nuclear threats—and therefore nuclear deterrence—did not play a clear and direct role in the outcome of the 1990 crisis, both sides since the early 1980s had recognized that nuclear disaster could result if they pushed each other too far militarily. Even conventional weapon attacks on civilian nuclear facilities could cause long-term disaster, as both recognized in the 1985 agreement not to attack each other's nuclear facilities. What changed *after* 1990 was the perception that India and Pakistan had nuclear weapon capabilities that were now affecting political and strategic decisions. Pakistanis, especially A. Q. Khan, had since 1984 overestimated the impact of nuclear deterrence on India, but now the belief in the bomb's talismanic deterrent effects had a real basis. General Beg stated his view in a 1992 interview shortly after his retirement:

> The balance of terror starts the moment the adversary realizes there is a threat from the other direction. In the case of weapons of mass destruction it is not the numbers that matter, but the destruction that can be caused by even a few. The strategy of terror starts working from the first notion that there is retaliation. The fear of retaliation lessens the likelihood of war between India and Pakistan. I can assure you that if there were no such fear, we would probably have gone to war in 1990.[106]

This belief may explain why Pakistani leaders ordered the assembly of at least one nuclear weapon in 1990, but it also reveals the danger of Beg's simplistic reliance on nuclear signaling. For if Beg intended to deter India in the crisis, his signal was not received in New Delhi.

In October 1990, President Bush informed Congress that he could no longer certify that Pakistan did not possess a nuclear explosive device. The Pressler Amendment sanctions were then invoked, cutting off economic and military aid to Pakistan. "From now on, for policy planning, both India and Pakistan have to consider each other 'de facto' nuclear weapon powers," K. Sundarji wrote.[107] This removed an important buttress for the restraint preferred by Rajiv Gandhi and other Indian prime ministers. Rajiv felt that the U.S. certification that Pakistan did *not* possess a nuclear explosive device helped keep Indian hawks at bay, even if India had reason to doubt that certification.[108] The Pressler sanctions removed the doubt.

In Pakistan, a new government would manage the confrontation. Benazir Bhutto's Pakistan Peoples Party (PPP) had been pushed from power in August and elections were called for October. In the elections, the thirteen-member Islamic Democratic Alliance, led by Nawaz Sharif and backed by the military establishment and the powerful president, defeated the PPP and came to power. The campaign had been particularly nasty and Benazir vowed revenge. Insofar as the military establishment doubted Bhutto's trustworthiness to maintain the nuclear program, the election results and the installation of Sharif as prime minister suggested that the program would be safe against American pressure to roll it back.

However, Sharif's early move to launch economic reforms and liberalization indicated the need to win international political-economic favor and to calm Indo-Pak relations in order to concentrate resources on economic development.

SECRET COMMITTEE TO PLAN INDIAN
RESPONSES TO NUCLEAR ATTACK, 1990

Pakistan's now undeniable nuclear capability prompted Indian officials to form in September a small, secret group to develop plans for ensuring that in the event of a nuclear attack on India, the government would continue to function and be able to deliver nuclear retaliation. The formation of this group was proposed by the scientific adviser to the minister of defense, V. S. Arunachalam, and was approved by V. P. Singh. The group included Arunachalam, R. Chidambaram of the Atomic Energy Commission, Arun Singh, General Sundarji (retired) and a few others, including K. Subrahmanyam.[109] Unlike the informal 1985 committee headed by Sundarji, this effort did not aim primarily to develop nuclear doctrine or promote weapon capabilities. Rather, it was predicated on a scenario in which India's top governmental echelon was gathered in one place, say the president's annual speech inaugurating a session of Parliament, and Pakistan dropped a nuclear weapon on the building, wiping out the civilian and military leadership. Given that India's Constitution calls for the prime minister to be elected by his or her peers in the Lok Sabha, how would succession be managed if the prime minister were killed or incapacitated? The president has constitutional authority to appoint a prime minister subject to Lok Sabha confirmation, but what would happen if this could not be effected? Who would then take over governmental authority? Who would be authorized to order a retaliatory nuclear strike? What would the new military chain of command be? How would orders for a nuclear retaliation be given and effected? What sorts of preplanning for nuclear operations should be prepared and conveyed to relevant military bases?

The committee held several meetings and made progress in designing on paper a framework for answering these questions. The group, which did not include active service chiefs, concluded that India need not be able to deliver an immediate nuclear riposte to an attacker but instead could effect deterrence through retaliation in a matter of days or weeks. Among its conclusions, the group called for designating air force units to receive nuclear devices and deliver them according to previously prepared orders that base commanders would possess under seal, to be executed upon authorization from surviving political authorities. No special emergency civilian chain of command was established. This would have required sustained involvement of top political leaders in formulating such plans and updating the Indian Constitution's succession provisions for the potential realities of nuclear war. Short of this, the secret committee assumed that in a nuclear war the Indian government could implement procedures already prepared for managing disasters.

Before this group could complete and present its work to the prime minister, V. P. Singh's government was engulfed in a political crisis emanating from Hindu-Muslim violence and agitation fueled by the resurgent BJP and the VHP.[110] Singh was toppled on November 7 and replaced by a short-lived government headed by Chandra Shekhar.

Once again nuclear policy was far from the forefront of political priorities. The planning group established by Arunachalam handed its conclusions to Narasimha Rao, who became prime minister after elections in May 1991, but the group ceased meeting. Some of the recommendations were implemented, but other important questions went unanswered, at least at the highest levels of the Indian government. Arunachalam in this period, as he had in the transitions between prime ministers since 1989, briefed President Venkataraman regularly on developments in the "strategic" programs with which the president had become familiar during his tenure as defense minister from 1982 to 1984.

LIMITED DEBATE ON DOCTRINE GROWS, 1990

As the strategic enclave continued to develop nuclear and missile capabilities, and officials like Arunachalam sought to rationalize Indian contingency plans for conducting nuclear operations, the seeds of a more traditional approach to nuclear doctrine were being sown among the small circle of Indian strategic analysts writing in newspapers. This discourse explicitly reflected the theories of Kenneth Waltz and other sanguine proponents of nuclear deterrence and pitted these theories against the heretofore dominant Indian approach. The most forceful voice among the pro-deterrence group belonged to K. Sundarji.

Sundarji wrote several short essays as part of a polemic with the eminent journalist Pran Chopra, who took a more indigenously Indian line. Chopra anticipated that Washington's inability to certify that Pakistan did not possess a nuclear weapon would prompt a renewed Indian push for the bomb. In a short, late-November essay in the *Hindu*, "The Nuclear Trap," he fretted that India and Pakistan would now begin a nuclear arms race that would subject both to economic sanctions and return Sino-Indian relations to their lower points of the 1960s and 1970s.[111] Once the arms race begins "it will be very difficult to curb it or its consequences," he argued.[112] Instead of embarking on this dangerous and costly course, Chopra recommended that India and Pakistan implement the earlier agreement not to attack each other's nuclear facilities and undertake other agreements to verify that neither was crossing the threshold of assembling or deploying nuclear weapons. More dramatically, he urged that India should "abandon its position that it cannot agree to nuclear abstinence so long as China does not destroy its nuclear arsenal. . . . It simply does not make sense any longer . . . for India to aim at catching up with the nuclear lead already built up by China in every way."[113]

Now retired, Sundarji rose to Chopra's bait and two weeks later countered that India and Pakistan would not engage in a nuclear arms race if and when they went overtly nuclear. Sundarji based his assertion on the distinction between "war-fighting" and "war-deterring." The former requires parity or, preferably, superiority across the range of nuclear weapon systems; the latter requires not parity but only an assured capacity to visit "unacceptable damage" on an aggressor.[114] Sundarji argued that India sought only deterrence and therefore would not be drawn into an arms race. However, this assumed naively that logic and strategy determine force postures in democracies (or any other state) and that domestic political compulsions would not drive India and Pakistan to seek parity with or superiority over each other. In the absence of cooperation and verification agreements, even the quest for parity leads to arms racing because neither side knows what the other has or is building once weaponization and deployments begin. In such a circumstance, worst-case assumptions can lead to overbuilding, which the opponent then tries to balance with new acquisitions in a rising spiral. (The desire for superiority, as opposed to parity, is inherently competitive.) Democracy exacerbates the potential for arms racing when opposition forces within the polity seize on apparent disparities and create political pressures on the government to build larger forces as a display of power and attention to national security. Countervailing considerations of cost can be politically argued, but the aura of insecurity caused by arms races—which is greater than under the nuclear ambiguity that existed for decades between India and Pakistan—tends to give the politically advantageous position to those who claim that security must be achieved at any cost. This is especially true when the true costs of nuclear weapons and delivery systems are not publicly known. This dynamic creates arms races. In later conversations, Sundarji recognized the possibility that deterrence theory could be violated by political expedience.[115]

Regarding China, Sundarji wrote that "there is no true clash of national interests between China and India, with India accepting Chinese sovereignty over Tibet. The border issue can and will be solved, but only through genuine give and take."[116] Such give and take, he argued, would be "more likely to take place with honour and no loss of face when there is genuine, mutual respect and mutual deterrence between the two countries." In other words, the Indian bomb would make China a more forthcoming negotiator. Finally, Sundarji denied that China was too far ahead for India to catch up in nuclear weaponization. All India needed, he wrote, is "a minimum deterrence . . . a retaliatory capability if deterrence fails, which can do unacceptable damage."[117] Sundarji did not define the quantitative and qualitative requirements for such a deterrent, but he bolstered his vague case by citing Kenneth Waltz: "As Kenneth Waltz writes, 'Why compare weapons with weapons when they are to be used not against each other but against cities that cannot counter them?' "[118]

The two writers continued their debate in three follow-up articles. Chopra asked why, if nuclear war is neither "fightable" or "winnable" as Sundarji acknowledged, India should not "first see whether it is also avoidable by means more affordable than the costly status of mutual deterrence."[119] Further, "How much will it cost India to reach such a nuclear level in relations with China that

India may . . . inflict on China unbearable damage in a second strike . . . ? Is that cost bearable for the Indian economy?" Chopra noted that "one never gets a clear answer to this question" from advocates of the Indian bomb.[120]

Sundarji countered that the requirement to deter China could not be avoided and that the cost of doing so would be "about one half to one per cent of the GDP."[121] He based this estimate on the erroneous belief that Britain and France spent "about ten per cent of their total defence budget" on building and maintaining their nuclear deterrents. In fact, France spent more than one-third of its defense budget in building its early nuclear arsenal in the early 1960s—and more than 51 percent of the defense procurement budget.[122] From 1963 to 1992, French nuclear forces consumed more than 30 percent of defense procurement budgets, and this figure did not include other costs associated with possessing nuclear weapons.[123] The Chopra-Sundarji debate did not resolve the extremely complicated and portentous issues involved, but it did illuminate them in constructive ways. As Sundarji concluded, "[T]here is a paucity of indigenous literature on the subject. . . . 'Thank you' to the pundits who have kept the debate alive, however imperfectly!"[124]

Over the next eight years, covered in the succeeding three chapters, the Indian debate occurred between the two poles represented by Sundarji and Chopra. The balance of internal power shifted to the Sundarji-Waltz side as the United States took the occasion of the cold war's end to lead the international community in tightening the nuclear nonproliferation regime in ways that both isolated and outraged India, prompting nationalistic demands that India should assert its power through nuclear weapons.

Ironically, Western-styled theories of deterrence and discourse on security were co-opted to validate this view. Realist international relations theory affected practice. Little detailed analysis occurred of India's specific regional and global security situation and the effect an overt nuclear weapon program would have on India's actual position. Nor did the bomb advocates assess why the United States and the Soviet Union had grossly exceeded the requirements of deterrence in building their enormous arsenals or whether denouncing nuclear war–fighting doctrines was enough to avoid such excess in South Asia. Waltz had recognized in a 1990 essay that "the United States and the Soviet Union have multiplied their weaponry far beyond the requirements of deterrence." He attributed this to "failure to appreciate the implications of nuclear weapons for military strategy and, no doubt, from internal military and political pressures in both countries."[125] Yet, writers like Sundarji and parties like the BJP ignored how this political pressure could lead India and Pakistan into an unwanted arms race. Prior to the Indo-Pak nuclear competition, no two democracies have ever undertaken nuclear competition against each other. Deterrence theorists have not factored the implications of this political variable into their calculations. Without saying so, the hawks essentially argued that what was good enough for the United States, China, and the other recognized nuclear powers, and what was prescribed by Realist theory, should be good enough for India.

CONCLUSION

In 1974 Indira Gandhi could plausibly, if not convincingly, declare that the detonation of a *"peaceful"* nuclear explosive device was consistent with India's principled position against nuclear weapons.[126] By the late 1980s, any significant public advance in the area of nuclear explosive capabilities would have destroyed the image Indians projected as world leaders in the cause of nuclear disarmament. India's postindependence mission of strengthening international morality and transforming the international system would have been repudiated, and with it the nation's moral credibility. However, the growing Pakistani nuclear threat and the ongoing Indian advances in nuclear weapon designs and ballistic missile development strained the elasticity of self-restraint. Thus, by the end of 1990, India and Pakistan possessed nonweaponized nuclear capabilities and they perceived deterrence to be operating. The secrecy and informality of nuclear decision making and the opacity of India's capabilities made India's nuclear "strategy" rather ad hoc, but Indian leaders could counter that this was no more dangerous than the highly elaborated doctrines and hair-triggered postures of the United States and the Soviet Union, which never allowed these superpowers to escape from the inherent contradictions of nuclear deterrence strategy.[127]

Still, India and Pakistan preferred not to cross the threshold to overt assembly and deployment of nuclear arsenals. While this could be interpreted as an exercise in hypocritical duplicity, India, to a significantly greater degree than less-ambivalent Pakistan, did in fact restrain itself. India's moral and cultural ambivalence toward nuclear weapons worked against "going nuclear," as did its interest in avoiding a rupture in relations with the United States and China. A succession of weak governments—four prime ministers between November 1989 and June 1991—and the polity's preoccupation with domestic affairs ruled out a dramatic departure in nuclear policy. Openly moving to build nuclear weapons would simply expose leaders to too many incalculable domestic and international reactions.

For Washington, the events of this period highlighted the growing likelihood of nuclear and missile proliferation and the waning leverage of the United States to stop it. The priority of driving the Soviet Union from Afghanistan had compromised what chance the United States had to block Pakistan's acquisition of nuclear weapons. When the Bush administration was compelled to invoke severe sanctions in 1990, it did so with little genuine belief that they would induce Pakistan to reverse course. The United States' leverage on India was weakened by the reality that the United States and the Soviet Union would not lead the world toward nuclear disarmament. This strengthened the political position of those in India who wanted nuclear weapons regardless of the state's normative stance against them, and it weakened those political leaders and intellectuals who thought nuclear weapons were immoral, excessively costly, and destabilizing.

TWELVE

American Nonproliferation
Initiatives Flounder

1991–1994

In 1991 India faced grave political, economic, and moral challenges that preoccupied leaders and citizens alike. To the extent that foreign policy won attention, it was dominated by Iraq's invasion of Kuwait and India's ineffective reaction to it. These issues dwarfed nuclear policy considerations.

However, by 1992 the Indian system began to rally as economic reforms raised hopes for the country's political-economic development and Indian leaders began to chart a foreign policy course more consonant with post–cold war global dynamics. Debates over nuclear policy reemerged as India, Pakistan, and the United States confronted the reality that South Asia now had nuclear weapon capabilities that would not be rolled back in the foreseeable future. By late 1993 it appeared that India might be willing to participate in global bans on fissile material production for explosive purposes and on nuclear weapon testing. However, 1994 brought disappointment as a U.S. initiative backfired in India and Pakistan, ending what had been the best (brief) chance of mutual accommodation on nuclear issues since the late 1970s. The Indian government led by Narasimha Rao did eschew overt weaponization in deference to India's internal values and interests and its international needs. However, as India sought to adapt to the evolving post–cold war international order by more openly interacting with the global political economy, Indian strategists increasingly began to argue that India should replicate the major powers' approaches to nuclear policy, too. This foreshadowed greater interest in building and deploying nuclear weapons as a means of exerting Indian influence. Indeed, the 1992–94 period culminated the initial weaponization process.

THE DOMESTIC MIRE, 1991

By mid-1990, V. P. Singh's opponents on the Right and Left were pulling his fragile government in opposite directions. Militant Hindus inflamed communal passions by campaigning to replace the Babri Mosque at Ayodhya with a Hindu temple. Meanwhile, caste conflict intensified, too, in reaction to the Singh government's
August 7 announcement that 27 percent of all jobs in the central government and
government-owned public sector enterprises would be "reserved" for people from
the socially and educationally "backward" classes.[1] The polity was becoming
more fractious and vengeful than at any time since partition. The Indian Army
had to be deployed to restore order several times. As a leading journalist, Prem
Shankar Jha, put it, "The six months from November 1990 to May 1991 were the
most dismal in independent India's forty-three year history."[2]

Amidst the turmoil, the Bharatiya Janata Party in November 1990 withdrew its
support for the government, causing V. P. Singh's Janata Dal to split. From the
rubble emerged Chandra Shekhar to form a government with the cynical backing
of Rajiv Gandhi and his 211 Congress party deputies and other followers.[3] Congress's support was conditional, and no one expected the Chandra Shekhar government to last.

By the end of January 1991, Rajiv began to unsettle the new government. In
March, the rug was pulled out and new elections called for May. The main combatants were Rajiv's Congress party, the BJP, and V. P. Singh's Janata Dal.

The election campaign centered on the social and political issues roiling the
country, but an even more portentous economic crisis loomed. At the beginning of
1991 India's foreign currency reserves had plunged below a month's import
requirements. The stock markets had plummeted. Consumer prices were rising
dramatically. The economy was more parlous than at any time since the 1960s
food crises, yet political conflict prevented parties from addressing the challenges.

Foreign policy did not escape electioneering. Saddam Hussein's invasion of
Kuwait in August 1990 prompted several Indian policy somersaults. First, the
Indian Foreign Minister embraced Iraq and tried to rally the Non-aligned Movement to plead for peace, in part because nearly two hundred thousand Indian
workers were trapped in Kuwait and Iraq. When Saddam rebuffed New Delhi's
pleas to evacuate Indian workers and the United States mobilized international
condemnation of Iraq, India joined in supporting sanctions. V. P. Singh shifted
course further in the fall and quietly agreed to allow U.S. aircraft to refuel in India.
Chandra Shekhar maintained that policy, but in January 1991 Rajiv attacked the
government's anti-Iraq line in an opportunistic play for Muslim votes.[4] Then, as
the air war against Iraq began, an Indian press photographer accidentally discovered and photographed a U.S. military transport refueling at Bombay airport.
Political groups across the Indian spectrum put the heat on the government, with
the notable exception of the BJP. Themes of anticolonialism fueled the fire. In

mid-February Chandra Shekhar was compelled to ask the United States to end the refueling in India. This had little effect on the war as it was within days from ending but it revealed Indian political sensibilities that were reflected in nuclear policy, too.

Rajiv's trumpeting of nonalignment pitted him against a BJP whose foreign policy plank deemed nonalignment a dead dogma and argued vaguely that India should seek instead to become a major power in a multipolar world. India should free itself from "the China/Pakistan obsession" and "promote international trade," a contributor to the Rashtriya Swayamsevak Sangh's (RSS) *Organiser* argued.[5] Better to develop a strong Hindu identity and "cultivate the several big powers of the new multi-polar world." The key here was economics. "A country's foreign policy is meaningless if it is not backed by an economy strong enough to be able to sustain it," said a leading BJP thinker, Jay Dubashi.[6]

Nuclear policy barely figured in the campaign.[7] Earlier, in February, Rajiv had expressed fear that the United States would use nuclear weapons in the Gulf war, compelling India "to convert our nuclear weapons capability into nuclear weapons capacity."[8] K. Sundarji added that the apparent American invocation of nuclear deterrence against Iraq confirmed "for the rest of the world that the possession of nuclear weapons is indeed the only coinage of power that the world recognizes as ultimate."[9] Yet, there was nothing new in such statements or in the BJP's repeated advocacy of the bomb. None of the electoral contestants found the issue resonant enough with the public to devote much attention to it.

The elections were scheduled for May 20, 22, and 26 (spread out as usual to allow management of the large number of polling stations and attendant security requirements). However, on May 21 tragedy struck India and the Nehru-Gandhi family once again. Campaigning in Tamil Nadu, Rajiv was assassinated horrifically when a bomb strapped to the body of a Sri Lankan Tamil girl was detonated as Rajiv leaned toward her to accept a garland along a campaign greeting line. The device blew up the girl, Rajiv, and a dozen others in a grizzly scene. The shock of the event forced the postponement of the second and third days of elections until June 12 and 15. The delay spawned a groundswell of sympathy for Rajiv, his family, and the Congress legacy. Congress took 226 seats in the Lok Sabha, enough to lead the formation of a government. The BJP did better than expected by most but less well than its own champions predicted, winning 119 seats, up from 86 in 1989 and 2 in 1984. Importantly, the party nearly doubled its national vote share, from 11 percent in 1989 to 20 percent.[10]

The Congress then formed a government backed by a combination of left wing and National Front parties and headed by Narasimha Rao. Seventy years old, taciturn, and uncharismatic, Rao had long been a stalwart in the Congress party establishment, known for his skill as a survivor and political problem solver. Rao's lack of a mass following did not inspire confidence among early prognosticators of this government's future.[11] However, the prime minister's first cabinet appointments displayed political acumen and the recognition that India needed officials of integrity and competence to solve its tremendous political and economic troubles.

The most important appointment turned out to be Dr. Manmohan Singh as Finance Minister. An outstanding economist of probity and decency he lost no time in devising the most radical reforms in Indian history. Within weeks the government devalued the rupee by more than 20 percent, toughened terms for imports, reduced export subsidies, and heralded plans for further measures to liberalize the economy and reduce the government's role in it.[12] Foreign investment was to be encouraged to fuel technological innovation and general modernization. "We want to be integrated with the world economy," Singh told *India Today*.[13]

GROPING FOR DIRECTION IN FOREIGN AND NUCLEAR POLICY, 1991

The imperative to integrate into the global economy militated against bucking the norms of the international nonproliferation regime. The scientists and technologists at BARC and the DRDO continued to enhance capabilities through their research and development, but attention was deflected from debating what India's public nuclear policy should be.

In late January 1991, Chandra Shekhar and Nawaz Sharif exchanged instruments to ratify the Indo-Pak agreement not to attack each other's nuclear facilities, to which the two countries had pledged in 1985 and agreed formally in 1988.[14] Ratification reflected a general effort by the two new prime ministers to improve Indo-Pak ties. The two had met in November 1990 at the fifth South Asian Association for Regional Cooperation summit in Male and had agreed to renew official talks between the two countries as well as to set up a telephone hot line between themselves with a pledge to use it frequently for communication.[15] A fourth round of foreign secretary talks occurred in Delhi in April, with progress on several confidence-building measures, including agreements to give advance notice of military exercises and maneuvers and steps to prevent airspace violations by military aircraft.[16]

In June, Pakistan proposed a five-power conference of Indian, Pakistani, American, Chinese, and Soviet representatives to facilitate an agreement by India and Pakistan to eliminate all weapons of mass destruction, which the United States, China, and the Soviet Union would guarantee. Washington had initiated the idea to overcome India's traditional rejection of bilateral Indo-Pak talks on the subject and to deal with India's concerns about China. China's role in the South Asian equation had become more acute in April when leaks from U.S. intelligence revealed that China had supplied M-11 missiles (or components) to Pakistan.[17] India would insist that in any conference China should put its strategic programs and policies affecting South Asia on the table—its assistance to Pakistan, its own missile deployments threatening India, and so on—and not merely guarantee a hypothetical agreement between India and Pakistan. When it was evident that China would not do more than guarantee an Indo-Pak agreement, American officials were not surprised when India rejected the proposal as a "propaganda exercise."[18] Because the conference was a Pakistani initiative that treated South Asia separately from global security issues and would not address China's nuclear deployments and supply of nuclear and missile technology assistance to Pakistan it was untenable for New Delhi.

Public opinion regarding nuclear policy at this time was confused. An October–November poll by the Indian Institute of Public Opinion showed that 50 percent of those surveyed "would like India to sign the NPT," while 81 percent "would like India to develop nuclear weapons for defence purposes."[19] Going nuclear, then, would have more easily won public support than nonproliferation, but the normative aversion to nuclear weapons remained.

The Gulf War and the dawning implications of the cold war's end made Indian commentators recognize that the "old shibboleths" of foreign policy needed to be discarded.[20] China should be dealt with afresh, free from the cold war constraints. Pakistan's importance to the United States had declined, and America's ascension as the leading global power dictated a vigorous Indian effort to "coexist with dignity with the US."[21] But the vestigial pulls of nonalignment and left-wing animus toward the United States prevented a major policy shift. By the end of 1991, commentators bemoaned the "unprecedented degree of drift in foreign policy."[22]

In the defense establishment other problems made nuclear policy less relevant. The economic crisis of 1991 and the implementation of economic restructuring made defense cuts the order of the day. On top of this, the decline of the Soviet Union imposed great uncertainties in the availability and rupee "payability" of military equipment and spare parts.[23] These cutbacks more moderately affected the missile program. The DRDO's budget did not shrink in rupee terms, although devaluation and inflation meant that in real terms it did drop briefly in 1991–1992.[24] As had been the case during the defense spending boom in the 1980s, now in the decline no strategy or even white paper existed to guide defense planning.

Economic reforms also raised new problems for the Atomic Energy Commission, prompting an interest in exporting nuclear technology to raise funds. The AEC's actual expenditures dropped from Rs. 514.97 crores in 1990–1991 to Rs. 488.89 crores in 1991–1992, a major fall when inflation and devaluation were reckoned. The government's determination to reduce direct investments and rely instead on private investments in the nuclear power sector put the brakes on new power projects. From 1990 to 1996, no new starts were made in nuclear power units.[25] The architect of these reforms, Finance Minister Manmohan Singh, had been one of the longest serving finance members of the Atomic Energy Commission; he understood how poorly this sector had performed and was now in a position to cut government losses and press the nuclear establishment to compete or wither. To compensate, the AEC announced in February 1991 that it would seek to export nuclear technology, expertise, plutonium reprocessing, and other services.[26] The nuclear establishment then made export overtures to Algeria, Cuba, Egypt, Syria, and Iran.[27] These states posed potential nuclear weapon proliferation threats in the eyes of the United States and other countries, setting up a clash between India's mercantile interest and the objectives of the nonproliferation regime.

The erosion of support for power programs naturally inclined the leaders of the establishment to try to increase its role in the national security realm. However, in the early 1990s neither the strategic enclave nor military nuclear hawks publicly used the budget crunch to press for overt nuclear weaponization. The nuclear establishment knew that the political-economic imperative to stay on the good side of international donors made the government unresponsive, say, to nuclear tests. Prime Minister Rao, who had expertise and leadership experience in foreign policy, neglected this domain in order to concentrate on reviving the economy. But those who did manage foreign affairs also got the message that economics were the highest priority of diplomacy. As a senior Ministry of External Affairs bureaucrat put it, "The economic content of diplomacy will now outstrip everything else."[28]

India desperately needed loans from the International Monetary Fund, other international financial institutions, and individual states to keep afloat. In September 1991, India won aid pledges totaling $6.7 billion from a meeting of international donors in Paris. Japan, Germany, and the United Kingdom provided the bulk of $2.2 billion in individual government funding—states that would react sharply if India tested or built nuclear weapons—while the Asian Development Bank and the World Bank would provide most of the balance.[29]

The Rao and Sharif governments kept up bilateral talks. Pakistan's Foreign Secretary Shahryar Khan came to New Delhi from August 18 to 20 and reiterated Pakistan's interest in normalizing relations.[30] In September an Indian military delegation led by Lieutenant General Satish Nambiar, director general of military operations, traveled to Pakistan to meet with counterparts to continue discussions on redeploying troops from the Siachen Glacier, the inhospitable high-altitude "front" where the two sides frequently exchanged fire. The two military delegations also agreed to try more actively to diminish firing across the Line of Control in Kashmir.[31] On October 17, Rao and Sharif held their first—albeit informal—face-to-face meeting at a gathering of the Commonwealth Heads of State and Heads of Government in Harare, Zimbabwe. Both leaders agreed that they should continue multilevel dialogues between their two governments and "redouble their efforts to find solutions to all outstanding issues."[32] Less than two weeks later, India and Pakistan conducted the fifth round of foreign secretary talks, where they agreed, after mutual recriminations over Kashmir, to organize expert discussions on a bilateral water project and a bilateral agreement to ban the development, production, and use of chemical weapons.[33]

However, the effort by Indian and Pakistani leaders to promote stability did not stop A. Q. Khan from once again injecting a discordant note. In a meeting with Pakistani business leaders to raise funds for a new research and development institute named for Pakistan's President Ghulam Ishaq Khan, the zealous hawk proclaimed once again that Pakistan was a nuclear power.[34] Khan boasted that his team of roughly six thousand engineers and scientists was now "manufacturing 350 million dollars worth of missiles and mines for the country." Khan also noted that the infamous Bank of Credit and Commerce International (BCCI) had donated Rs. 500 million (roughly $17 million) to the cause. Pakistan was not going to abandon its growing reliance on nuclear deterrence, even if it wanted relief from American sanctions.

Shortly after Khan's fund-raising speech, India's top defense scientist, V. S. Arunachalam, told Indian journalists that he estimated that Pakistan was now capable of producing ten nuclear bombs.[35] Following this statement, the vice president of the BJP, Krishna Lal Sharma, urged once again that India should acquire nuclear weapon capability to match Pakistan.[36] The BJP and other Indian commentators did not know that the state possessed a ready nuclear weapon capability but was keeping it under wraps for domestic and international political-economic reasons.[37]

A. Q. Khan's statements aside, Pakistan continued its peace offensive in November by sponsoring in the UN General Assembly a resolution to declare South Asia a nuclear-weapon-free zone.[38] The resolution begged important questions of verification, of whether China was in the region, and of how to address the presence of U.S. and other nuclear-armed ships and submarines in the Indian Ocean. Still, as a political tool the resolution hurt India badly when the Soviet Union voted for it. India reacted strongly, despite having been forewarned that the Soviet Union's genuine interest in nonproliferation would impel this vote.[39]

The Bush administration reentered the South Asian scene days after the UN vote, when Under Secretary of State for International Security Reginald Bartholomew traveled to Pakistan and India. Having been rebuffed in its effort to prompt the five-nation conference on the South Asian nuclear situation, the administration understandably had few other ideas to promote and was concentrating on events in Russia and the Middle East.[40] Bartholomew expressed Washington's growing realization that India would not sign the NPT in the foreseeable future. This represented a concession to India. Bartholomew urged India in kind to eschew helping other nations go nuclear, to refrain from nuclear tests, and to engage in regional discussions on nuclear problems.[41] Of most immediate concern, Washington pressed India not to go through with a proposed sale of a ten-megawatt research reactor to Iran. The Indian government soon acceded to American pressure and decided not to export the reactor, despite the objections of the Atomic Energy Commission.[42] However, the brief dustup over the reactor sale stirred anticolonial sentiments once again, distracting many Indian observers from the more important point that the United States was acknowledging that India (and Pakistan) were not about to give up their nuclear weapon capabilities anytime soon. This was a major, albeit understated change in U.S. nonproliferation diplomacy.

In December, Premier Li Peng became the first Chinese premier to visit India since before the 1962 war—a major symbolic advance in relations. The two governments agreed to institutionalize mechanisms for defusing tension along the border and signed three other agreements to enhance diplomatic representation in each other's country, to further space cooperation, and resume official border trade after a thirty-year hiatus.[43] High-level bilateral interactions between Indian and Chinese civilian and military officials then increased throughout the 1990s.

China's earlier announcement, in August 1991, that it finally would sign the Nuclear Non-Proliferation Treaty also signaled the potential beginning of Chinese self-restraint in assisting Pakistan's development of nuclear weapon capabilities. Winning complete implementation of this restraint would take years and embroil China, Pakistan, India, and the United States in several controversies later in the 1990s. Still, the Chinese move signaled Beijing's fledgling interest in participating constructively in the nonproliferation regime.

Thus, by the end of 1991, at the level of intentions the three regional nuclear protagonists—India, Pakistan, and China—showed an interest in stability and goodwill even if they were far from actually resolving fundamental disputes. For its part, the United States was moving to accommodate India's (and Pakistan's) categorical refusal to eliminate nuclear capabilities absent global nuclear disarmament. Instead, Washington was looking for more modest regional means to keep the nuclear programs in check. Most important, India preoccupied itself with overcoming domestic political-economic crises and winning the international goodwill required to revive its economy. Development of missiles and nuclear weapon capabilities continued autonomously behind the scenes, but the weaponeers knew that leaders would rebuff any desire they had to push across the threshold to overt nuclear weapon status.

MISSILE TESTS, SANCTIONS, AND TALKS, 1992

Nineteen ninety-two brought signs of progress on the domestic political-economic front, allowing resumed attention to foreign and nuclear policies. On January 1, India and Pakistan exchanged lists of each other's nuclear facilities, pursuant to the agreement not to attack them. Within days Pakistani media asserted that India's list was incomplete.[44] Weeks later Mark Hibbs reported in *Nucleonics Week* that India and Pakistan each omitted a uranium enrichment plant: Pakistan had built a second plant (in addition to Kahuta) believed to be in Golra, while India had built a new gas centrifuge enrichment plant near Mysore.[45] (K. Subrahmanyam later explained that while the Indian list did not name the Mysore enrichment plant, it did provide the coordinates of the plant's location at the same complex where the Atomic Energy Commission's Rare Earths Factory is sited.)[46] The symmetry of the apparent nondisclosures reflected decades of Indo-Pak relations and ongoing mutual suspicions that made even confidence-building measures sources of contention. India's wariness increased when China announced in early January that it would sell a 300-megawatt nuclear power plant to Pakistan to be located at Chasma, southwest of Rawalpindi.[47] While China increased assistance to Pakistan, Russia in late January announced that the deal to supply two power reactors to India had been "virtually scrapped."[48] India's AEC Chairman P. K. Iyengar said that if Russia would not provide both hardware and financing, India instead would construct four pressurized heavy-water reactors with indigenous technology.[49] As noted previously, the nuclear establishment actually preferred not to import Russian reactors.

Pakistan's and India's ongoing, albeit slow-motion, acquisition of nuclear and ballistic missile capabilities continued to alarm American officials. Robert Gates, now director of Central Intelligence, testified before Congress in January that the United States did not believe India or Pakistan maintained assembled or deployed nuclear weapons but that such weapons "could be assembled quickly."[50] The Bush administration continued to press India to join Pakistan and the United States, Russia, and China in a conference to seek regional constraints. In mid-January, British Foreign Secretary Douglas Hurd traveled to New Delhi to press against India's stone wall defense against regional nonproliferation measures.[51] As the *New York Times* reported, diplomats in New Delhi and Western capitals were "becoming increasingly frustrated by India's refusal either to discuss proliferation with them or to put forth ideas of their own."[52]

When President Bush met with Prime Minister Rao on January 31 at a UN Security Council Summit in New York, he urged India to reconsider its rejection of the five-nation regional conference proposal. Rao again demurred.[53] Beyond its well-known objections, the Indian government also feared that Indo-Pak nuclear constraints would prompt Washington to relieve sanctions on Pakistan. India had no interest in giving the United States a pretext for rearming Pakistan.[54] However, India did feel the pressure, recognizing its need for Western economic engagement. The Indians now proposed bilateral talks *with the United States* on nuclear issues.[55] The Bush administration eventually accepted and talks began later in 1992.

In early February, Pakistan's Foreign Secretary Shahryar Khan reportedly told editors of the *Washington Post* that Pakistan had the components and know-how to assemble at least one nuclear device. Khan added that this capability existed prior to Nawaz Sharif's election in October 1989 and that the new government "froze the program."[56] Over the ensuing weeks, Pakistani officials argued that Khan's statement had been taken out of context and that Pakistan's nuclear capabilities were entirely for peaceful purposes.[57] However, Indian politicians and commentators seized on Khan's admission to demand greater American pressure on Pakistan and to call for more robust Indian countermeasures. BJP President Murli Manohar Joshi declared that India "must waste no time to go nuclear."[58] This compelled the Rao government to reassure Parliament and the public that, in the words of an All India Radio broadcast, "India is fully prepared to meet any nuclear threat from Pakistan."[59] Defence Minister Sharad Pawar proclaimed ominously that if Pakistan was thinking of making a nuclear threat, "India's reaction would be to make Islamabad bear the burden of suffering for generations"—a clear reference to nuclear retaliation.[60] Pawar and Rao soon added that India did not want to "go nuclear" and was "firm in [its] resolve not to manufacture nuclear weapons [itself]."[61] Both leaders knew that DRDO and AEC teams had prepared the capability to quickly assemble nuclear weapons that could be delivered by air, but they continued to maintain the importance of not crossing the line to declare this capacity or deploy it. This "allowed" them to say that India did not possess nuclear weapons. R. Chidambaram, now the director of the Bhabha Atomic Research Centre and the leading force in the nuclear weapon design effort, echoed the Indian distinction when he told *Washington Post* reporter Steve Coll in March that India had not "stockpiled" or "deployed" nuclear weapons.[62]

It was precisely the unwillingness to clearly go nuclear that frustrated India's nuclear hawks. Thus, the indefatigable K. Subrahmanyam again entered the fray. In a long newspaper piece, Subrahmanyam used the reduction in defense budgets to urge open construction of "a minimum deterrent arsenal."[63] Whereas in 1970 Subrahmanyam had lambasted bomb advocates for underestimating the costs of deploying a nuclear arsenal, now he argued that nuclear weapons could facilitate cuts in conventional forces and rationalize security strategy in an era of resource constraints. He asserted problematically that a minimal arsenal of "a few scores of weapons and appropriate survivable mobile delivery systems" could be acquired for Rs. 10,000 crores (roughly $4 billion at 1992 rates) over "some seven years."[64] By comparison, defense expenditure in 1991–1992 was $6.7 billion.[65] Interestingly, Subrahmanyam argued that the requirements for such an arsenal had been made more manageable by India's improving relations with China. That improvement also allowed the reduction in conventional forces he recommended.[66] (After the May 1998 tests, Indian strategists would argue that conventional military budgets should *not* be reduced.) Like Sundarji and other bomb advocates, Subrahmanyam asserted that India need not try to match China's and Pakistan's nuclear capabilities but instead could stop at a basic, minimal deterrent force. By eschewing parity and "the spurious doctrines of counter-force," India could avoid the need for "extremely expensive multi-redundant command and control, communication and intelligence systems."[67] However, once again the "absence of a National Security Council set-up" prevented the government from undertaking "the comprehensive staff work" to rationalize defense strategy and move toward the sort of overt nuclear arsenal that Western models of deterrence prescribed.[68]

Events in May soon bespoke both the advance of India's missile capability and the difficulties it could cause with the United States. On May 5, India conducted another flight test of the short-range Prithvi missile. On May 11, the Bush administration imposed sanctions for two years on the Indian Space Research Organisation (ISRO) and the Russian space research organization Glavkosmos over a proposed sale to India of three liquid-hydrogen cryogenic rocket engines and technology for their construction. India and Russia had signed a reported $250 million contract for the engines in 1991.[69] The United States argued that the engines and, more important, the technology for their construction violated the Missile Technology Control Regime to which Russia had pledged to adhere. India reacted angrily, insisting that the technology was purely for the civilian purposes of the space program, specifically to launch communications satellites into geostationary orbit. The sanctions, coming on the heels of an April announcement by the Nuclear Suppliers Group that sixty-five classes of dual-use technology would be controlled for export to countries like India, portended growing efforts to crimp India's technological development.[70] American officials were less concerned about the rockets than the production technology, and less bothered by India's purchase than Russia's sale. That is, the United States feared that Russia's economic crisis and general bureaucratic breakdown could cause cash-driven sales of nuclear materials, weapons, missiles, and related technologies. The sanctions represented an early effort to persuade Russia to implement effective controls on its proliferation-sensitive agencies and enterprises. This did little to assuage Indian anger over the perceived colonial restrictions on the country's access to space and the manifold civilian benefits of the satellite age.

Ten days after the sanctions on India were announced, China tested a huge, one-megaton nuclear weapon when R. Venkataraman was conducting the first-ever visit by an Indian president to China. The visit represented the ongoing desire by both countries to improve relations, but to Indian observers the test symbolized China's haughty determination to set the terms.[71] It remains unknown whether top Chinese officials and the nuclear establishment consciously sought to send this intimidating message, but it is doubtful that Li Peng and other top officials whom Venkataraman met did not know of the test in advance.

Indian pride was soon salved, at least momentarily, when the DRDO conducted the second flight test of the Agni missile on May 29, in the presence of the chiefs of the army, navy, and air force staffs. *India News* celebrated the nearly five thousand engineers involved in developing the Agni, which represented, in Brahma Chellaney's words, India's nationalistic "quest for international respect and prestige."[72] Unfortunately for nationalist pride, despite the initial proclamations of a successful test, scientists soon acknowledged that the guidance system and other components failed and the missile burnt up in flight.[73]

If the Chinese nuclear test during President Venkataraman's visit signaled underlying Sino-Indian tensions, the Agni test signaled unresolved conflict in Indo-American interests. On the day the Agni flew east over the Bay of Bengal, American naval forces to the west, in the Indian Ocean, conducted their first-ever joint exercises with the Indian fleet. However, unlike the Indian president in China, the Americans were told in advance about the Indian test.[74] The American decision to proceed with the exercise indicated a desire to move the relationship forward despite the friction over the ISRO-Glavkosmos sanctions, India's missile program, and a trade dispute. As a senior Ministry of External Affairs official asked rhetorically, "If an Indo-US naval exercise is held on the same day that Agni is test-fired, does it not indicate the quality of the relationship?"[75]

Indeed, Washington was trying to recognize Indian sensitivities and deal with India as a rising power, not a poor supplicant to be bossed around. The State

Department issued only a short, muted criticism of the Agni test.[76] The Bush administration was no less concerned about proliferation; rather it concluded that the best way to interest India in constraining its nuclear and missile programs was to build a broader, more positive relationship. If the choice was between little progress on nonproliferation and *poor* relations with India and Pakistan, or little progress on nonproliferation and *good* relations with them, American policymakers preferred the latter.[77] Thus, by October 1992 the United States partially eased the ISRO sanctions and allowed shipment to India of supplies that had been in the pipeline prior to the imposition of sanctions.[78]

In June 1992, the United States and India acted on Rao's earlier proposal to conduct a bilateral dialogue on nonproliferation in lieu of the five-nation conference. In this meeting U.S. representatives acknowledged India's objections and requested alternative ideas for preventing a regional nuclear arms race. The Americans proposed for consideration agreements not to test nuclear weapons and to cease production of fissile material for weapons purposes. The Indian representatives did not reject these ideas. They offered to deliberate on alternative ways of convening a conference of India, Pakistan, China, the United States, Russia, and perhaps others to address regional and global security issues. However, when Foreign Secretary J. N. Dixit reported to the press this willingness to engage further with the United States along these lines, parliamentary critics attacked Prime Minister Rao for being too forthcoming with the Americans.[79] The balkiness of elected officials in dealing with this highly charged, symbolically laden issue foreshadowed a tougher Indian line in the next round of talks scheduled for November. As an American official later remarked, "[W]hat the Indians said they wanted and what they really wanted were not exactly the same."[80]

Rao was now personally more involved in international affairs than during 1991. He saw India's future tied more closely to integration with the West and greater involvement in Southeast Asia, whose postcolonial states were now booming economically. India established full diplomatic relations with Israel in February 1992 and sought closer affiliation with the states in the Association of Southeast Asian Nations (ASEAN) as potential trade partners that could help India achieve the kind of economic growth that had led China to be a rising power. Indeed, the Chinese path to power now appeared as a model. This model meant giving primacy to economic development while stabilizing India's relations with its closest neighbors. Only then would the world see India as a world player, not a South Asian Gulliver. Yet this nascent national strategy had not been elaborated formally, and military and nuclear policies had not been detailed to go with it. Nor had a political consensus been built around this economics-first strategy.

The domestic scene showed modest improvement in 1992, although major problems remained, including the aftermath of a scandal in the Bombay stock market in April. The foreign exchange crisis had passed thanks to emergency cuts in imports and to external financing from the IMF, the World Bank, and donor nations. Real growth in GDP was low at 2 to 3 percent for the first half of the year but picked up later. Inflation remained high early in the year but dropped below 10 percent by late summer.[81] Exports were starting to rise.[82] Politically, Rao in mid-1992 looked more solid than could have been predicted a year earlier. In July he calmed temporarily a tense confrontation between Hindus and Muslims in Ayodhya, and earlier he had brokered an agreement by insurgents in the northeastern state of Assam to end a four-year rebellion.[83] Just as important, the softspoken lawyer and part-time poet had taken charge of the Congress party and diminished the internecine conflicts that had bedeviled it for years.[84]

FOUR PILLARS OF NUCLEAR POLICY, AUGUST 1992

In August, the scientist who in many ways had been the leading manager of India's nuclear weapon and missile efforts since the mid-1980s, V. S. Arunachalam, stepped down as director general of the DRDO. Behind the scenes Arunachalam had been the primary liaison between the strategic enclave and successive prime ministers since the ascension of Rajiv Gandhi in 1984.[85] This reflected the key role of DRDO scientists and engineers in preparing the nonnuclear explosive components of bombs, the sophistication of which largely determined India's capacity to produce smaller, lighter, and more efficient weapons for delivery by aircraft and missiles. Arunachalam also had a good way with political leaders and international counterparts, as was seen in his relationship with U.S. defense leaders in the mid-1980s. After Indira Gandhi's refusal to authorize a nuclear test in 1983, he understood the Indian government's political, normative, and strategic interests in developing India's strategic capability without crossing the politically and internationally troublesome threshold to overt nuclearization.

Just as important, Arunachalam appreciated the imperative in India's volatile democracy of maintaining political accountability for the nuclear weapon enterprise. The committee he established with prime ministerial approval in 1990 was intended to elaborate procedures and plans for the management of nuclear forces in the event of a nuclear attack. Although this committee's work was never completed and not all of its tentative recommendations were adopted by the governments that succeeded V. P. Singh, it reflected the view that four pillars within the Indian system should check and balance nuclear policy: the political leadership, the ministerial bureaucracy, the scientific community, and the military. To maintain strict civilian control of nuclear policy, the first three pillars were to stand taller in the "system."

Arunachalam and most of India's strategic thinkers believed that four principles, as well, should guide nuclear policy. India should never use nuclear weapons first. Civilians should exert total control over the military in policy and plans. India should not engage in arms racing. And no single sector—partisan political leaders, the scientists, the bureaucracy, or the military—should be able to drive nuclear policy.[86]

These principles and the basic policy they represented evolved by default in the 1980s and early 1990s after the post-Pokhran lull. They reflected the essential

Indian belief that nuclear weapons were not instruments of war but were purely deterrents of last resort. As Subrahmanyam, Sundarji, and others had argued, this basic deterrent function did not require comprehensive, predesignated targeting plans or launch-on-warning operational plans as pursued by the United States and the Soviet Union. (However, operational planning for Prithvi or aircraft strikes required targeting well in advance of potential use.) The air force or other services as institutions did not need to be involved in policy formation. Only those few air force units responsible for carrying out orders needed to be informed of the nuclear response plans so that they could prepare the necessary military operations. Strategists in and outside the government would debate whether such a deterrent needed to be declared explicitly and deployed in peacetime, but India's elected leaders believed it did not, prior to the BJP's arrival in 1998. Deployment was eschewed in part because the weaponeers and prime ministers did not want to invite military and political pressures to build more than was necessary, and perhaps to use nuclear weapons.[87] "One thing we learned," a former nuclear establishment leader remarked, "is never to allow the military or the bureaucrats to have a role in the nuclear program. We knew if we started to develop an elaborate nuclear strategy and involved the military in it, we would end up like the United States—we would end up with 50,000 weapons and it would become boundless. We would lose control over the process."[88] Military leaders may not have appreciated this, but as long as the services knew that not each of them would get nuclear forces and missions, political leaders and the scientists could prevent a united military front from pushing them across the deployment threshold.[89]

However, the ad hoc nature of Indian nuclear policymaking precluded the institutionalization of the four principles and the checks and balances Arunachalam sought to effect. The tradition begun by Nehru and Bhabha continued: highly personalized, small-circle deliberations between prime ministers, their closest political advisers, and the scientists. Indeed, as long as efforts to institutionalize decision making were themselves conducted in this secret, personalized manner that the politicians preferred, the pattern could not be broken. The character and efficacy of nuclear policymaking depended on the personalities, perceptions, and political compulsions of a very few individuals.

PROLIFERATION PUSH, NONPROLIFERATION PULL, MORE POLITICAL TROUBLE, AUGUST TO DECEMBER 1992

On August 18, the Defence Research and Development Organisation, under its new leader, Abdul Kalam, conducted the first successful fully instrumented test of a longer-range, 250-kilometer version of the Prithvi missile. This was the ninth test overall of the Prithvi system and the second of the 250-kilometer variant. In commenting on the test and the new DRDO leader, W. P. S. Sidhu in *India Today* noted that the missile's value to the army remained doubtful given the lack of satellite or other reconnaissance capabilities to provide real-time target acquisition and given the already tight army budget.[90] Regarding Kalam, Sidhu reported the army's concern that the successor of the dynamic Arunachalam would be unable to keep the program from being retarded. This worry proved the dangers of prognostication: Kalam would win political support for major budget increases and would become a driving force for taking India across the nuclear threshold.

Kalam eventually would get the nuclear tests he sought but only after delays in the progress of the Prithvi, and more clearly, the Agni programs. Prime Minister Rao kept a foot on the Prithvi's brake, delaying deployment, while technological problems slowed the Agni's testing schedule, which Kalam tried to obscure by blaming budget shortfalls. Rao still wanted to concentrate on economic development and pursue diplomacy with Pakistan; for his part, Nawaz Sharif felt he could do business with Rao.[91] Yet, both men held weak grips on power. This inclined them to muddle along diplomatically and not take bold steps in the nuclear realm. Neither provocative moves like nuclear tests nor healing steps like a bilateral test ban appeared politically attractive to these weak leaders. Still, in 1992, following Arunachalam's departure, U.S. intelligence detected increased signs of activity at the Pokhran test site.[92]

Indian elites deepened their resistance to any attempt by the United States to persuade India to eliminate its core nuclear weapon capabilities. More than security concerns, issues of national identity and equity precluded such accommodation to outside pressure. K. Subrahmanyam revealed the racial sensibility at the heart of India's resistance. "What the world needs is for blacks in America to become 51 percent of the population," he told the author in 1992. "Then you will get rid of your nuclear weapons the next day, as South Africa has prepared to do."[93] To Subrahmanyam and other Indians, especially Brahmins, the nonproliferation regime represented an attempt by white nations to keep dark-skinned people like Indians from acquiring nuclear weapons.

Yet the Indian government, and to a lesser extent a few pundits, began to see the merit and perhaps the international political necessity of cooperating to negotiate global bans on nuclear weapon testing and production of fissile materials for weapons.[94] Experts such as Raja Ramanna believed that India could afford to place all its power reactors under International Atomic Energy Agency safeguards, a move that would demonstrate India's nuclear responsibility to the international community.[95] The BJP leader, Atal Behari Vajpayee, representing India at the Political and Security Council of the UN General Assembly, called in October for an immediate global freeze on the production of nuclear weapons and fissile material for weapons purposes.[96] This could have served as a basis for further bilateral talks between India and the United States, which were scheduled for November. However, the apparent Indian conciliation in the June talks had prompted a domestic backlash that turned the government toward a harder line in November. According to Mitchell Reiss, the Indian cabinet rejected the Foreign Ministry's initial paper for the November talks and forced India's delegate to read his new, tougher talking points to the prime minister before being dispatched to Washington.[97]

Unsurprisingly, American officials found the November talks extremely disappointing and doubted whether India would ever accept constraints on its nuclear program that did not apply to all countries.[98] The recently defeated Bush administration had in effect abandoned demands that India sign the NPT but found India unwilling or unable to countenance a corresponding shift in its approach to the nuclear problem. Indian leaders could not make up their minds on policy, while the weaponeers were intent on pursuing greater capabilities.

Indian interest in nuclear constraints diminished further in early December after NBC News reported that Pakistan had fabricated seven nuclear bombs in 1990, around the time of the Indo-Pak crisis over Kashmir.[99] Indian parliamentarians across party lines demanded that the government take the latest revelation into account and explain how India's nuclear policy would be adapted accordingly.[100] While some urged that India openly should build nuclear weapons, others disagreed. The consensus was that the government should convene an all-party meeting to discuss India's strategy.[101]

Within days, however, nuclear policy shrank from public concern: on December 6 Hindu militants mobilized by the Vishwa Hindu Parishad, the Rashtriya Swayamsevak Sangh, and other groups affiliated with the BJP destroyed the Babri Mosque at Ayodhya. The incident sparked communal riots around the country for weeks, leaving three thousand people dead.[102] Pakistani mobs attacked the Indian consulate premises in Karachi. The underlying and specific causes of the militants' action will be debated forever, as will the question of whether Rao and others could have done more to stop it. Of utmost importance from the standpoint of nuclear policymaking is that Indian politics had returned to the knife's edge after only a short period of relative stability in which the country tried to get its bearings in the changing world around it.

DOMESTIC PREOCCUPATIONS AND
NEW LEADERSHIP IN THE AEC, 1993

The Ayodhya catastrophe threw Rao back on the defensive in 1993. Preoccupied with domestic travails, the nation's top leadership gave little attention to nuclear policy.

The reins of the Atomic Energy Commission changed hands on January 31, when P. K. Iyengar retired as chairman, to be succeeded by Rajagopala Chidambaram. In his retirement address Iyengar articulated important themes in the Indian nuclear experience. "I was the first 'indigenous' scientist to become Chairman of the Atomic Energy Commission," he noted, "having acquired all my formal science education in India, unlike my predecessors."[103] Iyengar emphasized that his replacement, Chidambaram, was "indigenous," too, and shared "the same ideas of self-reliance, excellence and national honour."[104] Indigenousness bespoke the postcolonial narrative so central to the consciousness of the nuclear scientists and the nation. Iyengar continued: "To have been able to put together an atomic device in 1974, was the most exhilarating experience of my career."[105] Part of the pride in Pokhran derived from the defiance entailed by the secretive act: "It is not a surprise that the Pokhran experiment could be successfully carried out in a secretive manner, because of the small number of people involved, and the mutual faith they had, for a common purpose."[106]

From 1993 through at least 1998, R. Chidambaram would build on his early work on India's first nuclear explosive to seek the most powerful manifestation of human—and specifically Indian—power, the hydrogen bomb. Beyond the satisfaction of solving this scientific-technological puzzle, Chidambaram sought the recognition that had escaped him in 1974 when other scientists received the acclaim for the Pokhran blast and he was left unfairly in the shadows. A short, stocky man with an impish smile and no pretensions as a security strategist, Chidambaram the talented physicist would join Kalam in making the technological case for breaking India's nuclear self-restraint.

Portentously, the BJP shared Iyengar's and Chidambaram's interpretation of the bomb's national value. Ayodhya had bolstered the BJP's hopes of rallying the Hindu majority to bring the party to power. The party's principal spokesman, Kavel Ratna Malkani, wasted no time in expressing the narrative meaning the bomb held for the BJP. "We should go nuclear and sign the N.P.T. as a nuclear weapons state," he told the *New York Times* reporter Edward A. Gargan.[107] "The whole world will recognize us by our power." Malkani continued, "We don't want to be blackmailed and treated as oriental blackies. Nuclear weapons will give us prestige, power, standing. An Indian will talk straight and walk straight when we have the bomb."[108] Hardly the vision of Mahatma Gandhi or Jawaharlal Nehru, Malkani reflected thirty years of Indian political evolution and determination to resist the perceived colonialism of the nuclear age.

Yet India's resistance to formal constraints on nuclear activities was running afoul of the international community's renewed determination to roll back proliferation. Outsiders were less inclined to take seriously India's complaint about the discriminatory nature of the nonproliferation regime when the United States and Russia were rapidly scaling back their nuclear arsenals. Washington had unilaterally announced an end to fissile material production, and countries such as South Africa, Brazil, and Argentina were adhering to nonproliferation norms.[109] Progress in Sino-Indian diplomacy further undermined India's case against nuclear constraints. "Between India and China," Ashok Kapur noted, the nuclear issue "is not even on the table because neither country, for different reasons, sees the need to raise the issue."[110] Pakistan had further undermined the Indian position, perhaps cynically, by proclaiming that it would agree to the NPT or any other nuclear constraint that India would accept. As Subrahmanyam noted, India's "problem appears to be a total absence of cerebration on the subject and formulation of a credible declaratory policy."[111]

THE CLINTON ADMINISTRATION
UPDATES U.S. POLICY, APRIL 1993

Bill Clinton took the helm in Washington a novice in foreign and nuclear policy. He pledged in his campaign to pursue nonproliferation with great vigor, criticizing the Reagan and Bush administrations for departing from the more absolutist approach to the problem advocated by Congress and nonproliferation activists in the late 1970s. Early signs from the new administration suggested that a sanctions-heavy approach to India's and Pakistan's nuclear programs would hold. On February 24, CIA Director James Woolsey testified before Congress that "[t]he arms race between India and Pakistan poses perhaps the most probable prospect for future use of weapons of mass destruction, including nuclear weapons."[112] Woolsey added that both nations "could, on short notice, assemble nuclear weapons." Displaying firmness, the State Department signaled that it would seek to make permanent the two-year sanctions on ISRO and Glavkosmos over the cryogenic rocket deal.[113] At this time, Washington expected India to conduct a third test of the Agni missile in March.[114] However, for internal technical and political reasons, and no doubt foreign policy considerations, the test was delayed until February 1994, as discussed later in this chapter.

April provided the first major opportunity for the Clinton administration to define its rapidly evolving policy toward South Asia. In a legislatively mandated report to Congress, the administration announced a significant change in the U.S. approach that articulated what the Bush administration had practiced by late 1992. "Our objective is first to cap, then over time reduce, and finally eliminate the possession of weapons of mass destruction and their means of delivery," the report stated.[115] Instead of complete rollback and accession to the NPT, the Clinton administration sought incremental progress. The report also detailed diplomatic efforts and concrete proposals to encourage India and Pakistan to undertake confidence-building measures. Anticipating criticism that the new approach represented a retreat from nonproliferation, the report declared that "nonproliferation" is "*the* major issue in our relationship with both countries."[116] This statement, and the reality that some administration officials and prominent nonproliferation activists still emphasized the goal of completely rolling back India's nuclear capability, helped some Indian observers to argue that nothing had changed and India should resist *all* possible constraints on its capabilities.

Still, Washington's new line represented an emerging genuine acceptance among key government officials and nongovernmental experts that nuclear weapon capabilities would remain part of South Asian reality for the foreseeable future. The challenge now was to encourage India and Pakistan to capitalize on the basic deterrence they had achieved and to stop short of an overt weaponization process that could become destabilizing and subject both countries to costs and political difficulties that would divert them from more pressing needs.[117] To do this, the two states would have to engage each other on these issues directly and adopt formal agreements to preclude arms racing, such as bans on nuclear weapon testing and fissile material production for weapons as well as other confidence-building measures. Absent such measures, India and Pakistan would continue to assume the worst about each other's intentions and capabilities, providing fuel for political competitors to inflame nuclear policy and bilateral relations. And if instead of negotiating, India and Pakistan refused to explore such measures it would reveal the hollowness and perhaps the deceptiveness of Indian rhetoric.

Unfortunately, the absence of a U.S. ambassador in India made achieving progress in this direction more difficult. The Clinton administration had transferred the extremely able Thomas Pickering from the ambassadorship in New Delhi to Moscow, less than a year after he had arrived in India. The administration then hoped to name former Congressman Stephen Solarz to succeed Pickering, but the nomination was stalled and eventually dropped due to controversy over Solarz's and his wife's financial difficulties. The United States did not send an ambassador until August 1994, a long interlude that offended Indian sensibilities by suggesting the lack of importance the administration attached to the country.

RELATIONS WITH PAKISTAN STALL, BUT PROGRESS IS MADE WITH CHINA AND THE UNITED STATES, 1993

Indian and Pakistani leaders remained unwilling to take the perceived political risks to negotiate nuclear constraints. At the end of April, Pakistan again was shaken by political turmoil. President Ghulam Ishaq Khan displaced Prime Minister Nawaz Sharif by presidential fiat under Article VIII of the constitution, only to have the Supreme Court reinstate him in May. However, by July Sharif had been forced out and new elections called. In the meantime a caretaker government was appointed. Elections in October would return Benazir Bhutto to power with a thin and unstable majority. None of this boded well for Indo-Pak breakthroughs.

Meanwhile, Indian strategists resisted Indo-Pak negotiations because they would ignore the "China factor."[118] Since the mid-1980s, India had fixated on the Pakistani threat and Sino-Indian relations had been improving, thereby reducing the salience of nuclear weapons in that relationship. Yet China could be invoked to stall any serious nuclear diplomacy. At bottom, India lacked strategies to simultaneously pursue security vis-à-vis Pakistan and China and arms control diplomacy with the United States. As former Foreign Secretary Muchkund Dubey admitted, the Indian government had not devised disarmament initiatives—"Not in a planned way, not wholeheartedly."[119] And without Indian initiative, no progress on the subcontinent was possible.

Stasis reigned through the summer. Russia angered India in July by acceding to American pressure and canceling the ISRO-Glavkosmos contract. (However, in early 1994 American officials reached agreement with Russia to allow a small number of rocket engines—but not the technology for their construction—to be transferred to India in return for Russian commitments not to sell sensitive missile production technology.)[120] In July, Pakistan's interim president, Wasim Sajjad, called for Indo-Pak tension reduction talks, but India dismissed the invitation citing political uncertainties in Pakistan.[121]

In September 1993, India conducted two diplomatic forays bearing on nuclear policy. At the beginning of the month Prime Minister Rao traveled to Beijing, where the two governments signed an agreement to reduce troops and respect cease-fire lines along their disputed border.[122] (Indian and Chinese experts met in February 1994 to pursue implementation of the agreements, and reductions in troop levels did begin.)[123] "This is just what we had been wanting for a long time and the Chinese were stalling," K. Sundarji trumpeted.[124] Beyond signaling ongoing improvements in relations, the agreement allowed India to conserve already stretched military resources and diminished the need to plan for a two-front war. The BJP spokesman on foreign affairs, Brajesh Mishra, a former diplomat in Beijing who in 1998 would become principal secretary to Prime Minister Vajpayee, welcomed the accord but noted that it postponed final resolution of the border dispute.[125] Still, China's willingness to retrench militarily signified its indefinite acceptance of the status quo.

India conceived of its need for nuclear weapons as a counter to Chinese blackmail or aggression (or both), not as a means for Indian aggression to resolve the border dispute. If that was India's true strategic thinking, the accord with China, if implemented, would significantly reduce the threat of Chinese aggression, and therefore the "need" for Indian nuclear weapons. To be sure, India did not obtain assurance that China would stop assisting Pakistan's nuclear and missile programs. Yet this pointed back to the imperative to improve Indo-Pak security relations, a focus that Indian pundits and officials resisted. If Pakistan's strategic concerns could be allayed, China would find it more compelling to desist in aiding the Pakistani nuclear and missile programs. Though Indian security specialists would not admit it, the logic of addressing nuclear danger first and foremost at the Indo-Pak level was growing.[126]

A week after Rao's visit to China, Indian representatives to the third round of Indo-American nuclear talks dismissed Washington's renewed call for direct Indo-Pak dialogue on nuclear matters. India also continued to object to the five-nation conference idea. The Clinton administration urged India to suggest alternatives, especially in light of the improvement of Sino-Indian relations. Yet an Indian participant in the talks rejected the logic. "Whether our relations improve with China or not is irrelevant," he said. "The issue will remain that we are not going to agree to any discriminatory agreement. If several parties are talking and an agreement is reached, it should apply to all parties," meaning China, too.[127] Nevertheless, on an encouraging note, the Indians expressed potential interest in talks on regional security issues that would include China as a more equal participant, along with other major powers, perhaps Japan and Germany.[128]

Other issues in the discussions also raised hopes. The Tarapur reactors were again on the agenda, as the original 1963 U.S.-Indian fuel-supply contract was due to expire in October. France, the substitute supplier, had declared that it would no longer continue in this role because of its acceptance in 1992 of fullscope safeguarding requirements in any country to which it exported sensitive nuclear materials or technology. This posed the prospect once again of a fuel-supply crisis and an Indian threat to reprocess U.S.-origin spent fuel or use indigenous plutonium-uranium MOX fuel in the reactors, or resort to both measures. The American delegation reassured the Indians that it would try to find ways of preventing the closure of the reactors. U.S. officials added that this constructive approach would be abandoned and economic leverage exerted against India if it reprocessed the spent fuel originally supplied by the United States or abandoned safeguards on Tarapur spent fuel.[129] The two sides worked amicably on the issue and, ironically, soon turned to China as a substitute supplier. China had not accepted the Nuclear Suppliers Group's 1992 fullscope safeguarding requirement. Thus, it was free to provide low-enriched uranium fuel to India, which it began doing in 1995 as discussed in chapter 13.

Indian participants in the September talks also expressed interest in a global ban on fissile material production for explosive purposes. Under an American proposal, the treaty would apply to all states and would not force those that already had acquired weapon stocks to surrender them. Although it was not Washington's purpose, this would preserve India's (and Pakistan's) nuclear weapon options and still allow reprocessing of plutonium for fuel in the breeder reactor program under international safeguards. Thus, India joined with the United States in cosponsoring a December 1993 UN General Assembly resolution initiated by Canada urging the cessation of fissile material production for weapons purposes. This tentatively raised American hopes that progress was possible.[130] Indian officials also reportedly informed the Americans that the Prithvi missile would not be deployed imminently.[131] Unfortunately, the September 1993 talks were the last "serious discussions with the Indians on nuclear issues" through 1997, according to a key American participant.[132]

In November, India conducted two more tests of the Prithvi. Former Defence Minister Sharad Pawar declared that the missile would be deployed in 1994, although this was not confirmed.[133] A government official also announced that the medium-range Agni missile would be flight-tested again in January 1994.[134] These developments reflected the strong drive of DRDO head Abdul Kalam to push the strategic programs forward and across the threshold of an overt nuclear deterrent posture.

Having turned greater attention to South Asia, the Clinton administration now decided to do more than exhort the two antagonists. In November, State Department spokesman Mike McCurry declared that the Pressler Amendment no longer served U.S. nonproliferation objectives, signaling interest in replacing it with a non–country specific approach.[135] Administration officials felt that sanctions would fail to stop or roll back Pakistan's nuclear weapon program. They now wanted the flexibility to offer positive inducements instead if Pakistan would agree to undertake measures such as ending unsafeguarded fissile material production. Pressler precluded this.

Of course, the hint that Washington might relieve punitive pressure on Pakistan angered India. Indian officials and media had been alarmed already by an October 28 statement by Assistant Secretary of State for South Asian Affairs Robin Raphel that Kashmir was "disputed territory." The statement actually did not depart from past U.S. positions on Kashmir, but Indians were waiting to pounce on Raphel and she did not handle the matter well. The Indian government démarched Washington with a barbed inquiry "whether it is the United States' intention to question the territorial unity and integrity of India."[136] Indians mistrusted Raphel from the beginning, as she was the ex-wife of the former U.S. Ambassador to Pakistan Arnold Raphel, who had been killed with President Zia in 1988. She was perceived to be close to Benazir Bhutto and had been "only" a political counselor at the embassy in New Delhi before being elevated to the post of the United States' first-ever Assistant Secretary of State for South Asian Affairs. To Indians this seemed like an affront to the importance of the region.[137] Making matters worse, the rumors of American interest in revisiting the Pressler Amendment had sparked an intense debate in Pakistan over whether the government was planning to make secret concessions to the United States on the nuclear issue. This prompted Bhutto's government and the opposition to make increasingly bold statements in support of Pakistan's nuclear program.[138]

Indian nuclear policy remained static and ambiguous. Despite Congress party successes and BJP failures in recent state elections, the Rao government could not bring itself to take initiatives in Indo-Pak security and nuclear relations. If this befuddled American policymakers and Western-trained Indian analysts, the explanation was in the "Indian mind," according to K. Subrahmanyam. "To a question which to a westerner is capable of being answered only either in a clear yes or a clear no," the pundit explained, "the Indian answer very often is neither a full yes nor a full no, but a combination of both."[139] India's ambiguous nuclear posture was not as clear and robust as hawks advocated—a "yes"—but it was more than nothing—a "no." Any adversary would be uncertain that it could attack India without receiving a major nuclear counterblow, and this uncertainty on such a grave matter was adequate to deter. This existential approach to nuclear deterrence reflected the intuitive sense that the costs and risks of a more elaborate nuclear arsenal and doctrine outweighed any putative marginal benefits over the existing nonweaponized deterrent posture. Further clarity would require prime ministerial intervention in a system lacking institutions to coordinate such policies.

As Subrahmanyam noted, the prime minister "does not dare to do it because this is an issue which he himself does not want to think through."[140]

THE CLINTON GAMBIT FAILS, MARCH TO MAY 1994

Indian and Pakistani foreign secretaries met in early January 1994 for what would turn out to be the last time for three years. According to India's Foreign Secretary J. N. Dixit, Rao had instructed him to offer concrete proposals on confidence-building measures and political issues.[141] During the meeting, Dixit and his counterpart, Shahryar Khan, agreed that the two countries would prepare white papers on key issues of concern and proposals for next steps. India did so on six issues, including a proposal to extend the agreement not to attack each other's nuclear facilities to an agreement not to attack population centers. But before these papers could be presented to Islamabad, Pakistan submitted two papers of its own focusing on Kashmir. One proposed modalities for conducting a plebiscite in Jammu and Kashmir in accord with the 1948 UN Resolution on Kashmir. India viewed this as a nonstarter in light of the 1972 Simla Agreement's call for bilateral dialogue to deal with Kashmir. Pakistan suspended further talks, citing Indian misbehavior in Kashmir.[142] For Pakistan, Kashmir was the core issue upon which progress in all other areas hinged. For India, Kashmir was a problem that could be diminished with time by wearing down the insurgency.

As Indo-Pak relations again turned acrimonious, both countries resumed polishing their nuclear sabers with rhetoric and displays. On Republic Day, January 26, India paraded the Prithvi missile for the first time amidst the martial splendor of marching troops and trundling tanks. On February 19, the Agni missile took its third test flight—the second successful one. News of the test provoked thundering applause in the Parliament, as President Dr. S. D. Sharma proclaimed that efforts to restrict India's access to foreign technology required India "to rely even more on [its] talents."[143] By this time, U.S. intelligence estimated that India had enough weapon-grade fissile material for twenty to twenty-five nuclear weapons, several of which it could "assemble within a few days" and deliver by aircraft.[144] Indian sources suggest that around this time the strategic enclave had designs and components for five types of weapons, ranging from low-yield and fifteen-to-twenty-kiloton fission weapons to a boosted-fission weapon capability, although this could not be verified. These estimates did not comprehend the importance that the Indian scientists now attached to building a hydrogen bomb. Pakistan, according to secret U.S. estimates, had a strategically comparable stockpile of weapon-usable fissile material and possessed components for deliverable nuclear weapons that did not need to be tested in full-scale explosions.[145]

American officials sensed that the momentum of technological developments was pushing India and Pakistan to the edge of self-restraint. The CIA had estimated in early 1993 that India would "probably begin fielding the Prithvi with the Army and Air Force this year." This did not occur in 1993, but time was running out.[146] Major efforts had to be made now to persuade India and Pakistan to establish limits on their capacity to engage in a nuclear arms race. The Clinton administration had embraced global disarmament measures such as treaties to ban nuclear weapon testing and unsafeguarded fissile material production, giving American officials hope that common ground could finally be found with India. Pakistan's interest in ending American sanctions and rebuilding a security relationship with Washington suggested opportunities as well. Now was the time to move.

In March 1994, the Clinton administration unveiled a proposal to induce Pakistan to agree to ban unsafeguarded production of fissile materials (that is, no production at Kahuta or other facilities except under safeguards), in return for a one-time lifting of American sanctions to allow the delivery of twenty-eight F-16s that Pakistan had paid for but never received due to Pressler Amendment prohibitions. This would have left Pakistan with already produced stocks of bomb material as a deterrent. Washington would then try to persuade India to ban unsafeguarded production of fissile materials, offering as-then-undefined incentives as well as the Pakistani agreement to stop all production of bomb materials. Administration officials also sought to persuade India and Pakistan to head off a potential regional missile race by banning deployments of nuclear-capable systems. The third element of the administration's initiative was to convene an international conference of the five permanent members of the UN Security Council plus India, Pakistan, Germany, and Japan to consider regional and global arms control and disarmament proposals, with a special bearing on South Asia. This broadened group was intended to redress Indian criticisms of the previous five-nation conference proposal.

The three elements were not formally linked or dependent on each other. One sought to cap India's and Pakistan's nuclear weapon programs. The other sought to avoid a destabilizing missile competition and, in the case of Pakistan with its M-11s, a sanctions dispute with China. The international conference aimed to bolster overall Indo-Pak political and security relations and to connect South Asia more fully to the international security system.

The administration's initiative was daunting. Major obstacles had to be overcome in Washington, Islamabad, and New Delhi. The U.S. Senate, particularly Senators Pressler, Glenn, and others who had favored nonproliferation sanctions, would have to be persuaded to waive, at least on a one-time basis, the Pressler Amendment sanctions on Pakistan. Pakistan would have to accept heretofore intolerable inspections of the uranium enrichment plant at Kahuta, long a symbol of Pakistani sovereignty. The major inducement for this perceived surrender of the nuclear weapon program would be the supply of planes Pakistan had already paid for. India would have to abandon its traditional objection to any formal bilateral or regional nuclear constraints. And for doing so, India would receive as-yet-undefined inducements while watching Pakistan win possession of previously denied F-16 aircraft. For Washington to pull off this deal would be like making a triple bank shot in billiards on the same day as picking six winners at the race track—a combination of great skill and luck.

The administration recognized that China could augment the initiative's prospects by agreeing to participate fully in the proposed nine-power talks, not merely as a passive guarantor. This required Chinese willingness to consider constraints in fissile material production, cessation of assistance to Pakistan's nuclear and missile programs, and other steps of particular interest to India. In the course of a March meeting in Beijing, Deputy Assistant Secretary of State for Political-Military Affairs Robert Einhorn and Under Secretary of Defense Frank Wisner urged their Chinese counterparts to take a more forthcoming role in South Asia, arguing that it was in China's interest not to have two competitive nuclear and ballistic missile powers on its southern border.[147] But the Americans found the Chinese unreceptive to being drawn into regional nuclear affairs.[148] (However, Einhorn, a bookish-looking but tough diplomat, had been and would continue to make progress in gradually persuading China to live up to its commitments to the global nonproliferation regime.)

Still, the initiative's logic hinged on Pakistan. American officials felt that Pakistan was more susceptible to U.S. influence than India, because it had been a close ally and wanted the F-16s and other American military and security assistance. Indeed, in 1994, Pakistan faced an India whose prospects of becoming a major power looked greater than ever, leaving Pakistan with an interest in trying to bound India's nuclear weapon potential now instead of allowing its comparative strength to grow in the future.[149] Pakistan had declared that it was no longer enriching uranium to high levels, so Clinton administration officials thought Islamabad might agree to formalize that position and get something for it, namely the F-16s. The administration also seemed to think that if Pakistan would agree, India would become isolated regionally and globally and therefore would become more amenable to the proposals that, after all, would essentially legitimate the nuclear weapon option, even if this was not Washington's aim.[150] This may explain charitably why the administration did not detail positive inducements for India beyond an offer to discuss a range of scientific and technological cooperation.

The administration had to start the initiative somewhere, so it began at home in mid-March with private briefings of key congressional officials. Unfortunately, Senator Pressler immediately publicized his objections. Pressler then conducted a press conference for the Indian media in Washington at which he helped fuel Indian antagonism to the plan. The administration had not briefed Indian officials in Washington or New Delhi prior to the press reports on the initiative.[151] With this inauspicious send-off, Raphel traveled to New Delhi for meetings on March 24 to apprise Indian officials of the plan in anticipation of Deputy Secretary of State Strobe Talbott's scheduled trip to the region in early April. Raphel was the highest-level U.S. official to travel to India in the fourteen months of the Clinton administration, and she carried the baggage of her earlier statement that Kashmir was disputed territory. Making matters worse, Indian pundits had helped generate the public perception that Washington still sought nothing less than India's accession to the taboo NPT, making the new initiative seem a ruse. Unsurprisingly, Indian officials told Raphel they would not cap their nuclear program as part of a bilateral or regional plan.[152] Reversing leverage, they hinted that India would retaliate for the delivery of F-16s to Pakistan by deploying Prithvi missiles.[153]

Talbott arrived in the region the first week of April and began by meeting Prime Minister Rao. He dutifully presented the already battle-torn proposals for nuclear and ballistic missile controls and the nine-nation conference.[154] The Indian objections were now public knowledge, but Rao did not foreclose further discussions. Indeed, he agreed promisingly that experts from the two sides should explore the nine-nation conference proposal.[155] Talbott brought with him a formal invitation for Rao to conduct a state visit to Washington in May, and the Indian leader wanted to set as positive a tone as possible for that occasion.[156] Indian officials—if not the public—recognized that beneath the U.S. proposals lay the new foundation in Washington's nonproliferation policy, a willingness to live with India's nuclear weapon capability and not actively seek a rollback in the foreseeable future. Working with the administration to this end risked domestic controversies, but it had advantages over the two alternatives: going overt and building and deploying a nuclear arsenal that would repudiate India's long-standing norms and cause international backlash, or continuing to drift with an option policy that brought no relief from international pressure and technology denial.

Meanwhile, Congress's willingness to relieve sanctions on Pakistan as part of the deal remained suspect. Indeed, Senator John Glenn had been trying for several years to pass legislation augmenting existing nonproliferation sanctions by requiring the United States to block credit, credit guarantees, and other U.S. and international financial institutions' (i.e., World Bank and IMF) assistance to any country that, among other things, "detonates a nuclear explosive device." The Senate, with the Clinton administration's endorsement, had approved in January what would become known as the Glenn Amendment, or the Nuclear Proliferation Prevention Act of 1994. Glenn and others now pressed successfully for passage in the House as the Clinton administration appeared interested in alleviating sanctions on Pakistan. The tough new sanctions legislation was enacted into law on April 30.[157] The politics behind the legislation implied that the United States might not be able to deliver its part of the proposed bargain to Pakistan.

In any case, Benazir Bhutto's weak government could not withstand the political onslaught it could expect if it agreed to accept inspections on Kahuta and other now-sacred elements of the nuclear program. As a high-ranking Pakistani Foreign Ministry official explained in an interview, "Kahuta is the only symbol of sovereignty that we have left. You people took everything else."[158] Without reciprocal measures in India, Pakistan would not accept verification measures that could remove the ambiguity it valued in its nuclear deterrent. Talbott left the region with no agreement and many objections to the U.S. initiative. He also knew that India and Pakistan were not comfortable with their positions and the intensi-fied U.S. pressure.

The Indian nuclear and defense establishments and strategic community rec-ognized that Washington was more determined than ever to press for constraints, so they mobilized a counterattack that began prior to the Talbott visit and contin-ued after, anticipating the state visit by Narasimha Rao to Washington in mid-May. In early April, AEC Chairman Chidambaram made himself available for several interviews in which he reminded his audience that India was ahead of Pak-istan and China in the civilian applications of nuclear energy and that the major problem the establishment faced was lack of funds. (This belied other problems with the performance of the nuclear establishment itself—symbolized on May 13 when the containment dome of the under-construction Unit 1 of the Kaiga Atomic Power Plant collapsed. Had this accident occurred when the reactor was completed and operating, it could have been a major disaster.)[159] Chidambaram acknowledged that the recent plans to have 10,000 megawatts of installed power by the year 2000 would not remotely be reached, as only 1,720 megawatts of power were now on line.[160] Still, India's plutonium breeder program was rivaled only by Japan's and was a source of future electricity and prestige that should be protected against U.S.-led efforts to forestall plutonium reprocessing and use.[161] In an interview with Raj Chengappa of *India Today*, Chidambaram denounced the new U.S. nonproliferation push: "India has observed the longest moratorium on nuclear bomb explosions. So we don't have to take lessons on morality from the US or anyone else. . . . We are not in favour of any regional capping effort or hav-ing countries broker a deal between India and Pakistan on the nuclear ques-tion."[162] When asked whether India was still making bombs, Chidambaram replied evasively: "That's a pointed question. . . . Let me just say that we have built up an extraordinary range of knowhow and expertise on all aspects of nuclear technology. . . . There is now nothing India cannot do."

Abdul Kalam also joined the weaponeers' media campaign against the U.S. initiatives. Granting access to his government guest house in New Delhi to *India Today*'s Chengappa, the DRDO head celebrated the achievements of the ballistic missile program. The Prithvi missile was scheduled for induction into army and air force service in June. The Agni had been flight-tested successfully in February with a longer second stage intended to help achieve its proclaimed range of 2,500 kilometers, significantly farther than it actually had flown in either of its earlier test flights. Kalam emphasized that these programs had succeeded despite the nonproliferation regime's efforts to stymie them. In addition to leading India into "the rarefied strata of strategic missile competence," as Chengappa put it, DRDO had outmaneuvered the colonial Missile Technology Control Regime.[163] And to charges that the Agni was built with foreign help, Kalam answered, "Such a mes-sage is deliberately communicated because of racial prejudice where one group of people believes only they can do it."[164]

As the scientists rallied emotional support for their programs, military leaders more carefully hinted at their growing interest in possessing a nuclear deterrent. Top officers believed that Pakistan's nuclear capabilities required a clearer counter, and they offered elliptical public comments to this effect. In response to a question from *India Today* about the Prithvi missile's effectiveness, Air Chief Marshal S. K. Kaul said, "Right now, it's our declared policy to remain non-nuclear. With conventional heads it is at best a deterrent." Then, without breaking the code of military discretion regarding nuclear policy, he implied that the missile's real value was nuclear. "It gives us the ability to say: 'If you do something to us we can damn well do something to you.' If and when the situation changes and so do the options, then the vehicles are available."[165] The military services were still wary about allocating their budgets for these missiles, especially if they were to be limited only to conventional missions, but the DRDO under Kalam consciously had brought the services more deeply into the missile development program to help build a broader institutional coalition.

Rao got the message. In an April 13 speech before the Army Commanders Conference in New Delhi, he declared that India would reject any restrictions on its nuclear option. Instead, he said, India favored a firmly scheduled, time-bound, universal and nondiscriminatory approach to nuclear disarmament.[166] Domestic politics and institutional pressures along with skepticism over the prospects of eliminating the Pakistani nuclear threat made accession to the American proposals untenable. Washington's failure to offer positive inducements made the decision easier. As Rao's Cabinet Secretary Naresh Chandra put it to Mitchell Reiss: the United States "offered nothing!"[167]

The Clinton administration did not give up. It dispatched Robert Einhorn, State Department Office of South Asian Regional Affairs Director Michael Lemmon, and Arms Control and Disarmament Agency Deputy Assistant Director Norman Wulf to London for an unpublicized meeting on April 27 with N. Krishnan, a retired diplomat who had served as India's permanent representative to the United Nations in the mid-1980s, and Rakesh Sood. At the Indians' request, the two teams met at a hotel to avoid detection and press leaks. Based on Rao's recent meeting with Talbott in New Delhi, the Americans had hoped that some modest progress could be made at least in organizing the nine-power conference. But these hopes were dashed immediately when the Indian side said that all countries of relevance to nuclear issues, including Iran, Libya, and North Korea, should attend. This represented several steps backward from previous official discussions. The Americans ended the meeting quickly. As one of them explained, "The Ministry of External Affairs had pulled back. The meeting was a set up; the MEA leaked it to their press in advance so they could show that they were defying American pressure."[168] Looking back on this period two years later, a key American official observed that a chance for real progress had been lost. "We and the Indians were converging. We were prepared to tolerate a certain capability on their part," the official explained. "Both sides faced domestic constraints; we could not come out and say that we were abandoning the scripture of the NPT. But we were prepared to let them know we would just live with what they have and try to move on. That was all lost after the spring of 1994."[169] The 1993–1994 dialogue had motivated India to spin the wheels of nuclear arms control diplomacy, giving an impression of forward movement. In reality, the tires were digging deeper into a sandy rut.

Still, the Indian press and political circles were leery that the government might cave in to American pressures as Rao's visit to Washington approached. Noting this skepticism, the prime minister addressed the Rajya Sabha on May 3 and reaffirmed "a total national consensus" that India would not "accept any regional NPT arrangement."[170] Regarding U.S.-Indian diplomacy, Rao said, "There was not even a word about capping. How do you cap an experiment?" India did not have a nuclear weapon program, he suggested, but rather a peaceful program that was intended to keep it "abreast of times."[171]

Rao then turned to questions about the Agni. After the third test in February, the press had reported that the government had decided not to pursue the program further at this time. This led to charges that outside pressure was causing its abandonment. In fact, U.S. officials had been urging India to restrain the Prithvi and Agni programs lest it provoke a Pakistani response. But, according to an American official involved, the Rao government offered no promise of restraint on the Prithvi while stating elliptically that the Agni was only a "technology demonstrator."[172] Speaking to Parliament, Rao explained that the Agni "experiment" had been proved successful and therefore could be paused until all analysis was completed and future plans developed, which could take more than a year.[173] "It is not a missile. It signifies additional capabilities in the upgrading of our missile technology."[174] Then, like Shastri invoking Homi Bhabha in the controversial debate of November 1964, Rao explained that he had asked Kalam, "Is the experiment over?" The science adviser had said, "Yes, one phase of it is over."[175] Kalam's authority gave Rao cover. In fact, any pause in Agni development and testing at this time stemmed from technological problems that the DRDO leader was loath to admit. For his part, Rao preferred to avoid the thorny nuclear and missile issues and instead concentrate on India's overall development.

Rao recognized that India's greatest strategic imperative remained economic development. "If we cannot make . . . our economic sinews . . . strong," he said, India would have no "political clout . . . No one is going to take it seriously."[176] But "[i]f you are strong, if you are self-reliant, if the sinews of the economy are good," he declared, then the rest of the world will say, "Yes, here is a country which is doing business with us, at the same time influencing us."[177] To the prime minister, then, the debate on nuclear and missile policies could distract and divert India from its major objective. And in obtaining that objective, U.S. engagement in India was important.

CLINTON-RAO SUMMIT, MAY 1994

On May 17, Rao arrived in Washington for the first Indian state visit since that of Rajiv Gandhi in 1985. Both sides sought to emphasize the positive: India's concentration on economic development and the mutual interests in trade and investment. This was not simply mercantilism. American officials believed, like Rao and Finance Minister Manmohan Singh, that India's future security and well-being depended on an economics-first strategy. They wanted to encourage this line for its intrinsic merit and because they hoped it would diminish the role nuclear weapons and ballistic missiles played in India's strategic calculations. For their part, Indian leaders hoped that increased economic interaction would create a pro-India business lobby in the United States that could help reduce American pressure on contentious issues such as proliferation, human rights, and Kashmir.[178]

On May 18, Rao addressed a joint session of Congress, highlighting the opportunities for growing business and political ties between the world's two largest democracies. (Unfortunately many senators and congressmen did not attend, giving their tickets to spouses, friends, and interns, which insulted some of the visiting Indian team.) The sober, dignified prime minister sought to reassure his audience that India was neither a threat to peace nor an irresponsible nuclear actor. He mentioned India's support of bans on nuclear weapon testing and fissile material production for weapons purposes and urged further steps, including an agreement on "no first use" of nuclear weapons, to lead the world toward the elimination of nuclear weapons.[179]

Clinton and Rao addressed nuclear issues specifically in their private meeting on May 19, as did other officials from both sides in additional sessions. The United States continued to pursue proposals to cap India's nuclear and missile programs. The Indians neither accepted nor rejected these proposals, indicating a decorous stalemate. Rao did reportedly give Clinton a general assurance that India would not deploy ballistic missiles in the near term.[180] For his part, Clinton agreed to language in a joint statement that conveyed India's *and the United States'* commitment to the "progressive reduction" of weapons of mass destruction "with the goal of eliminating such weapons."[181] Administration officials acceded to this language reluctantly. They recognized that without a U.S. commitment to the goal of eliminating nuclear weapons, Rao would find it more difficult to constrain India's nuclear and missile programs.[182] Neither side played up the letter publicly; indeed, it was not mentioned in the American press.

Rao's visit went over well at home. The concentration on common interests signaled the kind of recognition as a budding major power that India craved. (American nonproliferation activists believed that this entailed a risk of misperception, insofar as the public downplaying of the nuclear issue could lead the Indian polity to conclude mistakenly that U.S. interests in restraint were waning.) The positive tone reflected Rao's steady political leadership and the acumen of the economics-first strategy he and Manmohan Singh were pursuing.

U.S. press coverage of the summit was minimal. The *Washington Post* reported the Clinton-Rao meeting on page 30, below a story on the Clinton administration's determination to support granting of Most Favored Nation trade status to China despite ongoing human rights and proliferation problems there.[183] The *New York Times* did not report on the meeting at all, running only a picture of Rao addressing the joint session of Congress on page 3.[184] Absence of controversy meant absence of news when it came to India, a situation Indian elites noted ruefully.

Around the time of Rao's visit, Indian sources reported that problems at two key manufacturers of the Prithvi and disagreements between them and the army would cause a delay, meaning that the Prithvi would not enter the armed forces in the near future.[185] A planned Prithvi test scheduled for May 14, the eve of Rao's departure for Washington had been postponed. This prompted political debate, with the government denying opposition parties' charges that the prime minister was delaying Prithvi user trials.[186] However, by August, the Indian Army commenced user trials of the Prithvi and reportedly ordered seventy-five missiles to be deployed later in the year.[187] Yet the missiles were not deployed during Rao's tenure—which ended in the spring of 1996—although flight tests continued. Nor was the Agni missile flight-tested again, although by the end of 1998 signs appeared that further flight tests would commence. In the Prithvi case, Rao wanted to avoid bold moves that would provoke Washington; the need for a major redesign kept the Agni out of sight. [188]

In the wake of the Rao-Clinton summit, India's representative to the Conference on Disarmament issued a statement in June supporting the prospective Comprehensive Test Ban Treaty (CTBT) as an important step toward nuclear disarmament.[189] This statement, and a subsequent September 1994 statement on criteria for the treaty's entry into force, indicated that India at this time accepted the basic direction of the treaty negotiations.[190] However, as the next chapter discusses, in late 1995 India would reverse course and link its endorsement of the CTBT to more demanding disarmament conditions.

Encouraged by these developments, the Clinton administration sought to bolster Indo-American relations further by organizing a series of cabinet-level official trips to India. Energy Secretary Hazel O'Leary was the first, traveling to India in July to promote commercial and government cooperation on energy and environmental projects. Her enthusiasm and deft interpersonal skills left a positive impression on Indian officials and the public, as both sides downplayed nuclear issues.[191]

Unfortunately, Pakistani politics did not allow nuclear passions to subside on the subcontinent. On August 23, Nawaz Sharif, who was now the opposition leader, traveled to Pakistan-controlled Kashmir and proclaimed:

> I confirm that Pakistan possesses [the] atomic bomb. . . . Prime Minister Benazir Bhutto was about to compromise on the nuclear programme at a time when India was preparing to make Azad Kashmir the target of aggression and suppress Kashmiris' struggle for their right to self-determination. . . . By bringing facts on the

record, I have not only pre-empted the Indian aggression against Azad Kashmir and the government's planned rollback, but made it clear to responsible International powers that Pakistan should be treated at par with India in the world community and in the region.[192]

This episode is instructive in the ways in which a Pakistani politician could use "the bomb." First, Sharif's aggressive advocacy of the bomb signified his strong leadership disposition. Second, it showed that he would provide greater protection to the Kashmiris in their struggle than Benazir Bhutto. Finally, it demonstrated both toughness toward India and defiant preservation of Pakistan's sovereignty and independence in the face of American colonial power. Sharif's statement was hardly a serious nuclear strategy, but it was good politics.

Indian observers understood all this, as the same domestic political dynamics obtained in their country. They anticipated that Benazir Bhutto would now take a "more combative policy towards India" to cover her flank.[193] Top Indian officials sought to downplay Sharif's patently political blast and avoid being distracted from their political-economic agenda in upcoming state elections. Rao told a Congress Parliamentary Party meeting, "You should not worry . . . [W]e are capable of defending ourselves. You go back to your constituencies and work for elections."[194] Yet India's opposition politicians also could not resist an opportunity, so they pressed the government for a tougher reaction to the Pakistani provocation. An Indian Foreign Ministry official responded in the Rajya Sabha as follows: "If the safety and security of the nation require deployment of conventional and non-conventional weapons on the border, the Government will not hesitate to do so."[195] This statement was as close as an Indian official had ever come to admitting possession of nuclear weapons.

Indeed, by the summer of 1994 India's nuclear weapon capability was significant, albeit secret and recessed from military control. Designs for air- and missile-deliverable fission weapons had been completed and their various components extensively tested. In all likelihood India also had the capability to assemble boosted-fission weapons.[196] American government specialists now stated the possibility that India could build thermonuclear weapons.[197] As the director of the Bhabha Atomic Research Centre put it confidently, "Other countries must realise that our nuclear capability is way ahead of Pakistan."[198] M. R. Srinivasan, former AEC Chairman, declared in an interview in the *Indian Express* that "[t]here are responsible persons who know we have the nuclear weapons capability. . . . There are no doubts in my mind about it." Although acknowledging that he had been "far from being hawkish on the nuclear question," Srinivasan now said, "We should have followed the Chinese example of open defiance and cultivation of force."[199] Raja Ramanna added that India had "more than enough" plutonium for its security needs.[200]

On the missile front, even if production and induction schedules had slowed, technological development continued. An army official stated in September that induction and deployment of the Prithvi should occur in mid-1995.[201] Later in the fall, the press reported that India was developing, with Russian assistance, a submarine-launched missile with a 300-kilometer range, dubbed Sagarika.[202] Although India would not be able to manufacture a submarine to deploy such a missile in the foreseeable future, the project indicated the defense establishment's intention to develop a suite of nuclear delivery systems. (In 1998 the *New York Times* would publish a front-page story "breaking the news" about this missile.)[203]

The small Indian strategic community's determination to resist constraints on India's nuclear and missile programs intensified in September when the Pentagon released the results of the first major U.S. nuclear posture review in fifteen years. The review was initiated in 1993 by then-Defense Secretary Les Aspin, who intended it to reexamine fundamental assumptions of U.S. nuclear doctrine and force posture. However, resistance by segments of the military and civilian defense bureaucracy caused Aspin's successor, William Perry, to accede to a much less ambitious review. The result was a "new" nuclear posture that essentially maintained the levels, force posture, and doctrine that had prevailed during the Bush administration. The United States would plan to rely on no fewer than the 3,500 deployed nuclear weapons envisioned in the 1992 START II agreement to reduce long-range nuclear arsenals, keeping an additional 2,400 operational but nondeployed weapons as a "hedge" against negative developments in the Soviet Union and a further 2,500 weapons without tritium and batteries as an inoperable reserve. Rather than devaluing significantly the role of nuclear weapons in the post–cold war environment, Clinton administration officials intimated that the United States would widen the role of nuclear weapons to deter or respond to chemical or biological weapon attacks against American interests.[204] Indian nuclear cognoscenti would berate visiting Americans over the Pentagon review for years.[205]

Indian animosity grew further in October when the United States announced that it would lift sanctions that had been triggered in 1993 by China's supply of M-11 missile-related equipment and technology to Pakistan, in return for Beijing's promise not to transfer further ground-to-ground missiles or missile-related technology to Pakistan or other states.[206] Some Indians interpreted the sanctions relief as another instance of American commercial interests in China superseding nonproliferation policies, and they juxtaposed this with ongoing American pressure on democratic India. On the other hand, if China truly would end its missile (and nuclear) assistance to Pakistan, India should welcome the move as the United States did. Yet Indian suspicions about Washington's favoritism toward China and China's perfidy in abetting Pakistan's military buildup outweighed any positive interpretation. (The Indians may have overlooked the possibility that the United States' cooperation with Chinese intelligence in prosecuting the Afghan war against the Soviet Union had reduced Washington's interest in pressuring China to desist from supporting Pakistan's nuclear program in the 1980s, and that this equation was changing in the 1990s.)[207] The Indian view that Washington was being duped at India's expense grew keener when China conducted its forty-first nuclear weapon test days after the sanctions had been relieved. Although China was conducting a final series of tests in anticipation of signing the prospective comprehensive test ban treaty, Indian officials took the event as one more reason to refuse constraints on India's nuclear program.[208]

CONCLUSION

As 1994 neared its end, India and the United States were heading for a period of truth on nuclear policy that neither really anticipated. The parties to the Nuclear Non-Proliferation Treaty were scheduled to meet in the spring of 1995 to determine whether the treaty should be extended, and if so, under what conditions and for how long. The United States was determined to make the extension indefinite. To facilitate this, the Clinton administration showed its disarmament bona fides by pressing for negotiations on treaties to ban nuclear testing and fissile material production for weapons purposes. These two treaties overlapped with the administration's scaled back objectives to persuade India and Pakistan to cap their nuclear weapon programs. For their part, Indian Foreign Ministry officials and other hawks felt that none of these American objectives was sufficient to induce them to constrain their own nuclear ambitions in the absence of a commitment by the nuclear weapon states to set a serious agenda for nuclear disarmament. At the same time, however, leaders like Rao and Manmohan Singh recognized that India's ultimate strength and security depended on economic growth and further integration into the world political economy. This argued for India's undertaking measures to preclude a nuclear arms race in South Asia, if not through bilateral negotiations, then through a larger forum of parties that would make equitable commitments. Hence India's tentative willingness in 1993 discussions with American officials to explore ways to cap the growth of India's nuclear weapon capabilities.

However, Indian leaders were caught between competing domestic and international forces and interests. This drove them back to the politically comfortable policy of retaining the nuclear option unconstrained. By the end of 1994 and early 1995, domestic politics took nuclear policy off the government's agenda. State elections loomed and Rao had neither the time nor the political interest to depart from the nuclear status quo. In December 1994, Rao's Congress party was defeated decisively in Karnataka and his home state of Andhra Pradesh. [209] In Karnataka the BJP made important inroads in the South by rising from five to forty seats. In March 1995, the trends continued as the BJP registered major gains in state elections in Gujarat and in Maharashtra, allied with the Shiv Sena, all at the expense of Rao's Congress party, which heretofore had controlled both states.[210]

Narasimha Rao had managed to calm what had been a dangerously volatile political situation in 1991 and post-Ayodhya in late 1992. He and Manmohan Singh had launched India on the most important and effective economic reforms in its history. Rao had tried to keep nuclear policy on an even keel, neither tipping into domestic controversy or international waves that could swamp the economic program. Yet, despite Rao's caution and the energetic efforts of the Clinton administration to slow, if not cap and freeze, India's and Pakistan's nuclear and ballistic missile programs, the momentum behind these programs grew. Political circumstances heading into 1995 reduced the prospects of formal constraints being adopted in the future.

THIRTEEN

India Verges on Nuclear Tests

1995—MAY 1996

The fitful U.S.-Indian discussions in 1994 brought India as close as it had come to limiting formally the potential for a regional missile and nuclear arms race. In May 1995, more than 170 countries, led by the United States, chose to extend indefinitely the Nuclear Non-Proliferation Treaty and pledged themselves to real progress on the treaties to ban nuclear weapon testing and fissile material production. India was now isolated and facing potential global treaties that the weaponeers and other hawks feared would foreclose India's nuclear weapon option. Instead of accommodating the world trend, India struck out defiantly against it on grounds that the NPT extension meant the eternal legitimation of nuclear weapons and the system of "nuclear apartheid."

With national elections looming, Narasimha Rao sought to head off opposition charges that he had held too tight a rein on the nuclear and missile programs. He authorized preparations for nuclear weapon tests, which were discovered by U.S. intelligence and leaked to the press in December 1995. This prompted a roaring national debate and signaled the transition to the third phase in the history of India's nuclear weapon program.

Rao, however, did not sanction the tests sought by the scientists. In the April 1996 elections he and the Congress party were driven from power, largely for domestic reasons. In May, the Bharatiya Janata Party formed a government that lasted only twelve days. In that brief period, Prime Minister Vajpayee secretly authorized nuclear weapon tests, and then quickly retracted the authorization. The BJP government fell and was replaced by a coalition of thirteen parties led by Deve Gowda. The scientists again pressed for tests and, indeed, secretly had placed at least one nuclear device in a test shaft at Pokhran. Gowda did not turn down the request but instead sought to delay a decision while the government attended to more pressing domestic matters.

FERMENT IN NUCLEAR POLICY AND
INDO-AMERICAN RELATIONS, 1995

Developments in 1994 had betrayed India's strategic confusion, both among political leaders and the public. The most detailed public opinion survey ever conducted on nuclear issues found in the fall of 1994 that 57 percent of "educated elites" supported India's policy of "keeping the nuclear option open." Thirty-three percent supported "acquisition of nuclear weapons," and 8 percent favored "renunciation of nuclear weapons."[1] Of those who favored acquiring nuclear weapons, 57 percent cited "threats from nuclear Pakistan," 49 percent sought the weapons "to improve India's bargaining power in world affairs," 38 percent sought weapons "to enhance India's international status," 27 percent cited "threats from other nuclear powers," and 18 percent sought an arsenal to rebuff "international pressures on India's domestic politics." Only 20 percent cited "threats from China." These data reflected both the primacy of the Pakistani threat in India's perceptions and the elite's hunger for international status and autonomy.

When asked under what circumstances India should renounce nuclear weapons, more than half of the respondents cited the international adoption of "a time-bound plan for global nuclear disarmament." Roughly 20 percent cited "a verifiable renunciation of Pakistan's nuclear option."[2] "Moral repugnance" motivated 46 percent of those who favored renunciation of nuclear weapons, while 41 percent cited the environmental danger of nuclear weapons production. Thirty-four percent said "India cannot afford nuclear weapons," and 29 percent said that nuclear weapons "do not address the primary threats to India's security, e.g., terrorism and insurgency."[3] When asked under what conditions India should *use* nuclear weapons, 44 percent of all respondents said "never," 33 percent said "if Pakistan were about to take Kashmir," and 23 percent said "if China were about to overwhelm India militarily."[4]

Most tellingly, the "nuclear issue" ranked very low in the ranking of public concerns. Only 6 percent said the issue was among their top five concerns. Communalism was the highest concern, followed by poverty, economic stability, terrorism, Kashmir, the General Agreement on Tariffs and Trade (GATT), and the nuclear issue. Only U.S. support to Pakistan and foreign exchange reserves ranked below the nuclear issue.[5] Just 17 percent of educated elites felt that they had "marginal" or "significant" influence on India's nuclear policy.[6]

The attentive public clearly supported both retaining the nuclear option *and* the "cause" of nuclear disarmament. Yet, it did not seem to have a clear view on the rationale and cost-benefit calculus that could or should guide policies to build, deploy, and potentially use nuclear weapons. This was reflected in the deterrent-negating belief that if India acquired nuclear weapons it should never use them.

In January 1995 India reached an agreement with China for the supply of low-enriched uranium fuel for the Tarapur reactors. China's willingness to solve the nagging fuel problem revealed good business sense and the continued improvement in the two states' relationship. As the *Times of India* editorialized, "This deal should be the first step toward promoting a meaningful India-China nuclear dialogue."[7] New Delhi and Beijing were still far from resolving their border dispute, but the positive trend suggested no acute security problem.

U.S. Defense Secretary William Perry visited Pakistan and India in January 1995, heralding Washington's interest to cooperate more closely with India on defense matters. The first American defense secretary to visit the region since 1988, Perry commended India's remarkable tradition of civilian control over the military and the two countries' evolving military-to-military contacts and technological cooperation. Perry pleased his hosts by not pushing the nuclear issue.[8] He deferred to Indian sensibilities and his own belief that a nuclear rollback was unfeasible on the subcontinent. "I told them," Perry recounted later, that "I'm going to acknowledge that you have a nuclear capability. The question is where do you go from here."[9] In his thoughtful, mild-mannered way, the secretary of defense urged India and Pakistan to adopt arms control and confidence-building measures to prevent instability. He also acknowledged India's concerns about Chinese nuclear weapons and the unresolved political issues between the two states.[10] This general, abstract discourse sat well with his Indian counterparts and the media.

Yet the Indian interest in avoiding actual arms control and confidence-building measures left Perry extremely discouraged, despite his smooth diplomatic veneer. "I left India and Pakistan with a profound sense of failure," Perry recounted. "This discussion had gotten nowhere. It was just a matter of time before both countries tested and deployed nuclear weapons. I never bothered going back."[11]

Ironically, the justly celebrated civilian control of the Indian military had contributed to the strategic indecision that Perry and Indian commentators now lamented. As the journalist Shekhar Gupta wrote, "In no other major democracy are the armed forces given so insignificant a role in policymaking as in India. . . . The Indian defence forces have time and again followed official decisions without even questioning their strategic and tactical soundness."[12] In the wake of Perry's visit, Indian strategists like former Air Force Commodore Jasjit Singh juxtaposed American strategic planning with India's decision-making procedures. "Unlike the United States," Singh wrote in the *Times of India*, "the framework for strategic thinking and planning is not based on long-term perspectives. . . . U.S. military officers deal with issues on the basis of their being an integral part of their government," but in India, "even the top military hierarchy" is not involved.[13] For those like Jasjit Singh—the director of the government-funded Institute for Defence Studies and Analyses—who urged a more robust nuclear and missile posture, the lack of integrated military-strategic planning undermined India. But for those like Arun Singh, who had worked in the inner circle of prime ministerial decision making, the military strategists did not understand how politicians dealt with concepts such as nuclear deterrence. "Politicians who lead precisely because they feel things felt by common people, or can portray themselves as having such feelings, are unlikely to know much about nuclear weapons, risk of nuclear war and what to do to reduce it," Singh explained to a seminar of Indian and American strategists. "Politicians don't have the time or interest to read . . . millions of learned words about nuclear weapons. If arguments seem useful to us, well, then maybe we will use them; if not we'll ignore them."[14] This resulted in indecision regarding whether to build a nuclear arsenal or whether to effect arms control, or how to combine both strategies.

Indian politicians in 1995, as before and since, cared more about persuading voters that their economic needs would be addressed. Prime Minister Rao and the Clinton administration understood this well. Thus, President Clinton dispatched Commerce Secretary Ron Brown to India on the heels of Perry's trip to show America's growing interest in India. Brown and his entourage of twenty-six corporate chief executives made commitments with Indian counterparts for $7 billion in economic projects.[15] If William Perry's foray into South Asia yielded no prospect of slowing the nuclear and missile buildup, the prospect of enhancing relations through commercial ventures looked promising. Both India and the United States at this time avoided addressing what would happen if India abandoned its restraint in the nuclear and missile realm.

Following the Perry and Brown visits, the second of an unusual series of nongovernmental meetings occurred among high-ranking former officials from India, Pakistan, China, and the United States. The January 1995 meeting of the so-called "Shanghai Initiative" was held in the beautiful Indian southwestern coast state of Goa.[16] At the end of four days of discussions, the twenty-two participants, including former leaders of the Indian and Pakistani nuclear programs and armies, agreed on a statement of objectives and steps the four governments should take.[17] According to the Pakistani newspaper *Dawn,* this included support for the goal of "total elimination of nuclear weapons with a time-frame"; exploration of modalities by which all nuclear weapon states could take their arsenals off hair-trigger alert status; declarations by India and Pakistan that they would not conduct nuclear weapon tests prior to a comprehensive test ban treaty coming into force; and voluntary moratoria on fissile material production for explosive purposes pending completion of a global ban on such production.[18]

Controversy erupted in Pakistan when the press reported on the alleged "secret negotiations" that had made "unusual progress" on nuclear disarmament in the region.[19] The government promptly (and accurately) declared, "We have nothing to do with the Goa conference."[20] This showed how sensitive "leaders" were to charges that Pakistan and India might actually reach agreements on these issues.

The Goa meeting's greatest value was to expose the underlying dynamics that made "agreements" at once difficult and possible, albeit at the unofficial level. The discussions revolved around "equity" in two senses of the term. First, and most obviously, participants from each state were not willing to depart from traditional lines if the others did not offer commensurate departures. The Indian participants would not agree to endorse reciprocal unilateral Indo-Pak cessation of fissile material production if the American participants did not strongly endorse the elimination of nuclear weapons. This need for equity was also recognized in an American public opinion poll in early 1995 that reported that 60 percent of respondents favored the goal of eliminating "all nuclear arms in the world" and only 37 percent favored the de facto U.S. government policy of retaining nuclear arms while "trying to keep others from having them."[21]

Equity needs affected the discussions in a second, perhaps more important, way. Each group revealed tensions between the desire for its nation to be regarded as "equal" to the others and the gnawing recognition of actual disparities in economic and military power. Within the international system states do not have equal power and status, but within polities and in the minds of individuals this inequality is unwelcome. The tension between international power imbalances and national and personal aspirations is especially acute in democracies where equity is a norm, and in states where the legacy of colonialism remains vivid. Popular sovereignty and political competition allow rivals to denounce politicians who would accept seemingly inequitable international agreements.

The Pakistanis evinced a palpable feeling of their state's inferiority vis-à-vis India and a desire to be regarded as equals to Indians and India. The Indians displayed occasional haughtiness and even rudeness toward Pakistani representatives but were diffident toward the Chinese both in direct conversations and in formal discussions. For example, the Indian side wanted China to declare specifically that it would not use nuclear weapons first against India, just as China had given a specific commitment to Russia. The Chinese side demurred patronizingly, saying that China had made a universal no-first-use commitment that of course applied to India. That was not the issue, though. The Indians wanted the recognition of equity that would come from a specific commitment. For their part, the Chinese insisted on remaining aloof from South Asia as a regional actor, demanding instead to be considered only as a global player. This reflected in part the desire for equal status with the United States. As nominal representatives of the world's leading power, the Americans did not feel the struggle for equity. Yet they recognized that failure to act on the others' equity needs would drive the other states to exercise power by saying no to measures the Americans thought to be in the regional, global, and American interest. "No" is power, especially for weaker states.

These were not issues of comparative military power and national security in the sense of protection against attack. In a session on ballistic missile threats, the Indian participants raised no concerns over China's missile capabilities vis-à-vis India, despite the fact that several of the Indians frequently wrote passionate articles in newspapers on the Chinese missile threat. When an American asked the Chinese participants to address India's concerns, a former high-ranking Indian foreign affairs official interjected, "China poses no threat to India." This fore-closed discussion. The American then pursued the matter during a break with a renowned Indian strategist, who said, "China is not a military threat. It is a polit-ical problem. India needs China to negotiate outstanding issues with it in a forth-right manner, and the Chinese will not do so unless India develops a greater nuclear and missile capability."[22] Should not a serious diplomatic approach to China on nuclear concerns be tried first? "Yes," the Indian said, "but our govern-ment won't do that."

Experienced Indian and Pakistani participants revealed the domestic political context of nuclear policymaking. "Politicians in the subcontinent are using nuclear capability for their own purposes. I don't think they understand the impli-cations. . . . In nuclear weapons they see a simplified approach to defense, the ulti-mate weapon," a Pakistani offered. "When things are falling apart it helps to pull a bogeyman out of the closet. You can tell people what you want them to believe because they are illiterate. If you invest in education, 80 percent of the problems will go away," said an Indian participant. "What is projected as a means of secu-rity is actually a means of ambition. What is sought as being in the ambition and honor of a country reflects the ambition of an individual," commented another Indian.[23]

Unofficial discussions such as the one at Goa often revealed much about the sources of official nuclear policy. On substance, at least in early 1995, progress was possible if interlocutors were politically free agents prepared for equity. Yet the world of officialdom was politically tangled, and issues other than national secu-rity interests pulled government leaders in opposite directions. As 1995 progressed, the tension grew and the equity sought by India—more solipsistically than other states—was not offered.

INDIAN NUCLEAR RESISTANCE HARDENS AS THE EXTENSION OF THE NPT APPROACHES, MARCH TO MAY 1995

By March 1995, the Indian strategic community was focusing intently on the pending international conference to review and vote on the extension of the Nuclear Non-Proliferation Treaty. The conference of parties to the treaty was scheduled for April and May at the United Nations in New York. India, as a nonsignatory, would not participate, but the conference posed an opportunity for and serious challenge to India's long-standing nuclear policies. If the non–nuclear weapon states, a huge majority of more than 170, could win firmer commitments to nuclear disarmament by the five nuclear weapon states, India's moral and diplomatic stance would be buttressed. If, however, the nuclear weapon states could rebuff disarmament demands and win instead a strong international con-sensus for maintaining the existing regime of nuclear haves and have-nots, the conference would be a major setback. In that case, India would find itself further isolated and under greater pressure to conform to international demands for banning nuclear weapon tests and the production of fissile material for explosive purposes, both of which would limit India's nuclear option.[24]

Prominent Indian commentators thus began questioning India's recently reaffirmed endorsement of bans on testing and fissile material production. Some of these were the same individuals who in Goa had favored not only the proposed global treaties but also bilateral Indo-Pak moratoria on testing and unsafeguarded fissile material production. Jasjit Singh, for example, now called the proposal for an Indo-Pak moratorium on fissile material production "a trap."[25] K. Subrahmanyam argued that India should still support a global treaty banning fissile material production for weapons purposes, but only if it was tied to demands that the nuclear weapon states reduce stocks of weapons, ban the use of nuclear weapons, and provide security assurances to nonnuclear states. He reminded readers that in any case years would be required before a fissile material production ban could be effected.[26]

The revived resistance to nuclear constraints reflected the fears of India's strategic enclave. Former chairman of the Atomic Energy Commission M. R. Srinivasan charged the Rao government with capitulating to U.S. efforts to "defang" India by supporting negotiations on the test and fissile material production bans.[27] Abdul Kalam publicly urged defiance of American pressures to slow or stop the deployment of the Prithvi missile. "We cannot go by the suggestions of other countries on such matters," he insisted.[28] Days after Kalam's statement, Minister of State for Defence Mallikarjun said in Abu Dhabi that Prithvi user trials "had been completed, [but] we have yet to take a decision on serial production."[29] The press and army officials rallied to Kalam's side against Mallikarjun.[30]

Indian concerns grew in early April when Prime Minister Benazir Bhutto visited the United States to urge relief of nonproliferation sanctions against Pakistan. President Clinton responded positively, saying that it seemed unfair to bar Pakistan from receiving twenty-eight F-16 fighters and other defense equipment that it had paid for but not received.[31] The administration's nonproliferation specialists blanched at the president's statement: they knew that Pakistan had moved to assemble nuclear explosive devices in 1990 comprehending that sanctions would follow and that the president was about to undo a hard-fought policy.[32] White House spokesman Mike McCurry tried to minimize the apparent upset by reminding reporters that "[t]he president can't lift the sanctions because first, they are enacted by Congress, and secondly, Pakistan has not abandoned its nuclear program."[33] Yet the president had just changed the executive branch's policy in response to the seeming equity of Bhutto's plea. As one adviser reportedly said in a White House meeting, "[T]his is one of those times when the president gets to be president. He said they should get their planes or their money back. That's our policy now."[34] Senator Hank Brown, a Republican from Colorado, pitched in by planning to pursue legislation that would partially relieve Pressler sanctions.[35] This prospect of resumed military aid deepened India's resistance to U.S. nonproliferation pressures. An April *Times of India* poll showed that 79 percent of urbanites surveyed believed that Pakistan's possession of nuclear weapons posed a "serious security threat to India." (Only 47 percent believed that China's nuclear status posed a threat, with 42 percent disagreeing.)[36]

On April 3, the BJP attacked the Rao government for "giving up" the nuclear option by succumbing to American pressure against the nuclear and missile programs. The party referred to congressional testimony by State Department official Robert Einhorn in March that the Prithvi missile had not entered serial production and that the Agni program was in a state "of suspended animation."[37] BJP leader Atal Behari Vajpayee declared that his party, unlike the government, would make nuclear weapons if it came to power. "The BJP is in favour of a nuclear weapon free world," the party's resolution stated, "but not for a world in which a few countries possess nuclear weapon and the rest are subject to their hegemony."[38]

Others seized on the capitulation theme, too. The Hindi daily *Dainik Jagran* editorialized, "Can't our government tell the United States in plain words that it has no right to meddle in our defence preparations nor can it tell India what to do or not do?"[39] The paper reminded readers that "[t]he Prithvi missile is the outcome of years of work by our scientists with outstanding brilliance and skill. . . . If we continue to tolerate unjustified foreign intervention in producing and using something we created with our own efforts and resources, would it not be severely damaging to our independence and sovereignty."[40] To constrain the Prithvi would be to devalue the scientists' prowess and give away the nation's jewels to the colonialists.

The normally dispassionate *India Today* summarized the disorientation caused by the imminent NPT meeting. Face facts, the magazine urged: "Ever since the Pokhran test in 1974, India's attitude towards nuclear strategy has been ambivalent if not downright schizophrenic. Secretly, New Delhi seemed to love the bomb and the power that accrued from it, while publicly it abjured the very thought of harnessing the atom for any other but peaceful purposes."[41] India needed its political parties to meet together and adopt a new, "long-term strategic planning" approach, *India Today* editorialized, "[i]nstead of making the nuclear-bomb issue a domestic political football game or using it for grandiose moralising abroad." The magazine argued that New Delhi should bargain constraints on the nuclear and missile programs for firmer disarmament commitments by the nuclear weapon states and greater access to American high technology.[42]

As the NPT extension vote on May 11 neared, India was isolated and the United States was at the apogee of its power. Indian officials knew it, too. The Non-aligned Movement had met in Bandung, Indonesia, in late April to consider an alternative proposal for a twenty-five-year extension of the NPT, but it could reach no consensus.[43] The United States and other international powers had recruited a clear majority in favor of indefinite extension. Major nonaligned states such as Indonesia, South Africa, Mexico, and Venezuela criticized the nuclear weapon states for not seriously pursuing nuclear disarmament, but they and most other states genuinely valued the treaty as a means to stop proliferation. This interest in nonproliferation, as much as U.S. pressure and cajolery, motivated support for indefinite extension. Rather than fight ineffectively and risk reprisals in UN debates on, say, Kashmir, or international support of India's economic reforms, the Indian government chose not to try to disrupt the NPT extension process.[44] Besides, India favored nonproliferation, just not at the expense of its nuclear option in a world where the declared nuclear weapon states clung to their arsenals.

After three weeks of debate, the president of the NPT conference, Jayantha Dhanapala, on May 11 declared without objection that a consensus existed among the 179 parties to extend the treaty indefinitely. Serious tensions remained over the questions of nuclear disarmament, technological assistance to nuclear programs in countries in good-treaty-standing like Iran, and the desire by Arab states (and others) to put greater pressure on Israel to join the NPT. But the benefits of the nonproliferation regime, the political and economic power of the strong, and the will of the majority prevailed in keeping these issues from blocking the treaty's indefinite extension.

The nuclear weapon states did make an accommodation that, paradoxically, gave impetus to India's subsequent moves to test nuclear weapons. At the behest of states in favor of nuclear disarmament, the conference adopted "Principles and Objectives for Nuclear Non-Proliferation and Disarmament." This document set benchmarks for evaluating the implementation of disarmament commitments under the treaty. Among them were completion of a Comprehensive Test Ban Treaty "no later than 1996"; immediate commencement and early conclusion of negotiations to ban fissile material production for explosive devices; and "determined pursuit by the nuclear-weapon States of systematic and progressive efforts to reduce nuclear weapons globally, with the ultimate goal of eliminating those weapons."[45] The explicit commitment by the nuclear weapon states suggested to Indian observers that the test ban and fissile material production ban would now be pursued as effectively as NPT extension had been. India had subscribed publicly to these potential treaties at a time when they did not appear likely. Now the treaty tide was rising, and Indian officials and commentators began to fear the nuclear program would be swamped.

POST-NPT DEFIANCE, MAY TO AUGUST 1995

The NPT extension conference left India more isolated than ever. Rather than conform with the international mainstream favoring nonproliferation, India became more defiant. It would at a minimum preserve the nuclear option. But to do this in the face of growing international pressure, India would have to show that its missile program would not be slowed. Additionally, the strategic enclave felt India would have to advance its nuclear weapon development, including conducting nuclear explosive tests, in order to hedge against a prospective international test ban treaty.

In late April, Indian sources had reported that an army unit in Hyderabad was created to induct and operate the first batch of Prithvi missiles.[46] In May, the Parliamentary Standing Committee on Defence recommended early deployment of the Prithvi.[47] The press joined the push. The *Indian Express* editorialized that the missile should already have been deployed and blamed the government for caving in to "the Americans, who never approved of a Third World country like India attaining mastery in missile technology."[48]

Rao got the message. On May 16, he told the Lok Sabha that the government was considering deploying the Prithvi and that "no amount of persuasion or pressure, which it is alleged is being brought on us, will make an iota of difference on the programme as conceived by us."[49] A week later, Minister for External Affairs Pranab Mukherjee met with top Clinton administration officials, including the president, in Washington and told them that India's deployment decision would depend on the evolution of the security environment in the coming months.[50] This formulation reflected the enormous domestic pressure weighing on the government and the conflicting interest in accommodating Washington. Clinton had not abandoned his effort to resolve the F-16 dispute with Pakistan, and India wanted to block it. Deploying the Prithvi might satisfy Indian domestic interests, but it also could open the door for the F-16s to go to Pakistan. This would cause political turmoil of its own within India. Thus, delaying Prithvi deployment seemed the least risky course.

India's political-security calculus became more complicated still when China conducted a nuclear test on May 15, just four days after the NPT extension. To attentive Indians, the Chinese test underlined the renewed and relegitimated determination of the nuclear weapon states to lord their arsenals over the rest of the world.[51] In March, China and India had completed another positive meeting to further confidence-building measures along the disputed border, including discussion of proposals on prior notification of military exercises and prevention of intrusions into each other's airspace.[52] However, the Chinese test, and subsequent revelations that China had shipped at least thirty M-11 missiles to Pakistan, heightened Indian insecurities.[53] Making matters worse, the Clinton administration, in the Indian view, seemed determined not to act on intelligence reports about the M-11s in order to avoid imposing legally mandated sanctions on China.[54] The administration concluded that it had not actually seen the missiles and, without such proof, should not impose sanctions.[55] Moreover, officials believed that quiet diplomacy would persuade China more effectively to cease such transfers. This further alienated India, which perceived a double standard in Washington's treatment of India and China in the missile realm.

Nevertheless, Sino-Indian bilateral relations continued positively when the two sides met again in August and agreed to further troop pullbacks from the eastern sector of their disputed border.[56] India raised the M-11 and nuclear test issues with the visiting Chinese delegation; the Chinese evaded the former but reassured India that it posed no nuclear threat to it.[57] In summing up the meeting, the *Business Standard* editorialized, "The normalisation of relations with China has been among the most outstanding Indian foreign policy successes of the last several years."[58]

However, Indian analysts began to draw a strategic lesson from the difference between Washington's dealings with China and India. "Why cannot we be like the Chinese?" Raja Mohan asked. "The effective combination of defiance and deal-making has been the hallmark of the Chinese approach to the United States in the recent years," he wrote.[59] Mohan recognized that China's power stemmed primarily from its growing economic strength. But China also exercised power through its seat on the UN Security Council, its possession of nuclear weapons, and its pivotal role in Asia. In contrast, India had allowed itself to be regionally bound by the tangle with Pakistan, and India's politics precluded the kind of deal making China undertook with the United States. To achieve China-like power, Mohan urged Indian leaders to move "towards a declared nuclear weapon status." This, "coupled with the deployment of the Prithvi missile and the renewed testing of the Agni, would mark the beginning of a national security strategy based essentially on self-help." Here, the erudite Mohan consciously referred to Waltzian international relations theory to augment his argument in India and the West. He argued that India must reorganize its national security establishment to rely less on domestically preoccupied politicians and more on military-security professionals. This represented a growing movement among elites to adopt American and Chinese patterns of thought and behavior as a means of achieving power and respect.

India's desire for greater leverage against the United States mounted in August when Senator Hank Brown announced that he would seek to pass an amendment to remove some of the Pressler sanctions on Pakistan.[60] The Senate had blocked his initial effort in early August, and Brown recognized that his legislation would not succeed if it called for shipping the held-up F-16s to Pakistan. The Clinton administration backed Brown and was now seeking a third party to buy the planes, enabling proceeds to go back to Pakistan as compensation. Clinton wrote Rao to reassure him that the partial relief of sanctions on Pakistan represented neither a threat to India nor a diminution of Washington's interest in relations with India.[61] Rao wrote back sharply that the Brown initiative would trigger an arms race.[62]

The issue strained Indo-American relations. New Delhi was still adjusting to the NPT extension and was under pressure regarding Prithvi production and deployment. At the same time Indian officials were trying to calm American and international investor concerns over the new state government of Maharashtra's attempt to renegotiate a multibillion dollar power supply contract with the American company, Enron.[63] To make matters worse, France had resumed nuclear weapon testing in the Pacific, and China had just conducted missile tests toward Taiwan. All of this deepened the sense that India must move decisively either to win U.S. and international favor or to assert its independent strength. As the former Indian diplomat A. Madhavan put it, "India has, sooner or later, either to flout [the U.S.-led nonproliferation regime] by going openly nuclear, or to accept it."[64]

PRELUDE TO NUCLEAR TESTS, AUGUST TO DECEMBER 1995

When Abdul Kalam assumed control of the Defence Research and Development Organisation in 1992, he inherited the leading role that Arunachalam had established in the strategic technology programs. Atomic Energy Commission Chairman R. Chidambaram remained a vital player. As explained by a then high-ranking official in New Delhi, "Kalam was the point person, but he and Chidambaram worked closely together, and if Kalam was not available you could accomplish what was necessary by dealing directly with Chidambaram. They were a team."[65] Kalam had been pushing relentlessly for serial production and deployment of the Prithvi missile, as well as for the development and testing of improved versions of the Agni. Reports emerged in late August that Kalam had "shut down 618 small and medium projects" in the DRDO in order to concentrate human and budgetary resources on large programs such as missiles, the Light Combat Aircraft, the Arjun tank, a laser weapons project, and an integrated electronic warfare project—all of which had high potential strategic value to the military.[66] Having worked to build a stronger, politically potent coalition with the armed forces, Kalam sought to overcome the Rao government's budgetary and policy constraints. Meanwhile, Chidambaram's team at BARC and their counterparts working on nuclear weapon designs at the DRDO had developed a range of deliverable fission weapons and one or more boosted-fission designs; plus, they were working on a thermonuclear design. The nuclear establishment's morale and budgets had become increasingly staked to the national security mission. The DRDO and BARC teams were coordinated by K. Santhanam of the DRDO, an intense, heavy-smoking man with an extraordinarily clever, biting wit and unconcealed resentment toward the U.S.-led nonproliferation regime.

Working through the press and political channels, the weaponeers had recently generated political interest in advancing the Agni program from a "technology demonstration" project to a deployable weapon system. In August, Defence Minister Achutan Nambiar had told Parliament that the Agni's further development was under consideration and depended on the strategic situation.[67] This belied important technical problems constraining the pace of the Agni's development. On August 30, the strategic analyst and pundit Brahma Chellaney had written that "the technical demands" of "a missile-based nuclear deterrent" could not "be met without testing" of nuclear weapons.[68] Reporting information that was not publicly available, Chellaney noted that "Indian scientists are capable of conducting hydro-dynamic and other advanced laboratory experiments involving computer modeling," but "full-scale testing would still be required to perfect reliable, missile-deliverable warheads." He then lambasted the current and past governments for lacking "a coherent nuclear strategy" and instead "playing to the gallery rather than grappling with issues related to the nuclear option." Indian counterparts believed that Chellaney's writings at this time often reflected information and positions provided by the top scientists.[69]

Indeed, by August 1995, army laborers were pumping water from shafts and making additional preparations for nuclear tests at the Pokhran site.[70] The details surrounding these activities remain murky. Since the early 1980s, the test site, including at least two vertical shafts, had been routinely maintained in case tests were to become necessary quickly to respond to a Pakistani nuclear test or other developments. According to former top-level scientists and policy advisers, the strategic enclave did not need explicit political authorization to maintain the site or make other test preparations. What did require authorization was the emplacement of devices in shafts, the sealing of shafts with devices in them, and the detonation of devices. Still, as one official involved at the time suggested, the extensive work now under way at Pokhran would not be happening if the scientists did not think they were going to be authorized to conduct tests.[71] It seems that Prime Minister Rao had responded to Kalam's and Chidambaram's requests and explicitly authorized preparatory work for nuclear tests, and perhaps even emplacement of devices in test shafts, without a firm decision actually to proceed to detonation of weapons. The scientists were given to assume that a test decision would follow.

According to the former official in New Delhi cited previously, the scientists had been pushing steadily for tests on three grounds: they needed to perfect and demonstrate their technological innovations; they believed that only full-scale explosive tests could validate their work, and therefore the nuclear deterrent; they needed explosive tests to both recruit and retain talented scientists and engineers in the nuclear and defense programs when higher-paying jobs awaited them in the commercial technology sector. Without full-scale tests, morale would fall and the nation would not find replacements for the aging cohort that had produced the first device in 1974.[72]

However, Rao and his advisers recognized that the scientists possessed no political or strategic expertise and therefore could not place their personal, institutional, and technical interests into the fuller context of the national interest.[73] Chidambaram acknowledged as much in a 1997 discussion. "I am not a strategist. Other people work on that . . . people like Subrahmanyam, Jasjit Singh, P. R. Chari," he said, naming no government officials but instead former officials now working in think tanks and writing for newspapers.[74] Available sources do not show whether Rao turned to these strategists, the scientists, or others for broader strategic advice at this point. It does not appear that a detailed threat analysis of Pakistan and China had been prepared with corresponding analyses of how developing nuclear weapons would affect these threats. Rao had considerable experience in foreign affairs, but he displayed little interest in details of nuclear policy. He innately disliked the notion of nuclear deterrence and tended to think of nuclear policy in moral terms.[75] He found the U.S. position on nonproliferation so hypocritical as to be immoral, but this did not lead him to embrace Indian reliance on nuclear weapons either. In authorizing test preparations, according to the aforementioned former official in New Delhi, the prime minister "did not have a nuclear deterrence strategy. He didn't think about when it will be used, against whom, or these questions of doctrine. He didn't think these things were useable, and he was not planning to use them, so why spend a lot of time thinking about such things?" Rather, India must keep its nuclear option open, and the scientists said this could not be done without testing. Still, Rao had not made up his mind finally to authorize actual tests.[76]

New Delhi's small strategic community bolstered the case for nuclear tests in a meeting on September 24 in which participants urged India to oppose prospective treaties banning nuclear testing and unsafeguarded fissile material production unless they were linked explicitly to a "time-bound framework" for nuclear disar-mament.[77] The group also called on the government to examine how the now "meaningless" nuclear option could be translated into "effective deterrence." This was an implicit call for testing. Furthermore, India should "continue developing longer range delivery systems" and proceed with "serial production and induc-tion" of the Prithvi. These positions no doubt reflected the views of the strategic enclave. Ominously for the Rao government, they echoed the rhetoric of the BJP.

The campaign for nuclear testing and further development of missiles received a further boost in September when the U.S. Senate passed the Brown Amend-ment, authorizing release of heretofore withheld military equipment to Pakistan. (The House concurred in late October.) To the Indians, the Brown Amendment and overall U.S. policy represented an important negative trend. An unattributed article in the *Business Standard* made the point: "The Indian DNA is anti-American. We are a proud civilisation. We have much to be proud about, just as we have a lot to be shameful about. But no Indian, however sympathetic to the US, can help but feel wounded" when U.S. officials ask India "to behave 'responsibly' in relation to the US arms package to Pakistan."[78] Indeed, according to "sources close to Rao," reported the *Times of India*, "the Brown amendment was the moment of truth" for the prime minister, who "till then had believed that the U.S. was genuinely inter-ested in non-proliferation."[79]

India expressed its growing resistance to U.S.-led arms control and nonprolif-eration initiatives in October 1995. In a statement to the United Nations, Atal Behari Vajpayee, serving on India's delegation to the General Assembly, declared that the indefinite extension of the NPT had "legitimised for all time . . . the divi-sion of the world into nuclear haves and have nots."[80] Vajpayee argued that by failing "even to discuss" commitments to eliminate their nuclear weapons "within a time-bound phased programme," the nuclear weapon states had raised the stakes involved in the test ban treaty negotiations. India now demanded more than it had earlier from the CTBT. In Vajpayee's words, the treaty now "must . . . contain a binding commitment on the international community, especially the nuclear weapon states," to "take further measures. . . towards the total elimination of nuclear weapons."[81] Moreover, Vajpayee argued, the treaty should not contain loopholes to allow subcritical or any other form of nuclear tests as the nuclear weapon states sought to have allowed under the treaty. The Indian weaponeers' long-standing resistance to proposals to impede their technological ambitions was boosted by a growing political determination to protest the way the United States was shaping the global nonproliferation regime in the aftermath of the cold war.

TEST PREPARATIONS EXPOSED—
ROILING DEBATE ERUPTS, DECEMBER 1995

By early fall 1995, Rao and his Congress party were politically endangered. A number of significant Congress politicians had been charged with corruption, and Rao himself was becoming tainted by the payoff miasma. The general feeling of party decline encouraged fractiousness. Economic growth, particularly in industrial sectors, had become impressive by Indian historical standards in 1994 and 1995, and exports grew, too. However, the general culture of high-level corruption and the government's political weakness now slowed the implementation of economic reforms. Investment in infrastructure improvements—electricity generation, roads, ports—lagged badly. Without a healthy infrastructure "circulatory system" the body would soon stop growing. These economic problems did not become center-stage political issues because they were complicated to average voters; however, they reflected political weakness and misgovernance that would become campaign themes.

The main challenge emanated from the BJP. BJP leaders saw great opportunity to replace the Congress as the only national party in a sea of smaller regional and ideological groupings. To win a majority, the BJP was abandoning hard-line Hindu-chauvinist rhetoric and portraying itself as a force for stability and anti-corruption.

The national campaign had begun for all intents and purposes by mid-1995. Nuclear policy still did not rival communalism, corruption, or employment, but the bomb became an element in the national image the BJP represented. The BJP's political narrative portrayed Congress as weak willed, meekly moralizing, and deferential to outside pressures trying to retard India's nuclear prowess and national strength. If elected, the BJP, on the other hand, would act decisively and display India's strength and scientific prowess in ways that would force the international community to give the nation its due. In this broader narrative context, nuclear policy had little to do with rigorous analysis of the military-security situation or projection of an effective national security strategy. Rather, the issue remained largely symbolic. The BJP's clear, proud line was more politically serviceable than Congress's.

With elections looming, any seasoned Indian politician would question the political implications of nuclear weapon testing. By allowing the scientists to accelerate test preparations in late summer, Rao had increased his options. He could quiet the strategic enclave by holding out the prospects of tests; he could outflank the BJP by testing if they mobilized popular sentiment on the nuclear issue; and, if he concluded that India could not afford the international consequences of nuclear tests, he could demonstrate that he had been prepared to conduct them but decided, reluctantly, that the national interest dictated restraint. Yet to manage the issue well required secrecy. If it became public, any number of forces, interests, and passions could determine policy, with the loudest voice not necessarily being the wisest.

Unfortunately, spotlights exposed the test preparations on December 15, 1995. Tim Weiner of the *New York Times* reported on page 1 that U.S. intelligence satellites had detected stepped-up activity at the Pokhran test site indicating India might be preparing to conduct a nuclear weapon test.[82] In qualifying the article's general assertion, Weiner added that "intelligence experts said they could not tell whether the activity involved preparations for exploding a nuclear bomb or some other experiment to increase India's expertise in making nuclear weapons." Although Weiner cited U.S. government sources, a nongovernmental nonproliferation expert had put him onto the story. When Weiner tried to pursue it with government officials he met resistance, as they did not want the information to leak. The State Department, informed by earlier American intelligence detection of stepped-up activity at Pokhran, was already mobilized and using quiet channels to press India not to conduct a test. Ambassador Frank Wisner returned to New Delhi from Washington just hours before the *Times* story broke and privately impressed upon officials close to Rao the problems that a test would cause. American officials knew that publicity would cause an uproar in India and make it more difficult for Rao to desist.[83] However, Weiner leveraged a vague comment of concern from one source to get clarification from another source in a different agency, going back and forth between government sources to build the sketchy story.[84] This background is significant because Indian commentators in the ensuing frenzy asserted that the U.S. government purposely planted the Weiner story.

The Indian government responded first by denying that it was preparing for a possible test. Hours later it called the *Times'* report "highly speculative."[85] Now a frenzy of activity and rhetoric began. The *Washington Post* reported on December 16 that American intelligence had detected unusually extensive activities at the test site.[86] The *Post*'s R. Jeffrey Smith added that "U.S. intelligence officials have said Indian scientists are trying to develop more powerful 'boosted' atomic arms as well as a hydrogen bomb." On Capitol Hill, the staff of Senator John Glenn, who had authored the 1994 Glenn Amendment to the Arms Export Control Act, reminded interested parties that a nuclear test automatically would trigger extensive sanctions against India, and against Pakistan if it followed suit. Pakistani officials reacted by saying they would test if India did.[87]

Shortly after news of the test preparations appeared in public, President Clinton called Prime Minister Rao to urge him not to proceed. According to a knowledgeable American official of the time, Rao said somewhat reassuringly that India would not act irresponsibly, but he offered no categorical commitment not to test.[88] American officials held their breath hoping that Rao would resist whatever temptations or pressures operated in favor of testing.

The Indian press and concerned elites reacted to the *Times'* report by calling it "an official plant" intended to pressure India "to give up its insistence on nuclear disarmament" and to reverse its recent tentative withdrawal of support for the test ban treaty.[89] Raja Ramanna called the American allegation "a big lie"—"They want to get us in trouble," he added.[90] The BJP issued a statement calling the reports a "ploy" by Washington to "coerce" India into signing the test ban treaty.[91] Jaswant Singh, the BJP's leading defense policy spokesman stated proudly that "India is not a colony to be bent or threatened into submission." He called on the government to "strengthen India's nuclear policies."[92]

Commentators noted the political dimension of the alleged test preparations and the debate. The *Hindustan Times* editorialized, "Mr. Narasimha Rao's Congress party stands a fair chance of winning if he undertakes fresh nuclear tests which would be widely seen by Indian voters as the act of a brave national hero."[93] The paper urged Rao not to be "inhibited" by the United States, nor to follow the BJP's demands for "weaponisation of the nuclear option." While "Rao does not have to conduct a nuclear test to justify the NYT story," the newspaper suggested he could argue that "he needs the tests for improving upon India's nuclear technology." If he did so, "he would have most of the nation behind him."

The government declared on December 18 that it would not succumb to external pressure.[94] For their part, top defense scientists generally stayed out of the highly charged debate, except to call for greater government support of "critical research programmes."[95] Military leaders remained publicly silent.

Opinion became more divided as the debate proceeded. All urged defiance of American pressure, while some called for conducting tests and others for restraint. The *Asian Age* editorialized that "[i]f India's scientists feel that they need to conduct a second test then they should go ahead with it. Washington may not approve, but Indians will applaud. Not only will [Rao] have stood by our scientists," the paper averred, "he will also have reasserted the fact that India's policies are built on just one foundation—independence."[96] However, the *Times of India* argued that India should not "abandon the mature stance of nuclear ambiguity in favour of a declared nuclear status."[97] Similarly, the *Business Standard* cited prospective economic sanctions as militating against an interest in testing.[98]

The most sophisticated analysts recognized that issues beyond politics and anticolonialism underlay the testing question. They now began parsing India's options. Raja Mohan wrote that the time was coming to close the "domestic nuclear debate" and decide on exercising the nuclear option. The pending Comprehensive Test Ban Treaty was forcing India to determine whether it could maintain a credible nuclear deterrent without testing or instead must conduct a "small number of tests that will allow India to impart credibility to its minimum deterrent posture." After this, Mohan argued, India could "join the CTBT as a declared nuclear weapon power."[99] K. Subrahmanyam, however, repeated his earlier arguments that India's first device had proved its scientists' know-how and the nation did not need to test now.[100] "Deterrence is mostly a matter of perception," he argued. "No country's animosity towards India is so intense as to compel that country to play the game of 'nuclear chicken,' " given

India's demonstrated nuclear capabilities. No serious analyst at this time argued that India required thermonuclear weapons that would necessitate a test program.

The government now moved to still the debate by having Foreign Minister Pranab Mukherjee categorically deny that India was preparing to conduct a nuclear test.[101] Indian officials knew that American intelligence probably would detect further activity. Thus, Mukherjee's statement likely reflected a genuine decision, otherwise India's credibility would have been damaged further. This is how Washington officials interpreted the matter, too, exhaling a collective sigh of relief.[102]

Rao's reaction to the furor appeared to flow from several considerations. A knowledgeable official in New Delhi at the time recounted that the prime minister did not hold formal group discussions of testing. "Rao was a great listener, not a great giver-away of what was in his mind," this former official said. "He talked with people one-on-one, people he trusted and respected, and then he decided."[103] Another Indian who discussed the issue later with Rao said the prime minister concluded that, given the international furor, it would be better to wait a couple of years until the Indian economy was stronger to withstand potential sanctions.[104] Yet another knowledgeable Indian official recalled that Rao was prepared to risk American dissatisfaction over nuclear tests but felt that it made more strategic sense to wait until the Indian economy was stronger and the missile program was more advanced.[105] Congress party leaders reportedly had concluded that inflation had contributed heavily to party losses in the late-1994 and early-1995 state elections, and Rao therefore asked his top economic advisers how nuclear tests in late 1995 would affect the economy. These advisers reportedly told him that sanctions would raise inflation.[106] This intensified Rao's doubts about conducting tests now. Thus, while Rao was willing in principle to authorize tests, he had not made up his mind that they were in India's interest. This reflected his general aversion to taking decisive action on difficult issues. Therefore, the government's announcement that tests were not planned did not represent a reversal, but rather an effort to stem the national and international debate.

While the debate continued, the focus shifted. Over the next months and years, as never before, the few participants in the nuclear debate would address real technological and doctrinal questions about what was necessary for deterrence. In the meantime, as a way of avoiding these harder, more recondite issues, a growing number of officials and commentators favored "a 'middle line' " policy of "abjuring a test, yet claiming nuclear weapon status" in a declaration at the Conference on Disarmament in Geneva, where the CTBT negotiations were occurring.[107] Such a declaration would signal self-professed global status and defiance of nonproliferation pressure and cause tumult in the international system. This would give India leverage in disarmament negotiations.

Jaswant Singh of the BJP provided an apt summary of where matters stood politically. "I don't think the government has gained any political mileage from this issue," he told the *Telegraph*.[108] "What has emerged is that the government has no policy on the issue at all. Silence is no policy, denial is no policy, nor is ambiguity a euphemism for policy." The reality was that even now, after the dramatic American "charges" and in the midst of an election buildup, "national security" did not have "the necessary political sex appeal," Singh noted. "The low attendance in Parliament when such debates are on is evidence enough. The issue has high appeal only when the bullets are flying."[109]

ELECTIONS AND THE BJP'S ABORTED ATTEMPT TO TEST, JANUARY TO MAY 1996

In early 1996, the run-up to elections dwarfed other national concerns. Yet India could not escape its critical role in the intense negotiations in Geneva on the Comprehensive Test Ban Treaty. The test ban talks raised vital national issues to the Ministry of External Affairs and the nuclear cognoscenti. Brahma Chellaney defined the issues well. He argued that if India wanted a credible deterrent, it must conduct tests "to perfect technical capabilities and convey a political message to other nuclear-armed states" *before* a test ban went into effect making tests much more politically difficult if not impossible.[110] By waiting, "India might have no choice ultimately but to cut its losses and surrender its long-held 'holy cow.' " Indeed, "If India has no intent or need to test, then it should not be concerned about a test ban." Other knowledgeable analysts such as P. R. Chari argued that it was already "too late for India to conduct the required series [of tests] before CTBT is negotiated. . . . [A] test series thereafter in the teeth of international opposition would become infinitely more difficult."[111] Both perspectives reflected the belief that the nuclear option was threatened. Kanti Bajpai argued boldly that nuclear weapons merely allowed Pakistan to "equalize" India and were "irrelevant" to dealing with the Kashmir insurgency and Pakistan's role supporting it. He thus suggested that India "should offer to give up its nuclear weapons capability," with the condition that the program would be resumed if Pakistan did not reciprocate within a year.[112] For its part, the Indian government in March 1996 declared in the Conference on Disarmament that it did "not believe that the acquisition of nuclear weapons is essential for national security."[113]

Having decided not to conduct tests prior to the elections, the Rao government demonstrated national prowess and strength by flight-testing the 250-kilometer variant of the Prithvi missile on January 27. The day before, during the Republic Day parade, a Prithvi missile on its mobile launch platform trundled down New Delhi's Rajpath, heralded by the announcer as the "pride of the nation."[114] Rao celebrated the launch by congratulating the scientists and engineers for their "selfless dedication" and promising that the Prithvi was "not the last significant milestone to be achieved" by the DRDO missile program.[115]

Still, people in New Delhi and Islamabad were preoccupied with internal problems. The Indian polity focused on investigations and corruption charges against

Congress party and BJP officials and the growing assertiveness of the judiciary in holding officials accountable. When nuclear issues arose in conversations, the focus was not on dangers from China or Pakistan or the threat of military conflict, but rather the U.S. campaign to overcome Indian objections to the test ban treaty and Washington's perceived tilt toward Pakistan in the form of the Brown Amendment.[116] The anticolonial narrative and the desire for greater recognition of India's demands for nuclear equity seemed most important.

In a conversation on his immaculate lawn in New Delhi, a BJP leader reflected on the strategic culture and security decision making of India. "Security is a very important issue," he said, "but to the average man, security relates to violence in a village or communal strife. We politicians can effect a tie between Pakistan and security or China and security—we can create rhetoric to win elections, as politicians do in all countries. But the people don't know anything about the CTBT."[117] The BJP, he added, criticized the "sheer ad hocism of Indian security policy." The problem stemmed from the absence of institutions. "We need someone to think these things through, but it is difficult to set up a National Security Council in a parliamentary system." This limited the military's preparation. "There is no training, no doctrine in our military on nuclear issues. The military has some officers training manuals on what to do if attacked by nuclear weapons, but there is no rudimentary command, control and information system."

When reminded that these issues were frequently debated in some detail in the English-language press, the BJP leader said, "Yes, but the English press is read by seven percent of the country. People read about sex, crime and corruption, but don't know anything about the CTBT." Even the Parliament paid little attention. "Not more than five percent of MPs are interested in these issues, still less would study them seriously. Our defence debates frequently must be adjourned for lack of a quorum," he lamented. Did this mean that the generally hawkish views expressed by national security pundits did not affect politicians? "We have to run for re-election every five years, so we are realistic. If we got swayed by what the papers write, we would not know what to do. Newspapers have a short half-life. That life is one reading, then the paper is what people eat off."

When asked whether the BJP would go through with its long-standing pledge to build and deploy nuclear weapons, this party leader said that "planks like this take on a life of their own in a party, just as certain planks do in your American parties, where when one wins an election it does not necessarily enact much of its platform." The BJP's tough nuclear position served a purpose, he noted wearily. "Pakistan and India are the only countries in the world now where you could organize public protests *for* the bomb. Atavism can be readily tapped here." All of this affected U.S. nonproliferation policy in ways that American officials failed to appreciate, in this man's view. "Whatever initiative the United States takes with South Asia on nonproliferation you carry baggage of centuries of history—colonialism, and then America's own role here including the USS *Enterprise* in 1971." Democracy complicated the problem. "We democracies take initiatives due to the compulsions of our domestic agenda," he noted. "The U.S. government feels a political compulsion to complete the CTBT by November 1996, your elections. So your leaders want to check off the CTBT box on their pad of paper. This is an occidental way of doing things." India, however, is different. "We take more time. If you push us on your schedule's compulsion, it will not help. It will harden us."

The United States pressed on in Geneva, and the Indian position did harden. Washington also in March reaffirmed that it would supply military equipment to Pakistan authorized under the Brown Amendment, notwithstanding intelligence reports that Pakistan had received five thousand ring magnets from China designed for use in enriching uranium at Kahuta.[118]

The eleventh Lok Sabha elections occurred in stages between April 27 and May 30, with the bulk of constituencies voting by May 7. The main combatants were the Congress party, the BJP, and a coalition of regional and small national parties under the rubric of the National Front–Left Front Alliance. The nuclear testing imbroglio had captivated the attention of security specialists and a segment of the national elite, but the manifestos of the major parties were "marked by the absence of a serious discussion of foreign policy and national security issues," as Raja Mohan noted.[119] Domestic political matters dominated debate as always: corruption, communalism, caste representation, economic globalization versus self-reliance, secular tradition versus Hindu nationalism.

The main contestants resorted to slogans and platitudes regarding nuclear policy. The Congress party downplayed nuclear issues. Without saying whether and under what conditions India should conduct nuclear tests or exercise its nuclear option, Congress focused on its principled objections to the CTBT and reiterated its position that India's nuclear program was dedicated to peaceful purposes.[120]

The BJP manifesto predictably evinced a bolder stance. "Though the BJP stands committed to a nuclear-free world," it stated, "we cannot accept a world of nuclear apartheid."[121] Thus the party declared it would "reevaluate the country's nuclear policy and exercise the option to induct nuclear weapons." Prejudging such a reevaluation, the party also declared it would not "agree to" the test ban treaty unless it contained a simultaneous agreement on the time-bound elimination of nuclear weapons. Regarding missiles, the manifesto said the party would "expedite the serial production of Prithvi and make Agni I operational for the deployment of these missiles." In addition, it would "hasten the development of Agni II," apparently referring to an effort then under way by the DRDO to develop a longer-range variant of the Agni missiles that had thus far been flight-tested at a range less than half the advertised 2,500 kilometers.

The BJP's language on exercising "the option to induct nuclear weapons" was vaguer than previous or subsequent statements by party leaders. This suggested an intention both to stifle potential domestic and international alarms and to give the party leeway in case it came to power. However, during the campaign BJP spokesmen sent conflicting signals. The party's general secretary, K. N. Govindacharya, declared in early April that a BJP government would test a nuclear weapon if it came to power.[122] This prompted a denial by another BJP spokesman, who said, "The issue of testing has not been discussed. . . . The policy is that we believe India should have its own nuclear deterrent. On testing, we have not taken a formal or official stand. That will be decided at the appropriate time."[123] After thirty-four years of advocating building the bomb, the party still had not developed a national security strategy detailed enough to determine whether nuclear testing was required. The party's de facto prime ministerial candidate, Vajpayee, intimated why—that the bomb was more a matter of national identity and international prestige: "India needs to regain its lost pride," he said in a speech on national television. "[T]he BJP alone can undertake the task of leading a reinvigorated, proud India to its rightful place in the comity of nations."[124]

With all but a handful of Lok Sabha seats decided by mid-May, the BJP won the largest tally with 186 seats. Congress and its allies won 138, its lowest total ever. The National Front took 113 seats, with 95 others going to regional parties and independents.[125] The question became which parties could build a coalition to obtain a majority of 273 to form a government. Because the BJP had won the largest tally, President Shankar Dayal Sharma on May 15 gave it the first opportunity to form a government. Atal Behari Vajpayee was sworn in as prime minister on May 16 and given up to fifteen days to win a vote of confidence for his government in the Lok Sabha. To survive, the BJP needed to persuade at least 75 heretofore nonsupporters in the Lok Sabha to support it. The challenge was daunting insofar as the Congress, the National Front, and others were determined to block the BJP from governing.[126]

Almost immediately, Vajpayee gave Kalam and Chidambaram the long-awaited signal to proceed with nuclear weapon tests. U.S. intelligence detected resumed activity in the spring of 1996, according to *Nucleonics Week*, prompting quiet démarches from the Clinton administration urging Indian officials to exercise forbearance.[127] What the United States did not know was that the Indian team at Pokhran had emplaced at least one nuclear explosive in a test shaft![128] The Indian scientists sought to seize the opportunity afforded by the BJP's nuclear hawkishness as quickly as possible, increasing preparations even before the BJP formed a government. Available sources leave it uncertain how many devices of what type they planned to test or how much technical detail they provided the prime minister.

However, the scientists were soon to be disappointed. Vajpayee, a reflective poet, was a man of propriety and respect for democracy. He thus took at least two advisers (but not many more, if any) into confidence about his authorization of the scientists to conduct nuclear tests and asked for their judgment on it. According to a knowledgeable source, Vajpayee recognized that he had the legal authority to authorize tests but was reminded by an adviser that the action would have major domestic and international consequences.[129] If the BJP did not survive the pending vote of confidence in the Parliament, a successor government would be left to deal with the consequences of an act that it had not authorized. Vajpayee contemplated whether it would be fair to impose this burden on a successor or whether it would be desirable to await the vote of confidence before moving ahead with tests. Vajpayee concluded that he should pause. He asked that the scientists be notified that no test would be conducted pending the outcome of the confidence vote. The Indian public and outside world, including the United States government, did not know of these developments. (At least two Indian journalists with good contacts in the defense science establishment knew of the retracted test authorization months later, as did the author.[130] American policymakers appeared to discount the likelihood of a quick decision to test, despite American intelligence detection of increased activity at the test site at this time.)[131]

The scientists wanted no delay, recalling the setback they suffered in late 1995. The situation was more urgent now that the test ban treaty was nearing completion. The scientists feared that it would be effected whether India signed it or not and that the weight of the international community would then lean so hard on India that no government would authorize nuclear tests. They had high confidence in their designs for fission weapons that could be fitted on the Prithvi or still more easily the Agni. But what they really wanted was the opportunity to demonstrate to the nation and the world their great leap forward to thermonuclear capability and to conduct other explosive experiments that would provide data for long-term computer-aided design activities in case no further tests were to be allowed. They also wanted to test their capacity to use non-weapon-grade plutonium in weapons, a capacity that would significantly increase India's potential stockpile of weapons, as discussed in chapter 15.

A security argument could have been made for testing before the CTBT shut the door. Yet this case was not made with any detailed strategic threat analysis and prescription, and no acute security threat existed. A strong national consensus insisted on maintaining the nuclear option, but practically no one—including the most versed and voluble analysts like Sundarji, Subrahmanyam, Jasjit Singh, Mohan, and Chellaney—argued that India needed more than fission weapons to maintain a viable deterrent. Nor was there a consensus on the need for explosive tests. The weaponeers and successive governments in the late 1980s and early 1990s had enough confidence from laboratory testing of weapon components to believe that their fission weapons would work without having to conduct full-scale explosive tests. On the other hand, the military services by now clearly preferred to see weapons tested if they were going to be required to deliver them in war.

On May 28, just twelve days after assuming power, the Vajpayee government lost the vote of confidence. The opposition united over political convenience and fears of potential BJP religious and cultural intolerance. A new coalition government comprising thirteen parties and backed from the outside by the Congress party took over. It was headed by the sixty-three-year-old H. D. Deve Gowda. Dubbed the United Front, the new government was destined for fractiousness. Gowda, until now chief minister of the small southern state of Karnataka, had no experience in foreign and national security policy. Indeed, he had little travel exposure to the outside world. As his coalition government formed by allocating cabinet posts among leaders of its dozen-plus constituent parties, the mosaic of India appeared vividly. The majority of new ministers were not Brahmins, and differences of language, caste, regional origin, and ideology abounded. The prime minister and the defence minister—the former wrestler and current Uttar Pradesh political heavyweight Mulayam Singh Yadav—did not share fluency in a common language. Similarly, Yadav and Abdul Kalam labored to communicate in Kalam's preferred English.

Gowda inherited a frustrated defense and atomic energy scientific leadership. The top three leaders of the strategic enclave—Kalam, Chidambaram, and Santhanam—had reacted angrily to being told that political propriety required putting off the tests until the BJP's confidence vote.[132] It is not clear whether Gowda had been informed of Vajpayee's earlier tentative authorization to test and its reversal.[133] In any case, the scientists soon renewed their request. Gowda demurred. According to a knowledgeable source, he did not say no, but he also did not feel that conducting nuclear tests was a high priority that required urgent attention. At some point in Gowda's tenure, probably late summer of 1996, the weaponeers removed the nuclear device(s) that had been emplaced at the test site for "a world record" period of time, according to one of the scientists involved.[134] Two years later, following the five nuclear explosions, Gowda said that "[a]s a prime minister I declined to give clearance for demonstrating India's nuclear capability not because of the likely reaction from the international community but because of concern for the economic situation."[135] A scientist who discussed the testing issue with him recalled that Gowda said in his native Kannada, "I don't like this. I want to make our people better."[136]

CONCLUSION

The indefinite extension of the NPT demonstrated to Indian politicians, pundits, and the strategic enclave that the U.S.-led nonproliferation regime was marching forward. The next two items on the regime's agenda—treaties to ban nuclear testing and unsafeguarded fissile material production—confronted India with unprecedented, difficult choices. To hold out against these treaties would further isolate the country and sharply diminish its international credibility. Yet to accede to them would amount to "capping" India's nuclear capability, which the strategic enclave, the small circle of security analysts, and the BJP did not want to do. If full-scale explosive testing was necessary to give confidence in India's nuclear weapons and recruit and train a new generation of scientists and engineers, it would become much more difficult in a test ban environment. Proving thermonuclear designs would be practically impossible without tests. Knowing this, and comprehending that the armed forces would be reluctant to rely on untested nuclear weapons, the weaponeers and the small strategic analysis community mobilized in late 1995 to persuade politicians to authorize tests before the window of opportunity closed.

In Narasimha Rao the scientists and engineers faced a prime minister with a traditional Indian aversion to nuclear weapons and nuclear doctrine and a determination to build India through economic growth and international engagement. In Deve Gowda they faced basically the same. The BJP had offered hope to the strategic enclave precisely because it was the only party to come to power in Indian history *without* a normative aversion to nuclear weapons. The BJP believed more in the norm of India as a great power in the *existing* international system than in the vision of India as a potential source for the moral *transformation* of the international system. Fifty years of experience suggested that moral suasion, self-restraint, and diplomacy would not induce the world's major powers to provide equitable dispensation on issues like nuclear disarmament. Overtly demonstrated and deployed nuclear and ballistic missile systems might provide more leverage. If not, a tested nuclear arsenal would provide strength against Pakistan, China, and the United States, and would deliver to Hindu India the international status it deserved as a great civilization and nation. This belief, more than anything else, explained the BJP leadership's initial inclination to say yes to the strategic enclave on nuclear tests.

Decision making remained ad hoc, the province of the prime minister, a handful of advisers, and the top leaders of the DRDO and the AEC. The scientists and engineers were the only people who knew all details of India's nuclear and missile programs. Prime ministers, cabinet secretaries, and principal secretaries knew only what the weaponeers told them, and this depended on personal relations and the extent to which the political leaders *wanted* to know details. Some pundits such as Subrahmanyam, Sundarji, Jasjit Singh, and Chellaney knew more because the scientists chose to inform them to help make the public case for nuclear testing and deployment of an arsenal. Parliamentarians, the nominal representatives of the people, were given almost no important information and exerted no real oversight of nuclear and strategic policy. Perhaps most remarkably, the top leaders of the armed forces played minimal roles in policy formation. As Deve Gowda put it in May 1998, "The decision to conduct the nuclear tests is not a military decision. It is a political decision . . . made by two or three persons in your cabinet."[137]

As the final two chapters discuss, the indigenous values and approaches to nuclear weapons and strategic decision making that led to India's remarkably self-restrained nuclear policies during the 1960s through the early 1990s now came under enormous pressure to change. Nationalist resistance to the pressures of the neocolonial nonproliferation regime and the national desire to win recognition as a major power mounted. In a world where the five permanent members of the UN Security Council possessed nuclear weapons and the dominant Realist school of international relations theory and practice assumed that countries of India's size, ambition, and strategic environment would seek nuclear weapons, it became more difficult for Indian elites to support the tradition of nuclear self-restraint.

FOURTEEN

India Rejects the CTBT

JUNE 1996–DECEMBER 1997

From June 1996 through March 1997, Indian nuclear policy remained in suspended animation. Final negotiations of the Comprehensive Test Ban Treaty posed an enormous challenge to the government, as the political class rallied cohesively against the treaty while the international community pressured India to sign it. Similarly, Indian weaponeers and many pundits continued to urge nuclear tests and the deployment of the Prithvi missile, while political-economic priorities and international considerations called for diplomatic magnanimity. The case for diplomacy was augmented by Chinese President Jiang Zemin's visit to South Asia in late 1996, which manifested Beijing's growing recognition of India's importance relative to Pakistan. Inder Gujral—first as foreign minister, then, after April 21, 1997, as prime minister—achieved major breakthroughs in relations with Bangladesh, Nepal, and Sri Lanka, as well as a resumption of direct high-level dialogue with Pakistan. By June 1997, talks yielded hopes of a genuine process for normalizing relations. Unfortunately, by September political uncertainties caused India to backtrack on Kashmir diplomacy, upsetting the politics of diplomacy in Pakistan.

During this period, India's new, magnanimous brand of diplomacy toward its smaller neighbors, which came to be known as the "Gujral Doctrine," and India's general political-economic progress prompted American leaders to raise India on Washington's agenda. Yet, as 1997 ended, national elections loomed again as India struggled for a clear sense of political direction. Nuclear policy became caught in an updraft caused by this political turbulence, rising hawkishly on currents that this chapter describes.

THE CTBT DENOUEMENT, JUNE TO SEPTEMBER 1996

Throughout the summer of 1996, nuclear policy revolved around the CTBT negotiations, which were entering their final stages. Practically no one except the strategic enclave and a handful of BJP leaders knew how close the government had come to conducting nuclear weapon tests in May. India continued to demand a time-bound framework for nuclear disarmament as part of the treaty, arguing that without this it would be merely a nonproliferation measure. Indian officials also objected to the treaty's allowance of so-called subcritical tests that do not have an explosive yield.[1] The United States and other nuclear weapon states wanted to reserve the right to conduct such tests to assess the reliability and safety of nuclear weapons in perpetuity. India and other critics alleged that such activities would allow ongoing nuclear weapon development, contrary to the spirit of the treaty.

India also found particularly repugnant the draft treaty's entry-into-force clause. Though it went through several iterations, the provision's basic idea was to make the treaty's implementation contingent on its ratification by a list of certain states. The criteria for including states on the list changed during the negotiations, but each time the list included India, Pakistan, and Israel.[2] These were the three main "targets" of the treaty in the eyes of the nuclear weapon states. Indian officials feared that treaty parties might use this clause to impose sanctions on India if it refused to sign. Though the United States in fact did not author the entry-into-force provision and disagreed with its British, Russian, and Chinese proponents, Indians tended to blame Washington for it.[3]

On June 20, India's ambassador to the Geneva talks, Arundhati Ghose, gave an important speech summarizing India's objections and disabusing American and other officials who thought that India could be pressured into going along with the majority now favoring the treaty.[4] Ghose, a fiery, bespectacled diplomat, argued that the CTBT as drafted reaffirmed the perpetuation of nuclear apartheid. India in 1995 had expressed its "dismay at the indefinite extension of the NPT because," in India's view, the treaty "sought to legitimise indefinite possession of nuclear weapons by five countries," Ghose said. "Today, the right to continue development and refinement of their arsenals is being sought to be legitimised through another flawed and eternal treaty."[5]

More remarkably, Ghose declared that "our national security considerations" will be "a key factor in our decision making."[6] This otherwise unexceptional invocation of national security actually signaled an innovation in India's nuclear diplomacy. Critics in New Delhi had frequently bemoaned the state's reliance on moral argumentation in nuclear affairs. They urged instead more hard-headed thinking and rhetoric about "national security." Pundits and arms control experts like the Ministry of External Affair's Rakesh Sood believed that the United States and others would pay more attention to Realpolitik presentations than to traditional moralism, whether or not India actually had a clear national security strategy. In her June 20 speech and others, Ghose followed close daily instructions from Sood, at a time when three changes in government during May and June left the ministry without top political leadership.[7] Ghose's speech also had been vetted by AEC Chairman Chidambaram, who welcomed the invocation of national security arguments to protect India's option to conduct nuclear tests.[8] Having twice come so close to getting their wish to test, the weaponeers would resist any move by political leaders now to sign the CTBT.

Of course, there were flaws in Ghose's case. The treaty had an "escape clause" allowing a signatory to withdraw after giving six months' notice and specifying "the extraordinary event or events" that it regarded as "jeopardizing its supreme interests."[9] This made the treaty less than eternal if India had justification for withdrawing from it. Similarly, as offensive as the entry-into-force clause appeared, no one could force India to join the treaty. Finally, while the treaty did not commit the nuclear weapon states to further steps toward nuclear disarmament, it clearly contributed to the goal, as India had acknowledged earlier in the negotiations. Banning nuclear tests is a necessary if not sufficient measure to end nuclear arms racing, to devalue nuclear weapons, and to facilitate disarmament. This was precisely why nuclear weapon establishments had fought against the treaty for decades.

India faced enormous international pressure to sign the treaty but even greater domestic pressure not to. This caused such severe strain on the government that it could not take on the added burden of actually conducting tests at this time—exactly what the scientists had feared.

Making matters worse, the nuclear establishment came under criticism for safety problems at nuclear power plants. On May 12, a fire reportedly erupted at the Narora power plant, prompting observers to call for serious independent monitoring of this and other plants.[10] The chairman of the Atomic Energy Regulatory Board (AERB), Dr. A. Gopalakrishnan, had recently warned of the deficiencies at older nuclear plants and expressed the need for greater independence of the regulatory body from the Department of Atomic Energy. As the system stood, Gopalakrishnan said, the AERB—the regulator—was "subservient to those whom he is supposed to regulate."[11] Controversy ensued when the Department of Atomic Energy notified the Berkeley-trained nuclear engineer that his contract would not be renewed, heightening perceptions of excessive secrecy and self-protection in the nuclear establishment.[12] This was the same Gopalakrishnan who in the mid-1980s had played a leading role in India's attempt to design a reactor for a nuclear-powered submarine until he was fired in November 1986 from his post as project general manager for Bharat Heavy Electronics Ltd.[13]

The Department of Atomic Energy—in all its endeavors—found itself caught in a vicious circle: government and parliamentary bodies criticized its large cost overruns and poor efficiency and then reduced government funding. This simply exacerbated the problems for which the establishment felt unfairly criticized.[14] Although budget figures are difficult to assess, Eric Arnett, an analyst at the Stockholm International Peace Research Institute, concluded that the Department of Atomic Energy's budget had declined by 70 percent in constant dollars since 1988.[15] Nonplan expenditures actually offset some of this decline, but, excluding inflation, total actual expenditures fell by roughly 29 percent between 1992–1993 and 1995–1996.[16] As of 1996, the target for nuclear power production by the year 2004 had been cut to 3,320 megawatts, down from the 10,000 megawatts planned in 1985 and the target of 5,300 megawatts announced in 1990.[17] With dwindling prospects in the nuclear power realm, the nuclear establishment placed increasing stock in its national defense mission. But here, too, it was hamstrung.

An unnamed nuclear official condemned India's nuclear policy as the worst of all worlds. "By not signing the CTBT you will invite international opprobrium, including sanctions," the official told the *Times of India*.[18] "As it is since 1975, the developed countries have stopped giving us vital technology, thus affecting our nuclear power generation, which, at the moment is pitiably low at 1700 Megawatt." But, the official continued, accepting this "pain" without seeking to "gain" from nuclear weapon tests "does not make any sense."[19]

China deepened the frustration by conducting its forty-fourth nuclear weapon test on June 7, days after agreeing in the Geneva negotiations to drop its insistence on retaining the right to conduct peaceful nuclear explosions under a test ban treaty. This followed a Chinese pattern of conducting nuclear tests immediately in the wake of "concessions" in international arms control and nonproliferation negotiations, and it rekindled Indian strategists' criticisms of New Delhi's approach. "Unlike China which sees the relationship between arms control and national security in a balanced perspective," Raja Mohan wrote, "India is obsessed with unrealisable goals of global disarmament."[20] In contrast, Mohan lamented, if India had "followed the much admired Chinese example, New Delhi could have announced a series of nuclear tests, at the end of which it could have considered signing the test ban treaty. Instead, India appears to have been deterred by its own fears."

Thus, those who saw nuclear weapons as a key to India's international power and security took little solace in the government's rejection of the test ban treaty. New Delhi stuck to its position as other negotiators scrambled to propose minor adjustments that might win India's support. Public opinion generally backed this defiance. Still, a few writers and intellectuals such as Praful Bidwai, Achin Vanaik, and Dhirendra Sharma urged signing the treaty as an important, albeit flawed, measure to augment nuclear disarmament. As Bidwai wrote, "Whatever the weaknesses of the present CTBT, it is indisputably a normative measure favouring nuclear arms reduction and disarmament, and a commitment not to conduct nuclear test explosions. This commitment is the least that India can demand of the world, and above all, of itself."[21]

On July 15, Foreign Minister Gujral gave a speech to Parliament reaffirming India's inclination to block consensus on the CTBT in Geneva. Because the Conference on Disarmament operates on a consensus basis, India could prevent the body from completing an otherwise agreed-to treaty. Gujral reiterated India's view that a test ban treaty would not contribute seriously to nuclear disarmament unless it were integrated into a time-specific agenda of further disarmament steps. He added that India was "willing to negotiate" what was a "reasonable time frame."[22] He concluded that "national security considerations will be the governing factor in our decision making" as long as "other countries in our region continue their weapon programs, whether openly or in a clandestine manner."[23]

In late July, U.S. Secretary of State Warren Christopher met with Gujral in Indonesia to try to reassure India that the treaty's entry-into-force provision would not lead to sanctions or other "punishment" if India refused to sign the treaty. The provision (Article XIV) specified that if the treaty had not entered into force within three years after it became open for signature, a conference of ratified parties would be convened to consider ways to accelerate the ratification process to facilitate entry into force. To India, this raised the specter of sanctions or other means to coerce India to join the treaty so it could enter into force. (Indeed, some Indians later cited fear of possible coercion from such a CTBT conference to justify the nuclear tests in May 1998.) Christopher's attempt to reassure Gujral in Jakarta reflected American officials' regrets that they had been unable to persuade first the United Kingdom, then China and Russia to alter the entry-into-force provision. The United States wanted India not to block the Conference on Disarmament in Geneva from reaching consensus on the treaty but accepted that India would not sign it in the near future.

Gujral had been unmoved in Jakarta, so Christopher tried again in a letter delivered to the foreign minister on August 9. The letter reaffirmed that although it was too late to change the treaty text, the United States categorically assured India that the treaty entailed no right or intention by parties to impose any coercive sanctions on India for not signing and ratifying it, now or later when treaty parties convened their conference.[24] The distinguished journalist Prem Shankar Jha noted at the time that history had taught India to be wary of U.S. commitments, recalling the unilateral "renegotiation" of the Tarapur fuel contract and the reversal of Reagan's promise to sell India a Cray XMP-24 supercomputer.[25] Yet he concluded that Christopher's offer represented a significant accommodation of India's position and an indirect acknowledgment of India's nuclear weapon capability. Moreover, Jha wrote, since "India's veto is not likely to block the proponents from [adopting the treaty at] the U.N. any way," India should take Christopher's offer and not prevent consensus in Geneva. American officials, for their part, saw that Gujral could have "pocketed" the U.S. assurance of noncoercion in return for not blocking in Geneva and still not sign the treaty.[26] However, American officials did not recognize how personally Indian leaders like Gujral took these negotiations. Gujral, a proud veteran of the independence movement, bridled at any appearance of colonial attitudes on the part of the world's great powers. In an interview he recalled with evident feeling that Secretary of State Christopher had treated him patronizingly in a phone call prior to their meeting in Jakarta and in their subsequent interactions.[27] Gujral remembered that when he traveled to New York for the early fall 1996 UN General Assembly meeting Christopher "refused to receive me, let alone share a meal." He continued, "[T]his is frequently the way you Americans treat Indians—unless we do something to make you stop and pay attention, you patronize us."

Politics, pride, and principle now prevailed over pragmatism. The CTBT had become a symbol of Indian resistance to hypocrisy and colonial coercion. A compromise based on nuance would have been misunderstood as a total surrender.

To stiffen the politicians' spines, DRDO head Abdul Kalam once again went public, giving a speech in which he urged the government to speed defense research programs and disregard American pressure. In an unusual breech of discretion, the defense science adviser told journalists on August 7 that he had submitted a proposal to the government to conduct additional development flights of the Agni missile.[28] Kalam welcomed any attention he could divert to the Agni. Except for the Prithvi, the other projects in the missile program had fallen way behind schedule. The Akash, Nag, and Trishul had not been fully validated in their flight tests to date and had not won military orders. The Prithvi was the only system that had been proved and ordered by the military (albeit reluctantly), but that had been done essentially before Kalam took over the DRDO.[29] Thus, the Agni was his priority, and he wanted to rally greater support to it.

Kalam's lobbying predictably generated press and elite support. The *Hindustan Times* editorialized in favor of resuming Agni tests.[30] The day after Kalam's volley, BJP foreign affairs spokesman Brajesh Mishra went further and insisted that "[w]e must conduct one or more nuclear tests in order to design nuclear warheads for our missiles."[31] Mishra would become an increasingly important shaper of India's nuclear policy. A group of strategic analysts and former officials issued a statement on August 9 calling for India to declare itself a nuclear weapon state.[32] Former Vice Chief of Naval Staff Admiral K. K. Nayyar declared it "essential to conduct a series of nuclear tests," as did Raja Mohan, arguing that India must "cross the psychological barrier."[33]

On August 14, India blocked consensus on the CTBT in Geneva. Pro-treaty forces in Geneva then proposed an alternative procedure for sending the treaty to the United Nations for a vote. India blocked this move, too, on August 20. However, Australia, encouraged by the United States and others, then initiated a plan to bypass the Conference on Disarmament and take the treaty directly to the UN General Assembly. India now began a more difficult campaign to keep the treaty from reaching the General Assembly or, if it arrived, to encourage amendments to it. However, Indian diplomats found few takers. The nation was isolated. The rest of the world appeared glad for the progress represented in the treaty, tired of seeking greater disarmament commitments from the nuclear weapon states and skeptical of India's credibility on the issue given its nuclear weapon and ballistic missile programs. Indeed, India's weaponeers and many pundits opposed the treaty precisely because they wanted India to conduct nuclear weapon tests.

On September 10, the UN General Assembly voted for the CTBT (as drafted in Geneva) by a margin of 158 to 3. Only India, neighboring Bhutan, and Libya voted against it. Pakistan did not vote against the treaty, but it also did not sign it.

NOW WHAT? SEPTEMBER TO NOVEMBER 1996

"India has hardly ever been so united internally, or so isolated internationally, as on the issue of the Comprehensive Test Ban Treaty," the *Times of India* noted. But, it asked, "[i]s the resolute stance we have taken against the . . . treaty really in the best long-term interests of the nation?"[34] To answer this vital question, it was necessary to specify the security or other interests India needed to protect and what kinds of nuclear and delivery-system capability and doctrine the state needed.

A handful of pundits had tried to answer these questions during the CTBT debate, as before, but a national consensus remained lacking. In the aftermath of the negotiations, the public debate intensified.

For its part, the government remained vague. As Foreign Minister Gujral told an interviewer from the *International Herald Tribune*, conducting another nuclear test "is not on our agenda in the immediate future. . . . We will continue our restraint but not surrender our option." When asked if India had nuclear weapons already, he replied, "Not to my knowledge. I don't think we have."[35] The latter comment revealed the limited distribution of information about India's true nuclear capabilities: only the top scientists, the prime minister, and perhaps his closest personal advisers knew, not the foreign minister. If the nuclear option must be retained, the government did not suggest when it should be exercised. "As to the 'right time,' " Gujral told Parliament, this would require "a bigger debate."[36] The government believed that India needed only the capacity to assemble and deliver quickly a nuclear retaliatory blow to an adversary, and such a capacity existed in the strategic enclave's undeclared possession of perhaps two dozen or more fission devices, which could be delivered by air force units that had by now practiced the necessary operations and perhaps by Prithvi missiles.[37] While this capacity was clearly adequate against Pakistan, India did not appear to have the means of delivering nuclear weapons to major Chinese targets. In any case, India did not officially declare China a military threat requiring nuclear countermeasures.

Raja Ramanna added his weight to those who thought that nuclear tests were unnecessary to maintain an adequate deterrent. In October he declared that a "plutonium bomb is sufficient enough to act as a deterrent and we have that capability" without the need for further tests.[38] What would require tests would be thermonuclear weapons. But, he asked, "[i]f the present capability is enough to produce bombs, why do you want thermo nuclear [sic] tests?" Instead of concentrating attention on nuclear weapons, he argued that India should devote itself to increasing nuclear energy production.

K. Sundarji echoed Ramanna in arguing that India needed only a "minimum nuclear deterrence," which could be achieved by the *survivable* deployment of about "15 weapons of about 20 kiloton yield each," against a country like Pakistan, "and about 30 such for even a larger country."[39] Sundarji did not say whether nuclear tests were required to effect such a deterrent, but he argued that if they were, India should do the tests and then sign the CTBT. "[I]t is in our interest if an effective CTBT is in place even if it is flawed," he concluded.

Yet, other voices in the debate wanted more. A prominent BJP figure, Mohan Guruswamy, asserted in October that "[t]o really be a credible nuclear power we need to develop, both bigger and miniaturised nuclear weapons and an array of delivery vehicles. [T]his means hydrogen bombs and tactical nuclear warheads, ICBMs and cruise missiles, and missile launching nuclear submarines and long-range bombers."[40] Guruswamy, who studied security strategy at Harvard's Kennedy School of Government in the early 1980s, did not address the expense, time, and strategic complications of such an arsenal, nor the doctrine that would guide it. Yet Guruswamy reflected a desire of an extreme segment of the polity and perhaps scientists like Kalam and Chidambaram to possess whatever the great powers did.[41]

Once again, K. Subrahmanyam tried to sort through India's nuclear alternatives. He argued that Western nuclear experience indicated that more nuclear tests were not necessary to build a deterrent based on fission weapons.[42] While "further refinement of the first generation weapons" might require explosive tests, such weapons would "be necessitated only in case a war fighting scenario with an identified enemy is envisaged." Yet, Subrahmanyam and almost all other Indian analysts rejected nuclear war fighting as immoral and unwinnable on the subcontinent. Those who argued for conducting nuclear tests, he suggested, wanted to develop thermonuclear weapons "in order to have a credible deterrent against China." Subrahmanyam rejected this as long as India was able to develop a missile capability that "can reach cities in Southern China"—that is, an improved Agni. "[C]an we think of contingencies," he asked, "in which China would risk its cities to retaliatory strikes even with 15–20 kiloton weapons?"

Subrahmanyam did not dismiss the China problem. "Irrespective of the state of relationship at any particular time," he argued, "India and China will constitute mutual challenges to each other" due to their size, their proximity, their civilizational identities, and their world ambitions.[43] In the near term, China's assistance to Pakistan's nuclear and missile programs would trouble India, as would the United States' perceived softness in punishing China for that assistance.[44] Thus he argued that India should "adopt a policy of directly befriending China and, at the same time," balancing China's power through "an Asian and global balance of power system." To do this, India must demonstrate its "will to power" and end the "vague" nuclear option policy by declaring itself "as an independent global player with a nuclear deterrent." But this did not require more than the capability to deliver fission weapons to a small number of Chinese targets under a strict no-first-use doctrine. Nor did it necessarily require mating nuclear warheads to missiles in advance.

If Subrahmanyam offered a coherent nuclear strategy, he also knew that it would not be adopted or even systematically debated if the government, including Parliament, did not make an unprecedented effort to address the issue seriously. Here he, and others, remained frustrated. Notwithstanding the drama of the testing and CTBT issues since December 1995, the government was simply too preoccupied with political-economic issues to initiate and manage a decisive, open review of nuclear strategy. Rejection of the CTBT kept the weaponeers' hopes alive and bought more time for the political leadership to weigh India's options.

Parallel to the Indian debate over nuclear strategy, India's relations with the United States and the United Nations continued to evolve. Immediately after the CTBT vote, the United States communicated its ongoing desire to improve relations with India. State Department spokesman Nicholas Burns reminded reporters after the CTBT vote that "the health of . . . Indo-US relations . . . has improved . . . over several years and we want to maintain that growth."[45] President Clinton said he believed that "we can find a way for the Indians to have their security concerns met" and thereby sign the CTBT.[46] (The president offered no strategy for doing this, however.) On September 31, the bilateral Defense Policy Group, which had been established during Defense Secretary William Perry's January 1995 trip to India, began two days of meetings in New Delhi on defense cooperation. The two sides purposely avoided discussing the CTBT issue and instead concentrated on broader strategic issues and perceptions. They also reportedly agreed to increase the scale and sophistication of their joint military exercises.[47]

In India, leaders and pundits recognized the need to reduce the anti-American fever generated by the CTBT debate. An unattributed column in the *Hindustan Times* noted that despite the "virulent anti-Americanism of the Indian elite," the United States is where they want "to send their sons and daughters to study" and the United States is the source of high technology and other material and intellectual achievements desired in India.[48] The Indian government took out a full-page ad in the *Washington Post* on October 2, in which Prime Minister Gowda commended the "remarkable improvement" in Indo-U.S. relations in recent years and highlighted India's growing market. The advertisement included a statement by Foreign Minister Gujral explaining India's position on the CTBT and saying an "emphatic no" to those who thought the issue had "strained relations" between the two countries.[49]

If the relationship with the United States looked to be rebounding, India was headed for a humiliating slap by the international community at the United Nations. In the General Assembly's meetings in October, a vote was scheduled to select five rotating members for two-year terms on the Security Council. India badly wanted the "Asian" seat, as did Japan. The body voted on October 21 and issued a stinging message to India: Japan won 142 to 40.[50] India's insistent effort to block the CTBT first in Geneva and then in New York had not been forgotten. Gujral acknowledged this to reporters, saying that after the CTBT negotiations, "I was under no impression we were going to win."[51] In a December parliamentary debate, Gujral said that if Parliament permitted him to sign the CTBT, then he would "promise them" permanent membership on the Security Council.[52]

When Bill Clinton was reelected in early November, Prime Minister Gowda congratulated him and renewed an invitation for the president to visit India at an early date. India's fiftieth anniversary as an independent state would be celebrated throughout 1997, and Gowda, on behalf of the Indian people, hoped Clinton would come to celebrate.[53] (Clinton soon indicated a desire to accept the invitation, but political uncertainties in India in 1997 compelled a postponement.)

Meanwhile, in Pakistan, President Farooq Ahmad Khan Leghari on November 5 exercised his constitutional prerogative and dissolved the National Assembly and dismissed Benazir Bhutto from the prime ministership. Among other reasons, Leghari cited widespread corruption and "extra-judicial killings" in Karachi. He called for general elections on February 3, 1997, and appointed an interim government.[54]

JIANG ZEMIN'S PIVOTAL VISIT
TO SOUTH ASIA, NOVEMBER 1996

On November 28, 1996, Jiang Zemin arrived in New Delhi for a state visit, the first Chinese president ever to do so. The visit symbolized China's growing respect for India and recognition that Beijing, for all its global and East Asian preoccupations, must attend to South Asian relations as well. The two governments signed four agreements, the most important of which was a measure to further the withdrawal of forces and enhance confidence building along the "Line of Actual Control" separating the two countries.[55] In a press conference, a Chinese foreign ministry spokesman denied that China had provided nuclear weapon technology or M-11 missiles to Pakistan but also declared that China would not sell advanced weapons to its neighbors.[56] The denial of past activities was false, but the statement about future activities, made on Indian soil and backed by recent American progress in nonproliferation diplomacy with China, offered some hope that Beijing actually would stem the flow of sensitive technology and assistance to Pakistan.

The most important development of Jiang's trip occurred in Pakistan. The Pakistanis were naturally concerned that Beijing was elevating its interest in India relative to Pakistan. The Chinese recognized this concern and offered positive reassurances to Pakistan, including a strong reaffirmation of cooperation in peaceful nuclear power projects. However, Jiang delivered a diplomatically veiled blow by calling for Pakistan and India to negotiate a settlement on Kashmir. This seemingly banal statement actually signaled that Beijing "no longer recognises [Kashmir] as an international issue, notwithstanding the UN resolutions," a Pakistani daily noted.[57] Pakistan always had sought international mediation on Kashmir, fearing that it could not stand up to India in direct talks. Now, erstwhile ally China was undercutting this position. Jiang essentially urged Pakistan to set aside the Kashmir issue and improve relations with India, much as China had successfully urged India to do regarding their own border dispute.[58]

Most Indian press commentary hailed the Jiang visit as a shift in China's regard toward India. Some, such as Brahma Chellaney, continued to bristle at China's haughtiness toward India and Beijing's strategy "to tie India down south of the Himalayas to prevent its rise as a rival."[59] But Jiang's message to the Pakistanis actually suggested China's interest in stabilizing Indo-Pak relations. China seemed interested in reducing stimuli for India's missile and nuclear programs and diminishing the salience of China's role in providing Pakistan with missile and nuclear weapon assistance.

If China's greater international power and rank bothered Indian strategists, Raja Mohan argued that the fault lay with India. "India's relative decline, vis a vis China, has arisen less from Beijing's advances, and more from New Delhi's stagnation," he wrote.[60] Mohan recognized that China's power derived from "average annual growth rates topping 10 percent," while "most international observers" doubted if India could "get its act together to launch itself on a path of sustained high economic growth rates." The imperatives for India therefore were to build cooperative relations with China, be patient on the border dispute, and attend to domestic reforms and regional stabilization so India could emerge as a major player. Regarding the nuclear issue, Mohan concluded that India has "whined too long" and "relied on actions of other States to resolve its nuclear dilemmas." Instead, he concluded vaguely, "India needs to take final decisions on defining its nuclear and missile posture that will help establish a stable deterrence between India and Pakistan on the one hand and between India and China on the other."

Mohan did not have in mind a step that Gowda announced shortly after Jiang's departure. On December 5, the Defence Ministry issued a report to Parliament stating that the government would not produce Agni missiles unless its security was threatened. Declaring that the Agni was a successful "re-entry technology demonstration project," the report said that a decision "to develop and produce a missile system based on Agni technology . . . can be taken at an appropriate time consistent with the prevailing threat perception and global or regional security environment."[61]

Indian security analysts quickly charged the government with buckling under U.S. pressure and speculated further that the move was a sop to China in the wake of the Jiang visit.[62] The BJP blasted the move, countering that "[d]evelopment and deployment of this missile should not be delayed or stopped under pressure."[63] Never mind that the Defence Ministry's statement accurately reflected the development strategy behind the Agni program and that producing a militarily useful intermediate-range missile would require significant technological advances over the model that had been flight-tested previously.

The government's announcement represented a rebuke of sorts to Abdul Kalam, and he fought back. On December 12, the *Business Standard* reported that a DRDO source had said little time would be required to assemble and prepare the Agni missile for launch if the government ordered it.[64] And on December 14, Defence Minister Mulayam Singh Yadav denied that the Agni program had been suspended.[65] The apparent confusion over the issue prompted the *Times of India* to editorialize against continued "adhocism" plaguing "the formulation of our national security policy."[66]

As 1996 came to an end, Indian strategic policy remained bedeviled by competing domestic and international interests and an incapacity to do more than muddle along. The national determination to resist the perceived colonial pressures and inequities of the CTBT negotiations expressed domestically rooted predilections, while the government's caution on nuclear testing and missile deployment reflected accession to international pressures. (To help keep the testing option open and palliate those who had been disappointed over the aborted test decision in May, the government in December extended Chidambaram's tenure as AEC chairman for another two years.) Even the progress with China frustrated those who wanted the state somehow to rise above its internal liabilities and be regarded as a major power. As former Defence Minister K. C. Pant noted, "China inspires awe far and wide. India, in contrast, is perceived as a soft state, a country wide open to external pressure and hesitant to take hard decisions."[67]

Yet domestic struggles in the political and economic realms contributed to indecision as they had since 1964. The thirteen-party ruling coalition remained a fractious mix of competing ideologies and interests—communists, regional parties, and free-marketeers. The economy, while achieving a decent growth rate of roughly 5 percent, still suffered serious structural and fiscal weaknesses.[68] The defense budget for 1996–1997 called for an increase of 3.4 percent, significantly lower than the rate of inflation.[69] This frustrated the service chiefs who saw their modernization needs going unmet, but as the *Hindu* noted, a rise in defense spending was not "feasible in the fast changing political and social context in this country."[70] The plain fact was that the nation of 938 million remained unavoidably challenged by its very size, diversity, poverty, and democratically expressed fractiousness. No nation on earth posed such a challenge of democratic governance. India's elected leaders could be forgiven their preoccupation with immediate, close-to-home priorities.

INDIA WINS GROWING INTERNATIONAL RECOGNITION, 1997

India's positive, if still inadequate, economic development since 1991 and the imperative of avoiding nuclear instability in the subcontinent prompted American foreign policy leaders to give the nation greater due. The potential threat that enigmatic China represented also caused some in Washington to see India as a possible source of balance in Asia.

In early January 1997, the Council on Foreign Relations issued a major report by an Independent Task Force on South Asia that had been convened to address U.S. policy options toward the region. The task force had been created at the instigation of Deputy Secretary of State Strobe Talbott, who welcomed outside assistance in shaping a more effective American approach to the difficult region. The twenty-eight-member task force's report expressed several major themes relevant to nuclear policy. It acknowledged that "India and Pakistan . . . have become de facto nuclear weapons-capable states and show no sign today of reversing course."[71] The task force believed that "India has the potential to emerge as a full-fledged major power in the coming decades," which led to the conclusion that instead of allowing nonproliferation policy to stifle American involvement with India, Washington should engage it and Pakistan "more rather than less."[72] This engagement should be on a host of economic, political, and other issues, as well as nuclear problems. Regarding the latter, the United States should seek to encourage India and Pakistan to establish a "more stable plateau for their nuclear competition." This plateau should be characterized by agreements not to test nuclear explosives, deploy nuclear weapons, and "export nuclear weapon- or missile-related material, technology, or expertise."[73] While many contributors recorded dissenting or qualifying views, almost all of them agreed with the fundamental point that progress in the region, as well as American interests, required an India-first strategy. This, as Raja Mohan noted, was "a major contribution" of the task force.[74]

The report stimulated scores of commentaries and references in India. Almost all were positive, although many cautioned that calls for greater Indo-American cooperation had been made before, only to be muted by subsequent disappointing events.[75] Remarkably, given India's international isolation on the CTBT issue, practically all Indian commentators concentrated only on steps the United States would have to take to draw India into a more productive relationship. Few addressed what India might need to do to make an effective strategic relationship with the United States.

THE GUJRAL DOCTRINE

Most Indian elites also gained confidence from the policies Foreign Minister Inder Gujral was effecting toward India's smaller South Asian neighbors. These policies won plaudits from the United States and others as well for indicating that India could become a constructive regional and global player. The "Gujral Doctrine" revolved around five principles, which were first enunciated in a September 1996 speech by Gujral at Chatham House, London, and then amplified in a mid-January 1997 speech in Colombo, Sri Lanka.[76] The basic idea was that India, as the region's great power, would act magnanimously in resolving heretofore contentious issues with the smaller states and create a regional norm and practice of noninterference in others' affairs. This new strategy evinced a much more cooperative tone and purpose than the 1983 "Indira Doctrine."

Gujral applied these principles in Bangladesh, Sri Lanka, and Nepal, without obstruction from the Indian polity. Perhaps most dramatically, India and Bangladesh on December 12, 1996, signed an agreement on Ganges River water sharing. This culminated years of on-again, off-again discussions and, more recently, unofficial "Track II" diplomacy.[77] The agreement showed how determined diplomacy could solve what had been regarded as an intractable problem.

Regarding Pakistan, Gujral's approach was more guarded. He did not include Pakistan in the list of states to which his doctrine applied, and several of its principles pointedly were not being applied by Pakistan's and India's intelligence services in their activities against each other. India did not mind if Pakistan was disturbed by its omission. Gujral sought to show that Pakistan would not bog India down in the region. Yet Gujral made it clear that he wanted to improve relations. He volunteered that India would ignore "needless provocations" from Pakistan and would not respond to Pakistani rhetoric on issues like Kashmir.[78] He also declared that India was ready for high-level talks with Pakistan after the Pakistani elections were held in early February.

The unusual decisiveness and tone of these overtures owed much to Gujral's intellect and character. Born in Jhelum, a city between Rawalpindi and Lahore in what is now the Pakistani part of Punjab, Gujral retained an affinity for the region and its culture. He participated in the independence movement against Great Britain from an early age, spending his first time in jail when he was ten. Rising through the Congress party, he was the minister for information and broadcasting at the time of the 1974 Pokhran blast, and then later joined the Janata Dal. Now, near the end of his career, the soft-spoken Gujral pursued a strategy to win India its desired place in the global order by first winning the confidence of its neighbors. Some of the initiatives he completed had been set in motion by Narasimha Rao and his foreign minister, Pranab Mukherjee, but Gujral had the courage and decisiveness actually to make the moves when others might have feared political backlash.[79] Indeed, the widespread public support for Gujral's diplomacy, including among some BJP leaders in private, suggested that the Indian polity was more amenable to visionary leadership than many politicians assumed in justifying their inaction.[80] Gujral's strategy also had the potential to reduce the external pressures and threats that Indian and Pakistani hawks cited to justify their ongoing desires for nuclear weapon and ballistic missile testing and development. All of this contributed to clear American respect for Gujral's efforts.[81]

SHARIF WINS IN PAKISTAN AND SIGNALS TALKS WITH INDIA, FEBRUARY 1997

Nawaz Sharif won a "thumping mandate" at the February polls in Pakistan and returned for his second "innings" as prime minister. Pakistan remained in dire economic and political straits. The political class felt that the nation faced its "last chance" and must get its house in order.[82] This required a lessening of tensions with India and reinvigoration of relations with the United States as a source of potential economic assistance and political support. Thus, during the campaign

Sharif displayed statesmanship by refraining from India-bashing. He sent private messages to interested Americans noting that if he were elected he would reach out to New Delhi.[83] By telling his countrymen in campaign speeches that he would seek talks with India, Sharif gave himself political space to do so if he were elected.

India noted this.[84] Sharif's decisive victory, paired with Gujral's generally supported foreign policies, raised hopes that the two countries actually could engage in productive talks leading to normalization of relations. Indians, of course, wanted to focus on avenues of cooperation in trade, cultural exchanges, and military confidence-building measures, while setting Kashmir aside. Pakistan, on the other hand, felt that Kashmir should not be set aside and must be addressed in tandem with less difficult issues. Yet, in private and in public statements, Pakistani leaders signaled a willingness not to make progress on Kashmir a *precondition* for progress on other issues.[85] This had been Jiang Zemin's message in December, and Sharif and his team were prepared to take some political risks to pursue this line.

When the Sharif government's willingness to be pragmatic in direct discussions of Kashmir was conveyed to experienced Indian political leaders of several parties they responded favorably, expressing the view that India should engage Pakistan across the board.[86] Indeed, two conservative political leaders suggested independently in interviews that India and Pakistan should each designate a single "plenipotentiary" to meet in secret and devise a road map for bilateral relations.[87] The interest in secret discussions, along with the Pakistani official's statement, indicated the political fear under which both sides operated, including on nuclear issues.

Meanwhile, the Indian nuclear power program remained stymied by budgetary limitations, lack of private investment, poor performance, and the general economic liabilities of nuclear power plants in the judgment of economic markets. On February 8, 1997, Prime Minister Gowda announced that the government intended to allow complete foreign ownership of nuclear plants on Indian territory.[88] The Indians hoped to stimulate France, Japan, and other countries with strong nuclear industries to reconsider their nonproliferation prohibitions on selling or building reactors in India. Gowda then traveled to Russia, where among other things, the two states announced agreement in principle for the sale of two 1,000-megawatt reactors to India for a price of $2.6 billion.[89] The "deal," which had been evolving for ten years, still required further project planning and financing arrangements.[90] Indian commentaries uniformly decried U.S. objections to the sale and seemed to urge the government to pursue it precisely to defy the United States. But some also questioned whether it made economic sense for India.[91] Indeed, in December 1997, when the United States temporarily indicated that it would not try to impede the deal on nonproliferation grounds, Indian commentators like Brahma Chellaney urged the Indian government not to pursue it but instead to invest in India's indigenous nuclear industry and spend hard currency to import natural-gas and other fossil-fueled plants, which could be completed more quickly.[92] (However, India and Russia continued their negotiations and in July 1998 signed a contract to prepare a Detailed Project Report predicated on Russia's agreement to provide 85 percent of the financing at 4 percent interest.[93] The Clinton administration by then had resumed criticizing Russia's proposed sale as especially inappropriate after the May 1998 Indian nuclear tests. This made it all the more appealing to India, whose cabinet approved the deal on September 9, 1998.)[94] All told, the Russian deal suggested the declining prospects of India's indigenous nuclear power program, making nuclear weapons work all the more attractive to Chidambaram and his colleagues.

On February 23, the DRDO conducted the sixteenth test launch of the Prithvi missile, the third of the 250-kilometer variant, and announced that the development phase of the missile was complete.[95] The test, coming so close upon Nawaz Sharif's swearing in, provoked concern in Pakistan that India would undermine Islamabad's professed interest in reducing tensions.[96] On March 4, Gowda told the Lok Sabha that the government would not abandon the Agni program. "We will give full support to the scientists working on this programme," he declared, revealing the source of pressure on him and the political support the public gave to the scientists.[97]

INDO-PAK TALKS RESUME AND
GOWDA PUSHED FROM POWER, MARCH TO APRIL 1997

In March 1997, the Indian and Pakistani polities prepared for the first talks between their foreign secretaries since January 1994. The mainstream press and elites in both countries indicated goodwill mixed with anxiety that political opportunists would somehow derail the process. As a Pakistani professor, Khalid Mahmud, wrote in the Rawalpindi *News*, the "climate of irrational frenzy and dogmatism conveniently nurtured by rival contenders for power" made improving ties with India treacherous.[98] Similarly, some Indian commentators bemoaned the "jingoism" in India that had accompanied the CTBT debate, preventing the "possibility of questioning whether the position was really in India's interest," as one journalist put it.[99]

The two foreign secretaries—Salman Haider of India and Shamshad Ahmad of Pakistan—began their talks on March 28 in New Delhi. Though circumspect, both used positive adjectives to describe the meetings. The talks focused primarily on developing the agenda and modalities for an anticipated process of bilateral dialogue, rather than on specific issues straightaway. The Pakistanis sought to establish working groups on key issues, including the important Kashmir dispute. They reportedly backtracked on earlier hints that mutual redeployment of forces from the Siachen Glacier could be considered separately from the larger Kashmir dispute.[100] India neither agreed to nor rejected the proposal for working groups.[101]

Unfortunately, political developments in India immediately overshadowed the talks. On March 30, the Congress party withdrew its support of Deve Gowda and the United Front. The Congress's president, Sitaram Kesri, an aged party insider, resented Gowda's handling of ongoing investigations into corruption charges against Congress officials, including Kesri himself. Moreover, zero-sum politics motivated Congress not to allow the United Front to remain successfully in power. As Raja Mohan commented, "Just as the Government . . . was beginning to make a mark on the economic and foreign policy fronts, Mr. Kesri pulled the rug from under its feet . . . [B]y the poor timing of his brinksmanship, he surely has undermined India's fledgling efforts to regain its standing in the world."[102] The United Front coalition of thirteen parties and the Congress struggled over the next two weeks to reconstruct a government without returning the nation to the polls.

As political negotiations continued, India's and Pakistan's foreign ministers—Gujral and Gohar Ayub Khan—met in New Delhi on April 9. The "ice-breaking meeting" proceeded well with both sides agreeing that slow and steady progress through dialogue should be pursued.[103] They agreed to release fishermen and boats and other prisoners detained by each other, and Gujral suggested that they pursue energy cooperation.

On April 20, the United Front, with Congress approval, selected the seventy-seven-year-old Inder Gujral to replace Gowda as prime minister, pending President Dr. S. D. Sharma's acceptance of a new United Front government. On April 21, Gujral was sworn in. The Congress party remained outside the government. Gujral immediately reassured national and international business leaders that he would maintain economic reforms and concentrate on improving infrastructure.[104]

The new prime minister continued the active diplomacy he had waged as foreign minister during the past year. On May 12, Gujral and Nawaz Sharif met at Male, in the island Republic of Maldives, the first time the prime ministers of the two states had met for substantive bilateral talks in eight years.[105] Gujral called Sharif "my old colleague and personal friend" and showed his magnanimity by speaking Urdu during part of the meeting.[106] Sharif reciprocated by saying of Gujral, "I like this man very much." The two prime ministers agreed to reestablish a hot line between their offices. This had been done previously but then quietly shut down after a fruitless 1989 meeting between Benazir Bhutto and Rajiv Gandhi, the last occasion on which prime ministers from the two countries met substantively.[107] Gujral and Sharif also agreed to ease travel and visa restrictions for citizens to go between the two countries. Importantly, they also deputed their foreign secretaries to address the contentious issue of a separate working group on Kashmir.[108] The Pakistanis believed that India would move positively on this issue as part of a "comprehensive mechanism" of bilateral working groups. While Indian diplomats hedged, the English-language press generally favored setting up a Kashmir working group.[109] Commentators in both countries heralded the Gujral-Sharif meeting. As the *Hindu* editorialized, "Mr. Gujral's stewardship of foreign policy . . . has ushered in a new phase of creative diplomacy focused primarily on the South Asian region."[110] All of this made subsequent developments more disappointing and seemingly unnecessary.

THREAT ASSESSMENTS AND THE PRITHVI, APRIL TO JUNE 1997

In April, the Ministry of Defence's annual report elicited commentary by invoking ongoing security threats from China, despite the recognized advance in confidence building following the Jiang visit. (Indeed, on May 22, India's Army Vice Chief of Staff V. P. Malik traveled to China for an eleven-day visit to boost military-to-military cooperation and confidence building.)[111] The report expressed concern over China's recent modernization of its "nuclear arsenal and missile capabilities" and its logistical improvements along the India-China border. The ministry also pointed to China's "position in the South-China Sea" and highlighted China's "strengthening defence relations with Myanmar," to India's east.[112] The ministry pegged India's development of "missile capability" to "the evolving security environment," specifically China's supply of M-11 missiles to Pakistan and assistance in Pakistan's "development of its indigenous missile programme."[113] These threats informed the report's criticism of the CTBT and a prospective treaty to ban unsafeguarded production of fissile materials.[114]

The Ministry of Defence's decorous bid for more resources was augmented by the Parliament's Standing Committee on Defence, which criticized the government for failing to fund a long-term defense strategy.[115] Part of the problem stemmed from personnel costs due to the excessive number of men kept under arms, itself a result of national employment needs and the use of army troops for internal security purposes. Whatever the causes, hawks bristled at India's inattention to defense. No wonder, Brahma Chellaney wrote, "India gets pushed around by nations that safeguard their security at all costs."[116] Yet, in a democratic nation where 52 percent of the people lived on less than $1 per day, political leaders could be excused for thinking that the internal security and political-economic challenges were more pressing.[117] Dismay over this reality prompted occasional intemperance, as when Chellaney argued that India, with its major overpopulation problem, suffered from "chronic impotence."[118]

Inder Gujral, for all his diplomatic efforts to raise India's regional and global stature, could not afford to neglect the strategic weaponeers. On May 31, he met with nuclear scientists at the Bhabha Atomic Research Centre and declared that India would not sign a fissile material production ban that was not tied to commitments by the nuclear weapon states to nuclear disarmament.[119] Gujral seemed to approach the prospective treaty as he had the CTBT, knowing the public supported defiance.[120] Yet his comments prompted a modest press debate on the issue. Most pundits celebrated the determination to resist any pressure to foreclose the nuclear option.[121] But others, such as K. P. Nayar recognized that despite the plaudits Gujral won from those who "equate negotiation with belligerence and diplomacy with defiance," the premature rejection of a prospective treaty was unwise. If, as Raja Ramanna and others believed, India already had enough plutonium for a minimum deterrent, signing such a treaty, assuming Pakistan would sign it, would preserve India's quantitative advantage over Pakistan while limiting the possibility of a potential nuclear arms race that all Indian leaders said they wanted to avoid. However, as Nayar noted, this was not the point of Gujral's statement. It was intended "to make the prime minister more popular at home in what may yet turn out to be an election year."

Within days Gujral found himself slightly singed by the military-technology flame. The *Washington Post* reported on June 3 that India had "deployed" less than a dozen Prithvi missiles to a military site in Jalandhar, just eighty miles away from Pakistan's major city of Lahore.[122] Pakistan reacted with alarm. The Pakistani press viewed the deployment as a "provocative act" intended to "reverse the process of rapprochement."[123] A. Q. Khan, as if on cue, declared, in the words of an interviewer, that "by the grace of God, Pakistan has proper and satisfactory arrangements to counter any enemy attack."[124] India immediately denied the *Post* story, triggering a spate of press denunciations of U.S. agencies for leaking information in order to block India's technology development, undermine the budding Indo-Pak dialogue, and otherwise damage India.[125]

Over the ensuing weeks, however, the story became more complicated. On June 11, Gujral traveled to Pune to watch the Indian Air Force unveil its new Russian-built Sukhoi-30 MK jet fighter and sat photogenically in the cockpit of one of the planes. With this suitably "strong" backdrop, the prime minister restated that "[w]e have not deployed the missile as misleadingly reported."[126] Gujral apparently meant to distinguish between "deployment" and "transfer and storage." Two days earlier the *Hindu* reported that India had "merely stored the Prithvi missiles at Jalandhar, not deployed them."[127] (To be deployed in a militarily significant way would require full complements of support equipment and units and movement to operational bases closer to the Pakistani border, given the missile's limited range.) Storage at Jalandhar was according to plans developed long ago by the army and the missile producers; they considered the transfer routine. According to K. K. Katyal in the *Hindu*, India had informed Washington of the storage plans two months earlier. However, according to the *Washington Post* and interviews with American officials, when U.S. intelligence detected the missiles' transfer, American officials quietly protested to Gujral. He at first denied the activity, and then looked into it. Gujral learned that the missiles were being moved as a routine matter and claimed that this was occurring without his prior knowledge or approval. Gujral comprehended the symbolic import of the missiles' placement so close to Pakistan and ordered the transfer to stop, pledging that he would keep the missiles from being deployed, according to the *Washington Post*.[128]

Now the problem became the report that Gujral had promised not to deploy the missiles. The Indian government took strong exception to this story and emphasized that India would not be pressured into such decisions. It was not deploying the missile because "there is no imminent threat."[129] This frustrated Indian hawks in several ways. They had welcomed the prospect that deployment of the Prithvi would compel Pakistan finally to take the M-11 missiles it had obtained from China out of their storage crates. This would then force the United

States to apply sanctions against China, something that those who focused on the China threat wanted to see.[130] More important, Gujral's reluctance to upset talks with Pakistan and stimulate Washington's ire showed that "[w]henever caught with their pants down, the Indians scamper for cover instead of asserting their right to secure themselves with the means of their choice," as Brahma Chellaney complained.[131] If India would not deploy the Prithvi, it was unlikely to move forward with the more strategically important Agni. Of course, in all of this rhetorical jousting over the Prithvi, few analyzed the costs and benefits of the system. Did its real utility as a conventional weapon delivery system outweigh the negative effects it could have in quickening an Indo-Pak nuclear arms race? The military utility was minimized by India's inadequate battlefield surveillance capabilities at the depths the Prithvi could fly. The potential arms race danger was exacerbated by both India's and Pakistan's lack of real-time surveillance capabilities and warning systems that would enable them to avoid getting drawn into nuclear exchanges based on worst-case projections of what the other side was doing or on faulty intelligence.

TIME magazine added fuel to the missile debate when it reported on June 30 that the CIA had detected in late 1995 that China was helping Pakistan build a factory to produce M-11 missiles, or variants of them, in Pakistan.[132] *TIME* reported that the White House and the State Department were treating the intelligence community's "Statement of Fact" about the missile plant in Rawalpindi "like a barrel of radioactive waste, refusing to schedule interagency meetings . . . even to discuss whether China should be penalized." The report put additional pressure on the Gujral government to strike a more robust tone in its nuclear and missile policies.

Still, neither India nor Pakistan wanted to short-circuit the still-promising dialogue between them. The two states' foreign secretaries met again June 20–23 in Islamabad. They announced a breakthrough agreement to "set up a mechanism, including working groups at appropriate levels, to address all . . . issues in an integrated manner."[133] These issues included most dramatically Jammu and Kashmir. This marked the first time since the 1972 Simla Agreement that the two sides agreed to direct dialogue focused on Kashmir.[134] A further round of foreign secretary talks was scheduled for September to pursue this and the other subjects. It would yield major disappointment.

GUJRAL UNDER PRESSURE, JULY TO OCTOBER 1997

Gujral adopted a tougher nuclear line in July, responding to domestic politics, pressure from the strategic enclave, and developments in Pakistan's missile program. On July 13 he told press interviewers that India's nuclear option was open and declared that the Agni program had not been shelved. The United States' recent conduct of a subcritical nuclear weapon test at the Nevada test site— allowed under the CTBT—had stirred India's righteous indignation. Gujral called the CTBT a "charade," allowing the nuclear weapon states to make "more sophisticated weapons . . . by different means."[135] Pakistan, too, had provoked India by test-firing a longer-range HATF-III missile that India (and others) believed was derived from Chinese technology. Gujral said India would keep China's assistance to Pakistan "in mind" as "we take care of our preparedness." He then said he would not rule out further tests of the Agni. "It depends on what the experts would say," he concluded.[136] The experts weighed in immediately. Representing the DRDO, Defence Minister Mulayam Singh Yadav on July 30 told Parliament that "[i]t has been decided to accord high priority to the next phase of the Agni programme."[137] In this next phase, efforts would be made to extend the missile's range, which thus far had fallen significantly short of the advertised 2,500 kilometers.

However, the nuclear establishment faced bad news on other fronts. The cabinet sought further cuts in funding, particularly at the nuclear fuel production complex at Hyderabad.[138] The *Telegraph* editorialized further that "India's entire nuclear power programme deserves evisceration [because] it costs the earth but provides not even a dream."[139] The paper noted that accounting for subsidized land, financing, and other costs, "India's reactors take far more out of the economy than they put in." This was a fair judgment given that nuclear plants provided less than 2 percent of national electricity supply. "Like much Nehruvian economic thinking," the newspaper concluded, "atomic energy has proven to be an expensive and potentially dangerous illusion." Of more material significance, the CIRUS plutonium-production reactor went out of service in September 1997 for major refurbishment.[140] This left Dhruva as the only dedicated source of weapon-grade plutonium.

The nuclear establishment could be forgiven its frustration over these developments. Indian scientists and technicians were on the verge of impressively completing two major repairs at the Rajasthan I and II power plants, which had long been shut down. RAPS-I had been plagued from the beginning by faulty Canadian-supplied components, and the problems at RAPS-II were so severe that Canadian advisers suggested that the most cost-effective option would be to write the reactor off.[141] However, the Indian nuclear establishment pressed on and innovated repair techniques in a massive undertaking that reportedly cost less than 7 percent of a Canadian bid for the job.[142] Yet repairing old reactors was not the same as building new ones.

Chidambaram now campaigned to keep India from falling into the "technology colonialism" trap by abandoning nuclear power or turning to foreign suppliers for it.[143] Here he revealed his ambivalence over the still-under-negotiation reactor deal with Russia. Money remained the problem. Russia still wanted 75 percent of the credit it would provide paid back in dollars (or other valuable commodities such as diamonds) and wanted quicker payment than India demanded.[144]

With the civilian nuclear power scenario so unrewarding, Chidambaram and his dozens of colleagues working on nuclear weapons took solace in their preparations of a hydrogen bomb design and other weapons for experimental testing.[145]

Once again they requested authorization to conduct nuclear weapon tests. Defence Minister Yadav later claimed that the scientists had prepared nuclear devices for testing in October 1997 and awaited only the last go-ahead from the government. However, Gujral had other strategic priorities. Beyond the primacy of political-economic progress, Gujral's concentration on raising India's regional and global standing through diplomacy militated against conducting tests. The prime minister had no trouble defying the demands of the nuclear weapon states, but it was another matter for a man of his background and principles to risk India's normative and diplomatic interests by testing nuclear weapons.

In September, Gujral declared that the Pokhran test was a "thing of the past" and India "does not want to make" nuclear weapons but merely to retain the option.[146] He made this statement the day after Nawaz Sharif had declared that Pakistan's nuclear weapon capability was an "established fact" and its "right as a sovereign nation."[147] Sharif was pursuing a new Pakistani tactic of insisting that the United States and others must simply learn to accept its nuclear weapon possession, abandoning any illusion of rolling it back through sanctions or other pressure. Indian officials reacted nonchalantly to Sharif's statement. Gujral said that Pakistan's "nuclear weapons programme is a well-documented fact" and that Sharif was taking this line due to nervousness about India's "burgeoning relationship" with the United States.[148] However, Gujral's understated rhetoric again rankled the strategic enclave and the security community. As Brahma Chellaney put it, India's focus on "scholastic issues, such as non-discrimination and morality" kept it "illogically" from adopting "rational self-interest, U.S.-style thinking."[149] Raja Mohan added that "[p]retending that the Indian nuclear programme is entirely peaceful convinces no one: such rhetoric will only convey the impression of deviousness on India's part."[150] Instead, India should do as Pakistan had done and signal that its "nuclear capability is here to stay."

But Gujral was fitfully pursuing a strategy that could alleviate the causes of insecurity. If dialogue with Pakistan could normalize relations, as it had begun to do with China, India's regional security and global status would improve. The nation then could focus on the internal development that ultimately would determine its strength.

Unfortunately, on September 18 the second round of foreign secretary talks since the Gujral-Sharif meeting in May ended at an impasse. Pakistan had focused the talks on Kashmir, specifically the modalities and agenda for the proposed working group that had been agreed to tentatively in June. Islamabad emphasized the need for a dedicated, high-level working group, while India reportedly maintained that a less formal discussion of Kashmir by the two foreign secretaries over time should be pursued.[151] The Pakistanis charged that India was retreating from the June agreement. Islamabad would not accept less than a separate formal working group.[152] Recognizing the impasse, the two sides issued a joint statement noting the "cordial atmosphere" of the talks and declaring that further discussions would be held.

India's apparent back-stepping on the Kashmir working group could be explained by political wariness on the part of an increasingly beleaguered coalition government.[153] For its part, Pakistan appeared to be looking forward to pending meetings between Nawaz Sharif and Bill Clinton, as well as between Gujral and Clinton. Pakistan would try to utilize the impasse to press Washington to become more involved in the Kashmir problem.

Clinton met separately with both leaders in New York in September. In a speech to the UN General Assembly, Sharif took the high ground by proposing once again a treaty "of non-aggression between India and Pakistan" and a bilateral agreement "for mutual and equal restraint in the nuclear and ballistic fields."[154] Sharif also invited UN and American initiatives to "help in resolving the Kashmir dispute." Gujral parried these traditional proposals in his speeches and meetings in New York. For his part, Clinton told Gujral in their September 22 meeting that the United States was "very careful not to interfere in any way with issues you [India] have with Pakistan." This pointed rejection of Pakistan's bid for direct U.S. diplomatic intervention on Kashmir relieved the Indians.[155] For Pakistan, Clinton renewed his intention to try to resolve the F-16 dispute because it is a "matter of justice."[156]

Indian commentators generally hailed the results of Gujral's meetings and the Clinton-Sharif meeting as a sign that Washington recognized the priority of relations with India.[157] This was true, but Gujral later revealed an anecdote that reflected the growing Indian feeling that nuclear weapons offered the means to achieve long-denied international respect. He recounted telling Clinton that an old Indian saying holds that Indians have a third eye. "I told President Clinton that when my third eye looks at the door into the Security Council chamber it sees a little sign that says, 'only those with economic wealth or nuclear weapons allowed.' I said to him, 'it is very difficult to achieve economic wealth.' " The implication was clear: nuclear weapons were relatively easy to build and detonate and could offer an apparent shortcut to great power status.[158]

PREPARING FOR "STRATEGIC DIALOGUE" WITH WASHINGTON, NOVEMBER 1997

The weaponeers did not rest while Gujral pursued diplomacy. In October, the Congress party urged the government to deploy Prithvi missiles.[159] More dramatically, Defence Minister Mulayam Singh Yadav—whose reliability is not certain—claimed that in October 1997 the "scientists had even tightened the last screw" in nuclear devices to be tested. Yadav told the *Times of India* that the scientists had conducted successful laboratory experiments in October and were awaiting final clearance for full-scale explosive tests. "At that time too, the government had discussed the pros and cons of global reactions, including economic sanctions. But it was felt that for the country's security, India should go nuclear," according to Yadav.[160] Yadav's account suggested he was more "in the loop" than most Indian defense ministers have been, which remains to be confirmed. (Inder Gujral, in a 1999 interview with the author, refused to comment on this and other questions related to nuclear testing.) Yet Yadav reportedly heeded the ministrations of Abdul Kalam: in early November the defense minister reiterated that the Agni missile program would not be restrained. Endorsing Kalam's call for a budget increase for the DRDO, Yadav said that funding constraints should not be allowed to interfere with defense preparedness.[161]

Around this time, Kalam was designated to receive India's highest civilian honor, the Bharat Ratna. Brahma Chellaney, whom Kalam reportedly had supplied with useful information on the nuclear and missile programs, gushingly heralded Kalam as one of "only two great scientific visionaries" in independent India's history. Homi Bhabha was the other. Chellaney contrasted Kalam's "vision and courage" with "a growing number of . . . upper-caste Hindus [who] have fallen victim to self-doubt and to the 'should-we-or-should-we-not' syndrome."[162] Here Chellaney added caste and communal politics to his earlier invocation of emasculation politics in an effort to push the Indian government toward a more militant nuclear policy. Bhabha and Kalam were non-Hindus, and many of the top leaders Chellaney accused of inaction were upper-caste Hindus, most typically South Indian Brahmins. Yet this insidious political attack ignored the fact that the three principal scientists behind the 1974 nuclear test—Ramanna, Iyengar, and Chidambaram—were upper-caste Hindus, as was the leader of the Defence Research and Development Organisation—Arunachalam—when the Prithvi missile and much of India's nuclear weapon capabilities were produced. Chellaney, echoing the BJP, urged India to achieve its rightful international place by exercising the strategic options prepared by "Dr. Bhabha's and Dr. Kalam's scientific endeavors." The award increased Kalam's standing and power within the polity, even if some observers believed the award was motivated in part to win favor with the large Muslim population in Uttar Pradesh, where Defence Minister Yadav was seeking reelection.[163] The government had frustrated Kalam's desire to conduct nuclear tests, but the Bharat Ratna was a glorious consolation prize.

Gujral recognized the pressure to test nuclear weapons and deploy missiles, but he again called for a broader perspective on India's national security needs. In a November 13 address to the National Defence College, he said that India had no desire to manufacture nuclear weapons unless it was forced to do so.[164] Gujral highlighted the primacy of reducing economic disparities around the world and increasing the "flow of wealth and technology" internationally. While he had the world's advanced economies in mind here, these were also his priorities for India.

On November 18 and 19, U.S. Secretary of State Madeleine Albright was slated to visit India as part of a brief tour of South Asia. Indian officials hoped to pick up Gujral's theme about technology cooperation and explore possibilities for greater U.S. engagement with India's nuclear establishment on safety and power projects.[165] Groundwork for the Albright meetings had been laid by Under Secretary of State for Political Affairs Thomas Pickering during an October trip to

India when he sought to initiate a "strategic dialogue" between India and the United States. Pickering, a highly respected diplomat who had served as ambassador to India, sought to encourage both sides to "listen" to rather than "talk at" each other.[166] The United States felt that the nomenclature of "strategic dialogue" represented a significant elevation of Washington's interest in India and hoped to encourage Indian officials to offer their ideas on specific means to flesh out the relationship. Yet the habits of nonalignment and wariness of the "sole remaining superpower's" intentions made Indians regard the American overture with a mixture of excitement and wariness.[167]

Albright did come to India in November (following stops in Bangladesh and Pakistan) but departed early to fly to Europe for emergency meetings on the crisis over Iraq's ejection of UN weapons inspectors. Although the importance of the Iraqi issue could not be denied, Indians once again felt that the nation's strategic importance remained tertiary to the Americans. Still, Indian commentators generally viewed the visit as another sign of progress in Indo-American relations.[168]

THE UNITED FRONT FALLS AND ELECTIONS ARE CALLED, NOVEMBER TO DECEMBER 1997

Little more than a week after Albright's brief visit, India once again thrust itself into domestic tumult. The Congress party had resumed unacceptable demands on the United Front, this time to drop ministers of the regional Dravida Munetra Kazhagam (DMK) party from the government. Rather than accede to this bullying, the United Front agreed that Gujral should offer his resignation to the president if Congress withdrew support of the United Front.[169] On November 28, Congress did the expected and Gujral resigned. President K. R. Narayanan accepted the resignation but asked Gujral to continue as prime minister until alternative arrangements were made. Negotiations within and among parties continued to see whether a new government could be formed, but on December 4, President Narayan dissolved the Lok Sabha and called for a new Parliament to be constituted by March 15, after elections. "The people of India need a reprieve from political instability," the president concluded.[170]

CONCLUSION

Nineteen ninety-seven marked India's fiftieth anniversary as an independent state. The nation duly celebrated and received international tributes for its maintenance of democracy in most difficult circumstances. Yet, Indians more than outsiders also recognized the nation's troubled condition. India had been born amidst tragedy with the hope of great promise. Now, fifty years later, much of the promise seemed unrealized. The horrors of communal violence had been replayed at Ayodyha. Democracy still obtained, but it was not of the ennobling kind. The people increasingly felt that they did not get the governance they deserved. Governments had fallen in rapid succession motivated in part by venal calculations of corrupt politicians. The growing assertiveness of an independent judiciary yielded some hope for self-correction, but few Indians felt that their current political situation was cause for celebration.

Economically, India had emerged from a true crisis in 1991 and had begun to enjoy relatively robust growth. Still, as the *Economist* noted in 1997, "Much of the developing world—especially in Asia—has left India far behind."[171] The subsequent collapse of East Asian economies in 1998 softened this judgment retrospectively, but for India's three hundred million illiterate adults and scores of millions of malnourished children comparisons with other states meant nothing. The nation needed at least $200 billion in new infrastructure investment over the next eight to ten years: power stations, expressways, ports, water treatment facilities, and so on. Without this, economic development would be stifled.

Infrastructure requirements bore on nuclear policy to the extent that much of the investment required for it would have to come from foreign sources, including governments and multilateral lending agencies. Such loans, aid, and investment could be sacrificed or limited if India violated international nonproliferation norms by, say, testing nuclear weapons. But financial constraints on the armed forces' modernization also led some to advocate nuclear weapons as a cost-saving strategy.[172]

To integrate the nation's economic and defense needs with nuclear policy required much better analysis and strategy development than the political system offered. Rejecting the CTBT won domestic plaudits, but the government was still torn over the narrow questions of whether to test nuclear weapons or to deploy Prithvi missiles. The scientists and many of their elite supporters clearly wanted to show their prowess, but they did not share their prime ministers' breadth of responsibilities. If one stepped back and sought to integrate nuclear policy into a larger national strategy the picture was more complicated. Into this situation came the Bharatiya Janata Party in 1998 with promises to effect the first-ever coherent strategy for national defense and nuclear policy.

FIFTEEN

The Bombs That Roared

1998

On May 11, 1998, India shocked the world when it tested three nuclear weapons at Pokhran, followed by two additional tests two days later. The momentum behind testing had built steadily since mid-1995, as described in the preceding two chapters. Now, the newly elected Vajpayee government boldly pushed India across the threshold of declared nuclear weapon status, carrying the country into the third phase of its nuclear history and perhaps ending its record of self-restraint. Pakistan followed on May 28.

A handful of Bharatiya Janata Party leaders made the decision to test. They did so without consulting other political parties who may have endorsed India's traditional aversion to nuclear weapons and without conducting a previously advertised strategic defense review. This chapter chronicles and analyzes the factors behind the decision to test and the rush of developments thereafter. It also explores how the U.S. government affected Indian calculations before the tests and reacted to India afterwards. Given the political interests of the BJP and the drive of the weaponeers, Washington probably could not have prevented India from testing in 1998.

Looking ahead from the standpoint of late 1998, it appeared that India would continue an ad hoc process of determining nuclear policy. Partisan political considerations, technological concerns, economic priorities, and international imperatives all remained important factors. Indian military leaders continued to be excluded from nuclear policymaking, and some officers privately agreed with American scientists' doubts regarding the claimed effectiveness of the Indian nuclear tests, particularly whether a two-stage thermonuclear explosion had occurred successfully. This chapter provides evidence to buttress these doubts. It also confirms that one of the devices India tested was composed of non-weapon-grade plutonium. This breakthrough would increase significantly the potential size of an Indian nuclear arsenal and has major implications for nuclear industry and the nonproliferation regime worldwide. Amidst these new and shifting technological realities, Indian and American leaders groped for a path that could lead them to reconciliation.

RUN-UP TO ELECTION 1998, JANUARY TO MARCH

On January 1, the Indian Election Commission announced that Lok Sabha elections would be held in four phases, beginning February 16 and running through March 7. The BJP hoped to extend its 1996 gains and win enough seats to form a government of its own, or at least to win enough coalition partners to withstand a vote of confidence and remain in power. Its main rivals were the United Front and the Congress, now led by Rajiv Gandhi's beautiful, Italian-born widow, who hoped to revive images of the Nehru-Gandhi dynasty.

This election, like all others before it, revolved around domestic political and economic issues. Atal Behari Vajpayee and other top leaders proclaimed that if elected the party would not pursue a divisive agenda but would accommodate the programs of regional parties with which it would likely need to form a coalition. The party downplayed its hard-core platform planks on domestic issues.[1] Yet the BJP's more ideologically committed base in the Rashtriya Swayamsevak Sangh (RSS) and the Vishwa Hindu Parishad (VHP) had to be encouraged, too. This left doubts regarding which elements of the party's relatively radical overall platform would be compromised by pragmatism and which would be acted upon after elections. For its part, Congress ran against the BJP's "ugly and fascist face in Indian politics" and against the ideological incoherence of the "rag-tag" United Front.[2] Congress claimed to represent "stability," "secularism," and a return to the successful economic modernization begun under the Rao government.

Foreign and security policies were not major issues in the campaign. Most parties generally had supported Inder Gujral's international efforts and did not exert themselves to call for major changes in them. Indeed, Gujral had consulted with the BJP and others on his major initiatives.[3]

The BJP sought to raise nuclear policy as a distinguishing issue. In mid-January, before the party produced its election manifesto, foreign policy spokesman Brajesh Mishra stated that the cornerstone of the BJP's defense and foreign policy strategies would be to defy international pressure and exercise the nuclear option. "[G]iven the security environment, we have no option but to go nuclear," he said, referring to China's nuclear and missile assistance to Pakistan.[4] He also charged obliquely that China was trying to *stabilize* the disputed border with India without actually *resolving* the issue. This was not enough for the BJP.[5]

In January Indian analysts digested the threatening implications of earlier U.S. reports of a new Pakistani ballistic missile, the Ghauri. Named for a twelfth-century Muslim invader who defeated the Indian ruler Prithviraj Chauhan, the

Ghauri (as yet unseen) surprised Indian analysts with its putative capability to deliver a nuclear warhead to most major Indian cities. Indians tended to underestimate Pakistan's strategic capabilities while overestimating its hostile intentions at this time. Indian analysts assumed "that Pakistan has received immense help from China in developing this missile," as a Rajasthan newspaper editorialized.[6] In fact, the United States would reveal in April that the help came from North Korea, not China. In any case, news of the Ghauri prompted renewed calls for reviving the Agni program.

Missiles aside, Pakistan was once again declining economically and politically. The estimable Pakistani columnist M. B. Naqvi summarized the situation: "Islamabad is caught in a no-win situation created by the snowballing external debts, low production, a low growth rate, smaller exports, high inflation and big budget and balance of payments deficits."[7] Making matters worse, Naqvi wrote, "both major parties" were "consciously cynical in offering populist programmes they have no intention of implementing," while bending "over backwards to cultivate the goodwill of generals" and "obscurantist" Islamic leaders. Internationally, Naqvi noted that the United States "dislikes" Pakistan's "nuclear programme, missile development plans, Kashmir policy and refusal to normalise relations with India until the Kashmir dispute is resolved." Naqvi also fretted that China was "actually unhappy" over Pakistan's Afghanistan policy, "its unrelenting confrontationist stance vis-a-vis India and its perceived promotion of Islamic fundamentalist forces." In short, Naqvi aptly concluded, "on one side, Pakistan faces a possible collapse and on the other, its elites show no capability to resolve any of its many crises."

These Pakistani realities should have been part of any Indian strategic assessment. Nuclear-armed missiles no doubt posed a threat to India. Yet Pakistan's internal weakness, ill-equipped air force, and frustrated "allies" in Beijing and Washington suggested that Islamabad was in no position to fight. Pakistan needed to cut its losses by finding a way to normalize relations with India. To effect this, however, Prime Minister Sharif needed face-saving measures from New Delhi on Kashmir. India was disinclined to oblige. Nationalist sentiments in an election season suggested instead that India should seek "a preponderance of power," in one pundit's words, so that it could impose rapprochement on its terms.[8] Yet this heightened Pakistan's interest in nuclear weapons and ballistic missiles as the only means to prevent India from achieving a preponderance of power. Inder Gujral comprehended the need to reassure Pakistan that it could live securely with a powerful India, but his innings were nearly over.

On February 22, Prime Minister Gujral, in a lame duck role, stated that India was prepared to discuss Jammu and Kashmir with Pakistan "in the same way" that the other seven issues agreed to for bilateral talks in June 1997 would be addressed.[9] This seemed to represent a return to the more forthcoming Indian position of June 1997. However, the BJP dashed whatever hope Gujral's apparent shift elicited in Pakistan. On February 25, during a campaign rally in Mumbai, candidate Vajpayee declared that a BJP government would "take back that part of Kashmir that is under Pakistan's occupation."[10] The audience erupted with thunderous applause. Pakistan responded that the BJP was making the atmosphere "foul and unsuitable" for dialogue.[11]

If Pakistan assumed the worst from a prospective BJP government, American and Indian analysts thought that domestic and international political considerations could moderate the BJP's approach to nuclear policy. The BJP's campaign manifesto, issued on February 3, seemed to mark "a significant easing of the party's nuclear stand," as Raja Mohan noted.[12] The manifesto said vaguely that the BJP would "re-evaluate the country's nuclear policy and exercise the option to induct nuclear weapons." It also called for the "development of the Agni series of ballistic missiles with a view to increasing their range and accuracy." The manifesto did not comment on nuclear tests. When party president L. K. Advani was asked whether the BJP would conduct nuclear tests, he admitted his lack of expertise on the subject and said that experts told him that "nuclear tests may not be necessary for India to induct nuclear weapons."[13]

However, in early March Atomic Energy Commission Chairman R. Chidambaram tipped the weaponeers' hand in a largely unnoticed interview with an Indian journalist. Chidambaram began innocuously by saying that "we are prepared . . . , but it is [for] the policy makers to decide whether to go nuclear or keep the options open."[14] He was then asked whether computer simulations were adequate to develop nuclear weapons. Chidambaram responded, "[T]hen what was the use of some countries going for 2,000 explosions?" This was a good rhetorical question: one could argue that many of the American and Russian tests were not necessary and that the computing power available in the 1990s would have reduced the "need" for many of the tests conducted in the 1950s, '60s, '70s, and '80s. Yet Chidambaram effectively used the U.S. and Russian testing experiences to argue that nuclear explosions were necessary to increase the database for conducting computer simulations: "Higher the database, better the simulations," he said. Obviously Chidambaram believed that full-scale nuclear tests were necessary. "[I]f you are weak, people will try to take advantage of it," he summarized. Chidambaram came as close to publicly advocating nuclear weapon tests as any serving Atomic Energy Commission chairman had.

In early March the election results arrived. The Bharatiya Janata Party earned 26 percent of the popular vote and with its allies won 250 seats, leaving them 22 shy of a majority. The Congress and its allies won 166, an improved performance that owed much to Sonia Gandhi's campaigning. The United Front won 98, with a few dozen going to splinter parties and independent candidates.[15] President Raman Narayanan gave the BJP the opportunity to form a government. After almost two weeks of negotiating with regional parties, the BJP formed a majority coalition and Atal Behari Vajpayee again was sworn in as prime minister on March 19. However, he led a fractious group of fourteen parties.

THE BJP'S MIXED NUCLEAR SIGNALS AND
THE SECRET ORDER TO TEST, MARCH TO APRIL

In his earliest public statements, Vajpayee struck a moderate tone on nuclear policy, seeming even to backtrack from the BJP manifesto. Asked when India should incorporate nuclear weapons into its arsenal, he said, "There is no time frame. We are keeping the option open, and if need be, that option will be exercised."[16] On March 20, the new defense minister, sixty-eight-year-old George Fernandes, said that the government would not be afraid to induct nuclear weapons but also would not rush into it: "We have not said we are going in for nuclear weapons. Instead, through a first ever strategic defence review we will examine our security and threat perceptions and in light of that decide on induction of nuclear weapons."[17] Fernandes said further, "I don't think we need to test [nuclear weapons] at this point of time. We did a good job in Pokhran in 1974. . . . The world knows India has the capacity and the capability. We don't need to perform for others." Fernandes had been one of the few critics of the 1974 Pokhran blast, and his incarnation now as defense minister showed the vagaries of Indian politics. He was leader of a small labor-oriented party that gave the BJP precious Lok Sabha votes by allying with it. In return for this, the BJP had to find a place for him in the cabinet. He was an incongruous choice for the defense post—a self-described "pacifist"—but it was one of the few suitably prominent positions open as the BJP formed its cabinet.[18]

Unfortunately, Fernandes, like defense ministers before him, did not know what he was talking about because the prime minister had not informed him of nuclear policy. Thus, Indians and foreign observers could be misled by Fernandes's utterances. Moreover, Vajpayee himself had appeared to soften the position on "going nuclear." President Narayanan notably omitted any mention of nuclear policy in his March 25 speech opening the Lok Sabha. Even a rather extreme voice, Mohan Guruswamy, the Harvard-trained BJP defense specialist, said, "We don't know" when asked whether the government would carry out nuclear tests. "Simulation could perhaps do the job. But a decision on this will be taken after consultations with appropriate authorities," Guruswamy said.[19] These sounded like signals of patience if not moderation.

In fact, despite Vajpayee's and Fernandes's apparent dithering over nuclear tests, the prime minister had consulted with Abdul Kalam days before he was sworn in and with Chidambaram on March 20.[20] Such meetings by a new prime minister and top officials were routine, but given the experience of May 1996 when Vajpayee had authorized the scientists to move forward with tests and then ordered them to pause, it is reasonable to think that the subject of tests came up now. It is also reasonable to think that Vajpayee told the scientists that he would be inclined to authorize tests after his government won a vote of confidence. The new government's moderate *public* line on nuclear policy reflected several dynamics. First, no one but Vajpayee, Jaswant Singh, Brajesh Mishra, perhaps L. K.

Advani, and certainly Kalam, Chidambaram, and a handful of other top scientists knew what "the government" actually was intending to do. Everyone else, including cabinet ministers, was just guessing. Second, Vajpayee and others in the know were determined not to alarm their coalition partners or the opposition before a pending confidence vote.

The BJP-led coalition prevailed narrowly in the March 28 confidence vote, 275 to 260. Now it could pursue its agenda. On the key challenge of economics, new Finance Minister Yaswant Sinha announced that overall economic growth had slowed to 5 percent in 1997–1998, agricultural output had fallen by 2 percent, and industry continued to be "in doldrums."[21] The budget deficit was alarmingly high at 6 percent of GDP. This made it less likely that defense modernization would receive long-denied funding.[22] By overstating the mess it was inheriting the new government hoped it would not be blamed for economic difficulties and would be acclaimed if the economy improved. Politically, the government retreated from pledges to (re)build the Ram Temple at Ayodhya and repeal Article 370 of the Constitution, out of deference to coalition partners that did not share its more radical Hindutva agenda. Yet this increased the need for moves to satisfy the BJP's hard-line base.

The least controversial area for asserting the BJP's uniqueness was national security. National security policy was not salient to the Indian masses, while the elites who did follow these issues generally agreed that "reforms" were needed. This gave the government leeway. The BJP had promised to conduct the nation's first-ever strategic defense review and to form an effective National Security Council. There was no mass-based countervailing political pressure against toughening security policy. This made it politically low risk. Thus, to make the new government's mark, it is reasonable to assume that shortly after winning the confidence vote Vajpayee authorized Kalam and Chidambaram to prepare for nuclear tests. If strategic considerations had been paramount, the decision could have awaited a defense strategy review and still enabled the scientists to act prior to the anticipated entry into force of the test ban treaty in late 1999.

PAKISTAN TESTS GHAURI MISSILE, APRIL

On April 6, Pakistan tested the Ghauri missile. The mobile, medium-range missile reportedly was launched near Jhelum in northeastern Punjab and flew southwest perhaps 800 kilometers to Baluchistan. Pakistan claimed the missile had a possible range of 1,500 kilometers with a payload of 700 kilograms.

The missile's existence had been reported in 1997, and Pakistani sources had hinted it would be tested around the time of the Republic Day parade on March 23. Still, the test shocked India and frustrated the United States. Secretary of State Madeleine Albright had written a personal letter to Prime Minister Nawaz Sharif a week earlier urging him to postpone any missile tests until after the new Indian government had time to settle into office and, hopefully, renew dialogue with Pakistan.[23] Pakistan apparently did not reply to Albright's letter. The Ghauri test spoke for itself. Albright did not appreciate this bellicose response, but the U.S. government kept the existence of her letter from becoming public.

The Ghauri test caught India, unlike the United States, by surprise, despite Fernandes's claims to the contrary.[24] India lacked constant spy satellite coverage of Pakistan, and the Indian Remote Sensing satellites that passed over the subcontinent in regular orbits did not detect preparations or the launch itself.[25] The lack of intelligence on the test and the general Indian contempt for Pakistan's technical capabilities caused some in India to assert that the test was a hoax.[26] Others argued that if it was not a hoax, Pakistan must have obtained the missile from China. When U.S. officials suggested that North Korea, not China, had provided the Ghauri—or its components—many Indian journalists and analysts thought that the United States was covering up once again for China by shifting the blame to North Korea.[27]

The Ghauri test twisted the Indian security narrative in several disturbing ways. First, if the Ghauri truly could achieve its advertised range and Pakistan could deploy a nuclear warhead atop it most of India's major cities were vulnerable to Pakistan for the first time. India had assumed—mistakenly—that its indigenous scientific-technological superiority over Pakistan rendered Pakistan's nuclear and missile programs troublesome but not really a threat to India's existence. Leaders of the strategic enclave—and others—superciliously denied that India competed with Pakistan. Instead they insisted that China was the concern that drove India's strategic technology acquisitions. Yes, Pakistan had some inaccurate, unreliable HATF missiles, and, yes, they had received some M-11 missiles from China, but India had a robust indigenous capability that made its strategic programs superior to anything Pakistan could produce. Now, however, the Ghauri surpassed any systems India had ready to deploy. The Agni had not been tested in four years. The DRDO's calls to begin testing the Agni II indicated that the first Agni series needed to be improved upon. This would take time even after Agni flight-testing resumed.

Defence Minister Fernandes responded lamely that India "doesn't have reason to feel worried about the Ghauri test, and what Pakistan has or is doing. The Prithvi is there, in adequate numbers. It can take care of our security."[28] This was true as far as it went. Given Pakistan's lack of strategic depth, the Prithvi or Indian aircraft could deliver enough nuclear weapons to destroy Pakistan's major cities. Yet this Indian capability was not new. What was new was *Pakistan's* apparent capacity to target India's largest cities. India could not meaningfully "improve upon" its capacity to destroy/deter Pakistan. But Pakistan did have room for "improving" its capacity to threaten and deter India.

Indian opinion shapers also failed to recognize that Pakistan feared that the BJP would fundamentally change the subcontinent's security narrative. Former Indian Foreign Secretary S. K. Singh wrote that Pakistan had tested the Ghauri to coerce India to "settle the Jammu and Kashmir issue on their terms."[29] This assessment missed the mark. Surely Pakistan *desired* to settle Kashmir on its terms, but Pakistani leaders felt their country was in grave trouble now and declining relative to India. Pakistani leaders believed the BJP's pledges to induct nuclear weapons. They saw the nuclear and missile programs as last-resort protection. The Ghauri test was in part to signal that the BJP could not realize Vajpayee's campaign pledge to "take back that part of Kashmir that is under Pakistan's occupation."[30] Pakistanis wanted to show that they would not be cowed. Nuclear weapons and ballistic missiles were great equalizers.

To be sure, these programs also pushed ahead due to the zealotry and drive of men like A. Q. Khan, whom the politicians in Islamabad were hesitant to control. Competition between Khan's laboratories and the Pakistan Atomic Energy Commission now helped fuel the Pakistani missile program. Each organization was developing its own missile systems and vying for funding and political authority to conduct tests. The Ghauri was Khan's system, and his rivals at the PAEC had another system—the Shaheen—that they had wanted to test in March or April. When they experienced difficulties, Khan beat them to the punch and won permission to launch the Ghauri.[31] Pakistani leaders did not rein in either group because they truly feared the BJP. Indian officials and commentators seemed not to be aware that Pakistan had competing missile programs that could speed the pace of innovation in Pakistan.

TEST PREPARATIONS ACCELERATE AND THE GOVERNMENT CONTINUES MIXED SIGNALS, APRIL 10 TO MAY 10

On April 10, Vajpayee announced the formation of a three-person task force to prepare recommendations for the constitution of a National Security Council. The task force was chaired by former Congress government Defence Minister K. C. Pant (who had quit the Congress party in late January). It included Institute for Defence Studies and Analyses Director Jasjit Singh and Deputy Chairman of the Planning Commission Jaswant Singh. Governmental and nongovernmental strategic analysts, economic experts, and others were slated to give inputs to the task force. Once formed, the NSC was then to undertake India's first-ever strategic defense review (SDR), analyzing "the military, economic and political threats" to the country.[32] A key question was whether to give the military a greater role in policymaking. Some felt that this "would create friction amongst the three services on the one hand and between the defence ministry and the services on the other," as Mohan Guruswamy noted.[33] Yet the military backgrounds of Jasjit Singh (air force) and Jaswant Singh (army) suggested that the new task force would at least keep an open mind about a greater military role.

By proposing to create a workable National Security Council that would then conduct a strategic defense review, the BJP conveyed that nuclear policy would follow a well-prepared national security strategy. Or so it seemed. In fact, although the precise dating of the decision to conduct nuclear tests remains uncertain, the latest publicly mentioned date—April 10—still put the decision many months before the definition of a national security strategy. (Some reports stated that Vajpayee authorized nuclear weapon tests on April 8, 9, or 10.[34] Kalam said D-day was set for thirty days from April 10.[35] This dating made the decision seem to come in response to Pakistan's Ghauri missile test, but there is reason to think that the tests were authorized earlier, shortly after the March 28 confidence vote. Ambiguity about the timing of authorization may stem from the fact that at least three steps in the testing process must be approved by the prime minister: emplacement of a device[s] in the test shaft[s], plugging the shaft[s], and actual detonation of the device[s]. The basic decision to proceed toward testing was most likely conveyed to the weaponeers in late March, with authorization of the key steps in the process following.)[36] In any case, by early April—before work began on a national security strategy—a core group of "100 odd scientists and engineers" plus army laborers hurriedly toiled in the Thar Desert of Rajasthan to prepare for nuclear tests.[37] The scientists were not surprised by Vajpayee's authorization, but they were nonetheless elated.

Pakistan's Ghauri test assuaged any doubts Vajpayee might have had. The BJP's historic toughness on national security would have seemed hollow if the government did not respond decisively to the new Pakistani threat. Nevertheless, the Indian decision to test was not strategically vetted. The government did not consult the nation's strategic experts. Nor did it take input from coalition partners or economic experts, although in 1996 the Finance Ministry reportedly had estimated the potential cost of international sanctions to be on the order of $3 billion. A handful of politicians instigated by a handful of scientists with little experience in international affairs was pushing India across a portentous strategic threshold whose implications they did not fully appreciate.

Whatever Vajpayee's and the scientists' strategic acumen, they expertly avoided detection. On April 14, a high-level U.S. delegation led by Permanent Representative to the United Nations Bill Richardson arrived in New Delhi for meetings with Vajpayee and other Indian officials. The visit represented Washington's growing regard for India in anticipation of President Clinton's planned visit to the region in November.[38]

The two sides discussed Pakistan's Ghauri test and its implications. The Indians privately found the Americans insensitive to their concerns. According to an Indian official privy to the talks, Ambassador Richardson lamented the Ghauri test and the prospect of further missile competition between India and Pakistan but reiterated that the United States had a special security relationship with Pakistan, too, and could not simply take India's "side" on the issue.[39] Whether or not Richardson actually said this in New Delhi, days later in Islamabad he reportedly told Nawaz Sharif that the Clinton administration considered Pakistan "a strategic friend and ally."[40] News reports also stated that Richardson told the Pakistanis that he understood the steps they had to take to ensure their defense.[41] This revived India's nightmares about U.S. favoritism toward Pakistan at a time when

New Delhi was determined to rise above comparisons with Pakistan and was looking for evidence that Washington might give India greater due against the "China-Pakistan axis." Washington had been speaking of a new "strategic dialogue" to connote the raised importance of bilateral relations with India, but now Richardson spoke in similar terms about dialogue with Pakistan, devaluing what the Indians thought the United States was offering them. "The people in New Delhi are feeling a cold anger toward the U.S.," a source with good contacts in Indian government circles noted after Richardson's visit.[42]

Indian and American officials later disputed whether the Indian side misled the Americans into thinking that nuclear tests were not planned. The Indians insisted that they never denied such plans, while the Americans said that the discussions led them to conclude that no tests were imminent and that any such decision would await the results of the strategic defense review.[43] "I was there," a U.S. official stated in an interview, "and I'm telling you that there are ways that responsible officials can talk to one another without giving away secret plans but nonetheless protecting your counterparts from being set up. That's what you do if you are serious about a positive relationship. And the Indians didn't do it."[44] In the Americans' view, the Indians had to know that the positive agenda for improving relations would be undone by nuclear tests. The Indians did nothing in the meetings to minimize the pending damage.[45]

Before Richardson left New Delhi, A. Q. Khan once again fueled India's fire. On April 15, he declared that Pakistani teams were ready and able to conduct nuclear weapon tests as soon as they could "get permission from the government."[46] He added self-aggrandizingly that Pakistan was the only country in the world where, in the words of *Dawn*, "one institution, his own Khan Research Laboratories, had developed both nuclear and missile systems." Unbeknownst to Indian observers, Khan was campaigning in a pitched battle with the Pakistan Atomic Energy Commission to win primacy in funding and recognition for strategic systems.

Pakistan's growing strategic capability now acutely concerned India's military. At a five-day army commander's conference, Army Chief of Staff General V. P. Malik declared that a "strategic deterrent to counter the emerging nuclear and missile challenges was the need of the hour," according to a state television account.[47] The army also needed significantly greater financial resources to modernize its forces, Malik added. This required greater army control over its budget, which the military hoped would result from the formation of a National Security Council that would give the armed forces a greater role in defense planning and policy implementation. Both points—the call for a strategic deterrent and for greater military autonomy vis-à-vis civilian bureaucrats—were unusually bold for a serving military leader to make in public.

Another indicative but little-noted event occurred in late April when scientists at the Bhabha Atomic Research Centre told journalists that they were making preparations to protect the public against the effects of a nuclear attack on India.[48]

The scientists reportedly said they had developed medicine that would control diseases and infections associated with a major nuclear explosion or meltdown. They also described protection measures such as urging people to "stay indoors" in radiation-afflicted areas. The timing of this workshop for journalists could have reflected several considerations. The Ghauri test had raised the threat of Indian cities being subjected to Pakistani nuclear attack, and BARC could have wanted to allay public concerns. BARC leaders also knew that they were preparing to conduct nuclear tests and could have been trying to obviate any public concern over unintended fallout or the consequences of ensuing escalation of tensions. "All told," according to the Hindi-language *Navbharat Times,* "the scientists' view was that in the event of a nuclear bomb being dropped on our territory the history of Hiroshima and Nagasaki would not be allowed to repeat itself."[49]

Meanwhile, a BJP foreign affairs leader, Nagendra Nath Jha, signaled that the government still had not decided on the necessity of conducting nuclear tests. "It is possible to induct nuclear weapons without testing them," he said. Indeed, this was "one way of circumventing the US law" on nuclear testing.[50] In any case, he suggested, a National Security Council would help make these decisions. If this BJP official did not know what his government actually was doing, outsiders could be forgiven for believing that a nuclear decision would follow, not precede, the formation of a National Security Council. Little did Nath Jha and most other Indian officials know.

On April 27, the *New York Times* reported on the front page that U.S. intelligence sources were concerned that India was building a sea-launched missile with Russian assistance.[51] Indian sources had reported on the Sagarika missile's development as early as 1994, but American officials now were especially watchful in the wake of the Ghauri missile test and Russia's assistance to Iran's missile program.[52] Details of the Sagarika remained obscure. India possessed no submarines capable of launching land-attack missiles, and India's nascent program to build a nuclear-powered ballistic-missile submarine was probably at least a decade away from fruition. Defence Minister George Fernandes told reporters shortly *before* the *Times* report that "there are three versions of the Prithvi including a sea version."[53] Fernandes did not mention Russian assistance here, and misled his interlocutors insofar as the Sagarika was not simply a variant of the Prithvi. Evidently the missile was to be released from a submarine and then to rise through the water, after which an engine would ignite to take the missile on a trajectory to targets up to 350 kilometers away.[54] Whatever the Sagarika's technological or military features, it pointed to the Indian defense scientists' desire to develop the full suite of strategic weapons associated with being a major military power. Like Bhabha's plans for nuclear power in the 1950s, the defense scientists were working now on a missile for which no delivery platform could be built indigenously for at least a decade, and then at extraordinary expense. However, the very prospect of building a sea-based nuclear weapon system could increase the navy's interest in nuclear weapons. This would create more political and bureaucratic support for the weaponeers. Once each service obtained an interest in nuclear weapons, the requirements for greater numbers, diverse systems, and budgets would grow enormously.

However, for every seemingly bellicose sign emanating from India, a reassuring diplomatic signal also could be found. In late April, Sino-Indian dialogue continued with a pathbreaking visit to India by top Chinese military officers, including, for the first time, the Chinese chief of general staff. This reciprocated a trip India's Army Chief of Staff Malik had taken to China in 1997 when he was vice chief. Beyond bolstering military-to-military relations, the Indian and Chinese brass planned to pursue further demarcation of the Line of Actual Control between the two countries, which small numbers of Chinese troops reportedly had crossed "unintentionally" in 1997.[55] On April 30 and May 1, India's Foreign Secretary K. Raghunath met with American officials in Washington to further the budding strategic dialogue and prepare for President Clinton's planned trip to the subcontinent. In response to direct questions on nuclear policy, Raghunath gave no hint of the nuclear tests that were about to come.

Before Raghunath arrived home, unnamed DRDO scientists told the press that the government had approved work to develop and deploy a full-fledged missile system based on the results of the Agni missile's technology demonstration phase.[56] The DRDO sought to increase the missile's range and accuracy to make it militarily useful and to convert it to an all-solid-fuel rocket system. It appeared that India was mobilizing the Agni as *the* response to the Ghauri. This led observers inside and outside India to downplay further the likelihood of immediate nuclear weapon tests.

On May 3, George Fernandes launched an extraordinary rhetorical attack on China. Days after China's army chief completed his historic visit to India, Fernandes called China the "potential threat number one" facing India.[57] He elaborated on this theme several times in the ensuing two days, reflecting his longstanding animus toward China for invading Tibet almost forty years earlier. Fernandes's fusillade upset not only China but also Vajpayee, the Ministry of External Affairs, and many others. (The BJP's hard-line fraternal organization, the RSS, supported Fernandes's alarm.)[58] The Ministry of External Affairs issued an elaborately reassuring statement to China on May 6.[59]

People could be excused for wondering which voices represented the Indian government position. The tests that were about to come only heightened the perplexity. There was an explanation: Fernandes did not know the nuclear tests were pending when he jabbed at China. Like Raghunath in Washington, he was another high-level Indian official out of the loop in a government that had no integrated strategy.

BLASTS AND SHOCKWAVES—I, MAY 11 TO 13

At 3:45 P.M. on May 11, almost twenty-four years to the day since India conducted its first nuclear test, the desert ground near Pokhran shook again. India's strategic enclave simultaneously detonated three nuclear devices. Shock waves rippled through the test area, cracking walls in a nearby village and shaking the edifice of the international nonproliferation regime. The scientists exulted. Minutes later the phone rang at Prime Minister Vajpayee's official residence. Principal Secretary Brajesh Mishra received the message that the deed was done. He went to an adjoining room and notified Vajpayee, Home Minister L. K. Advani, Finance Minister Yashwant Sinha, Planning Commission Deputy Chairman Jaswant Singh, and George Fernandes. According to *India Today*, Advani, the firebrand leader of the BJP was seen wiping away tears.[60]

As in 1974 only a handful of officials knew of the tests beforehand, and even fewer participated in deliberations over whether and when to conduct them. Vajpayee, Mishra, and Jaswant Singh participated in the relevant deliberations with the top scientists. Advani's and Sinha's roles remain unclear. Fernandes was told only two days before the event, while the three military service chiefs and the foreign secretary were informed on May 10. President K. R. Narayanan was informed the night before the tests. Vice President Krishna Kant was also informed. The cabinet secretary apparently was kept out of the loop, unlike in 1996.[61] Whereas in 1982 and 1983 Ramanna and Arunachalam had involved Defence Minister Venkataraman and the cabinet and principal secretaries in deliberations over the proposal to conduct nuclear tests before presenting the idea to Indira Gandhi, the vetting now was more circumscribed.

The government's first public announcement of the tests offered few details. The scientists soon declared that they had detonated a "fission device with a yield of about 12 kilotons, a thermonuclear device with a yield of about 43 kilotons, and a sub-kiloton device."[62] Outside analysts subsequently disputed the claimed yields and the thermonuclear nature of the one device. In India the announcement of the tests drove people into the streets to celebrate with dance and fireworks.

The tests were an immediate triumph for the tenuous new government. In its few weeks in office it had experienced the tribulations of holding together a fractious coalition. The Tamil AIADMK (All-India Anna Dravida Munetra Kazhagam) regional party—with its eighteen vital Lok Sabha seats—had been particularly troublesome, resisting Vajpayee's effort to oust one of its central government ministers who had been charged with corruption. Others had expressed frustration that the government was failing to live up to its campaign pledges on political and economic issues. As the *Times of India* put it, "the predominant image" in April and early May "was of a weak-kneed government, exhibiting resistance to change."[63] This image changed in the afterglow of the tests. The explosions would increase "Vajpayee's credibility and infuse India with a great sense of confidence and pride," former Foreign Secretary J. N. Dixit declared.[64] "Nothing better could have happened," said former Indian Air Force Chief of Staff Air Chief Marshal N. C. Suri.[65] Indeed, a quick public opinion poll in six major cities showed that 91 percent approved the tests.[66]

Official statements and comments from Indian officials propounded several themes in the twenty-four hours following the tests. The tests "have established that India has a proven capability for a weaponised nuclear programme," an official press statement proclaimed on May 11. "They also provide a valuable database which is useful in the design of nuclear weapons of different yields for different applications and for different delivery systems." These data could then enable Indian scientists to conduct "sound computer simulation" that "may be supported by sub-critical experiments if considered necessary," the statement continued. Furthermore, the tests would help to train and motivate a new generation of scientists and engineers who had not participated in the 1974 blast, according to Indian sources.[67]

The government said that "the nuclear environment in India's neighbourhood" had necessitated the tests to "provide reassurance to the people of India that their national security interests are paramount." In a May 11 letter to President Clinton, Vajpayee stated that the threat from China motivated the tests: "We have an overt nuclear-weapon state on our borders . . . a state which committed armed aggression against India in 1962."[68] Brajesh Mishra explained, "We had to show a credible deterrent capability not only to the outside world, but to our own people."[69]

Anticolonial motivations also appeared explicitly and implicitly in the tests' aftermath. "Who are the Americans to tell us how to take care of our security concerns?" a BJP official asked a *Hindu* reporter.[70] Mishra took pains to say that "[t]he tests were not directed at the US," but it was clear that the scientists and the nationalistic government did mean to send a message to Washington and the Indian people that the nation could not be pushed around.[71] Colonialism was dead— again.

Yet India remained officially committed to "the goal of a truly comprehensive" ban on all underground nuclear testing. George Fernandes said that the tests enabled India now to "pursue, with credibility and greater conviction, our long-term campaign to rid the world of nuclear weapons."[72]

The tests shocked the U.S. government and expert community, but not in ways that Indians may have hoped. Most American officials saw New Delhi's performance before and after the tests as highly amateurish. These feelings, of course, were magnified by the embarrassment of the Clinton administration's failure to anticipate and detect the pending tests, which critics in Washington considered amateurish, too.

Top Clinton administration officials learned of the tests from the media following the Indian government's official announcement—not from U.S. intelligence agencies. They scrambled to react. "We are deeply disturbed by this announcement," State Department spokesman James P. Rubin declared.[73] The Clinton administration tried to contain the damage by urging Pakistan to wait before responding in kind to India's tests. Over the next two weeks the United States would try to isolate India internationally and cajole Pakistan.

American officials barely contained their personal anger and professional dismay at India's actions. "Secretary Albright believes it was appalling that Indian diplomats left the administration with anything but the impression that there would be nuclear tests this week," spokesman Rubin told reporters on May 12.[74] "The Indians lulled us into thinking that they were not going to undertake any precipitous action in the nuclear area without a careful review of their options," another official told the *Washington Post*.[75]

However, American taxpayers were spending more than $27 billion per year for intelligence services precisely to detect things like nuclear weapon test preparations. If diplomats did not perceive the signs, surely spy satellites should have, argued many. Chairman of the Senate Intelligence Committee Richard C. Shelby called the episode "a colossal failure" that betrayed a "dreadfully inadequate job" by the intelligence community.[76] The day after the tests, it emerged that U.S. satellites had at midnight Washington time detected "clear-cut" evidence of test preparations six hours before the devices were detonated. However, CIA satellite intelligence analysts were home sleeping because they had not been put on alert.[77] CIA Director George Tenet quickly appointed an independent panel to review the failure. Whatever the particularities of the tactical intelligence failure at this time, the central fact was that the United States never had possessed detailed intelligence on India's nuclear capabilities and policymaking to rival the intelligence it had on Pakistan.[78]

At this stage, the implications of the Indian tests for U.S. and international security were unclear. Defense Secretary William Cohen spoke for many when he predicted on May 12 that the tests would cause "a chain reaction. . . . There will be other countries that see this as an open invitation to try to acquire this technology."[79] Interestingly, if Cohen's argument was valid, it seemed to endorse the view of disarmament activists (and India) that the possession of nuclear weapons by a few countries—including the five declared nuclear powers—helped motivate others to want the same thing. From a security-centric logic, India's tests did not really threaten any other country besides Pakistan, and if Pakistan followed suit, it would not pose a plausibly serious security threat to any other state except theoretically Israel, which already had nuclear weapons. But from the standpoint of status and politics, India's tests could be assumed to make nuclear weapons more attractive to others. This is the very logic that in reverse direction makes disarmament by the recognized nuclear weapon states a necessary condition for persuading others to give up nuclear weapon ambitions. Cohen and other officials worried about the proliferation domino problem, but they continued to reject the implication that the nuclear weapon states must model the behavior they urge upon others.

Much of Washington's fear centered on Pakistan. Nawaz Sharif and other officials said they were not surprised by the Indian tests, given their worst-case assumptions about the BJP. They declared they would take "necessary steps for addressing Pakistan's legitimate security concerns."[80] Sharif wisely bought time to consider Pakistan's options and evaluate how the United States and the international community would punish India and offer rewards for Pakistani restraint now. He would judge the political dynamic within his own country to determine how much leeway he had. However, from the beginning, Pakistan's nuclear scientists and engineers itched to reciprocate. While Army Chief of Staff Jehangir Karamat reportedly counseled restraint, other national security officials demanded a show of strength. Politicians across the spectrum demanded firmness. Benazir Bhutto, now in opposition, called for the government to launch "a preemptive military strike," if possible, "against India's nuclear capability."[81] President Clinton, British Prime Minister Tony Blair, and other international leaders offered strategic reasons and political-economic incentives for not testing, but Pakistani leaders felt compelled to match India and suffer the dire economic consequences of sanctions.

Indian officials did not worry greatly about Pakistan's reaction. If Pakistan truly had nuclear weapon capabilities, they would conduct tests. This would ameliorate India's international isolation. If Pakistan actually could not produce and detonate nuclear weapons, their weakness would be exposed. In any case, Indians did not believe Pakistan had enough weapon-usable fissile material to engage in a testing competition with India. This reduced the potential downside of the Indian tests, in the view of Indian specialists.[82]

China took a day to react and then on May 12 stated tersely that it was "seriously concerned."[83] However, when Vajpayee's letter to Clinton appeared (by leak) in the *New York Times*, Beijing's tone changed. Not appreciating being blamed as the cause of India's tests or the 1962 war, the Chinese now declared that the tests showed "outrageous contempt" for the international community and should be strongly condemned. George Fernandes's verbal assault had disturbed the Chinese, but the Indian Foreign Ministry and other officials had tried to calm things. Now, days later, the tests and Vajpayee's letter called India's intentions into question. New Delhi soon began backpedaling to reassure China that it valued the ten-year-old process of constructive dialogue and meant no harm. But backpedaling did not say much about India's forward strategy.

BLASTS AND SHOCK WAVES—II, MAY 13 TO 28

On May 13, India shocked its own people and the international community by declaring it had conducted two more nuclear tests. The government announced that the two "sub-kiloton" blasts occurred at 12:21 P.M. and were intended "to generate additional data for improved computer simulation" and other nuclear weapon experiments.[84] "This completes the planned series of tests," the government declared, reiterating vaguely that it was prepared to "consider adhering to some of the undertakings in the CTBT." Indeed, several well-informed strategists in New Delhi thought the government would quickly announce a decision to sign the CTBT. This would dampen the international outcry over the tests and exploit the public euphoria in India to avoid domestic questioning of joining the recently vilified treaty.[85]

The second round of tests occurred as President Clinton, in Berlin, was preparing to sign an order implementing U.S. sanctions against India pursuant to the 1994 Nuclear Proliferation Prevention Act. The law called for sweeping economic penalties, but because it had never been applied and because the United States wanted to avoid sanctions that would unintentionally undermine its own interests, the administration planned to take the allowed thirty days to determine exactly how to apply the sanctions.[86] Some were applied now, but the full array would emerge later, as discussed later in this chapter.

The May 13 tests showed the Indian weaponeers' determination to execute their weapons-development testing plans before the international community could exert its potential influence on the government. They bunched the experiments together in a preapproved two-day series to be executed without interruption. Yet, the management of Indian diplomacy revealed the potential liabilities of excessive secrecy. Indian diplomats around the world, including Ambassador Naresh Chandra in Washington, did not know of the second round of tests. Between May 11 and 12, these uninformed diplomats easily could have made unwitting statements to the press and foreign governments suggesting the tests were over, only to have their nation's credibility undermined by the May 13 tests.

Prime Minister Vajpayee further alarmed the international community when he gave his first interview since the tests. "We have a big bomb now," he declared to *India Today,* suggesting an ominous triumphalism.[87] Speaking to party workers the same day, Vajpayee said his government "will not hesitate to use these weapons in self-defence."[88] Other officials moved to correct the impressions left by the prime minister. The government retracted the "big bomb" statement, and *India Today* deleted it from the published version of the Vajpayee interview, although transcripts with the offending phrase already had been distributed by the prime minister's office.[89] Then, on May 18, the prime minister's office "modified" Vajpayee's statement about not hesitating to use nuclear weapons in self-defense. The government wanted to remove the impression that Vajpayee meant to contemplate defending India through *first use* of nuclear weapons. "India will not be the first to use nuclear weapons against anyone," the prime minister's office now insisted.[90] Observers could be forgiven for wondering if the Indian government knew what it was doing.

Meanwhile, in Washington, Congress and others questioned whether the Clinton administration knew what *it* was doing. Many blasted the administration for failing to detect the tests in advance. In Senate committee hearings on May 13 and 14, senators called for the United States to compel India to roll back its nuclear program completely.[91] In the frenzy, experienced administration officials such as Robert Einhorn urged senators "to be realistic about what can be achieved in the near term."[92] This did little to mollify Congress and other critics. Yet the critics failed to ask whether and how the United States could have persuaded the BJP government not to test even if the test preparations had been detected. Perhaps the United States could have used advanced warning to mobilize those BJP coalition partners who did not share the party's attraction to the bomb, but then the issue would have been transformed into a colonial fight. Nationalistic impulses probably would have prevailed politically.

The administration's pique at Indian leaders and Congress's implicit assumption of U.S. power over India reflected a fundamental perceptual gap. Clinton administration officials genuinely felt that they had elevated India to a prominent place in the U.S. foreign policy agenda. President Clinton was due to visit the region in November. Secretary of State Albright had agreed to urge cabinet secretaries to visit South Asia throughout 1998.[93] The United States was eager to develop a "strategic dialogue" with India. Furthermore, Washington's diplomacy with China included intense, albeit quiet, pressure to cease supplying sensitive technology to Pakistan, recognizing India's concerns. Given these exertions, administration officials expected openness and disclosure from their Indian counterparts. The two governments and peoples were not adversaries; they were increasingly close friends. They had differences, particularly on nuclear policy. Yet the Americans believed that *both* sides now were taking steps not to increase tensions over nuclear issues, while expanding areas of positive cooperation. This is why administration officials reacted so angrily to the unwillingness of their Indian counterparts to give some warning of the tests.[94]

However, Indian officials saw matters differently. They perceived that Washington put much greater stock in relations with Beijing, to the point where the United States seemed to indulge China's nuclear and missile cooperation with Pakistan. A high-level Indian official spoke of a "U.S.-China-Pakistan axis" against India.[95] When reminded that the Clinton administration finally had convinced Beijing to implement fully its nonproliferation commitments, this official scoffed. India welcomed greater U.S. interest and the prospect of a Clinton visit, but Indian officials still felt that the nonproliferation issue was highly adversarial. If India was defending its nuclear sovereignty against an American assault, Indian leaders were not about to warn Washington of the tests. This was ironic: Indian leaders intended the tests to display India's autonomy and security but were somehow afraid that they would not be able to withstand U.S. pressure had Washington been warned. This combination of defiant assertiveness and diffident timidity may have been a price paid for the colonial experience. In any case, New Delhi's handling of pretest diplomacy undermined whatever increase in international respect India sought from the tests.

Differences of opinion existed within the Indian government and political organizations over the importance of ties with the United States. In a conversation shortly after the May 11 tests, an Indian official used a golf metaphor to express goodwill: "President Clinton is on his homeward nine, and he and we want it to be a good one. We don't want to put sand traps in his way."[96] This official stated that the Indian government knew that the United States would impose sanctions: "they are part of the American legal system, and yours is a law abiding country." The challenge now was for Washington and New Delhi to accept what India had done and move forward. However, more militant and less internationalist voices in India urged a harder, more defiant line.

Even as the Indian public maintained its visceral celebration of the nuclear tests, doubts began to emerge over their implications. Sanctions loomed. The rupee's value immediately began to fall against the dollar. Money was being pulled from Indian stocks, and economic growth would be impaired.[97] English-language newspapers charged the government with exploiting the tests for partisan advantage and representing India in an unseemly manner.[98] A commentator in the *Indian Express* wrote that the government was "like a virgin on Viagra and not quite knowing what to do with its new-found power."[99] Several groups numbering in the scores and hundreds protested in New Delhi and other cities, decrying the tests on moral grounds and as a diversion of resources when people lacked electricity, education, and other basic needs. The protests were much smaller than the celebrations, but they indicated an undercurrent of doubt.

The *Times of India* noted in a May 14 editorial that "[f]or a nation which in the normal course cannot agree on anything," the widespread support for the tests "was startling."[100] Yet the paper said that by testing now India had "restored parity" with Pakistan in "an equation which was earlier very unequal" in India's favor. Moreover, if the "*real* adversary was China," the tests came when India had achieved a solid conventional military footing against China along the northern border. India's "well-established" ability to make dozens of fission bombs was also "known where it matters" and provided "deterrence enough even if a China-Pakistan axis was in the making." Instead of solving a real security problem, the paper charged that Vajpayee was trying "to establish a new myth in the place of Nehru's discredited one"—a myth of "India as a producer of not just atom, but hydrogen bombs." This would give Vajpayee "the only chance of saving his floundering minority government, . . . giving it a focus which was large and immediate; the ultimate Quick Fix solution." Yet, the efficacy of such a fix was illusory, the newspaper argued. The Indian people "are at a low point in our history. We feel vulnerable as a people due to continuing political uncertainty; our self-esteem is at its nadir because of the venality and corruption of politicians on open display every day." The "liberalised economy," as well, was a cause of domestic insecurity and frustration. In this situation, the *Times of India* concluded, "A drowning man will grasp even a thermonuclear device to stay alive. And he isn't going to think of the consequences."

As in 1974 and 1975, the public began to show signs of not appreciating attempts to divert it from woes that politicians otherwise were failing to redress. Behind the scenes, at least one crucial supporter of the government in the Lok Sabha viewed the tests as an enormous and unnecessarily costly mistake of which he had not been forewarned.[101] This portended political difficulties ahead for a government that still had a thin coalition-dependent majority.

Fears that the BJP would undermine India's interests and normative self-regard grew when Home Minister L. K. Advani declared that "Islamabad should realise the change in the geo-strategic situation in the region" and "roll back its anti-India policy, especially with regard to Kashmir."[102] A week later, on May 25, Advani declared that India would undertake "hot pursuit" to chase insurgents from Kashmir back into Pakistan.[103] This was an aggressive face that the Indian polity did not wear comfortably, and it appeared to be hardened by the nuclear tests. Vajpayee seemed to recognize the moral problem when he reminded Parliament on May 27 that India would "continue to reflect a commitment to sensibilities and obligations of an ancient civilization, a sense of responsibility and restraint."[104]

The government announced on May 21 that it was voluntarily undertaking a moratorium on further nuclear tests. Brajesh Mishra, who appeared to have been a strong advocate of conducting the tests, told journalists that India would now like to translate the moratorium into "a formal obligation" through negotiations with the United States and other relevant parties.[105] Officials publicly did not explain what India would try to negotiate on a treaty that 149 sovereign states already had signed. In private they alluded to seeking the same sort of secret arrangement the United States reportedly had made with France to facilitate its joining the CTBT: technical assistance and cooperation with U.S. nuclear weapons laboratories to enhance computer simulation and other experimental capabilities to maintain the "reliability" of nuclear weapons.[106] This dovetailed with the government's May 11 statement that referred to the weaponeers' ongoing interest in computer simulation and subcritical experiments. However, this was a nonstarter in Washington: to provide such assistance to a non–nuclear weapon state as defined by the NPT would violate the treaty. India appeared to drop this bid in subsequent interactions with the United States.

On May 27, Vajpayee went to the Lok Sabha for the first parliamentary debate on nuclear policy since the tests. Opposition leaders unleashed a volley of pointed questions and criticisms. Indrajit Gupta, a Communist who had been Interior Minister in the United Front governments, declared, "The nuclear tests are a great achievement for India, no doubt, but we can't even supply ordinary drinking water and electrical power to the people of this country."[107] He wondered, "Where does all this lead to?" P. Chidambaram, the respected finance minister of the United Front governments, joined others in accusing the new government of "inventing" a security threat to justify the tests.[108] Chidambaram noted bellicose government statements prior to the tests and complained, "[I]f anybody asks why, where is the threat, they are branded as a traitor. That is the depth of your political cynicism."[109] Of course, cynicism abounded, including amongst the critics now. Congress party leader Natwar Singh declared that not a "single incident" had occurred in recent months to suggest a deterioration in the security environment, ignoring the Ghauri test, just as P. Chidambaram ignored the possible value of nuclear deterrence.[110] Singh's broader point was that the government had concocted a security pretext for conducting tests largely for political gain, when the nation's long-standing, self-restrained nuclear option policy, and the capabilities behind it, were adequate to deter foreign threats. Former Prime Minister Chandra

Shekhar said that bombs were no substitute for economic strength—it was easy to make a bomb but difficult for the nation now to face its consequences.[111]

Vajpayee listened in silence, apparently dismayed by the attacks.[112] Eventually BJP ministers, parliamentarians, and other government supporters rose to the debate. Many tempered earlier comments and retreated from jingoism, including George Fernandes who joined others in finding more subdued ways to argue that the regional security environment justified the tests. Most agreed that India should continue to pursue constructive dialogue with China, although this should not deter India from enhancing its strategic capabilities. Government supporters appeared to have the wind knocked from their sails, but they still blew hot about their patriotism and the need for India to take its rightful place under the sun.

Like many parliamentary debates on nuclear policy stretching back to 1964, this one did little to develop a consensus on what India's nuclear policies and strategy should be. All participants, including from the BJP, acknowledged that the technological achievement owed not to one political party but to a string of governments who supported the development of the nuclear option dating from the 1950s. The debate also yielded general recognition that government ministers' heated rhetoric before and after the tests had undermined India's credibility. Looking ahead, though, the respected journalist Pran Chopra argued that neither the tests nor subsequent developments evidenced a coherent strategy for reducing as well as deterring threats over the long term. If " 'why now?' was answered unsatisfactorily," Chopra concluded, " 'what next?' was not even addressed properly by the Government."[113]

On May 28, the day after the debate, Pakistan at once complicated and simplified the Indian challenge of deciding "what next?" Pakistan conducted five claimed nuclear tests of its own. This is discussed below after examining the technical and related doctrinal questions raised by India's tests.

WHAT DID INDIA TEST AND WHY?

Indian scientists declared that they had tested a total of five nuclear devices. In a press conference in New Delhi on May 17, the four lead scientists received kudos and offered a few details about the tests. Abdul Kalam and R. Chidambaram, as the leaders of the DRDO and AEC, respectively, received top billing, followed by K. Santhanam of the DRDO and Anil Kakodkar, the director of BARC. Pictures of them posing awkwardly but happily at the podium appeared in newspapers around the world. Brief adulatory profiles of Kalam and Chidambaram ran in Indian and international papers. They invariably extolled the Muslim bachelor Kalam's Spartan lifestyle and interest in Hindu culture, as well as his pure Indianness.[114] "I am completely indigenous," Kalam exclaimed, distinguishing himself from other scientists who were trained in the West. Chidambaram received slightly less attention, as usual, because he lacked Kalam's drive for public self-promotion and was a less colorful figure. Still, this modesty was a virtue. A *Times of India* profile described the physicist as "self-effacing to a fault," disdainful of heavy security protection, and doting as a grandfather.[115] Chidambaram's scientific qualifications and skills were indeed impressive. Though he never received the public recognition of Ramanna and Iyengar, and now Kalam, Chidambaram arguably was the leading scientific mind behind India's nuclear weapon capabilities. Still, the moniker "father of the bomb" went to Kalam. (BARC director Kakodkar tried to give additional credit where it was due by mentioning other key contributors: M. S. Ramakumar, director of the Nuclear Fuel and Automation Manufacturing group, who shaped critical nuclear components; S. K. Gupta of the Solid State Physics and Spectroscopy Group, who contributed to the design and assessment of the devices; D. D. Sood, director of the Radiochemistry and Isotope group, who led the effort to supply the various nuclear materials used in the devices; G. Govindraj, associate director of the Electronics and Instrumentation Group, who set up the field instrumentation for the tests.)[116]

The press conference clarified the extensive role of the DRDO in the nuclear weapon program, which the Indian public and much of the outside world had not appreciated before. Beginning with the 1974 Pokhran experiment and then intensifying during the 1980s, India's nuclear weapon capabilities owed as much to the DRDO's scientists and engineers as to the nuclear scientists in the AEC. Developing deliverable weapons required reductions in size and weight and improvements in the symmetry (simultaneity) of the high-explosive systems required to compress the fissile cores of weapons. The DRDO concentrated on these problems. The DRDO also "ruggedized" nuclear weapons for safer handling and potential delivery to targets and performed the necessary engineering to allow them to be mounted on aircraft and missiles. It devised means to protect aircraft systems against electromagnetic interference. Thus, Kalam correctly explained that the DRDO and the Department of Atomic Energy had "effectively and efficiently coordinated and integrated their respective technological strengths in a national mission."[117] This had begun in 1982 with the close collaboration between Ramanna and Arunachalum, although it took the 1998 tests to expose these developments to public view.

Chidambaram announced that the thermonuclear, or hydrogen, bomb achieved a yield of 43 kilotons. He said that it purposely had been kept at this relatively low yield in order to prevent damage to "neighbouring villages" and radiation venting.[118] As earlier, he described the other May 11 tests as a 12-kiloton fission device that was significantly lighter and more compact than the 1974 device and a 0.2-kiloton-yield device of unspecified composition. The two May 13 tests had reported yields of 0.2 and 0.6 kilotons. The scientists provided no details on the fissile materials used in the devices or the depths of the devices' burial before detonation. After the press conference, two of the leading technical figures— BARC Director Kakodkar and S. K. Sikka, a longtime research partner of Chidambaram's—prepared a note for the May 1998 BARC Newsletter in which the yield of the thermonuclear device was stated as 45 kilotons and that of the fission device as 15 kilotons; the three smaller devices were described as "experimental," with yields of approximately 0.2, 0.5, and 0.3 kilotons. (*India Today* reported in October that the scientists subsequently said the May 11 fission bomb yield was 20 kilotons and the hydrogen bomb 25 kilotons.)[119]

Western experts expressed doubts about the claimed yields of the May 11 tests and even the occurrence of the two May 13 tests. After months of analyzing seismological and crater data, the University of Arizona's Terry Wallace published in September 1998 a detailed paper concluding that the combined yield of the May 11 tests was between 10 to 15 kilotons.[120] Wallace also concluded that the yield of the 1974 test had been less than 5 kilotons. In an earlier article he had argued that even if the 1974 blast had the claimed yield of 12 kilotons, the May 11, 1998, yield was "2.1 to 2.2" times greater, making it less than 30 kilotons and more likely "20 kilotons at most."[121]

Chidambaram and others heard of these doubts and bristled at the lack of respect, according to a source in the Indian science establishment.[122] The scientists knew that the 1974 Pokhran device's yield was disparaged quietly in international weaponeer circles, and they did not want to be subjected to doubts by American scientists again. Chidambaram chose to explode the three May 11 devices simultaneously in part to mask their seismic signal so that outsiders would find it more difficult to evaluate the yields of each one.[123] (The Indian press reported a variety of other reasons for simultaneity: "a gap in the blasts could have resulted in the loss of valuable data for the shock waves travel in mili-seconds," the *Times of India* reported. The *Hindu* said "the devices were located at a lateral distance of around one kilometer . . . to prevent accidental explosions." *India Today* said "they feared that the shock released from the hydrogen explosion could damage the other shafts.")[124]

In private, Chidambaram exclaimed that "the Americans" and other outsiders did not know the characteristics of the geological formations at the test site and so had little basis for their interpretations of the seismic data. He said that his team had deployed multiple accelerometers around each test shaft and obtained reliable data from them.[125]

In the September 10, 1998, issue of the Indian journal *Current Science*, three authors from the Bhabha Atomic Research Centre published a technical paper attempting to debunk the American seismologists' low estimates of the May 11 test yields. The Indians—none of whom is a seismologist—argued that the simultaneity of the May 11 explosions had distorted the seismographic signals registered at international stations located to the east and west of the test site, causing them to register lower-than-correct values. Stations to the north and south, they argued, had more accurate readings, and their average produced values indicating a yield of 58 kilotons plus or minus 5 kilotons.[126]

The key datum for evaluating the debate over the seismographic interpretations of the 1998 tests is the yield of the 1974 test. Thus, the BARC authors based their calculation in part on the 1974 Pokhran blast's "known yield of 13 kt." This assumption was vital because the 1974 data provided a benchmark for calibrating the geological character of the Indian test site, as the Indian scientists acknowledged. It was possible to assess the yield of the 1998 tests by comparing their seismographic signal with that of the 1974 test. The Indian scientists' claimed yield(s) of the 1998 tests were valid only if the 1974 test yield was very close to 14 kilotons.[127] Hence the BARC team's reiteration that the 1974 yield was 13 kilotons. However, two former nuclear establishment leaders acknowledged previously to the author that the 1974 yield had been "much lower," in one man's phrase, or "8 kilotons" in P. K. Iyengar's words. This badly undermined the foundation on which the BARC team's 1998 claim rested, although this was not acknowledged in India because the lower yield of the 1974 test was never publicly admitted.[128]

The most triumphant achievement for the weaponeers—and perhaps India— was the thermonuclear device. Thus, the scientists grew angry at those in the international community who questioned whether they really had done it. In the first few days after the tests, Western intelligence sources and others suggested that a boosted-fission weapon, not a true thermonuclear device had been detonated.[129] Having heard this, Chidambaram on May 17 took pains to emphasize that the 43-kiloton blast came from a "thermonuclear," or "hydrogen bomb," not a boosted-fission device. "We used a fission trigger and a secondary fusion," he said. "A boosted-fission device does not have a secondary stage."[130] Chidambaram added that the strategic enclave had designed a boosted-fission weapon but decided not to test it.[131] In later interviews he reversed himself and stated that the primary stage of the thermonuclear device was a boosted-fission device whose radiation then detonated the secondary, fusion stage.[132] A close colleague of Chidambaram explained the apparent contradiction by saying that Chidambaram had been flustered by the flurry of questions at the May 17 press conference and had misspoken—the primary was indeed a boosted-fission device.[133]

India plausibly possessed the materials required for boosted-fission and thermonuclear weapons. Boosted-fission weapons require tritium while hydrogen bombs require lithium-6 deuteride. BARC reportedly began separating lithium-6 in the mid-1980s, which could then be inserted into reactor cores and transmuted by irradiation into tritium or could be mixed directly with deuterium to form the solid lithium-6 deuteride. BARC also had begun extracting tritium from reactor heavy water earlier.[134] According to a Mumbai-based journalist, S. Gopi Rethinaraj, a team at BARC had developed a "pioneering" method of extracting significant quantities of tritium from CANDU-reactor heavy water.[135] Using a liquid phase catalytic exchange process, the pilot plant at BARC apparently began operating in 1997. Although Rethinaraj, citing the BARC team, claimed that the process was original, it actually had been patented by Canadian scientists in the 1980s. The details of the process were available in public literature. Moreover, Canadian experts on the process had discussed it with BARC scientists and engineers, most recently at a meeting sponsored by the International Atomic Energy Agency at the Chalk River nuclear complex in Canada in 1994.[136] Indian domestic law does not allow foreign entities to extend patents in this area to India, and it appeared that the new Indian plant was based on the method patented in Canada. Whatever the derivation of India's new tritium extraction capability, it gave the nuclear establishment a vital ingredient for thermonuclear weapons. When asked by Rethinaraj whether BARC was stockpiling tritium, Chidambaram said, "No comment."

If it was reasonable to assume that the nuclear establishment had the necessary materials for a thermonuclear device, the question was whether it could design an effective two-stage device with such a relatively low yield. Many American nuclear weapon specialists doubted this, noting that the first U.S. hydrogen bombs had enormous yields—more than one megaton—and that it took much experimentation and testing to be able to control the second stage to obtain reliably lower yields.[137] However, others, including one of the United States' early premier weapon designers, Theodore Taylor, said that in the forty-plus years since the first hydrogen bombs were developed, enormous quantities of theoretical and practical information had become public through literature and international conferences. In his view, it would be foolish to think that India's talented scientists could not do what they said they had done.[138] As Harold Agnew, the former director of the Los Alamos National Laboratory put it, building a hydrogen bomb is "not a giant step if you have smart people and understand the basics."[139] For its part, the U.S. intelligence community concluded that the Indian team had attempted to detonate a two-stage hydrogen bomb but that the second stage had failed to ignite as planned.[140]

Ultimately, radiochemical analysis of debris at the test site would provide the most accurate way of assessing the composition and yields of the nuclear explosive devices. Indian teams have conducted such analyses.[141] If they make the data available to other scientists, the questions about the May 11 and 13 blasts can be answered definitively. In the meantime, India's political and military leaders—and the international community—must choose whether to take the scientists at their word. In making this judgment, it can be recalled that the current leaders of the Indian nuclear establishment still insist that the yield of the 1974 test was significantly higher than former leaders of this establishment have acknowledged privately.

Beyond testing a thermonuclear device, the Indian scientists may have pursued another portentous breakthrough. Press accounts hinted that the "low yield" device tested on May 11 was composed of non-weapon-grade plutonium. Subsequent interviews by the author with knowledgeable Indian sources confirmed this, although the exact composition of the tested material remains unclear from public sources.[142]

Plutonium is classified as weapon-grade if its concentration of the isotope plutonium-239 is greater than 93 percent. So-called reactor-grade plutonium has a significantly smaller concentration of plutonium-239—typically 65 to 70 percent in the spent fuel of India's CANDU reactors. It is possible that the non-weapon-grade plutonium tested in 1998 had a mix of isotopes intermediate between weapon-grade and reactor-grade. Such plutonium can easily be produced in a

CANDU reactor by irradiating some of the fuel for a shorter period than that characteristic of a commercial operation.

The use of non-weapon-grade plutonium in weapons has several potential liabilities. For example, the higher concentrations of isotopes other than plutonium-239—particularly plutonium-240 and plutonium-238—increase the risks that a weapon will explode with less than its designed yield. These isotopes have high rates of spontaneous fission that produces neutrons that could initiate the neutron chain reaction prematurely, that is, before the plutonium core has been fully compressed by the surrounding conventional high explosive. As a result, most of the plutonium will remain unfissioned by the time thermal expansion of the core causes the chain reaction to terminate. Isotopes other than plutonium-239 also have higher rates of alpha particle emission and electromagnetic radiation. This may cause the high explosive to degrade and raise radiation exposure to workers during weapon fabrication, respectively.

Despite these difficulties, nuclear weapon designers in the United States and elsewhere learned how to make effective weapons from non-weapon-grade plutonium. (The United States in 1962 conducted a test of an explosive composed of reactor-grade plutonium, and in 1977 American officials privately persuaded French and Japanese officials and nuclear experts that reactor-grade plutonium could function in weapons. This information was imparted to help persuade France not to go through with a contract to build a plutonium reprocessing plant in Pakistan.) The problem of excess heating of the high explosive due to alpha particle emission can be redressed by increasing the conduction of heat from the plutonium core to the outside of the weapon. Radiation can be blocked by adding shielding at warhead fabrication facilities. The problem of preinitiation due to spontaneous neutron fissioning can be solved several ways. Perhaps most important, "boosted" fission weapons can be designed to be virtually immune to the problem of premature initiation. That is, reactor-grade plutonium can be used to produce the low-yield fission explosion needed to fuse the mixture of deuterium and tritium in such weapons. The above considerations are reflected in the recent unclassified guidance issued by the U.S. Department of Energy that reactor-grade plutonium can be used to make nuclear weapons at all levels of technical sophistication.[143]

While proponents of nuclear power in Japan and elsewhere have been reluctant to acknowledge the weapon applications of reactor-grade plutonium, there is no reason to doubt that Indian nuclear scientists have long grasped the explosive reality. Indeed, the potential weapon utility of reactor-grade plutonium is greater in India than has been commonly appreciated. The Canadian CANDU reactor design on which most Indian nuclear plants are based yields spent fuel with a lower concentration of plutonium-238, which is the most troublesome heat-producing isotope in spent fuel. The smaller amount of plutonium-238 reduces the need to design the weapon so that the heat produced by the decay of this isotope does not cause the temperature inside the weapon to rise too high. Indian scientists and engineers would also comprehend that boosted-fission weapons largely obviate the preinitiation problem.[144]

Indian weaponeers had several motives for building and testing non-weapon-grade plutonium weapons. India's stockpile of separated weapon-grade plutonium produced by the CIRUS and Dhruva reactors was probably around 250 to 300 kilograms by 1998.[145] Depending on assumptions about weapon designs, this stockpile could "fuel" perhaps fifty weapons. Such an arsenal would be more than enough to deter and/or destroy Pakistan as a functioning state but might not seem sufficient to fulfill theoretical requirements to deter both Pakistan and China. Scientists like Chidambaram recognized that political leaders in New Delhi could be inclined or pressured into signing a treaty to end unsafeguarded production of fissile materials. Such a treaty would legitimate India's existing stock of weapon-grade plutonium but would require international safeguards on any further separation, storage, and use of plutonium. Thus India's potential arsenal of weapon-grade plutonium would be capped. However, if India's initial explosive experiments with non-weapon-grade plutonium gave confidence that this material could be used for bombs, then India's prospective arsenal would be significantly larger. If the plutonium was reactor-grade, then India's entire stockpile of this material, recently estimated roughly to be 600 kilograms as of the end of 1998, could be used directly in weapons.[146] If the plutonium was of intermediate composition, a large amount of such material could be created by mixing the stockpiles of weapon- and reactor-grade plutonium. In either case the stockpile of weapon-usable material would be enlarged, making a fissile-material production cutoff treaty more palatable.

The international implications of India's experiment depend partially on whether India used reactor-grade or greater-than-reactor-grade plutonium in its test(s), and whether the tests were effective enough to allow India to make weapons from this material. If reactor-grade plutonium were used—as opposed to a mix of isotopes closer to weapon-grade—then the Indian test could signal a potentially grave warning to the international security system. Countries with plutonium reprocessing plants and/or stockpiles of reactor-grade plutonium should then be seen to be much closer to possession of nuclear weapons than previously acknowledged. This includes Japan, Germany, the Netherlands, Switzerland, and Belgium, and also South Korea and Taiwan. The latter two have occasionally expressed interest in reprocessing their spent fuel; moreover, South Korea, like India operates CANDU reactors as well as light-water reactors.

The international security implications of France's and the United Kingdom's plutonium reprocessing services provided to non-nuclear-weapon states should also then come under closer scrutiny. To be sure, all such countries that are party to the NPT have put their plutonium stockpiles and separation plants under international safeguards. Yet, if they elected to leave the NPT or clandestinely to divert this material to military uses, they could do so with greater confidence that they could produce nuclear weapons. For its part, India's desired reputation as a responsible peaceful user of nuclear technology could be undermined by the revelation that plutonium derived from nuclear electricity generation were to be used in weapons, further weakening the likelihood of international cooperation in the civilian applications of nuclear power. But, again, from India's standpoint, international cooperation had been largely refused since 1974. There was little to lose.

The Indian scientists and engineers achieved a second breakthrough in the 1998 tests by proving the effectiveness of deuterium-tritium (DT) neutron initiators to trigger fission explosions. The weaponeers had been working on such initiators for years to replace the original initiator design that relied on beryllium and polonium. The earlier model posed significant obstacles to building deployable weapons insofar as polonium's short, 138-day half-life meant that initiators would have to be replaced frequently, preventing effective deployments or on-the-shelf readiness. The initiator breakthrough was reported obliquely in the press statement written by K. Santhanam after the May tests. The relevant sentence read, "BARC has also worked out several new concepts like long shelf life of device components and optimisation of the yield-to-weight ratio."[147]

More important than questions of bomb composition and whether India actually possessed hydrogen bombs were the questions of why its scientists wanted to develop them and what the state proposed to do with them. Previous chapters note that Indian strategists and military officials had not stated that India required hydrogen bombs for deterrence, with the recent exception of armchair strategists like the BJP's Mohan Guruswamy. "There is no need for fusion (hydrogen weapon) or enhanced yield fission (tritium) warheads," K. Sundarji wrote in a recent representative statement.[148]

Indeed, there is no evidence that the "requirement" to develop and test thermonuclear weapons came from anyone but the scientists themselves, continuing the process of scientific "push" begun by Homi Bhabha. For scientists like Chidambaram (and Edward Teller before him), the H-bomb held a great attraction as a capability to be mastered. The H-bomb is widely perceived as the ultimate achievement of mastery over the atom's power. The scientist or scientists who acquire it go down in history. If Ramanna and Iyengar were lionized for being the fathers of India's atomic bomb, Chidambaram could win his due as the father of the H-bomb. Moreover, arch rival Pakistan, even with China's help, was unlikely to be able to build H-bombs. India's capacity to do so would put Pakistan in its place.

Yet nuclear weapons are supposed—in both senses of the term—to serve strategic purposes. To have a strategic purpose the Indian H-bomb required a doctrinal context. But no such doctrine had been developed and decided officially in India prior to the production of the H-bomb. *After* the tests, the Institute for Defence Studies and Analyses convened India's leading strategists—serving and retired defense officials, academics, Foreign Ministry officials, and journalists. They declared, "[T]here is now an urgent need for India to both develop a nuclear doctrine and ensure that the success of the tests is not frittered away as did happen after the 1974 nuclear implosion," according to a *Times of India* account.[149]

The gathered experts all had participated for years in debating the adequacy of the "nuclear option," or "nonweaponized deterrence," or "recessed deterrence," or "minimum deterrence." These doctrinal approaches ranged in their economic and technical demands and their conceptions of India's deterrence requirements. They were still the main courses on the menu from which Indian officials would now choose. None of the heretofore debated doctrines envisioned or required thermonuclear weapons, yet these weapons now had to be reckoned with *post facto*. It was likely that the most radically pronuclear analysts would adapt by finding strategic imperatives for these superweapons.

Still, the prime minister had no specific doctrine in mind when he authorized the tests. As his office stated on May 18, "Our mindset is not in favour of a war. We wanted a nuclear deterrent. We conducted the tests. Fullstop."[150] This reflected a not untenable view that nuclear weapons are primarily political devices and that the mere possession of a deliverable few was adequate to deter. But, again, the government did not address the need for hydrogen bombs.

Beyond the prime minister's general declaration, Indian officials offered little detail on the vital related issue of command and control. Kalam declared that "India has command-and-control systems in different forms at present." He added that "[w]e have to consolidate [them] and we are progressing towards that."[151] Would India continue its long-standing avoidance of allocating nuclear weapons and command-and-control roles to the military? The BJP's Guruswamy answered that nuclear weapons would not be transferred to the military services: "These are not weapons to be issued to the existing services. . . . It's undesirable that [a nuclear command should] come under any one service. They get into competition."[152] Defence Minister George Fernandes said that this was "a matter that needs to be discussed at great length."[153] So, too, he added, "the question arises as to under what circumstances nuclear weapons can be used. And which units then may have to use them. More vitally, whether there will be any resultant restructuring of our armed forces." Good questions; Fernandes was asking them without answers, more than a month after the tests.

To be sure, the United States proceeded similarly in the 1940s and 1950s: doctrine and strategy followed capabilities. China, as well, developed nuclear doctrine only long after it had acquired the weapons. Yet India had the "benefit" of fifty years of other states' experiences and decades of its own relatively open debate on nuclear doctrine. If the BJP had been correct in its call for a first-ever strategic review, then its strategic seriousness was undermined by the conduct of the tests before the determination of strategy. Hydrogen bombs without strategic and operational doctrines and delivery systems are political devices and symbols of power. They are not usable military instruments of security.

Moreover, if hydrogen bombs were somehow strategically necessary for India and the May 1998 test was not a success, then a policy driven by national security imperatives would call for further tests. Faced with technical doubts about India's nuclear weapons, strategists and military leaders who saw these weapons as security instruments would object to signing the Comprehensive Test Ban Treaty even after the May tests. They would take some comfort from India's capacity to conduct computer simulation experiments but would still want the validation of explosive tests. Indeed, posttest inteviews with former top-ranking military officers indicated that the armed forces did not feel that enough testing had been done to give them confidence that Indian nuclear weaponeers could produce reliable, deliverable nuclear weapons.[154] These former officers and others added that the military's views on testing were not being sought by the political leadership in determining India's position on further testing and the CTBT.

However, if India's final decision makers saw nuclear weapons, particularly H-bombs, more as political devices—at the global and domestic levels—then it would be acceptable in terms of security to sign the CTBT. Of course, the nuclear scientists' insistence that the H-bomb worked perfectly spared political leaders from making a trade-off between security and political considerations. As long as ongoing technical needs could be met through computer simulations and subcritical testing, there was little tension between these categories of interest. The evidence gathered here suggests, tentatively, that the thermonuclear weapon experiment did not succeed but that India could have high confidence in its fission weapon capabilities without further explosive testing. Therefore, if security imperatives drove the design and testing of an H-bomb, India would not satisfy its security interest by signing the CTBT. However, if personal and symbolic political interests motivated the H-bomb effort, then signing the treaty would not undermine security.

PAKISTAN TESTS, MAY 28

On May 28 Pakistan did the expected and simultaneously detonated a reported five nuclear devices in a tunnel under the Ras Koh mountain range near Chagai in Baluchistan. The mountain turned white. "Today, we have settled a score," Nawaz Sharif declared over national television.[155]

U.S. analysts immediately questioned the claimed number of devices tested and their yield. A. Q. Khan had declared that the largest device had a yield of thirty to thirty-five kilotons. Dr. Samar Mubarakmand, the Oxford-trained physicist who headed the program for the Pakistan Atomic Energy Commission, said the total yield for the day's tests was forty to forty-five kilotons. (In explicating the primary role that Atomic Energy Commission scientists and engineers played in the program, Mubarakmand and others diminished A. Q. Khan's relentlessly self-promoted standing as "father" of the bomb. Indeed in a videotape of Prime Minister Sharif's visit to the test site recorded in early June, Mubarakmand stood and walked next to Sharif while Khan was relegated to the side.) U.S. analysts citing seismographic data estimated that the total yield of the Pakistani blasts was between nine and twelve kilotons.[156] If accurate, this estimate puzzled intelligence officials who felt they had a good understanding of Pakistan's capabilities. The design(s) they believed Pakistan possessed should have resulted in higher yields if five weapons had functioned properly.[157] If only one device had been detonated, instead of five, the result appeared less strange. The claim of five tests also raised doubts why Pakistan would consume so much precious weapon-grade fissile material at one time, limiting the state's "reserve" stockpile for further tests in the event the first results suggested the need for changes of design. The political psychology of Pakistan's claims, however, was anything but strange given Pakistan's drive for parity with India. The stated number of tests—five—and their yield suspiciously matched India's advertised accomplishment.

News of the Pakistani tests came as the Indian Lok Sabha met for a second day of debate on nuclear policy. Politicians seemed genuinely surprised, and the House erupted in shouting and finger wagging as opposition parliamentarians accused the government of harming the nation's security by provoking a nuclear arms race. "A new situation has arisen," Vajpayee said soberly to the body. "The house should think about it deeply and seriously. We may have differences in our house, but if the challenge is from the outside, we should give the message that . . . the country is together."[158] While some heeded the prime minister's call, others continued in uproar. Debate was called off and rescheduled for the following day. As one junior BJP parliamentarian remarked getting into his car, "We are ready for war."[159] An opposition Janata Dal leader, S. Jaipal Reddy, betrayed the risk beneath India's two-week period of triumphalism: "India had a decisive military edge over Pakistan. We must remember that an atom bomb is a great equalizer. With this test, the edge that India had has been wiped out."[160] It was as if the nation's political elite had thought Pakistan could not or would not rise to meet the Indian challenge and that nuclear arms racing was not serious business.

The small number of serious security specialists in India understood that Pakistan would test. One of India's most respected journalists, Shekhar Gupta, wrote, "[W]e can heave a sigh of relief. Now Pakistan's Western friends have no choice to impose on it the same sanctions that they have inflicted on us."[161] This was comparative suffering as solace. Gupta exclaimed that "[w]e must not let our Pakistan obsession distract us from the fundamentals of our long-term nuclear and foreign policy framework." The nuclear program, he continued, "was never meant, and should never be seen, to be directed only at Pakistan." Instead, "rightly or wrongly," India has "looked at nuclear weapons as an essential prerequisite for a larger role on the world stage besides giving us a deterrent against China." Yet, by opening up the region's nuclear closet, the Indian government had allowed Pakistan to rise to its level and relegate India once more in the world's eyes to a regionally troubled state. Pakistan could now exploit international concern over regional instability to draw greater attention to the Kashmir dispute, the internationalization of which India doggedly sought to avoid.

On May 30, Pakistan detonated another nuclear device—this came two days after the first tests, just as India's second explosions had. And now, Pakistan's claimed total was six, to India's recent five. Pakistan had always desired to be a match for India—nuclear weapons appeared as the means, at least symbolically.

PICKING UP THE PIECES, JUNE TO JULY

Before the Pakistani tests, the Vajpayee government told Parliament, "India shall not engage in an arms race. India shall also not subscribe [to] or reinvent the doctrines of the Cold War."[162] After the tests, the issue was less under India's control. Nor did the government move quickly to engage Pakistan in a search for stability. Rather, the priority was to redress India's international isolation.

The international community was not responding to India's nuclear bid for great international status and power. Much of the world did not join the United States in imposing economic sanctions. Yet, almost all states downgraded their regard for India. Japan and others proposed various international working groups to address the proliferation threat in South Asia. International opprobrium over India's (and Pakistan's) nuclear ambitions was not going away, even if states refrained from sustained public criticism. India's hopes for a permanent seat on the UN Security Council had never looked poorer. To assess and reaffirm bilateral relations with key states, Vajpayee dispatched emissaries to Paris, London, Moscow, and other major capitals.

Like it or not, India recognized that the United States had to be addressed. In early June, Vajpayee wanted to send his friend and trusted adviser Planning Commission Deputy Chairman Jaswant Singh as an envoy to Washington. But more nationalistic elements within the government and the BJP's fraternal organizations resisted this. They felt that India should part ways with the United States rather than subject itself to Washington's criticisms and demands. For their part, some still-angry Clinton administration officials preferred to let India stew in its own sanction-warmed juices rather than welcome an emissary from the BJP. Uncertain whether high-level American officials would agree to meet with Singh, New Delhi was reluctant to request such meetings. If they were turned down, hard-liners in the BJP as well as opposition leaders from the Left would broadcast the slight to embarrass the government. Singh, an erudite, elegant, and proud man from an eminent Rajasthani family, was prepared to take political risks to restore ties with the United States. He comprehended that to achieve greatness India must integrate itself fully into the international political economy. This could not be done without good relations with the United States. Top Clinton administration officials ultimately recognized Singh's outstanding character and the need to move forward with the Vajpayee government.[163] At a meeting in early June they decided to inform the Indians that Singh would be received by Strobe Talbott on June 12 in his capacity as acting secretary of state, while Madeleine Albright was traveling in Europe.

Singh prepared to travel to the United States knowing that Clinton administration officials remained piqued. Washington's joining with the other permanent members of the UN Security Council to enumerate steps India and Pakistan should take, including signature of the CTBT without conditions, appeared as a precondition for resumed diplomacy with India. If this tough attitude toward India persisted, Singh worried, there could be little progress. "If you hold a gun to a country's head and say 'sign on the dotted line,' then it makes things very difficult," he said.[164] "No sovereign country would do this." Indeed, the U.S. and international reaction to the Indian tests revived colonial nightmares for Singh and others. "This country has had a long history of colonial domination," he explained. "It's only fifty years free from it. Now, fifty years down the line we are not prepared to accept another form of colonialism."[165] Singh was "ready to sit with an American of equivalent rank and address these issues and the CTBT." However, he said, "if you say first I must crawl—India must crawl before we can talk with you—then it reminds us of Amritsar," a reference to the 1919 episode in which British General Sir Michael O'Dwyer ordered that any Indian passing along the street where an Englishwoman recently had been molested must crawl. In referring to Amritsar, Singh echoed the legacy of colonialism that consciously or subconsciously had affected India's nuclear development and policy from 1948. This legacy—fifty years after independence—informed both the decision to conduct tests and the government's perspective on the process of engaging the international community afterwards.

The Singh-Talbott talks on June 12 rededicated the Indian and American governments to improving ties. Neither side released details other than to say that Singh presented why India felt it had to conduct the nuclear tests and Talbott explained why the tests caused a major setback in India's relations with the United States and the international community. Both recognized that the tests had reinstated nuclear issues as the major obstacle that had to be negotiated before bilateral relations could move forward again. The tone of the meeting encouraged both officials that they as individuals, and hopefully their governments, were prepared to work cooperatively. Singh was moved by Talbott's willingness to continue the meeting for two and one-half hours, running into the time Talbott was scheduled to be at his son's graduation. This level of personal attention and respect to India mattered greatly, as had its absence in earlier episodes. Singh and Talbott agreed to launch a process of talks with each heading his government's representation.

On June 18, the Clinton administration announced the sanctions it would impose on India and Pakistan. Earlier sanctions in May already had caused the postponement of $1.17 billion in international lending to India. By June 9, the rupee's value had fallen 6 percent against the dollar from mid-May. The major Indian stock index had fallen 400 points, more than 10 percent, after Standard & Poor's had downgraded its outlook on India. Moody's was about to lower India's credit rating.[166] Among the additional sanctions Washington now announced were termination of new commitments of U.S. government credits and credit guarantees for export financing, investment guarantees, and agricultural credits. India had been one of the top five countries benefiting from U.S. investment guarantees, receiving on average $300 million annually in such support. U.S. bank loans and credits to the Indian and Pakistani governments were now blocked, although in a concession to the U.S. (and Indian) banking industry, loans to the private sector were not affected. The United States would ban export of all nuclear- or missile-related dual-use items and now presume denial for all other dual-use exports.[167] The United States estimated the total direct impact on India at $2.5 billion, and on Pakistan at $1.5 billion. The sanctions also would entail indirect costs. Still, the administration sought to remind Congress and others that sanctions alone would not compel changes in India's and Pakistan's nuclear policies. The administration would require greater flexibility in providing positive inducements as well. This meant that Congress would need to revise its approach to sanctions, allowing executive branch discretion in lifting them selectively commensurate to changes in India and Pakistan. (Congress obliged in October 1998, and on November 6 President Clinton invoked the authority granted to him by the Brownback Amendment to waive some of the posttest sanctions on India and Pakistan, restoring Export-Import Bank, Overseas Private Investment Corporation, and Trade Development Agency programs in both countries.)[168]

Singh and Talbott met again on July 9 and 10 in Frankfurt, Germany, with top arms control and nonproliferation advisers Robert Einhorn of the State Department and Rakesh Sood of the Ministry of External Affairs. From July 21 to 24, Talbott, Einhorn, National Security Council official Bruce Riedel, Vice Chairman of the Joint Chiefs of Staff General Joseph W. Ralston, and Assistant Secretary of State for South Asian Affairs Karl Inderfurth conducted further meetings in India and Pakistan. Interviews with knowledgeable sources indicated that the United States sought Indian accession to the CTBT, a moratorium on fissile material production for explosive purposes pending negotiation of an international treaty, Indian agreement not to flight-test missile systems other than the Prithvi and Agni, and a commitment not to deploy missiles and nuclear weapons. Washington also sought Indian and Pakistani assurances that they would not export sensitive materials, equipment, or know-how to other countries. American officials argued that these steps coincided with India's own security interests and would enable the Clinton administration to seek the removal of sanctions on India. This in turn would allow President Clinton to go forward with his planned visit to India (and Pakistan) and would help rebuild other states', including China's, confidence in India. With this confidence, previously planned cooperation in energy development and other important economic activities could be pursued again. For his part, Singh reaffirmed India's interest in converting its de facto testing moratorium into a de jure commitment, including accession to the CTBT. But he emphasized that the BJP government faced many domestic difficulties in taking this step and urged American receptivity to an incremental process leading to signature of the treaty. He also noted that the government was now preparing the strategic defense review that would show that India had no intention of engaging in an arms race and would seek only a minimum nuclear deterrent capability that would be managed responsibly.[169]

However, to avoid an arms race would require putting limits on the numbers and types of nuclear weapons and delivery systems India (and Pakistan) could build. Otherwise the political and strategic temptation would always exist to assume that the other side was building more and then to increase one's own arsenal. Partisan politics would exacerbate this tendency to build up rather than control the nuclear and missile programs. Arms limitations also would require imposing political and strategic discipline on the weaponeers. In the summer of 1998, India's weaponeers wanted to develop and deploy missiles with greater than twice the range of the Agni, build nuclear-powered ballistic-missile submarines, and generally acquire the most widely recognized trappings of military-technological power.[170] They recognized it would take time, but they had been reluctantly patient since 1964 as political leaders and technological obstacles restrained them. Pakistan's weaponeers had similar desires. By the end of 1998, American negotiator Talbott and his Indian and Pakistani counterparts had achieved little progress in effecting arms control agreements. Even if a modest breakthrough were to occur in the eighth round of talks with India, scheduled for January 1999, and India and Pakistan were to sign the CTBT, neither South Asian government appeared ready to impose limits on the future research and development programs of their respective nuclear and missile establishments.

Thus, the early post-Pokhran-II period ended with India's political leaders unable or unwilling to impose clear limits on the ambitions of the weaponeers, who wanted to produce an ever-larger gamut of nuclear weapons and delivery systems. For its part, the United States was unable or unwilling to offer the kinds of inducements that would make such limitations more politically palatable for India. The Comprehensive Test Ban Treaty's ratification by the United States and entry into force remained uncertain. India's most ambitious strategists called for further nuclear tests, perhaps reflecting the desire by the weaponeers and the military to answer doubts about the effectiveness of the thermonuclear weapon design. Meanwhile, as before, the Indian polity remained fixated on domestic political, economic, and communal travails that threatened the BJP's hold on power. Left-leaning elements within the society questioned the morality and priorities reflected in "nuclearism." Whatever the future held, the tests of 1998 had not freed India from its central dilemmas.

CONCLUSION

If India's nuclear tests did not appear to serve many of India's objectives, how can they be explained?

The tests were a bold statement and bid for Indian power in the international system. But the public declarations of government officials betrayed the absence of a coherent, analytically buttressed national security strategy. The driving forces behind the tests—the scientists and engineers—could claim no expertise in military-strategic affairs or international relations, nor any deep understanding of how nuclear weapons would affect India's relations with Pakistan, China, the United States, and others over the mid and long terms.

Indian officials wanted the tests to serve or at least not detract from seven objectives: to win recognition of India as a major power; to catch up to China in terms of status and strategic deterrence; to reassert technological and strategic superiority over Pakistan; to bolster the expertise, morale, and recruitment of BARC and the DRDO; to strengthen national defense at low cost while maintaining civilian control over nuclear policy; to maintain moral standing as an advocate of nuclear disarmament; and to boost the BJP government's internal position.[171]

Yet most of these objectives were not served, except the satisfaction of the weaponeers' interests. (In November, Chidambaram received another two-year extension as chairman of the Atomic Energy Commission. Chidambaram received the nation's second-highest civilian award, the Padma Vibhushan. Kakodkar and Santhanam received the third-highest, the Padma Bhushan, and M. S. Ramakumar and Satinder Kumar Sikka of BARC and Virender Singh Sethi of the Terminal Ballistics Research Laboratory in Chandigarh each received the states's next highest honor.)[172] As of late 1998, the international community did not increase its respect of India or grant it greater influence. Pakistan had practically matched India in effective nuclear power and recast India not as the preeminent South Asian state but as part of an unstable Indo-Pak dyad whose conflict over Kashmir and potential nuclear and missile competition must be managed above all else. The demonstration of nuclear weapon capabilities perhaps gave India and Pakistan political and psychological confidence to revive bilateral diplomacy, but as before, the fate of such diplomacy would depend more on political will than on nuclear strength. Indian strategists and the military did not call for cuts in defense spending, but rather increases.[173] Civilians hoped to keep nuclear weapons from being allocated to the military, but it appeared more difficult to prevent greater military participation in nuclear policymaking. India lost much of the moral credibility it had as a champion of disarmament in the eyes of other states. The BJP government continued to be beleaguered. An October 1998 poll of two thousand urban voters showed that support for the nuclear tests fell to 44 percent from the 91 percent registered in May.[174] In November elections in four states, the BJP suffered remarkable defeats, blamed largely on the rise in onion prices, which meant more to voters than demonstrations of nuclear prowess.

To Indian and international security specialists, the objective of enhancing security vis-à-vis China was most important, not least because it conformed with Realist expectations of what a state in India's environment should do. Yet Indian strategists before and shortly after the May tests failed to say how the display of nuclear capability would warm China's intentions toward India or add capabilities that India could use in any meaningful way against China. Security derives from the balance between one's own intentions and capabilities and the intentions and capabilities of one's rivals. The tests did nothing to enhance China's intentions toward India; if anything, they set them back after ten years of progress. The tests helped increase India's nuclear capabilities, but a nuclear weapon buildup would undermine its economic growth on which all else depended. Moreover, according to the Rand Corporation sinologist Jonathan Pollack, China had been seeking to "sharply curtail" any military rivalry with India to avoid "an enormous diversion from longer-term security challenges in East Asia."[175] If India now provoked Beijing to pay more attention to the nuclear and missile equation, India could not hope to match China's capacity to modernize and expand its arsenal. In early July a BJP official admitted as much: "We do not seek parity with China; we don't have the resources, and we don't have the will. What we are seeking is a minimum deterrent."[176]

But to deter what and when? By the late 1990s Indian conventional forces were clearly capable of successfully defending against Chinese conventional attack.[177] If they were not, India's insistence that it would not use nuclear weapons first in a conflict would be self-defeating, as it would presume that China could overwhelm India conventionally without recourse to nuclear weapons and New Delhi would let this happen rather than use nuclear weapons first. In this case, why possess these weapons at all? If the need for nuclear weapons rested on deterring Chinese nuclear threats or attack, not conventional aggression, then the case was weak. Given China's hierarchy of security interests and its insistence that it would not use nuclear weapons first, it was implausible that China would instigate either a conventional war or nuclear threat against India over the border. India could repulse the conventional attack, and a Chinese nuclear threat would destroy Beijing's international credibility and subject it to severe counterpressures from the United States and Russia, among others. India and the Sino-Indian border dispute were not important or threatening enough to China to risk this, especially with the all-important question of Taiwan's future unresolved. As K. Subrahmanyam wrote after the May 1998 tests, it "is not a question of Chinese aggression or military threat."[178]

Of course, India could welcome a robust minimal deterrent arsenal as a hedge against future Chinese aggression. Yet, here the requirement would be to ensure that India deployed a force that could survive a putative Chinese nuclear first strike and deliver a counterattack against valued Chinese targets. In 1998, however, India was far from developing and producing missiles that reliably could reach major Chinese targets, and even further from deploying a survivable submarine-based arsenal. Moreover, the idea of India's escalating a conflict in, say, Arunachal Pradesh, to a nuclear attack on Chinese cities, with attendant Chinese counterstrikes on Indian cities, would not be credible. By conveying hostility toward China now, the BJP government probably heightened Chinese interest in devising plans and capabilities to target India's nuclear infrastructure and potential deployment bases to threaten the survivability of India's possible arsenal and weaken the deterrent. India still might achieve a survivable minimal deterrent in the coming decades, but by pursuing it without greater priority on building a more cooperative security relationship with China, New Delhi would raise the costs and requirements of a sufficient arsenal. If the Chinese threat was low in 1998 but could be much greater in the next decades, India needed to evaluate carefully the costs and benefits of a new, seemingly more bellicose approach to China at this time against alternative strategies. Even if India feared that it would be compelled to join the CTBT and therefore had to test in 1998 to hedge against a future Chinese threat, a case could be made that joining the CTBT without testing would have increased India's leverage to extract international support in the event China became aggressive against India. India could then threaten to withdraw from the treaty if its needs were not met. In any case, India proceeded without a carefully considered national security strategy.

If most of India's declared objectives for conducting the tests had not been served, it was possible that the new government and the scientists simply miscalculated. More likely, still, other less explicit intuitions, desires, and aims motivated them. These could have stemmed from both foreign and domestic considerations.

Externally, the end of the cold war deprived India of its Soviet patron and left the United States as the dominant global power, with China as an ascendant major power. India had aspired to this status for itself since independence. After the Communist revolution in China, the two Asian giants started on roughly equal footings and perceived themselves in a development race—economically, technologically, politically, and, after 1962, militarily. Both India and China wanted to be recognized within Asia and the broader global community as the premier state. By the mid-1990s it appeared that China had won the race. This could have alarmed Indian officials so much so that they saw nuclear weapons and ballistic missiles as equalizers—symbolic counters more than military-strategic ones.

Jaswant Singh put it this way in an interview with National Public Radio in the United States: "All that we have done is give ourselves a degree of strategic autonomy by acquiring those symbols of power . . . which have universal currency."[179] India's colonial experience—still vivid to its older leaders—toughened the will to sacrifice for autonomy and recognition. As Singh put it:

> We cannot have a situation in which some countries say, "We have a permanent right to these symbols of deterrence and of power, all of the rest of you . . . do not have that right. We will decide what your security is and how you are to deal with that security." A country the size of India—not simply a sixth of the human race, but also an ancient civilization—cannot in this fashion abdicate its responsibility.[180]

This desire for international standing and autonomy explained the nuclear tests better than a specific security explanation. However, it missed a major reality that many Indians recognized—including Prime Ministers Rao, Gowda, and Gujral—a reality that ultimately pointed back to domestic dynamics. Namely, the source of major power in the new global system is economics. At the end of the twentieth century, China is seen as an emerging great power because of its economic growth, not its nuclear arsenal. The rankings of countries like Germany, Japan, South Korea, and others in the international system depend on their economic status. France has nuclear weapons but no longer gets treated as a major power whom others must accommodate. Indeed, the impetus for European powers to seek political-economic integration stems largely from awareness that power and well-being derive from economics. Narasimha Rao and many Indian officials and commentators understood this reality and declared that India's greatest strategic priority must be sustained high-level economic growth. To the extent that acquiring a nuclear arsenal distracts or even retards India from building economic strength, it will be a grave strategic error.

Yet this, too, misses a decisive factor in India. India's *domestic* weaknesses made the economic route to international power and status seem less attractive to the BJP than the nuclear weapons route. Sustaining robust economic growth for long enough to catch up even to the smaller states of Southeast Asia has looked like a daunting challenge for India. Catching and surpassing China or the other recognized major powers has looked more difficult still. If an economic grand strategy to achieve global power and status appeared fraught with severe domestic political difficulties and delays, nuclear weapons offered a very simple shortcut. A hundred highly motivated scientists and engineers spending a few tens of millions of rupees (at marginal pricing) to build nuclear warheads could go out secretly to the desert and within six weeks deliver shots heard round the world. Given the apparent global currency of nuclear weapons, a government and polity could think that this would achieve long-denied recognition as a major power. And domestically, compared with the rancorous difficulties of adopting effective economic reforms, going nuclear was extremely easy. As a Vajpayee aide put it, "Narasimha Rao's policy of 'nothing but the economy' has been modified to read 'security first and the rest will follow.' "[181] Nuclear weapons would somehow provide a shortcut to economic development.

Of course, this "strategy" is marred by a major flaw. Nuclear weapons are a devalued currency precisely because the rest of the world's leading actors have determined that economic strength and political stability are greater measures of power. Economy first and the rest will follow. The five recognized nuclear weapon states still cling to their arsenals, but the rest of the international community sees this as a problem, not a source of respect. Those who confer status see India's attempt to take a shortcut to major power as a detour. The powerful states and societies that bestow rank in 1998 see India as a poor country that has counterproductively diverted its energies to nuclear weapons while failing to strengthen its economic, educational, and political sinews.[182]

Taking a shortcut to international power and status allowed Indian leaders to give the nation what they thought it wanted. Vajpayee made the general point:

> Millions of Indians have viewed this occasion as the beginning of the rise of a strong and self-confident India. I fully share this assessment and this dream. India has never

considered military might as the ultimate measure of national strength. It is a necessary component of overall national strength. I would, therefore, say that the greatest meaning of the tests is that they have given India *shakti*, they have given India strength, they have given India self-confidence.[183]

Yet India is a more complicated nation than this. It has grappled with the meaning and challenges of the nuclear age more openly than perhaps any other state. Ironically, the man who presided over the production of India's first nuclear bomb, Raja Ramanna, reminded his countrymen why they had been ambivalent about these weapons. "If India thinks that just by exploding a bomb it has become a great country," Ramanna said, "she is wrong."[184]

Exploded Illusions of the Nuclear Age

The foregoing narrative chronicles the important developments, debates, and decisions affecting India's nuclear weapon policy from 1947 through 1998. It provides answers to the three questions formulated at the beginning of the study: Why has India developed its nuclear weapon capability when it has and the way it has? What are the factors that keep India from stopping or reversing its nuclear weapon program? What effects has the United States had on India's nuclear intentions and capabilities?

This history explodes a number of illusions, many of them Indian. For example, although Nehru made moral aversion to nuclear weapons a dominant theme in the Indian national narrative, he also expressed interest in having a nuclear weapon option for India. India's nuclear activities have not been as "pure" as Indian conventional wisdom suggests—even if moral considerations have had an unusually material impact on Indian policy. In another illusion, Indian nuclear scientists beginning with Homi Bhabha built a reputation as men of great prowess and technical self-reliance, when in fact many of Bhabha's and his successors' claims proved hollow. The strategic enclave, notwithstanding its talents, depended extensively on foreign technology and know-how, and required more time than commonly recognized to produce effective nuclear weapons. Yet another illusion is that nuclear weapons offered a shortcut to great power status in the modern world. By the early 1990s, it became more apparent that economic strength and political stability were the primary sources of usable power, not nuclear weapons. Thus, India's scientists, engineers, and ardent nationalists were frustrated in their desire to rocket India into great power status in part because their enterprise required a more robust economy and stable polity for a launching pad. Other

Indian illusions emerged and were shattered during the fifty years chronicled in this volume, and the account here will stimulate debate over them.

Yet the history of India's nuclear policymaking has exposed larger illusions in American international relations theory and nuclear nonproliferation policy. The first is that external security concerns universally and decisively determine states' nuclear policies. The second is that proliferation and "nonproliferation" are two sides of the same coin, and therefore to reverse nuclear proliferation it is sufficient to "flip" the circumstances that caused it initially. To the extent that security concerns are seen as the primary cause, this means that improving a state's security conditions should lead to "nonproliferation." The same illusory logic holds that if particular domestic factors lay behind a state's acquisition of nuclear weapons, altering those original factors in the aftermath of proliferation should lead to reversal. The third major illusion is that democracy's international security benefits tend automatically to support nonproliferation objectives.[1] Insofar as no nation has debated more democratically than India whether to acquire or give up nuclear weapons, India's rejection of the nonproliferation regime may convey lessons about how other democracies will deal with this issue, too. Finally, perhaps the grandest illusion of the nuclear age is that a handful of states possessing nuclear weapons can secure themselves and the world indefinitely against the dangers of nuclear proliferation *without* placing a higher priority on simultaneously striving to eliminate their own nuclear weapons, too.

This concluding chapter explores how India's nuclear history suggests four alternative propositions to the illusions just listed. Namely,

1. Domestic factors, including individual personalities, have been at least as important as the external security environment in determining Indian nuclear policy and that of other states.
2. Proliferation is an essentially different process from "unproliferation"—a state's decision to stop and/or reverse acquisition of nuclear weapon capabilities. In democracies especially, the acquisition of nuclear weapons so changes the politics within the state that removal of the original proliferation stimuli is not sufficient to cause unproliferation.
3. Open, democratic debate may inhibit decisions to make nuclear weapons, but democracy as it is practiced today appears to obstruct efforts to control and eliminate nuclear weapons once they have been acquired.
4. If reversing the spread of nuclear weapons is an important goal and the promotion of democracy is desirable, then averting the potential clash between these two objectives requires clearer commitments to eliminating nuclear weapons from all states.

These propositions—and the phenomena they reflect—are interrelated but distinguishable. They have emerged from and apply to the history of Indian nuclear decision makers. It must be left to other scholars and analysts to explore how this history and analysis helps explain and predict the behavior of other states.

ILLUSION 1:
SECURITY CONCERNS DECISIVELY DETERMINE PROLIFERATION

Until 1998, Indian leaders insisted that their state was not seeking to build or deploy a nuclear arsenal. Instead, they advocated global nuclear disarmament. Still, the preceding narrative showed the many twists and turns of India's nuclear history: Bhabha's and Nehru's hope to launch India into the upper ranks of modern, powerful states; Bhabha's plans in the mid-1950s to acquire weapon-grade plutonium, kept free from international safeguards; Nehru and Bhabha's subtle invocation of India's latent nuclear weapon capability as a deterrent, in 1960; Lal Bahadur Shastri's compromise with Bhabha to allow initial work on *peaceful* nuclear explosives in the aftermath of China's nuclear test in 1964. Then Bhabha's successor, Vikram Sarabhai, tried to stop studies on nuclear explosives and Indira Gandhi concentrated on domestic challenges while India struggled to effect a Nuclear Non-Proliferation Treaty that would commit the world to nuclear disarmament. The course twisted back in early 1968 when a handful of scientists and engineers took the initiative to reinvigorate nuclear explosive design work. In late 1970 and 1971, Indira Gandhi indicated that India was interested in conducting peaceful nuclear explosions. In 1972, after victory over Pakistan in the 1971 war, she opted to proceed toward conducting a nuclear explosion, which occurred finally in 1974, without benefit of a clear national security strategy.

The second phase of India's nuclear history began after May 1974 and it entailed a protracted period of fitful self-restraint. No further nuclear tests were conducted, despite the hopes and expectations of the strategic enclave. Indira Gandhi evinced moral, political, and geopolitical doubts about building nuclear weapons. Her successor, Morarji Desai, steadfastly rejected further nuclear tests on moral grounds and did nothing to bolster the nuclear establishment that was now suffering under international isolation brought about after the 1974 test. When Indira Gandhi returned to power in 1980, she confounded American and some Indian expectations by not dramatically advancing the nuclear weapon effort. In late 1982 or early 1983 she secretly authorized a second nuclear test but changed her mind after twenty-four hours. Indira's son Rajiv succeeded her in late 1984 and demonstrated great ambivalence toward the bomb. Espousing the cause of nuclear disarmament, he insisted India did not want to build nuclear weapons, rebuffed the pleas by some military leaders for the bomb, and generally did not rise to news that Pakistan was steadily acquiring nuclear weapon capability. However, he did knowingly allow the strategic enclave to enhance nuclear weapon designs and technology without taking the major step of conducting nuclear tests or building an arsenal.

And so it went through the early 1990s until, beginning around 1995, the internal debate in India began to shift more decisively in favor of "exercising the nuclear option," leading India toward the third phase of its nuclear history and the tests of 1998.

Security concerns indubitably created conditions that "allowed" Indian decision makers to develop nuclear weapon capabilities. Had China not defeated India in the 1962 war and acquired nuclear weapons in 1964, India might not have built upon the nuclear weapon capabilities made possible by the projects planned and initiated in the 1950s. Had India not declared its possible nuclear weapon ambitions in the early 1960s, Pakistan might not have pursued countervailing nuclear weapon capabilities, which in turn intensified India's motivations to build nuclear weapons in the 1980s and 1990s, although India still eschewed a clear commitment to produce a nuclear arsenal. By the 1990s, Pakistan and China combined to heighten India's security concerns, as Beijing assisted Pakistan's nuclear weapon and missile programs.

Still, domestic—more than international security—factors must be recognized to answer why India began developing the bomb option in the 1950s, and why it moved in fits and starts through the 1960s, '70s, '80s, and '90s. Just as important, domestic factors explain why India through early 1998 did not declare itself a nuclear weapon power and deploy a nuclear arsenal. These factors can be specified and categorized in an intellectually and practically manageable way that explains Indian behavior and may predict other states' behaviors. These factors operated more decisively in India than in other declared or threshold nuclear weapon states because India is the only one that has debated publicly its decision to "go nuclear." Even though actual decisions generally have been made in secret, and very few individuals understood the details of India's program, decision makers were electorally accountable to a public that knew "going nuclear" was an active option.

The central domestic factors determining India's perceived national interest regarding nuclear weapons can be summarized as follows.

The strategic enclave of scientists/technologists has driven India's quest for nuclear weapon capability. Beginning with Homi Bhabha in the late 1940s, leading scientists and engineers pressed political leaders to accelerate the development and demonstration of nuclear weapon capabilities. This process peaked once in 1974 when the top scientists persuaded Indira Gandhi to authorize the nuclear test at Pokhran. Atomic Energy Commission and Defence Research and Development Organisation scientists subsequently pressed for additional tests and other steps to develop a nuclear arsenal. Their influence peaked again in the 1995–1998 period, culminating in the test of a thermonuclear device that had no articulated strategic or doctrinal necessity but that capped the careers of retirement-aged scientists. History suggests that even if India signs the Comprehensive Test Ban Treaty, Indian weaponeers will continue to press for unending programs to refine nuclear warheads and, more important, extend the range and diversity of missile systems.

In pressing the nuclear accelerator the weaponeers have exploited but not systematically redressed general concerns about the security environment and India's standing in the broader global system. The technologies and promise provided by the weaponeers have assumed great symbolic importance for the nation. Indeed, the scientists and their artifacts represent modernity, international rank, and transcendence of the colonial past. They have attracted politicians to support their cause. This has generated political-economic momentum behind nuclear and ballistic missile technology. This momentum has been difficult to arrest completely because the technical issues are highly complicated and arcane, making it difficult for other actors to enter the debate effectively. Decision making has occurred among small circles of actors operating in tight secrecy without formal checking and balancing mechanisms, even as an open, largely symbolic debate occurred in the polity. The importance of the strategic enclave is reflected further, and perhaps paradoxically, in India's self-restrained response to the nuclear stimuli provided by China in the 1960s and Pakistan in the 1970s and 1980s. The leaders of the AEC and the DRDO have been rather uninterested in building a military nuclear arsenal. The scientists have sought to prove their brilliance and prowess and give India the measure of great international status and strength without risking the loss of institutional autonomy that would occur if a truly military arsenal were created. Developing and testing prototype weapons satisfies the creative urges of designers; serial production is not interesting, even if it would be central to a military-security strategy for nuclear weapons. Many of the top scientists and engineers also worried that the costs and security risks of an arms race would grow if the program were militarized. Prime ministers shared this view.

India's national identity and normative aspirations have shaped nuclear policy choices. India's national identity is constructed around the determination to be an independent, great state that transcends its colonial past and is morally superior to its colonizers and the dominant states of the international system. India's attachment to democracy reflects its founders' determination to show that the Indian people, despite their numbers, poverty, and colonial past, could rule themselves with dignity and freedom even while many other developing nations, including China, could not.

Two vital norms coexist uneasily within this national identity: one, India should achieve major power status in the international system and, two, India should demonstrate moral superiority over the world's dominant states, which have been perceived as exploitative, overly militarized, and insensitive to the needs and aspirations of the world's majority of poor people. These two norms have clashed in the nuclear policy arena. Acquisition and demonstration of nuclear weapon capabilities could plausibly fulfill the norm of achieving great power status in an international system led by nuclear weapon states, but possession of nuclear weapons also could undermine the moral norm. India's two great moral exemplars, Mahatma Gandhi and Jawaharlal Nehru, have been perceived to represent humanity's and India's moral campaign against nuclear weapons—even if Nehru actually was more ambivalent than commonly perceived. This has complicated India's quest for major power status through military might. Only the Bharatiya Janata Party has favored the "great power" norm to the exclusion (almost) of the moral-superiority-through-nuclear-self-restraint norm. Yet it, too, has framed its policies in normative terms, not arguing for nuclear weapons merely on narrow grounds of national defense.

Rather than resolve the tension between India's dual norms, leaders, at least up to 1998, acted ambivalently and ambiguously. They sought the power and prestige associated with nuclear weapon capability, while insisting that India preferred nuclear disarmament and would not build nuclear weapons. By the 1980s, Indian leaders and the strategic enclave were walking a fine, ethically tenuous line distinguishing between possessing nuclear weapon capabilities and the overt assembly and deployment of a nuclear arsenal. Given India's demonstrated nuclear weapon capabilities, its normative stance for nuclear disarmament often has been considered hypocritical. Indeed, Indian security pundits and the strategic enclave have called for disarmament knowing that the nuclear weapon states would not oblige, thereby giving normative cover for India to pursue nuclear weapons. Yet many Indians have insisted that the emphasis on disarmament reflects a strategic judgment that India would be more secure in a world without nuclear weapons and that India has gained political power through its moral purposefulness. Indians have trumpeted that their self-restraint in not deploying a nuclear arsenal has proven both their moral bona fides and the seriousness of their calls for nuclear disarmament.[2] Even after the May 1998 tests, Prime Minister Vajpayee reinvoked India's normative calls for nuclear disarmament and equivocated on the question of going forward to deploy nuclear weapons. A small covey of India's most bellicose strategists has bristled at this moralistic approach and urged an unmitigated pursuit of amoral Realpolitik, but even after May 1998 this position has represented only a small minority within the polity.

The key representative of India's identity and norms has always been the prime minister. This means that his or her personal beliefs and rhetoric about nuclear weapons have mattered enormously. Since Nehru, the great majority of prime ministers have genuinely believed in and espoused the norm against acquiring nuclear weapons, even as many hedged their bets by allowing the development of nuclear weapon capability. Morarji Desai was perhaps most adamant in applying the moral norm to restrain the nuclear complex, but Rajiv Gandhi and Narasimha Rao also exhibited restraint. Prime Minister Vajpayee invoked the norm of great power status and the grammar of security strategy in explaining the 1998 tests, but no strategic defense review had been undertaken to inform this rhetoric.

The Indian public has been amenable to its leaders' unresolved expression of the dual norms. It tolerated the emphasis on the moral aversion to nuclear weapons just as it celebrated the nuclear explosions in 1974 and 1998. This amenability has stemmed in part from the low salience of nuclear issues in the average citizen's life.

Barring a clear and present threat of attack from Pakistan or China, the public has not demanded that leaders give up the moral position against nuclear weapons and deploy an arsenal. Pakistan's acquisition of nuclear weapons with Chinese assistance pushed public opinion toward more robust policies in the 1980s and 1990s, but the public remained confused over whether and how nuclear weapons could be used by India to deal with this threat. By departing from the nuclear option policy, the BJP may have exposed itself to political criticism on behalf of the "violated" moral norm, especially if more salient economic and international costs result from the break.

The institutional apparatus of Indian national security policymaking has inhibited deployment of a nuclear arsenal. Fear of military usurpation of democratic political authority has motivated political leaders to control nuclear decision making with little input from military-strategic experts. Through 1998, institutions and procedures had not been formed to allow the military to participate extensively in the decision-making process. Prime ministers and the scientific leaders of the nuclear establishment have concluded that the militarization of nuclear policy would lead to excessive demands for resources and risks of arms racing that, in the end, would not make the state any more secure than it is without a deployed nuclear arsenal.

Other nuclear weapon states have ceded the doctrinal and operational direction of nuclear policy to specialists operating within dedicated national security institutions. India has not done this. The role of the administrative system of the Indian state has contributed to this exclusion of the military and security specialists from decision making. The Indian Administrative Services (IAS) comprises the elite cadre of state managers in India, including the leaders of the Ministry of Defence. The IAS's position stems from the Indian government's belief that talented generalists can and should manage state institutions, including the defense apparatus that in other states is the province of military and civilian specialists.[3] In addition, some military officers and others believe that the Indian caste system has contributed to the exclusion of the military from nuclear policymaking. As the former vice chief of naval staff K. K. Nayyar put it, "The scientific community, and especially the nuclear community . . . are all Brahmins," and the military rank below them in the caste structure. "This explains the shabby treatment that I as a serviceman feel we are given at times in the armed forces."[4]

Additional domestic considerations help explain the slight institutional role of military experts in nuclear policymaking. The deployment of operational nuclear forces would undermine the strict control civilians (elected political leaders and scientists) have exercised over Indian nuclear policy. The delivery of nuclear weapons to prescribed targets under time pressures requires preplanning, a certain amount of delegated command authority, and extensive exercises. As the executors of these operations, military leaders must have a say in how they are prepared. These operational necessities therefore would bring the military into policymaking, prescribing conditions that would have to be met to satisfy doctrinal objectives. This potentially would erode the complete control of political leaders over policy and the relative autonomy enjoyed by the nuclear and defense science establishments. Complicating matters further, the deployment of a nuclear arsenal would force Indian civilian and military leaders to decide which armed service—the army, the air force, and eventually perhaps the navy—should control and operate the arsenal, or whether a special service would be created for this task. India's leaders have preferred to avoid these operational and interservice control problems by stopping short of actually building and deploying a nuclear arsenal.[5] This has frustrated certain recent military leaders, and it may or may not be rational in military terms. Yet it reflects the domestic imperatives and peculiarities of the Indian policy.

Nine months after coming to power, the BJP in December 1998 formed a National Security Council to be headed by the prime minister and to include the ministers of defense, external affairs, finance, and home affairs—the core of the Cabinet Committee on Political Affairs. The prime minister's principal secretary, Brajesh Mishra, was named national security adviser, in a move that conformed to traditional patterns of Indian decision makers. The NSC was to be complemented by a Strategic Policy Group comprising the cabinet secretary, the three service chiefs, and secretaries of key ministries. This body was slated to conduct a strategic defense review benefiting from inputs from a large National Security Advisory Board made up of former officials, pundits, and analysts representing expertise in military and security affairs, economics, science, and technology. Many of the individuals cited frequently in this volume—Subrahmanyam, Mohan, J. N. Dixit, Jasjit Singh, Chellaney—were included in this advisory body. However, initial Indian commentaries suggested that the new institution did not represent significant change from past approaches, as no single entity emerged with the power, expertise, and military staffing envisioned by those who advocated a more robust mechanism for long-term strategy making and implementation.

Economic constraints have added importantly to the mix of values and interests that have motivated Indian leaders to refrain from building and deploying a nuclear arsenal. The greatest costs associated with nuclear forces arise from delivery vehicles and command and control systems. The preceding chapters chronicle Indian leaders' awareness that building a robust nuclear arsenal would require unacceptable sacrifices of investment in other military or civilian sectors. Economic considerations explicitly contributed to nuclear self-restraint in the 1964 debate, in Sarabhai's policies throughout the 1960s, in Prime Minister Indira Gandhi's 1968 declaration that India would not produce nuclear weapons, in Rajiv Gandhi's 1985 rejection of military calls for developing and deploying a missile-based deterrent, and in ongoing nuclear policy debates. Indeed, India has violated or revised the maxim that no price is too high to pay for protecting national security. China, with a very different political system and moral-political ideology, chose to make this sacrifice. Pakistan, too, has chosen to invest a much larger share of its gross domestic product in the military than has India.[6] Through 1998 India had not followed suit in part because a greater premium has been placed on internal over external security. Democratic accountability has reinforced this sense of priorities among political leaders, unlike in China and Pakistan. The BJP rhetorically at least rejected this constraint, but it remains to be seen how the coalition government it leads will reconcile domestic political-economic priorities with desires for greater military strength.

Lastly, international pressures and sanctions on technology imports following the 1974 test also have limited India's interest in developing and deploying nuclear weapon capabilities. These external factors have worked two ways: the nonproliferation regime has impeded the technological development of the Indian nuclear program, while the desire to avoid further international political and economic recriminations caused Indian leaders to choose a policy of self-restraint at least through 1997. These external sources of self-restraint should not be minimized. They in some ways balance the external motivations *for* building nuclear weapons. Military leaders and many strategic analysts favor rigorous weaponization—conducting further nuclear weapon tests, integrating warheads with delivery systems, exercising nuclear weapon delivery operations, and otherwise preparing and planning for the actual use of nuclear weapons in short order. Such activities, however, could elicit international pressures that political leaders thus far have preferred to avoid. Yet, in both directions—pressures to weaponize and pressures not to—external factors have mixed with manifold domestic factors that are at least as influential. Moreover, as will be discussed further in this chapter, internal interests have deepened India's determination not to eliminate nuclear weapon capabilities. Thus, India's decades-long position on the plateau of the nuclear option—above the plain of zero nuclear weapons, and below the plain of a full-fledged arsenal—must be understood as a product of internal and external factors.

In sum, this study suggests six major factors to explain why and to what extent India—and perhaps other states—seeks nuclear weapon capability, *in addition to the commonly agreed variable of military insecurity.* Two of these factors have fostered the building of nuclear weapons:

* the normative/national identity interest in achieving major power status; and
* the push by the strategic enclave.

The other four factors have motivated Indian decision makers to stop short of building and deploying a nuclear arsenal:

* the normative interest in positioning India as morally superior to the international system's major powers who possess and threaten to use nuclear weapons;
* the absence of an institutional apparatus for defining and implementing national security strategy with significant military input;
* economic constraints and the priority given to nonmilitary and nonnuclear expenditures of national resources; and
* international pressure imposing high political-economic costs if India were to build and deploy a nuclear arsenal.

Most of these factors bear the influence of India's postcolonial identity and democratic system of government. India might have acted differently had one or several of these factors not obtained. For example, had there been no charismatic Homi Bhabha with a close relationship to Nehru, the early momentum and prestige associated with the nuclear program would have been lacking. If India had not been animated by the normative goal of transforming the international system and demonstrating moral superiority over its former colonizers and the leading states in the international system, India would have been less self-restrained in the nuclear realm. Had India's civilian leaders not been determined to minimize the authority of the military, greater impetus would have been given to building and deploying nuclear weapons, at least after the mid-1980s. Had India not been a democracy, priority to the economic needs of the poor masses might have been diminished, as in China and Pakistan. Thus, each of the factors culled from this historical narrative must be considered important.

The history of India's nuclear policymaking suggests that Structural Realism points in the right general direction by predicting that states in an anarchical international structure in which major rivals possess nuclear weapons will likely seek such weapons for themselves. Yet this general compass direction is not precise enough to keep policymakers, scholars, or attentive citizens from getting lost. To answer not only why states seek nuclear weapons but also when and how they will do it requires greater sensitivity to "unit" or state preferences in time than structural theory allows. In fairness the most careful proponents of Structural Realism claim that the theory aims only to predict and explain general outcomes and does not address particular processes and behaviors. Some theorists, such as Ashley Tellis, argue that the leading model of Structural Realism cannot "predict what the characteristic behaviors of any entity would be when confronted by the specific situations abstracted in the models" but that improvements in the theory can and should be made to enable predictions about particular state behavior.[7] Yet, despite such disclaimers, many theorists and policymakers have not hesitated to apply structural theory to specific cases. Here the abstractness and timelessness of the approach can render it misleading and not particularly useful.

At bottom, prevalent Western, or more accurately, American-originated theories of Structural Realism, rational choice, and nuclear deterrence—each of which informs the other—cannot explain why and how India's nuclear policy developed from 1947 to 1964. Nor can they explain why India waited thirty-four years after China's first nuclear weapon test to declare that it had countervailing nuclear weapons. If and when India finally deploys a survivable nuclear arsenal, it will conform to these theories, but the theories will not explain why it took India this long or what were the actionable causes. In the long view of human history or the distant perspective of international political theory, the particulars of Indian decision making may not matter. But for the eight American administrations, the thirteen Indian prime ministers, and the countless other officials, scholars, and citizens who have tried to understand and shape Indian nuclear policy between 1948 and 1998, history has not seemed so overdetermined.[8] Alternate actions and policies—in India and the United States—could have been undertaken. The particularity of decisions and their timing have mattered. Understanding these particularities may help policymakers, scholars, and citizens of the future to interact more effectively with India and other states.

Of course, it can be argued that domestic factors merely reflected decision makers' perceptions and toleration of different levels of security risks. In other words, nuclear restraint occurred when security threats were not perceived to be grave, and nuclear "activism" occurred when security threats were seen to be severe. However, this points back to the primacy of subjective individual and state-level processes of perception, not the external environment. More tellingly, leading Realist theorists such as Kenneth Waltz and practitioners such as Henry Kissinger (who also shaped international relations theory in this domain in the 1950s and '60s) have perceived that India would or should have built a survivable, retaliatory nuclear arsenal *long ago* given its threat environment.[9] Similarly, even if Realist precepts could explain the 1974 nuclear test, the absence of follow-up tests for twenty-four years cannot be explained by these same precepts. If Indian behavior since 1964 has run counter to the expectations of the security-based model, the model's real-time utility is suspect. India after 1998 may finally do as this model predicted long ago, but internal causes, again, will weigh at least as heavily as the external security environment.

The inclusion of factors beyond national security considerations will prompt objections that this approach is not parsimonious. Yet the domestic focus projected here is more accurate and illuminating than a single-factor explanation. No reductive theory can adequately explain or predict state decisions to seek nuclear weapon capabilities, but a set of factors can be specified as essential in determining such decisions. Again, theorists such as Kenneth Waltz have acknowledged the need for state-level analyses to explain specific policies, but this has not prevented loose assumptions that the international system decisively shapes the formation of particular policies. To be useful, theorists and analysts must specify more accurately how key individuals and groups in India have identified, constructed, and followed the state's "national interest" in nuclear policy.

Moreover, the social science quest for parsimony, modeled after the natural sciences, seems an unnecessary and unhelpful conceit when the subject is nuclear proliferation.[10] In the proliferation problematic, the set of current and potential cases that must be addressed is small enough that particular, fine-grained assessments of each can be undertaken. This set includes four categories of states as described more fully in the next section—the five recognized nuclear weapon states; India, Israel, and Pakistan; other current or prospective aspirants to nuclear weapons; and states that have abandoned nascent nuclear weapon programs and joined the international nonproliferation regime.[11] Practically and theoretically, it does not seem rational or wise to limit the search for causes of proliferation among such a manageable set of states to one variable when additional factors may be able to explain and predict much more.

ILLUSION 2:
NONPROLIFERATION IS THE FLIP-SIDE OF
THE PROLIFERATION COIN

Proliferation can be defined as a state's decision to acquire nuclear weapons or nuclear weapon capabilities. Nonproliferation has been defined in two ways. The first encompasses a state's decision to forego the initial acquisition of nuclear weapons or related capabilities outside of international safeguards. The second definition refers to a state's decision to eliminate or roll back existing nuclear weapon capabilities and put all relevant facilities and materials under international safeguards. The former definition is most aptly encompassed by the term nonproliferation, as it connotes the nonexistence of proliferation. The latter category is better defined as *unproliferation,* as it signifies the undoing or reversal of previously acquired capabilities and activities. (Unproliferation has much in common with *arms control* and *disarmament,* terms normally applied to the five recognized nuclear weapon states.)

Nonproliferation applies to the 180-plus states that have signed and implemented the Nuclear Non-Proliferation Treaty as non–nuclear weapon states without having had to abandon acquired nuclear weapon capabilities. This includes states such as Australia, Germany, Italy, Japan, Sweden, and Switzerland, whose capabilities and/or intentions took them partway down the path toward nuclear weapons before they changed course and joined the NPT by the time the treaty entered into force in 1970. Unproliferation encompasses states like South Africa, North Korea (tentatively), Belarus, Kazakhstan, and Ukraine that built or inherited nuclear weapons after the international nonproliferation regime came into effect and then agreed to relinquish them. Unproliferation also covers states such as Argentina, Brazil, South Korea, and Taiwan that, in varying degrees, sought to produce nuclear explosives after 1970 but decided to stop these efforts before they came to fruition. Iraq was pursuing a major nuclear weapon acquisition program, despite its legal obligations under the NPT, and was stopped forcibly.

Today, the major unproliferation challenges are India, Israel, Pakistan, Iran, Iraq, and North Korea. (Iraq and North Korea are significantly restrained but must remain under watch.) The first three have acquired nuclear weapons or the capacity to assemble them quickly and are not party to the NPT. Iran is a party to the NPT but is believed to be seeking capabilities for producing nuclear weapons. Thus, "unproliferation" as applied to India, Israel, Pakistan, and, less clearly, Iran requires that these states stop and reverse their acquisition of nuclear weapons. This requirement amounts to nuclear disarmament (or less comprehensively, arms control). Thus, the challenge is similar to that of persuading the five legally recognized nuclear weapon states to further reduce and then eliminate their nuclear arsenals. The Nuclear Non-Proliferation Treaty accepts for the time being the possession of nuclear arsenals by the United States, Russia, China, France, and the United Kingdom. However, Article VI of the treaty links disarmament with unproliferation and nonproliferation by calling for the nuclear weapon states "to pursue negotiations in good faith on effective measures relating to cessation of the nuclear arms race at an early date and to nuclear disarmament." Thus, the discussion that follows regarding India's approach to unproliferation relates more broadly to the challenge of nuclear arms reductions and disarmament.

No detailed theory of nonproliferation or unproliferation has been developed yet. However, policymakers and scholars believe that knowing the sources of proliferation can augment nonproliferation and unproliferation policies. This belief rests on the proposition that to achieve unproliferation it is necessary and perhaps sufficient to remove the causes of proliferation.[12] Insofar as theorists and policymakers emphasize that states seek nuclear weapons for security, they assume that unproliferation can and will be achieved if a state's security circumstances improve.

However, this common and influential assumption suffers from two major flaws, as the preceding chapters demonstrate. First, the phenomenon of unproliferation is essentially different from the phenomenon of proliferation. The process of proliferation changes the state that undertakes it. The building of nuclear weapons and related capabilities creates new interests, bureaucratic actors, beliefs, perspectives, and expectations within a state. The exact nature of the changes depends on the form, history, culture, and milieu of the state. Democracies are most greatly affected by these changes because the material, ideological, psychological, and institutional effects of acquiring nuclear weapons are more widely and openly diffused into the polity. The key point is that the phenomenon of proliferation seriously complicates the challenge of unproliferation. Rollback does not occur by simply rewinding and erasing the processes that led a state to proliferate.

A second key flaw is revealed by the insight that there is no single cause of proliferation. Thus, removing security threats will be insufficient to stimulate unproliferation. Other variables play important causal roles. It may be possible to prompt a state to adopt unproliferation policies without major changes in the surrounding security environment. Alternatively, changes in the security environment may be insufficient to bring about unproliferation, as long as other factors remain.

The Indian case illuminates these two flaws and yields a potentially important insight that is discussed more fully below: namely, *democracy may inhibit state decisions to eliminate existing nuclear weapon capabilities.* Before describing and explaining this phenomenon, however, it is useful to summarize the other factors that have kept India from stopping or reversing its nuclear weapon program.

It should be noted at the outset that no state has abandoned a nuclear weapon program without claiming that its security or at least its international situation had changed.[13] Leaders in South Africa, Argentina, Brazil, Ukraine, and, tentatively, North Korea concluded that nuclear weapons were not advantageous to their international interests when they decided to abandon nuclear weapon capabilities and programs. North Korea's 1994 agreement to freeze its nuclear weapon acquisition program also appeared to reflect a desire to improve its relations with the United States and the broader international community. To be sure, domestic interests motivated leaders in these states to adhere to nonproliferation norms. In the cases of South Korea and Taiwan, interests in maintaining good relations with the United States outweighed the value of seeking nuclear weapons.

In India, too, security concerns significantly affect the debate over unproliferation and arms control. India will require Pakistani reciprocity in any formal steps to constrain or reverse its nuclear weapon capabilities. Similarly, India will require major improvements in the relationship with China, if not Chinese nuclear disarmament, before India will formally limit or roll back its nuclear weapon and ballistic missile capabilities. Yet, until 1995, the "security" arguments against unproliferation in India tended to be rather vague and rhetorical. And, despite these arguments, other factors have been at least as important in the unproliferation debates in India from the 1960s through 1998.

The domestic sources of India's resistance to unproliferation can be described under four categories.[14]

The Symbolic Import of Nuclear Weapon and Missile Capability.   By detonating nuclear bombs in 1974 and 1998, India demonstrated that it could do what only the five recognized major powers had done. The Indian achievement was even greater as it came against such odds and obstacles. In the words of Raja Ramanna, "India is the only developing country to have achieved such stupendous success in the field [of atomic energy] despite innumerable pressures and all sorts of discouragement from various nations."[15] The Indian press and public have continued to glorify the achievements of the nuclear and ballistic missile establishments. To constrain or surrender symbolically laden weapon capabilities would repudiate one of India's greatest perceived postcolonial achievements. Unless and until substitute symbols of scientific prowess are created and promoted by India's leaders, unproliferation will represent antimodernism. In the present circumstances, this makes it psychologically and politically untenable for a nation with India's history and aspirations to unproliferate.

Repudiation of the Legacy of Colonialism.   The preceding chapters show how Indians equate the nonproliferation regime with colonialism and racism. Thus, many Indians tar proponents of more restrained nuclear policies with invidious and intimidating language. In urging India to block the nuclear test ban treaty in Geneva, the former foreign secretary, A. P. Venkateswaran, brutally attacked proponents of a less confrontational approach in racially laden terms: "Alas, some of our own analysts are guilefully Uncle-Tomming such a course of action on the servile argument that we should not displease the great powers."[16] Another prominent nuclear hawk added a sexual dimension to this debate. Noting that American "nonproliferation missionaries" pressed India to sign the Comprehensive Test Ban Treaty and support a treaty to ban unsafeguarded production of fissile materials, Brahma Chellaney argued that accession to these "self-castration measures" would leave India as a "nuclear eunuch."[17] In a subsequent attack on India's self-restrained nuclear policy, Chellaney likened India's "nuclear option" to "chronic impotence," and decried national leaders for leaving the nation "naked."[18] The character of this debate—prevalent since the mid-1960s—makes it increasingly difficult for Indian political leaders to advocate nuclear restraint, let alone a roll-back of the Indian nuclear program. As long as resistance to unproliferation is identified with defying colonialism, racism, and emasculation, it will be difficult to overcome.

Nuclear Weapon Capabilities as Political Devices. No Indian election has been decided on nuclear policy. Nor, with a few important exceptions including the 1964 and 1995-to-1998 periods, has political pressure compelled leaders to *advance* the nation's nuclear weapon and missile capabilities. However, nuclear policy, especially since 1974, has become a potentially explosive political device deterring leaders from undertaking measures to restrain and roll back nuclear capabilities. Indian political leaders fear that to abandon nuclear capabilities would be political suicide. They have been afraid even to adopt arms control measures that would limit the growth of these capabilities without requiring their abandonment. This was seen in late 1998 as government leaders such as Jaswant Singh expressed the state's interest in signing the CTBT but were politically intimidated from doing so.

Unquestionably, "the bomb," as a means of providing both security and status, has evoked strong visceral support among the Indian populace. Yet the public has not specifically defined what constitutes "the bomb" or exactly what nuclear capability is required to satisfy it or the national interest. The political debate has taken place within the parameters of not abandoning the bomb and not bankrupting the country to pursue it. Certain parties such as the Jana Sangh cum Bharatiya Janata Party have used advocacy of nuclear weapons as a rallying cry. They have put their adversaries on the defensive by portraying nuclear weapons as guarantors of Indian sovereignty, security, prowess, and power and denouncing as "soft" those who do not favor "the bomb." This has been largely a symbolic exercise. In any case, public opinion and therefore partisan politics limit India's willingness to undertake unproliferation, whatever the security circumstances facing the country.

The Nuclear and Missile Establishments as States within the State. The powerful role of the strategic enclave in propelling the development of nuclear weapon capabilities and aspirations in India is described throughout this book. The nuclear and missile establishments have pushed India to the threshold of a decision to deploy a nuclear arsenal, even if they have not yet been able to cross this threshold. While the strategic enclave's role in India's proliferation has been tempered by higher authorities, the enclave has greater power to prevent *un*proliferation policies—arms control as well as complete rollback. The strategic enclave has resisted unproliferation policies regardless of India's security environment. As long as this enclave's achievements stand for India's postcolonial modernity and prowess, and as long as its performance and expenditures remain protected against open scrutiny and debate, it will be a major force against unproliferation.

Of course, it can be argued that other sources of resistance to unproliferation, including security concerns, have been so great that the strategic enclave's particular role has not been particularly significant. Yet the preceding chapters offer specific instances where the weaponeers did shape policy. Homi Bhabha in the mid-1950s determined India's position to block stronger international controls over plutonium separation plants and resultant stockpiles of the material. The Atomic Energy Commission significantly influenced the government's turnabout in the mid-1990s on a prospective treaty to ban unsafeguarded fissile material production, and on the test ban treaty. Indeed, the government's hinted willingness after the 1998 tests to contemplate joining the test ban treaty and negotiating a fissile material production ban owed in part to the nuclear establishment's reduced resistance, which political leaders and Foreign Ministry officials negotiated with AEC leaders.

The absence of independent institutions of scientific and technical expertise that could check and balance the work of the strategic enclave has undermined Indian decision makers.[19] Political leaders and the press have lacked scientific, technical, and economic data and analyses to question the self-interested claims of the nuclear and missile establishments. This institutional shortcoming is not unique to India, but that does not lessen its significance. Without independent bodies of technical expertise to evaluate the data, capabilities, and proposals of the strategic enclave, India will be less likely to undertake arms control and unproliferation.

ILLUSION 3:
DEMOCRACY FACILITATES NONPROLIFERATION

The nonsecurity attachments just discussed will profoundly affect India's receptivity to unproliferation proposals, even if the security environment improves. This stems in large part from two facts: India is a democracy and the state's nuclear weapon capabilities are widely, albeit incompletely, known. Public awareness of India's nuclear weapon assets means that to constrain or abandon these capabilities would be to give up something of perceived value. Democracy means that decisions to do so must be popularly supported. In India, the democratic process provides the medium through which political and bureaucratic actors express the four previously described domestic factors inhibiting unproliferation. Leaders cannot ignore or overwhelm these factors as they could conceivably in a nondemocracy.

Because India is the state that has most democratically debated whether to pursue unproliferation, its experience may have implications for other cases. To assess fully the effects of democracy on states' dispositions to roll back publicly known nuclear capabilities it is necessary to analyze thoroughly cases where rollback has occurred since the nuclear nonproliferation regime went into effect in 1970. Space here allows only an illustrative reference to the South African and Ukrainian cases, and still briefer mentions of the North Korean, South Korean, Taiwanese, and Brazilian and Argentine cases. The aim is to stimulate other scholars to test how the presence or absence of democracy has affected state decisions to abandon nuclear programs after 1970—the year when the norm and attendant regime of nonproliferation entered into force.

South Africa is a most important case—the only country that built nuclear weapons and then verifiably destroyed them in order to join the nuclear nonproliferation regime. South Africa began secret research on uranium enrichment in the 1960s, and in 1971 under the aegis of the minister of mines began preliminary investigations into the feasibility of producing nuclear explosives.[20] At least two key South African officials have said that the nuclear weapons program started in 1974, before security challenges were felt to be acute.[21] Only a handful of scientists and government decision makers were involved in these decisions, and the scientists leading the effort did not consult with the South African Defense Force.[22]

Security imperatives explained neither the beginning nor the end of South Africa's nuclear bomb program. To be sure, in his bold March 24, 1993, announcement that South Africa had in 1990 and 1991 destroyed a nuclear arsenal of at least six devices, President F. W. deKlerk explained that the security threats that ostensibly had motivated their construction were gone.[23] However, other factors loomed at least as large. Internationally, deKlerk sought to end South Africa's isolation and to reenter the international trading and political community. President deKlerk concluded that joining the NPT was a necessary means to this end. Domestically, the prospect of apartheid's end and the emergence of a black-led government motivated the white regime to ensure that a black government did not inherit nuclear weapons.[24]

Whatever South Africa's motivations, deKlerk's decision in 1990 to begin dismantling its nuclear weapons and to join the NPT was made secretly outside of democratic processes. Indeed, the nondemocratic nature of the decision made it easier. Because the nuclear program was so secretive, the polity—white, colored, and black—was not attached to it. The country experienced no loss in power, status, or military security. Instead, it perceived only the gain of ending international isolation. Nuclear disarmament occurred before the polity even knew bombs had been built, and it was presented as a fait accompli.

Ukraine is another unproliferation success story, albeit of a unique kind. Ukraine did not build the nuclear warheads left on its soil after the collapse of the Soviet Union; nor did Ukraine then possess the infrastructure to command and control them. However, Ukraine theoretically had the expertise and technological wherewithal eventually to operate these weapons, unlike Kazakhstan and Belarus, whose nonproliferation decisions are for this reason and space considerations not considered here.

Ukrainian leaders faced real decisions in transferring nuclear weapons back to Russia. These decisions occurred in stages from 1991 to 1994 as Ukraine underwent its transition to independence and as the Ukrainian Rada (Parliament) emerged as an inexperienced political force in the newly democratic state. During this period democracy played its complicating role in unproliferation.

The new president of Ukraine, Leonid Kravchuk—the former Communist Party chief of ideology—had agreed in December 1991 to allow removal of all tactical nuclear weapons from his state's soil, but in March 1992 he publicly suspended the transfers. Domestic politics and mistrust of Russia had intervened. After Washington increased its pressure and Moscow its positive inducements, Kravchuk agreed to resume facilitating the transfers. However, the Rada soon intervened to block implementation of the May 1992 Lisbon Protocol, under which Ukraine, Belarus, and Kazakhstan agreed to cooperate in the removal of strategic nuclear weapons to Russia. This agreement required the Rada's ratification. From the summer of 1992 to early 1994, at the Rada's instigation Ukraine balked at ratifying the Lisbon Protocol, START I, and its earlier commitment to join the NPT as a non–nuclear weapon state. Ukrainian government leaders and more emphatically the Rada wanted stronger security guarantees from the United States and Russia and more compensation for "giving up" the nuclear weapons Ukraine had inherited. Competing political factions and interests pulled the knot of issues tighter. Nationalists resisted "nonproliferation" even though the Ukrainian military lobbied against the nuclear option, preferring instead to concentrate resources on basic social services for troops and conventional weaponry. As a senior adviser to the then defense minister told Sherman Garnett, according to Garnett's paraphrase, "nuclear weapons were not a serious military issue at all, but rather part of the 'political maneuvering' over power."[25]

Ultimately, the Rada in several votes spanning from February to November 1994 ratified the NPT and the START I Treaty, a (weak) trilateral American-Russian-Ukrainian agreement on security guarantees and financial compensation. A number of important security, financial, and political-psychological issues affected the Rada's deliberations, but the point is that the emergence of democracy greatly complicated unproliferation decision makers. Had Ukraine's new government been unconstrained by the Parliament, the initial agreements they made would have been implemented more directly and smoothly. Had the Rada been more established when these decisions were made, there is no telling what would have happened.

North Korea's decision in October 1994 to freeze its plutonium production and separation as part of the framework agreement negotiated by the United States was made by a nondemocratic regime. North Korean leaders, unaccountable to their citizenry, agreed, as part of a complicated package of quid pro quos, to freeze and eventually abandon whatever nuclear weapons their scientists may have produced without the public's knowledge that any weapons had existed. Taiwan, too, had a nascent nuclear weapon program despite being a party to the NPT.[26] At key junctures in the mid-1970s and in 1985 and 1988, the United States managed to persuade Taiwan's nondemocratic leadership to desist from suspect plutonium production and separation activities and to dismantle proliferation-sensitive apparatuses. A similar process resulted in South Korea's suspension of plans to reprocess plutonium as part of a strategy to obtain a nascent bomb-acquisition option in the mid-1970s. The United States' capacity to persuade Taiwan and South Korea to desist from plutonium reprocessing was no doubt augmented by its role as a strategic protector of both states. Moreover, it is possible that Taiwan, North Korea, and South Korea would have made similar unproliferation decisions had they been democracies, yet the facts are that the authoritarian leaderships of these states reversed their nuclear programs in ways that have not occurred in democracies beyond Argentina and Brazil since the nonproliferation regime's entry into force in 1970.

Argentina and Brazil present complicated cases for assessing the role of democracy in unproliferation. Both countries, in an adversarial dyad for decades, clandestinely pursued nuclear explosive capabilities before pledging to join the nonproliferation regime in the 1990s. The motivations and dynamics of each nuclear program are beyond the scope of this book, but it can be said that Argentina's and Brazil's mutual transitions to democracy did facilitate their decisions to abandon their quests for nuclear explosive capabilities. Indeed, the fact that these nuclear programs were initiated and conducted secretly by military regimes became important issues in the struggle for democracy. Democrats, particularly in Brazil, saw the nuclear programs as symbols of what they despised in these military regimes. Thus, the democrats were unlikely to continue these programs once democratization took hold. Other factors played important roles, too, but Brazil and Argentina represent at least partial counterexamples to the argument posited here that democracy reduces the likelihood of states' rolling back or even significantly constraining publicly known nuclear weapon programs.

India's leaders do not have the freedom to maneuver that leaders of South Africa, North Korea, South Korea, Taiwan, Belarus, Kazakhstan, and Ukraine had. In contrast with countries that have abandoned nuclear weapon capabilities, Indian leaders would have to undertake unproliferation in full view of the public, through processes that would take considerable time and debate. India would relinquish perhaps dozens of weapons, a significant quantity of separated plutonium, and the "keys" to facilities from which foreign inspectors have always been excluded. The prospects for this are highly doubtful given the domestic attachments and interests now tied to nuclear weapon capabilities. Moreover, that most citizens and many leaders appear to think that nuclear weapons would never be used reduces the polity's motivation to get rid of them. Whatever the substantive merits of arms control measures—and, more ambitiously, unproliferation—

opportunistic political parties would mobilize powerful symbolic arguments to undermine a government pursuing such measures.

The problem extends beyond India. Seven of the eight recognized and threshold nuclear weapon states are democracies: the United States, the United Kingdom, France, and Russia among the recognized nuclear weapon states, and India, Israel, and Pakistan.[27] These states and their polities appear to have even greater attachments to nuclear weapons than does India, which has maintained strong public support for nuclear disarmament. Whereas India's "reliance" on nuclear weapons has been as much symbolic and political as military, the recognized nuclear weapon states perceive their security to be based on their arsenals and have achieved major power status at least in part through them. Whatever the validity of security arguments for retaining nuclear weapons in these states, the long-standing nuclear powers see their nuclear arsenals as measures and guarantees of their global status. Indeed, the United Kingdom, France, and Russia now cling to nuclear weapons as arguably the last vestiges of this status. These states may require greater adjustments to prepare themselves to undertake their non-proliferation commitments to roll back their own nuclear arsenals. Competing political actors in these states may question the patriotism and leadership of those who would give up these symbols of great power. Opposition parties would no doubt seize the opportunity to seek political gain by resisting such moves. The "strategic enclaves" within these states will defend their budgets, jobs, and status, and their political representatives will fight to retain the economic benefits of investments in nuclear forces. Democracy gives voice and power to groups that will press their material, political, and psychological attachments to nuclear weapons regardless of changes in the international security environment. If India's approach to nuclear policy sometimes appears contradictory and confusing, it is arguably no less so than the post–cold war nuclear doctrines and disarmament policies of the United States, the United Kingdom, France, and Russia.[28]

These observations and propositions regarding democracy and unproliferation are not meant to disparage democracy or recommend authoritarianism. Rather, they are to suggest further research into the ways in which democracy affects nuclear policymaking. Such research may conclude that the correlation between nondemocratic decision makers and nuclear rollback is accidental and that no causal link exists between government forms and unproliferation decisions. Conversely, further research may indicate tendencies within democracies that must be addressed if such states are to eliminate nuclear weapons. It could be argued, for example, that the problem is not democracy per se, but rather the way in which democracies thus far have managed nuclear policy. That is, perhaps nuclear policy has been so shrouded in secrecy and left so dependent on the judgments of a few insulated military and scientific establishments that the virtues of democracy have not been adequately applied to nuclear policymaking.

On another level, it is possible that the focus on unproliferation and nuclear disarmament is misplaced—that nuclear weapons are salutary and therefore that the nuclear-armed democracies' apparent aversion to disarmament is both wise and harmless. It could be argued that nuclear weapons deter war at acceptable levels of cost and risk and that, therefore, disarmament would not serve national and international interests. However, even if this were true, it would pose a major problem for the international system. For the nonproliferation regime today is highly valued as a foundation of the international security system; and the cornerstone Nuclear Non-Proliferation Treaty does call for serious progress toward nuclear disarmament. If this regime, which has been led by the United States, is not to be displaced or discarded, nuclear weapons cannot be accepted forever, or even for the foreseeable future.

Thus, if nonproliferation is to remain a major goal, it appears necessary to pay greater attention to the myriad attachments nuclear-armed democracies have to these weapons and to devise leadership and public education strategies to break them. Democracy always has been supposed to require hard work and serious public education—its benefits do not come automatically or passively. The recent literature on the "democratic peace," which argues that democracies are highly unlikely to war against each other, may encourage laxity, as if the hard work is done once democracy has been widely achieved.[29] To the extent that nuclear weapons are an international problem and that the analysis here about democracies and unproliferation cannot be dismissed, further research, public education, and action on the predicament are necessary.

ILLUSION 4: EQUITABLE DISARMAMENT IS UNNECESSARY FOR NONPROLIFERATION

For the international community, particularly the five recognized nuclear weapon states, India represents a nettlesome, frequently hypocritical and frustrating gadfly. India may be induced to limit the pace and scope of its nuclear weapon and missile development and deployments, but India will not curtail them without concomitant progress in global nuclear disarmament. In arguably the grandest illusion of the nuclear age, many policymakers and security specialists in the nuclear weapon states resist the proposition that global nuclear disarmament and unproliferation are linked. It is worth exploring briefly how the Indian experience illuminates this illusion.

Two narratives and causal relationships link India's (and other states') nuclear policies to the global disarmament process. One narrative pertains to national security, the other to politics. India argues that its policies to acquire nuclear weapons and ballistic missiles derive from the threat it faces from China. The foregoing chapters identify the weakness, incompleteness, and unanswered implications of this argument but acknowledge that perceived security threats from China and Pakistan added impetus to India's nuclear program. The China factor thus connects India (and Pakistan) to the chain of declared nuclear weapon states. China's possession of a nuclear arsenal is linked historically to perceived threats from the United States and Russia. Russia and the United States in turn link their arsenals to threats from each other, from China, and potential rogue actors. Thus, by the nuclear weapons states' own logic, security dynamics partially—and sometimes speciously—link the policies of India (and therefore Pakistan) to those of the established nuclear weapon states.

Ironically, many otherwise security-conscious American specialists and officials debunk the actuality or importance of this chain. American officials maintain that nuclear weapons are indispensable for U.S. security, as Russians insist they are for Russian security, and Frenchmen say nuclear weapons are for French security, and so on. Yet officials and security specialists from the five nuclear weapon states often argue that their arsenals and policies do not bear on India's nuclear needs or policies. As one former American nonproliferation policymaker put it, "There is no connection between 'vertical proliferation' and 'horizontal proliferation' "—that is, between the accretion of nuclear weapons by the five established nuclear weapon states and the spread of nuclear weapons to countries like India.[30] While arguable, the same analysis should raise questions about the security rationale for French and British nuclear weapons, to name just two examples. What threats of nuclear attack (or other attack) do France and the United Kingdom face from Russia, the United States, or China? If such threats can be plausibly argued, would they not be addressed by proposals for verifiable and equitable nuclear disarmament, something that the five established nuclear weapon states have not seriously discussed? India certainly is not alone in exaggerating security rationales for its nuclear weapon endeavors, and India's connection of its nuclear policies to those of the "major powers" is no more dubious than many of the arguments proffered by the recognized nuclear powers. More to the point, the unproliferation challenge is not to determine whether the nuclear arsenals of the established nuclear weapon states cause others to *acquire* nuclear weapons but instead to determine whether the possession of these arsenals undermines efforts to persuade states like India to *abandon* their nuclear capabilities.[31] Here the policies of the United States, Russia, China, France, and the United Kingdom do bear directly on the attitudes and interests of India and therefore Pakistan.

However, the security narrative is not most important to India in any case. The most important narrative is political. Most polities, but especially democracies, insist on equity in their international relations, at least among states that they regard as their peers. This is particularly true of large postcolonial democracies whose purposes and internal legitimacy were founded on the achievement of independence and equity. Perceptions matter here. In practical reality, international agreements and arrangements may not be symmetrical or identically balanced, but they nonetheless may serve each party's important interests. Conversely, agreements that apply identical obligations to all parties may require unequal sacrifices or bestow unequal advantages between parties. Not every international agreement, arrangement, or treaty distributes costs and benefits equally, or even equitably, and yet states continue to participate in international regimes.

However, in a democracy the challenge is to persuade the polity that a given international action or agreement is equitable, whatever its specific terms, and that the overall international system tends toward equity even if this or that agreement is uneven. This is not easy because opposition parties in democracies will seize on perceived inequities to accuse officeholders of surrendering national dignity and interest to foreign advantage seekers. In the United States this could be seen in the Senate's 1998–1999 debates on the Global Climate Change Treaty, the Comprehensive Test Ban Treaty, and other measures. In Russia, the Duma's resistance to ratifying the START II Treaty reveals this dynamic.

Indians see nuclear policy as part of a political narrative whose central theme is India's desire to be regarded as an equal among the world's few major powers. Nuclear nonproliferation and arms control initiatives directed at India always have been perceived through the equity lens. This narrative is more gripping in India and other once-dominated states than the national security narrative in which the nuclear weapon states tend to describe and rationalize their nuclear policies. India's competitive, mass politics will not allow Indian leaders to take *fundamental* steps toward unproliferation in the absence of perceived equitable measures by the nuclear weapon states. This means that whatever the security justification for the nuclear arsenals in the United States, Russia, China, the United Kingdom, France, and Israel, the failure of these states to heed the political imperative to pursue nuclear disarmament seriously will limit how far India, and therefore Pakistan, will go in constraining its nuclear and missile development. Anything less will be seen as inequitable and therefore unacceptable.

Politics—democratic politics—tie the future of the global nonproliferation regime to progress in creating the conditions for nuclear disarmament. Among democracies, if not other states, achieving greater equity in the global nuclear order will be a necessary condition for meeting the nonproliferation regime's disarmament obligations. Policymakers and scholars reading from the international security narrative often dismiss the linkage of disarmament and proliferation/unproliferation as softheaded—as if the aspiration for equity is less real than, say, the balance of armored divisions or missiles between states. American and world history suggest otherwise, as do the rivers of blood that have flowed over campaigns for equity. The downplaying of the equity dynamic in nuclear politics is doubly ironic insofar as American foreign policymakers promote democracy precisely because equity is seen as a good—because they believe that states that achieve relative equity will be more stable and peace loving. Democracy is a means to equity. Yet, when it comes to global nuclear policy, American (and other) officials devalue equity as a cause of action.

To be sure, most of the world has accepted the security arguments made in behalf of a nonproliferation regime that allows five states to retain nuclear weapons while keeping them from others. Most states lack the ambition, scientific and technical base, and security interests to acquire nuclear weapons. They therefore welcome the international regime's prevention of nuclear weapon spread to their neighbors. Some non–nuclear weapon states complain that the equity promised in NPT's Article VI has not been delivered, but the salience of nuclear issues is not great enough in these states to make the matter worth pressing aggressively. Others accept that the nuclear weapon states have more challenging security environments and roles than other states. To them, the dichotomy between the nuclear haves and have-nots is commensurate with their circumstances and therefore not inequitable. Others are too weak to resist U.S.-led international pressure to support the global nuclear regime, including even pressure to roll back nascent nuclear weapon programs. But India, Pakistan, and Israel have not accepted these arguments; they are strong and unthreatening enough to resist unproliferation pressures without triggering international coercion against them. Others may join these three states in the future, especially if the norms and equities of the nonproliferation regime are not reaffirmed, and the will to strengthen its enforcement is weakened.

In the wake of the May 1998 tests, international frustration may mount given that the nonproliferation regime's promise of nuclear disarmament is not being realized despite the absence of obvious needs for deployed nuclear weapons in the post–cold war era. That is, nuclear weapons now seem necessary only to counter other nuclear weapons, not to deter or fight conventional wars among the existing nuclear powers, who no longer appear to have an interest in attacking one another. The weakened necessity for nuclear weapons may make key non–nuclear weapon states less supportive of a nonproliferation regime that perpetuates the possession of these devices by the five major cold war powers. Some theorists, policymakers, and citizens may question whether stopping the spread of nuclear weapons is desirable, but a strong American and global consensus holds that it is. Similarly, the post–cold war promotion of democracy—which is meaningless without concomitant endorsement of equity—renders a dichotomous global nuclear regime untenable over time. If this is so, the need for a more patently equitable approach to nuclear unproliferation and disarmament emerges from the Indian nuclear experience, shattering a central illusion of the nuclear age.

Still, the last word must be directed toward India's responsibilities for overcoming its disillusionment with the nuclear age. India has shown that the actions of states depend greatly on "who" they are, what their people need, what they believe in, and what they aspire to be. This explains much of what India has done in the nuclear realm, often in a self-restrained fashion. It also explains less restrained moments such as the May 1998 tests that brought India into closer alignment with the very powers, practices, and inequities it had traditionally deplored. Yet India's identity, needs, and aspirations are precisely what may be undermined by investing national energies and resources in nuclear weapons. These weapons do not provide what the Indian people need or reflect who they are.

India is well positioned to assume a major place in the twenty-first century. This will be a world in which economic capacity is the determining source of power and the real value of nuclear weapons continues to decline.[32] However, to realize its potential, India must escape from the colonial framework within which it has perceived nuclear diplomacy and adopt the sort of pragmatism that in the mid-1990s engendered promising economic reforms. Pragmatic action, as opposed to idealistic posturing, requires a willingness to make decisions that achieve progress if not perfection and to compromise some long-held demands in return for similar concessions by others, even if the net result falls short of the "right and pure." It requires the kind of statesmanship and public education that the Indian people have missed in recent decades. Self-confident states and leaders make compromises and educate their people to support them. With a more pragmatic approach to tactics, India could lead the international community in helping to avoid and reduce the dangers of deployed nuclear arsenals. Having not yet completely followed the path of the nuclear weapon states, India can now more than ever be a force of change in the international system. This would be the ultimate legacy of a remarkable fifty-year history of nuclear policy in India.

Afterword

The first edition of this book chronicled India's nuclear policy through the end of 1998. The narrative recorded how internal factors largely shaped India's policy. This afterword focuses on the evolution of India's international security environment since 1998 and on New Delhi's efforts to shape it, recognizing Indian arguments that security factors compelled the nuclear tests of May 1998. This is not to diminish the importance of internal factors. Rather, the aim is to explore whether the evolution of India's nuclear policy since 1998 reveals discontinuities from the earlier narrative. Do military security considerations appear to be determining India's nuclear policy more decisively than political, institutional, normative, and technological factors?

As 1998 ended, the BJP-led government resolved not to repeat the history that followed India's first detonation of a nuclear device, in 1974. India would now move decisively forward from the May 1998 nuclear tests and develop and deploy a sophisticated nuclear arsenal with attendant nuclear doctrine and command and control systems. The resultant nuclear deterrent would stabilize security relations with Pakistan and strengthen India's position vis-à-vis China. By downplaying the moralism of its traditional diplomacy and speaking the language of Realpolitik, India would compel the United States and the international community to abandon sanctions and sanctionary attitudes toward India as a nuclear power. At the same time, India would invalidate the charges of international and domestic critics who fretted that India and Pakistan would stumble into an excessively costly and destabilizing arms race.

However, this assertive optimism begged many questions raised throughout the fifty years of history chronicled in this book.

Would India overcome its long-standing ambivalence and confusion regarding national security strategy? Could it actually plot a clear course for improving its security relationships with both Pakistan and China? Would nuclear weapons play a central role here?

Would India alter its traditional reluctance to establish robust institutions for devising nuclear strategy and policy? Would the military be integrated into nuclear policymaking?

Could India simultaneously develop and deploy a ballistic-missile-based nuclear arsenal and engage its adversaries in measures to avoid excessively costly and destabilizing arms racing?

Would Indian leaders create institutions to check and balance the claims and demands of the nuclear and missile technological establishments?

Would overt nuclear capabilities improve India's global influence?

LAHORE, FEBRUARY 1999

On February 20, 1999, Prime Minister Vajpayee took a bus to Pakistan. The prosaic mode of transport added irony to the poetic statesman's mission, taken at the invitation of Prime Minister Nawaz Sharif. India and Pakistan possessed relatively high-tech nuclear weapons, but establishing a bus connection between Delhi and Lahore would herald a breakthrough in their relations. Nawaz Sharif embraced Vajpayee at the Pakistani end of the line.

Two days of ceremonies and meetings yielded several agreements and a lofty statement of mutual purpose called the Lahore Declaration. The two sides agreed to hold periodic meetings at the foreign minister level and to move toward facilitating cross-border travel. The foreign secretaries signed a Memorandum of Understanding committing them to hold consultations on security concepts and nuclear doctrines "with a view to developing measures for confidence building in the nuclear and conventional fields, aimed at the avoidance of conflict." They agreed to notify each other in advance of ballistic missile flight tests and to undertake national measures to reduce the risks of accidental or unauthorized use of nuclear weapons. Both also pledged not to conduct further nuclear test explosions "unless either side . . . decides that extraordinary events have jeopardised its supreme interests."[1] This agreement gave hope that India and Pakistan would fulfill their 1998 pledges not to engage in a nuclear and missile arms race and to be uniquely self-restrained stewards of nuclear arsenals.

The Lahore Declaration framed the two nations' purpose. Invoking a shared "vision of peace and stability between the two countries, and of progress and prosperity for their peoples," the two governments recognized that "the nuclear dimension" of their relationship "adds to their responsibility for avoidance of conflict between the two countries." On this basis they agreed to "intensify their efforts to resolve all issues, including the issue of Jammu and Kashmir," and to "refrain from intervention and interference in each other's internal affairs."[2]

The publics in both countries reacted enthusiastically. For years government officials and pundits had insisted that "the people" would cast aside any Indian or Pakistani leader who would bid openly for peace. The widespread celebration over the Lahore drama and text put the lie to these assumptions. Indians close to Prime Minister Vajpayee confided that the Lahore initiative reflected his personal desire to make peace with Pakistan. The bold diplomacy appeared to confirm Vajpayee's belief that nuclear weaponry was vital for Indian power and self-defense but would not be regarded as an instrument of coercion. Indeed, the bomb could facilitate peace. A former leader of the Indian nuclear establishment explained: "Despite what you Americans say, the bomb gives us the confidence to make peace."[3] The public response to Lahore in both India and Pakistan, just nine months after the nuclear tests, lent credence to this view.

The Lahore summit was not the only sign of the new diplomatic and strategic environment created by the 1998 nuclear tests. Days after Vajapyee left Lahore, Indian diplomats traveled to Beijing to resume the Sino-Indian dialogue that had been suspended since the tests. President K. R. Narayanan declared in his February 22 speech in Parliament that India "seeks to strengthen and deepen" its "historic and friendly relations with China."[4] Meanwhile, China's defense minister was in Islamabad calling upon Pakistani counterparts. The regional environment had been upset by nuclear blasts, and now that the dust had settled, the actors were moving to chart the new terrain.

Of course the new terrain was contiguous to the old: Indian and Pakistani missile and bomb designers continued improving their wares. On April 11, as the BJP-led coalition government was crumbling, DRDO engineers in Orissa launched an enhanced version of the Agni missile on its first test flight. The Agni II, with an all-solid-fuel propulsion system, reportedly traversed 2,000 kilometers in what Indian officials deemed a successful mission. This was the fourth test overall for the Agni system, which previously had not achieved a range beyond 1,000 kilometers. Unlike after the 1998 nuclear tests, Indian leaders handled the pre- and post-Agni test diplomacy in sober, reassuring terms. Prime Minister Vajpayee insisted that the test was "not meant for aggression against any nation. . . . [It] is a purely defensive step."[5] India notified Pakistan two days prior to the test in accord with the Lahore agreement and also forewarned its fellow major powers: China, the United States, Russia, the United Kingdom, France, Germany, and Japan.

Pakistan wasted little time in showing that "anything India can do, we can do better." On April 14 it fired the Ghauri II missile. According to the Khan Research Laboratory (KRL), the improved missile had a range of up to 2,300 kilometers, surpassing the Agni II's announced range. The Pakistan foreign office put the Ghauri II's range at 1,500 kilometers.[6] A day later Pakistan test-launched a second missile, the Shaheen. The twin tests were intended to do India "one better." They also reflected the portentous reality that Pakistan had two competing missile programs managed by rival institutions. The Ghauri was the pride of the Khan Research Laboratories and its erstwhile director, Dr. A. Q. Khan. The Shaheen missile program was run by the Pakistan Atomic Energy Commission. The Ghauri program reportedly benefited from major inputs from North Korea, while the Shaheen missiles' parentage lay in China. Competition between the two Pakistani institutions increased momentum to develop, test, and eventually deploy greater numbers of missiles. Foreign assistance complicated the prospects of controlling these programs. (In March 2001, the military government of Pakistan sought to limit these competitive tendencies by restructuring the missile and nuclear programs. A new National Defence Complex was established, encompassing the Khan Research Laboratories and the Pakistan Atomic Energy Commission's nuclear weapon and missile activities. In the process, the government retired Dr. A. Q. Khan and the PAEC Chairman, Dr. Ashfaq Ahmad.)[7]

At Lahore the political leaders of Pakistan and India had seemed to set a course for diplomatic normalization of relations. Yet individuals and institutions in India, Pakistan and China had developed deep interests and power through building and displaying (and in the case of China, selling) the most awesome weapons known to man. Skillful political leaders might channel the national self-confidence derived from these weapons into bold initiatives to make peace with neighbors, but to succeed they would have to pull all of their states' major institutional actors into a common harness.

KARGIL WAR AND ITS IMPLICATIONS, MAY–JULY 1999

Unfortunately, not all centers of power in Pakistan shared the spirit of the Lahore Declaration. Key military leaders at General Headquarters in Rawalpindi bristled at the lofty, conciliatory rhetoric and the intimations of pending rapprochement. General Pervez Musharraf had been appointed chief of army staff in October 1998. He was known as a commando with experience in unconventional operations and mountain warfare. Musharraf in turn appointed Lt. Gen. Mohammad Aziz Khan as chief of general staff, another figure known for his determination to exert military pressure on India in Kashmir. Musharraf subsequently revealed that Nawaz Sharif had briefed him in advance on the Lahore Declaration, but that Musharraf did not support it. "I did know there's a Declaration," he told the *Hindu*'s editor Malini Parthasarathy after the October 1999 coup that brought him to power, "but I did object to it."[8] Musharraf could not abide "the lack of emphasis on Kashmir." He felt that Nawaz Sharif at Lahore surrendered Pakistan's leverage for extracting Indian concessions in Kashmir.

Thus, while Sharif and Vajpayee and their diplomats charted a path toward diplomatic reconciliation, Musharraf and his aides planned a bold incursion of forces across the Line of Control in the Kargil sector of Kashmir. These men had developed similar plans years earlier and had advocated exercising them in the 1996–1998 period, only to be turned down by Army Chief of Staff General Jehangir Karamat.[9] The aim was to infiltrate forces by stealth—regular Army units and irregular militants all disguised as freedom fighters—and have them take strategic positions at mountainous high points in Indian-controlled territory before they could be detected. From there multiple objectives could have been pursued, though it remains uncertain what the actual plan was. The forces could have cut the Srinagar-Leh highway, thereby isolating Indian forces on the Siachen Glacier and increasing Pakistan's leverage to negotiate an Indian withdrawal from it. More broadly, the forceful alteration to the status quo was meant to upset India and alarm the international community into trying to broker a diplomatic compromise of the Kashmir dispute.

Nawaz Sharif reportedly was briefed on the plan at least once, in January 1999, before the Lahore summit, and approved it.[10] It was unclear whether Sharif understood that this military foray would sunder the reconciliation process begun at Lahore. Indeed, the record does not indicate what exactly he thought would be accomplished. Clearly, important elements within Pakistan felt that overt nuclearization made the subcontinent safe for low-intensity military conflict. Men such as Musharraf and Aziz preferred this mode of activity over diplomatic rapprochement. Sharif may have thought that Lahore-style diplomacy and military aggression were not incompatible, but even his supporters did not credit him with intellectual or strategic acumen.

Pakistani-backed infiltrators were first detected by shepherds in the Kargil area on May 3, according to the subsequent Kargil Review Committee assessment.[11] In a highly proficient and well-planned operation, albeit with a tenuous logistics train, 1,700 fighters made their way into the Indian-controlled sector.[12] By mid-May the battle was joined. What became known as the Kargil war raged from May to mid-July and involved fierce, sometimes hand-to-hand combat. Four hundred seventy-four Indian soldiers were killed and 1,109 wounded.[13] Pakistani and mujahideen casualty figures were not released, in part because Pakistan maintained that its forces were not involved. India's Kargil Review Committee claimed that the "lowest estimate of regular Pakistan Army casualties is 700 killed" and that 243 "militants" were killed and 156 injured.[14]

Kargil was the first "televised" war between India and Pakistan. Unlike the Gulf War in 1991, where televised displays of precision air strikes sending bombs down elevator shafts gave American audiences (if not others) the sense that warfare now resembled computer games with relatively little risk of casualties to the "good guys," the Kargil war was a brutal encounter. Viewers saw fearsome scenes of battle and close-ups of their fallen countrymen. Yet the Indian public did not shrink from the cause. It rallied to it. The government fueled the sense of national determination by breaking with tradition and sending the bodies of dead soldiers back to their home villages for final rites. This action heightened the national resolve to redeem the fallen by prevailing in the conflict. If the specter of nuclear weapons was supposed to inhibit states from escalating conflicts, the Indian public at least did not seem to fear this eventuality and temper its support of the war.

Yet Indian leaders were mindful of the danger in at least two ways. They were determined to drive the infiltrators back and "win" the war, but they could not know what military actions would be necessary to achieve this. If winning required attacks across the Line of Control into Pakistani-held Kashmir, how would Pakistan respond? How did Pakistani leaders define the threshold between conventional conflict and escalation to nuclear threats? Beyond the danger of escalation to the point of nuclear threats and possible use of nuclear weapons, Indian leaders also worried that the international community would see the war as proof that India and Pakistan could not responsibly manage nuclear forces. Were this to occur, India's strategy of winning international respect and power as a nuclear-weapon state would be undermined.

The Indian government addressed these concerns ably. The BJP-led coalition had lost a vote of confidence in April and now served in a caretaker capacity until elections scheduled for October. Although political survival depended on winning the war with as few casualties and setbacks as possible and offered opportunity for bloodlusty rhetoric, Vajpayee and his closest advisors displayed statesmanly restraint throughout. They had been betrayed personally by Pakistan's violation of the Lahore spirit and damaged politically by the successful incursion, yet they did not overreact. Vajpayee insisted in government councils that Indian forces would not attack across the Line of Control. Military commanders felt that the prime minister was tying a hand behind their backs. Still, Vajpayee did not bend in his determination to drive the infiltrators out by fighting only on territory recognized as Indian. He resolved not to let the conflict in the mountains of Kashmir escalate into a nuclear crisis. New Delhi made sure that the international community understood that statesmanship and nuclear stewardship lay behind this position. Principal Secretary and National Security Advisor Brajesh Mishra declared in June that India's restraint "will drive home the point that a nuclear India can and does act in a responsible manner."[15]

As in earlier Indo-Pak crises in 1987 and 1990, the actual level of nuclear threat overhanging the Kargil conflict remained uncertain. During the conflict, Pakistani officials on May 31 issued veiled nuclear threats in an apparent bid to intimidate India.[16] On June 30 Indian Defence Minister George Fernandes noted that "Pakistan's threat that it may go for the ultimate option of using nuclear weapons in the event of a full-scale war should not be taken casually coming as it does from the responsible leaders of that country."[17] Months after the fighting, the British minister of state for foreign affairs, Peter Hain, said, "We know the two countries came very close to a nuclear exchange over it."[18] Knowledgeable American officials considered that an overstatement but did say privately that intelligence detected signs "related to missile activities" in Pakistan and "conventional force movements in India" that "made us nervous" about possible escalation.[19] In January 2001, Army Chief of Staff General Sundarajan Padmanabhan told an interviewer that Pakistan had "activated . . . some of the areas where they had carried out tests earlier of one of their missiles."[20] Still, it is probable that during the conflict no one knew what exact steps, if any, both Pakistan and India were or were not taking to ready nuclear weapons for use in the conflict. The uncertainty was conducive to a host of possibilities ranging from confidence that escalation was not occurring, to mutual deterrence, to worst-case assumptions that could have driven escalation.

Whatever the degree of actual nuclear threat, the Kargil conflict did debunk two Indian assertions about the benefits of overt nuclearization. Indian hawks had insisted after the 1998 nuclear tests that the open display of weapon capabilities did not change underlying realities. This assertion missed the important point that until Pakistan tested nuclear weapons, only a handful of military officers and scientists were privy to the nation's capabilities: these capabilities were unproved to the nation's military establishment and polity at large. After the tests, everyone knew that Pakistan had workable nuclear weapons. This knowledge significantly raised the military's confidence in the nuclear deterrent. Pakistan's military brass was then emboldened to initiate aggression in Kargil because it believed that nuclear deterrence would prevent India from escalating to the point of a major conventional war. To be sure, the Kargil conflict was contained, and concerns over escalation may have contributed to this outcome. But this was little solace for India. Indian strategists now had to contend with the possibility that Pakistan would rely on nuclear deterrence to inhibit Indian reactions to Pakistan's prosecution of low-intensity conflict in Kashmir.

India won as much or more diplomatically through the war as it did militarily. The biggest gain occurred with the United States. Washington quietly began urging India and Pakistan to de-escalate the conflict on May 24.[21] On May 27, the State Department summoned Pakistan's ambassador, Riaz Khokhar, and bluntly conveyed that Pakistan had initiated the conflict and should rectify it by ordering the infiltrators to withdraw. This message was so tough that Khokhar returned on June 1 to protest its tone and substance, under instructions from Islamabad.[22] Washington was not yet publicly assigning blame for the fighting. Officials believed that a quick solution would be easier to obtain through private remonstrances to Islamabad. U.S. officials also contacted other governments, including China's, to urge them to entreat on Pakistan and India to keep the conflict from escalating.

With no sign that the conflict was abating, the United States in early June increased the pressure on Pakistan.[23] On June 5 Nawaz Sharif received a letter from President Clinton whose contents were leaked to the press. It called for Pakistan to "take steps to defuse the crisis and respect the Line of Control."[24] Sensing pressure and looking for wiggle room, Pakistani officials sought to deflect blame by arguing that the Line of Control in the Kargil area was not delineated.[25] The U.S. National Security Council official responsible for South Asia, Bruce Reidel, countered that "we think the Line of Control has been demarcated over the years. . . . It has been clear and those who infiltrated from the Pakistani side to the Indian must go back."[26] Privately, American officials showed a Pakistani diplomat a long document that an Indian and a Pakistani lieutenant general had signed years earlier delineating the Line of Control.[27]

The U.S. position was evolving in ways that heartened India and shook Pakistan. Washington was blaming Pakistan and, what was more important, categorizing the Line of Control as a de facto border that should not be violated. This position seriously undermined the traditional Pakistani argument that all of Kashmir was disputed territory. By investing the Line of Control with sanctity, the United States seemed to be suggesting that the LoC would be the basis for any resolution of the dispute and that Pakistan should forget about "winning" the part of Kashmir now controlled by India. President Clinton further aligned the United States behind India's position by calling Vajpayee on June 14 to express appreciation for India's restraint in the fighting to drive the intruders back across the Line of Control.

Despite the mounting evidence, many in India doubted that the United States truly was siding with India. Influenced by decades of anticolonial history and mistrust of U.S. priorities in South Asia, Indian commentators and politicians suspected a trap. A U.S. official recounted that Indian counterparts still feared that Washington's traditional "evenhandedness" would somehow lead it to find a "compromise" that would give Pakistan some gain from the perceived unprovoked aggression. Such Indian doubts appeared even in the writing of the sophisticated and well-informed commentator Raja Mohan. On June 4 an American official called Mohan and chided him gently for failing "to break the code" of U.S. diplomacy on Kargil.[28] The official laid out "in political science" terms the U.S. assessment of what Pakistan was doing in Kashmir, what those actions portended about general developments in Pakistan, and how these were problematic from the standpoint of American, Pakistani, Indian, and global interests. He then explained why India's self-restrained reactions thus far demonstrated an important overlap with U.S. regional security interests. U.S. interests and the facts on the ground in South Asia pointed to compatibility between New Delhi and Washington. There was no trick; the United States was lining up with India on the merits. Moreover, it was not asking India for a quid pro quo in other areas, including nonproliferation. Two days after this conversation, a key Indian foreign ministry official called the American at home and said that Mohan had related the earlier conversation to him. Would the American be willing to repeat the message to this official and a colleague from the Prime Minister's Office who was sitting with him? The American obliged, inferring that the two Indians were likely to brief the prime minister.

The public and private diplomacy eventually registered. On June 23 the *Hindustan Times* reported that the "Indian foreign policy establishment believes that there has been a 'paradigm shift' in the U.S. policy toward India."[29] Gone were the days of the 1971 Indo-Pak war and the tilt toward Pakistan. The United States appeared finally to comprehend and respect India's virtue and strategic importance.

After a series of phone calls and letters between President Clinton and Prime Minister Sharif, Clinton increased the pressure on Pakistan by dispatching Marine General Anthony Zinni, commander in chief of U.S. Central Command,

and Gibson Lanpher, deputy secretary of state for South Asia, to Rawalpindi for talks on June 24–25. Zinni was key, a straight-talking, formidable man sent to talk general to general with Pakistan's powerful brass. On the afternoon of June 24, Zinni met at General Headquarters in Rawalpindi with Army Chief of Staff General Pervez Musharraf and his top military colleagues. "There were no civilians, and the lowest-ranking guy there was a brigadier who was taking notes," according to a participant.[30] Zinni told Musharraf that Pakistan's military position was untenable and that the nation was isolated internationally. If the intruders were not withdrawn Pakistan would be defeated, but more, its relationship with the United States and the rest of the world would suffer enormously.[31] Musharraf did not challenge Zinni's assessment. Instead, he tried to suggest face-saving conditions, such as U.S. mediation over Kashmir, that might make it possible for Pakistan to ask the intruders to withdraw. Zinni responded that his orders from the president were not to negotiate. "My mandate is Kargil, not Kashmir," he said repeatedly. The president sent him to insist that Pakistan withdraw without conditions. Musharraf seemed to realize the gravity of the problem Pakistan now faced. Late in the meeting he implied that perhaps Pakistan could talk to the intruders and persuade them to withdraw. But he said that he alone could not make such a decision—this was the province of Pakistan's prime minister. Zinni mentioned that the prime minister had not responded to Clinton's request that Sharif meet with Zinni and Lanpher; the two Americans were going to go back to their hotel to pack for departure. This was about 4 P.M. When Zinni arrived at his room at the Marriott Hotel in Islamabad, he received a phone call from Musharraf saying that Sharif had set an appointment for the Americans at 11 A.M. the following morning, June 25.

Zinni and Lanpher arrived at the prime minister's palatial residence and noted that Sharif had gathered the top civilian and military leaders of the country in the room. "It was like a meeting of the corporate board," a participant recalled. "Everyone who mattered was there." Sharif evidently meant to implicate all his potential critics or rivals in any decision that followed. In the meeting, Nawaz Sharif, like Musharraf earlier, bemoaned that Pakistan was being wrongly maligned, his hands were tied, and some involvement by the United States to mediate the long-running Kashmir dispute would be needed if Sharif was to persuade the infiltrators to leave. Zinni responded again, "It's not Kashmir, it's Kargil we're here to talk about." Sharif put great stock in his personal rapport with Bill Clinton and hoped that the president's friendship and instincts as a negotiator would lead him to help extricate Sharif from the dire situation. Once again, Zinni stated that the U.S. position was unequivocal. Sharif asked, "What do you want me to do?" Zinni replied, "Withdraw." Sharif said vaguely that "perhaps we can talk to the intruders and ask them to leave."

Looking for the worm in the mango, some in India suggested that the Zinni visit amounted to U.S. mediation of the Kashmir crisis, which Pakistan wanted all along.[32] Once again, Clinton administration officials declared that the U.S. was "not a mediator" in the dispute.[33] (Indeed, in a subsequent conversation with Foreign Minister Jaswant Singh, Deputy Secretary of State Strobe Talbott made light of India's aversion to any hint of U.S. mediation by joking, "Jaswant, I don't care how many times you ask me, we won't mediate Kashmir. Stop asking me.")[34]

The end of the crisis came on July 4. Nawaz Sharif, like many Pakistani leaders before him, clung to the hope that the American president somehow would save him. So he pressed President Clinton to receive him in Washington, which Clinton duly did on the guarantee that the meeting would not be a negotiation but rather an announcement of Pakistan's decision to withdraw. The two leaders met for several hours at Blair House, across Pennsylvania Avenue from the White House. At one point, during a break, Clinton called Vajpayee in New Delhi to apprise him of the situation. After their meeting Clinton and Sharif issued a joint statement. It declared the need for both Pakistan and India to reaffirm the Line of Control. On this basis, "it was agreed between the President and the Prime Minister that concrete steps will be taken for the restoration of the Line of Control in accordance with the Simla Agreement."[35] The vague and passive construction could not hide that Pakistan was withdrawing the infiltrators. It can only be guessed why the Pakistani prime minister sought to end the conflict in Washington, with an agreement with a president whose state was not a belligerent. An additional line in the joint statement gave a hint. "The President said he would take a personal interest in encouraging an expeditious resumption and intensification of . . . bilateral efforts" between India and Pakistan to resolve "all issues dividing India and Pakistan, including Kashmir." Pakistan's longstanding desire was to "internationalize" the Kashmir dispute and bring the United States into it as a mediator. This vague statement by the president provided the only fig leaf Nawaz Sharif could find to hide the defeat that he and the architects of the Kargil incursion had wrought.

If Kargil improved India's relationship with the United States, New Delhi also took heart from China's reactions to the conflict. Indians remembered that China had sided rhetorically and diplomatically with Pakistan in the 1965 and 1971 wars. In the spring of 1999, China and Pakistan remained close; India only months earlier had angered Beijing by blaming nuclear weapon tests on the threat posed by China. Indian leaders obviously had not anticipated the major conflict now raging with Pakistan and the related possibility that they would want China to take a benign role. Fortunately for New Delhi, Beijing obliged.

As the fighting in Kargil intensified in early June, China, while bemoaning the danger of regional instability, took a noncommittal public stance.[36] Pakistan predictably sought to garner more forceful support from China. Foreign Minister Sartaj Aziz announced that he would travel to Beijing on June 11. The Chinese Foreign Ministry appeared to lower Islamabad's expectations by declaring, "China sincerely hopes that both India and Pakistan would . . . continue efforts to settle their disputes peacefully through dialogues and negotiations so as to prevent the situation from further deteriorating."[37] In a further hint that Beijing would not side with Pakistan, the government announced that it would receive Foreign Minister Jaswant Singh for an earlier scheduled visit to follow on the heels of Sartaj Aziz's emergency trip.

The Pakistani foreign minister received little solace in Beijing. Li Peng, the chairman of the Standing Committee of the Chinese parliament, reportedly told him that Kashmir was a "complicated affair" and that China "sincerely" hoped that Islamabad and New Delhi would exercise restraint.[38] Such evenhandedness from Pakistan's stalwart ally could not have been reassuring.

Indian Foreign Minister Jaswant Singh received a decidedly better reception during his two days of talks in Beijing beginning June 14. Notwithstanding the war in Kargil, Singh and his counterparts focused on bilateral and global issues. Singh declared that China was not a security threat to India and that both states should reinvigorate their relationship on the basis of the *Panchsheel* principles enunciated in 1954.[39] The Chinese Foreign Ministry spokesperson echoed this declaration, stating that upholding the five principles of peaceful coexistence and not "regarding each other as a threat" were the "prerequisite for the growth of Sino-Indian relations." The two states capped the meeting by announcing that they would initiate a bilateral "security dialogue" and formal talks to clarify the Line of Actual Control along their disputed border. The security dialogue promised to be the first such mechanism for dealing directly with the two states' wideranging foreign policy and national security concerns. With its announcement, India now added a Chinese component to the suite of "strategic dialogues" it had formalized recently with the United States, France, and Russia. Not only had China rejected the opportunity to press Pakistan's case over the Kargil conflict, the Beijing government had elevated the plane of Sino-Indian relations. Thus, when Nawaz Sharif made a last desperate foray to China in late June, he found no salvation and had little recourse but to go to Washington and "surrender."

The Kargil war ended as had previous wars, with an Indian victory. The overt nuclear weaponization of the subcontinent had not prevented a major military conflict; it probably even had encouraged Pakistani leaders in their aggressive gambit. Yet the shadow of nuclear escalation also probably helped preclude the temptation by either side to escalate. To the extent that the United States, China, and the broader international community helped contain the conflict, it could be said that their fear over the potential for nuclear escalation helped motivate them to act energetically. Yet the conflict itself revealed an essential vulnerability of nuclear deterrence. Any form of deterrence relies on the assumption that antagonists are rational actors who will seek to minimize risk. Pakistani decision making leading into the Kargil conflict raised important questions about this assumption. Do conflicting interests within the institutions of power impair calculations? What happens when the nominal leader is not highly capable and informed? Do protagonists who subscribe to holy war and celebrate martyrdom weigh risks differently than models of deterrence assume? The diplomacy at Lahore indicated that both Pakistan and India recognized the special dangers associated with a nuclear standoff and were prepared to establish and act upon "rules of the road" to prevent conflict and manage differences in favor of stability. Kargil offered at least some evidence to the contrary.

UNOFFICIAL DRAFT NUCLEAR DOCTRINE, AUGUST 1999

In August 1999, the prospect seemed to dwindle that India, and therefore Pakistan, would develop a realistic, stabilizing nuclear doctrine. India's National Security Advisory Board released a Draft Report on Indian Nuclear Doctrine. The BJP-led government had created the board to advise the newly formed National Security Council. The board included former officials, strategic analysts, and pundits, many of whom had been leading advocates of a more hawkish nuclear policy for decades. Neither the board nor the draft doctrine represented actual government policy, but the document's release by National Security Advisor Brajesh Mishra gave it an official patina.

Issued on August 17, the document called for "a doctrine of credible minimum nuclear deterrence" under which nuclear weapons would be used for "retaliation only."[40] A "triad of aircraft, mobile land-based missiles and sea-based assets" would be built and deployed to carry the deterrent force that was to be "fully employable in the shortest possible time." A "robust command and control system" and "effective intelligence and early warning capabilities," including space-based assets, were envisioned to manage the force. Emphasizing the Indian tradition of civilian control over nuclear policy, the document stated that "the authority to release nuclear weapons for use resides in the person of the Prime Minister of India, or the designated successor(s)." The latter clause implied the need to revise the Indian Constitution or otherwise formalize a chain of command that had not been specified in existing Indian law.

The advisory board did not offer any realistic assessment of how many weapons were required, when the envisioned triad of weapon platforms could be built, and at what cost. However, two of the leading figures on the board, K. Subrahmanyam and Bharat Karnad, posited elsewhere that India's deterrent required 150 or 325 (or more) weapons, respectively.[41] The draft doctrine and imprecations surrounding it resembled Homi Bhabha's fanciful visions of India's nuclear future. Once again, grandiosity and technical optimism were not balanced by realistic analysis.

For example, the "necessity" of a triad—land-, air- and sea-based nuclear forces—was not explained. From a prestige standpoint, a triad would equate India with the United States and Russia. But strategic and economic cases could be made that a triad was unnecessary. France and the United Kingdom had abandoned triads and were moving toward purely sea-based nuclear forces. China's triad was more nominal and symbolic than real: China's sole ballistic-missile submarine was practically inutile, while China's air-delivery capability was primitive.[42] Land-based missiles made up the only reliable leg of Beijing's deterrent force.

In calculating the requirements of a deterrent, force survivability is a key criterion. Yet survivability can be achieved in several ways. Nuclear forces can be dispersed and hidden—under water or on mobile land-based platforms—denying an opponent knowledge of targets that need to be destroyed to negate one's second-strike deterrent. China was following this concealment strategy with its land-based force, and there was reason to think it would serve India, especially against Pakistan. Yet, with few exceptions, Indian analysts did not question the problematic assumption that a submarine-based force was both necessary and sufficient to ensure survivability of the deterrent.[43] Nor did they examine whether India had the economic and technological resources to build submarines of sufficient quality and quantity to have an "always ready" force that could stay ahead of developments in antisubmarine warfare.

The draft nuclear doctrine did not designate states that were deemed targets of India's deterrent—for example Pakistan and China—but it did say that "the system" would contain "an integrated operational plan." This language invoked the sort of operational planning practiced by the United States and the Soviet Union. These plans choreographed launches of air-based, land-based, and sea-based nuclear forces to arrive sequentially on thousands of previously determined targets. For example, missile-delivered warheads were to clear paths through air defenses, enabling bombers to proceed to targets unimpeded by defenses and free from the blast effects of the earlier weapons. Integrated operational plans increase the certainty of destroying adversary targets, but they accomplish this goal through overkill and limiting the range of options available to political leaders who may wish for flexibility in a crisis. None of this comported with Indian capabilities or the political leadership's traditional philosophy of deterrence. But it fit great-power aspirations, at least in Cold War terms.

The draft doctrine also reflected the historical inwardness of Indian nuclear policy and rhetoric. It sought to give Indian audiences a feeling of strength, technological prowess, and great power assertiveness, with little regard for the document's potential to stimulate countermoves by adversaries. Pakistan, for example, interpreted India to be declaring the intention to conduct an open-ended, aggressive nuclear and missile arms race. U.S. officials noted the absence of mention of China and Pakistan and inferred that the authors meant to develop a nuclear arsenal geared toward deterring the United States. The document increased wariness about Indian intentions rather than inspiring confidence in building a constructive relationship with it. Had India magically possessed the technical capabilities to overwhelm Pakistan's and China's potential responses to a more aggressive Indian posture, their reactions to it would have mattered less. Unfortunately, as in 1974, India was unprepared for the response its declarations could engender.

In fairness, when questioned, authors of the draft doctrine acknowledged that it was "perfunctory," a vision for a "thirty-year course of activity."[44] The document was a product of a disharmonious group: the venerable K. Subrahmanyam chaired the project, but a few younger hawks within the group seemed intent on pushing him from his perch as India's grand strategist. They intimated that he had become too dovelike and that it was time for a new generation to assert itself.[45] Collectively the authors seemed to care less about how foreigners would react to the document than about forcing the government of India to be bold and reject the ambiguity and passivity of the past. Moreover, the draft doctrine was only that—a draft. Plenty of time existed for correction and refinement.

BEHIND-THE-SCENES NUCLEAR PLANNING

The public urgings of the National Security Advisory Board belied the actual approach being taken by the small circle of officials responsible for setting India's nuclear policies.[46] This disparity between rhetoric and reality, too, repeated historical patterns. The prime minister, the foreign and defense ministers, and technical advisors had a deeper appreciation of the competing imperatives and interests that had to be weighed in decisions about nuclear weapons, ballistic missiles, and operational doctrines. They apprehended that national economic infrastructure and development must be India's greatest strategic priority. The ambitious agenda of nuclearization proffered by the NSAB would entail significant economic and political opportunity costs. Indian decision makers preferred to minimize controversial public debate over nuclear policy in India's fractious democracy. Pursuing the NSAB's recommendations would unleash many disputes over the nature of the threat from Pakistan and China, India's technical and economic capacities, civil-military relations, moral norms, and much else. These were difficult issues, and nuclear policy was not a priority of the electorate.[47]

Technological realities and "ideological" preferences also made real decision makers unlikely to embrace the NSAB's vision. Informed policymakers could not avoid doubting India's fiscal wherewithal and scientific-technical capacity to build, deploy, and manage the kind of nuclear force recommended by the NSAB. Reasonable public estimates posited that India held about three hundred kilograms of separated weapon-grade plutonium at the end of 2000. This was enough for approximately fifty fission weapons, or only 33 percent of the number advocated by Subrahmanyam.[48] (The actual stockpile could have been higher, though, if the Madras nuclear power reactors were being run to produce weapon-grade plutonium that would be separated at the nearby Kalpakkam reprocessing plant. This was conceivable after 1998, but not subject to confirmation from public sources). The nuclear establishment had not proved warhead designs more sophisticated and powerful than a 20-kiloton explosive, though this was enough to kill hundreds of thousands in an urban attack. India had one steady leg of the desired triad of delivery systems—modified attack aircraft—but the land-based missile leg remained under development, and the sea-based leg was even further from maturity. The Agni II, with a range of two thousand kilometers, had been tested only twice by early 2001. Though its all-solid-fuel propulsion system represented a major improvement over the Agni I, even this most advanced Indian missile's range would fall at least a thousand kilometers short of threatening Bei-jing, Shanghai, and all but one or two major Chinese cities. Cruise missiles that could be launched from surface ships were closer to hand, thanks in part to Russ-ian assistance, but these lacked range to be highly valuable against China. The nuclear-powered ballistic missile submarine on which India's strategists rested their ultimate hopes was a glimmer in optimists' eyes.

Beyond technical questions, India's moral norms, political sensibilities, and in-tuition also ran counter to the NSAB's vision of deterrence. Indians traditionally rejected the U.S. and Soviet vision of nuclear weapons as war-fighting instru-ments. The U.S. and Soviet conception of nuclear deterrence required the capac-ity to respond with nuclear weapons to any level of aggression and to have an arsenal large enough, diverse enough, and rapidly employable enough to domi-nate each level of escalation from tactical exchanges up to massive attacks involv-ing thousands of weapons. In this view, only dominance in the ability to fight a nuclear war and preparedness for first use guarantee deterrence. Indians had tended to reject this approach as unrealistic, excessive, and immoral. They had regarded war-fighting doctrines of deterrence to be a pathology of militaristic ab-straction that neglects the cost-benefit analysis that political leaders would actu-ally undertake. Instead, Indians had seen nuclear weapons as political means to provide their possessor with strategic autonomy, political power and prestige, and an amorphous destructive capacity that inspires great caution on the part of any adversary. Possession of nuclear weapons strengthens a state's resolve to resist po-tential blackmail. It gives the state confidence that adversaries will conclude that coercion or aggression cannot provide gains that outweigh the potential conse-quences of nuclear retaliation. Achieving these salutary effects does not require more than a relatively small, survivable force that could inflict great damage on an aggressor with enough likelihood to make an adversary decide not to gamble. The relatively calm Indian approach to deterrence stemmed also from the belief that the disputes with Pakistan and China were not so great as to motivate either adversary to risk massive loss of life and societal wherewithal.[49]

At the end of 2000 it appeared that India's political leaders still concluded that at least for the next five or ten years the nation would be better off with a recessed force of dispersed and hidden nuclear weapons than with an immediately launch-ready arsenal as envisioned by the NSAB. (The longer term was uncertain.) Under this model, warheads, most likely air-deliverable fission bombs in the near term, would be secured under civilian control separate from the aircraft config-ured to deliver them. As intermediate-range missiles came on line, the warheads developed for them, too, would be stored separately under civilian control. (The necessity of deploying warheads mated to delivery systems would arise only when decision makers opted to put nuclear weapons at sea.) Small units, most likely from the air force, were designated to cooperate with the defense scientific-technical establishment in mating weapons to delivery systems under orders from the prime minister or his designees. The Department of Atomic Energy would control nuclear weapon cores; the Defence Research and Development Organisation would control the non-nuclear weapon assemblies into which nuclear cores must be integrated; the military would control delivery systems. These units would conduct the exercises necessary to minimize the time required to integrate weapons and perform nuclear retaliatory operations upon civilian command.[50]

The modest, uncoiled force preferred by Indian leaders comported with India's insistence that it would not strike first with nuclear weapons in a conflict. As Jaswant Singh put it,

> The U.S., Russia, the U.K., France and China developed their nuclear weapons as weapons of war. Most nuclear-weapon powers follow doctrines of first use, and all of them envisage tactical or sub-strategic roles for their nuclear weapons. The Indian thinking is different, principally because we have discarded the Cold War reference frame of nuclear warfighting. In our view, the principal role of nuclear weapons is to deter their use by an adversary. For this, India needs only that strategic minimum which is credible. With the policy of "retaliation only," survivability becomes critical to ensure credibility.[51]

This stance placed a premium on dispersing and hiding India's retaliatory assets so that no adversary would have confidence that it could destroy India's capacity to retaliate.

Indian military leaders, like those in the United States, Russia, and other states, questioned this politically imbued notion of deterrence. By training and mission, they argued that nuclear weapons should be seen as military instruments. After the 1998 tests a few retired military officers—representing each of the three services, interestingly—offered public arguments for relatively large, diverse nuclear arsenals that would be deployed, targeted, and commanded by military officers under the general direction and ultimate authority of the highest political leadership.[52] This predilection was natural. Any military's job is to plan to fight and win wars against whatever adversaries and weapons it might face. To the military, deterrence may be a condition that arises from military balances. But deterrence is not an objective in the sense of a desired mutually-affecting condition. Military planners seek to devise strategies and means to prevent their state from being deterred in the event of a conflict. They prefer to have options to win. If the enemy is deterred, fine, but a military should try to avoid finding its own state deterred.

This natural military predilection appeared in early 2000 when Army Chief of Staff General V. P. Malik and Defence Minister George Fernandes publicly declared that nuclear weapons had not made war "obsolete" and that India was prepared to fight and win a "limited war at a time and place chosen by the aggressor" while preventing escalation to nuclear conflict.[53] This pronouncement was explicitly intended to counter lessons that Pakistan or others might have drawn from the Kargil conflict. Military leaders worried that Pakistan had "felt that its overt nuclear status had ensured that covert war could continue and aggression across the Line of Control could be carried out while India would be deterred by the nuclear factor."[54] The Indian government's decision not to allow the military to hit targets beyond the Line of Control buttressed this perception. To counter it, the Indian military should be provided the resources to develop and implement strategies to dominate at any stage of the escalation ladder. Fernandes and Malik sought to warn Pakistan that India would be so prepared. They sought to encourage Indian leaders to provide the necessary resources.

Yet declaring that limited war could be fought and won short of nuclear escalation raised the question "How?" Fernandes stated that India needed "to ensure that a conventional war, if imposed upon us in the future, is kept below the nuclear threshold."[55] But the uncomfortable reality was that at some point up the escalation ladder, one comes to a nuclear rung. The two states with the most experience elaborating force structures and doctrines to fight at each rung of the ladder—the United States and the Soviet Union—never persuasively demonstrated that they would not move up to the nuclear rungs and that if they reached the first such rung—tactical nuclear weapons—they would not escalate further. To suppose otherwise required believing that the other side would submit to being dominated. Both sides refused to contemplate this situation. Thus, both emphasized the willingness and capability to escalate up the nuclear ladder, showing that they would not be deterred. This escalatory bias is the essential risk of a nuclear standoff.

Insofar as India lacked tactical nuclear weapons and eschewed them in keeping with no-first-use, Fernandes' and Malik's pronouncements had gaping holes. Unless India could wield such overwhelming conventional military power that it could defeat Pakistan at purely conventional stages of the conflict ladder, the Indian military would need to acquire the means to fight in a nuclear environment, including perhaps tactical nuclear weapons. No doubt Malik and Fernandes meant to say that India did have the means to defeat Pakistan at any level of conventional conflict. Yet this presupposed that Pakistan would not jump to a nuclear rung. Even with conventional dominance, India could not guarantee that nuclear escalation would not occur. Neither man addressed this problem.

However, Lt. Gen. (ret.) V. R. Raghavan did. With characteristic perspicacity, he called the Fernandes speech "another instance of insufficient understanding of the grave risks involved. . . . The choice of keeping the war limited cannot entirely be in Indian hands. The threshold of tolerance which triggers the adversary's nuclear weapons choice will always remain a matter of conjecture." Raghavan concluded that when "nuclear weapons are there for the asking, a war, however limited, is a huge strategic liability."[56]

The tension between military logic and the strategy of deterrence favored by political leaders became still more apparent in late 2000 and early 2001 with the ascent of a new Indian army chief of staff, General Sundararajan Padmanabhan. In his first public statements, Padmanabhan stated that he would focus on making the army ready to fight nuclear wars.[57] When read carefully, the statements highlighted the need for tactics and equipment to enable the general's ground forces to withstand Pakistani battlefield nuclear attacks and keep fighting. Padmanabhan assumed that India would not have tactical nuclear weapons and would not be the first to use any nuclear weapons. Indeed, in a January 2001 interview with Raj Chengappa, the general clarified that he was "not for one moment suggesting that we are going to be indulging in nuclear war fighting."[58] Yet Padmanabhan's rhetoric echoed that of Fernandes, Malik, and others who seemed to be getting caught in the military logic of nuclear weapons. As V. R. Raghavan noted, this position suggested a shift in "the stated Indian policy of nuclear weapons being merely defensive and deterrent instruments." According to Raghavan, Padmanabhan's earliest remarks confirmed "the doubts in and outside of India on the degree of coordination that exists in security matters" and revealed deep tension between "military commanders and the nuclear establishment" and between "the defence chiefs and the Cabinet."[59] In fact, the positions of these actors was more harmonized in private government councils than occasional public statements may have suggested.

However, this harmony did not mean that the military services had escaped from the natural tendency to compete with each other for nuclear roles, missions, and budgets. The army chief of staff's bid for a greater nuclear role reflected frustration that the Indian Air Force had heretofore been regarded as the nuclear service. This perception stemmed from the fact that India's extant nuclear capability relied on delivery by aircraft, a capability that had been first tested under operational conditions in May 1994.[60] Padmanabhan sought to downplay the notion of competition by saying,

> There is no fight between the Army, Navy and the Air Force on this. As and when the Navy gets a launcher with a nuclear weapon capability, they are probably the best suited. Today, I do not have something that can launch a nuclear weapon as far as it should. The Air Force has. But the point is . . . is the launcher everything? It is about the weapon. The weapon is controlled by the top-most authority in the government. It is the Prime Minister who will decide on the nuclear weapon.[61]

Interservice competition could not be dismissed so easily, but the general's remark did point to the political leadership's determination to keep nuclear explosives under civilian control away from delivery systems.

The government recognized, at least conceptually, a need to structure greater interservice coordination and better civilian-military interface within the defense bureaucracy to manage India's evolving nuclear posture. To this end, Arun Singh was tapped to chair a Task Force on Higher Defence Management. Singh's role was telling. His performance under Rajiv Gandhi made him arguably the most respected civilian defense policymaker in Indian history. In 1990 he had been drawn out of "retirement" to head at least one secret panel to devise plans for managing retaliation to a possible Pakistani nuclear attack. This service not only reflected his outstanding talent and temperament, but also highlighted the small, informal network of people relied upon to shape Indian nuclear policy. Singh's Task Force now recommended creation of a chief of defence staff (CDS) who would be a "four star" officer selected from the top echelon of the air force, army, or navy.[62] The CDS would serve as an umpire helping to sort out and rationalize the three military services' requests for forces and budgets. Instead of each service leaving it to the civilian ministry of defence leadership to arbitrate relatively unfiltered parochial requests, the proposed CDS system would yield more militarily informed recommendations to civilian decision makers. The CDS would be the "single-point military advisor" to the civilian leadership regarding nuclear policy. He would be the principal conduit of communications to and from the civilian leadership to the military services, and would coordinate military deliberations regarding nuclear weapons delivery systems and operational plans. The government still had not acted upon Singh's recommendations as of April 2001, but reportedly was inclined to do so. Yet meaningful implementation of the recommended reforms would require overcoming famous bureaucratic inertia.

India's political leaders always had dreaded the prospect of competition between the military services and their collective bid for a greater role in nuclear policy. Because of this fear (detailed in earlier chapters) India's leadership, more than any other state's, had excluded the military from such a role. The overt nuclear weaponization of India since 1998 necessarily opened avenues for military officers to participate in operational planning to ensure that India could execute nuclear reprisal against a nuclear aggressor. Yet these avenues had remained circumscribed. Political leaders and the scientific establishment insisted that the military not be given peacetime possession of nuclear weapons. As the Agni II missile and other technologies became available, the political leadership would find it more difficult to avoid making momentous decisions about military roles and missions in nuclear policy. Deployment of nuclear weapons at sea would force the government to transfer possession to the military. Yet if the past was prologue to the foreseeable future, India's political leaders would take a more cautious and reserved approach to building, deploying, and operating the nuclear arsenal than some military leaders and outside analysts preferred.

To help resolve these tensions, Indian experts for more than a decade had urged the constitution and empowerment of a National Security Council. However, inertia, bureaucratic turf battles, and the general preferences of prime ministers to control information and decision making on such sensitive matters prevented this development. The BJP in 1998 said it would break the pattern and create an effective NSC. Two years later, though, the NSC still did not integrate military professionals and their advice into decision making.[63] The body lacked both a robust and talented staff and the support of the foreign affairs and defense bureaucracies. As in 1990, the NSC tended to neglect the strategic policy group and the National Security Advisory Board that were intended to inform and assist it. The fact that the national security advisor, Brajesh Mishra, was also the powerful principal secretary to the prime minister reaffirmed the traditional pattern of India's nuclear history. Prime ministers were sovereign over nuclear policy. They viewed nuclear weapons as political instruments. They saw budgetary, political, and strategic dangers in allowing the military to define uses and missions for nuclear weapons. The evolution of the National Security Council, along with the implementation of defense reorganization, would indicate whether and how political, scientific, and military interests were being integrated. As of early 2001, these indicators remained ambiguous.

THE CTBT AND NUCLEAR TESTING

The tension between the wishful recommendations of the NSAB and the more sober approach to nuclear weaponization pursued by government insiders could be seen as India decided whether to sign the Comprehensive Test Ban Treaty (CTBT). The impetus for signing came largely from U.S.-Indian diplomacy. Many of the sessions in the Jaswant Singh-Strobe Talbott dialogue centered on the CTBT. The United States urged India to formalize Prime Minister Vajpayee's repeated declaration that India would turn its de facto moratorium on nuclear testing into a de jure commitment. Foreign Minister Singh repeatedly told his interlocutors that the BJP government was trying to develop "a national consensus" in favor of signing the treaty.

However, Singh and his colleagues did little publicly to build such a consensus throughout 1999 and 2000. The best chance had been in the early aftermath of the nuclear tests. In January 1999, U.S. officials felt that Singh had determined that signing the treaty would serve India's overall strategic interests and that the polity would accept it. The Lahore summit made the political environment still more hospitable. However, the Indian government still could not bring itself to act. Then, in April, the BJP-led coalition lost its majority, and elections were called for October. Signing the CTBT would have constituted a major political gamble in this period. The Kargil conflict severely wounded the treaty's prospects thereafter.

In October 1999, national elections brought the BJP back to power at the head of a stronger coalition. Yet any hopes that the fresh mandate might give Vajyapee and Singh confidence to sign the CTBT were dashed by political developments in Washington. On October 12, the U.S. Senate voted not to ratify the treaty. The Vajpayee government did not publicly exploit the Senate's rebuff of the treaty and argue that India no longer need to consider signing it. Rather, Jaswant Singh suggested that the Senate's action established a model of "disaggregated" decision making that India could follow. India, like the United States, could sign the treaty and then decide separately whether to ratify it, and still later whether to deposit the instrument of ratification.[64] However, privately both governments knew the Senate's action removed any incentive for the Indians to breathe life into a treaty that could more comfortably be left for dead. New Delhi and Washington continued decorously to speak as if it were still alive. Washington wished India would sign, while New Delhi pretended that it might. Neither wanted their position on the CTBT to sunder the relationship.

From the beginning, the notion of developing a national consensus on this matter deserved scrutiny. A national political consensus was almost impossible to create on any issue in India, especially one as symbolically laden as the CTBT. Important decisions almost always required the government to act with the support of a narrow plurality or majority, not a consensus. Vajpayee and Jaswant Singh had not even achieved a consensus on the CTBT within their own party, the BJP.[65] If the government truly believed that India should sign the treaty, as it told the United States, then the quest for a consensus was self-defeating. More likely, the Vajpayee government had not made up its mind whether India should sign the treaty. Like previous governments' policies of nuclear ambiguity, the Vajpayee government's position on the CTBT somewhat satisfied conflicting interests and retained maximum flexibility. Vajpayee and Foreign Minister Singh could partially mend the rift in Indo-American relations by saying they wanted to sign the treaty; they could keep India's hawks and strategic enclave calm by not signing it and therefore not foreclosing further nuclear tests. The CTBT "option" resembled the "nuclear option" strategy of the 1974–1998 period.

Behind-the-scenes realities in the nuclear and defense science establishment also complicated the government's calculus. Throughout 1999 international experts continued to doubt the Indian scientists' claims about the yields and effectiveness of the devices tested in May 1998. Most important, analysts argued that evidence did not support the claim that the thermonuclear device achieved a 43-kiloton yield. Indian diplomats who met with American counterparts complained that the international debate over India's test results impaired the government's effort to generate support for signing the CTBT.[66] India's defense science establishment resented the questioning of their achievements. Military commentators and politicians and at least one former top nuclear scientist doubted that the existing test data were sufficient to enable India to build a nuclear arsenal without more testing.[67]

Although the nuclear establishment and the military wanted more tests, the government's freedom to conduct more tests was severely constrained by its repeated pledges at the highest levels that India would maintain a moratorium on nuclear testing. This betwixt-and-between posture resembled earlier periods. Not signing the CTBT, but declaring that India would not conduct more tests, was akin to not signing the NPT in 1968 and saying that India would not build nuclear weapons. All options were open, but India would minimize its international isolation by conveying good intentions. The scientists and engineers would refine their weapons and prepare devices for future tests. Little pressure existed within the polity to sign the treaty, notwithstanding the imprecations of a dedicated but small peace and disarmament movement in the country.[68]

PRESIDENT CLINTON VISITS INDIA, MARCH 2000

Ever since Hillary and Chelsea Clinton traveled to the subcontinent in 1995, Bill Clinton made it known that he keenly desired to make a presidential visit to

India. As recounted earlier, he had planned to go in 1997, only to be delayed by the collapse of the Indian government, and then again in 1998, only to be forestalled by the nuclear weapon tests. When the Jaswant Singh-Strobe Talbott talks began in June 1998, a prospective presidential visit to India became a subtext in the dialogue and, gradually, its central point. Talbott, an Oxford classmate of the president, knew that Clinton wanted enough diplomatic progress to justify a state visit to India. The foreign policy establishment in Washington, particularly its nonproliferation wing, would question the Clinton administration's "rewarding" India with a presidential visit if India did not satisfy key American demands in the wake of the nuclear tests. Meanwhile, in New Delhi, Prime Minister Vajpayee and Foreign Minister Singh wanted theirs to be the first Indian government since 1978 to receive an American president. Such a visit would validate the BJP at home and abroad.

By late 1999, Clinton's term in office was nearly over. Both sides felt some urgency in setting a date for the state visit. The Talbott-Singh talks had gone twelve rounds, with little progress on any of the American nonproliferation demands. The United States had received some satisfaction that India would implement measures to prevent the export of sensitive nuclear and strategic technologies, but little progress on requests that India impose a moratorium on production of fissile materials for weapons and define the limits of its prospective nuclear arsenal. The Comprehensive Test Ban Treaty was still the focal point of diplomacy. Paradoxically, the prospective Clinton visit made it more difficult for the Vajpayee government to develop a political consensus for the CTBT. Politicians and pundits accused the government of preparing to sign the treaty to induce a Clinton visit. This charge hit the always sensitive nerve of anticolonialism. Elements of the left and right insisted that India should never sell Indian sovereignty for a mere visit by the American leader.

Although New Delhi was unable or unwilling to commit on the CTBT, Clinton continued to press his desire to schedule a visit. He believed that the stakes went well beyond arms control and nonproliferation. The U.S.-Indian relationship always had been defined by Cold War exigencies; he wanted now to build a relationship that reflected India's intrinsic importance as a leading democracy with great economic potential. Meanwhile, Clinton's bureaucracy was becoming increasingly concerned over the risk of major conflict in the subcontinent. The Kargil war, the October 1999 military coup in Pakistan, and the December 1999 hijacking of an Indian civilian airliner by Pakistan-based terrorists suggested dangerous trends. The growth of violent Islamic militant groups in Pakistan and Kashmir exacerbated the sense of impending crisis. The good will of the Lahore summit was gone. New Delhi and Islamabad were now exchanging nothing but recriminations. American government and outside analysts averred that the risk of war was higher than it had been in the past decade, approaching a probability of 40–60 percent.[69] The increased salience of nuclear weapons in the subcontinent raised the stakes further.

Long- and short-term interests therefore dictated that the president should do whatever he could to build trust and calm the situation in the subcontinent. Other American officials could try to convey the urgent need for Indian and Pakistani leaders to change course, but, as one U.S. official put it, "Only the president could deliver the message in a way that would stick."[70] Thus, in late January 2000, Washington and New Delhi formally announced March dates for a Clinton state visit. Building relationships and preventing war became the central rationale for the trip.

The new rationale did not spare the Clinton administration from preserving the international nonproliferation regime's norm against granting legitimacy to new nuclear powers. As Strobe Talbott told Raja Mohan in an interview prior to Clinton's visit,

> If the issues we discuss under the rubric of non-proliferation were relevant only to India and the United States, they would be much easier to solve. Where our objectives diverge is in the impact of these matters on third countries. . . .[W]e saw the May 1998 nuclear tests as not directly threatening to the U.S. itself, but as damaging to the global non-proliferation regime in which all of us have a major stake. We are concerned that since May 1998, there is a greater danger of the spread of nuclear weapons, and we're convinced that's contrary to everyone's security, yours or ours included.[71]

If the United States granted India the benefits it sought as a nuclear weapon power, Washington would undermine the nonproliferation regime and break faith with countries such as Japan, Germany, South Africa, Sweden, Argentina, and Brazil that chose not to build nuclear weapons. Thus, the United States and others continued to block transfers of nuclear and other strategic technologies to India. Some sanctions were maintained. Undersecretary of State John Holum, the top State Department official responsible for nonproliferation policy, insisted that the United States did not "acquiesce in or accept" India's nuclear capability.[72]

Many in India nevertheless believed that the pending presidential visit proved that defiant demonstration of nuclear weapon prowess had won India the long-denied global respect it was due. Proponents of this view also could cite the U.S. Congress's October 1999 decision to grant the president authority to lift all sanctions imposed on India and Pakistan following their 1998 nuclear tests and to waive permanently the Symington and Pressler amendment sanctions that had been applied to Pakistan since 1990 and earlier. In passing the Brownback amendment to the defense appropriations bill (dubbed Brownback II), Congress criticized the "broad application" of export controls barring U.S. technology to Indian and Pakistani government agencies and private companies suspected of involvement in either country's nuclear or missile programs.[73] Washington appeared increasingly reluctant to allow nonproliferation policies to interfere with business and better relations with India and Pakistan.

However, it was misleading to argue that India's nuclear assertiveness caused

Washington to pay India greater respect. Clinton would have visited earlier if India had not conducted the nuclear tests in 1998. India's democracy and economic potential, as manifested most dramatically by its thriving information technology sector, were the principal attractions. Relatedly, Clinton and members of the U.S. Congress were influenced by the wealthy and increasingly politically assertive Indian American community. By the late 1990s, Indian Americans were on a per capita basis the single wealthiest "ethnic" group in the United States, including whites.[74] As the high-tech economy flourished in the United States, the disproportionate role of Indian Americans in this sector became the subject of media coverage that elevated political leaders' awareness of the money, and therefore influence, located in the community. The U.S.-India Business Council and the India Interest Group augmented the ministrations of politically mobilized Indian Americans by educating politicians about the business opportunities in India's growing economy. In short, the politically mobilized wealth of Indian Americans, and the attraction of the Indian economy, explained growing American attention to India more than nuclear bombs did.

Astute Indian commentators understood this. Writing prior to Clinton's visit, Raja Mohan called on his society to

> shed many of the grand illusions that have gripped it since Pokhran-II and come back to the basics that must guide national strategy. The greatest recent illusion has been the notion that nuclear weapons are a short-cut to great power status. India will never get there, however many nuclear weapons it might choose to build. India can gain the much-vaunted influence on the world stage only when it can effect a rapid economic advancement of its people.[75]

To be sure, the U.S. and other governments would have paid less serious attention to South Asia if it were not a potential nuclear flash point. Nuclear weapons did concentrate American minds and mobilize the government. Yet this focus of attention was primarily negative. Concerns about India's nuclear program and its implications for U.S. interests kept the president throughout 2000 from waiving the full range of sanctions that Congress had authorized him to. The perception of South Asia as a nuclear flash point also impelled the president to decide to stop briefly in Pakistan to meet with General Musharraf at the end of his South Asian visit. Many in India objected to this visit as a symbol of the Indo-Pak equation that they so detested.

Clinton's long-awaited sojourn in India began on March 21. Through word, deed, and the venues selected for visitation, the president identified the sources from which he believed India's current and future greatness would spring. After an arrival ceremony at Rashtrapati Bhawan (the presidential palace), Clinton visited the Gandhi Memorial and celebrated the Mahatma's role not only in creating independent, democratic India, but also in inspiring the American civil rights movement. President Clinton and Prime Minister Vajpayee then met and issued a "vision statement" outlining the goals and principles of a renewed Indo-

American relationship. The statement centered on the term and concept of "partnership" as the basis for building cooperation on the range of issues confronting the two states bilaterally, regionally, and globally. The statement declared that "India and the United States share a commitment to reducing and ultimately eliminating nuclear weapons" but acknowledged that "we have not always agreed on how to reach this common goal."[76] The document obligatorily stated the U.S. "belief" that "India should forgo nuclear weapons" and the contrary Indian position that "it needs to maintain a credible minimum nuclear deterrent." Notwithstanding this core difference, both states reaffirmed their "respective commitment to forgo further nuclear explosive tests [and to] work together and with others for an early commencement of negotiations on a treaty to end the production of fissile materials for nuclear weapons." Both pledged to "work together to prevent the spread of dangerous technologies [and not to] engage in nuclear and missile arms races." These platitudes, albeit constructive, were all that the two states had to show for two years of intensive diplomacy on nuclear issues.

The state dinner on March 21 revealed tension between the old anticolonial sensitivities that had bedeviled Indo-American relations for decades and the new confidence of a rising power. President K. R. Narayanan rebuked Clinton for stating that the subcontinent was "the most dangerous place in the world today." Narayanan called Clinton's description "alarmist" and warned that it would only encourage those who wanted to foment violence, meaning Pakistan.[77] This statement reflected India's strategic interest in keeping the United States and other outsiders from intervening in Kashmir issues. But more, Narayanan's rebuke and subsequent declaration that the evolving global village would not be run by "one headman" betrayed anticolonial resistance to American power. What was new, however, was the reaction of many Indians to Narayanan's bristly words. Commentators criticized the Indian president's *impolitesse.* Indian officials allowed that Narayanan's speech had not been cleared by the government and that he had discarded government-prepared remarks.[78] In earlier years, a similar rebuke of the American president would have been more widely celebrated as an act of anticolonial defiance. For its part, the United States wisely chose not to respond.

On March 22, Clinton addressed the two houses of the Indian Parliament. In the impressively crafted speech, the president focused on the greatness common to India and the United States: their "liberty," "diversity," and shared "aspiration for a more humane and just world."[79] Clinton said that every country, including the United States, was "tempted to cling to yesterday's definition of economic and military might" as the measures of greatness. However, he argued, "True leadership for the United States and India derives more from the power of our example and the potential of our people."[80] He then elaborated on the role that economic development must play for India to reach its fullest potential and power.

Clinton painstakingly and respectfully acknowledged that "only India can determine its interests" in the nuclear realm.[81] Yet he pointed out that "from South America to South Africa, nations are foreswearing [nuclear] weapons, realizing

that a nuclear future is not a more secure future. Most of the world is moving toward the elimination of nuclear weapons. That goal is not advanced if any country, in any region, moves in the other direction." Predictably, this statement met
with silence. His audience continued to insist that only equitable nuclear disarmament could turn it away from seeking what Foreign Minister Singh had called
"those symbols of power . . . which have universal currency."[82] Clinton knew this,
so he continued by urging India to recognize the dangers that lay ahead on the
nuclear route. He said that only years of "direct dialogue" between the United
States and the Soviet Union in the Cold War had given each side the necessary
understanding of the other's "capabilities, doctrines and intentions."[83] Safely
managing these forces required "billions of dollars on elaborate command and
control systems." (Here Clinton understated the true combined U.S.-Soviet expenditures on nuclear command and control which surpassed one trillion dollars.)
Even with all this effort and expense, "we learned that deterrence alone cannot be
relied on to prevent accident or miscalculation." In a pointed reminder to Indian
politicians, he added that "in a nuclear standoff, there is nothing more dangerous
than believing there is no danger." This cautionary tone could not have contrasted more with the sanguine, almost insouciant character of the National Security Advisory Board's draft nuclear doctrine.

With the exception of the nuclear passage, Clinton's oratory elicited a famously
enthusiastic response. At the end of the speech, parliamentarians rushed the well
of the House, clamoring to shake the president's hand. In the twenty-two years
since the last American president's visit, India had changed, as had the world
around it. The celebratory sense of India's potential and the desire for a new
partnership between it and the world's leading power obscured the hard realities
that leaders from both sides would face when they returned to their quotidian
duties. But the momentary relief did give a glimpse of a future that could be
achieved.[84]

The vast majority of observers celebrated Clinton's visit and what it represented for the future of India and of Indo-American relations. *Outlook* magazine
summarized the reaction well: "Spontaneous gestures of warmth rather than
planned diplomatic manoeuvres is what has made the Clinton visit a hit in this
country. . . . Perhaps no other head of state visiting India has managed to catch
the public's fancy the way Clinton has."[85]

American officials, too, deemed the visit a success. Recognizing that atmosphere and tone matter greatly in Indo-American relations, they took comfort in
the enthusiastic reception the president received on every stop. The previous
months of diplomacy had dampened expectation of major substantive breakthroughs, so administration officials sought to lower the standards for grading the
trip in policy terms. "On the security agenda," a top official explained to reporters on the president's plane leaving India,

> we had no expectation. We said so to many of you before we left, that in the context
> of this trip the Indians were [not] going to . . . take any steps. It's not possible for

them to do that, politically. I would hope that in the aftermath of the trip, that the process of building a consensus in India—for example, signing the CTBT—will be strengthened. I hope the discussion of the future of their nuclear program will increase. But these are obviously issues that, ultimately, India has got to decide.[86]

American officials retained thin hopes that the visit to India could lead to concrete results in the run-up to Prime Minister Vajpayee's reciprocal visit to the United States, which occurred in September 2000. However, these hopes, too, proved chimerical. No breakthroughs occurred on nuclear or other contentious issues. Disappointment was shared, though, as Indians found that their nation's prominence in the American body politic still lagged far behind their aspirations, notwithstanding recent gains. After some maneuvering assisted by prominent Indian Americans, Vajpayee was invited to address a joint session of Congress. Yet the American media paid almost no attention. The *New York Times* wrote nothing on the speech, memorializing it only in a picture on page A18. In 1994 Narasimha Rao had received similar treatment when the *Times* did not report on his speech to a joint session of Congress. However, his picture at the lectern ran on page A3. Trivial perhaps, but if nuclear weapons were to earn India standing as a great power, Indian leaders may have miscalculated twenty-first-century currency rates.

CHINA

Indian diplomacy in 1999 and 2000 suggested that brandishing nuclear strength was meant to serve protean purposes. Nuclear prowess gave the Vajpayee government confidence and domestic political credit to invest in diplomacy to stabilize the Pakistan front, as was attempted at Lahore. Nuclear assertiveness created newfound respect for India in Washington, as Indians saw it. India's growing importance also drew the heads of state from France, Germany, Japan, and the United Kingdom to meet with Vajpayee. China was a more delicate challenge; India approached it with less self-assurance than it displayed toward its other interlocutors.

With barely disguised contempt, China had rebuked India for invoking it as the cause of the 1998 nuclear tests. China joined the United States in cosponsoring UN Resolution 1172, which condemned the Indian and Pakistani nuclear tests and called upon them "immediately to stop their nuclear weapon development programs."[87] The resolution urged all states to prevent export of "equipment, materials or technology that could in any way assist" the Indian and Pakistani nuclear and missile programs. Hypocrisy abounded here. China shamelessly overlooked its own violation of the spirit and law of the nonproliferation regime in assisting Pakistan's nuclear and missile programs. In 1997, following Jiang Zemin's important visit to South Asia, the United States had urged and detected Chinese restraint in assisting Pakistan's missile program. But following the Indian nuclear tests of 1998, "the Pakistanis called on their old friends to show loyalty and we saw problems in the missile proliferation area again in late 1998 and 1999," an American official noted.[88] "This prompted us to go to the Chinese in early 2000 and warn them that U.S. sanctions" were looming again on the horizon.

Indian officials and analysts were not sure how to deal now with China.[89] Some, such as K. Subrahmanyam, argued that India should press China directly and through the United States to end its assistance to Pakistan's nuclear and missile programs.[90] China's willingness to desist in this behavior would address a material Indian security problem and signify general respect for India's legitimate interests. Others insisted that China and India were destined to rivalry and that the core problem for India was the "Chinese attitude . . . that India has no leverage, and can be taken for granted."[91] In the words of Brahma Chellaney, "Beijing treats India as a country to be threatened, belittled and kept in check."[92] India must therefore confront "the inbuilt sense of superiority of the Chinese," as the former foreign secretary, A.P. Venkateswaran, argued.[93]

Perhaps the most direct and succinct statement of Indian objectives vis-à-vis China was offered privately by a highly respected government advisor. India needed China to

> acknowledge that we have legitimate rights and interests and there cannot be a meaningful relationship unless such an acknowledgement is unequivocal and public. China must show signs of abandoning its specific policy to use Pakistan as its "counter-irritant" in its relationship with India. China will have to show signs that it intends to build a bilateral relationship not governed by its own third party requirements. China will have to show signs that it considers an improvement in Sino-Indian relations as important or at least meaningful to China.[94]

Yet these were largely political objectives. Sophisticated nuclear weapons and reliable means of delivering them to Chinese targets conceivably could redress a specific military strategic threat, but a weapon-heavy approach would engender more hostility in the otherwise manageable relationship. Thus, Foreign Minister Jaswant Singh declared in June 1999 that India did not regard China as a threat. "The threat chapter is over," he said, "the Pokhran chapter is behind us."[95] The Ministry of Defence's annual report for 1998–1999 stated that India did not regard China as "an adversary."[96]

Indeed, the most careful study yet done of the military-strategic equation between India and China concluded that "there are almost no circumstances under which Chinese use of nuclear weapons as warfighting instruments become either plausible or advantageous in the context of a conventional conflict with India."[97] India's conventional military resources along the Himalayan frontier, especially its tactical air superiority, rendered a Chinese offensive impractical. The author, Ashley Tellis, concluded further that China could not effectively use tactical nuclear weapons to overcome the geographic and conventional military balance that made aggression along the disputed border a fool's errand.[98]

China was highly unlikely to run the geopolitical and military risks of aggression or blackmail against India. Yet, if it did, India faced a hugely problematic challenge to develop and deploy a nuclear arsenal to deter such risk-taking without triggering Chinese counterdevelopments that would negate India's gain. China began its quest for nuclear weapons in the mid-1950s to deter the United States, but fifty years later still had not overcome the American capacity to negate this deterrent by destroying or decisively crippling the Chinese force in a first strike. The capability gap between China and the United States was greater than that between India and China, but India faced a practically insurmountable challenge in trying to overcome China's nuclear advantage.

Fortunately for New Delhi, China did not pose the sort of direct threat that nuclear weapons were necessary to meet. As Army Chief of Staff General S. Padmanabhan put it, "The level of confrontation, the level of tempers and the tendency to jump off the edge is much less with China" than with Pakistan.[99] To be sure, China was modernizing its nuclear arsenal, but this modernization was due to technological momentum and Sino-American dynamics. China possessed a more menacing nuclear arsenal than India could, but it was a residual of Beijing's standoff with the United States more than a threat directed at India.

Thus, the Vajpayee government in 1999 and 2000 concentrated on diplomatic means to address the realistic challenge of persuading Beijing to treat India with greater respect and fashion a relationship predicated on durable stability. Chinese leaders, grudgingly perhaps, accepted that their interest, too, lay in stabilizing the South Asian front. Beijing faced more acute problems in Tibet, in preventing Taiwanese movement toward independence, and in containing American assertiveness in Northeast Asia. Within South Asia, Chinese analysts also began to comprehend the danger of Kashmir and the spread of militant Islam, terrorism, and narcotics trafficking from Pakistan and Afghanistan into the troubled Xinjiang province of China.[100] On these and other issues, "China and India have more common interests than differences," a Chinese commentator declared.[101]

If conflicting interests and perceptions drove China to augment Pakistan's nuclear and missile programs, and India to test nuclear weapons in 1998, New Delhi and Beijing now sought to prevent their differences from deepening. In April 1999, delegations to the Joint Working Group met in Beijing, the eleventh such meeting but the first since the 1998 nuclear tests. China signaled conciliation by arranging for the Indian delegation's leader, Foreign Secretary K. Raghunath, to meet with high-level government and party leaders, including Vice Premier Qian Qichen and Foreign Minister Tang Jixuan. Both sides expressed willingness to intensify dialogue to resolve the boundary dispute, and both downplayed the accusatory rhetoric that surrounded the 1998 nuclear tests.

Months later, the Kargil war between India and Pakistan provided a dramatic occasion for testing China's true willingness to strengthen relations with India. As recounted above, China's refusal to side with Pakistan and its determination, announced during the conflict, to begin a strategic dialogue with India showed that Beijing was recalculating its interests in ways more favorable to India. Following the Indian elections of October 1999, China and India resumed their dialogue in late November with a meeting of experts in New Delhi to discuss the border dispute.

In January 2000, Pakistan's chief executive, General Pervez Musharraf, who had displaced Nawaz Sharif in an October 12, 1999 coup, traveled to Beijing. This was Musharraf's first foreign visit since taking power, reflecting Pakistan's dependence on China. Chinese President Jiang Zemin and other officials reaffirmed their support for Pakistan. However, in declaring that the "mutual understanding and support of the two countries are due to adhering to the five principles of peaceful co-existence," Jiang invoked the same formulation that China was using to guide relations with India. This equation could not have comforted Pakistan.[102] Whether or not China continued to provide clandestine assistance to Pakistan's nuclear and missile programs, Beijing's overall policy seemed to give greater due to India than in previous decades.

January also exposed the simmering issue of Tibet in Sino-Indian relations. As long as the Dalai Lama and other Tibetan Buddhist leaders lived in India, Beijing worried that India could allow the Tibetans to inflame demand for autonomy from China. If India were to exploit this Chinese vulnerability, Beijing could reciprocate the ill will through relations with Pakistan, support for insurgents in northeastern India, or other acts. Conversely, if India restrained the Tibetan Buddhists from agitating against China (at least on Indian soil), Beijing had an interest in rewarding such behavior. Mutual reassurance offered Beijing and New Delhi a Realpolitik win-win, notwithstanding the morality of the Tibetan cause. Thus, when a fourteen-year-old Tibetan boy regarded by the Dalai Lama *and* China as the seventeenth Karmapa escaped to India after a harrowing trek out of Tibet, Beijing warned India not to grant him political asylum.[103] Chinese authorities feared that the Dalai Lama and other Tibetan activists would be emboldened toward greater agitation with the arrival of this top young leader of Tibetan Buddhism, who could potentially be a candidate to succeed the Dalai Lama. India parried that no request for asylum had been made. Over the ensuing months New Delhi demonstrated that it would not allow Tibetan issues to derail Sino-Indian relations.[104]

More diplomatic reassurance came in February 2000 when Principal Secretary and National Security Advisor Brajesh Mishra declared in Munich that India was "not, definitely not, attempting to catch up with China in the number of delivery systems or warheads."[105] This statement made a virtue out of a necessity insofar as India had little prospect of producing enough fissile materials, warheads, or long-range missiles to catch up with China. Yet it spotlighted how Indian rhetoric had changed from the May 1998 nuclear test period and even the August 1999 draft nuclear doctrine. Scientists and engineers would work as hard as they could to strengthen India's nuclear and missile capabilities, but top decision makers seemed more aware than ever that diplomacy (and a favorable conventional military balance in the Himalayas), not nuclear weaponry, was the key to Sino-Indian security.

In early March, just before President Clinton's arrival in India, Chinese and Indian officials met in Beijing for the first of the "security dialogues" planned during Jaswant Singh's June 1999 visit to Beijing. The timing reflected the growing triangularity of Sino-Indian-American relations, especially as seen from China. Beijing noted that influential Americans, particularly from the Republican party, portrayed democratic India as a potential partner in containing Communist China. Clinton's high-profile visit alarmed Chinese officials, who suspected that the president's agenda had more to do with containing China than the White House let on.[106] Thus, China welcomed the opportunity on March 6–7 to assess Indian perceptions of the pending presidential visit and, more broadly, to explore whether India shared China's interest in promoting global multipolarity. During the meetings the two sides shared their analyses of global trends and an array of issues in which Indian and Chinese interests overlapped. When the discussion turned to nuclear weapons, the Chinese representative called for India to adhere to UN Security Council Resolution 1172. The Indian delegation, led by long-time arms control and disarmament advisor Rakesh Sood, countered that India had a sovereign right to determine its own security needs and argued that China's assistance to Pakistan's nuclear and missile programs was a major reason why India had to augment and test its nuclear weapons.[107] The Indian team returned home feeling that China was adjusting to the reality that India would not roll back its nuclear capabilities and that beneath the obligatory rhetoric on the issue, Beijing was taking India more seriously.

The reinvigoration of Sino-Indian relations hit a peak in late May when President K. R. Narayanan visited China. Narayanan had been India's ambassador to China in the mid-1970s. He came now to put relations on a firm footing of "friendship and brotherhood," reflecting that China is India's "most important neighbour."[108] In their talks, Narayanan and Jiang Zemin declared that their two states were not political rivals and that both wished to effect a more multipolar world as an alternative to American dominance of the international system. Beijing hoped that New Delhi might join it and, where appropriate, Russia in blocking expressions of American unilateralism. Each recognized that the other would seek its own good relations with Washington. Yet the prospect of solid Sino-Indian relations and harmony in advocating multipolarity could make Washington more attentive to each of the Asian states.

In their direct discussion, Narayanan and Jiang did not raise the nuclear issue, another welcome sign for India. Jiang did highlight the problem of Tibet, expressing concern that the Karmapa's presence with the Dalai Lama in India could foment anti-Chinese activities there. Narayanan reportedly reassured Jiang on this score.[109] On the border dispute, Jiang reiterated China's counsel of "patience" in dealing with a problem "left over by history." Narayanan responded cleverly that problems inherited from history "must not be left over for history."[110] India would press for more forthcoming Chinese diplomacy on the border dispute.

Both sides concluded that important momentum had been imparted to Sino-

Indian relations. According to Indian analysts, four major trends were noted. First, China displayed genuine warmth toward the Indian president, an intangible that India longed to see from the often haughty Chinese. Second, Chinese leaders seemed to acknowledge India's growing economic and political importance, granting India a prominence that heretofore had been denied. Third, Chinese leaders appeared more willing than before to engage openly on matters of tension, including the border dispute. Finally, Chinese leaders eschewed polemical discourse on the nuclear issue.[111] Indians were not alone in seeing progress. As one Chinese writer concluded,

> The Sino-Indian border dispute, though still complex, has seen positive progress. . . . China and India have more common interests than differences, and both intend to establish a constructive partnership oriented toward the future. . . . The BJP is the only party in India which can afford to make a certain breakthrough on border issues without incurring accusation from the opposition. . . . If both China and India would seize this opportunity, it is possible to achieve such breakthroughs on border issues.[112]

South Asia remained a tertiary concern for most Chinese leaders, and few analysts focused on the region. However, those who did recognized a mutual interest in bilateral progress.

In July 2000, Chinese Foreign Minister Tang Jiaxuan traveled to New Delhi where he and counterpart Jaswant Singh agreed to speed the pace of negotiations to clarify the Line of Actual Control separating the two nations.[113] The prospect of more forthcoming Chinese interest in these negotiations prompted respected Indian commentators such as Raja Mohan and Lt. General (ret.) V. R. Raghavan to acknowledge that India's position on the border dispute needed to become more pragmatic. As Raghavan argued, "This would involve moving away from old inflexible positions. It would also mean a political consensus on revisiting the Indian Parliamentary resolution on regaining all lost territories. Territories are meaningful if they provide security and homelands to people, or vital resources to the nation. When neither is involved, the border settlement should be viewed in the strategic context of ending the prospect of conflict and building lasting partnerships."[114] To this end, in November the two sides for the first time exchanged maps of the 545-kilometer middle section of the disputed border.

The apparent momentum of Sino-Indian relations gained more thrust with the January 2001 visit of the powerful Li Peng to India. Beijing signaled its desire to take the relationship to a new level by dispatching Li for nine days with an agenda that went beyond the usual meetings in Delhi and included trips to the Taj Mahal, Mumbai, Bangalore, and Hyderabad. Indian officials described the tone of the official talks as "very cordial, and friendly, even relaxed," rather effusive for diplomatese. China's official media called the visit a "complete success."[115] In talks with Vajpayee, Li welcomed the intensification of dialogue to clarify the Line of Actual Control dividing India and China. The two leaders expressed hope that the process would be completed quickly, a departure from the long-standing Chinese counsel of patience.[116] When Vajpayee was asked about the contentious issue of China's supply of nuclear and missile technology assistance to Pakistan, the prime minister said, according to the *Hindu*, that "when old ties were taking new shape and new relations were being formed, 'such contradictions will come and we have to deal with them.'"[117] This statement implied a mutual recognition that China was recalculating its interests in South Asia, including its material support to Pakistan's nuclear weapon and missile capabilities. The United States in early 2000 believed that China had adopted proliferation restraint toward Pakistan.[118] Still, Indian officials noted warily in private that China refused to acknowledge its seminal role in Pakistan's nuclear weapon program. Without such acknowledgement, India remained suspicious that China could resume violating its nonproliferation obligations.

Indians recognized that some of China's recent forthcoming diplomacy stemmed from Beijing's determination to resist U.S. hegemonism.[119] The arrival of a new Republican administration in Washington made Beijing more anxious to give India incentives not to join with the United States in containing China.

India displayed its own goodwill by holding off a long-planned second test of the Agni II missile until Li Peng was leaving India. The missile had been readied on its launch pad in Orissa for some time, and United States officials expected the test to occur on the weekend of January 13–14. India waited until January 17 when Li had ended his scheduled visit.[120] The Agni test became a Rorschach test for Indian commentators. The government announced that the test had been held off until Li departed. An unsigned editorial in the *Times of India* needled that the "Agni II has been tested during Li Peng's visit to India, just as the Chinese carried out a major nuclear test during President Venkataraman's visit to China [in 1992]." Brahma Chellaney opined that the test reflected "India's growing confidence that the China-reachable missile was tested while Li was still on Indian soil."[121] Later reports clarified that the test occurred two hours before Li's plane actually departed, a temporal proximity that left India's intentions in this regard ambivalent, inasmuch as the countdown sequence could not have been sped up or slowed at the last minute to match Li's precise moment of departure. China refused to be provoked and took little public note of the test.

RUSSO-INDIAN COOPERATION AND INDIA'S ONGOING TECHNICAL PROBLEMS

The Agni II test reportedly satisfied its makers: they said the missile hit almost exactly on target and the mock nuclear warhead (minus the fissile material core) detonated at the intended altitude.[122] Abdul Kalam's successor as science advisor to the defence minister, Dr. V. K. Atre, declared that the Agni II would be "inducted" into the military by the end of 2001 with nuclear warheads.[123] Even if this proved true, India would not have a certified missile system with a range that would constitute a militarily effective deterrent against China (as opposed to a politically effective one).[124] India's conventional forces also needed modernization and neither the military nor political leadership believed that the indigenous research and development establishment could provide weapons of sufficient quality and quantity in a timely manner. Meanwhile, India's nuclear power program had improved its performance, but political leaders and the nuclear establishment acknowledged the need for international cooperation to meet electricity demands.[125]

To help meet all of these needs, no outside supplier of hardware and know-how stood more willing and able than Russia. Geopolitics and history added impetus to the technological and financial imperatives drawing Russia and India closer.

In late 1998 India and Russia moved smartly to revive old ties and make new deals. Prime Minister Yevgeny Primakov traveled to India in December to begin the renewal. Primakov was one of Russia's most experienced foreign policy strategists, and he believed that Russia had undermined its international power by focusing too much on relations with the United States and the West in recent years. He sought to balance Washington's increasingly preponderant power by strengthening Russia's ties with China and India. In New Delhi, Primakov met with President Narayanan and Prime Minister Vajpayee to prepare the ground for a "strategic partnership" that would update the landmark Treaty of Peace, Friendship and Co-operation signed in 1971, and less heralded agreements of 1993 and 1994.[126]

In mid-June 2000, Foreign Minister Singh traveled to Russia to intensify the courtship by planning a visit to India by the newly elected Russian president, Vladimir Putin. Defence Minister George Fernandes arrived in Moscow days later to meet with Russian defense officials and Putin to sketch contracts for Indian purchase of major Russian weapon systems. Putin greeted Fernandes with a charming sales pitch. Declaring Russia to be "the closest, dearest and best friend of India," the former KGB officer promised to help India become "a strong and defence-capable nation."[127] Russian officials acknowledged India's concerns that Russia's extensive arms supplies to China could undermine Indian interests. India especially worried about Russia's assistance to China's FC-1 jet fighter that Pakistan wanted to acquire.[128] Behind the general bonhomie of these meetings, the two states were haggling intensely over prices and terms of the cooperation.[129]

In October 2000 Putin traveled in India to consummate the new relationship. The *India Today* headline—"Arming of India"—described the dowry.[130] Russia agreed to sell India 150 Su-30 fighters for $2 billion, 310 T-90 main battle tanks for $450 million, the refitted Gorschkov aircraft carrier for $550 million. The Sukoi fighters would be built in India, while a portion of the T-90 tanks also would be assembled there. The new deals added to already extensive cooperation: Russia in October delivered to India the *INS Sindhushastra*, an attack submarine with a complement of short-range cruise missiles. The missiles, and ongoing assistance from Russian engineers, would help India "indigenously" design and build longer-range cruise missiles that could launch nuclear weapons from surface ships or, eventually, submarines.[131] Russian technicians also were reportedly assisting India to design its problem-plagued nuclear-powered ballistic-missile submarine that was envisioned as the ultimate foundation of an "invulnerable" deterrent.[132] Putin also signed a Memorandum of Understanding to intensify bilateral cooperation in "the peaceful uses of atomic energy." The full extent of the cooperation was secret but, among other things, it included further progress in the long-in-the-works deal under which Russia would build two 1,000-megawatt power reactors in Tamil Nadu and possibly help in constructing two additional reactors and supplying fuel for the Tarapur reactors.[133]

The new arrangements revealed much about both countries. Russia under Putin was reasserting its global influence and restocking its treasury by exploiting its only competitive industrial capacities. Russia had lost its traditional position in India, and the United States had largely filled the vacuum in political-economic and diplomatic terms. The conventional weapons sales to India represented a bid to regain lost ground. The assistance to India's missile and nuclear programs carried the competition to new territory, consciously defying nonproliferation norms championed by the United States. Russia was saying, in essence, that if the United States made its own rules in expanding NATO and bombing Serbia, Russia would follow its own preferences in augmenting India's strategic programs. Moscow did not disavow its participation in the international nonproliferation regime, but it was challenging some of the terms.[134] The strategic and commercial interests of the hard-pressed nation left it disinclined to worry over the niceties of regulations pushed by rich states that were treating Russia as a fallen power.

For its part, India's eagerness to obtain Russian technology revealed mismanagement of defense policy and, more, the failings of the defense and nuclear technology establishments. India's defense procurement had ebbed and flowed dramatically, betraying strategic confusion, political inattention, and economic travails. The arms import binge of the early 1980s had given way to a crash diet, leaving the military services desperate for modern replacements in the late 1990s. The long gestations of indigenously produced systems such as the Arjun tank and the light combat aircraft delayed reckoning with the services' needs. In the wake of the Kargil war, it became obvious that the state continued to depend on foreign defense technology. According to one retired admiral writing in October 2000, "Nearly 70 per cent of weapons and equipment in the Navy and the Air Force, and 60 per cent in the Army is of Soviet/Russian origin." The admiral joined quieter voices in the military in complaining that "despite their routine publicity hype" the Defence Research and Development Organisation "has failed to produce a single product of consequence to replace foreign acquisitions."[135] The same was largely true for the nuclear establishment. To approach advertised levels of electricity production from nuclear power plants, India needed foreign help. Given fifty years of history, it was also reasonable to wonder whether Russian expertise would be used discretely to correct imperfections in the design and fabrication of India's thermonuclear weapon prototype.

There was nothing inherently wrong or dishonorable in seeking the range of cooperation India was now procuring from Russia. The United Kingdom, Israel, China, and others relied heavily on foreign assistance in their nuclear and conventional military spheres. It only required overcoming the national and scientific pride that had made India so insistent on indigenous development of strategic technologies. That this occurred in 2000 reflected, ironically, the self-confidence and realism that had grown after the 1998 nuclear tests. India had proved itself and joined "the club"; now it could get down to business. The global attention, foreign reserves, and sense of national prowess gained from India's world-class information technology sector made Indian pride less dependent on self-reliance in defense technology.

CONCLUSION

This chapter began with central questions emergent from the 1998 nuclear tests and the long history that led to them. The intervening two years offered at least partial tentative answers.

India did begin to plot a course for improving its security relationships with both Pakistan and China. The Lahore summit of 1999, and even more boldly, the tentative initiative begun in late 2000 to seek dialogue with Kashmiris and perhaps Pakistan to resolve the conflict there, suggested India's determination to stabilize relations with Pakistan. The intensifying diplomacy with China seemed to put relations between those two states on a more positive course than had been followed since the mid-1950s. A coherent strategic logic lay behind these developments: India would seek durable stability and peace with its two neighbors through diplomacy that allowed for give and take.

India did not in this period develop and use robust institutions for devising and implementing nuclear policy. The vaunted National Security Council remained marginal; proposals for integrating military officers into nuclear policymaking had not been enacted fully. Nuclear policy remained tightly controlled by the prime minister and those he sought for counsel. However, this political control was not necessarily a defect. Nor was it to say that India lacked an operational nuclear doctrine and a command and control system that would enable the state to retaliate against Pakistani use of nuclear weapons, which was the only feasible contingency. Rather, the point is that India's management of nuclear policy, however sensible, still ran counter to the pattern expected by the dominant Realist school of national-security thinkers.

India continued its slow-motion development and testing of missiles but failed to engage its competitors in diplomacy to limit the possibility of an arms race.

Indian leaders did not create institutions to check and balance the claims and demands of the nuclear and missile-technology establishments. The 1998 stars A. P. J. Abdul Kalam and R. Chidambaram were retired from the Atomic Energy Commission and the DRDO, and India's political leaders seemed less inclined to encourage hero-worship of their successors, but the AEC and DRDO still remained free from technically expert scrutiny. Kalam reportedly continued to wield influence in New Delhi. The nuclear establishment had rid itself of even nominal independent oversight when, in April 2000, it removed plutonium production reactors and reprocessing facilities controlled by the Bhabha Atomic Research Centre from the purview of the Atomic Energy Regulatory Board.[136] Political leaders still had no independent means of evaluating the inputs they received from the strategic enclave, be they claims about the effectiveness of past or current projects; assessments of the impact of arms control measures on India; or the costs, performance, and timely production of prospective weapons systems.

India's global influence did grow since 1998 as seen in the state's interactions with the established great powers. This increased influence arguably was the greatest motive behind the nuclear weapon effort in the first place. Yet, it was not self-evident that nuclear weapons were *the* cause, or even an important driver, of this progress. For one thing, after the May 1998 tests, India kept a low nuclear profile. It conducted no new nuclear explosive tests. Laboratory developments and experiments were kept quiet. The Agni missile was tested only twice, though future tests were likely. As far as the world could tell, no nuclear weapons were operationally deployed. The only real public display of nuclear "might" was the rhetorical imprecation of the National Security Advisory Board, and this was quickly devalued by the government, whose discussions of nuclear policy were much more demure. Nuclear weapons as physical phenomena did not shape this period.

Yet nuclear weapons as psychological assets probably did much to launch India into its largely successful interactions with the outside world. The government still avoided making hard decisions, but Indian leaders and politicians gained confidence from the nuclear tests and the notion that India was a nuclear power for all to see. The confidence came more from the act of defying the international community than from the material accomplishment in the Rajasthan desert. The latter was modest by world-class standards. India had asserted its national "self" in terms set not by the weak and the irrelevant, but by the strong and the great. This defiant act emboldened Indian leaders to deal with other powers as self-perceived equals. Ironically, if not tragically, India's strengthened national identity came through mimicking the once-derided big powers. The civilian leadership still insisted on a rather unique, politically sagacious and relatively moral approach to nuclear weapons, but India was abandoning its mission as an agent of change in the international system.

If India became more confident in approaching other major powers, why did the others deal more forthcomingly with India? The most demonstrable reasons were money and balance-of-power politics in which, again, nuclear weapons figured slightly. The Clinton administration had elevated India in its priorities long before 1998. India was a great emerging market; it had a world-class information technology sector; Americans of Indian origin were achieving great prominence and wealth and exerting their influence through the political process. Nuclear issues and worries over the Indo-Pak conflict increased the overall level of Washington's engagement, but not the balance of positive to negative. France saw an opportunity to sell nuclear reactors and advanced conventional arms to India. Russia was desperate to sell arms and nuclear technology and saw India as an important partner for balancing American and Chinese influence. China wanted to stabilize its southern flank, increase trade, and, most of all, keep India from getting drawn into an American bloc to contain China. Indeed, the single largest common denominator in the new relationships with China, Russia, and France was the determination to counteract the United States' dominant and "arrogantly" manifested global power. India's nuclear weapon capability played no positive role in attracting these powers to it, and only a marginally small role in motivating China to take India more seriously. Rather, India was taking itself more seriously, and others responded in kind.

This assessment—no doubt arguable—goes back to the central questions of this book: why did India, and why do other states, seek nuclear weapon capabilities, and why do they resist giving them up? The traditional answer is that national security concerns determine nuclear policies. However, defining national security as a largely material-military problem does not explain much of Indian history from 1947 to 1998 and is only a little more telling for the period from late 1998 to early 2001. But if "security" is seen as a psychological-political condition, then India's acquisition of nuclear weapons has much to do with it. It may help to analogize from individual behavior here. One may say that an individual is "secure," referring to a physical situation. He lives in a crime-free neighborhood, in a safe house; or he has a large bank account to ensure his material well-being. This is security in the material sense. But "security" also can connote that a person is confident: he is secure in himself, self-assured, with no chip on his shoulder. A secure person is one who feels comfortable about his or her identity—physical appearance, ability to make good friends, and so on. One does not obtain this latter type of security by hiring a security firm, an analog to the military acquisition of nuclear weapons. It is possible that India, as a state and society, derived this sort of self-confidence and assurance from acquiring nuclear weapon capabilities because these capabilities were believed to be esteemed by the ranks of states India wanted to join. Entering these ranks, speaking this language, and possessing this currency engendered national confidence. This could be called "security."

"Security," then is a conflated concept. In addition to being a military or physical aspiration or condition, as the dominant discourse emphasizes, security should be recognized as a broader psychological-political phenomenon. Security is not just the stuff of military strategy and geopolitics; it is an anthropological construct. The Indian experience suggests that this understanding would enhance the international community's ability to manage the ongoing challenges of nuclear proliferation, arms control, and disarmament.

India's Nuclear Infrastructure

Name/Location of Facility	Type and Capacity: Gross Design (NET) Output[a]	Completion or Target Date	IAEA Safeguards
Power Reactors: Operating			
Tarapur 1	Light-water, LEU and MOX 210 (150) MWe.	1969	Yes
Tarapur 2	Light-water, LEU 210 (160) MWe.	1969	Yes
Rajasthan, RAPS-1, Kota	Heavy-water, natural U 220 (90) MWe.	1972	Yes
Rajasthan, RAPS-2, Kota	Heavy-water, natural U 220 (187) MWe.	1980	Yes
Madras, MAPS-1, Kalpakkam	Heavy-water, natural U 235 (170) MWe.	1983	No
Madras, MAPS-2, Kalpakkam	Heavy-water, natural U 235 (170) MWe.	1985	No
Narora 1	Heavy-water, natural U 235 (202) MWe.	1989	No
Narora 2	Heavy-water, natural U 235 (202) MWe.	1991	No
Kakrapar 1	Heavy-water, natural U 235 (170) MWe.	1992	No
Kakrapar 2	Heavy-water, natural U 235 (202) MWe.	1995	No

Name/Location of Facility	Type and Capacity: Gross Design (NET) Output[a]	Completion or Target Date	IAEA Safeguards
Power Reactors: Under Construction			
Kaiga 1	Heavy-water, natural U 235 (202) MWe.	1998	No
Kaiga 2	Heavy-water, natural U 235 (202) MWe.	1998	No
Rajasthan, RAPS-3, Kota	Heavy-water, natural U 235 (202) MWe.	1999	No
Rajasthan, RAPS-4, Kota	Heavy-water, natural U 235 (202) MWe.	1999	No
Power Reactors: Planned and Proposed			
Tarapur 3	Heavy-water, natural U 500 (450) MWe.	2004	No
Tarapur 4	Heavy-water, natural U 500 (450) MWe.	—	No
Kaiga 3	Heavy-water, natural U 235 (202) MWe.	—	No
Kaiga 4	Heavy-water, natural U 235 (202) MWe.	—	No
Kaiga 5	Heavy-water, natural U 235 (202) MWe.	—	No
Kaiga 6	Heavy-water, natural U 235 (202) MWe.	—	No
Rajasthan, RAPS-5, Kota	Heavy-water, natural U 500 (450) MWe.	—	No
Rajasthan, RAPS-6, Kota	Heavy-water, natural U 500 (450) MWe.	—	No
Rajasthan, RAPS-7, Kota	Heavy-water, natural U 500 (450) MWe.	—	No
Rajasthan, RAPS-8, Kota	Heavy-water, natural U 500 (450) MWe.	—	No
Koodankulam 1	Russian VVER Light-water, LEU 1000 (953) MWe.	—	Yes
Koodankulam 2	Russian VVER Light-water, LEU 1000 (953) MWe.	—	Yes
Research Reactors			
Apsara BARC, Trombay	Light-water, medium-enriched Uranium, pool type, 1 MWt.	1956	No
CIRUS BARC, Trombay	Heavy-water, natural U 40 MWt.	1960	No

Name/Location of Facility	Type and Capacity: Gross Design (NET) Output[a]	Completion or Target Date	IAEA Safeguards
Dhruva BARC, Trombay	Heavy-water, natural U 100 MWt.	1985	No
Kamini IGCAR, Kalpakkam	Uranium-233 30 kWt.	1996	No
Zerlina BARC, Trombay	Heavy-water, variable fuel, 100 Wt, decommissioned.	1961	No
Purnima 1 BARC, Trombay	Fast neutron, critical assembly, zero power, decommissioned.	1972	No
Purnima 2 BARC, Trombay	Uranium-233 .005 kWt, dismantled	1984	No
Purnima 3 BARC, Trombay	Uranium-233	—	No
Breeder Reactors			
Fast Breeder Test Reactor (FBTR) IGCAR, Kalpakkam	Plutonium and natural U 40 MWt.	1985	No
Prototype Fast Breeder Reactor (PFBR) IGCAR, Kalpakkam	Mixed-oxide fuel, 500 MWe, planned.	2008	No
Uranium Enrichment			
Trombay	Pilot-scale ultracentrifuge plant; operating.	1985	No
Trombay	Laser enrichment research site.	early 1980s	No
Rattehalli (Mysore)	Pilot-scale ultracentrifuge plant; operating.	1990	No
Center for Advanced Technology, Indore	Laser enrichment research site.	1993	No
Reprocessing (Plutonium Extraction)			
Trombay	Medium-scale, 50 tHM/y; operating.	1964/ 1985	No
Tarapur (Prefre)	Large-scale, 100 (25) tHM/y; operating.	1977	Only when safeguarded fuel is present.
Kalpakkam	Laboratory-scale, operating.	1985	No
Kalpakkam	Large-scale, two lines, 100 tHM/y each; under construction.	1998/ 2008	No

Name/Location of Facility	Type and Capacity: Gross Design (NET) Output[a]	Completion or Target Date	IAEA Safeguards
Uranium Processing			
Rakh, Surda, Mosaboni	Uranium recovery plant at copper concentrator; operating.		N/A (Not Applicable)
Jaduguda, Narwpahar, Bhatin	Uranium mining and milling; operating.		N/A
Hyderabad	Uranium purification (UO_2); operating.		No
Hyderabad	Fuel fabrication; operating.		Partial
Trombay	Uranium conversion (UF_6); operating. Fuel fabrication.		No
Tarapur	Mixed uranium-plutonium oxide (MOX) fuel fabrication; operating.		Only when safe-guarded fuel is present.
Heavy-Water Processing			
Trombay	Pilot-scale; operaional.		—
Nangal	14 t/y; operating.	1962	—
Baroda	67 t/y; intermittent operation.	1980	—
Tuticorin	71 t/y; operating.	1978	—
Talcher phase 1	62 t/y; suspended.	1980	—
Talcher phase 2	62 t/y; suspended.	1980	—
Kota	100 t/y; operating.	1981	—
Thal-Vaishet	110 t/y; operating.	1991	—
Manuguru	185 t/y; operating, under expansion.	1991	—
Hazira	110 t/y; operating.	1991	—

ABBREVIATIONS

HEU   =   highly enriched uranium
LEU   =   low-enriched uranium
nat. U   =   natural uranium
MWe   =   millions of watts of electrical output
MWt   =   millions of watts of thermal output
kWt   =   thousands of watts of thermal output
tHM/y =   tons of heavy metal per year
MOX   =   mixed natural U and plutonium oxide fuel

[a] The gross design capacity of the reactor is its original power rating, while the net operating capacity refers to *current* output as reported for the latest operational use. See *Nuclear Engineering International: 1997 World Nuclear Industry Handbook*.

NOTES

INTRODUCTION

1. Much of this section is informed by Raj Chengappa, "The Bomb Makers," *India Today*, June 22, 1998, and by interviews by the author with former high-ranking officials of the Indian Atomic Energy Commission.

2. Itty Abraham has offered a precise and useful definition of the "strategic enclave":

The guided missile and nuclear programs in India . . . constitute a "strategic enclave." This enclave is defined as a subset of the Indian military-security complex—specifically, the set of research establishments and production facilities that are responsible for the development of these new programs. It is "strategic" because the end product of the efforts forms the most advanced technological means toward the goal of national security and represents the currency of international prestige and power today. It is an "enclave" because institutionally, spatially, and legally, the high-technology sectors of space and nuclear energy are distinct and different from the existing structure of the Indian military-security complex.

"India's 'Strategic Enclave': Civilian Scientists and Military Technologies," *Armed Forces and Society* 18, no. 2 (Winter 1992): p. 233.

3. For the twenty-five devices figure, see Mark Hibbs, *Nucleonics Week*, June 11, 1998, p. 15. Regarding weapon-grade plutonium stocks, the Indian science reporter R. Ramachandran has written in some detail that India in 1998 possessed on the order of 250 kilograms of separated weapon-grade plutonium, enough for 30 to 35 weapons in his view. R. Ramachandran, "Pokhran II: The Scientific Dimensions," in *India's Nuclear Deterrent: Pokhran II and Beyond,* ed. Amitabh Mattoo (New Delhi: Har-Anand, 1999), p. 36. This estimate fits within the lower bound of the inventory provided in David Albright, Frans Berkhout, and William Walker, *Plutonium and Highly Enriched Uranium, 1996* (New York: Oxford University Press, 1997), p. 269.

4. The Prithvi is a liquid-fueled mobile missile that comes in two models. The army version has a range of 150 kilometers and carries a payload of up to 1,000 kilograms; the air force version has a range of 250 kilometers with a payload of 500 kilograms. R. R. Subramanian, "India's Nuclear Weapon Capabilities: A Technological Appraisal," in *Nuclear Non-Proliferation in India and Pakistan: South Asian Perspectives,* ed. P. R. Chari, Pervaiz Iqbal Cheema, and Iftekharuzzaman (New Delhi: Manohar, 1996), p. 28.

5. Office of the Secretary of Defense, *Proliferation: Threat and Response* (Washington, D.C.: U.S. Government Printing Office, 1996), p. 36. For a similar French view, see Thérèse Delpech, *L'Heritage Nucleaire* (Paris: Espace Internationale, 1997), p. 21.

6. In a representative formulation,

> States secure their survival by accumulating military force they can use, singly or in combination with other states, against states wishing them ill. In an anarchical system force is the final arbiter. . . . The importance of force means that in an anarchical system units are arranged in accordance with the power they possess, not the authority or legitimacy they claim to have. . . . The key question in an anarchical system is how a state maintains its own security and risks the security of others.

Benjamin Frankel, "The Brooding Shadow: Systemic Incentives and Nuclear Weapons Proliferation," *Security Studies* 2, nos. 3-4 (Spring/Summer 1993): p. 43. For the leading presentation of Structural Realism as applied to nuclear weapons, see Kenneth N. Waltz, *The Spread of Nuclear Weapons: More May Be Better,* Adelphi Paper Series, no. 171 (London: International Institute for Strategic Studies, 1981), and "Nuclear Myths and Political Realities," *American Political Science Review* 84, no. 3 (September 1980). See also Michael M. May, "Nuclear Weapons Supply and Demand," *American Scientist* 82 (November-December 1994): pp. 533-534.

Numerous scholars recently have sought to critique, modify, or supplant Structural Realism with theoretical approaches that take much greater account of domestic factors. However, these scholars thus far have not applied their approaches to the nuclear proliferation/nonproliferation problem. See, for example, Peter B. Evans, Harold K. Jacobson, and Robert D. Putnam, eds., *Double-Edged Diplomacy* (Berkeley and Los Angeles: University of California Press, 1993); Peter J. Katzenstein, ed., *The Culture of National Security* (New York: Columbia University Press, 1996); Richard Rosecrance and Arthur A. Stein, eds., *The Domestic Bases of Grand Strategy* (Ithaca, N.Y.: Cornell University Press, 1993); and Jack Snyder, *Myths of Empire: Domestic Politics and International Ambition* (Ithaca, N.Y.: Cornell University Press, 1992).

7. This is the most obvious condition that would prompt nuclear "balancing." Other distributions of capabilities within the international system also could predictably stimulate nuclear weapon acquisition: to balance an adversary's (or adversaries') superior conventional forces; to provide cover for waging offensive aggression; to substitute for conventional forces.

8. Bradley Thayer, "The Causes of Nuclear Proliferation and the Utility of the Nuclear Nonproliferation Regime," *Security Studies* 4, no. 3 (Spring 1995): pp. 491-492. Alternatively, India or other states in its security environment should be expected to seek external help in balancing an adversary's power.

9. These assumptions are predicated on Western models of rational choice:

> [W]e assume that national decisions of such magnitude as acquiring a nuclear capability or using such a capability in a war are made by a single, dominant leader

who is an expected utility maximizer. . . . Each of these decisions [must involve,] among other things, a serious calculation of the advantages and disadvantages of the acquisition of nuclear weapons.

Bruce Bueno de Mesquita and William H. Riker, "An Assessment of the Merits of Selective Nuclear Proliferation," *Journal of Conflict Resolution* 26, no. 2 (June 1982): pp. 287, 292. In the modern era of technocratic government, the serious calculation of advantages and disadvantages is presumed to entail the systematic collection and analysis of data bearing on the costs, technical feasibility, military utility, and domestic and international effects of acquiring nuclear weapons.

10. "[D]eterrence without second-strike forces will not work." Kenneth N. Waltz, "Thoughts about Virtual Nuclear Arsenals," *Washington Quarterly* 20, no. 3 (Summer 1997): p. 155.

11. China is the only clear nondemocracy. Pakistan is included here as a democracy on the narrow ground that it has recently elected its civilian leaders.

12. For a detailed assessment of U.S. policy in South Asia from 1947 to 1965 see Robert J. McMahon, *The Cold War on the Periphery: The United States, India, and Pakistan, 1947–1965* (New York: Columbia University Press, 1994). See also William J. Barnds, *India, Pakistan, and the Great Powers* (New York: Praeger, 1972); and Dennis Kux, *India and the United States: Estranged Democracies* (Washington, D.C.: National Defense University Press, 1992).

13. Stephen P. Cohen, *The Indian Army* (Berkeley and Los Angeles: University of California Press, 1971), pp. 173–174.

14. Ibid., p. 173.

15. Ibid., pp. 174–175.

16. Among the few notable exceptions are Dagobert L. Brito, Michael D. Intrilligator, and Adele E. Wick, eds., *Strategies for Managing Nuclear Proliferation* (Lexington, Mass.: Lexington Books, 1983); Bueno de Mesquita and Riker, "An Assessment of the Merits of Selective Proliferation"; Frankel, "The Brooding Shadow: Systemic Incentives and Nuclear Weapons Proliferation"; Stephen M. Meyer, *The Dynamics of Nuclear Proliferation* (Chicago: University of Chicago Press, 1984); George Quester, *The Politics of Nuclear Proliferation* (Baltimore: Johns Hopkins University Press, 1973); Scott D. Sagan, "Why Do States Build Nuclear Weapons? Three Models in Search of a Bomb," *International Security* 21, no. 3 (Winter 1996/1997); Thayer, "The Causes of Nuclear Proliferation"; and Waltz, *The Spread of Nuclear Weapons: More May Be Better.*

17. On the U.S. nuclear weapon program, see, among others, Richard Rhodes, *The Making of the Atomic Bomb* (New York: Simon & Schuster, 1986); Thomas B. Cochran, William M. Arkin, Robert S. Norris, and Milton M. Hoenig, *Nuclear Weapons Databook*, Vol. 1, *U.S. Nuclear Forces and Capabilities* (Cambridge, Mass.: Ballinger, 1984); and Thomas B. Cochran, William M. Arkin, Robert S. Norris, and Milton M. Hoenig, *Nuclear Weapons Databook*, Vol. 2, *U.S. Nuclear Warhead Production* (Cambridge, Mass.: Ballinger, 1987). On the British nuclear weapon program, see Margaret Gowing, *Britain and Atomic Energy, 1939–1945* (London: Macmillan, 1964). On the French nuclear weapon program, see Lawrence Scheinman, *Atomic Energy Policy in France under the Fourth Republic* (Princeton, N.J.: Princeton University Press, 1965). On the French, British, and Chinese nuclear programs, see Robert S. Norris, Andrew S. Burrows, and Richard W. Fieldhouse, *Nuclear Weapons Databook*, Vol. 5, *British, French, and Chinese Nuclear Weapons* (Boulder, Colo.: Westview Press, 1994). On the Chinese nuclear weapons program, see also John W. Lewis and Litai Xue, *China Builds the*

Bomb (Stanford, Calif.: Stanford University Press, 1988). On the Soviet nuclear weapon program, see David Holloway, *Stalin and the Bomb: The Soviet Union and Atomic Energy, 1939–1956* (New Haven, Conn.: Yale University Press, 1994). In addition, hundreds of journal articles and books describe and analyze the evolution of nuclear strategy and operations. Among the most illuminating of these are McGeorge Bundy, *Danger and Survival* (New York: Vintage Books, 1990); Ashton B. Carter, John D. Steinbruner, Charles A. Zraket, eds., *Managing Nuclear Operations* (Washington, D.C.: Brookings Institution, 1987); Lawrence Freedman, *The Evolution of Nuclear Strategy* (New York: St. Martin's Press, 1981); Fred Kaplan, *The Wizards of Armageddon* (New York: Simon & Schuster, 1983); Janne E. Nolan, *Guardians of the Arsenal* (New York: A New Republic Book, 1989); and Scott D. Sagan, *The Limits of Safety* (Princeton, N.J.: Princeton University Press, 1993).

18. Avner Cohen, *Israel and the Bomb* (New York: Columbia University Press, 1998); Shai Feldman, *Israeli Nuclear Deterrence: A Strategy for the 1980s* (New York: Columbia University Press, 1982).

19. Mitchell Reiss, *Bridled Ambition* (Washington, D.C.: Woodrow Wilson Center Press, 1995); David Albright, "South Africa's Secret Nuclear Weapons," *ISIS Report* 1, no. 4 (May 1994); Waldo Stumpf, "South Africa's Nuclear Weapons Program: From Deterrence to Dismantlement," *Arms Control Today* 25, no. 10 (December 1995/January 1996).

20. Among many volumes and journal articles, see Akhtar Ali, *Pakistan's Nuclear Dilemma* (Karachi: Pakistan Economist Research Unit, 1984); Ashok Kapur, "A Nuclearizing Pakistan: Some Hypotheses," *Asian Survey* 20, no. 5 (May 1980); Zalmay Khalizad, "Pakistan and the Bomb," *Survival* 21, no. 6 (November/December, 1979); Steve Weisman and Herbert Krosney, *The Islamic Bomb* (New York: Times Books, 1981); and Zahid Malik, *Dr. A. Q. Khan and the Islamic Bomb* (Islamabad: Hurmat, 1992). In addition, the author has done extensive archival research and interviews on the Pakistani program.

21. Reiss, *Bridled Ambition.*

22. Leonard S. Spector, *Nuclear Proliferation Today* (New York: Random House, 1984); Leonard S. Spector, *The Undeclared Bomb* (Cambridge, Mass.: Ballinger, 1988); Leonard S. Spector, *Nuclear Ambitions* (Boulder, Colo.: Westview Press, 1990); Quester, *The Politics of Nuclear Proliferation.*

23. Ashok Kapur, *India's Nuclear Option* (New York: Praeger, 1976); Shyam Bhatia, *India's Nuclear Bomb* (Ghaziabad: Vikas, 1979).

24. Brahma Chellaney, *Nuclear Proliferation: The US-Indian Conflict* (New Delhi: Orient Longman, 1993).

25. Itty Abraham, *The Making of the Indian Atomic Bomb,* (London: Zed Books, 1998).

26. Among them, G. S. Bhargava, "India's Nuclear Policy," *India Quarterly* 34, no. 2 (April–June 1978); P. R. Chari, *Indo-Pak Nuclear Standoff* (New Delhi: Manohar, 1995); Chari, Cheema, and Iftekharuzzaman, *Nuclear Non-Proliferation in India and Pakistan: South Asian Perspectives*; Brahma Chellaney, "The Challenge of Nuclear Arms Control in South Asia," *Survival* 35, no. 3 (Autumn 1993); Brahma Chellaney, "South Asia's Passage to Nuclear Power," *International Security* 16, no. 1 (Summer 1991); Neil Joeck, "Nuclear Proliferation and National Security in India and Pakistan," unpublished manuscript, Berkeley, Calif., 1986; Onkar Marwah, "India's Nuclear and Space Programs: Intent and Policy," *International Security* 2, no. 2 (Fall 1977); G. G. Mirchandani, *India's Nuclear Dilemma* (New Delhi: Popular Book Services, 1968); Brigadier Vijai K. Nair (ret.), *Nuclear India* (New Delhi: Lancer International, 1992); A. G. Noorani, "Indo-U.S. Nuclear Relations," *Asian Survey* 21, no. 4 (April 1981); Shrikant Paranjpe, *US Nonproliferation Policy in Action: South Asia* (New Delhi: Sterling, 1987);

K. K. Pathak, *Nuclear Policy of India* (New Delhi: Gitanjali Prakashan, 1980); R. L. M. Patil, *India—Nuclear Weapons and International Politics* (Delhi: National, 1969); T. T. Poulose, ed., *Perspectives of India's Nuclear Policy* (New Delhi: Young Asia, 1978); T. T. Poulose, ed., *Nuclear Proliferation and the Third World* (New Delhi: ABC, 1982); Paul F. Power, "The Indo-American Nuclear Controversy," *Asian Survey* 19, no. 6 (June 1979); N. Ram, "India's Nuclear Policy," paper prepared for the Thirty-fourth Annual Meeting of the Association of Asian Studies, April 2–4, 1982, Chicago; Bhabani Sen Gupta, *Nuclear Weapons? Policy Options for India* (New Delhi: Sage Publications India, 1983); N. Seshagiri, *The Bomb! Fallout of India's Nuclear Explosion* (Delhi: Vikas, 1975); Sampooran Singh, *India and the Nuclear Bomb* (New Delhi: S. Chand & Co., 1971); *Institute for Defence Studies and Analyses Journal* 3 (July 1970); Roberta Wohlstetter, *"The Buddha Smiles": Absent-Minded Peaceful Aid and the Indian Bomb* (Los Angeles: Pan Heuristics, 1977).

27. Mirchandani, *India's Nuclear Dilemma,* is an exception in this regard.

28. *Atomic Energy Act, 1962,* art. 3(c).

29. In separate interviews, four former chairmen of the Indian Atomic Energy Commission and a former minister of state in the Ministry of Defence all made this point about the lack of informative files and the reliance on oral instructions.

CHAPTER ONE

1. T. T. Poulose, "India's Nuclear Policy," in Poulose, *Perspectives of India's Nuclear Policy,* p. 102.

2. Demands for Grants, *Lok Sabha Debates,* 2d ser., July 24, 1957, col. 4954. Among other statements see also Nehru's New Delhi press conference of September 17, 1961:

> We are opposed to atomic bombs, hydrogen bombs, and all that breed. That is not an empty statement for us to make because we will be in a position—we have the competence and the equipment—to make them. Yet, we have said we will not go that way at all. If we had tried hard enough we might have made them. We are probably apart from the three big countries, among two or three others which are so advanced in this matter—maybe one or two countries in Europe and one or two in Asia. We have deliberately said we will not make them.

3. Chellaney, *Nuclear Proliferation: The U.S.-Indian Conflict,* p. 9; Kapur, *India's Nuclear Option,* p. 107.

4. Dorothy Newman, ed., *Nehru: The First 60 Years,* vol. 2 (New York: John Day, 1965), p. 264.

5. See P. N. Haksar, *India's Foreign Policy and Its Problems* (New Delhi: Patriot, 1989), p. 98; Nehru's speech, "The Plan Is the Country's Defence," March 21, 1956, in *Jawaharlal Nehru's Speeches,* vol. 3 (Delhi: Ministry of Information and Broadcasting, 1958), pp. 38–43.

6. Interview by author, January 23, 1996, New Delhi.

7. Cited in Francine R. Frankel, *India's Political Economy, 1947–1977* (Princeton, N.J.: Princeton University Press, 1978), p. 3.

8. The other two sectors put under government monopoly were the manufacture of arms and ammunition and the railways. Ibid., p. 77.

9. *Jawaharlal Nehru's Speeches,* vol. 1, September 1946–May 1949 (Delhi: Ministry of Information and Broadcasting, 1949), pp. 24–25; Nehru cited in Pathak, *Nuclear Policy of India,* p. 5.

10. Interview by author with former Atomic Energy Commission engineer, August 1997.

11. Robert S. Anderson, "Building Scientific Institutions in India: Saha and Bhabha," Occasional Paper No. 11, Centre for Developing-Area Studies, McGill University, Montreal, Canada, 1975, p. 14. The scholar Itty Abraham posited that in the early 1940s Bhabha deduced that these and other scientists were secretly working on a nuclear weapon project when he stopped receiving replies from them to his mail. Bhabha then made a list of scientists he would have gathered if he were trying to make an atomic bomb and compared this list with the list of now-quiet correspondents. The lists overlapped extensively, leading Bhabha to conclude that his international colleagues were engaged in a secret bomb-building effort. Electronic correspondence with the author, September 21, 1995.

12. Anderson, "Building Scientific Institutions in India," p. 31.

13. Sir John Cockcroft, "Homi Jehangir Bhabha, 1909–1966," pt. 4, *Proceedings of the Royal Institution* 41, no. 191 (1967): p. 412.

14. Mirchandani, *India's Nuclear Dilemma*, p. 223.

15. The quote appears in M. G. K. Menon, "Homi Jehangir Bhabha, 1909–1966," pt. 5, *Proceedings of the Royal Institution* 41, no. 191 (1967): p. 428.

16. Wohlstetter, *"The Buddha Smiles,"* p. 20.

17. Menon, "Homi Jehangir Bhabha, 1909–1966," p. 428.

18. For examples, see G. Venkataraman, *Bhabha and His Magnificent Obsessions* (Hyderabad: Universities Press India, 1994).

19. Menon, "Homi Jehangir Bhabha, 1909–1966," p. 429.

20. Bhabha's aristocratic nature and spending habits exacerbated tensions between himself and important left-leaning figures such as Krishna Menon and the physicist Meghnad Saha. Former high-ranking Indian defense scientist, interview by author, April 1997.

21. Venkataraman, *Bhabha and His Magnificent Obsessions*, p. 178. According to Venkataraman, Indira Gandhi told an Indian audience in 1968 that she and her father met Bhabha when they were all traveling on the same ship in 1937.

22. In the United States, the authors of the Acheson-Lilienthal plan and other leading Manhattan Project scientists initially downplayed the importance of nuclear power for nonmilitary applications, recognizing the weapons proliferation problem and the fact that the United States had abundant alternative sources of electricity. For a good summary of the American debate over nuclear power in this period, see P. M. S. Blackett, *Fear, War, and the Bomb: Military and Political Consequences of Atomic Energy* (New York: Whittlesey House, 1949), pp. 102–108.

23. See, for example, Meghnad Saha, "Science in Social and International Planning, With Special Reference to India," *Nature*, February 24, 1945, pp. 221–224; Blackett, *Fear, War, and the Bomb*, p. 106.

24. For early analyses of costs, technological challenges, and implications of nuclear power, see Sam H. Schurr, "Economic Aspects of Atomic Energy as a Source of Power," *Bulletin of Atomic Scientists* 3, no. 4–5 (April–May 1947): p. 125, and David Lilienthal, "Atomic Energy and American Industry," *Bulletin of Atomic Scientists* 3, no. 11 (November 1947): p. 339.

25. *Constituent Assembly of India (Legislative Debates)*, 2d sess., vol. 5, April 6, 1948, p. 3315.

26. Ibid., p. 3323.

27. Itty Abraham, "Towards a Reflexive South Asian Security Studies," in *South Asia Approaches the Millennium*, ed. Marvin G. Weinbaum and Chetan Kumar (Boulder, Colo.: Westview Press, 1995), p. 34.

28. *Constituent Assembly of India (Legislative Debates)*, vol. 5, April 6, 1948, p. 3323.

29. Ibid., p. 3324.

30. Ibid., p. 3328.

31. Ibid., pp. 3332–3333, emphasis added.

32. Ibid., pp. 3333–3334, emphasis added.

33. Abraham, *The Making of the Indian Atomic Bomb*, p. 61.

34. Anderson, "Building Scientific Institutions in India," pp. 2, 33.

35. Ibid., p. 40.

36. Ibid.

37. Ibid. See also George Greenstein, "A Gentleman of the Old School: Homi Bhabha and the Development of Science in India," *American Scholar* 61 (Summer 1992): pp. 409–419.

38. Greenstein records that Bhabha in his correspondence addressed Nehru as "My Dear Bhai," which translates in this context as "My Dear Brother." Nehru addressed Bhabha, "My Dear Homi." "A Gentleman of the Old School," p. 418.

39. Bhatia, *India's Nuclear Bomb*, p. 43.

40. Ibid., p. 88.

41. Abraham, *The Making of the Indian Atomic Bomb*, pp. 78–81.

42. McMahon, *The Cold War on the Periphery*, p. 181.

43. Ibid., p. 182.

44. Ibid., p. 24. When India and Pakistan became independent in 1947, the princely state of Jammu and Kashmir consisted of a majority Muslim population ruled by a Hindu maharajah. The maharajah chose to accede neither to India nor Pakistan at the time of partition, and the English governor-general, Lord Mountbatten, could not resolve the matter. In the fall of 1947, five thousand tribesmen from Pakistan's Northwest Frontier Province captured several towns in Jammu and Kashmir. To obtain military assistance from India to rebuff the incursion, the maharajah had to sign an Instrument of Accession to India, which he did on October 26, 1947. While India argued with some cause that the accession was legal, Pakistan disputed it. Pakistan cited that India provided an assurance that "the question of accession should be decided in accordance with the wishes of the people of the State [and this could be] settled by a reference to the people." This was taken to mean a plebiscite, despite later Indian protestations that no such specific mechanism was agreed on to determine the wishes of the people of Jammu and Kashmir. See A. Appadorai and M. S. Rajan, *India's Foreign Policy and Relations* (New Delhi: South Asian Publishers Private, 1985), pp. 80–81, 94; quotation taken from p. 80.

Events continued with Pakistan dispatching regular forces into Jammu and Kashmir to solidify a hold on the western part of the state. India countered with army troops, and war ensued. Ultimately the United Nations brokered an agreement to end the fighting. Two resolutions—one of August 13, 1948, the second of January 6, 1949—called for a cease-fire, a truce, and a plebiscite. The cease-fire was effected as of January 1, 1949. The truce has not been formally implemented to this day. Nor has a plebiscite been held.

45. McMahon, *The Cold War on the Periphery*, p. 64.

46. Ibid., p. 69.

47. Cable from Dulles sent by Consulate General Istanbul to the State Department, May 26, 1953, cited in Kux, *Estranged Democracies*, p. 106.

48. Minutes of June 1, 1953, NSC meeting, cited in Kux, *Estranged Democracies*, p. 106.

49. McMahon, *The Cold War on the Periphery*, p. 168.

50. Sarvepalli Gopal, *Jawaharlal Nehru, A Biography*, vol. 2 (London: Jonathan Cape, 1979), p. 184.

51. Nehru to his chief ministers, November 15, 1953, *Jawaharlal Nehru: Letters to Chief Ministers*, vol. 3 (New Delhi: Jawaharlal Nehru Memorial Fund, 1986), p. 441, cited in Kux, *Estranged Democracies*, p. 109.

52. Ibid.

53. As Robert McMahon noted, however, "the strategic vision that animated U.S. plans for Pakistan remained curiously inchoate and inconsistent." U.S. officials did not and could not say precisely how a weak and tumultuous Pakistan could help stabilize the Middle East or prevent Soviet incursions southwards. McMahon, *The Cold War on the Periphery*, p. 175.

54. Kux, *Estranged Democracies*, p. 111.

55. Appadorai and Rajan, *India's Foreign Policy and Relations*, p. 229.

56. Kux, *Estranged Democracies*, p. 114.

57. "The Plan Is the Country's Defence," March 21, 1956, in *Jawaharlal Nehru's Speeches*, vol. 3, p. 40.

58. Ibid.

59. Ibid., p. 41.

60. Ibid.

61. Eisenhower, speech to the General Assembly of the United Nations, December 8, 1953, White House Press Office.

62. "Control of Nuclear Energy," speech to the Lok Sabha, May 10, 1954, in *Jawaharlal Nehru's Speeches*, vol. 3, p. 254.

63. Ibid., p. 255.

64. Ibid., p. 257.

65. Krishna Menon, statements to the First Committee of the United Nations, November 17, 22-23, 1954, reprinted in J. P. Jain, *Nuclear India*, vol. 2 (New Delhi: Radiant, 1974), pp. 4-12.

66. The Indian draft read as follows:

> That the inspection and safeguard provisions should be reasonable and ensure that any aid given by the Agency is not used directly for furthering a military purpose. The inspection and safeguards should not, however, be so rigorous as to give the Agency a hold on the economic life of the country through control of fissionable material or lead to the development of an unhealthy situation in which States in the world receiving aid from the Agency are put into a different class from those who do not go to the Agency for aid.

From a statement by Prime Minister Nehru in reply to a question in the Lok Sabha, May 4, 1956, in ibid., pp. 37-38.

67. Bhabha developed the three-phase plan between late 1954 and its formal acceptance in 1958. See Venkataraman, *Bhabha and His Magnificent Obsessions*, p. 158; Wohlstetter, *"The Buddha Smiles,"* p. 56.

68. Abraham, *The Making of the Indian Atomic Bomb*, p. 73.

69. Ibid., p. 74.

70. Raja Ramanna, *Years of Pilgrimage* (New Delhi: Viking Penguin Books India, 1991), p. 61. For a full and insightful treatment of this conference see Abraham, *The Making of the Indian Atomic Bomb*, pp. 74-75.

71. Ramanna, *Years of Pilgrimage*, p. 61.

72. Homi J. Bhabha, "The Role of Atomic Power in India and Its Immediate Possibilities," paper submitted to the First International Conference on the Peaceful Uses of Atomic Energy, August 1955, in Jain, *Nuclear India*, vol. 2, p. 17.

73. Statement by Bhabha in 1953, quoted in Wohlstetter, *"The Buddha Smiles,"* p. 39.

74. Statement by Bhabha at the First International Conference on the Peaceful Uses of Atomic Energy, August 1955, in Jain, *Nuclear India*, vol. 2, p. 21. See also Bhabha's statement at the Second IAEA General Conference, September 26, 1958, in ibid., p. 87.

75. Ibid.

76. Abraham, *The Making of the Indian Atomic Bomb*, p. 85.

77. The Colombo Plan was an initiative by the wealthier Commonwealth nations to aid the development of poorer Commonwealth states in South and Southeast Asia. The U.S. contribution was heavy water to moderate the reactor.

78. The Canadian-Indian agreement on nuclear cooperation was signed on April 28, 1956, calling for Canada to supply half of the initial natural uranium fuel and India the rest. India's preference for natural uranium fuel is often explained by an ideological determination to remain self-sufficient. Yet, as the former chairman of the Indian AEC, Homi Sethna, told the author in a January 29, 1996, interview in Mumbai, "The basic reason we chose the Canadian technology was that we didn't have enough foreign exchange. It had nothing to do with ideology. We had to choose this technology and fabricate our own fuel because we couldn't afford to do it any other way." In their first supply relationship, the United States in 1956 agreed to sell India 18.9 metric tonnes of heavy water. This agreement, like the Canadian-Indian agreement, had no formal safeguards, reflecting the relative American insensitivity to proliferation risks. This would cause controversy in 1974 when the plutonium used in India's nuclear test was recognized to have been produced in the CIRUS reactor moderated by U.S.-supplied heavy water. See Chellaney, *Nuclear Proliferation: The US-Indian Conflict*, p. 6.

79. Abraham, *The Making of the Indian Atomic Bomb*, p. 121.

80. Other reactor technologies and fuels, such as light-water reactors, produce relatively little plutonium-239, and instead produce higher quantities of plutonium-240, a reactor-grade fuel that, while explosive, is not preferred for weapons use.

81. Wohlstetter, *"The Buddha Smiles,"* p. 55.

82. Ibid., pp. 63–64, and Homi Sethna, interview by author, February 26, 1997, Mumbai. Sethna added that India overbuilt the plant in terms of scale and safety features:

> Normally you engineer something 2 to 3 times over the safety margin. We put the safety factor at this plant to 8 to 10 times greater so that even if we made glaring mistakes it wouldn't show up. We did make some boo-boos, but this is to be expected. The biggest problem was not to achieve criticality in the plant [from having too much plutonium too close together in a neutron-slowing solution, which could engender a spontaneous chain reaction]. We didn't know what quantity would achieve criticality—those numbers weren't available in the literature— so we were super safe. We never kept more than 500 grams together.

83. Article XII of the draft IAEA statute, in Jain, *Nuclear India*, vol. 2, p. 38.

84. Statement by Bhabha at the Conference on the IAEA Statute, September 27, 1956, in ibid., p. 44.

85. IAEA Statute, Article XII (A.5), signed October 23, 1956, in ibid., p. 78.

86. Statement by Bhabha at the Conference on the IAEA Statute, October 22, 1956, in ibid. p. 72.

87. Bhabha, September 27, 1956, statement at the Conference on the IAEA Statute, in ibid., p. 44.

88. Glenn Seaborg, interview by author, June 17, 1996.

89. Bhabha, September 27, 1956, statement at the Conference on the IAEA Statute, in Jain, *Nuclear India*, vol. 2, pp. 45–46.

90. Bhatia, *India's Nuclear Bomb*, p. 101.

91. In 1958 the Atomic Energy Commission would be restructured and empowered to set and execute policy without seeking assent of the cabinet.

92. State Department, memorandum of conversation, February 3, 1956, *Foreign Relations of the United States, 1955–1957*, vol. 20 (Washington, D.C.: Government Printing Office), p. 308.

93. Secretary of Defense to the Secretary of State, memorandum, February 24, 1956, ibid., p. 347.

94. State Department, memorandum of conversation, February 3, 1956, ibid., p. 309.

95. Wohlstetter, *"The Buddha Smiles,"* p. 30.

96. The number of Indian scientists and engineers appeared in ibid., p. 28. The reference to Indian use of declassified U.S. Purex reprocessing plans appeared in ibid., p. 63. In addition, Canada trained 263 Indian scientists and engineers prior to 1971. Anderson, "Building Scientific Institutions in India," p. 101.

97. Wohlstetter, *"The Buddha Smiles,"* p. 32. The proposal to supply India with heavy water was made just in case India's own Nangal heavy-water plant failed to operate sufficiently. This turned out to be the case.

98. Smith, memorandum for file, September 14, 1955, *Foreign Relations of the United States, 1955–1957*, vol. 20, p. 1981, cited in Peter A. Clausen, *Nonproliferation and the National Interest* (New York: HarperCollins College, 1993), p. 34.

99. Lewis Strauss to President Eisenhower, August 30, 1956, p. 2, Joint Committee on Atomic Energy files, International Affairs, India, National Archives.

100. As the U.S. Representative for International Atomic Energy Agency Negotiations, Ambassador Morehead Patterson, told the Atomic Industrial Forum in April 1955, "In underdeveloped areas the availability of atomic power will not ease the basic problem of finding capital for economic development." Wohlstetter, *"The Buddha Smiles,"* p. 38.

101. M. R. Srinivasan, "An Appraisal of India's Civil Nuclear Power Programme," paper presented at the Asia Society and the Japan Institute of International Affairs conference on Civilian Nuclear Power and Technology, New York, June 19–21, 1996, p. 2. Srinivasan was the chairman of the Indian Atomic Energy Commission from 1987 to 1990.

102. I. M. D. Little, "Atomic Bombay? A Comment on 'The Need for Atomic Energy in the Underdeveloped Countries,' " *Economic and Political Weekly* (Bombay), November 29, 1958, p. 1483, cited in Wohlstetter, *"The Buddha Smiles,"* pp. 46–47.

103. Thomas W. Graham, "The Economics of Producing Nuclear Weapons in *N*th Countries," in *Strategies for Managing Proliferation: Economics and Political Issues*, ed., Dagobert L. Brito, Michael D. Intriligator, and Adele E. Wickes (Lexington, Mass.: Lexington Books, 1983), p. 15.

104. Bhabha said at the Second IAEA General Conference, September 26, 1958, "that a nuclear power station of 150 or even 250 MW could be installed [in the Bombay grid] and could without difficulty be operated at a high load factor." in Jain, *Nuclear India*, vol. 2, p.87.

Wohlstetter, *"The Buddha Smiles,"* p. 48, cited Bhabha's use of the 80 percent load factor assumption.

105. By comparison, American and European reactors typically now operate at 75–80 percent load factors, although this rate was achieved slower than had been advertised and planned.

106. K. S. Jayaraman, "Cash Crisis Halts Nuclear Power in India," *Nature* March 21, 1996, p. 188.

107. Rahul Tongia and V. S. Arunachalum, "India's Nuclear Breeders: Technology, Viability, and Options," *Current Science* 75, no. 6 (September 25, 1998): pp. 549–558.

108. Anderson, "Building Scientific Institutions in India," p. 69. In March 1958 Bhabha announced the formation of a new Atomic Energy Commission to replace the body established in 1948. Now, with Bhabha as chair, the commission had full executive and financial powers to formulate and implement policies for the Department of Atomic Energy and to prepare the department's annual budget, all subject to the approval of the prime minister. The chairman had final power to formulate and implement policy, except where finances were concerned; if he differed with the commissioner responsible for finances, the matter would be submitted to the prime minister for resolution. Bhatia, *India's Nuclear Bomb,* p. 100.

109. *Lok Sabha Debates,* 2d ser., July 24, 1957, col. 4949.

110. Abraham, "India's 'Strategic Enclave': Civilian Scientists and Military Technologies," p. 242, citing research and development statistics, Department of Science and Technology, Government of India.

111. Bhabha, statement at the Third IAEA General Conference, September 25, 1959, in Jain, *Nuclear India,* vol. 2, p. 91.

112. In the 1957 Lok Sabha election, the Congress party won 75 percent of the seats, with 47 percent of the vote, and controlled every state but Kerala, where the Communist Party won. Indian Institute of Public Opinion, "The Indian People in Transition, March 1975 to March 1977," *Monthly Public Opinion Surveys* 22, nos. 5–6, April–May 1977, p. 3.

113. Ibid.

114. Nehru quoted in Mirchandani, *India's Nuclear Dilemma,* p. 230.

115. Ibid.

116. *Lok Sabha Debates,* 2d ser., July 24, 1957, col. 4954.

117. Ibid.

118. Menon, "Homi Jehangir Bhabha, 1905–1966," p. 434.

119. Bertrand Goldschmidt, *The Atomic Complex* (La Grange Park, Ill.: American Nuclear Society, 1982), p. 185.

120. Mirchandani, *India's Nuclear Dilemma,* p. 231.

121. India would not begin constructing the facility required to separate plutonium that could in turn be used in a bomb until 1961. Additionally, projected timelines like this simply seemed to assume with no experiential basis that all necessary design work and component construction would fall into place easily.

122. Bhatia, *India's Nuclear Bomb,* p. 114.

123. Cockcroft, "Homi Jehangir Bhabha, 1905–1966," p. 421. Cockcroft did not provide a specific date for Bhabha's private remarks but seemed to indicate they were in the early 1960s.

124. Glenn T. Seaborg, *Stemming the Tide* (Lexington, Mass.: Lexington Books, 1987), p. 309. This program was first put under the auspices of the Livermore National Laboratory's Division of Military Application, reflecting the fact that peaceful nuclear explosives and weapons used essentially the same technology. In 1961, a separate Division of Peaceful

Nuclear Explosives was created for public relations purposes to distinguish between military and peaceful uses of atomic energy.

125. Ibid., p. 310.

126. Seshagiri, *The Bomb! Fallout of India's Nuclear Explosion*, p. 85.

127. Kenneth D. Nichols, *The Road to Trinity* (New York: Morrow, 1987), p. 9.

128. Ibid., p. 351.

129. Ibid.

130. Ibid.

131. Ibid., p. 352.

132. Nichols acknowledged this but pointed out that the Indians ultimately contracted with Westinghouse's rival, General Electric. Ibid.

133. The reactor went critical in 1972, moderated with heavy water from Canada, the United States, and the Soviet Union. Sometimes the acronym RAPP is used for the two power plants at this site (Rajasthan Atomic Power Plant).

134. "Setting Up Nuclear Power Plant," *Statesman*, February 3, 1961, p. 1.

135. Ibid.

136. H. Venkatasubbiah, "Atomic Power Programme," *Hindu*, February 3, 1961, p. 1.

137. Ibid.

138. "India's Drive for Atomic Power," *Times of India*, August 20, 1961.

139. "What Price Power," *Hindustan Times*, August 23, 1961.

140. Ibid.

141. Ibid.

142. "Misplaced," *Times of India*, March 29, 1961.

143. Some parliamentarians did express concerns about the cost of the nuclear program. But in an August 10, 1960, Lok Sabha discussion of the annual report of the Department of Atomic Energy, Nehru rebuffed them, saying India would be able to produce nuclear power more cheaply than the United States or the United Kingdom. "I think no other department of the Government of India has had this unanimous appreciation," he concluded. See *Jawaharlal Nehru's Speeches*, vol. 4, September 1957–April 1963 (Delhi: Government of India, Ministry of Information and Broadcasting, 1964), pp. 435–440.

144. Leonard Beaton and John Maddox, *The Spread of Nuclear Weapons* (New York: Praeger, 1962, for Institute for Strategic Studies), p. 144.

145. Mirchandani, *India's Nuclear Dilemma*, p. 235.

146. H. Venkatasubbiah, "Atomic Power Programme," *Hindu*, February 3, 1961, p. 1.

147. Pathak, *Nuclear Policy of India*, p. 30.

148. Abraham, *The Making of the Indian Atomic Bomb*, pp. 114–120.

149. Mirchandani, *India's Nuclear Dilemma*, pp. 15–16.

150. Kux, *Estranged Democracies*, p. 192.

151. Frankel, *India's Political Economy*, p. 158.

152. Bhatia, *India's Nuclear Bomb*, p. 115.

153. Ibid., pp. 117–118.

154. Quoted in ibid., p. 118.

155. M. J. Akbar, *Nehru: The Making of India* (London: Viking Penguin Group, 1988), no references to Bhabha or atomic energy; Michael Brecher, *Nehru, A Political Biography* (London: Oxford University Press, 1959), one reference to the Department of Atomic Energy; Sarvepalli Gopal, *Jawaharlal Nehru: A Biography*, vol. 2, 1947–1956 (London: Jonathan Cape, 1979), two mentions of Bhabha, none of atomic energy or nuclear weapons; vol. 3,

1956–1964 (London: Jonathan Cape, 1984), one mention of the AEC, three footnote references to Bhabha, and no references to nuclear weapons; Frank Moraes, *Jawaharlal Nehru: A Biography* (New York: Macmillan, 1956), no significant discussion of atomic energy; Stanley Wolpert, *Nehru: A Tryst with Destiny* (New York: Oxford University Press, 1996), two references to Bhabha, one to atomic energy.

156. The former high-ranking Indian official P. N. Haksar wrote, "For India, at any rate, the problems of foreign policy in the coming years are essentially the problems of a domestic nature. An incoherent country cannot pursue a coherent foreign policy." Haksar, *India's Foreign Policy and Its Problems*, p. 98.

157. *Constituent Assembly of India (Legislative Debates)*, vol. 2, no. 5, December 4, 1947, p. 1260.

158. Appadorai and Rajan, *India's Foreign Policy and Relations*, p. 262.

159. Ibid., p. 264.

160. Quoted in Ibid., p. 266.

161. Quoted in Ibid., p. 267. This statement was particularly ironic in light of regular Indian attacks on U.S. policies toward Pakistan in precisely the zero-sum terms Nehru disparaged here.

162. Ibid., p. 273.

163. Memorandum of conversation between AEC Chairman John McCone and V. S. Emelyanov, November 19, 1960, in *U.S. Nuclear Non-Proliferation Policy, 1945–91*, ed. Foran, no. 00701.

164. Nehru reportedly told his intelligence staff in 1952 that all Indian resources would be required to defend a hostile frontier with China. Ibid., p. 49.

165. A. Appadorai, ed., *Select Documents on India's Foreign Policy and Relations, 1947–1972*, vol. 1 (Delhi: Oxford University Press, 1982), p. 459.

166. Appadorai and Rajan, *India's Foreign Policy and Relations*, p. 116.

167. Tariq Ali, *An Indian Dynasty: The Story of the Nehru-Gandhi Family* (New York: G. P. Putnam's Sons, 1985), p. 99.

168. Appadorai and Rajan, *India's Foreign Policy and Relations*, p. 117.

169. In 1956–1957, China built a road in one of the disputed regions, Aksai Chin in Ladakh. In 1958, Indian personnel entered the disputed region of Barahoti in Tibet. In 1959, Chinese troops crossed into the third disputed area, near the village of Longju in northeast India. Ibid., p. 121.

170. In 1959, China apparently proposed a deal whereby India would waive its claim on Aksai Chin in the northwest and China would grant India's position regarding the disputed eastern territory. Nehru reportedly declared, "If I give them that, I shall no longer be Prime Minister of India—I will not do it." Ibid., p. 127. Ironically, in 1996, according to Sunil Dasgupta, an *India Today* editor, "India's efforts to normalize the border issue with China resolves [sic] around giving up Indian claims on Aksai Chin in the northwest in return from some concessions in the northeast," the essence of the arrangment Nehru turned down in 1959. Sunil Dasgupta, "Economic Engagement in South Asia: Towards an Effective Nonproliferation Policy," draft manuscript, April 1996, p. 23.

171. Cohen, *The Indian Army*, p. 176.

172. Norris, Burrows, and Fieldhouse, *Nuclear Weapons Databook*, vol. 5, p. 331.

173. Ibid.

174. Mirchandani, *India's Nuclear Dilemma*, p. 12.

175. Ibid., p. 13.

176. Norris, Burrows, and Fieldhouse, *Nuclear Weapons Databook*, vol. 5, p. 332.

177. Mirchandani, *India's Nuclear Dilemma*, p. 13.

178. Ibid.

179. Ibid., p. 15.

180. Ibid., p. 17.

181. George C. McGhee to the Secretary of State, memorandum, "Anticipatory Action Pending Chinese Communist Demonstration of a Nuclear Capability," September 13, 1961, Nuclear Non-Proliferation Freedom of Information Act (FOIA) files, India, National Security Archive, Washington, D.C.

182. Appadorai and Rajan, *India's Foreign Policy and Relations*, p. 137.

183. Kux, *Estranged Democracies*, p. 203.

184. Quoted in Ibid., p. 204.

185. M. Y. Prozumenschikov, "The Sino-Indian Conflict, the Cuban Missile Crisis, and the Sino-Soviet Split, October 1962: New Evidence from the Russian Archives," *Cold War International History Project Bulletin*, nos. 8–9 (Winter 1996/1997): p. 251.

186. Ibid., p. 252, quoting official Soviet document.

187. Ibid., p. 253.

188. Ibid., p. 254.

189. Ibid., p. 255.

190. Ibid., p. 265, citing *Pravda*, November 5, 1962.

191. Kux, *Estranged Democracies*, p. 207.

192. China still occupies 14,000 square miles captured in 1962. Sumit Ganguly, correspondence with the author, December 14, 1996.

193. Quoted in Steven A. Hoffmann, *India and the China Crisis* (Berkeley and Los Angeles: University of California Press, 1990), p. 165.

194. Ibid., pp. 225–226.

195. McMahon, *The Cold War on the Periphery*, pp. 290–297.

196. Hoffmann, *India and the China Crisis*, pp. 223, 230.

197. The leading pro-bomb force in Indian politics, the Jana Sangh later became the Bharatiya Janata Party.

198. Quoted in Mirchandani, *India's Nuclear Dilemma*, p. 22. Nehru offered a more robust, albeit indirect, indication of how India must develop its strength when he told the Standing Committee of the National Development Council on January 18, 1963, "War is undoubtedly governed by [scientific advance]. It is not governed by Rajput chivalry; Rajput chivalry is very good; it gives spirit to the man but it is not real war. Real war is governed by scientific advance." Among other things, Nehru clearly had in mind advances in atomic energy know-how and capabilities. *Jawaharlal Nehru's Speeches*, vol. 4, September 1957–April 1963, p. 164.

199. Bhatia, *India's Nuclear Bomb*, pp. 108–109.

200. Quoted in Mirchandani, *India's Nuclear Dilemma*, p. 23.

201. An extremely brief summary of the Kashmir dispute's origins appears in note 44 of this chapter.

202. MacMahon, *The Cold War on the Periphery*, p. 266.

203. Ibid., p. 300.

204. Ibid., p. 297.

205. Ibid., p. 308.

206. Kux, Estranged Democracies, p. 154, citing *Foreign Relations of the United States, 1955–1957*, vol. 8, pp. 25–27.

207. Kux, ibid., p. 154.

208. U.S. National Security Council, Operations Coordinating Board, memorandum, "Outline Plan of Operations with Respect to India and Nepal," February 27, 1957, p. 1, in *U.S. Nuclear Non-Proliferation Policy, 1945–1991,* ed. Virginia I. Foran (Alexandria, Va.: National Security Archive/Chadwyck-Healey, 1991), no. 00290.

209. Ibid., p. 2.

210. Ibid.

211. Ibid., p. 16.

212. Ibid.

213. Kux, *Estranged Democracies,* pp. 146–148. Bilateral U.S. aid to India grew from $92.8 million in 1956 to $364.8 million in 1957, compared with $162.5 million and $170.7 million respectively for Pakistan. McMahon, *The Cold War on the Periphery,* p. 258.

214. Kux, *Estranged Democracies,* p. 149.

215. Ibid., p. 166.

216. Ibid.

217. Ibid., p. 167.

218. Ibid., pp. 167–168.

219. Ibid., pp. 168–169.

220. Ibid., p. 169, quoting letter from Assistant Secretary of State G. Lewis Jones to Ambassador Ellsworth Bunker, July 13, 1960.

221. "Setting Up Nuclear Power Plant," *Statesman,* February 3, 1961; H. Venkatasubbiah, "Atomic Power Programme," *Hindu,* February 3, 1961.

222. Wohlstetter, *"The Buddha Smiles,"* pp. 82–86.

223. Atomic Energy Commission, memorandum of record, November 13, 1959, p. 1, Joint Committee on Atomic Energy files, International Affairs, India, National Archives.

224. Ibid., p. 2.

225. Dwight A. Ink, general manager of the AEC, to John McCone, chairman of the AEC, memorandum, February 15, 1960, in Foran, *U.S. Nuclear Non-Proliferation Policy, 1945–1991,* no. 00625.

226. Secretary of State Dean Rusk to U.S. Embassies, airgram, circular CG-769, March, 3, 1961, in Foran, *U.S. Nuclear Non-Proliferation Policy, 1945–1991,* no. 00755.

227. McGhee to Rusk, "Anticipatory Action Pending Chinese Communist Demonstration of a Nuclear Capability," p. 1, September 13, 1961, FOIA files, India, National Security Archive, Washington, D.C.

228. Ibid., pp. 2–3.

229. Ibid., p. 3.

230. Ibid., p. 2.

231. Ibid., p. 2.

232. Ibid., p. 3.

233. Ibid., p. 4.

234. Ibid.

235. Ibid., p. 5.

236. Secretary of State Dean Rusk to State Department Executive Secretary Lucius Battle, memorandum, October 7, 1961, Nuclear Non-Proliferation Policy, FOIA files, India, National Security Archive, Washington, D.C.

237. Kux, *Estranged Democracies,* p. 186.

238. Quoted in Ibid., p. 190.

239. Quoted in Arthur M. Schlesinger Jr., *A Thousand Days, John F. Kennedy in the White House* (Boston: Houghton Mifflin Co., 1968), p. 526.

240. Kux, *Estranged Democracies,* p. 198.

241. John K. Galbraith, *Ambassador's Journal* (Boston: Houghton Mifflin Co., 1969), p. 327.

242. Ibid., p. 455.

243. McMahon, *The Cold War on the Periphery,* pp. 297-298, recorded that Defense Secretary Robert McNamara estimated that $150-300 million per year over three years would be manageable for the United States and adequate for India. Indian military officials, on the other hand, were seeking $1.6 billion in assistance over the same period.

244. Ibid., p. 303.

245. Agreement for Cooperation between the Government of the United States of America and the Government of India Concerning the Civil Uses of Atomic Energy, signed in Washington, August 8, 1963, and entered into force October 25, 1963, Article VII, reprinted in Chellaney, *Nuclear Proliferation,* pp. 318-327.

246. Chellaney, *Nuclear Proliferation,* p. 26.

247. Ibid., p. 17.

248. Ibid.

249. Quoted in Wohlstetter, *"The Buddha Smiles,"* p. 86.

250. Ibid., p. 87.

251. Ibid.

252. Secretary of Defense to the President, memorandum, "The Diffusion of Nuclear Weapons with and without a Test Ban Agreement," February 12, 1963, p. 1, in Foran, *U.S. Nuclear Non-Proliferation Policy, 1945-1991,* no. 00941. This memo pointed out importantly that delivery systems incur by far the greatest costs in producing usable nuclear weapons and that a "small force" deployed on aircraft and medium-range missiles "would cost around two billion dollars."

253. Ibid., p. 2.

254. Ibid., attachment.

255. Ibid., p. 4.

256. Ibid., p. 3, emphasis added.

257. Ibid.

258. Mirchandani, *India's Nuclear Dilemma,* p. 240.

CHAPTER TWO

1. Homi J. Bhabha, "The Implications of a Wider Dispersal of Military Power for World Security and the Problem of Safeguards," in *Proceedings of the Twelfth Pugwash Conference on Science and World Affairs,* January 27-February 1, 1964, Udaipur, India, p. 75.

2. Ibid.

3. Ibid., pp. 75-76. Bhabha's case would have been even stronger if China had nuclear weapons.

4. Ibid., p. 76.

5. Ibid., p. 77.

6. Ibid., p. 78.

7. Ibid.

8. Ibid., pp. 78–79.

9. Statement by Bhabha at the Conference on the IAEA Statute, September 27, 1956, in Jain, *Nuclear India*, pp. 45–46.

10. See Kapur, *India's Nuclear Option*, p. 193.

11. Mitchell Reiss, *Without the Bomb: The Politics of Nuclear Proliferation* (New York: Columbia University Press, 1988), pp. 206–207.

12. This was agreed to by President Johnson on February 8, 1964. Kux, *Estranged Democracies*, p. 229.

13. Ibid., pp. 229–231.

14. Ibid., p. 230.

15. Mirchandani, *India's Nuclear Dilemma*, p. 242.

16. Kapur, *India's Nuclear Option*, pp. 193–194. Kapur did not cite his source for Nehru's marginal note. Nevertheless, it is consistent with Nehru's views described in chapter 1.

17. Frankel, *India's Political Economy*, p. 242.

18. Ibid., pp. 241–243.

19. Pathak, *Nuclear Policy of India*, p. 39.

20. India was operating the reactor at low burn-up rates, maximizing the quantity of weapon-grade plutonium in the spent fuel.

21. Homi J. Bhabha, "Development of Atomic Energy in India," All India Radio address, August 3, 1964, in Jain, *Nuclear India*, vol. 2, p. 146.

22. Ibid., pp. 147–148. The plutonium separation plant had been completed in April 1964. The Indian Department of Atomic Energy press release announcing its completion emphasized misleadingly, like Bhabha, that "[t]he plant was designed and built entirely by the staff of the Atomic Energy Establishment at Trombay." Indian DAE press release, appended to American Consulate (Bombay) to the Department of State, airgram no. A-253, April 29, 1964, p. 2, Nuclear Non-Proliferation Policy, FOIA files, India, National Security Archive, Washington, D.C. See also Donald L. Fuller (scientific attaché, American Embassy, New Delhi) to State Department, airgram no. A-964, "Trombay and Atomic Energy in India," March 16, 1965, Nuclear Non-Proliferation Policy, FOIA files, India, National Security Archive, Washington, D.C.

23. "India and the Bomb," *Statesman*, August 24, 1964.

24. Ibid.

25. Ibid.

26. Mirchandani, *India's Nuclear Dilemma*, p. 242.

27. "Bhabha: India Can Make Atom Bomb in 18 Months," *National Herald*, October 5, 1964.

28. Three weeks earlier Bhabha had told an IAEA meeting in Vienna that "India welcomed" the opportunity to conduct "atomic explosions in civil engineering works . . . so long as such explosions were subject to international supervision." Statement by Bhabha at the Eighth IAEA General Conference, September 17, 1964, in Jain, *Nuclear India*, vol. 2, p. 157.

29. Mirchandani, *India's Nuclear Dilemma*, p. 25. On October 6, India's ambassador to the United States, B. K. Nehru, asked for the U.S. secretary of state to say publicly that "India like Communist China has potential to produce nuclear weapons but as good citizen of world India has no intention of producing nuclear weapons." Nehru asked further that the United States commend India for its policy, "which contrasts with course being followed by Chicoms." State Department to U.S. Embassy (New Delhi), cable no. 744, October 6,

1964, p. 1, Nuclear Non-Proliferation Policy, FOIA files, India, National Security Archive, Washington, D.C.

30. Inder Malhotra, "India's Response to Chinese Nuclear Threat," *Statesman*, October 9, 1964.

31. Ibid.

32. Ibid.

33. Ibid.

34. Ibid.

35. U.S. Embassy (New Delhi) to State Department, cable no. 1203, October 17, 1964, p. 1, Nuclear Non-Proliferation Policy, FOIA files, India, National Security Archive, Washington, D.C.

36. Mirchandani, *India's Nuclear Dilemma*, p. 26.

37. Seaborg, *Stemming the Tide*, p. 113.

38. Quoted in ibid., pp. 115-116.

39. "Nath Pai Wants to Produce the Bomb," *Indian Express*, October 19, 1964.

40. Ibid.

41. Indira Gandhi, then minister for information and broadcasting, and Krishna Menon publicly defended Shastri's peaceful-uses-only line at this time. "India's 'Atoms for Peace Policy' Defined," *Indian Express*, October 23, 1963; " 'Folly for India to Explode Nuclear Device,' " *Patriot*, October 24, 1963.

42. *Hindustan Times*, October 19, 1964, quoted in Bhatia, *India's Nuclear Bomb*, p. 116.

43. U.S. Embassy (New Delhi) to the State Department, airgram no. A-411, "India's Nuclear Policy in the Wake of ChiCom Nuclear Detonation," October 23, 1964, in Foran, *U.S. Nuclear Non-Proliferation Policy, 1945-1991,* no. 01016.

44. Ibid.

45. U.S. Arms Control and Disarmament Agency, memorandum for members of the Committee of Principals, "Revision of Appendix 4 of the paper entitled 'The Indian Nuclear Problem: Proposed Course of Action,' dated October 13, 1964," November 19, 1964, p. 2, Nuclear Non-Proliferation Policy, FOIA files, India, National Security Archive, Washington, D.C. The revised appendix appearing in the November 19 memo (from which the quotation in the text is taken) derived from a National Intelligence Estimate approved on October 21, 1964, according to the covering letter by William C. Foster, director of the Arms Control and Disarmament Agency.

46. Ibid., pp. 1-2.

47. Homi J. Bhabha, All India Radio address, October 24, 1964, in Jain, *Nuclear India*, vol. 2, p. 159.

48. Ibid. Bhabha was using a rounded-up 5:1 rate of rupee to dollar exchange. One lakh equals 100,000 rupees, which equaled $20,000 by Bhabha's conversion and $21,500 by the then official exchange rate of 4.75 rupees to one dollar.

49. Ibid.

50. Ibid., p. 160.

51. Ibid., p. 161.

52. "A Temptation for Many—Atomic Bomb Will Cost Only 17 Lakhs: Bhabha," *Hindustan Times,* October 25, 1964; "Low Cost of Nuclear Weapons—'Temptations' to Other Nations," *Hindu*, October 27, 1964.

53. "India Urged to Produce Atom Bomb," *Times of India*, October 26, 1964.

54. Quoted in Poulose, "India's Nuclear Policy," p. 105.

55. See "India Split over Deterrent," *Guardian* (London), October 29, 1964, and "Indian Cabinet Being Urged to Test A-Bomb," *Times* (London), October 28, 1964.

56. "India & the Bomb," *Indian Express,* October 28, 1964.

57. Ibid.

58. U.S. Embassy (New Delhi) to Secretary of State, cable no. 1323, October 29, 1964, p. 1, in Foran, *U.S. Nuclear Non-Proliferation Policy 1945–1991,* no. 01031.

59. Ibid., p. 2.

60. Ibid., p. 2.

61. For a detailed analysis of this period see Frankel, *India's Political Economy,* pp. 246–266.

62. U.S. Arms Control and Disarmament Agency, National Intelligence Estimate paper, "The Indian Nuclear Problem: Proposed Course of Action," October 13, 1964, app. 3, "Economic Factors," p. 1, Nuclear Non-Proliferation Policy, FOIA files, India, National Security Archive, Washington, D.C.

63. Ibid.

64. Ibid. The analysts pointed out that additional sums could have been hidden in non-DAE accounts.

65. Frankel, *India's Political Economy,* p. 256.

66. Ibid., p. 251.

67. Ibid., p. 260.

68. Ibid.

69. Ibid., pp. 264–265.

70. U.S. Embassy (New Delhi) to Secretary of State, cable no. 1323, October 29, 1964, p. 3, Nuclear Non-Proliferation Policy, FOIA files, National Security Archive, Washington, D.C.

71. Ibid.

72. Robert Rochlin, U.S. Arms Control and Disarmament Agency, memorandum, "Comments on Non-Proliferation Background Papers of December 12, 1964," December 31, 1964, p. 2, Nuclear Non-Proliferation Policy, FOIA files, National Security Archive, Washington, D.C.

73. U.S. Embassy (New Delhi) to Secretary of State, cable no. 1323, October 29, 1964, p. 3, Nuclear Non-Proliferation Policy, FOIA files, National Security Archive, Washington, D.C. There appear to be two versions of this cable. The one cited here, bearing the same number as the earlier cited cable, is longer and more detailed.

74. Raja Ramanna, interview by the author, January 28, 1996, Bangalore.

75. U.S. Arms Control and Disarmament Agency, National Intelligence Estimate paper, "The Indian Nuclear Problem: Proposed Course of Action," October 21, 1964, revised appendix 4, p. 2, Nuclear Non-Proliferation Policy, FOIA files, India, National Security Archive, Washington, D.C. The intelligence estimate did not quantify "large number of specialists working on plutonium metallurgy."

76. Inder Malhotra, "Russia's New Rulers Silent on Chinese Bomb," *Statesman,* October 30, 1964.

77. Ibid.

78. See Gordon H. Chang, "To the Nuclear Brink: Eisenhower, Dulles, and the Quemoy-Matsu Crisis," *International Security* 12, no. 4 (Spring 1988), reprinted in *Nuclear Diplomacy and Crisis Management,* ed. Sean M. Lynn-Jones, Steven E. Miller, and Stephen Van Evera (Cambridge, Mass.: MIT Press, 1990), pp. 200–227.

79. Malhotra, "Russia's New Rulers Silent on Chinese Bomb," *Statesman,* October 30, 1964.

80. Ibid. On the same day the *Hindustan Times* ran a piece also bearing Bhabha's influence. The article listed a host of "breakthrough" accomplishments by the Atomic Energy Establishment at Trombay and concluded that "[a]lthough China's nuclear explosion has generated a psychological fear in Asia and elsewhere, the Indian atomic scientists have taken the bang in stride. Their confidence stems from the knowledge that they could have developed an atom bomb 18 months ago." This dubious claim went unchallenged, as it had been for years. "Indian Achievements in A-Energy Development," *Hindustan Times*.

81. Romesh Thapar, "In the Shadow of the Bomb," *Economic Weekly*, October 31, 1964, p. 1741.

82. Ibid.

83. Ibid.

84. Ibid.

85. Ibid.

86. Ibid.

87. Ibid.

88. Ibid., p. 1742.

89. Mirchandani, *India's Nuclear Dilemma*, p. 27.

90. Ibid., p. 27.

91. K. Rangaswami, "Leaders Reject Demand for Atom Bomb," *Hindu*, November 9, 1964, p. 1.

92. "AICC and the Bomb," *Economic Weekly*, November 14, 1964, p. 1793.

93. "AICC Keeps Rationing Issue Still Open," *Hindustan Times*, November 9, 1964, p. 1.

94. Rangaswami, "Leaders Reject Demand for Atom Bomb," p. 1.

95. Ibid.

96. Cited in "AICC and the Bomb," *Economic Weekly*, November 14, 1964, p. 1793.

97. Rangaswami, "Leaders Reject Demand for Atom Bomb," *Hindu*, p. 1.

98. Ibid., p. 8.

99. Ibid., p. 1.

100. Ibid.

101. "AICC Keeps Rationing Issue Still Open," *Hindustan Times*, November 9, 1964, p. 1.

102. "An Indian Bomb," *Times of India*, November 10, 1964. Other papers offered various additional arguments against the bomb: "A Nuclear Testing Zone in India," *Statesman*, November 11, 1964; "The Bomb," *Hindu*, November 10, 1964; "That Bomb," *Indian Express*, November 10, 1964.

103. Quoted in Bhatia, *India's Nuclear Bomb*, p. 112.

104. *Economic Weekly*, November 14, 1964, p. 1.

105. B. G. Verghese, "Atomic Energy for Peaceful Purposes—Bhabha Favours Policy," *Times of India*, November 18, 1964. Bhabha himself wrote an article that appeared in the *National Herald* on November 22 recounting Nehru's leadership of the Indian nuclear program. He concluded characteristically by saying, "If today India is in the proud position of being able to say in the face of the Chinese test explosion that she could have done the same if she wanted to, but has chosen not to, it is due entirely to the unfailing support and wise guidance given by Jawaharlal Nehru to our atomic energy programme." Bhabha did not explain how India could have conducted a nuclear test at this point. Homi Bhabha, "India's Atomic Energy Programme," *National Herald*, November 22, 1964.

Bhabha also discussed his views on nuclear issues with the Canadian high commissioner in New Delhi on November 11. According to a U.S. State Department cable relaying a Canadian official's summary of the discussion, Bhabha emphasized India's decision "to confine its nuclear program to peaceful use of nuclear energy although it could make bomb." Bhabha hoped that "China would not be given any special recognition or added status because of this accomplishment that would not at same time be given to those countries which have the capability to produce nuclear weapons but have decided not to do so." Moreover, Bhabha urged that "if admitted to UN, Communist China would not be given 5th permanent security council seat unless similar recognition were to be accorded India." U.S. Embassy (New Delhi) to State Department, cable no. 1463, November 14, 1964, pp. 2–3, Nuclear Non-Proliferation Policy, FOIA files, India, National Security Archive, Washington, D.C. In a follow-up cable two days later, the embassy added that the Canadian high commissioner had asked Bhabha whether he was considering nuclear explosives for a Plowshare program: "Bhabha replied definitely not." U.S. Embassy (New Delhi) to State Department, cable no. 1471, November 16, 1964, p. 1, Nuclear Non-Proliferation Policy, FOIA files, India, National Security Archive, Washington, D.C.

106. *Times of India*, November 18, 1964.

107. "India's Efforts to Enter N-Club," *Dawn* (Karachi), November 21, 1964. See also V. V. R. Sharma, "India's Capability to Produce Nuclear Weapons Haunts Pakistan," *Times of India*, November 9, 1964.

108. "PM Rejects Plea for Change in Atoms-for-Peace Policy," *Hindustan Times*, November 24, 1964.

109. For an inside critique of the governmental process, see Congress party MP Vidya Charan Shukla, *Lok Sabha Debates*, 3d ser., vol. 35, no. 6, November 23, 1964, col. 1338.

110. Rangaswami, "Leaders Reject Demand for Atom Bomb," *Hindu*, p. 1.

111. *Lok Sabha Debates*, November 23, 1964, col. 1295.

112. *Lok Sabha Debates*, 3d ser., vol. 35, no. 7, November 24, 1964, cols. 1534, 1553.

113. The one exception was J. B. Kripalani, a veteran Independent opposition figure who urged seeking help from the West to counter China. He doubted that Bhabha's estimate of the cost of producing a nuclear weapon was any more accurate than his claim that "atomic energy will be manufactured more cheaply than the thermal and hydraulic electricity." Moreover, he doubted that the nuclear establishment had the capacity to "experiment and manufacture an atom bomb," given its dependence on U.S. and Canadian help. Ibid., cols. 1486–1487.

114. See U. M. Trivedi, ibid., col. 1511.

115. *Lok Sabha Debates*, November 23, 1964, col. 1240.

116. Ibid., col. 1242. In fact, the Soviet Union and China were becoming bitter rivals at this time.

117. *Times of India*, November 21, 1964.

118. *Lok Sabha Debates*, November 23, 1964, col. 1280.

119. Ibid., col. 1301.

120. Ibid., col. 1309.

121. Ibid., col. 1313.

122. Ibid., col. 1320.

123. Ibid., col. 1317.

124. *Lok Sabha Debates*, November 24, 1964, cols. 1478–1479.

125. Ibid., col. 1480.

126. Ibid., col. 1481.

127. Ibid., col. 1521.

128. Ibid., cols. 1532–1533.

129. Ibid., col. 1512.

130. Ibid., col. 1513.

131. Ibid., col. 1517.

132. Stephen I. Schwartz, ed., *Atomic Audit*, (Washington, D.C.: Brookings Institution, 1998). On the question of delivery system needs and costs for India, the U.S. Arms Control and Disarmament Agency estimated in 1964 that India could procure and operate a fleet of twenty U.S. or Soviet medium-range bomber aircraft for $20 million per year, or a fleet of twenty long-range bombers (Soviet Bisons or U.S. B-52s) for $60 million per year. This estimate begged questions of the availability of these planes, the costs of training crews, and so on. U.S. Arms Control and Disarmament Agency, National Intelligence Estimate paper, "The Indian Nuclear Problem: Proposed Course of Action," October 13, 1964, app. 3, p. 2. As other government analysts noted at the time, however, such forces would be highly vulnerable on the ground and in the air, and other expensive systems would have to be developed to provide warning and command and control capabilities. See, for example, Henry S. Rowen, "The Indian Nuclear Problem," Department of Defense, background paper, December 24, 1964, pps. 3–4, Nuclear Non-Proliferation Policy, FOIA files, India, National Security Archive, Washington, D.C.

133. Mathur, *Lok Sabha Debates*, November 23, 1964, col. 1309, and also Vidya Charan Shukla, col. 1338.

134. Masani, ibid., col. 1249.

135. Lewis and Xue, *China Builds the Bomb*, p. 70.

136. Ibid., p. 108. This amounted to more than 100 percent of China's 1957 and 1958 defense budgets.

137. Mathur, *Lok Sabha Debates*, November 23, 1964, col. 1300.

138. Nath Pai's colleagues and the press ("Threat Posed by Chinese Atom Bomb," *Times of India*, November 24, 1964, p. 1) believed him to be arguing for an effort to produce nuclear weapons, but during the November 27 Lok Sabha debate he argued that he was being misinterpreted. "I never said that we should manufacture. All I pleaded was that it cannot be a policy to say that we shall not produce." *Lok Sabha Debates*, 3d. ser., vol. 35, no. 10 (November 27, 1964), col. 2297.

139. *Lok Sabha Debates*, November 23, 1964, col. 1315.

140. Ibid.

141. Ibid.

142. Ibid., col. 1318.

143. *Lok Sabha Debates*, November 24, 1964, cols. 1561–1568, translated from Hindi by Raman Srinivasan.

144. Shastri, cited and translated in Mirchandani, *India's Nuclear Dilemma*, p. 34.

145. "Atom Bomb Policy Not Inflexible, Says PM," *Hindustan Times*, November 25, 1964, p. 1.

146. It is difficult to quantify the support behind this and other positions. A U.S. Embassy airgram to the State Department dated December 31, 1964, recorded that three leading Congress party officials had separately told embassy officials that a majority of

Congress MPs supported acquisition of "the bomb." However, the report also noted that other Congress officials disagreed with this assessment. "Whatever the numerical count of the hawks may be, however, there is little doubt that they are formidable force within Congress." U.S. Embassy (New Delhi) to State Department, airgram no. A-660, "India and the Chinese Bomb: The Search for Alternatives," dated December 31, 1964, pouched January 5, 1965, p. 6, Nuclear Non-Proliferation Policy, FOIA files, India, National Security Archive, Washington, D.C.

147. For this analysis of Congress party positions, see the airgram (no. A-499) from U.S. Embassy (New Delhi) to the State Department, "[Redacted] Views on India and the Bomb," November 27, 1964, in Foran, *U.S. Nuclear Non-Proliferation Policy, 1945–1991,* no. 01050.

148. "Shastri's Stand on Bomb Issue," *Times of India,* November 27, 1964, p. 1.

149. Ibid.

150. Quoted in *National Herald,* November 28, 1966.

151. *Lok Sabha Debates,* November 27, 1964, col. 2292.

152. According to Inder Malhotra, "[T]he present pronouncements on nuclear policy are Mr. Shastri's own, based more on intuition and political instinct than on expert advice and analysis." Inder Malhotra, "Significance of Mr. Shastri's Lok Sabha Speech," *Statesman,* November 27, 1964.

153. *Lok Sabha Debates,* November 27, 1964, translated from the Hindi by Pravin Kumar.

154. "Nuclear Race Will Ruin Country's Economy—Shastri's Firm Stand: Many M.Ps. Plead for Change in Policy," *Hindu,* November 28, 1964, p. 1. American scholars, too, overlooked this shift. For example, see Frank E. Couper, "Indian Party Conflict on the Issue of Atomic Weapons," *Journal of Developing Areas* 3 (January 1969): pp. 191–206.

155. Each of these headlines appeared in November 28, 1964, editions. A few subsequent Indian commentators, however, recognized that Shastri's November 27 statement did mark an important shift in Indian policy. See, for example, Paranjpe, *US Nonproliferation Policy in Action: South Asia,* p. 21, and "Mrs. Gandhi Informs Giri of Blast," *Times of India,* May 19, 1974, p. 5.

156. "P.M. Rejects Bomb Demand," *Times of India,* November 28, 1964. According to Inder Malhotra's article "Significance of Mr. Shastri's Lok Sabha Speech," *Statesman,* November 27, 1964, Shastri after his November 24 Lok Sabha speech sent "an urgent message to Dr. Homi J. Bhabha to furnish precise estimates of nuclear costs."

157. "P.M.: Bhabha against Making A-Bomb," *National Herald,* November 28, 1964, p. 1.

158. "PM Refuses to Budge on Bomb," *Hindustan Times,* November 28, 1964.

159. Ibid.

160. However, a December 31, 1964, U.S. Embassy (New Delhi) airgram to the State Department noted "an almost universal feeling . . . that India must continue to develop her nuclear technology. While many of those urging this might not be prepared to state explicitly that such a development should be pursued against the eventuality of India's being obliged to produce a bomb of her own, it is what they mean." U.S. Embassy (New Delhi) to State Department, airgram no. A-660, "India and the Chinese Bomb: The Search for Alternatives," December 31, 1964, p. 8, Nuclear Non-Proliferation Policy, FOIA files, India, National Security Archive, Washington, D.C. This was true of the rising Congress party star K. C. Pant, for example, who recognized that developing peaceful nuclear explosives was tantamount to a bomb but involved lower cost and risk. Yet, the Indian press and, still more removed, the public did not make this connection.

161. See, for example, C. P. Srivastava, *Lal Bahadur Shastri, Prime Minister of India 1964–66: A Life of Truth in Politics* (Delhi: Oxford University Press, 1995). Srivastava makes no mention of Bhabha, nuclear policy, or atomic energy.

162. Raja Ramanna, interview by the author, January 28, 1996, Bangalore. In his autobiography, *Years of Pilgrimage*, p. 74, Ramanna uncertainly and vaguely dated his assignment as beginning "sometime later" than Shastri's January 1965 visit to Trombay to inaugurate the reprocessing plant. He added that "there was little discussion on this subject." Other authors such as Kapur, *India's Nuclear Option*, p. 194, have used the acronym SNEP for Subterranean Nuclear Explosion Project. Kapur wrote that Shastri authorized this project in December 1965 following a note from Bhabha received in November 1965. However, the evidence marshaled here indicates that the move came in late 1964. Homi Sethna, in a January 29, 1996, interview, said, "We formed a small group at the end of 1964, beginning of 1965. That's when we started paper studies of what it would take to do a PNE."

163. Raja Ramanna, interview by the author, January 28, 1996, Bangalore.

164. Homi Sethna, interview by the author, February 26, 1997, Mumbai.

165. The early January 1965 annual session of the Congress party, according to the *Times of India*, January 11, 1965, entailed "the most ruthless criticism of the Government [by the rank and file] ever to be witnessed at a Congress session." Cited in Frankel, *India's Political Economy*, p. 265.

166. Although American officials and analysts underestimated the importance of Shastri's November 27 statement and overestimated India's technical preparedness to make nuclear explosives, analysts understood the political dynamic affecting Indian decision making. For example, an Arms Control and Disarmament Agency memorandum opined that in any decision to produce nuclear weapons,

> political considerations will weigh heavily, much more so than they did when Nehru formulated the Indian position and maintained it thereafter. One reason for this is that the new Shastri government is much more subject to the political pressures of the day than its predecessor under Nehru. To stay in power it must reach out for support and be on the popular side of national issues to a much greater extent than the Nehru government.

U.S. Arms Control and Disarmament Agency, National Intelligence Estimate paper, "The Indian Nuclear Problem: Proposed Course of Action," October 13, 1964, app. 2, "Political Factors Related to Indian Nuclear Weapons Policy," p. 3.

167. K. C. Pant recalled in an interview by the author, February 28, 1997, New Delhi, that "[t]here is no one in this country who could have had such influence on the government as Bhabha. He was very persuasive."

CHAPTER THREE

1. L. P. Singh, *India's Foreign Policy: The Shastri Period* (New Delhi: Uppal, 1980), p. 39.

2. See A. G. Noorani, "India's Quest for a Nuclear Guarantee," *Asian Survey* 7, no. 7 (July 1967): pp. 490–502. The summary here draws on Noorani's account and additional contemporaneous press reports.

3. Quoted in Seaborg, *Stemming the Tide*, pp. 115–116.

4. Noorani, "India's Quest for a Nuclear Guarantee," p. 491, citing the *Times* (London), December 5, 1964.

5. Ibid., citing the *Hindu*, December 7, 1964.

6. Iqbal Singh, " 'Nuclear Shield' Move May Lead to New Problems," *Patriot*, December 7, 1964, p. 1.

7. This was confirmed in a U.S. State Department telegram from Secretary of State Dean Rusk to Governor Averill Harriman, February 27, 1965, p. 2, FOIA files, India, National Security Archive, Washington, D.C.

8. Noorani, "India's Quest for a Nuclear Guarantee," p. 492.

9. Ibid.

10. K. C. Khanna, "Shastri on Way Home," *Times of India*, December 7, 1964, p. 1.

11. *Lok Sabha Debates*, November 23, 1964, cols. 1256–1257.

12. Ibid.

13. In a meeting of the interagency Committee on Nuclear Non-Proliferation, chaired by the State Department's Ambassador Thompson, March 17, 1965, U.S. officials debated providing India with a more explicit security guarantee than was offered by President Johnson on October 18, 1964. The stronger of two alternate options would have had the president state that "all free countries in Asia may be sure that nuclear aggression by Peiping against their territory would be met by the United States with a prompt response. Since US military power to effect such a response is beyond doubt, Peiping will not be able to conclude that its own interests would be served by nuclear aggression." The statement would have continued by emphasizing the United States' objective of finding a way "to halt the nuclear arms race" and would have specified several measures to this end, including a complete nuclear test ban and a cutoff of fissile material production for use in weapons. In the U.S. government debate, the Joint Chiefs of Staff argued against the stronger security guarantee language and opposed committing the United States to a complete test ban, a fissile material production ban, and "a formal undertaking to stop the spread of nuclear weapons." Others questioned the desirability or feasibility of a stronger guarantee and Congress's willingness to support it. The matter was referred for further discussion. State Department, memorandum, "Assurances for India," prepared for the Tenth Meeting of the Committee on Nuclear Non-Proliferation, March 17, 1965, and "Informal Minutes of the Tenth Meeting of the Committee on Nuclear Non-Proliferation," March 17, 1965, Nuclear Non-Proliferation Policy, FOIA files, India, National Security Archive, Washington, D.C.

14. Frankel, *India's Political Economy*, pp. 265–270.

15. "Strong Plea for an Indian bomb," *Statesman*, January 8, 1965.

16. K. Rangaswami, "Atom Bomb to Meet China's Threat," *Hindu*, January 8, 1965.

17. Ibid.

18. "Strong Plea for an Indian Bomb," *Statesman*, January 8, 1965.

19. Ibid.

20. Thomas F. Brady, "Shastri Opposes A-Bomb for India," *New York Times*, January 10, 1965.

21. Ibid. Shastri's formulation obscured the reality that he had authorized Bhabha's request to work on nuclear explosives for *peaceful* purposes.

22. "Atom for Peace but No Firm Line against Bomb," *Indian Express*, January 7, 1965.

23. "Strong Plea for an Indian Bomb," *Statesman*, January 8, 1965.

24. Ibid. Politically, it was interesting that Desai took the lead in defending Shastri's line. Desai had wanted to succeed Nehru and could therefore be seen as a major rival of

Shastri. Yet he stayed true to his principled opposition to the bomb and, rather than undermine Shastri, covered the prime minister's flank.

25. "The Bomb and All That," editorial, *Hindu,* January 11, 1965, emphasis added. See also "The Bomb Again," editorial, *Statesman,* January 8, 1965.

26. Quoted in Mirchandani, *India's Nuclear Dilemma,* p. 35.

27. In 1964 the AEC organized an international Plowshare Symposium. That summer, at the Third UN Conference on the Peaceful Uses of Atomic Energy, the United States trumpeted the uses of PNEs with a major scientific paper, a film, and an exhibit. Glenn Seaborg, *Stemming the Tide,* p. 321.

28. The prospect of using PNEs for major excavation projects was limited by the Partial Test Ban Treaty's prohibition of radioactive fallout that could migrate across international borders. By 1965 this (not insurmountable) constraint, plus the growing realization that PNEs were actually uneconomical, began to elicit strong reservations about the program within the United States. These doubts eventually doomed the program by the mid-1970s. Ibid., pp. 346–350.

29. United States Atomic Energy Commission, "Discussion Paper on Prospects of Intensifying Peaceful Atomic Cooperation with India," forwarded to Ambassador Llewellyn E. Thompson, November 23, 1964, p. 4, FOIA files, India, National Security Archive, Washington, D.C.

30. Ibid., p. 4.

31. Ibid.

32. Deputy Under Secretary of State Llewellyn E. Thompson to Secretary of State Dean Rusk, memorandum, "Review of Non-Proliferation Policy," December 4, 1964, p. 1, cover attachment to Defense Department staff study, "U.S. Nuclear Assistance to Pacific-Asian Countries," Nuclear Non-Proliferation Policy, FOIA files, National Security Archive, Washington, D.C.

33. U.S. Defense Department staff study, "U.S. Nuclear Assistance to Pacific-Asian Countries," p. 12.

34. Ibid., p. 2.

35. Ibid., p. 4.

36. Ibid., p. 5.

37. Ibid., p. 7.

38. Ibid., p. 11.

39. Ibid.

40. Ibid.

41. Ibid., p. 18.

42. Ibid., p. 17.

43. Daniel Ellsberg, then an official on McNaughton's staff, correspondence with the author, May 30, 1996. Ellsberg's recollection of the broad course of this episode was offered before the McNaughton staff study became publicly available in 1998, and is corroborated by the study. For his part, McNamara, in a June 1996 interview with the author did not recall the episode.

44. Deputy Under Secretary of State Llewellyn E. Thompson to Secretary of State Dean Rusk, memorandum, "Review of Non-Proliferation Policy," December 4, 1964, p. 2, cover attachment to Defense Department staff study, "U.S. Nuclear Assistance to Pacific-Asian Countries."

45. State Department to U.S. Embassies in New Delhi, Karachi, and London, January 12, 1965, p. 1.

46. Ibid., p. 2., and J. W. Joyce, "Preliminary Report on Visit of J. B. Wiesner and J. W. Joyce to India, January 14–20, 1965," January 27, 1965, p. 1, Central Files of the Department of State, Records of Ambassador at Large Llewellyn Thompson, 1961–1970, RG 59, National Archives.

47. Ibid., p. 1.

48. Dr. Wiesner, U.S. Embassy (New Delhi), to Secretary of State, cable no. 2054, January 21, 1965, p. 2, FOIA files, India, National Security Archive, Washington, D.C.

49. State Department to John Palfrey at U.S. Embassy (New Delhi), cable, January 21, 1965, in Foran, *U.S. Nuclear Non-Proliferation Policy, 1945–1991*, no. 01100. This cable also noted that the U.S. intelligence community believed that "[e]xpenditures for a modest weapons program (up to testing first device) would total no more than $30–40 million" and that "[g]iven present facilities, believe India could produce and test first nuclear device one to three years after decision to do so."

50. Joyce, "Preliminary Report," p. 1.

51. State Department to John Palfrey at U.S. Embassy (New Delhi), cable, January 21, 1965, p. 1.

52. Ibid.

53. Ibid., p. 2, emphasis added.

54. Sethna, interview by author, February 26, 1997, Mumbai.

55. Bhabha also had sought meetings with Averill Harriman and National Security Adviser McGeorge Bundy, but they were both out of town. State Department to U.S. Embassies in New Delhi, Karachi, and Tel Aviv, February 26, 1965.

56. U.S. Department of State, memorandum of conversation, February 22, 1965, p. 1, in Foran, *U.S. Nuclear Non-Proliferation Policy, 1945–1991*, no. 01108. Participating in the conversation were B. K. Nehru, ambassador of India; Homi Bhabha, secretary of the Department of Atomic Energy, India; George Ball, under secretary of state; Robert Anderson; and David T. Schneider.

57. Ibid.

58. Ibid., p. 2. The existing record does not allow a detailed assessment of the extent to which Soviet assistance actually contributed to China's nuclear weapon program. Major cooperation began in 1955, but by June 1959 the Soviet Communist Party Central Committee had notified the Chinese Communist Party Central Committee that the Soviets would not provide technical details or working models of atomic bombs. By 1960, all Soviet advisers and technicians working in China on nuclear weapons and energy had been withdrawn. Still, according to Lewis and Xue, two Soviet weapons specialists inadvertently left behind fragments of documents pertaining to implosions that did help Chinese nuclear weapon designers. *China Builds the Bomb*, pp. 160–161. See also Norris, Burrows, and Fieldhouse, *British, French, and Chinese Nuclear Weapons*, pp. 330–337.

59. U.S. Department of State, memorandum of conversation, February 22, 1965, emphasis added.

60. Ibid., p. 3.

61. Ibid.

62. Donald Fuller, scientific attaché, U.S. Embassy (New Delhi), to Department of State, airgram no. A-964, "Trombay and Atomic Energy in India," March 16, 1965, p. 6,

Nuclear Non-Proliferation Policy, FOIA files, India, National Security Archive, Washington, D.C.

63. Ibid., p. 7.

64. Ibid., p. 8. According to former Atomic Energy Commission Chairman Homi Sethna, the explosion resulted from a nitric acid excursion and bent the metal of the vessel containing the material, but was not major. Interview by author, February 26, 1997, Mumbai.

65. Ibid.

66. Ibid., p. 9.

67. Ibid., p. 10.

68. The draft of the letter was appended to a memorandum from Lewellyn E. Thompson, acting deputy under secretary of state, to members of the Committee on Nuclear Non-Proliferation, "Progress Report and Minutes of the Tenth Meeting of the Committee," March 29, 1965, Nuclear Non-Proliferation Policy, FOIA files, India, National Security Archive, Washington, D.C. The other six areas of potential cooperation were as follows: "US-Indian Exchange in the Field of Thorium Recycle"; "Joint Study Regarding How India Might Utilize Its Uranium and Thorium Resources Most Effectively"; "Fast Reactor Exchange"; "Maritime Reactors"; "Desalting"; "Assistance in the Design and Construction of Particle Accelerator."

69. Ibid., p. 3 of the draft letter.

70. Ibid.

71. Ibid., p. 4.

72. AEC Chairman Glenn Seaborg to Joint Committee on Atomic Energy Chairman Chet Holifield, correspondence, April 30, 1965, Joint Committee on Atomic Energy files, International Affairs, India, National Archives.

73. Ambassador Chester Bowles to William J. Handley, correspondence, April 12, 1965, p. 1, Nuclear Non-Proliferation Policy, FOIA files, India, National Security Archive, Washington, D.C.

74. William J. Handley to Ambassador Chester Bowles, correspondence, May 7, 1965, p. 1, Nuclear Non-Proliferation Policy, FOIA files, India, National Security Archive, Washington, D.C.

75. Ibid. "Ploughshare" is an alternate spelling of "Plowshare" used by some writers and in some documents.

76. Then-National Security Adviser McGeorge Bundy, in a note written to the author just prior to Bundy's death, said that he did not recall whether Bhabha requested a nuclear device from the United States but "would not have been surprised if he had." Note read to the author by Bundy's secretary, October 3, 1996. Myron Kratzer, then an official of the U.S. Atomic Energy Commission and deeply involved in interactions with India, also did not recollect a request by Bhabha for a Plowshare device. Kratzer, in correspondence with the author, wrote, "If Bhabha raised the proposition of a device with us [in Bombay in January, 1965] or later in Washington, I'm sure we would not have taken it seriously and would have dismissed it so quickly as to leave no lasting impression with us." Correspondence, July 26, 1996, p. 5.

77. Rowen, "The Indian Nuclear Program," Department of Defense, background paper, pps. 3–4. The referenced Indian military study was not made public in India.

78. Ibid., pp. 4–5.

79. Former Atomic Energy Commission scientist, interview by author, May 1997.

80. Briefing memorandum from Phillips Talbot to Ball, regarding February 22 meeting with Dr. Homi Bhabha, February 20, 1965, p. 1, FOIA files, India, National Security Archive, Washington, D.C.

81. A conversation between Indian Ambassador to the United States B. K. Nehru and Director of the U.S. Arms Control and Disarmament Agency William Foster on November 3, 1964, reflected the challenges facing Indian officials and the inadequacy of American responses. Nehru told Foster that "the genuine psychological advantages which the Chinese had obtained in Southeast Asia by virtue of their explosion" might cause "political pressures within India [to] build up so that it would be politically impossible to resist proposals for an Indian bomb."

Foster's limp response must have provided little assurance:

I told the Ambassador we understood the pressures which might build up and yet his government must recognize that if India were to make the decision to produce nuclear weapons, this would be a long step toward proliferation of such weapons throughout the world. It seemed to us a much better decision, both from the viewpoint of best utilization of economic resources and indeed the security of the world, to devote the Indian influence to non-proliferation.

U.S. Arms Control and Disarmament Agency, memorandum of conversation between B. K. Nehru and William C. Foster, "Chinese Nuclear Explosion," November 3, 1964, pp. 1–2, Nuclear Non-Proliferation Policy, FOIA files, India, National Security Archive, Washington, D.C.

82. Henry Kissinger, *The Troubled Partnership* (New York: McGraw-Hill, 1965), p. 154.

83. Five U.S. government committees were involved in assessing the implications of the Chinese test. Lindsey Grant to National Security Adviser McGeorge Bundy, memorandum, "U.S. Government Committees Considering Implications of the Chicom Nuclear Capability," December 31, 1964, Nuclear Non-Proliferation Policy, FOIA files, National Security Archive, Washington, D.C.

84. U.S. Arms Control and Disarmament Agency, paper, "Non-Proliferation of Nuclear Weapons," November 9, 1964, pp. 2–3, in Foran, *U.S. Nuclear Non-Proliferation Policy, 1945–1991*, no. 01040.

85. Ibid., p. 9.

86. Background paper, "Value and Feasibility of a Nuclear Non-Proliferation Treaty," authorship unstated, December 10, 1964, pp. 1–2, in Foran, *U.S. Nuclear Non-Proliferation Policy, 1945–1991*, no. 01070.

87. Ibid., pp. 12–13.

88. Ibid., p. 13.

89. Ibid., p. 13.

90. State Department, "Background Paper on National Attitudes towards Adherence to a Comprehensive Test Ban Treaty and to a Non-Proliferation Agreement," December 12, 1964, pp. 2–4, in Foran, *U.S. Nuclear Non-Proliferation Policy, 1945–1991*, no. 01078.

91. Ibid., p. 11.

92. U.S. Embassy (New Delhi) to State Department, airgram no. A-1101, "India and the Nuclear Bomb," April 20, 1965, p. 2, Nuclear Non-Proliferation Policy, FOIA files, India, National Security Archive, Washington, D.C.

93. The committee consisted of Chairman Roswell L. Gilpatric, Robert A. Lovett, Dean Acheson, John J. McCloy, Arthur H. Dean, George B. Kistiakowsky, James A.

Perkins, Herbert F. York, Allen W. Dulles, Glenn Seaborg, Arthur K. Watson, William Webster, and Alfred B. Gruenther. Staff director was Spurgeon Keeny Jr.

94. Roswell L. Gilpatric, chairman, "A Report to the President by the Committee on Nuclear Proliferation," January 21, 1965, p. 1, Nuclear Non-Proliferation Policy, FOIA files, National Security Archive, Washington, D.C.

95. Ibid., p. 2.

96. Ibid., p. 5.

97. Ibid., p. 17.

98. Ibid., p. 11.

99. Ibid., p. 12.

100. Ibid., pp. 11–12.

101. Statement by the Indian representative (Chakravarty) to the Disarmament Commission, May 4, 1965, in U.S. Arms Control and Disarmament Agency, *Documents on Disarmament, 1965* (Washington, D.C.: U.S. Arms Control and Disarmament Agency), p. 148.

102. The United States, the United Kingdom, Canda, France, and Italy; the Soviet Union, Bulgaria, Czechoslovakia, Poland, and Romania; Brazil, Burma, Ethiopia, India, Mexico, Nigeria, Sweden, and the United Arab Republic.

103. K. C. Pant, interview by author, February 28, 1997, New Delhi. Pant recalled watching Trivedi and Sarabhai argue vehemently over India's nuclear policy during a dinner in Geneva. Trivedi favored and Sarabhai opposed building the bomb.

104. Statement by Indian representative (Trivedi) to the Eighteen Nation Disarmament Committee, August 12, 1965, in U.S. ACDA, *Documents on Disarmament, 1965*, pp. 335–336.

105. U.S. ACDA, *Documents on Disarmament, 1965*, pp. 533–534. The other two called for treaty effectiveness and the support for regional nuclear-weapon-free zones.

106. U.S. Embassy (New Delhi) to State Department, cable no. 2055, January 21, 1965, p. 2, in Foran, *U.S. Nuclear Non-Proliferation Policy, 1945–1991*, no. 01102.

CHAPTER FOUR

1. Barnds, *India, Pakistan, and the Great Powers*, p. 194.

2. Hari Ram Gupta, *India-Pakistan War, 1965*, vol. 1 (Delhi: Hariyana Prakashan, 1967), pp. 62–65.

3. Ibid., p. 65.

4. Barnds, *India, Pakistan, and the Great Powers*, p. 199.

5. Kux, *Estranged Democracies*, pp. 234–235. Also, Gupta, *India-Pakistan War*, vol. 1, pp. 54–56.

6. Kux, *Estranged Democracies*, pp. 241–242.

7. Ibid., p. 241.

8. Ibid., p. 243.

9. Barnds, *India, Pakistan, and the Great Powers*, p. 185.

10. Ibid., p. 194.

11. U.S. Embassy (Karachi) to Secretary of State, cable no. 462, November 18, 1964, p. 2, Nuclear Non-Proliferation Policy, FOIA files, Pakistan, National Security Archive, Washington, D.C.

12. "The Brown Bomb," *Guardian* (Manchester), March 11, 1965, p. 10.

13. Ibid.

14. Ibid. This is a rather famous quote, although people who repeat it often assume it was made much later than 1965.

15. Kux, *Estranged Democracies*, p. 235.

16. Barnds, *India, Pakistan, and the Great Powers*, p. 203.

17. Barnds dated the attack on September 5. Kux, *Estranged Democracies*, p. 237, and Gupta, *India-Pakistan War*, vol. 1, p. 143, dated it on September 6.

18. Kux, *Estranged Democracies*, p. 236.

19. Barnds, *India, Pakistan, and the Great Powers*, p. 206.

20. Ibid., p. 207.

21. Ibid.

22. Gupta, *India-Pakistan War*, vol. 1, p. 20. The casualty figures were through November 16, including skirmishes that followed the cease-fire.

23. Ibid.

24. Gupta recorded that Pakistan lost 475 tanks destroyed, disabled, or captured compared with 128 destroyed or damaged Indian tanks, and 73 Pakistani aircraft downed compared with 28 Indian. Ibid.

25. "Tashkent Declaration," January 10, 1965, Articles II and VII, in Appadorai, *Select Documents on India's Foreign Policy and Relations*, vol. 1, pp. 388–389.

26. Ibid., Article I. India wanted to negotiate a no-war pact at Tashkent, but Pakistan declined.

27. Ibid., Article I.

28. Hari Ram Gupta, *India-Pakistan War, 1965*, vol. 2 (Delhi: Hariyana Prakashan, 1968), p. 62.

29. Barnds, *India, Pakistan, and the Great Powers*, p. 211.

30. Gupta, *India-Pakistan War*, vol. 2, p. 63.

31. Ibid., p. 62. However, Shastri's favorability rating had soared in the immediate aftermath of the war. Indian Institute of Public Opinion, *Monthly Public Opinion Surveys* 14, no. 11, #167 (August 1969): p. 8.

32. Gupta, *India-Pakistan War*, vol. 2, p. 105.

33. MP letter quoted in Mirchandani, *India's Nuclear Dilemma*, p. 39.

34. Mirchandani, *India's Nuclear Dilemma*, p. 40.

35. Quoted in ibid., pp. 40–41.

36. Anthony Lukas, "Indian Rules Out Secret Atom Test," *New York Times*, November 30, 1965.

37. Ibid.

38. Ibid.

39. Frankel, *India's Political Economy*, p. 293. Twenty-eight percent was from foreign aid and 13 percent from deficit financing.

40. Kux, *Estranged Democracies*, p. 254.

41. "Tarapur Atomic Power Project," *Financial Express*, January 25, 1966, p. 8.

42. Interviews by author with three former high-ranking Atomic Energy Commission officials.

43. Interviews by author, January 28 and 29, 1996, in Bangalore and Mumbai, respectively.

44. Reiss, *Without the Bomb*, p. 325 n. 42, stated, based on a 1986 interview with a former senior Atomic Energy Commission official, that "Indira Gandhi was unaware of SNEP and Sarabhai canceled it on his own authority."

45. However, before Bhabha departed for Europe and while Indira Gandhi and Morarji Desai were campaigning among Congress party elites for the prime minister's post, Bhabha had a long discussion of nuclear issues with K. C. Pant, a leading Congress figure. Pant did not recall that Bhabha described specific preparations for work on a peaceful nuclear explosive but rather that Bhabha conveyed the importance of selecting a prime minister who would strongly support Bhabha's overall nuclear program. Interview by author, February 28, 1997, New Delhi.

46. Sethna's appointment was announced on February 15. Mirchandani, *India's Nuclear Dilemma*, p. 247.

47. Once Sarabhai was tapped, he was delayed in assuming the post officially until a routine financial investigation was completed. This took an unusually long time due to Sarabhai's numerous and complicated holdings. Homi Sethna, interview by author, February 26, 1997, Mumbai.

48. Ramanna, *Years of Pilgrimage*, p. 75.

49. Ibid.

50. Ibid. Ashok Kapur added some detail to the account, without providing sources to enable checking. He suggested that one faction urged the appointment of Dr. Prakash, an AEC director who, Kapur says, favored the peaceful nuclear explosives project. "Another view argued that no scientist should have independent charge of the AEC." Kapur, *India's Nuclear Option*, p. 195.

51. Ibid. Sarabhai and his family controlled major enterprises in the glass, chemical, pharmaceutical, textile, and oil industries. See Padmanabh K. Joshi, ed., *Vikram Sarabhai: The Man and the Vision* (Ahmedabad: Mapin, 1992).

52. Sarabhai seemed to hint at his divergence from Bhabha's views on nuclear explosives when he paid tribute to Bhabha on January 25. Sarabhai referred to the growing perception that Bhabha had favored the manufacture of an atomic bomb. But, Sarabhai said, India's policy was in fact a national one, created by Nehru and followed by Shastri, that confined the use of atomic energy to peaceful purposes. Sarabhai appeared to be trying to finesse Bhabha's bomb advocacy and bring Bhabha posthumously into line with the policy that Sarabhai favored. "Bhabha Was Firm Believer in Atom-for-Peace Policy," *Financial Express*, January 26, 1966, p. 8.

53. In Joshi, *Vikram Sarabhai*, p. 121.

54. Homi Sethna, interview by author, February 26, 1997, Mumbai.

55. Statement by the Indian representative (Trivedi) to the ENDC, February 15, 1966, in U.S. ACDA, *Documents on Disarmament, 1966*, p. 20.

56. Ibid., p. 17.

57. Rusk, quoted in Seaborg, *Stemming the Tide*, p. 367.

58. Ibid. President Johnson had earlier, on January 27, proposed a seven-point arms control program. Cited in Mirchandani, *India's Nuclear Dilemma*, p. 123.

59. Secretary of State to the President, memorandum and attached study, S/P-66–34-UNNC4, received March 16, 1966, cover memo drafted March 3, 1966, by Deputy Under Secretary of State Alexis Johnson, "Possible Assurances and Nuclear Support Arrangements for India," Policy Planning Council, Subject and Country files 1965–1969, box 727, National Archives. The study was the basis for a paper submitted to the president for consideration at a June 9, 1966, National Security Council meeting, "The Indian Nuclear Weapons Problem: Current Issues," forwarded by Acting Secretary of State George Ball to the president, June 7, 1966, FOIA files, India, National Security Archive, Washington, D.C.

60. Secretary of State to President Johnson, memorandum, "Possible Assurances and Nuclear Support Arrangements for India," p. 1.

61. Ibid.

62. State Department study S/P-66–34-UNNC4, p. 1, quoting from National Intelligence Estimate 4–66, "The Likelihood of Further Nuclear Proliferation," January 20, 1966. The U.S. intelligence community at this time tasked the American Embassy in New Delhi to search for signs of Indian efforts to acquire or test nuclear explosives or relevant components. Analysts noted that "[e]lectronic neutron generators and high-quality detonators—components likely to be used in the first Indian nuclear device—are readily available on the open market in Western Europe." U.S. Department of State to U.S. Embassy (New Delhi), airgram no. A-256, "Possible Indian Nuclear Weapons Development," March 29, 1966, p. 2, FOIA files, India, National Security Archive, Washington, D.C.

63. Ibid., p. 2.

64. Ibid., p. 5.

65. The alternatives were discussed in ibid., pp. 5–7.

66. State Department study S/P-66–34-UNNC4, p. 9.

67. Ibid.

68. Ibid.

69. Ibid., p. 10.

70. Ibid.

71. Ibid., p. 8. As noted in chapter 3, sixteen months earlier U.S. Atomic Energy Commission officials believed that providing a Plowshare device would "deter" India from embarking on a device development program of its own.

72. Ibid.

73. Ibid., p. 11, emphasis in original.

74. Ibid.

75. Ibid., p. 12.

76. Ibid., p. 12.

77. Department of State to U.S. Embassy (New Delhi), telegram, stamp no. 26616, July 28, 1966, p. 2, FOIA files, India, National Security Archive, Washington, D.C. This telegram makes reference to the May 24 telegram cited in the following note.

78. Department of State to U.S. Embassy (New Delhi), telegram no. 13982, May 24, 1966, p. 1, FOIA files, India, National Security Archive, Washington, D.C.

79. Ibid.

80. Ibid.

81. Ibid., p. 4.

82. Ibid., p. 5.

83. Mirchandani, *India's Nuclear Dilemma*, p. 43.

84. Ibid.

85. Ibid.

86. Ibid., and K. C. Pant, interview by author, February 28, 1997, New Delhi. Pant understood that the technology development that he and Bhabha advocated could be used to make weapons.

87. Mirchandani, *India's Nuclear Dilemma*, p. 44.

88. *Lok Sabha Debates,* oral answers, 3d. ser., vol. 55, no. 56, May 10, 1966, col. 15712.

89. Ibid.

90. Ibid., col. 15713.

91. Ibid., col. 15714.
92. Mirchandani, *India's Nuclear Dilemma,* p. 45.
93. *Lok Sabha Debates,* May 10, 1966, col. 15716.
94. Ibid.
95. Ibid.
96. Quoted in Mirchandani, *India's Nuclear Dilemma,* p. 46.
97. Ibid., p. 47.
98. Ibid.
99. Homi Sethna, interview by author, February 26, 1997, Mumbai.
100. Warren Unna, "Peking's Bomb Agitates India," *Washington Post,* May 12, 1966.
101. Ibid.
102. Statement by the Indian representative (Trivedi) to the ENDC, May 10, 1966, in U.S. ACDA, *Documents on Disarmament, 1966,* p. 284.
103. Sarabhai's appointment was announced on May 26. Mirchandani, *India's Nuclear Dilemma,* p. 248.
104. Vikram Sarabhai, press conference, June 1, 1966, in Jain, *Nuclear India,* vol. 2, p. 179.
105. Ibid., pp. 179–180.
106. "A-Bomb Alone Not Enough for Security: Sarabhai," *Hindustan Times,* June 2, 1966; "Stress on Development of Electronics Industry," *Financial Express,* June 2, 1966, p. 1.
107. Kapur, *India's Nuclear Option,* p. 195.
108. Interview by author, January 28, 1996, Bangalore. Raja Ramanna referred to the project using the acronym SNEPP (Study Nuclear Explosion for Peaceful Purposes) while Ashok Kapur used the acronym SNEP (Subterranean Nuclear Explosion Project).
109. Interview by author, January 29, 1996, Mumbai.
110. Ramanna, *Years of Pilgrimage,* p. 75.
111. Kapur, *India's Nuclear Option,* p. 195.
112. Interview by author, January 29, 1996, Mumbai.
113. Interview by author, January 28, 1996, Bangalore.
114. Ibid.
115. Ramanna, *Years of Pilgrimage,* pp. 75–76.
116. Interview by author, January 29, 1996, Mumbai.
117. Interview by author, January 28, 1996, Bangalore.
118. Former Minister of State for Defence Arun Singh, interview by author, March 1, 1997, New Delhi.

CHAPTER FIVE

1. The treaty is titled the Treaty on the Non-Proliferation of Nuclear Weapons, with a hyphen, although nonproliferation is now commonly spelled without the hyphen.
2. Mirchandani, *India's Nuclear Dilemma,* p. 49.
3. Ibid., pp. 49–50.
4. Pant, quoted in ibid., p. 51.
5. K. C. Pant, interview by author, February 28, 1997, New Delhi. See also a May 1966 conversation between U.S. Embassy officials and Pant in U.S. Embassy (New Delhi) to State Department, airgram no. A-1078, "Indian Nuclear Policy on the Eve of the Third Chinese Communist Explosion," May 13, 1966, p. 3, Nuclear Non-Proliferation Policy, FOIA files, India, National Security Archive, Washington, D.C.

6. C. S. Jha, *From Bandung to Tashkent* (Madras: Sangam Books, 1983), p. 300. The committee consisted of the cabinet secretary, defense secretary, home secretary, secretary of the Department of Atomic Energy, secretary to the prime minister, and foreign secretary.

7. Statement by the Indian representative (Trivedi) in the First Committee of the United Nations, October 31, 1966, in Jain, *Nuclear India*, vol. 2, p. 186.

8. Ibid., p. 187.

9. Ibid.

10. These three objectives were embodied, respectively, in Articles I, II, and III of the NPT. See Mohamed I. Shaker, *The Nuclear Non-Proliferation Treaty: Origin and Implementation, 1959–1979*, 3 vols. (New York: Oceana, 1980).

11. Seaborg, *Stemming the Tide*, p. 198.

12. Mirchandani, *India's Nuclear Dilemma*, p. 52.

13. Major General D. Som Dutt, *India and the Bomb*, Adelphi Paper Series, no. 30 (London: International Institute for Strategic Studies, 1966), p. 1.

14. Ibid.

15. Ibid.

16. Ibid., p. 2.

17. Ibid., p. 3.

18. Ibid.

19. Ibid., p. 5.

20. Ibid., p. 6.

21. Ibid.

22. Ibid.

23. Ibid., p. 6.

24. Ibid., p. 4.

25. Ibid.

26. Ibid.

27. Ibid.

28. Ibid., p. 7, referring to Leonard Beaton, "Capabilities of Non-nuclear Powers," in *A World of Nuclear Powers?* by the American Assembly (New York: Prentice Hall, 1966).

29. Ibid., p. 8.

30. Ibid., p. 9.

31. As a former Ministry of Defence official remarked to the author in a February 1997 discussion, "[T]his is typical of all Indian discussion on this subject—even up to today. Assessments tend to be inward looking and ignore perceptions or effects in the world outside."

32. "The communication of an anti-hegemonistic message to the world is necessary to ensure our own people that no matter what happens, India shall not be run by others ever again. Only Indians understand this need." Raj Krishna, "Proliferation," *Indian Quarterly* 22, no. 3 (July–September 1966): pp. 287–288.

33. General J. N. Chaudhuri, *Arms, Aims, and Aspects* (Bombay: P. C. Manaktala & Sons, 1966), p. 257.

34. Pathak, *Nuclear Policy of India*, p. 56.

35. Kapur, *India's Nuclear Option*, p. 196.

36. Mirchandani, *India's Nuclear Dilemma*, p. 250.

37. Ibid. India's second reprocessing plant, built at Tarapur, did not begin trial runs until 1979 and full-scale operations until 1982.

38. Kuldip Nayar, *India after Nehru* (Delhi: Vikas, 1975), p. 92.

39. Ibid., p. 89.

40. Mirchandani, *India's Nuclear Dilemma*, p. 52.

41. Ibid.

42. Ibid., p. 53.

43. Ibid.

44. Ibid.

45. Ibid.

46. Frankel, *India's Political Economy*, p. 356, for these and election figures below.

47. Ibid., p. 361.

48. Ali, *An Indian Dynasty*, p. 163.

49. An August-September poll by the Indian Institute of Public Opinion showed Indira Gandhi's favorability rating at its nadir, with a weighted score of 101 compared to 170 in May 1966. However, she would rebound 10 points by February 1968, and 30 points by August 1969. Indian Institute of Public Opinion, *Monthly Public Opinion Surveys* 14, no. 11, #167 (August 1969): p. 9.

50. Cited in Seaborg, *Stemming the Tide*, p. 356.

51. Ibid., p. 357.

52. Ibid., p. 356.

53. Cited in Mirchandani, *India's Nuclear Dilemma*, p. 137.

54. Ibid.

55. Seaborg, *Stemming the Tide*, p. 255. Sarabhai went on to insist that each nation should decide whether to develop peaceful nuclear explosives unimpeded by the nonproliferation treaty.

56. Cited in Mirchandani, *India's Nuclear Dilemma*, p. 134.

57. Ibid. This proposal reflected the U.S. Atomic Energy Commission's technology-promotion preference. The Arms Control and Disarmament Agency had sought to preclude any transfer of peaceful nuclear explosive capability to other nations. See Seaborg, *Stemming the Tide*, pp. 307–351 and 364–366.

58. Mirchandani, *India's Nuclear Dilemma*, pp. 135–136.

59. Foreign Minister M. C. Chagla, Lok Sabha Debates, March 27, 1967, in Jain, *Nuclear India*, p. 191.

60. Ibid.

61. Shri Balraj Madhok, in ibid.

62. Ibid.

63. Jha, *From Bandung to Tashkent*, p. 301.

64. Ibid.

65. Seaborg, *Stemming the Tide*, pp. 372–373, emphasis in original. Indicating the relatively low salience of nuclear policy in India, B. K. Nehru in his autobiography did not refer to the subject. B. K. Nehru, *Nice Guys Finish Second: An Autobiography* (Delhi: Viking Penguin India, 1997).

66. U.S. Defense Department, memorandum of conversation, "Meeting between the Secretary of Defense and Mr. L. K. Jha, Tuesday, 18 April at 10 a.m.," p. 2, in FOIA files, India, National Security Archive, Washington, D.C.

67. Ibid., p. 3.

68. Ibid.

69. Mirchandani, *India's Nuclear Dilemma*, p. 144.

70. Quoted in ibid., p. 143.

71. Jha, *From Bangdung to Tashkent*, p. 303. The *Hindu*, May 6, 1967, reported Prime Minister Gandhi saying, "We for our part may find ourselves having to take a nuclear decision any moment, and it is therefore not possible for us to tie our hands. . . . And it is not only our security but the future of our industry which is at stake."

72. Jha, *From Bangdung to Tashkent*, p. 303.

73. Jha stated that after his departure from the foreign secretary's post in August, 1967, the Ministry of External Affairs suggested "some re-examination of India's attitude toward the NPT." Ibid. Kuldip Nayar wrote that Jha's successor, Rajeshwar Dayal, argued that "since making the bomb would be too costly for India, it would be better to sign the treaty and get the promised assurance of protection from both Washington and Moscow against nuclear attack." Nayar, *India after Nehru*, p. 131. However, Nayar added that Indira Gandhi had not been convinced.

74. Statement by the Indian representative (Trivedi) to the ENDC, May 23, 1967, in U.S. Arms Control and Disarmament Agency, *Documents on Disarmament, 1967* (Washington, D.C.: U.S. Arms Control and Disarmament Agency), p. 235.

75. Ibid., p. 234.

76. Ibid. He added without explanation that "a weapon has many characteristics which are not present in a peaceful device." In any case, Trivedi personally believed India should develop nuclear explosives capability. K. C. Pant, interview by author, February 28, 1997, New Delhi.

77. Ibid., p. 235.

78. The draft appeared in Shaker, *The Nuclear Non-Proliferation Treaty,* vol. 3, pp. 946–950.

79. Ibid., p. 947.

80. Statement by the Indian representative (Trivedi) to the ENDC, September 28, 1967, in U.S. ACDA, *Documents on Disarmament, 1967*, p. 435.

81. European states with nuclear industries had formed EURATOM, a regional institution for regulating and promoting nuclear development, and they wanted to avoid the double burden of accepting bilateral safeguards overseen by the IAEA. This ultimately was done.

82. The security guarantee, UNSC Resolution 255, was passed on June 19, 1968, by a 10-to-0 vote, with Algeria, Brazil, France, India, and Pakistan abstaining. Seaborg noted that the guarantee "added nothing, except perhaps a note of urgency, to the Security Council's existing obligations." Seaborg, *Stemming the Tide*, p. 373. Seaborg overestimated the solace to India.

83. See Shaker, *The Nuclear Non-Proliferation Treaty,* vol. 3, for successive drafts.

84. Mirchandani, *India's Nuclear Dilemma*, p. 149.

85. Ibid.

86. Ramanna, *Years of Pilgrimage*, p. 75.

87. The account here derives from interviews with former high-ranking Indian defense and atomic energy officials in July and September 1997.

88. As described in chapter 7, the rudimentary 1974 device relied on a neutron initiator in the core.

89. R. Chidambaram and C. Ganguly, "Plutonium and Thorium in the Indian Nuclear Programme," *Current Science* 70, no. 1 (January 10, 1996): p. 25.

90. Interviews by author with three former high-ranking Atomic Energy Commission officials, 1996 and 1997.

91. Interview by author, September 1997.

92. Nayar, *India after Nehru*, p. 121.

93. Norris, Burrows, and Fieldhouse, *British, French, and Chinese Nuclear Weapons*, p. 334.

94. Interviews by author with former high-ranking Atomic Energy Commission officials, 1995 to 1998.

95. Statement by Prime Minister Indira Gandhi, Lok Sabha, April 24, 1968, in Jain, *Nuclear India*, vol. 2, pp. 201–202.

96. This meeting, at an unspecified date, was reconstructed by Rodney Jones on the basis of interviews with participants. Rodney Jones, "India," in *Non-Proliferation: The Why and the Wherefore*, ed. Jozef Goldblat (Philadelphia: Taylor & Francis, 1985), pp. 111–112.

97. Ibid., p. 112.

98. The vote was 95 to 4, with 21 abstentions.

99. "Had Bhabha not died in that plane crash on Mont Blanc in 1966, the decision against signing the NPT would probably have been a formality; . . . the possibility of Bhabha being overruled on key nuclear issues by any Prime Minister, not to mention bureaucratic faction, could be considered exceedingly remote." N. Ram, "India's Nuclear Policy" (paper presented at the thirty-fourth annual meeting of the Association of Asian Studies, Chicago, April 2–4, 1992), p. 16.

100. Jha, *From Bandung to Tashkent*, p. 307.

101. This was true even though Indian parliamentarians perceived China to be a threat to India. However, Indian parliamentarians' opinions of China had "gone up" in the "last year or two," and the major reasons Indian parliamentarians cited for their unfavorable views of China were "internal instability, disorder, chaos; Cultural Revolution, Red Guard movement; power struggle between factions or top leaders." Only 16 percent of the Indian parliamentarians cited China's "increasing aggressiveness, militarism [or] expansionist policies." Indian Institute of Public Opinion, *Monthly Public Opinion Surveys* 14, nos. 2–3, #158–159 (November–December 1968): pp. 25, 31, 32.

102. Ramanna, *Years of Pilgrimage*, p. 94.

103. Homi Sethna, interview by author, January 29, 1996, Mumbai.

104. Interview by author, September 1997.

105. Seaborg recorded that the Arms Control and Disarmament Agency director, William C. Foster, advised officials meeting in the White House on March 27, 1968, that "a high Indian official told him they would eventually sign." Seaborg, *Stemming the Tide*, p. 375. A State Department memorandum to the president recommended "no dramatic steps to discourage the Indians from starting a nuclear weapons program; this is because we have been unable to devise anything dramatic which would not cost us more than any anticipated gain." Secretary of State Dean Rusk to the President, cover page of memorandum, "Report to the President on the Indian Nuclear Weapons Problem," July 25, 1966, Nuclear Non-Proliferation Policy, FOIA files, India, National Security Archive, Washington, D.C.

CHAPTER SIX

1. Frankel, *India's Political Economy*, p. 388.

2. Ali, *An Indian Dynasty*, p. 165.

3. Frankel, *India's Political Economy*, p. 429. Indira Gandhi's grouping would later become known as Congress (I) for Indira.

4. Ali, *An Indian Dynasty*, p. 169.

5. Frankel, *India's Political Economy*, p. 455. Her party received 43 percent of the popular vote, compared with the undivided Congress party's 40.7 percent in the 1967 elections.

6. Ibid., p. 456.

7. Ibid.

8. Ibid., pp. 458–459.

9. K. C. Pant, interview by author, February 28, 1997, New Delhi.

10. Dhirendra Sharma, *India's Nuclear Estate* (New Delhi: Lancers, 1983), p. 90. The Programme Analysis Group had been operating informally since 1968.

11. K. Subrahmanyam, interview by author, March 21, 1998, New Delhi.

12. Purnima stands for Plutonium Reactor for Neutronic Investigations in Multiplying Assemblies. It also means "full moon" in Hindi.

13. P. K. Iyengar, "Twenty Years after Pokhran," *Indian Express*, May 18, 1994, p. 11.

14. Homi Sethna, interview by author, February 26, 1997, Mumbai.

15. V. Venkateswaran, "India's Place on the Nuclear Map," *Hindu*, May 22, 1974, p. 4.

16. U.S. Embassy (New Delhi) to State Department, airgram no. A-811, "Indian Atomic Energy and Space Plans," March 30, 1967, Nuclear Non-Proliferation Policy, FOIA files, India, National Security Archive, Washington, D.C.

17. According to a former high-ranking official, Sarabhai directed the new complex to be built at Kalpakkam to diminish the role of Sethna, who was based at BARC. Interview by author, September 1997.

18. This reactor ultimately went critical in 1985, but it did not operate until at least 1987.

19. U.S. Consul (Madras) to State Department, airgram Madras A-16, July 12, 1971, p. 3, Nuclear Non-Proliferation Policy, FOIA files, India, National Security Archive, Washington, D.C.

20. A June 1970 U.S. government memorandum noted that "A Pulsed Critical Facility" was under construction at Trombay; however, further discussion of the facility is redacted in the declassified memorandum. U.S. Embassy (New Delhi) to State Department, airgram no. A-329, "India's Nuclear Program," June 16, 1970, p. 18, Nuclear Non-Proliferation Policy, FOIA files, India, National Security Archive, Washington, D.C.

Iyengar, in an April 24, 1997, interview with the author, in Tokyo, explained that had a full-blown reactor been built, it would have been done at Kalpakkam, but Purnima was a simpler boot-strapped project built in a hurry.

21. P. K. Iyengar, "Twenty Years after Pokhran," *Indian Express*, May 18, 1994. Iyengar argued that the reactor was useful for neutron spectroscopy, his research specialty. Interview by author, April 24, 1997, Tokyo.

22. Iyengar, correspondence with the author, April 16, 1999.

23. In the April 24, 1997, interview, Iyengar said, "Sarabhai worried or suspected that people were trying to push him into explosives. He knew that a pulsed reactor was significant—that a bomb is a big pulse."

24. Ibid.

25. Homi Sethna, interview by author, February 26, 1997, Mumbai.

26. Iyengar confirmed this, saying in the April 24, 1997, interview that "there was no question of getting formal approval—there was no budget needed."

27. Homi Sethna, interview by author, February 26, 1997, Mumbai.

28. Bhatia, in *India's Nuclear Bomb*, p. 141, wrote that Sarabhai approached Prime Minister Gandhi in 1968 to say that preparations for a nuclear test could begin if the government wished, and asked for funds to build what would become the Purnima reactor. "Sarabhai's request was readily agreed to by the Prime Minister after informal consultations with some colleagues in the cabinet. The cost for building Poornima was never disclosed, but its funding was 'hidden' within the budget of the experimental breeder reactor being built at Kalpakkam near Madras." Bhatia's account does not square with Iyengar's and Sethna's recollections that Sarabhai resisted this project and that the prime minister did not specifically approve it.

29. P. K. Iyengar, "Twenty Years after Pokhran," *Indian Express*, May 18, 1994, and interview by author, January 30, 1996, Mumbai.

30. Sampooran Singh, *India and the Nuclear Bomb* (New Delhi: S. Chand & Co., 1971), p. 133. Kapur, in *India's Nuclear Option*, p. 168, wrote that this occurred "during February and March."

31. N. Seshagiri, *The Bomb!* p. viii. Seshagiri stated that "nuclear explosives engineering" was Sarabhai's preferred term for peaceful nuclear explosives.

32. The *Times of India*, May 19, 1974, p. 7, reported that an "expert group" had been set up on August 2, 1970, to "study technological and cost aspects of going nuclear." This seemed to have been in response to the parliamentary request of March, but, again, it is not certain whether this was the same study in which Seshagiri participated.

33. Correspondence of Milton Leitenberg to Rodney Jones, June 16, 1993.

34. Interview by author, October 17, 1998, Madison, Wisc.

35. Seshagiri, *The Bomb!* p. ix.

36. Ibid.

37. Indian Institute of Public Opinion, *Monthly Public Opinion Surveys* 17, no. 3, #195 (December 1971): p. 49.

38. Indian Institute of Public Opinion, *Monthly Public Opinion Surveys* 15, no. 12, #180 (September 1970): p. 14.

39. Ibid., p. 19.

40. Ibid., p. 14.

41. Ibid., p. 13. Jana Sangh members among respondents still favored going nuclear by a margin of 74 to 26 percent, as did "New" (Indira Gandhi faction) Congress party members by a 51 to 49 percent margin. Education and income did not drastically alter respondents' views, while there was a major geographic divergence. In Delhi, 75 percent favored going nuclear even at major costs, while the numbers were 42 percent in Bombay, 28 percent in Calcutta, and 34 percent in Madras.

42. Peter Hazelhurst, "Atom-Bomb Urged for India," *Times of London*, May 11, 1970. Also on May 10 the Indian Council for World Affairs and the Institute for Defence Studies and Analyses held a seminar where a consensus emerged in favor of developing nuclear weapons. Singh, *India and the Nuclear Bomb*, p. 102.

43. Singh, *India and the Nuclear Bomb*, p. 102.

44. *Times of India*, May 22, 1970, p. 18.

45. Singh, *India and the Nuclear Bomb*, p. 107.

46. Government of India, Atomic Energy Commission, *Atomic Energy and Space Research: A Profile for the Decade 1970–80* (Bombay: Government of India, Atomic Energy Commission, July 1970). The plan was announced on May 25 but published two months later. The *Times of India* reported the announcement on page 9, reflecting the relative unimportance of the

topic in a time of political turmoil. "Plan for 2,700 MW of Nuclear Power by 1980 Urged," *Times of India,* May 26, 1970, p. 9.

47. Seshagiri, *The Bomb!* p. ix. "First Nuclear Explosion by India," *Times of India,* May 19, 1974, p. 1, also cited Sarabhai's May 17, 1970, statement as heralding the plan that would culminate in the Pokhran blast.

48. Beyond general fiscal constraints, planners noted that India's existing thermal power plants were operating well below nominal capacity and that priority should be given to improving the efficiency of the existing power infrastructure before investing in costly new capacity. R. Rama Rao, "India's Nuclear Progress—A Balance Sheet," *India Quarterly* 30, no. 4 (October/December 1974): p. 244.

49. "Plan for 2,700 MW of Nuclear Power by 1980 Urged," *Times of India,* May 26, 1970, p. 9. These figures changed by the time the Sarabhai Profile was actually published in July, as discussed later in this chapter. The dollar figures derive from the pre-December 1971 exchange rates of 7.5 rupees to 1 dollar, according to the World Bank, *Economic Developments in India: Achievements and Challenges* (Washington, D.C.: World Bank, 1995), p. xiii.

50. Each of the two reactors was designed and built to produce 210 megawatts, but problems with their steam generators forced them to be down-rated to 160 megawatts each.

51. See for example, Subramanian Swamy, "A Weapons Strategy for a Nuclear India," *India Quarterly* 30, no. 4 (October/December 1974): pp. 271–275.

52. Government of India, Atomic Energy Commission, *A Profile for the Decade 1970–80,* p. v.

53. Ibid., p. iv.

54. The 1970 profile slightly corrected the misleading assumption of the 1950s that increased provision of power would directly raise per capita gross national product. "A correlation [between per capita energy consumption and per capita GNP] does not necessarily signify a direct cause and effect relationship." Ibid., p. 4.

55. Ibid., p. 3.

56. Ibid., p. 4.

57. Ibid., p. 7. This assumed, optimistically, that the plutonium-producing reactors would operate at a 75 percent load factor and that reprocessing of spent fuel would occur quickly and optimally, with minimal material losses. These and other assumptions proved extremely overoptimistic.

58. These included natural-uranium fuel fabrication facilities, heavy-water production facilities, plutonium reprocessing and waste treatment plants, and uranium enrichment capability. Ibid., pp. 9–10.

59. Ibid., p. 11.

60. Ibid., pp. 11–12.

61. Ibid., p. 13. The plan acknowledged that in the case of "several items" the cost estimates were "*ad hoc.*"

62. In 1968–1969, India spent Rs. 10,033.19 million on defense. The 1970–1971 figure was slated to be Rs. 10,151.51 million. Singh, *India and the Nuclear Bomb,* p. 150. The GNP-related figure is taken from K. N. Reddy, J. V. M. Sarma, and Narain Sinha, *Central Government Expenditure: Growth, Structure, and Impact (1950–51 to 1977–78)* (New Delhi: National Institute of Public Finance and Policy, 1984), pp. 62, 66.

63. The 1970–1971 DAE budget was Rs. 92 crores (920 million), or $150 million. However, this was a marked increase over the 1969–1970 revised budget estimate of Rs. 63.16 crores. Singh, *India and the Nuclear Bomb,* p. 151.

64. Ibid.

65. Angathevar Baskaran, "India's Space Programme: A Study of the Accumulation of Technological Capabilities" (Ph.D. diss., University of Sussex, U.K., 1996), p. 53.

66. Homi Sethna, interview by author, February 26, 1997, Mumbai.

67. Government of India, Atomic Energy Commission, *A Profile for the Decade 1970-80,* p. 29.

68. Ibid., p. 31.

69. A few basic data suggest that there are important distinctions between the space and missile programs: the first ballistic missile, the Defence Research and Development Organisation's Prithvi, uses liquid fuel, undesirable for operational purposes, but necessary due to its derivation from the Soviet-supplied SAM-2 missile. Yet ISRO developed solid-fuel rockets. As Angathevar Baskaran argued, "The organisations have been miles apart due to organisational and personal rivalries and also due to the conscious effort of ISRO not to get entangled with military activities due to the fear of deviating from the development oriented objectives set by Sarabhai." Baskaran, "India's Space Programme," p. 316.

70. Government of India, Atomic Energy Commission, *A Profile for the Decade 1970-80,* p. 55.

71. Ibid., pp. 40-41. The government's plan called for spending on space Rs. 31.10 crores from 1969 to 1974, while the Sarabhai Profile called for Rs. 62 crores from 1970 to 1975.

72. U.S. Embassy (New Delhi) to State Department, airgram no. A-329, June 16, 1970, p. 10, Nuclear Non-Proliferation Policy, FOIA files, India, National Security Archive, Washington, D.C. This report also stated that "India could almost certainly produce a respectable test blast within a year of a GOI decision to do so. However, India does not presently have sufficient nuclear material, or facilities not under safeguards for its manufacture, to launch a serious weapons-making effort." Ibid., p. 9.

73. The plan was not approved until after the 1971 elections. But the actual DAE budget did not meet the proposed levels. Instead, the following expenditures occurred: 1971-1972, Rs 105 crores; 1972-1973, Rs. 126 crores; 1973-1974, Rs. 110 crores; 1974-1975, Rs. 96 crores. Rama Rao, "India's Nuclear Progress," p. 251.

74. R. Chidambaram presented a brief paper at a March 1970 International Atomic Energy Agency panel on peaceful nuclear explosives, describing Indian interest in using such explosives for mining copper ore. R. Chidambaram, "India," in *Peaceful Nuclear Explosions,* proceedings of a panel held in Vienna, March 2-6, 1970 (Vienna: International Atomic Energy Agency, 1970), IAEA-PL-388/27, pp. 9-10. According to P. K. Iyengar, Chidambaram and another BARC scientist, George Verghese, had gone to the United States in the late 1960s to observe an Atomic Energy Commission Plowshare test. Interview by author, April 24, 1997, Tokyo.

75. Bhabhani Sen Gupta, *Nuclear Weapons? Policy Options for India* (New Delhi: Sage, 1983), p. 5. Rama Rao, in "India's Nuclear Progress," p. 248, suggested that in late 1970 or early 1971, Sarabhai ordered exploration of possible sites for conducting peaceful nuclear explosions. Other sources, as discussed below, indicated that site exploration did not begin until late 1972.

76. Ibid.

77. Singh, *India and the Nuclear Bomb,* p. 94.

78. Ibid., p. 100.

79. Ibid., p. 132.

80. K. Subrahmanyam, "The Path to Nuclear Capability," *Institute for Defence Studies and Analyses Journal* 3 (1970): p. 100.

81. "The Indian Government behaves as though . . . no nuclear threat from China exists." K. Subrahmanyam, "Options for India," *Institute for Defence Studies and Analyses Journal* 3 (1970): p. 117

82. Ibid., p. 102.

83. Cited in Poulose, "India's Nuclear Policy," p. 107.

84. Subrahmanyam, "Options for India," p. 108.

85. Ibid., p. 103.

86. V. P. Dutt, *India's Foreign Policy* (New Delhi: Vikas, 1984), pp. 215–216.

87. Subrahmanyam, "Options for India," p. 107.

88. Ibid., p. 108.

89. Plutonium is classified as weapon-grade if its concentration of the isotope plutonium-239 is greater than or equal to 94 percent, with 5 percent plutonium-240, and 1 percent plutonium-241 in the balance. Plutonium is classified as reactor-grade if its PU-239 concentration is greater than or equal to 70 percent, with 25 percent PU-240, 5 percent PU-241, and less than 1 percent PU-242. It is now known, but was not appreciated in India at the time of Subrahmanyam's writing, that the reduced yield and reliability associated with the use of reactor-grade, rather than weapon-grade, plutonium in early implosion weapons such as the Nagasaki bomb can be largely if not wholly obviated by using more sophisticated designs to make reliable, high-yield fission and fission-fusion nuclear weapons using such reactor-grade plutonium. However, the use of weapon-grade plutonium is more straightforward, and the production of such material in special reactors and associated reprocessing plants is a well-developed technology, in line with what Subrahmanyam was recommending.

90. Subrahmanyam, "Options for India," p. 109. In 1974, India did use reprocessed spent fuel from CIRUS to build the 1974 device and did suffer harmful cessation of assistance from Canada.

91. K. Subrahmanyam, "Costing of Nuclear Weapons Programme," *Institute for Defence Studies and Analyses Journal* 3 (1970): p. 84.

92. He seemed to envision annual expenditures growing over seven to nine years to an annual level of Rs. 400 to Rs. 500 crores ($533–666 million), or roughly four to five times what the Atomic Energy Commission was spending in 1970. Subrahmanyam, "Options for India," p. 112. By contrast, Sampooran Singh asserted that India could produce "a small high-quality nuclear force" for "Rs. 2,300 crores over a period of ten years," roughly half of Subrahmanyam's estimate. Singh, *India and the Nuclear Bomb*, p. 117.

93. "[T]hose who criticise the U.N. estimates are not talking in terms of a credible deterrent, but of an obsolete weapon system of the '50s, which will not prove credible in the '70s let alone in the '80s." Subrahmanyam, "Costing of Nuclear Weapons Programme," pp. 87–88.

94. Subrahmanyam, "Options for India," pp. 109–110.

95. Schwartz, ed., *Atomic Audit*, p. 1.

96. Subrahmanyam, "Options for India," p. 110.

97. Indian Institute of Public Opinion, *Monthly Public Opinion Surveys* 16, nos. 11–12, #191–192 (August–September): p. 53. The majority of those who opposed going nuclear cited cost and alternative priorities as their primary reasons. Sixty-three percent disagreed with the proposition that "China will never use nuclear weapons against India." Ibid., p. 61.

98. Ibid.

99. U.S. Aide-Mémoire, August 16, 1970, declassified by the Bureau of Oceans and International Environmental and Scientific Affairs, September 19, 1980, reprinted in Chellaney, *Nuclear Nonproliferation*, app. D, pp. 350–351.

100. Chellaney, *Nuclear Nonproliferation*, p. 36.

101. Bhabhani Sen Gupta, in *Nuclear Weapons?* p. 5, quoted articles to this effect in the *Daily Telegraph* of London on July 27 and the *Christian Science Monitor* on August 31.

102. *Times of India*, June 7, 1971, quoted in Sen Gupta, *Nuclear Weapons?* p. 5.

103. Cited in Wohlstetter, *"The Buddha Smiles,"* p. 117.

104. Quoted in ibid.

105. Ibid., p. 118.

106. The *Hindu*, May 20, 1974, drew on an interview with Sarabhai's successor, Homi Sethna, to aver that "had Dr. Homi Baba [sic] been alive, this would have become a reality long ago. But Dr. Baba's [sic] death held up the experiment. Dr. Vikram Sarabhai, who succeeded Dr. Baba [sic] devoted most of his time for space and electronic research. When he took over, he [Sethna] gave the green signal." Another reporter for the *Hindu*, V. Venkateswaran, reported similarly two days later. "India's Place on the Nuclear Map," *Hindu*, May 22, 1974, p. 4.

P. K. Iyengar believed that India would have conducted a nuclear explosion even if Sarabhai had remained alive and in the AEC leadership: "Mrs. Gandhi was personally interested in this. She wanted to demonstrate—'don't take us for granted.' Her attitude was to demonstrate India's place in the world. . . . So the demonstration would have happened even had Sarabhai stayed alive." Interview by author, April 24, 1997, Tokyo.

107. Interview by author, February 26, 1997, Mumbai.

108. Ramanna, *Years of Pilgrimage*, p. 88.

CHAPTER SEVEN

1. Sumit Ganguly, *The Origins of War in South Asia: The Indo-Pakistani Conflicts since 1947* (Boulder, Colo.: Westview Press, 1986), p. 116.

2. On the broader context of Soviet-Indian relations, see Robert C. Horn, *Soviet-Indian Relations: Issues and Influence* (New York: Praeger, 1982).

3. Appadorai and Rajan, in *India's Foreign Policy and Relations*, p. 281, discuss an April 2, 1971, letter by Soviet President Nikolay Podgorny to Pakistani President Yahya Khan urging a stop to the repression in the east.

4. Ibid.

5. Satish Kumar, "India and Pakistan," in *Indian Foreign Policy: The Indira Gandhi Years*, ed. A. K. Damodaran and U. S. Bajpai (New Delhi: Radian, 1990), p. 138.

6. Kux, *Estranged Democracies*, p. 293; Henry Kissinger, *White House Years* (Boston: Little, Brown, 1979), pp. 713–715. The Chou invitation was in response to a December 16, 1970, message from President Nixon requesting that China receive such an emissary.

7. This was done as a "one-time exception" to the 1967 policy barring such exports to both India and Pakistan.

8. The military supply to Pakistan became still more troublesome when, in June 1971, the State Department declared that all arms aid would be suspended due to Pakistan's repression in the east. However, the State Department had misspoken, and arms already

loaded on ships for delivery to Pakistan were allowed to be conveyed. India did not accept Washington's explanations of the snafu. Kux, *Estranged Democracies,* pp. 293–294.

9. Ibid., 295.

10. Kumar, "India and Pakistan," p. 138.

11. "Treaty of Peace, Friendship and Co-operation between the Republic of India and the Union of Soviet Socialist Republics," August 9, 1971, Article IX, in *Select Documents on India's Foreign Policy, 1947–1972,* vol. 2, ed. A. Appadorai (Delhi: Oxford University Press, 1985), p. 139.

12. Appadorai and Rajan, *India's Foreign Policy and Relations,* p. 281.

13. Kissinger, *White House Years,* pp. 842–918.

14. Ibid., p. 878.

15. Raymond Garthoff, *Détente and Confrontation: American-Soviet Relations from Nixon to Reagan,* rev. ed. (Washington, D.C.: Brookings Institution, 1994), p. 301. Garthoff wrote:

[I]n contrast to the assessments of the Department of State and the CIA, Kissinger and Nixon believed India's aim was to dismember Pakistan and end West Pakistan as an independent state. . . . [O]ther participants have described it as an *idée fixe* of them both throughout the crisis. Similarly, they believed, contrary to evidence, that the Soviet Union must also want West Pakistan to be destroyed. They then interpreted developments in terms of those prejudgments.

16. Kux, *Estranged Democracies,* p. 302; Kissinger, *White House Years,* pp. 885–889.

17. Kux, *Estranged Democracies,* p. 302.

18. Garthoff, *Détente and Confrontation,* p. 304 and note 36.

19. Kissinger, *White House Years,* p. 905.

20. Ibid.

21. Ibid., p. 906.

22. Garthoff, *Détente and Confrontation,* p. 305.

23. Ibid. The navy still had not been told its mission.

24. Kissinger, *White House Years,* p. 911. Without irony, Kissinger noted that the "Chinese message was not what we expected." Contrary to his imagination, neither the Soviet Union nor China saw the Indo-Pak conflict as more than a regional affair. The only ambiguous move China had made was to increase military alert levels along the Chinese-Indian border from December 8 to 16, an unexceptional step given the circumstances. Garthoff, *Détente and Confrontation,* p. 316.

25. Garthoff, *Détente and Confrontation,* p. 309.

26. Ibid.

27. Ibid.

28. Appadorai and Rajan, *India's Foreign Policy and Relations,* p. 104. See also General K. M. Arif (ret.), *Working with Zia: Pakistan's Power Politics, 1977–1988* (Oxford: Oxford University Press, 1995), p. 36.

29. "[T]here has been no indication that China played an active role in advising or assisting Pakistan in the 1971 crisis," wrote Raymond Garthoff in *Détente and Confrontation,* p. 314.

30. K. Subrahmanyam wrote that "had India possessed nuclear weapons the *Enterprise* would not have steamed into the Bay of Bengal . . . in what appeared from New Delhi to constitute atomic gunboat diplomacy." K. Subrahmanyam, "India: Keeping the Option

Open," in *Nuclear Proliferation: Phase II,* ed. Robert M. Lawrence and Joel Larus (Lawrence: University of Kansas Press, 1974), p. 122.

31. Ali, *An Indian Dynasty,* pp. 174-175.

32. Thomas P. Thornton, "U.S.-Indian Relations in the Nixon and Ford Years," in *The Hope and the Reality: U.S.-Indian Relations from Roosevelt to Reagan,* ed. Harold A. Gould and Sumit Ganguly (Boulder, Colo.: Westview Press, 1992), pp. 101-102.

33. Dutt, *India's Foreign Policy,* pp. 88-89.

34. On Diego Garcia, see Ajoy Sinha, *Indo-US Relations* (New Delhi: Janaki Prakashan, 1985), pp. 63-70.

35. "U.S. Foreign Policy for the 1970s: Shaping a Durable Peace," report to Congress, May 3, 1974, *Department of State Bulletin* 68, no. 1749 (June 4, 1973): pp. 791-792.

36. Ibid., p. 792.

37. Thornton, "U.S.-Indian Relations in the Nixon and Ford Years," pp. 107-108.

38. Dutt, *India's Foreign Policy,* p. 90.

39. Prime Minister Indira Gandhi, address to the "One Asia Assembly," February 6, 1973, quoted in Appadorai and Rajan, *India's Foreign Policy and Relations,* p. 567.

40. Ibid., pp. 571-573.

41. Dutt, *India's Foreign Policy,* p. 218.

42. Ibid.

43. Appadorai and Rajan, *India's Foreign Policy and Relations,* pp. 575-576.

44. *Times of India,* March 23, 1973, quoted in Sen Gupta, *Nuclear Weapons?* p. 16.

45. Ali, *An Indian Dynasty,* p. 176.

46. Frankel, *India's Political Economy,* p. 515.

47. Ibid., p. 493.

48. Nayar, *India after Nehru,* p. 217.

49. Ali, *An Indian Dynasty,* p. 177.

50. Inder Malhotra, *Indira Gandhi* (London: Hodder and Stoughton, Coronet Open Market edition, 1991), p. 154.

51. Frankel, *India's Political Economy,* p. 504.

52. Nayar, *India after Nehru,* pp. 202-213; Malhotra, *Indira Gandhi,* pp. 145-146.

53. Frankel, *India's Political Economy,* p. 477.

54. Nayar, *India after Nehru,* p. 198.

55. Ibid., pp. 202-203.

56. Frankel, *India's Political Economy,* pp. 479-483.

57. Ibid., p. 518.

58. Ibid., pp. 483-484.

59. *Lok Sabha Debates,* 5th ser., vol. 11, no. 5, March 17, 1972, cols. 130-131.

60. Reported in *Link,* May 7, 1972, p. 9.

61. Ibid. "He said the first five or six processes in the production of atomic energy and production of the bomb were the same. . . . The production of 50 atom bomb would cost 10 crore rupees ($13 million) and that of 50 hydrogen bombs Rs. 15 crores ($19.4 million)."

62. Ibid.

63. Ibid.

64. *Link,* May 21, 1972, p. 40.

65. Ibid., p. 39.

66. *Lok Sabha Debates,* 5th ser., vol. 20 no. 3, November 15, 1972, col. 49.

67. Rama Rao, "India's Nuclear Progress," p. 251. The budget then declined to Rs. 110 crores in 1973–1974 and Rs. 96 crores in 1974–1975.

68. Homi Sethna, interview by author, January 29, 1996, Mumbai. Written orders were required to implement decisions, for example, to engage Ministry of Defence employees in the digging of the hole in which the device was placed.

69. Homi Sethna, interview by author, February 26, 1997, Mumbai.

70. Bhatia wrote in *India's Nuclear Bomb*, p. 144, that the nuclear establishment completed theoretical calculations for an implosion device test by December 1972.

71. Homi Sethna, interview by author, February 26, 1997, Mumbai. Six sites were explored, in the south, north, and west of India.

72. "N-Test Decision Taken in 1971, says J. Ram," *Indian Express*, May 19, 1974, p. 1; Ajit Bhattacharjea, "Politics and the Test," *Times of India*, May 22, 1974, p. 4.

73. "Trombay Plutonium Used for Blast," *Hindu*, May 20, 1974.

74. Interview by author, February 26, 1997, Mumbai. According to Sethna, on that day Prime Minister Gandhi and Sethna and his wife flew to the nuclear establishment at Trombay and discussed the peaceful nuclear explosive project en route. The discussion continued over lunch at Trombay and culminated with the prime minister's authorization of the Atomic Energy Commission to fabricate a device and prepare for an explosion experiment.

75. Ramanna, *Years of Pilgrimage*, p. 90.

76. Government of India, Ministry of Information and Broadcasting, *India: A Reference Manual, 1976* (Delhi: Government of India, Ministry of Information and Broadcasting, 1976), pp. 437–438.

77. Interview by author with former high-ranking official, September 1997. The journalist K. C. Khanna reported that the test was the work of "[a]t least 56 scientists and technicians from BARC, with P. K. Iyengar as co-ordinator." K. C. Khanna, "India's First Atomic Blast," *Times of India*, May 21, 1974, p. 4.

78. Lewis and Xue, *China Builds the Bomb*, p. 186.

79. Bhatia, *India's Nuclear Bomb*, p. 144. Reiss reported in *Without the Bomb*, p. 228, that "a small number of chemical explosions" were conducted in March, based on a June 1986 interview with a "former senior Atomic Energy Commission official."

80. "Twenty Years after Pokhran," *Indian Express*, May 18, 1994, p. 11.

81. Anonymous, interview by author, July 1996.

82. Ibid.

83. Ramanna, *Years of Pilgrimage*, p. 88.

84. Ibid., p. 90.

85. Ibid. The U.S. Atomic Energy Commission published a textbook on polonium, including methods for its extraction, in 1956, which would have been available to the Indian scientists. See Harvey V. Moyer, ed., *Polonium* (Oak Ridge, Tenn.: U.S. Atomic Energy Commission Technical Information Service Extension, 1956).

86. Interview by author with two former high-ranking Indian Atomic Energy Commission officials, 1997.

87. Homi Sethna, interview by author, February 26, 1997, Mumbai. Manhattan Project scientists and engineers also experienced great difficulties in designing a polonium-beryllium initiator. Richard Rhodes, *Dark Sun* (New York: Simon & Schuster, 1995), pp. 187–188.

88. Lillian Hoddeson, Paul W. Henriksen, Roger A. Meade, and Catherine Westfall, *Critical Assembly: A Technical History of Los Alamos during the Oppenheimer Years, 1943–1945* (Cambridge: Cambridge University Press, 1993), p. 119.

89. (Rajya Sabha) *Parliamentary Debates,* written answers to questions, 86th sess., vol. 86, no. 4, November 15, 1973, cols. 138-139.

90. Kapur, *India's Nuclear Option,* p. 198.

91. Ibid. Kapur dated the meeting "on or around February 15."

92. Ramanna, *Years of Pilgrimage,* p. 89.

93. Homi Sethna, interview by author, January 29, 1996, Mumbai.

94. Rodney Jones recalled that after his April 13, 1978, interview with Indira Gandhi he "took away an impression that Mrs. Gandhi did not consider the Canadian cut-off as highly probable." Personal correspondence with the author, September 10, 1996. See also G. K. Reddy, "Nuclear Energy Only for Peaceful Use: PM Allays Bhutto's Fears," *Hindu,* May 24, 1974, p. 1.

95. Frankel, *India's Political Economy,* p. 523, quoting Kuldip Nayar, "Accommodating Various Interests," *Statesman,* April 24, 1974.

96. Frankel, *India's Political Economy,* pp. 526-527.

97. Ibid., p. 527.

98. Ibid.

99. Quoted in Ibid., p. 532.

100. Ibid., p. 533.

101. Former Ministry of Defence official, interview by author, June 19, 1996.

102. Frankel, *India's Political Economy,* p. 529, quoting from All India Congress Committee, "Resolution on Political Situation," *Congress Marches Ahead-10,* p. 16.

103. Raja Ramanna, interview by author, January 28, 1996, Bangalore.

104. Ramanna, *Years of Pilgrimage,* p. 89.

105. Ibid. The author tried to elicit P. N. Haksar's recollection in a February 20, 1996, phone conversation, but Haksar, then eighty-three years old and ailing, insisted that "certain traditions" and probity required him to maintain confidentiality. He did volunteer, however, that "scientists are a very poor evaluator of a very complex phenomenon called politics." In a later phone conversation, he expressed dismay at this "obsession with power, this quest for power. What is it good for? It is not food, the people cannot eat it."

106. Jones, "India," p. 114.

107. In his April 13, 1978, interview with Mrs. Gandhi, Rodney Jones asked about the possible political considerations of her decision. She said, "How could it have been political? There were no elections coming up. There was no way for it to serve a political purpose." However, when Jones added that "the explosion would not have been relevant to the election anyway—people in the villages would not understand it," Mrs. Gandhi responded, "You would be surprised. Of course, they would not understand the PNE as such. But they would understand India's achievement and that it was done despite the big powers trying to prevent India. It would have been useful for elections. But we did not have any." Personal correspondence with the author, September 10, 1996.

108. Raja Ramanna, interview by author, January 28, 1996, Bangalore.

109. Rama Rao, "India's Nuclear Progress," p. 251. The 13 percent drop, to Rs. 96 crores, or roughly $83.4 million at the 1974 exchange rate, did not take inflation into account, meaning the cut was still sharper. This compared to an annual Central Budget of roughly Rs. 5,700 crores, or $40.9 billion.

110. Interviews by author with former high-ranking Atomic Energy Commission and defense officials, January 1996 and September 1997. One termed the Ramanna-Indira

relationship "extra-familiar," meaning more coequal and friendly than the formal hierarchy would indicate.

111. Sen Gupta, *Nuclear Weapons?* p. 4.

112. Neil Joeck, "Nuclear Proliferation and National Security in India and Pakistan," p. 129.

113. Ibid.

114. Rodney Jones, correspondence with author, September 10, 1996. Jones wrote that he asked her specifically whether China's possession of nuclear weapons was a motivating factor for the PNE.

115. Interview by author, April 1997.

116. Pokhran (or Pokharan) is typically cited as the locale of the PNE. Actually the smaller village of Lokhari is closer to the test site. See Shubhabrata Bhattacharya, "Another Nuclear Blast at Pokhran?" *Sunday* (Calcutta), May 9–15, 1982.

117. Lewis M. Simons, "India Explodes A-Device, Cites 'Peaceful Use,' " *Washington Post*, May 19, 1974, p. A1.

118. See, for example, Prime Minister Gandhi's statement before the Lok Sabha on July 22, 1974 (*Lok Sabha Debates*, 5th ser., vol. 41, no. 1, "Statement re: Underground Nuclear Experiment"). See also her interview with *Newsweek*, in June 1974, cited in *Times of India*, May 28, 1974, p. 8: "There is a difference between a nuclear country and a nuclear weapons country; we are not a nuclear weapons country; we don't have any bombs."

119. "Neighbours Need Have No Fears: Mrs. Gandhi," *Times of India*, May 26, 1974, p. 1.

120. "First Nuclear Explosion by India," *Times of India*, May 19, 1974, p. 1.

121. Cited in Mirchandani, "India and Nuclear Weapons," in Poulose, *Perspectives of India's Nuclear Policy*, p. 53.

122. Bernard Weinraub, *New York Times*, May 20, 1974, p. 1, in an article headlined "Atom Test Buoys Indians' Morale."

123. *Hindu*, May 19, 1974. The editorial concluded, "[T]hough it is India's policy not to go in for nuclear weapons, its explosion of a nuclear device adds a new and important dimension to its defence capability. India has crossed the nuclear threshold."

124. T. V. Parasuram, "New Member in the Club," *Indian Express*, May 28, 1974, p. 4.

125. Weinraub, "Atom Test Buoys Indians' Morale," *New York Times*, May 20, 1974, pp. 1, 6.

126. "We Can Make It," *Janata*, May, 1974.

127. Lewis M. Simons, "A-Blast Temporarily Muffles Gandhi Critics," *Washington Post*, May 20, 1974, p. A18. Simons continued prophetically: "By exploding the nuclear device, she took the steam out of an issue the Jana Sangh and other rightists had been pushing for years—and grabbed the glory for herself. But such glory is likely to be shortlived. As the brutally hot summer wears on and food prices climb, the man in the street and the village lane will cease to find comfort in his country's nuclear capability."

128. Mirchandani, in Poulose, *Perspectives of India's Nuclear Policy*, p. 64. The Jana Sangh pressed Mrs. Gandhi to go further and manufacture nuclear weapons. Jana Sangh leader L. K. Advani asserted, "The demand for an atom bomb is no longer confined to a section or sections which can be termed a lobby. It is the nation's demand." Mirchandani, in ibid., p. 65.

129. Ibid., p. 64.

130. "Total Irresponsibility," *Statesman Weekly,* May 25, 1974, p. 8:

[W]hat on earth is all this for? Potential defence it may no doubt be said. But defence against whom? Surely not against Pakistan, unless somebody even more daft intends to supply that country with "nukes." Even more surely not against China, unless somebody still more daft than all supposes that Tom Thumba rockets would compete with a Lop Nor. Then what? One can only suppose plain conceit. India can make it, therefore let it be made.

131. George Fernandes, "India's Bomb and Indira's India," in *George Fernandes Speaks,* ed. George Mathew (New Delhi: Ajanta, 1991), p. 358.

132. Ibid., p. 363.

133. Indian Institute of Public Opinion, *Monthly Public Opinion Surveys* 19, no. 8, #224 (May 1974). The poll was conducted in early June.

134. Bernard Weinraub, "India Becomes 6th Nation to Set Off Nuclear Device," *New York Times,* May 19, 1974, p. 18.

135. "Blast Is Topic of the Day," *Times of India,* May 20, 1974, p. 1. This was ironic inasmuch as Sarabhai had resisted a nuclear weapon effort and only reluctantly grew to support the peaceful nuclear explosive project and Sethna, though a bomb advocate, had little technical involvement in building the device. Interview by author with former high-ranking Atomic Energy official, September 1997.

136. Kushwant Singh, "Explosion in the Desert: Meet the Scientists," *Illustrated Weekly of India,* July 14, 1974.

137. Ibid., p. 6.

138. "We Can Make It," *Janata,* May 1974.

139. Reiss, *Bridled Ambition,* p. 213 n. 8. Reiss cited an interview with a U.S. government official in stating that "[t]he explosion caused debris to vent into the atmosphere." Other U.S. government sources confirmed this to the author on April 18, 1996.

140. Weinraub, "Atom Test Buoys Indians' Morale," *New York Times,* p. 6.

141. See, for example, Indian Institute of Public Opinion, *Monthly Public Opinion Surveys* 15, no. 180, (August 1970): p. 13: "A majority (54 [percent]) would not go in for the Bomb if the cost carries drastic cuts in the developmental expenditure."

142. Singh, "Explosion in the Desert," p. 8.

143. Ibid. Twenty-three years later, Sethna elaborated that "we didn't put any money into the experiment to speak of. Even the hole digging was done using camels. It was cheap." Interview by author, February 26, 1997, Mumbai.

144. Seshagiri, *The Bomb!* p. 7.

145. "PM Reiterates Stand on Nuclear Weapons," *Times of India,* May 28, 1974, page 8, citing an interview Mrs. Gandhi gave to *Newsweek.*

146. Weinraub, "India Becomes 6th Nation to Set Off Nuclear Device," *New York Times,* May 19, 1974, p. 18.

147. Ramanna, *Years of Pilgrimage,* p. 91; Bhatia, *India's Nuclear Bomb,* p. 146; Reiss, *Without the Bomb,* p. 228; David Albright and Mark Hibbs, "India's Silent Bomb," *Bulletin of the Atomic Scientists,* September 1992, p. 28; Peter Clausen, *Nonproliferaton and The National Interest* (New York: HarperCollins College, 1993), p. 124. Shubhabrata Bhattacharya, "Another Nuclear Blast at Pokhran?" *Sunday,* May 9–15, 1982, p. 15, said that "[t]he atomic bomb tested by India at Pokhran in 1974 had a destructive power of 15,000 to 20,000 tons of TNT."

148. R. Chidambaram and Raja Ramanna, "Some Studies on India's Peaceful Nuclear Explosion Experiment" paper presented to the IAEA Technical Committee on the Peaceful Uses of Nuclear Explosions, January 20–24, 1975, paper no. IAEA-TC-1-4/19 (Vienna: International Atomic Energy Agency), p. 421.

149. Simon Winchester, "India's Big Blast Shrinks a Bit," *Manchester Guardian*, printed in the *Washington Post*, June 23, 1978, p. A20.

150. Yogi Aggarwal, *Sunday Observer* (Bombay), August 30, 1981, reprinted in U.S. Consul (Bombay) to Secretary of State, cable no. R041104Z, September 1981, Nuclear Non-Proliferation Policy, FOIA files, India, National Security Archive, Washington, D.C.

151. Chidambaram and Ramanna, "Some Studies on India's Peaceful Nuclear Explosion Experiment," p. 435.

152. Government of India, Department of Atomic Energy, *Annual Report of the Department of Atomic Energy, 1974–1975*, p. 61.

153. In the question-and-answer period following the Chidambaram and Ramanna presentation to the IAEA, they were asked, "What was the discrepancy between the calculated and actual yield of the explosion?" The respondent replied, "I do not have this information." Chidambaram and Ramanna, "Some Studies on India's Peaceful Nuclear Explosion Experiment," p. 436.

154. Homi Sethna, interview by author, January 29, 1996, Mumbai.

155. P. K. Iyengar, interviews by author, January 30, 1996, Mumbai, and June 21, 1996, New York.

156. Another scientist involved in the project explained that the data gleaned from the radio-chemical analysis were problematic and made detailed conclusions on yield problematic. Interview by author, February 26, 1997, Mumbai.

157. Terry C. Wallace, "The May 1998 India and Pakistan Nuclear Tests," *Seismological Research Letters*, September 1998, p. 3, <http://www.geo.arizona-edu/geophysics/faculty/wallace/ind.pak/>.

158. P. K. Iyengar, interview by author, June 21, 1996, New York.

159. P. N. Haksar, interview published in *Blitz*, August 10, 1974, reprinted in Haksar, *India's Foreign Policy and Its Problems*, p. 193.

160. Weinraub, "India Becomes 6th Nation to Set Off Nuclear Device," p. 1. The historical record at the time suggests that the U.S. government should not have been surprised that India would conduct a nuclear test. A 1972 U.S. government memorandum, NSSM 202, according to its principal drafter, Dennis Kux, "concluded that the odds were better than 50–50 that India would explode a device over the next five years. After the NSSM was sent to the NSC, nothing more was heard until after the test." Kux, *Estranged Democracies*, p. 325.

161. Kux, *Estranged Democracies*, p. 315. See also Thornton, "U.S.-Indian Relations in the Nixon and Ford Years," p. 112.

162. The ranking of nonproliferation and the Indian nuclear test among Kissinger's concerns is perhaps reflected in his memoir covering this period, *Years of Upheaval*, where neither the 1974 Indian PNE nor the general problem of proliferation is discussed. Henry Kissinger, *Years of Upheaval* (Boston: Little, Brown, 1982).

163. Secretary of State Kissinger testified at hearings on the Export Reorganization Act of 1976 before the Senate Committee on Government Operations that "[w]e deplored [the Indian test] strongly, and we have made it clear to India that we saw no need for it. . . . We

objected strongly, but since there was no violation of U.S. agreements involved, we had no specific leverage on which to bring our objections to bear." Senate Committee on Government Operations, *Export Reorganization Act of 1976: Hearings before the Committee on Government Operations,* 94th Cong., 2nd sess., March 9, 1976, p. 793.

164. "Contract of Sale of Enriched Uranium between the United States Atomic Energy Commission Acting on Behalf of the Government of the United States of America and the Government of India," May 17, 1966.

165. Letter from Dixy Lee Ray to Homi Sethna, June 19, 1974, in Chellaney, *Nuclear Proliferation,* app. F, pp. 360–361; letter from Dixy Lee Ray to Homi Sethna, September 16, 1974, ibid. p. 365; letter from Homi Sethna to Dixy Lee Ray, September 17, 1974, ibid., p. 366.

166. The congressional sanction against U.S. support for Indian loans by the World Bank was lifted in 1977.

167. Interview by author with U.S. official who traveled with Kissinger on this visit, January 1998.

168. Kux, *Estranged Democracies,* p. 328.

169. Ibid.

170. Briefing memorandum to Secretary of State Kissinger from Assistant Secretary of State Alfred L. Atherton Jr. and Policy Planning Staff Director Winston Lord, "Visit to India: Special Proposals in the Nuclear Field," October 19, 1974, State Department General Records, Policy Planning Staff Director's files, RG 59, box 369, National Archives.

171. Ibid., p. 2.

172. Ibid., attachment no. 2.

173. Ibid.

174. U.S. State Department, Bureau of Intelligence and Research, intelligence note, "India: Uncertainty over Nuclear Policy," June 13, 1974, p. 4, in FOIA files, India, National Security Archive, Washington, D.C.

175. Interview by author, January 1998.

176. "Pakistan Bars 'Blackmail,'" *New York Times,* May 20, 1974, p. 6.

177. Quoted in Appadorai and Rajan, *India's Foreign Policy and Relations,* pp. 578–579.

178. Ibid., p. 580. The Indo-Pak talks resumed in September but made no progress.

179. Leonard S. Spector, *Nuclear Proliferation Today* (New York: Vintage Books, 1984), p. 74.

180. Moynihan, quoted from an interview, in Kux, *Estranged Democracies,* p. 315.

181. Spector, *Nuclear Proliferation Today,* pp. 34–35.

182. Kapur, *India's Nuclear Option,* p. 219.

183. See *New Times,* no. 21, May 1974, pp. 13, 15.

184. Statement by Prime Minister Indira Gandhi to the Lok Sabha, July 22, 1974.

185. Kapur, *India's Nuclear Option,* p. 223.

186. Ibid., p. 232.

187. Robert L. Beckman, *Nuclear Non-Proliferation* (Boulder, Colo.: Westview Press, 1985), p. 229.

188. Ibid.

189. Homi Sethna and P. K. Iyengar, interviews by author, January 29, 1996, and January 30, 1996, respectively, Mumbai.

190. In an interview shortly after the PNE, Atomic Energy Commission Chairman Homi Sethna offered no plan for follow-up engineering experiments or applications. Reiss, *Without the Bomb,* p. 231.

191. Statement by Prime Minister Indira Gandhi to the Lok Sabha, July 22, 1974.

192. Indian Institute of Public Opinion, *Monthly Public Opinion Surveys* 19, no. 11, #227 (August 1974): p. 6.

193. Indian Institute of Public Opinion, *Monthly Public Opinion Surveys* 23, no. 12, #276 (September 1978): p. 8.

194. "The modest nuclear explosion carried out by India today is only the first in the series of similar tests." G. K. Reddy, "India Explodes Nuclear Device Underground," *Hindu*, May 19, 1974, p. 1.

195. Interview by author, September 1997.

196. Ibid.

197. China, like India, achieved the technology necessary to wield nuclear weapons before developing doctrine to guide potential use. See Lewis and Xue, *China Builds the Bomb*.

CHAPTER EIGHT

1. In April 1974, Senator Abraham Ribicoff released an internal report to the U.S. Atomic Energy Commission, decrying the inadequate attention and effort being paid to preventing weapons-usable nuclear materials from being diverted from power plants and other facilities into the hands of unauthorized persons or groups. *Congressional Record*, 93d Cong., 2d sess., 1974, 120, pt. 9: pp. 12353–12359. See also Mason Willrich and Theodore Taylor, *Nuclear Theft: Risks and Safeguards* (Cambridge, Mass.: Ballinger, 1974), and John McPhee, *The Curve of Binding Energy* (New York: Ballantine Books, 1973).

2. Fred Iklé, interview by author, April 22, 1998.

3. The Nuclear Suppliers Group guidelines were not made public until 1978 when the International Atomic Energy Agency published them in a circular entitled "Communications Received from Certain Member States Regarding Guidelines for the Export of Nuclear Materials, Equipment or Technology," INFCIRC/254, February 1978.

4. Chellaney, *Nuclear Proliferation*, p. 64.

5. K. Subrahmanyam, "Bomb—The Only Answer," reprinted in Indian Institute of Public Opinion, *Monthly Public Opinion Surveys* 26, nos. 5–6, #305–306 (February–March 1981): p. 9.

6. Frankel, *India's Political Economy*, p. 535, quoting from *Statesman*, November 27, 1974.

7. Frankel, *India's Political Economy*, p. 537.

8. Ibid., p. 539.

9. Quoted in ibid., pp. 545–546. Six years later, the Shah Commission Report on the Emergency offered a more accurate assessment when it concluded that the prime minister had been motivated by narrow, selfish political considerations and had "sacrificed the interests of the many to serve the ambitions of a few." Shah Commission Report on the Emergency, quoted in Ali, *An Indian Dynasty*, p. 186.

10. Frankel, *India's Political Economy*, p. 546.

11. Ibid., p. 557.

12. Speech of Finance Minister H. M. Patel, introducing the 1977–1978 budget, June 17, 1977, in *Speeches of Union Finance Ministers, 1947–48 to 1984–85* (Government of India, Ministry of Finance, Department of Economic Affairs, October 1984), p. 425.

13. Statement by M. R. Srinivasan, January 4, 1976, cited in *Foreign Broadcast Information Service-Middle East and Africa* (FBIS-MEA), 76–4, January 7, 1976.

14. Interviews by author, January 28, 1996, Bangalore, and January 29, 1996, Mumbai.

15. Memorandum from State Department Policy Planning Staff Director Winston Lord and Assistant Secretary of State for Near East Asia Alfred L. Atherton Jr. to Secretary of State Kissinger, "Nuclear Dialogue with India," August 19, 1975, p. 1, in General Records of the Department of State Policy Planning Staff, Director's files, Winston Lord, RG 59, entry no. 5027, stack 250, row D, compartment 7, shelf 7, box no. 369, National Archives.

16. Ibid., p. 1.

17. Ibid., p. 2.

18. Ibid., pp. 2–3.

19. Ibid., p. 3.

20. Ibid, emphasis added.

21. Bharat Wariawalla, "Nuclear Option Is an Illusion," *Indian Express,* December 16, 1997, asserted, "A month after Pokhran our European and American donors at the Aid India Club meeting in Paris in June 1974 asked us some blunt questions regarding our nuclear policy. The upshot was that we called off the series of nuclear explosions we had planned."

22. Quoted in Shirin Tahir-Kelhi, "Pakistan's Nuclear Option and U.S. Policy," *Orbis* 22, no. 2 (Summer 1978): p. 371.

23. Draft memorandum for President Ford from Secretary of State Kissinger regarding "U.S. Policy on Military Supply for South Asia," prepared by Alfred L. Atherton Jr., January 28, 1975, pp. 2–3, in General Records of the Department of State Policy Planning Staff, Director's files, Winston Lord, RG 59, entry no. 5027, stack 250, row D, compartment 7, shelf 7, box no. 369, National Archives.

24. Ibid.

25. Ibid., p. 3.

26. The full text of the three-paragraph Pakistani note was attached to a memorandum from State Department Policy Planning Staff Director Winston Lord to Arms Control and Disarmament Agency Director Fred Iklé, February 20, 1975, in General Records of the Department of State Policy Planning Staff, Director's files, Winston Lord, RG 59, entry no. 5027, stack 250, row D, compartment 7, shelf 7, box no. 369, National Archives.

27. Kux, *Estranged Democracies,* p. 332.

28. Munir Ahmad Khan, "Bhutto and Pakistan's Nuclear Programme," *Frontier Post,* April 4, 1995, p. 1.

29. Ibid. In March 1976, France and Pakistan also signed an agreement for French construction of a 600-megawatt pressurized water reactor to be built at Chashma.

30. Zahid Malik, *Dr. A. Q. Khan and the Islamic Bomb* (Islamabad: Hurmat, 1992), p. 59. This generally fawning biography of A. Q. Khan contains many details presented in ways that suggest that it was heavily informed, if not written, by Khan himself.

31. Ibid., p. 60.

32. Ibid., p. 62.

33. "Report of the Inter-ministerial Working Party Responsible for Investigating the 'Khan Affair,' " Government of the Netherlands, October 1979. A Dutch court found Khan guilty on October 31, 1983, of attempting to obtain classified information on uranium enrichment technology and sentenced him *in absentia* to four years' imprisonment. This conviction was overturned on appeal in 1985 on the grounds that Khan was not properly served with a summons. *Financial Times,* July 16, 1986. On U.S. intelligence assessments,

see, for example, U.S. State Department, "The Pakistani Nuclear Program," June 23, 1983, p. 4., FOIA files, Pakistan, National Security Archive, Washington, D.C.

34. Malik, *Dr. A. Q. Khan and the Islamic Bomb*, p. 63. As the Pakistani nuclear program progressed, A. Q. Khan cultivated the mythology that he was its father and guiding spirit. This understated the role played by Munir Ahmad Khan through 1992 in coordinating all of the activities that go into producing a nuclear weapon.

35. Zulfikar Ali Bhutto, testimony before the Supreme Court of Pakistan, reprinted in P. K. S. Namboodiri, "Pakistan's Nuclear Posture," in *Nuclear Myths and Realities*, ed. K. Subrahmanyam (New Delhi: ABC, 1981), pp. 145–146.

36. U.S. State Department, "The Pakistani Nuclear Program," June 23, 1983, p. 6, FOIA files, Pakistan, National Security Archive, Washington, D.C. On June 22 and 23, 1984, Leslie Gelb reported learning from U.S. intelligence sources that in 1983 China provided Pakistan the design of the nuclear bomb used in China's fourth nuclear test. Leslie Gelb, "Pakistan Tie Imperils U.S.-China Nuclear Pact," *New York Times*, June 22, 1984, p. 1; Leslie Gelb, "Peking Said to Balk at Nuclear Pledges," *New York Times*, June 23, 1984, pp. 3, 9.

37. Dutt, *India's Foreign Policy*, pp. 219–220.

38. Then-Pakistani Ambassador to the United States Yaqub Khan indicated during an April 20 lunch with State Department Policy Planning Staff Director Winston Lord that, according to Lord, "Peking had coordinated its moves with his [Yaqub's] government," as "Peking had always told Islamabad that it would never move toward India . . . except in the wake of Pakistani moves." Winston Lord to Secretary of State Kissinger, memorandum of conversation with the Pakistani Ambassador, April 22, 1976, p. 2, in General Records of the Department of State Policy Planning Staff, Director's files, Winston Lord, RG 59, entry no. 5027, stack 250, row D, compartment 7, box no. 369, National Archives.

39. Correspondence from Prime Minister Bhutto to Prime Minister Gandhi, March 27, 1976; from Gandhi to Bhutto, April 11, 1976; from Bhutto to Gandhi, April 18, 1976; and joint statement by Pakistan and India, May 14, 1976, all in *Pakistan Horizon* 29, no. 1 (First Quarter, 1976): pp. 194–198.

40. *Foreign Assistance Act of 1961, U.S. Code*, vol. 22, sec. 669 (1976).

41. Anticipating the direction of congressionally driven policy, Secretary of State Henry Kissinger traveled to Islamabad in August 1976 to press Prime Minister Bhutto to cancel the French-Pakistani plans to build the reprocessing plant. Kissinger offered the supply of American A-7 jet fighters as an inducement. When Bhutto declined, Kissinger reportedly advised him, according to General K. M. Arif, that if elected, the Democrats would "make a horrible example of you." Arif, *Working with Zia*, p. 366. According to a U.S. official traveling with Kissinger, the secretary of state was "surprised by Bhutto's absolute determination to go forward with the nuclear program," while Bhutto appeared surprised by the U.S. determination to try to stop it. Interview by author, January 1998, Washington, D.C.

42. India did not share the U.S. interpretation, arguing that the 1956 agreement did not exclude using heavy water for *peaceful* nuclear explosives and that the United States was wrong to reinterpret the agreement fifteen years later. The State Department previously had calculated mistakenly that the U.S.-supplied heavy water had evaporated and therefore was not "implicated" in the Pokhran blast. When the State Department corrected this analysis in August 1975, nonproliferation activists in the Senate seized on the correction as an example of executive branch laxity. See Kux, *Estranged Democracies*, pp. 340–341.

43. Memorandum on nuclear dialogue with India from State Department Policy Planning Staff Director Winston Lord and Assistant Secretary of State for Near East Asia Alfred L. Atherton Jr. to Secretary of State Kissinger, April 3, 1976, in General Records of the Department of State Policy Planning Staff, Director's files, Winston Lord, RG 59, entry no. 5027, stack 250, row D, compartment 7, shelf 7, box no. 369, National Archives.

44. Jimmy Carter, "Address on Nuclear Policy to the United Nations," May 13, 1976.

45. The declassified files of the then director of the State Department Policy Planning Staff indicated that by mid-1976 the Ford administration was devoting considerable attention to the nonproliferation problem. A Non-Proliferation Working Group (NPWG) was created with Winston Lord as coordinator. Numerous studies, papers, and policy recommendations were produced, culminating in Ford's October 28, 1976, statement.

46. Memorandum from State Department Policy Planning Staff Director Winston Lord to Secretary of State Kissinger, October 22, 1976, in General Records of the Department of State Policy Planning Staff, Director's files, Winston Lord, RG 59, entry no. 5027, stack 250, row D, compartment 7, shelf 7, box no. 367, National Archives.

47. Quoted in Michael J. Brenner, *Nuclear Power and Non-Proliferation* (Cambridge, U.K.: Cambridge University Press, 1981), p. 115.

48. Indira Gandhi, national radio broadcast, January 18, 1977, reprinted in Sharda Paul, *1977 General Elections in India* (New Delhi: Associated, 1977), p. 4.

49. S. Devadas Pillai, ed., *The Incredible Elections: 1977* (Bombay: Popular Prakashan, 1977), p. 37.

50. The other major forces were the two rival Communist parties (the pro-Soviet CPI and the pro-China CPI-M) and the Congress for Democracy, which split from Mrs. Gandhi's Congress upon the February 2 defection of then-Agriculture Minister Jagjivan Ram.

51. All the manifestos, including the one quoted here (from p. 163), appeared in Paul, *1977 General Elections in India*, pp. 100-221.

52. H. T. Ramakrishna, *Elections 77* (Tiptur: Lalitha Prakashana, 1977), p. 121.

53. By August, the Janata front, including the Congress for Democracy, held 302 of 544 seats, according to "Yes, To Mid-Term Poll," *India Today*, August 1-15, 1979, p. 10.

54. The national Emergency was lifted on March 22 by proclamation of the acting president. Six days later the external Emergency, in effect since the 1971 Indo-Pak war, was also lifted.

55. Interview by author, January 29, 1996, Mumbai.

56. Morarji Desai, press conference, March 24, 1977, *FBIS-MEA*, March 25, 1977, pp. S3-S7.

57. Mirchandani, "India and Nuclear Weapons," in Poulose, *Perspectives of India's Nuclear Policy*, pp. 65-66.

58. *Hindustan Times*, May 17, 1977.

59. Quote from Don Oberdorfer, "Carter Willing to Ship India Uranium Fuel," *Washington Post*, May 25, 1977, p. 1.

60. See, for example, Pathak, *Nuclear Policy of India*, pp. 194-198; Margaret Alva, "Janata's Foreign Policy: A Critique," in *Janata's Foreign Policy*, ed. K. P. Misra, (New Delhi: Vikas, 1979), p. 17; and Ashok Kapur, "Janata Government's Nuclear Policy," in Poulose, *Perspectives of India's Nuclear Policy*, pp. 174-180.

61. Paul F. Power, "The Indo-American Nuclear Controversy," *Asian Survey* 19, no. 6 (June 1979): p. 585.

62. Agence France-Presse, March 18, 1977, in *FBIS-MEA*, March 18, 1977, p. S2.

63. Dhruva began operation ten years later, in August 1985, and then was shut down due to technical difficulties, before resuming full operations in 1988.

64. Kux, *Estranged Democracies,* p. 349, quoting interview with Robert Goheen.

65. Ibid.; author interview with Goheen, December 6, 1995, Princeton; and personal correspondence with Goheen, March 3, 1998.

66. The Nuclear Regulatory Commission issued the export license on June 28, 1977.

67. Uncorrected transcript of Lok Sabha, short notice question period, July 13, 1977, Government of India, Department of Atomic Energy, col. 14098.

68. Ibid., col. 14100.

69. Ibid., col. 14101.

70. Ibid., col. 14102.

71. Ibid., col. 14103.

72. Ibid., col. 14105.

73. Ibid., col. 14108.

74. Ibid.

75. "No More Tests," *Times of India,* July 16, 1977. The editorial failed to mention that Desai had ruled out a white paper on the subject.

76. *Indian Express,* July 15, 1977; *Patriot,* July 15, 1977.

77. On December 22, Desai told the Rajya Sabha that India was committed "not to explode any nuclear device for peaceful purposes or make any nuclear weapons." "Nuclear Research without Explosions," *Indian and Foreign Review,* January 1, 1978, p. 7.

78. Mirchandani, "India and Nuclear Weapons," in Poulose, *Perspectives of India's Nuclear Policy,* p. 66.

79. Maharaj K. Chopra, "Nuclear Rights versus Nuclear Realities," *Organiser,* October 10, 1977, p. 7.

80. Ibid.

81. Ibid., p. 12.

82. S. C. Gangal, in Misra, *Jamata's Foreign Policy,* p. 40.

83. Interviews by author with former high-ranking Pakistani atomic energy, finance, and foreign policy officials, 1992, 1993, and 1996, Islamabad.

84. Ibid.

85. Interview with former high-ranking Indian official, February 7, 1998.

86. Beckman, *Nuclear Non-Proliferation,* pp. 299–300.

87. Robert F. Goheen, "U.S. Policy toward India during the Carter Presidency," in Gould and Ganguly, *The Hope and the Reality,* p. 121.

88. Section 128 of the *Atomic Energy Act* as amended by the *NNPA, U.S. Code,* vol. 42, sec. 2157 (1997).

89. Ibid., sec. 2156.

90. Ibid., sec. 2158.

91. Ibid.

92. Richard P. Cronin, "U.S. Uranium Fuel Exports to India: A Case Study," in *Congress and Foreign Policy, 1980* (Washington: U.S. Government Printing Office, 1981), pp. 91–92.

93. Senator John Glenn, in *Nuclear Non-Proliferation Act of 1977: Hearings of the U.S. Senate Subcommittee on Energy, Nuclear Proliferation, and Federal Services,* Committee on Governmental Affairs, 95th Congress, 1st sess., hearing of May 6, 1977, p. 239.

94. Ibid. Glenn did not mention India explicitly here.

95. Ibid., p. 63, hearing of April 1, 1977.

96. Beckman, *Nuclear Non-Proliferation,* p. 330.

97. U.S. Senate Committee on Governmental Affairs, *Legislative History of the Nuclear Non-Proliferation Act of 1978, H.R. 8638 (Public Law 95-242),* Subcommittee on Energy, Nuclear Proliferation, and Federal Services, January 1979, p. 817.

98. Leonard Weiss, interview by author, June 9, 1995, Washington, D.C. Weiss was staff director of the Senate Governmental Affairs Committee Subcommittee on Energy, Nuclear Proliferation, and Federal Services and a key drafter of the NNPA. The remaining quotes in this paragraph are from this same interview.

99. Senator John Glenn, in *Nuclear Non-Proliferation Act of 1977: Hearings of the U.S. Senate Subcommittee on Energy, Nuclear Proliferation, and Federal Services,* Committee on Governmental Affairs, 95th Congress, 1st. sess., hearing of April 1, 1977, p. 43.

100. Nye testimony in ibid., p. 242, hearing of May 6, 1977.

101. Leonard Weiss, interview by author, June 9, 1995.

102. Section 131 of the *Atomic Energy Act* as amended by the *NNPA, U.S. Code,* vol. 42, sec. 2160 (1997). The U.S. would accept foreign spent fuel only if both houses of Congress do not object and if the president submits a detailed plan for such disposition or storage.

103. Power, "The Indo-American Nuclear Controversy," p. 583. The 1963 agreement stipulated that no special nuclear materials produced in the Tarapur reactor would be used for atomic weapons or other military purpose, which implied verification inspections of the material wherever it sat.

104. U.S. Senate Committee on Governmental Affairs, *Legislative History of the Nuclear Non-Proliferation Act of 1978, H.R. 8638 (Public Law 95-242),* Subcommittee on Energy, Nuclear Proliferation, and Federal Services, January 1979, p. 704.

105. Goheen, "U.S. Policy toward India during the Carter Presidency," p. 125.

106. Quoted in ibid., p. 124. No such letter was sent, although Carter and Desai maintained an earnest correspondence.

107. Kux, *Estranged Democracies,* p. 355.

108. Indian Institute of Public Opinion, *Monthly Public Opinion Surveys* 23, no. 5, #269-270, (February-March 1978): p. 4.

109. Ibid.

110. Ibid. Respondents were evenly divided in their concern about the spread of nuclear weapons—29 percent were concerned, 25 percent were not, while 47 percent had no opinion on the issue. The pollsters noted that proliferation was "not easily comprehensible to the common man."

111. Kux, *Estranged Democracies,* p. 355.

112. Atal Behari Vajpayee, "Continuity and Change—FM on Foreign Policy," *India News,* May 22, 1978, p. 5.

113. Kux, *Estranged Democracies,* pp. 355-56. In 1980 India received $1.285 billion in International Development Assistance, of which the U.S. provided $347 million. Goheen, "U.S. Policy toward India during the Carter Presidency," p. 124.

114. "The Ides of March," *India Today,* March 1-15, 1978, pp. 6-7. Indira Gàndhi had split the Congress party in January 1978, as she had in 1969. Her new faction was dubbed the Congress (I), with the "I" representing Indira.

115. "Playing the Wrong Tune," *India Today,* March 16-31, pp. 10-11.

116. Address by Indian Prime Minister Desai before Special Session of the General Assembly, June 9, 1978, quoted in Reiss, *Without the Bomb,* p. 235.

117. Memorandum from Secretary of State Cyrus Vance to President Carter, "Prime Minister Desai's Visit to Washington," p. 2, undated, FOIA files, India, National Security Archive, Washington, D.C.

118. Ibid., pp. 2–10.

119. Minutes of President Carter's Meetings with Prime Minister Desai, June 13, 1978, FOIA files, India, National Security Archive, Washington, D.C.

120. Ibid., pp. 2–3.

121. Ibid., p. 7.

122. Ibid. In an interesting aside, Desai misread the Pakistani military regime and predicted erroneously that Zulfikar Ali Bhutto would not be hanged. Ibid., p. 8.

123. Minutes of President Carter's Meetings with Prime Minister Desai, June 14, 1978, p. 15., FOIA files, India, National Security Archive, Washington, D.C.

124. Kux, *Estranged Democracies*, p. 358.

125. Quoted in ibid., p. 359.

126. "Anxiety Sets In," *India Today*, January 1–15, 1978, pp. 12–13, and "Torn with Strife," *India Today*, April 1–15, 1978, pp. 10–11.

127. "Anxiety Sets In," *India Today*, January 1–15, p. 13.

128. Delhi Domestic News Service, June 17, 1978, in *FBIS-South Asia (SA)*, June 19, 1978, p. S2.

129. G. K. Reddy, "Opposition Assails PM's Nuclear Policy," *Hindu*, June 20, 1978.

130. Pathak, *Nuclear Policy of India*, pp. 36–37.

131. Jay Dubashi, "A Perennial Problem," *India Today*, June 16–30, 1978, pp. 62–63.

132. Jay Dubashi, "Vicious Circle of Confusion," *India Today*, November 16–30, 1978, pp. 72–73.

133. Interview by author with former high-ranking Indian official, August 1997.

134. Ramanna, *Years of Pilgrimage*, pp. 97–100.

135. Previously there had been three departments within the Ministry of Defence: Department of Defence; Department of Defence Production; Department of Defence Supplies. The Department of Defence Research and Development was created upon Ramanna's arrival.

136. Ramanna, *Years of Pilgrimage*, p. 100.

137. According to a news report, Ramanna in August 1978 was so frustrated at Desai's dismissal of the Pokhran test as "politically motivated" that he contemplated quitting his new posts. "Blasting the Scientists," *India Today*, August 16–31, 1978, p. 54.

138. From the reply to the discussion on Baron Nuclear Explosions, July 26, 1978, *Selected Speeches of Morarji Desai, 1977–1979* (New Delhi: Ministry of Information and Broadcasting, 1986), p. 93.

139. Ibid., pp. 93–94. See also *Lok Sabha Debates*, 6th. ser., vol. 19, no. 10, December 1, 1978, col. 372.

140. *Selected Speeches of Morarji Desai, 1977–1979*, p. 93.

141. Statement in Rajya Sabha, July 31, 1978, in ibid., p. 95.

142. At this time in the test ban treaty negotiations the Soviet Union was prepared to join the United States in banning peaceful nuclear explosions.

143. Statement in Rajya Sabha, July 31, 1978, in *Selected Speeches of Morarji Desai, 1977–1979*, p. 97.

144. Power, "The Indo-American Nuclear Controversy," p. 588.

145. Robert F. Goheen, interview by author, December 6, 1995, Princeton, N.J.

146. Interview by author, January 20, 1998, New Delhi. Goheen noted that Desai's deep resistance to the inequitable NPT would have precluded India's signing the treaty.

147. Indian Institute of Public Opinion, *Monthly Public Opinion Surveys* 23, no. 12, #276 (September 1978): p. 10. As usual, respondents in Delhi were significantly more hawkish on nuclear policy than in the other cities: 20 percent there supported Desai's position, while 65 percent opposed it. This contrasted with Bombay (35/48), Calcutta (40/46), and Madras (41/45).

148. Ibid., emphasis added.

149. K. N. Ramchandran, "Sino-Indian Relations," in Misra, *Janata's Foreign Policy,* p. 200.

150. Indian Institute of Public Opinion, *Monthly Public Opinion Surveys* 24, no. 1, #277, (October 1978): p. 4.

151. Ibid.

152. Personal correspondence with author, March 3, 1998.

153. R. Rama Rao, "Bear Hugs and Bruises," *India Today,* April 1–15, 1979, p. 20. The Indians described the Chinese incursions into Vietnam as "massive armed attack."

154. See, for example, Swadesh Rana, "The Islamic Bomb," *India Today,* June 1–15, 1979, pp. 88–89.

155. See, for example, Inderjit Badhwar, "Confused Preferences," *India Today,* September 16–30, 1979, pp. 55–59.

156. For an analysis of India's overall defense policy, see Chris Smith, *India's Ad Hoc Arsenal* (New York: Oxford University Press, 1994).

157. U.S. Embassy (New Delhi) to Secretary of State, cable no. 7195, April 1979, p. 1, FOIA files, India, National Security Archive, Washington, D.C.

158. Ibid., p. 2. This overlooked the American invocation of the Symington Amendment.

159. Carter quoted in Kux, *Estranged Democracies,* p. 362. In a June 4, 1979, letter to Desai, Carter noted, "We have reached agreement on SALT but I will not be satisfied until the end of that road is reached and nuclear weapons are no longer part of the world's armories." Letter from President Jimmy Carter to Prime Minister Morarji Desai, June 4, 1979, in FOIA files, India, National Security Archive, Washington, D.C.

160. Draft State Department background briefing, January 1979, p. 1, FOIA files, India, National Security Archive, Washington, D.C.

161. Power, "The Indo-American Nuclear Controversy," p. 594. For an Indian debate over this committee and Desai's overall policy, see *Lok Sabha Debates,* 6th ser., vol. 19, no. 10, December 1, 1978, cols. 361–376.

162. Sreekant Khandekar, "Images India," *India Today,* May 16–31, 1979, pp. 100–101.

163. "Tragedy of Errors," *India Today,* July 16–31, 1979, p. 12.

164. C. Subramaniam, "India's Defence Strategy in the Next Decade," quoted in Raju G. C. Thomas, *Indian Security Policy* (Princeton, N.J.: Princeton University Press, 1986), p. 121.

165. "India to Keep 'Nuclear Options,' "*New York Times,* July 28, 1979.

166. "Reassurance on Nuclear Policy Likely Soon," *Statesman,* August 17, 1979, p. 1.

167. Ibid.

168. Goheen, "U.S. Policy toward India during the Carter Presidency," p. 129.

169. Letter from Ambassador Robert F. Goheen to Senator Paul Sarbanes, December 11, 1979, pp. 1–2, in FOIA files, India, National Security Archive, Washington, D.C.

170. The summary here draws heavily from Garthoff, *Détente and Confrontation*, pp. 977–1075.

171. Statement quoted in Kux, *Estranged Democracies*, p. 367.

172. Dilip Bobb, Chhotu Karadia, with Inderjit Badhwar, "The Super Power Game," *India Today*, February 1–15, 1980, p. 10.

173. Kux, *Estranged Democracies*, p. 368.

174. Following Gandhi's election, Zia called her to offer congratulations and express hopes that normalization of relations could be "expedited." Zia reported that she had replied positively. Kuldip Nayar, interview with Zia-ul-Haq, " 'Learn a Lesson from History,' " *India Today*, February 16–29, 1980, p. 85.

175. Ibid., p. 86.

176. Ali, *An Indian Dynasty*, p. 208.

177. Indian Institute of Public Opinion, *Monthly Public Opinion Survey* 25, nos. 4–5, Blue Supplement (March 1980).

178. Indian Institute of Public Opinion, *Monthly Public Opinion Surveys* 25, no. 7, #295 (April 1980): p. 3.

179. Ibid., p. 4.

180. *India Today*, December 16–31, 1979, p. 67.

181. Dipa Jaywant, "Bleak Prospects," *India Today*, February 1–15, 1980, p. 65.

182. Ibid.

183. Ibid. The Baroda heavy-water plant remained shut down following its explosion in 1977, just four months after commissioning, and it was not due to be back on line until later in 1980. "P.M. for Peaceful Nuclear Tests in National Interest," *Times of India*, March 14, 1980, p. 1.

184. Jay Dubashi, "The Stalemate Persists," *India Today*, April 1–15, 1980, p. 29.

185. Jay Dubashi, "A Blueprint for Frustration?" *India Today*, August 16–31, 1980, pp. 70–71.

186. Ibid.

187. "P.M. for Peaceful Nuclear Tests in National Interest," *Times of India*, March 14, 1980, p. 1.

188. Ibid.

189. A month later, she responded to parliamentary concerns over Pakistan's uranium enrichment program by saying, "While we do not have all we would like to have in the defence sphere, we are trying to strengthen ourselves." She then alluded to an Atomic Energy Commission effort to develop uranium enrichment capacity. Spector, *Nuclear Proliferation Today*, p. 43.

CHAPTER NINE

1. See testimony of U.S. Deputy Secretary of State Warren Christopher in Senate Committee on Foreign Relations and Committee on Governmental Affairs, *The Tarapur Nuclear Fuel Export Issue: Joint Hearings*, 96th Cong., 2d sess., June 18–19, 1980, p. 69.

2. Indira Gandhi, letter, December 1980, quoted in Ram, "India's Nuclear Policy," p. 51.

3. Smith, *India's Ad Hoc Arsenal*, p. 111.

4. Don Oberdorfer, "U.S., Pakistan Progressing on New Aid Plan," *Washington Post*, April 22, 1981, p. 1.

5. Kux, *Estranged Democracies*, p. 383.

6. Smith, *India's Ad Hoc Arsenal*, p. 111.

7. Judith Miller, "Cranston Says India and Pakistan Are Preparing for Nuclear Testing," *New York Times*, April 28, 1981, p. 1.

8. Rahul Bedi, "Pokhran Full of N-Test Talk," *Indian Express*, May 5, 1981, p. 1. In 1996, two Lawrence Livermore National Laboratory experts analyzed the Cranston and Bedi reports against commercial satellite imagery and concluded that preparations consistent with a potential nuclear explosive test had indeed occurred at this time. Vipin Gupta and Frank Pabian, "Investigating the Allegations of Indian Nuclear Test Preparations in the Rajasthan Desert," *Science & Global Security* 6 (1996): pp. 101–189.

9. Sethna, comments from May 5 speech at Kurukshetra University, quoted in "Pak N-Blast Any Time after June: Sethna," *Hindustan Times*, May 6, 1981, and reported in U.S. Embassy (New Delhi) to Secretary of State, cable no. 09095, May 1981, FOIA files, India, National Security Archive, Washington, D.C. The *Agence France-Presse* carried a report on April 28 that Indian officials had declined to confirm or deny the U.S. report of test preparations near Pokhran. *FBIS-SA*, April 28, 1981, p. E1.

10. *India News*, January 5, 1981, p. 2.

11. Raja Ramanna, interview by author, March 20, 1998, New Delhi.

12. Ramanna, *Years of Pilgrimage*, pp. 108–109.

13. K. Subrahmanyam, interview by author, March 22, 1998, New Delhi.

14. Yogi Aggarwal, "India Makes Another Bomb," *Sunday Observer*, August 31, 1981, reprinted in U.S. Consul (Bombay) to Secretary of State, cable no. 3265, September, 1981, in FOIA files, India, National Security Archive, Washington, D.C.

15. Aggarwal cited "some sources" at BARC who suggested that the yield of the 1974 PNE was "as low as 2,000 tons (2 kilotons) of TNT," not the twelve kilotons reported in India and elsewhere.

16. Ibid., p. 2.

17. Ibid.

18. Ram, "India's Nuclear Policy," p. 7.

19. Subrahmanyam, *Times of India*, April 26, 1981, reprinted in U.S. Embassy (New Delhi) to Secretary of State, telegram no. 08521, April 28, 1981, p. 1, in FOIA files, India, National Security Archive, Washington, D.C.

20. Ibid., p. 6.

21. Ibid.

22. Ibid., p. 7.

23. Ibid.

24. Stuart Auerbach, "Arms for Pakistan Spur Gandhi's Fears, Hawks' Calls for A-Weapon," *Washington Post*, May 3, 1981, pp. A25–26, citing articles in *Times of India, Bombay Daily*, and *Statesman*.

25. Ibid.

26. Indian Institute of Public Opinion, *Monthly Public Opinion Surveys* 26, no. 10, #310 (July 1981): p. 8.

27. Ibid., p. 7.

28. Lieutenant General K. Sundarji, ed., "Effects of Nuclear Asymmetry on Conventional Deterrence," *Combat Papers* (Mhow), no. 1 (April 1981), and "Nuclear Weapons in Third World Context," *Combat Papers* (Mhow), no. 2 (August 1981).

29. For an analysis of the evolution of military thinking about nuclear weapons, see W. P. S. Sidhu, "The Development of an Indian Nuclear Doctrine since 1980" (Ph.D. diss., Emmanuel College, University of Cambridge, 1997); Bhabani Sen Gupta, "India's Nuclear Challenge," *India Today,* June 16–30, 1981, p. 54.

30. Address by Vice Admiral M. R. Schunker, in *Nuclear Shadow over the Sub-Continent,* ed. Colonel Pyara Lal (New Delhi: United Service Institution of India, 1981), p. 2.

31. Amiya Kumar Ghosh, *India's Defence Budget and Expenditure Management in a Wider Context* (New Delhi: Lancer, 1996), pp. 111, 134.

32. Smith, *India's Ad Hoc Arsenal,* p. 129, and Ravi Rikhye, *The Militarization of Mother India* (New Delhi: Chanakya, 1990). Rikhye reported that the Mirage 2000 cost Rs. 42.5 crores per plane "without the promised engine and radar, and without weapons," compared with the Rs. 30 crores Pakistan paid for American F-16s with all components and weapons. A knowledgeable Indian Ministry of Defence official reported in correspondence with the author (April 21, 1998) that the contracted price for the Mirage 2000s was less than half what Rikhye claimed. Another knowledgeable former Indian official added that the Mirage 2000s were necessary to match Pakistan's acquisition of the American F-16s and that India had tried to obtain cheaper MiG-29s from the Soviet Union, only to be told by Soviet Defense Minister Dmitry Ustinov that the plane did not exist. Only after India had completed negotiations for the contract with France for the Mirages did the Soviets acknowledge the MiG-29's existence and offer to sell it to India. Had the availability of the MiG-29 been known earlier, this former Indian official argued that India would not have bought the overpriced Mirages. Interview by author, March 1998.

33. Interviews by author with former high-ranking army and air force officials, March 19–20, 1998, New Delhi.

34. Quoted in Sidhu, "The Development of an Indian Nuclear Doctrine," p. 202.

35. J. N. Dixit, *Anatomy of a Flawed Inheritance, Indo-Pak Relations, 1970–1994* (Delhi: Konark, 1995), p. 65.

36. Ibid., pp. 65–66.

37. Ibid., p. 71.

38. Cited in Sidhu, "The Development of an Indian Nuclear Doctrine," p. 203.

39. See, for example, "Waiting for the Next Round," *Statesman,* December 17, 1981, p. 8.

40. Inder Malhotra, *Indira Gandhi,* p. 266.

41. Indira Gandhi, September 1981 interview with *AGE* magazine, quoted in U.S. Embassy (New Delhi) to Secretary of State, June 1982, cable no. 11254, p. 16, in FOIA files, India, National Security Archive, Washington, D.C.

42. "Pak Boast about Bomb," *Hindu,* November 29, 1981, p. 2.

43. Indira Gandhi, quoted in July 10, 1981, Indian press, cited in U.S. Embassy (New Delhi) to Secretary of State, June 1982, cable no. 11254, p. 16, in FOIA files, India, National Security Archive, Washington, D.C.

44. In his 749-page autobiography, Reagan did not mention India or Indira Gandhi. *Ronald Reagan, An American Life* (New York: Simon & Schuster, 1990).

45. Interview by author with former Reagan administration official, July 14, 1998.

46. Kux, *Estranged Democracies,* p. 380.

47. Ibid., p. 385.

48. Former Ambassador to India Harry Barnes, interview by author, January 26, 1998.

49. Ibid. and Kux, *Estranged Democracies,* p. 387.

50. P. C. Alexander, *My Years with Indira Gandhi* (New Delhi: Vision Books, 1991), p. 86.

51. Peter A. Clausen, *Nonproliferation and the National Interest* (New York: HarperCollins College, 1993), pp. 157–158.

52. Ram, "India's Nuclear Policy," p. 93, citing a U.S. document presented to Indian negotiators on April 16, 1981.

53. Ibid., p. 94. The Indians had reason to doubt that Malone could make this assurance viable, given the likely outcry of the U.S. Congress.

54. Eric Gonsalves, interview by author, March 19, 1998, New Delhi.

55. Ram, "India's Nuclear Policy," p. 91, emphasis added.

56. Interview by author with former high-ranking Indian Ministry of Defence official, April 1998.

57. Inder Malhotra, interview by author, September 26, 1997. As *Nuclear Fuel* reported in its February 16, 1981, edition, Raja Ramanna had recognized the difficulty of switching to MOX fuel at Tarapur, and Sethna himself acknowledged the challenge of scaling up MOX fuel production. See Brahma Chellaney, *Nuclear Proliferation*, p. 133.

58. Delhi Domestic News Service, interview with Homi Sethna, December 1, 1982, in *FBIS-SA*, December 7, 1982, p. E2.

59. Ibid.

60. In late March 1981, three boys and a woman died and ten others were injured in an explosion and fire at the Nuclear Fuel Complex in Hyderabad when waste was being unloaded for open-air burning. "Paying for Negligence," *India Today*, April 16–30, 1981, p. 100.

61. *Agence France-Presse*, Hong Kong, October 26, 1981 in *FBIS-SA*, November 4, 1981, p. E3.

62. U.S. Embassy (New Delhi) to Secretary of State, cable no. 11254, June 1982, p. 2, in FOIA files, India, National Security Archive, Washington, D.C.

63. Ibid., p. 6.

64. Ibid.

65. Ibid., p. 4.

66. T. N. Ninan with Prabhu Chawla, "High Hopes, Little Power," *India Today*, August 31, 1982, p. 80.

67. Ibid., p. 83.

68. Ibid.

69. Mark Tully and Satish Jacob, *Amritsar: Mrs. Gandhi's Last Battle* (London: Jonathan Cape, 1985), p. 60.

70. Inder Malhotra, *Indira Gandhi*, p. 250.

71. Delhi Domestic News Service, January 22, 1981, in *FBIS-SA*, January 22, 1981, p. E1.

72. "At the end of 1981, the future of the party system seemed bleak, because there was no early prospect of the Opposition parties seeking unity in order to give the country a viable alternative." Indian Institute of Public Opinion, *Monthly Public Opinion Surveys* 27, nos. 2–3, #314–315 (November–December 1981): pp. 4–5.

73. "Mrs. Gandhi Bounces Back," *India Today*, April 1–15, 1981, p. 27.

74. Harry Barnes, interview by author, January 26, 1998.

75. Inderjit Badhwar, "Breaking the Ice," *India Today*, August 31, 1982, p. 69.

76. Kux, *Estranged Democracies*, p. 389.

77. Bhattacharya, "Another Nuclear Blast at Pokhran?" pp. 12–15.

78. Delhi Domestic News Service, May 13, 1982, in *FBIS-SA*, May 14, 1982, p. E1.

79. Christophe Jaffrelot, *The Hindu Nationalist Movement in India* (New York: Columbia University Press, 1996), pp. 315–316.

80. Pran Chopra, "Our Nuclear Nightmare," *Indian Express*, April 26, 1982, p. 6. Chopra had attended the Centre for Policy Research meeting that later resulted in the volume by Bhabani Sen Gupta, *Nuclear Weapons?*

81. Ibid.

82. Chellaney, *Nuclear Proliferation*, p. 134.

83. Indira Gandhi, interview with Steve Patton, *U.S. News & World Report*, January 23, 1982, in *Prime Minister Indira Gandhi, Statements on Foreign Policy, January–March 1982* (New Delhi: Government of India, 1982), pp. 25–26.

84. Interview by author, January 26, 1998.

85. Indira Gandhi, cited in Kux, *Estranged Democracies*, p. 390.

86. "Breaking the Ice," *India Today*, August 31, 1982, p. 67.

87. Interview by author, January 26, 1998.

88. Indian Institute of Public Opinion, *Monthly Public Opinion Surveys* 27, no. 10, #322 (July 1982). Seventy percent of respondents in Bombay, Calcutta, Madras, and Delhi considered the visit important. Sixty percent thought it would improve relations (7.3 percent "very much," 53 percent "somewhat"), while 26.6 percent though it would remain about the same.

89. Ibid., p. 12.

90. Ibid., p. 10.

91. Dixit, *Anatomy of a Flawed Inheritance*, p. 72.

92. "Press Report on Alleged Indian Military Plans—'Figment of Imagination'—Envoy," *India News*, December 27, 1982, p. 1.

93. "India Said to Eye Raid on Pakistani A-Plants," *Washington Post*, December 20, 1982, p. 1.

94. "Press Report on Alleged Indian Military Plans—'Figment of Imagination'—Envoy," *India News*, December 27, 1982, p. 1.

95. Delhi Domestic News Service, December 20, 1982, in *FBIS-SA*, December 21, 1982, p. E1.

96. Sidhu, "The Development of an Indian Nuclear Doctrine," p. 331.

97. Interview by author with former high-ranking Ministry of Defence official, March 21, 1998, New Delhi.

98. Sidhu, "The Development of an Indian Nuclear Doctrine," p. 331.

99. Interviews by author with three former high-ranking air force and Ministry of Defence officials, March 19–21, 1998, New Delhi.

100. Interview by author with former high-ranking air force official, March 19, 1998, New Delhi.

101. Interview by author, March 21, 1998, New Delhi.

102. Interview by author, March 20, 1998, New Delhi.

103. Interview by author, March 29, 1998.

104. Munir Ahmad Khan, correspondence with the author, January 1, 1998.

105. "The Crash of '83," *India Today*, January 31, 1983, p. 18.

106. Ibid., p. 20.

107. The other members in 1983 were Ramanna, Professor S. Dhawan (chairman of the Space Commission and ISRO), the industrialist J. R. D. Tata, and, representing the Ministry of Finance, R. N. Malhotra.

108. Interview by author with former colleague of Rao Sahib, April 10, 1998.

109. Interview by author, March 19, 1998, New Delhi.

110. G. K. Reddy, "Opposition to Assail PM's Nuclear Policy," *Hindu*, June 20, 1978, wrote that the Atomic Energy Commission was actively considering alternative test sites, "including one in the Andaman and Nicobar islands."

111. Sidhu, "The Development of an Indian Nuclear Doctrine," p. 129, and interviews by author with former high-ranking Indian officials, March 1998. Sidhu's account was the only one in the extant literature.

112. Interviews by author with former high-ranking Indian officials, March 1998.

113. Raj Chengappa, "The Bomb Makers," *India Today*, June 22, 1998, p. 44, reports such speculation.

114. Harry Barnes, interview by author, January 26, 1998, Atlanta.

115. Phone interview by author, February 20, 1996.

116. Interview by author with former high-ranking official, March 1998.

117. Delhi Domestic News Service, April 20, 1983, in *FBIS-SA*, April 20, 1983, p. E1.

118. Baskaran, "India's Space Programme," p. 54.

119. Ibid., p. 90.

120. Dhawan had been director of the Indian Institute of Science at Bangalore and was a contemporary and friend of Sarabhai, sharing the latter's devotion to a peaceful-use-only space program.

121. The Scout used solid propellant, which was also the fuel on which the Indian space program concentrated at the time (as opposed to liquid-fuel systems). The American rocket also had a one-meter diameter, which made it, unlike larger rockets, one that the Indian technologists could produce. Baskaran, "India's Space Programme," p. 101.

122. Ibid., p. 102.

123. Amarnath K. Menon, "Pyre in the Sky," *India Today*, June 16–30, 1981, p. 73.

124. Sidhu, "The Development of an Indian Nuclear Doctrine," p. 257.

125. Ibid., p. 251.

126. Baskaran, "India's Space Programme," pp. 320–321.

127. Interview by author, March 1998.

128. Sidhu, "The Development of an Indian Nuclear Doctrine," pp. 259–260; V. S. Arunachalam, interview by author, March 4, 1998; A. P. J. Abdul Kalam with Arun Tiwari, *Wings of Fire* (Hyderabad: Universities Press, 1999), pp. 113–117.

129. V. S. Arunachalam, interview by author, March 4, 1998.

130. Ibid.

131. Ibid.

132. Leonard S. Spector, *The Undeclared Bomb* (Cambridge, Mass.: Ballinger, 1988), p. 102.

133. The fact that the Agni uses the originally civilian SLV-3 engine indicates the ways in which technology and personnel can be dual use and the Indian space program can serve the missile program. However, it is incorrect to say that the space program began with missiles in mind or that the civilian and military programs are indistinguishable.

134. Sidhu, "The Development of an Indian Nuclear Doctrine," pp. 265–266.

135. Ibid., p. 268.

136. Baskaran, "India's Space Programme," p. 330.

137. Interview by author, March 4, 1998.

138. Interview by author with former high-ranking air force official, March 19, 1998, New Delhi.

139. Indira Gandhi, interview with *Le Monde*, March 3, 1983, in *Prime Minister Indira Gandhi, Statements on Foreign Policy, January–April 1983* (New Delhi: Government of India, Ministry of External Affairs, 1983), p. 27.

140. Milton R. Benjamin, "U.S. Is Delaying Nuclear Exports to India," *Washington Post*, June 23, 1983.

141. William Claiborne, "Shultz Promises Parts for India's Reactor," *Washington Post*, July 1, 1983.

142. "Mrs. Gandhi Reiterates India's Policy of Using Nuclear Power for Peaceful Purposes Only," *India News*, August 1, 1983, p. 1.

143. Ibid.

144. Gary Milhollin, "Dateline New Delhi: India's Nuclear Cover-Up," *Foreign Policy*, no. 64 (Fall 1986): p. 167.

145. This was an unlikely scenario given that the reactor was restarted in 1985.

146. S. H. Venkatramani, "On the Map," *India Today*, August 15, 1983, p. 91.

147. Cited in Milhollin, "Dateline New Delhi," p. 173.

148. Leonard S. Spector (with Jacqueline R. Smith), *Nuclear Ambitions* (Boulder, Colo.: Westview Press, 1990), p. 73, citing three Indian press accounts of the Comptroller and Auditor General report.

149. Ibid., p. 37.

150. Ibid.

151. Gary Milhollin, "Asia's Nuclear Nightmare: The German Connection," *Washington Post*, June 10, 1990, p. C2.

152. In addition to the previously mentioned Praful Bidwai article on the mysterious supply of heavy water, *India Today* also noted that "doubts have been expressed in several quarters about the procurement of the heavy water." S. H. Venkatramani, "On the Map," August 15, 1983, p. 91.

153. The Wisconsin Project, *Risk Report* 1, no. 2 (March 1995); Spector, *Nuclear Ambitions*, p. 73. More broadly, the nuclear power program continued to suffer. In response to a parliamentary inquiry in April 1983, the government reported that the Tarapur power reactors had operated at 40 percent capacity in 1982–1983, and the Rajasthan reactors at 14 percent. The Rajasthan power station had operated at a deficit of Rs. 911.51 lakhs between 1973 and 1981, or roughly $1 million (at 1981 currency rates). *Lok Sabha Debates*, 7th ser., vol. 37, no. 39, April 27, 1983, cols. 159–160.

154. Quoted in Sidhu, "The Development of an Indian Nuclear Doctrine," p. 67.

155. Dilip Bobb, "Sphere of Suspicion," *India Today*, October 15, 1983, pp. 54–55. The Sri Lankan government feared that India's southern state of Tamil Nadu was harboring and aiding terrorists operating in Sri Lanka. Bangladesh bristled as India erected a barbed-wire fence along the border.

156. Ibid., p. 57.

157. Alexander, *My Years with Indira Gandhi*, p. 66.

158. Dilip Bobb, "Sphere of Suspicion," *India Today*, October 15, 1983, p. 58.

159. *Indian Express*, cited in ibid.

160. Dilip Bobb, "Sphere of Suspicion," *India Today,* October 15, 1983, p. 63.

161. Sidhu, "The Development of an Indian Nuclear Doctrine," p. 124.

162. Ibid., p. 140.

163. A. Q. Khan, interview with *Nawa-e-Waqt,* February 10, 1984, in *Dr. A. Q. Khan on Pakistan Bomb,* ed. Sreedhar (New Delhi: ABC, 1987), p. 57.

164. Ibid., p. 69.

165. Ibid.

166. Shri Indrajit Gupta, *Lok Sabha Debates,* 7th. ser., vol. 46, no. 22, March 23, 1984, col. 337.

167. Ibid., col. 341.

168. Ibid., cols. 343–346.

169. Professor Saifuddin Soz, in ibid., col. 356.

170. Dr. Karan Singh, in ibid., col. 368.

171. *Lok Sabha Debates,* 7th ser., vol. 46, no. 22, March 23, 1984, col. 402.

172. Shri R. Venkataraman, in ibid., col. 398.

173. Ibid.

174. Ibid.

175. Ibid., col. 399.

176. Ibid.

177. Dr. Subramaniam Swamy, in ibid.

178. Shri R. Venkataraman, in ibid., col. 400.

179. Cited in Kanti P. Bajpai, P. R. Chari, Pervaiz Iqbal Cheema, Stephen P. Cohen, and Sumit Ganguly, *Brasstacks and Beyond* (New Delhi: Manohar, 1995), p. 143.

180. *Lok Sabha Debates,* 7th ser., vol. 46, no. 27, March 30, 1984, col. 395.

181. Indira Gandhi, statement to Lok Sabha, March 28, 1984, quoted by Foreign Minister Narasimha Rao, *Lok Sabha Debates,* 7th ser., vol. 46, no. 27, March 30, 1984, col. 398.

182. Bajpai et al., *Brasstacks and Beyond,* p. 144.

183. Indira Gandhi had made this argument in January, according to Kux, *Estranged Democracies,* p. 396.

184. Ibid., p. 398.

185. International Institute for Strategic Studies, *Strategic Survey, 1984–85* (London: International Institute for Strategic Studies, 1985), p. 140.

186. Tully and Jacob, *Amritsar: Mrs. Gandhi's Last Battle,* p. 80.

187. Ibid., p. 140.

188. Ibid., p. 185.

189. Ibid., pp. 183–184.

190. Ibid., p. 180.

191. Ibid., pp. 194–197.

192. Ibid., p. 209.

193. Zia "did not openly support the Sikhs and we have found no evidence he gave them covert help. In fact he did the very reverse; he set out on what he called a 'peace offensive.' " Ibid., p. 212.

194. In the aftermath of Operation Bluestar, the former vice chief of the army staff, Lieutenant General S. K. Sinha, publicly attacked the government for downgrading the status of military officers relative to civil service officers throughout the Indian civil service rankings, a reflection of the overall devaluation of military inputs into policymaking. S. K. Sinha, *Statesman,* June 25, 1984.

195. *Nawa-e-Waqt,* October 5, 1984, translated in U.S. Embassy (Islamabad) to Secretary of State, cable no. 080951Z, October 1984, p. 2, in FOIA files, Pakistan, National Security Archive, Washington, D.C.

196. See, for example, "Appraise Soberly," *Indian Express,* October 15, 1984, p. 6. The American Embassy in New Delhi reported intense Indian governmental inquiries as to the validity and implications of the Pakistani news report, adding that American diplomats denied the provision of a U.S. nuclear umbrella while refusing to confirm or deny that Reagan had sent a letter to Zia. U.S. Embassy (New Delhi) to Secretary of State, cable no. 120104Z, October 1984, p. 2, in FOIA files, India, National Security Archive, Washington, D.C.

197. Hinton's comment was cited in U.S. Embassy (Islamabad) to Secretary of State, cable no. 120926Z, October 1984, p. 2, in FOIA files, Pakistan, National Security Archive, Washington, D.C.

198. Don Oberdorfer, "Pakistan Concerned about Attack on Atomic Plants," *Washington Post,* October 12, 1984.

199. Ibid.

200. Interview by author with U.S. official familiar with this history, March 26, 1998.

201. Interview by author, March 19, 1998, New Delhi.

202. Ibid.

203. Quoted in Oberdorfer, "Pakistan Concerned about Attack on Atomic Plants."

204. "US Bid to Brand India as Aggressor Assailed," *Times of India,* October 16, 1984. See also William K. Stevens, "India Worried by U.S. Links to Pakistanis," *New York Times,* October 21, 1984, for a detailed account of Indian concerns and denials.

205. Sidhu, "The Development of an Indian Nuclear Doctrine," p. 136.

206. *Foreign Report,* December 13, 1984, pp. 1-2.

207. K. Sundarji, *Blind Men of Hindoostan* (New Delhi: UBS, 1993), p. xiv.

208. Ibid., p. xv.

209. Sidhu, "The Development of an Indian Nuclear Doctrine," p. 106, citing official Indian data.

CHAPTER TEN

1. Ali, *An Indian Dynasty;* Hari Jaisingh, *India after Indira* (New Delhi: Allied, 1989).

2. A phrase used by a former Atomic Energy Commission official to describe Rajiv.

3. Interview by author, 1996.

4. *Los Angeles Times,* February 21, 1985, cited in Neil Joeck, "Tacit Bargaining and Stable Proliferation in South Asia," *Journal of Strategic Studies* 13, no. 3 (September 1990): p. 86.

5. Rajiv Gandhi, broadcast to the nation, November 12, 1984, in *Rajiv Gandhi: Selected Speeches and Writings,* vol. 1, October 31, 1984–December 31, 1985 (New Delhi: Ministry of Information and Broadcasting, 1987), p. 5.

6. Ibid., p. 6.

7. Interview by author, August 1997.

8. Ramanna, *Years of Pilgrimage,* p. 115.

9. Interview by author with former Rajiv Gandhi adviser, March 1998.

10. Ibid.

11. Inderjit Badhwar, "Explosive Links," *India Today,* March 31, 1985, p. 74.

12. Spector, *Nuclear Ambitions,* p. 91.

13. The editor of *Hurmat* (circulation 7,000) was Zahid Malik, who later wrote the fawning biography *Dr. A. Q. Khan and the Islamic Bomb*.

14. *Hurmat,* March 14, 1985, translated and reprinted in Sreedhar, *Dr. A. Q. Khan on Pakistan Bomb,* pp. 80, 86. For an Indian interpretation of this interview, see P. K. S. Namboodiri, "Pak Nuclear Capability," *Times of India,* May 11, 1985.

15. U.S. and Pakistani sources debate whether Zia actually pledged in writing or verbally, or both, not to enrich uranium above 5 percent. A former leader of the Pakistan Atomic Energy Commission told the author that Zia had orally pledged to U.S. Ambassador Deane Hinton that Pakistan would not enrich above 5 percent and that the United States tried to persuade the Pakistani government to initial the minutes of this discussion. Zia was then advised not to put this pledge in writing and, according to this former official, did not. Interview by author, January 20, 1996, Islamabad.

16. Michael Armacost, interview by author, April 16, 1998, Washington, D.C.

17. Inderjit Badhwar, *India Today,* March 31, 1985, p. 74.

18. Reply to debate in the Lok Sabha, April 10, 1985, in *Rajiv Gandhi: Selected Speeches and Writings,* vol. 1, p. 294.

19. Quoted in Bhabani Sen Gupta, "Ambivalent Stand,"*India Today,* May 31, 1985, p. 116.

20. Interview by author with former U.S. arms control official, July 13, 1998.

21. Ibid.

22. G. K. Reddy, "Nuclear Option Open if Pak. Gets the Bomb," *Hindu,* May 5, 1985.

23. Ibid.; "India to Review Nuclear Policy, Gandhi Says," *Washington Post,* May 5, 1985.

24. "India to Review Nuclear Policy, Gandhi Says," *Washington Post,* May 5, 1985.

25. G. K. Reddy, "Nuclear Option Open if Pak. Gets the Bomb," *Hindu,* May 5, 1985.

26. "Stern Steps against Hoarders: P.M.," *Times of India,* May 6, 1985, p. 1.

27. Stephen Philip Cohen, "The Reagan Administration and India," in *The Hope and the Reality,* ed. Harold A. Gould and Sumit Ganguly (Boulder, Colo.: Westview Press, 1992), p. 143.

28. Kux, *Estranged Democracies,* p. 402.

29. Ibid.

30. Fred Iklé, interview by author, April 22, 1998, Washington, D.C.

31. Interview by author, April 16, 1998, Washington, D.C.

32. Steven R. Weisman, "His Visit Nearing, Gandhi Faults U.S.," *New York Times,* June 5, 1985.

33. U.S. Embassy (New Delhi) to Secretary of State, cable no. 051134Z, June 1985, reporting on Gandhi's predeparture interviews with American media.

34. Ibid.

35. Ibid.

36. Warren Donnelly, "India and Nuclear Weapons," Congressional Research Service Issue Brief, Washington, D.C., January 5, 1988, p. 3, citing *Le Monde,* June 5, 1985.

37. Interview by author with former high-ranking defense official, March 1998.

38. Roberta Wohlstetter, "The Pleasures of Self-Deception," *Washington Quarterly,* Autumn 1979, p. 58.

39. Inderjit Badhwar and Madhu Trehan, "A Fresh Look," *India Today,* July 15, 1985, p. 50.

40. Ibid., p. 53.

41. "U.S. and India Doubtful on Any Arms Deal Soon," *New York Times,* June 14, 1985, p. 5.

42. Arunachalam found open doors at General Electric, Grumman, Northrop, and Lockheed facilities, as well as I.T.T. and Control Data Corporation headquarters. Nayan Chanda, "Arms for Friendship," *Far Eastern Economic Review*, September 26, 1985, pp. 34–35.

43. Fred Iklé, interview by author, April 22, 1998, Washington, D.C.

44. American officials concluded that the XMP-14 could perform the requisite meteorological functions but that it would not jeopardize the cryptographic systems that the National Security Agency sought to protect. Kux, *Estranged Democracies*, p. 410.

45. Spector, *Nuclear Ambitions*, p. 332 n. 25.

46. *Foreign Assistance Act of 1961*, sec. 620E(e) (1985).

47. *Hindustan Times*, July 14, 1985, quoted in U.S. Embassy (New Delhi) to Secretary of State, cable no. 1609302, July 1985.

48. BJP resolution quoted in "India Must Make N-Bomb: BJP," *Times of India*, July 22, 1985.

49. "India Can Meet Pak. N-Threat: Minister," *Times of India*, August 8, 1985.

50. " 'India Can Develop Delivery System,' " *Statesman Weekly*, August 3, 1985.

51. Khurshid Alam Khan, quoted in "India Must Make N-Bomb: BJP," *Times of India*, August 8, 1985.

52. "India Can Meet Pak. N-Threat: Minister," *Times of India*, August 8, 1985.

53. "India Not to Have Nuclear Umbrella," *Times of India*, August 9, 1985, p. 1.

54. Swaminathan S. Aiyar, "Dhruva an N-Bomb Spinner," *Indian Express*, August 10, 1985, p. 1.

55. Albright and Hibbs, "India's Silent Bomb," p. 28.

56. In the second half of 1985 (or early 1986) India's Tarapur reprocessing plant began separating plutonium from spent fuel from the unsafeguarded Madras I reactor. This entailed transporting the spent fuel some 1,000 miles from the reactor to the reprocessing facility. Spector, *Nuclear Ambitions*, p. 320 n. 25. CIRUS also was unsafeguarded, but it, unlike Dhruva, was "encumbered" by the pledge to Canada that CIRUS would be used only for peaceful purposes.

57. Ibid.

58. Michael Knapik and Mark Hibbs, "German Firm's Beryllium Export to India May Have Violated U.S. Laws," *Nucleonics Week*, Special Report, January 30, 1989.

59. Ibid.

60. "Shadow of an Indian H-Bomb," *Foreign Report* (London), December 13, 1984, pp. 1–2; Federal Intelligence Service, Federal Republic of Germany, "India: Possible Revision of Nuclear Policy," April 1, 1985, cited in David Albright and Tom Zamora, "India, Pakistan's Nuclear Weapons: All the Pieces in Place," *Bulletin of the Atomic Scientists*, June 1989, p. 25.

61. Interviews by author with former high-ranking atomic energy officials, 1997–1998.

62. Albright and Zamora, "India, Pakistan's Nuclear Weapons: All the Pieces in Place," p. 25.

63. G. K. Reddy, "Containment of Pak. Bomb Threat," *Hindu*, August 11, 1985.

64. Ibid.

65. Ibid.

66. Ibid.

67. Michael Armacost, interview by author, April 16, 1998, Washington.

68. Ibid.

69. K. Subrahmanyam, "Politics of Shakti," *Times of India*, May 26, 1998.

70. Interview by author, March 7, 1999, New Delhi.

71. K. Sundarji, interview by author, March 19, 1998, New Delhi. K. Subrahmanyam, "Politics of Shakti," *Times of India,* May 26, 1998, wrote that only one copy of the report existed and that Sundarji personally delivered it to Rajiv Gandhi, whereupon it "vanished into thin air."

72. Interview by author with former high-ranking atomic energy official, March 20, 1998, New Delhi.

73. Interview by author, March 9, 1999, New Delhi.

74. K. Sundarji, Interview by author, March 19, 1998; *India Today,* December 31, 1990.

75. Interview by author, March 9, 1999, New Delhi.

76. Interview by author with former high-ranking Ministry of Defence official, March 22, 1998, New Delhi.

77. K. Subrahmanyam, "Politics of Shakti," *Times of India,* May 26, 1998.

78. K. Subrahmanyam, "Indian Nuclear Policy—1964–98 (A Personal Recollection)," in *Nuclear India,* ed. Jasjit Singh (New Delhi: Knowledge World, 1998), p. 41.

79. Interview by author with former high-ranking Ministry of Defence official, March 22, 1998, New Delhi.

80. Interview by author, March 20, 1998.

81. Interview by author, January 1996.

82. Albright and Hibbs, "India's Silent Bomb," p. 29.

83. "Let Pak Make Bomb; India Won't," *Hindustan Times,* November 29, 1985.

84. Interview by author, March 11, 1999, New Delhi.

85. Bajpai et al, *Brasstacks and Beyond,* pp. 155–156.

86. Ajay Kumar, "Getting into Gear," *India Today,* January 15, 1986, p. 137.

87. Ibid.; interviews by author with former Indian officials and correspondence from Munir Ahmad Khan, January 1, 1998.

88. Ramesh Thakur, *The Politics and Economics of India's Foreign Policy* (New York: St. Martin's Press, 1994), p. 104.

89. Dilip Bobb, "The New Offensive," *India Today,* February 15, 1986, p. 96.

90. Quoted in Jaisingh, *India after Indira,* p. 128.

91. Arun Singh, interview by author, August 19, 1996, Airlie, Va.

92. Bajpai et al., *Brasstacks and Beyond,* p. 27.

93. Ibid., p. 29.

94. Ibid., p. 30.

95. *Times of India,* September 15, 1986, cited in ibid., p. 157.

96. *Chatan,* August 31, 1986, reprinted in Sreedhar, *Dr. A. Q. Khan on Pakistan Bomb,* p. 144.

97. Bob Woodward, "Pakistan Reported Near Atom Arms Production," *Washington Post,* November 4, 1986.

98. *Times of India, Statesman,* and *Hindustan Times* respectively, cited in Bajpai et al., *Brasstacks and Beyond,* p. 159.

99. "The Declaration for a Nuclear-Weapon Free and Non-Violent World," signed by Prime Minister Rajiv Gandhi and the General Secretary of the Communist Party of the Soviet Union, Mikhail S. Gorbachev, New Delhi, November 27, 1986, in *Rajiv Gandhi: Selected Speeches and Writings,* vol. 2, January 1, 1986—December 31, 1986 (New Delhi: Ministry of Information and Broadcasting, 1989), pp. 333–334.

100. "Gandhi Praises New Zealand's Anti-Nuclear Stand," *Reuters,* October 17, 1986, dateline Auckland, New Zealand, October 17.

101. Bajpai et al., *Brasstacks and Beyond*, p. 33.

102. Interview by author with meeting participant, March 1998.

103. Bajpai et al., *Brasstacks and Beyond*, p. 34.

103. Nayar claimed, and Khan denied, that the interview was planned, and therefore a premeditated signal to India. Nayar said he had visited Pakistan annually for the preceding four years and each time requested an interview with Khan, only to be refused. In 1987, however, Mushahid Hussain told Nayar that Khan would see him, indicating, by Nayar's account, that Khan was prepared for the interview. *India Today,* March 31, 1987, p. 73. Khan told the American analyst Neil Joeck that he had merely received Hussain to accept an invitation to his wedding and spoke with the accompanying Nayar on an impromptu basis. Neil Joeck, *Maintaining Nuclear Stability in South Asia,* Adelphi Paper Series, no. 312 (London: International Institute for Strategic Studies, 1997), p. 21.

104. A. Q. Khan interview with Kuldip Nayar, *Observer* (London), March 1, 1987, quoted in Joeck, *Maintaining Nuclear Stability in South Asia,* p. 39.

106. Joeck, *Maintaining Nuclear Stability in South Asia,* p. 21.

107. *Dawn,* January 27, 1987, quoted in Bajpai et al., *Brasstacks and Beyond,* p. 3.

108. Sumit Ganguly, "Mending Fences," in *Crisis Prevention, Confidence Building, and Reconciliation in South Asia,* ed. Michael Krepon and Amit Sevak (New Delhi: Manohar, 1996), p. 13.

109. Ibid.

110. Bajpai et al., *Brasstacks and Beyond,* p. 43.

111. "India Raises Spending for Military by 43%," *New York Times,* March 1, 1987.

112. "Saving Cash," *India Today,* March 31, 1988, p. 171.

113. Arun Singh, interview by author, August 19, 1996.

114. "Bharatiya Janata Stand," *Times of India,* January 20, 1987, p. 16.

115. Delhi Domestic News Service, March 2, 1987.

116. B. G. Deshmukh, "The Inside Story," *India Today,* February 28, 1994, p. 62.

117. Ibid.

118. "Minister Says No Current Plans for Indian Nuclear Bomb," *Patriot,* March 14, 1987, p. 5.

119. G. K. Reddy, "Major Decision This Year on Nuclear Option," *Hindu,* international edition, March 14, 1987.

120. Dilip Bobb and Ramindar Singh, "Pakistan's Nuclear Bombshell," *India Today,* March 31, 1987, p. 73.

121. Ibid.

122. Ibid., p. 75.

123. Ibid.

124. Ibid., p. 76.

125. Interview by author with former high-ranking Ministry of Defence official, March 22, 1998.

126. Ibid.

127. Ibid. and Dilip Bobb and Ramindar Singh, "India-Pakistan Nuclear Weapons Issue Discussed," p. 76.

128. Interview by author, March 19, 1998, New Delhi.

129. Bobb and Singh, "India-Pakistan Nuclear Weapons Issue Discussed," p. 76.

130. Ibid., p. 80.

131. Tom Diaz, "Gandhi Warns U.S. Is 'Soft' on 'Islamic Bomb' Threat," *Washington Times,* March 27, 1987, p. 1.

132. "President Warns India Can Make Nuclear Bomb," *Times of India*, March 30, 1987, p. 1.

133. "India Announces Review of Nuclear Policy," *Reuters*, March 27, 1987.

134. K. C. Khanna, "Setbacks to Atomic Energy," *Times of India*, September 16, 1986.

135. U.S. Embassy (New Delhi) to Secretary of State, cable no. 022414, "India's Nuclear Energy Program," September 1986, p. 15, in FOIA files, India, National Security Archive, Washington, D.C.

136. K. C. Khanna, "Setbacks to Atomic Energy," *Times of India*, September 16, 1986. This judgment was validated by the detailed assessment of U.S. officials in India, as recorded in the long report cited at ibid.

137. U.S. Embassy (New Delhi) to Secretary of State, cable no. 022414, "India's Nuclear Energy Program," September 1986, p. 23, in FOIA files, India, National Security Archive, Washington, D.C.

138. Ibid., pp. 27-29. U.S. government analysts enumerated many other difficulties, including safety and environmental protection liabilities that had resulted in several cases of large numbers of workers being exposed to excessive radiation.

139. Ibid., p. 6. The actual expenditures of the Department of Atomic Energy—plan and nonplan—reflected these difficulties: 1985-1986 Rs. 961.72 crores ($780 million); 1986-1987, 1,102.62 crores ($862 million); 1987-1988, 1,110.09 crores ($856 million); 1988-1989, 1,051.92 crores ($726 million); 1989-1990, 1,178.14 crores ($710 million). Figures provided by the Institute of Peace and Conflict Studies, New Delhi. Dollar figures are at the official exchange rate for each year.

140. Gary Milhollin, *Heavy Water in India: A Study* (Washington, D.C.: Wisconsin Project on Nuclear Arms Control, 1986); Milhollin, "Dateline New Delhi," pp. 161-175.

141. K. Subrahmanyam, *Times of India*, February 5, 1986, reprinted in U.S. Embassy (New Delhi) to Secretary of State, cable no. 12356, February 1986.

142. Ibid. In 1987 the Soviet representative at the UN Disarmament Commission confirmed that a European firm bought from Soviet sources many small lots of heavy water—allowing the purchases to fall below the threshold of IAEA safeguard requirements—and then consolidated them to be shipped to "a nation of proliferation concern," namely India. Shekhar Gupta, "The Nuclear Heist," *India Today*, July 31, 1987, p. 103.

143. *Indian Express*, September 11, 1986.

144. Interviews by author with numerous Indian scientists, academics, diplomats, and journalists.

145. India declined the Soviet offers until 1988, when the two countries agreed on a deal whereby the Soviet Union would construct two 1,000-megawatt reactors. This arrangement then lay dormant until 1997, as discussed in chapter 11.

146. Ramanna, *Years of Pilgrimage*, p. 109.

147. Ibid.

148. Interview by author, March 1998.

149. Inder Malhotra, "Worsening the Mess," *Times of India*, February 5, 1987.

150. Interview by author with former high-ranking Atomic Energy Commission official, June 20, 1996.

151. Ibid.

152. Jaisingh, *India after Indira*, p. 41.

153. Nilova Roy, "Gandhi Loses Critical State Election," *Washington Post,* June 19, 1987.

154. Jaisingh, *India after Indira,* p. 104.

155. V. P. Singh had been finance minister until January 1987, when Rajiv shifted him to the defense portfolio in a move many believed was intended to curtail Singh's investigations into charges of corruption involving the prime minister and his circle.

156. Quoted in "China Lauds P.M.'s Foreign Policy," *Statesman Weekly,* August 3, 1985, p. 6.

157. Hoffmann, *India and the China Crisis,* p. 231.

158. Ibid.

159. "Tibetan Says PRC Nuclear Weapons Aimed at India," *Patriot,* March 10, 1987, p. 1. Such reports continued to emerge. In mid-July Indian sources said China had deployed seventy medium-range and twenty short-range missiles outside of Lhasa. K. Subrahmanyam commented that China had deployed such missiles in Tibet from the early 1970s and the Indian government's attitude had been "to live with it." UNI, "Defence Expert Says Bomb Required against PRC," *Telegraph* (Calcutta), July 15, 1987, p. 5. Regarding China's denial, see "China Denies Deployment of Missiles on Border, Directed toward India," *News India,* August 17, 1987.

160. Stephen P. Cohen, correspondence with author, July 27, 1998.

161. Delhi Domestic News Service, April 27, 1987, in *FBIS-Near East and South Asia (NESA),* April 28, 1987, p. E1.

162. Hoffmann, *India and the China Crisis,* p. 231.

163. Richard M. Weintraub, "India-China Border Tensions Rise," *Washington Post,* May 27, 1987, p. A16.

164. Hoffmann, *India and the China Crisis,* p. 233.

165. *Washington Post,* August 19, 1987; *Reuters,* "India, China Reducing Troops along Border."

166. The talks began in 1981.

167. Delhi General Overseas Service, in *FBIS-NESA,* November 20, 1987.

168. UNI, "Defence Expert Says Bomb Required against PRC," *Telegraph* (Calcutta), July 15, 1987, p. 5.

169. Arun Singh, interview by author, August 19, 1996.

170. Ibid.

171. Interview with Egyptian journalist, published in *Al-Jumhuriyah,* December 3, 1987, in *FBIS-NESA,* December 10, 1987, p. 44.

172. On the Indian rejection, see " 'Mutual Inspection of Nuke Plants Impossible,' " *News India,* August 28, 1987. On the U.S. attempt to revive the proposal, see Steven R. Weisman, "India Rejects Idea for Nuclear Ban," *New York Times,* October 11, 1987.

173. Steven R. Weisman, "India Rejects Idea for Nuclear Ban," *New York Times,* October 11, 1987.

174. Remarks of Prime Minister Rajiv Gandhi at the White House, October 20, 1987 (White House transcript, photocopy), p. 3.

175. Transcript of Rajiv Gandhi press conference with the U.S. press, October 20, 1987 (White House transcript, photocopy), pp. 4–5.

176. Ibid., p. 6.

177. Editorial, *Hindustan Times,* cited in U.S. Embassy (New Delhi) to Secretary of State, cable no. 25952, October 1987, in FOIA files, India, National Security Archive, Washington, D.C.

178. U.S. Embassy (New Delhi) to Secretary of State, cable no. 27419, November 1987, p. 1, reporting on press coverage of Prime Minister Gandhi's statement in Parliament on his recent foreign travel, in FOIA files, India, National Security Archive, Washington, D.C.

179. "India Should Go Nuke—Vajpayee," *News India,* December 11, 1987.

CHAPTER ELEVEN

1. K. Subrahmanyam, "Politics of Shakti," *Times of India,* May 26, 1998, and interview by author, July 17, 1998. The "two dozen" figure is probably high.

2. Donnelly, "India and Nuclear Weapons," p. 7.

3. R. Adam Moody, "The Indian-Russian Light Water Reactor Deal," *Nonproliferation Review* 5, no. 1 (Fall 1997): p. 117.

4. Marvin Miller, personal correspondence with author, reporting on visits to Indian nuclear facilities and officials in Bombay and Trombay, December 12, 1988, to January 5, 1989, p. 6.

5. Interview by author, April 1997.

6. Moody, "The Indian-Russian Light Water Reactor Deal," pp. 117–119.

7. Interviews by author with former high-ranking officials, 1997–1998; Marvin Miller, report, December 12, 1988, to January 5, 1989, p. 12.

8. Interview by author, May 1998.

9. Interview by author with former Ministry of Defence official, September 1998.

10. Richard Sale, "India Said to Upgrade Nuclear Arsenal," *United Press International,* March 20, 1988.

11. Interview by author, March 19, 1998, New Delhi.

12. Interview by author, March 10, 1998.

13. Schwartz, *Atomic Audit,* p. 29.

14. Shekhar Gupta, "Shooting Ahead," *India Today,* March 31, 1988, p. 171.

15. Lieutenant General (retired) Harwant Singh, "Prithvi's Accuracy," *Vayu* 4 (1994): p. 30.

16. Ibid.

17. Interview by author, March 19, 1998, New Delhi.

18. Interview by author, March 19, 1998, New Delhi.

19. Sidhu, "The Development of an Indian Nuclear Doctrine," pp. 332–333, reported accordingly that the air force "had to be virtually coerced into placing orders for the conventionally armed missile." Corroborated by interview by author with former high-ranking air force officer, March 19, 1998.

20. Interview by author, March 19, 1998.

21. P. R. Chari, interview by author, May 6, 1998.

22. Raymond L. Garthoff, *The Great Transition* (Washington, D.C.: Brookings Institution, 1994), p. 735. Foreign Minister Shevardnadze privately had told Secretary of State George Shultz of Moscow's determination to withdraw back in September 1987, conditioned on American cooperation in negotiations on facilitating the withdrawal and a transition to a post-Soviet regime in Afghanistan that would prevent the emergence of a radical Islamic fundamentalist regime there. Ibid., p. 730.

23. Spector, *Nuclear Ambitions,* p. 101.

24. *Washington Post,* November 19, 1988.

25. Hedrick Smith, "A Bomb Ticks in Pakistan," *New York Times Magazine*, March 6, 1988, p. 38.

26. Rajiv Gandhi, speech at the inaugural session of the SAARC Summit, Islamabad, December 29, 1988, in *Rajiv Gandhi: Selected Speeches and Writings, 1988*, vol. 4 (New Delhi: Ministry of Information and Broadcasting, 1989), p. 416, and Thakur, *The Politics and Economics of India's Foreign Policy*, p. 49.

27. UN General Assembly, Document A/S-15/12, India, letter, May 20, 1988 (New York, 1988).

28. Zafar Iqbal Cheema, "Nuclear Diplomacy in South Asia during the 80s," *Regional Studies* 10, no. 3 (Summer 1992): p. 60.

29. Rajiv Gandhi address at the Non-Governmental Organizations Conference "Towards a Nuclear Weapon-free and Non-violent World," New Delhi, November 14, 1988, in *Rajiv Gandhi: Selected Speeches and Writings, 1988*, pp. 364–374.

30. Thakur, *The Politics and Economics of India's Foreign Policy*, p. 78.

31. Ibid., pp. 78–79.

32. Sidhu, "The Development of an Indian Nuclear Doctrine," p. 233.

33. Prem Shankar Jha, *In the Eye of the Cyclone* (New Delhi: Viking, 1993), p. 53.

34. Ibid., p. 78.

35. Dixit, *Anatomy of a Flawed Inheritance*, p. 125.

36. Ibid.

37. Spector, *Nuclear Ambitions*, p. 103.

38. Mushahid Hussain, "Missile Missive," *India Today*, March 15, 1989, p. 129.

39. As of 1990 this supplier cartel included the United States, Canada, the United Kingdom, France, West Germany, Italy, Japan, Spain, Belgium, Luxembourg, and the Netherlands.

40. Janne E. Nolan, *Trappings of Power* (Washington, D.C.: Brookings Institution, 1991), p. 117.

41. See, for example, Chellaney, *Nuclear Proliferation*, pp. 206–289.

42. Barbara Crossette, "India Reports Successful Test of Mid-Range Missile," *New York Times*, May 23, 1991, p. A9.

43. Ibid.

44. Dilip Bobb with Amarnath K. Menon, "Chariot of Fire," *India Today*, June 15, 1989, p. 32.

45. Ibid., p. 28.

46. Rajiv Gandhi, statement on the Agni launch, May 22, 1989, in *Rajiv Gandhi: Selected Speeches and Writings, 1989*, vol. 5 (New Delhi: Ministry of Information and Broadcasting, Government of India, 1991), p. 139.

47. Bobb with Menon, "Chariot of Fire," p. 28.

48. Rajiv Gandhi, statement on the Agni launch, May 22, 1989, in *Rajiv Gandhi: Selected Speeches and Writings, 1989*, pp. 139, 138.

49. Russian Federation: Foreign Intelligence Service Report, 1993, reprinted in *FBIS*, JPRS Report, *Proliferation Issues*, March 5, 1993, p. 27.

50. Arun Singh, "Nuclear Deterrence: An Indian Perspective," unpublished paper, August 1996, p. 6.

51. Chellaney, *Nuclear Proliferation*, p. 268, emphasis added.

52. Cited in Nolan, *Trappings of Power*, p. 1.

53. Kux, *Estranged Democracies*, p. 430; Chellaney, *Nuclear Proliferation*, p. 282.

54. David B. Ottaway, "Bush Administration Debates Sale of Missile-Testing Device to India," *Washington Post,* May 28, 1989, p. A8.

55. Kux, *Estranged Democracies,* p. 431.

56. Ibid., p. 429.

57. Quoted in Sidhu, "The Development of an Indian Nuclear Doctrine," pp. 223-224.

58. Seymour Hersh, "On the Nuclear Edge," *The New Yorker,* March 29, 1993, p. 61, and interviews by author with U.S. officials.

59. Robert Oakley, interview by author, January 14, 1998.

60. Ibid.

61. Jha, *In the Eye of the Cyclone,* p. 10.

62. Ibid., p. 81.

63. Inderjit Badhwar, "Clear Choices," *India Today,* November 15, 1989, pp. 24-25; Raj Chengappa, "Dull Documents," November 30, 1989, pp. 157-158.

64. Singh made the offer on December 5, as cited in Spector, *Nuclear Ambitions,* p. 329.

65. Telephone interview by author with participant in the meeting, July 9, 1998.

66. This episode was related by a former Ministry of Defence official, not Mehra, and comports well with other information gained from independent sources regarding this period.

67. Interview by author, March 8, 1999.

68. V. P. Singh, interview with *Hard Talk,* the BBC, June 26, 1998.

69. Ibid.

70. Statement to Parliament by Prime Minister Narasimha Rao on the National Security Council, May 16, 1995, in Jaswant Singh, *National Security* (New Delhi: Lancer, 1996), pp. 90-93.

71. Hersh, "On the Nuclear Edge," pp. 56-73. Hersh's article contained errors and exaggerations, including, for example, the assertion, p. 59, that in the 1987 Brasstacks exercise "General Sundarji . . . integrate[d] India's special weapons, including tactical nuclear bombs, into the day-to-day field maneuvers of the troops."

72. Devin T. Hagerty, "Nuclear Deterrence in South Asia," *International Security* 20, no. 3 (Winter 1995/1996): pp. 79-114; Shai Feldman, "Is There a Proliferation Debate?" *Security Studies* 4, no. 4 (Summer 1995): p. 791; and numerous Indian and Pakistani accounts.

73. Sumit Ganguly, *The Crisis in Kashmir* (New York: Cambridge University Press and the Woodrow Wilson Center Press, 1997), p. 98.

74. Shirin Tahir-Kheli, "Lessons for the Future: The Gates Mission to India and Pakistan," unpublished report to the Rockefeller Foundation, New York, August 19, 1993, p. 4.

75. Dixit, *Anatomy of a Flawed Inheritance,* p. 128.

76. I. K. Gujral, interview by author, March 9, 1999, New Delhi.

77. See also Dixit, *Anatomy of a Flawed Inheritance,* p. 129.

78. Hagerty, "Nuclear Deterrence in South Asia," p. 98; Hersh, "On the Nuclear Edge," March 29, 1993, p. 64.

79. Robert Oakley, interview by author, January 14, 1998. Oakley sought to disabuse Beg and President Khan of illusions that Iranian support would be decisive in any way in combat against India.

80. Cited in Hagerty, "Nuclear Deterrence in South Asia," p. 99.

81. Ibid.

82. Ibid.

83. Ibid.

84. Ibid., p. 98.

85. Michael Krepon and Mishi Faruqee, eds., "Conflict Prevention and Confidence-Building Measures in South Asia: The 1990 Crisis," Occasional Paper no. 17, Henry L. Stimson Center, Washington, D.C., 1994.

86. The two countries' foreign ministers met twice in New York on April 10 and 15 to try to calm the situation, but these and other occasional efforts to downplay aggressive intentions did not succeed in resolving the crisis.

87. Interviews by author with then-U.S. Ambassador to Pakistan Robert Oakley and then-National Security Council official Richard Haass, January 14 and 23, 1988, respectively.

88. Krepon and Faruqee, "Conflict Prevention and Confidence-Building Measures in South Asia: The 1990 Crisis," pp. 30–31; Hersh, "On the Nuclear Edge," p. 64; interviews by author with American officials, 1997 and 1998; and extrapolation from the fact that after the invocation of the Pressler Amendment in October 1990, U.S. officials demanded that, among other things, Pakistan destroy or render useless nuclear weapon cores then believed to be in its possession. The then-Chairman of the Pakistan Atomic Energy Commission Munir Ahmad Khan acknowledged in a March 1998 interview with the author that the PAEC would have been mobilized if nuclear weapons were to be prepared, but he denied specifically that this had occurred in the spring 1990 crisis.

89. Reiss, *Bridled Ambition*, p. 188.

90. Dr. Samar Mubarakmand, quoted in Amit Baruah, "Pak Scientists Fight for Credit," *Hindu*, June 3, 1998, p. 13.

91. Seymour Hersh, "On the Nuclear Edge," p. 94, asserted that three additional alarming activities were detected: "Sometime in May . . . an orbiting American satellite relayed photographs of what some officials believed was the evacuation of thousands of workers from Kahuta"; "satellite and other intelligence later produced signs of a truck convoy moving from the suspected nuclear-storage site in Balochistan to a nearby Air Force base"; and, finally, intelligence detected that Pakistan "had F-16s prepositioned and armed for delivery—on full alert, with pilots in the aircraft." These latter three assertions have been contested by the U.S. ambassador and military attachés then stationed in Pakistan and must be doubted. Then-U.S. Air Force attaché Colonel Don Jones, in Krepon and Faruqee, "Conflict Prevention and Confidence-Building Measures in South Asia: The 1990 Crisis," pp. 21–22.

92. Hersh, "On the Nuclear Edge," p. 67.

93. As recalled by Oakley, interview by author, January 14, 1998.

94. Ibid.

95. Ibid.

96. Ibid.

97. Dixit, *Anatomy of a Flawed Inheritance*, p. 137.

98. Richard Haass, interview by author, January 23, 1998; William Clark, interview by author, June 12, 1998.

99. J. N. Dixit wrote that "there is no truth at all" to "speculations" that "India and Pakistan were on the brink of a nuclear war." Dixit, *Anatomy of a Flawed Inheritance*, p. 132.

100. Interview by author, March 8, 1999, New Delhi.

101. Interview by author, January 23, 1998.

102. Hagerty, "Nuclear Deterrence in South Asia," pp. 107–108.

103. Ibid., p. 108.

104. For military details that buttress this conclusion, see numerous statements by former U.S. Army and Air Force attachés in Pakistan and India in Krepon and Faruqee, "Conflict Prevention and Confidence-Building Measures in South Asia: The 1990 Crisis," pp. 20–23.

105. Quoted in Sidhu, "The Development of an Indian Nuclear Doctrine," p. 223.

106. Interview by the author, September 1992, Rawalpindi.

107. K. Sundarji, "Declare Nuclear Status," *India Today,* December 31, 1990, p. 163.

108. Interviews by author with U.S. officials of this period.

109. Without reference to his participation in the 1990 committee, about which he would not comment, Arun Singh in a general discussion of Indian nuclear policy said that he was unaware of Pakistan's move to assemble nuclear weapons in May 1990 until he read the Hersh and Stimson Center accounts in 1994. This reaffirmed the conclusion that Indian leaders in the 1990 crisis did not see it in nuclear terms, for presumably Singh would have been informed of this dimension of the crisis when he joined the committee in the fall of 1990.

110. Jaffrelot, *The Hindu Nationalist Movement in India,* pp. 414–417.

111. Pran Chopra, "The Nuclear Trap," *Hindu,* November 29, 1990, reprinted in Pran Chopra, *The Crisis of Foreign Policy* (Allahabad: Wheeler, 1993), p. 180.

112. Ibid.

113. Ibid., pp. 181–182.

114. K. Sundarji, " 'In the Nuclear Trap': Wrong Assumptions," *Hindu,* December 11, 1990, reprinted in Chopra, *The Crisis of Foreign Policy,* p. 183.

115. K. Sundarji, interview by author, February 8, 1994.

116. K. Sundarji, " 'In the Nuclear Trap': Wrong Assumptions," p. 184.

117. Ibid.

118. Ibid., p. 185.

119. Pran Chopra, "The Year of the Bomb?" *Hindu,* December 28, 1990, reprinted in Chopra, *The Crisis of Foreign Policy,* p. 189.

120. Ibid.

121. K. Sundarji, "Minimum Nuclear Deterrence—Where Third World Differs from the West," *Hindu,* January 11, 1991, reprinted in Chopra, *The Crisis of Foreign Policy,* p. 197.

122. U.S. State Department to U.S. Embassy (New Delhi), telegram no. 2296, May 24, 1966, p. 2, in FOIA files, India, National Security Archive, Washington, D.C., and Camille Grand, "A French Nuclear Exception?" Occasional Paper no. 38, Henry L. Stimson Center, Washington, D.C., 1998, p. 3.

123. Grand, "A French Nuclear Exception?"

124. K. Sundarji, "Minimum Nuclear Deterrence—Where Third World Differs from the West," p. 199.

125. Waltz, "Nuclear Myths and Political Realities," *American Political Science Review* 84, no. 3 (September 1990): p. 741.

126. Her claim would have been more credible if the scientists had elaborated further scientific or engineering benefits from such explosives, which they did not do seriously.

127. On these contradictions, see Robert Jervis, *The Illogic of American Nuclear Strategy* (Ithaca, N.Y.: Cornell University Press, 1984). On the dangers of U.S. and Soviet opera-

tional practices, see Bruce G. Blair, *The Logic of Accidental Nuclear War* (Washington: Brookings Institution, 1993).

CHAPTER TWELVE

1. Jha, *In the Eye of the Cyclone*, p. 133.

2. Ibid., pp. 240–241.

3. Prabhu Chawla and Harindar Baweja, "How Long Will It Last?" *India Today*, November 30, 1990, p. 22.

4. Shahnaz Anklesaria Aiyar, "Goofing Around," *India Today*, March 31, 1991, p. 47.

5. Prafull Goradia, "Wanted a New Foreign Policy for India—Non-alignment Obsolete," *Organiser*, January 13, 1991, p. 10.

6. Jay Dubashi, "Why India Has Ceased to Count," *Organiser*, February 3, 1991, p. 2.

7. For example, the mainstream weekly *India Today* and the RSS's *Organiser* from late 1990 through mid-1991 did not mention nuclear policy in their coverage of Indian politics.

8. "Rajiv Fears Use of N-Arms," *Hindustan Times*, February 12, 1991, p. 20.

9. K. Sundarji, "The Threat of Nuclear Strike is Real," *Hindu*, February 3, 1991, p. 4.

10. Jha, *In the Eye of the Cyclone*, p. 255; "What the Results Mean," *India Today*, July 15, 1991, p. 40. V. P. Singh's Janata Dal, the leading element of the National Front, fared miserably, dropping from 141 seats in 1989 to 55.

11. Ibid., *India Today*, July 15, 1991, p. 35.

12. Sundeep Chakravarti with Zafar Agha and Shahnaz Anklesaria Aiyar, "Bold Gamble," *India Today*, July 31, 1991, p. 23.

13. Ibid., p. 24.

14. Delhi Domestic News Service, January 27, 1991, *FBIS-NESA*, January 28, 1991, p. 80.

15. Dixit, *Anatomy of a Flawed Inheritance*, p. 140.

16. Ibid., p. 143.

17. Chellaney, *Nuclear Proliferation*, p. 253. China in 1991 agreed not to defy MTCR controls, but claimed that M-11 missiles with ranges of less than 300 kilometers did not fall under them. Nolan, *Trappings of Power*, pp. 115, 121.

18. Raj Chengappa, "A Sudden Cooling," *India Today*, July 15, 1991, p. 104.

19. Indian Institute of Public Opinion, *Monthly Public Opinion Surveys* 37, nos. 8–9, #440–441 (May–June 1992): p. 21.

20. Shahnaz Anklesaria Aiyar, "Goofing Around," *India Today*, March 31, 1991, p. 47.

21. Ibid., p. 49.

22. Shekhar Gupta with Shahnaz Anklesaria Aiyar, "Blundering Along," *India Today*, December 15, 1991, p. 27.

23. Shekhar Gupta, *India Redefines Its Role*, Adelphi Paper Series, no. 293 (London: International Institute for Strategic Studies, 1995), p. 5.

24. DRDO expenditures for 1992–1993 were Rs. 1,1488.29 crores, up from Rs. 1,280.76 in 1991–1992.

25. Srinivasan, "An Appraisal of India's Civil Nuclear Power Programme," p. 5.

26. *Nuclear News*, March 1991, p. 56; Neel Patri, *Nuclear Fuel*, May 1991, pp. 8–9.

27. Ibid., and *Nucleonics Week*, July 18, 1991, p. 3; *New York Times*, November 18, 1991, p. A4.

28. Shahnaz Anklesaria Aiyar, "A Decisive Shift," *India Today*, August 31, 1991, p. 108.

29. James Clad, *Christian Science Monitor*, September 25, 1991. The IMF also approved another $1.8 billion in credits.

30. J. N. Dixit, *Anatomy of a Flawed Inheritance*, p. 152.

31. Ibid., p. 154.

32. Ibid., p. 156.

33. "Foreign Secretaries Hold Talks in Islamabad," *India News*, November 16–31, p. 5.

34. *Dawn*, October 22, 1991, p. 1, *FBIS-NESA*, October 25, 1991, p. 56.

35. All India Radio, November 10, 1991, *FBIS-NESA*, November 13, 1991, p. 50.

36. All India Radio, November 10, 1991, *FBIS-NESA*, November 14, 1991, p. 51.

37. Interviews by author with former high-ranking Indian nuclear and defense officials.

38. Nawaz Sharif statement to the Qatari News Agency, in *FBIS-NESA*, November 15, 1991, p. 46.

39. Gupta with Aiyar, "Blundering Along," p. 28.

40. Kux, *Estranged Democracies*, p. 444, notes that no U.S. cabinet level officer traveled to South Asia in the first two years of the Bush administration. Secretary of State James Baker did not mention India in his autobiography and mentioned Pakistan glancingly in a discussion of China. James A. Baker with Thomas M. DeFrank, *The Politics of Diplomacy* (New York: G. P. Putnam's Sons, 1995).

41. "Visit of U.S. Under-Secretary of State to India," *India News*, November 16–30, 1991, p. 6; Gupta with Aiyar, "Blundering Along," p. 28.

42. K. K. Katyal, *Hindu*, November 30, 1991, p. 9; Mark Hibbs, *Nucleonics Week*, January 30, 1992, pp. 16–17.

43. Thakur, *The Politics and Economics of India's Foreign Policy*, p. 81.

44. All India Radio, January 9, 1992, in *FBIS-NESA*, January 10, 1992, p. 24.

45. Mark Hibbs, *Nucleonics Week*, February 26, 1992, pp. 9–10.

46. K. Subrahmanyam, *Economic Times*, January 8, 1993, p. 8.

47. "Pakistan, India Exchange Lists of Nuclear Facilities," *Washington Post*, January 2, 1992; Radio Pakistan Network, February 22, 1992, in *FBIS-NESA*, February 24, 1992, p. 73. Pakistan was already building an unsafeguarded nuclear reactor at Khushab that could produce plutonium for weapons.

48. Ann Machlachlan, Rauf Siddiqi, and Neel Patri, *Nucleonics Week*, January 23, 1992, p. 3.

49. *Nuclear Engineering International*, February 1992, p. 8.

50. Quoted in Albright and Hibbs, "India's Silent Bomb," p. 27.

51. *New York Times*, January 22, 1992.

52. Ibid.

53. A. Balu, "Prime Minister Enunciates Global Approach to Stop Nuclear Proliferation," *India News*, January 16–31, p. 1.

54. Steve Coll, "U.S. Nuclear Diplomacy in South Asia Faces Obstacles," *Washington Post*, February 8, 1992.

55. K. K. Katyal, "Talks between Prime Ministers of India and Pakistan," *India News*, February 1–15, 1992, p. 2.

56. Coll, "U.S. Nuclear Diplomacy in South Asia Faces Obstacles," *Washington Post,* February 8, 1992.

57. Numerous citations in *FBIS-NESA,* February 10–11, 1992.

58. Steve Coll, "India Pressured on Bomb," *Washington Post,* February 9, 1992, p. A23.

59. All India Radio, February 8, 1992, in *FBIS-NESA,* February 11, 1992, p. 43.

60. All India Radio, February 11, 1992, in *FBIS-NESA,* February 12, 1992, p. 49.

61. All India Radio, February 19, 1992, in *FBIS-NESA,* February 19, 1992, p. 56; *India News,* March 1–15, 1992, p. 1.

62. Steve Coll, "India Faces Nuclear Watershed," *Washington Post,* March 7, 1992, p. A19.

63. *FBIS-NESA,* March 2, 1992, p. 65.

64. This cost estimate assumed that such an arsenal would be built in a geopolitical vacuum and that the United States and other countries would not impose serious economic penalties on India for building a nuclear arsenal. It also neglected the costs of building a sophisticated command and control and communications and intelligence infrastructure.

65. Institute for Defence Studies and Analyses data—Rs. 163.47 billion, divided by IMF rupee conversion rate of 24.52.

66. *Hindustan Times,* in *FBIS-NESA,* March 2, 1992, p. 66.

67. Ibid.

68. Ibid., p. 65.

69. "Space Programme Has No Military Aim Says India," *India News,* May 1–15, 1992, p. 1.

70. Chellaney, *Nuclear Proliferation,* p. 195.

71. See for example, K. Subrahmanyam, "An Indo-Pakistan Nuclear Restraint Regime," (paper prepared for the Forty-Second Pugwash Conference on Science and World Affairs, Berlin, September 11–17), pp. 10–12.

72. " 'Agni'—India's First Intermediate Range Ballistic Missile," *India News,* May 16–31, p. 8; Chellaney, *Nuclear Proliferation,* p. 275.

73. *Observer* (Delhi), January 4, 1993, p. 3.

74. Correspondence with Indian Ministry of External Affairs official, August 5, 1998.

75. Quoted in Shekhar Gupta with W. P. S. Sidhu, "Cautious Manoeuvres," *India Today,* June 30, 1992, p. 34.

76. Ibid., p. 35.

77. Author's contemporaneous discussions with American State Department and National Security Council officials.

78. "US Quietly Lifts Embargo on ISRO," *Economic Times,* October 25, 1992.

79. Reiss, *Bridled Ambition,* p. 200.

80. Correspondence with former high-ranking U.S. official involved in talks with India, July 26, 1998.

81. Suman Dubey, "Indian Economy Shows Signs of Recovery," *Wall Street Journal,* September 8, 1992, p. A13.

82. Ibid.

83. Sanjoy Hazarika, "India Reports Insurgents in Assam Have Agreed to End Their Four-Year Rebellion," *New York Times,* January 16, 1992.

84. Jefferson Penberthy, "Rao's Surprising Rule," *TIME* (international), August 31, 1992, p. 12.

85. Interviews by author with several former high-ranking Indian officials, 1996 through 1998.

86. Interviews by author with participants in the 1990 committee to review Indian nuclear defense policies, March 1998, New Delhi.

87. Interview by author with former high-ranking atomic energy official, April, 1997. Other former high-ranking atomic energy, defense, and political officials echoed this view in numerous interviews and discussions with the author between 1992 and 1998.

88. Interview by author, April 23, 1997. This also preserved the autonomy of the scientists and engineers in the strategic enclave.

89. Rivalries between the services explain much of U.S. nuclear policy and the acquisition of scores of nuclear weapons and dozens of delivery systems as the air force, navy, and army vied for nuclear missions and budgets. See, for example, Schwartz, *Atomic Audit.*

90. W. P. S. Sidhu, "Tactical Gap," *India Today,* September 15, 1992, pp. 158–159.

91. Interviews by author with Pakistani officials in Islamabad and Washington, 1992.

92. Interview by author with knowledgeable U.S. defense analyst, December, 1998.

93. K. Subrahmanyam, interview by author, September 1992, New Delhi. Subrahmanyam referred to South African President F. W. deKlerk's decision to abolish South Africa's nuclear weapons as apartheid was ending.

94. Interviews by author with more than a dozen former high-ranking Indian officials, strategic analysts, and pundits, September 1992, New Delhi.

95. "India and IAEA Safeguards," K. Subrahmanyam, *Economic Times,* October 16, 1992.

96. *India News,* October 16–31, 1992, p. 1.

97. Reiss, *Bridled Ambition,* pp. 200, 224 n. 80.

98. Ibid., p. 220.

99. Gautam Adhikari, "Pak Has N-Bombs It Can Drop Any Time," *Times of India,* December 3, 1992, p. 1.

100. All India Radio, December 3, 1992, in *FBIS-NESA,* December 4, 1992, p. 50; All India Radio, December 4, 1992, in *FBIS-NESA,* December 10, 1992, p. 43.

101. "India Should Have Deterrant [sic] to Pak Nuclear Threat: RS," *Economic Times,* December 4, 1992, p. 14.

102. *New York Times,* January 24, 1993, p. 2.

103. P. K. Iyengar, "Forty Years with Atomic Energy," farewell address, February 4, 1993, in *Collected Scientific Papers of Dr. P. K. Iyengar,* vol. 5, compiled and edited by M. R. Balakrishnan (Bombay: Bhabha Atomic Research Centre, Library and Information Services Division, 1993), p. 80.

104. Ibid., p. 82.

105. Ibid., p. 85.

106. Ibid., p. 88.

107. Edward A. Gargan, "Demands Growing for an India That's Truly Hindu," *New York Times,* January 24, 1993, p. A2.

108. Ibid.

109. Ashok Kapur, "Nuclear Disarmament," *Indian Express,* January 14, 1993, p. 8.

110. Ibid.

111. "Bombs in Sub-continent," *Economic Times,* February 1, 1993.

112. Prepared testimony of Director of Central Intelligence James Woolsey, Senate Governmental Affairs Committee (Washington, D.C., February 24, 1993, photocopy), p. 12.

113. "US May Impose Permanent Curbs on ISRO," *Indian Express,* February 1, 1993, p. 1.

114. "Upgraded Agni Missile to Be Test Launched in March," *Observer* (Delhi), January 4, 1993, p. 3.

115. U.S. State Department, "Report to Congress: Progress toward Regional Nonproliferation in South Asia" (April 1993, photocopy), p. 2.

116. Ibid., emphasis added.

117. A widely noted description of the nuclear situation in South Asia as "nonweaponized deterrence" and a set of recommendations on steps to stabilize this situation appeared in George Perkovich, "A Nuclear Third Way in South Asia," *Foreign Policy,* no. 91 (Summer 1993).

118. Jasjit Singh, panel discussion, All India Radio, August 8, 1993, in *FBIS-NESA,* August 11, 1993, p. 32.

119. Muchkund Dubey, in ibid.

120. Reiss, *Bridled Ambition,* p. 195.

121. C. Raja Mohan and Peter R. Lavoy, "Avoiding Nuclear War," in *Crisis Prevention, Confidence Building, And Reconciliation in South Asia,* ed. Michael Krepon and Amit Sevak (New Delhi: Manohar, 1996), p. 45.

122. Lena H. Sun, "China, India Sign Accord to Ease Border Dispute," *Washington Post,* September 8, 1993, p. 1.

123. U.S. State Department, Report to Congress: Update on Progress toward Regional Nonproliferation in South Asia (April 1994, photocopy), p. 8.

124. Shekhar Gupta with Sudeep Chakravarti, "Vital Breakthrough," *India Today,* September 30, 1993, p. 38.

125. Ibid., p. 42.

126. For example, Brahma Chellaney acknowledged that "a nuclear rivalry with Pakistan would not only be strategically and militarily disadvantageous to India but would be inconsistent with its long-term security interests and ambitions in the region." "Regional Security and the Diffusion of Advanced Weapons and Technologies to India, Pakistan, and China," report, Centre for Policy Research, New Delhi, July 1994, p. 4.

127. Aziz Haniffa, "U.S. Ends Push for 5-Nation Parley," *India Abroad,* September 24, 1993.

128. Interview by author with U.S. government official, July 24, 1998.

129. Reiss, *Bridled Ambition,* p. 201.

130. Interviews by author with American officials involved in the talks, September 1993.

131. "Missile Developments, India," *The Nonproliferation Review* 1, no. 3 (Spring/Summer 1994): p. 163.

132. Interview by author, May 12, 1997.

133. "Nuclear Developments, India," *The Nonproliferation Review* 1, no. 3 (Spring/Summer 1994): p. 161.

134. Ibid.

135. Cited in All India Radio General Overseas Service, November 29, 1993, in *FBIS-NESA,* November 30, 1993, p. 67.

136. Quoted in Susumu Awanohara, "Clinton's New Line," *Far Eastern Economic Review,* December 23, 1993, p. 22.

137. Interviews by author with Indian journalists and diplomats, 1993–1996.

138. "Sharif: PPP Stalling Nuclear Programme," *Muslim,* November 18, 1993, p. 12; Naeem Qamar, "Sharif Urges Maintaining Nuclear, Kashmir Policies," *Nation,* November 19, 1993, p. 12.

139. K. Subrahmanyam, "Narasimha Strategy," *Economic Times,* October 1993.

140. Ibid.

141. Dixit, *Anatomy of a Flawed Inheritance,* p. 174.

142. Sumit Ganguly, "Mending Fences," in Krepon and Sevak, *Crisis Prevention, Confidence Building, And Reconciliation in South Asia,* p. 13.

143. *Hindu,* March 5, 1994, p. 9.

144. High-ranking U.S. official, quoted in Reiss, *Bridled Ambition,* p. 185.

145. Interview by author with knowledgeable U.S. government official, August 2, 1998. This official noted that public accounts uniformly underestimated Pakistan's inventory of highly enriched uranium and that the asymmetry between Pakistan's and India's holdings of weapon-usable materials was not strategically significant.

146. Admiral William O. Studeman, acting director of Central Intelligence, written answers to questions for the record from the Senate Governmental Affairs Committee Hearing, February 24, 1993, in Senate Committee on Governmental Affairs, *Proliferation Threats of the 1990s: Hearing, Committee on Governmental Affairs* (Washington, D.C.: U.S. Government Printing Office, 1993), p. 155.

147. Einhorn was already in Beijing on other business, and decided to stay over when he learned that Wisner was coming also on non-South Asian business. Although South Asia was not the express or central purpose of their meetings with Chinese officials, they recognized that China's role in facilitating the conference was important. Robert Einhorn, interview by author, July 31, 1998.

148. Reiss, *Bridled Ambition,* p. 204.

149. See Najam Sethi, "Rethinking Nuclear Policy," *Friday Times,* March 31, 1994.

150. Contemporaneous interviews with key U.S. officials working on the initiative, March 1994.

151. Reiss, *Bridled Ambition,* p. 204.

152. John F. Burns, "India Rejects U.S. Bid for Nuclear Pact with Pakistan," *New York Times,* March 26, 1994.

153. Ibid.

154. The debates in Washington, Islamabad, and New Delhi, as well as the unsuccessful diplomacy with China, forewarned Talbott that the initiative was doomed and he proceeded on his mission reluctantly, according to interviews with several U.S. officials involved in the process, March and April 1994. Pakistan's Chief of Army Staff General Malik Abdul Waheed had visited Washington prior to Talbott's mission and told American officials that the F-16s were a woefully inadequate inducement. Robert Einhorn, interview by author, July 31, 1998.

155. Robert Einhorn, interview by author, July 31, 1998.

156. Raj Chengappa, "Nuclear Dilemma," *India Today,* April 30, 1994, p. 44.

157. "Legislative History of the Nuclear Proliferation Prevention Act of 1994 (NPPA)," fact sheet provided by Senator Glenn's staff, July 1998.

158. Interview by author, June 1994, Islamabad.

159. Raj Chengappa, "Ominous Accidents," *India Today,* June 30, 1994, pp. 88–96, detailed this accident and other recent major operational, technical, and health problems associated with the nuclear power program managed by the Nuclear Power Corporation.

160. *Hindustan Times,* April 2, 1994, p. 12, in *FBIS-NESA,* April 8, 1994, p. 44.

161. All India Radio, April 6, 1994, in *FBIS-NESA,* April 6, 1994, p. 38.

162. Raj Chengappa, "Nuclear Dilemma," *India Today,* April 30, 1994, p. 46.

163. Raj Chengappa, "The Missile Man," *India Today,* April 15, 1994, p. 66.

164. Ibid., p. 71.

165. Ibid., p. 69.

166. All India Radio, April 13, 1994, in *FBIS-NESA,* April 14, 1994, p. 44.

167. Reiss, *Bridled Ambition,* p. 205.

168. Interview by author, May 14, 1998.

169. Interview by author, September 4, 1996.

170. Prime Minister Rao, reply to discussion of Defence Ministry matters, Rajya Sabha, May 3, 1994, in *Narasimha Rao: Selected Speeches,* vol. 3, July 1993–June 1994 (New Delhi: Ministry of Information and Broadcasting, 1995), p. 175.

171. Ibid., p. 176.

172. Correspondence with U.S. official, July 7, 1998.

173. *Narasimha Rao: Selected Speeches,* vol. 3, p. 178.

174. Ibid., p. 177.

175. Ibid.

176. Ibid., p. 181.

177. Ibid., p. 182.

178. Dilip Bobb, "A Quiet Triumph," *India Today,* June 15, 1994, pp. 45–47.

179. Address to Joint Session of Congress, May 18, 1994, in *Narasimha Rao: Selected Speeches,* vol. 3, p. 484.

180. Dilip Bobb, "A Quiet Triumph," *India Today,* June 15, 1994, p. 47.

181. Joint Statement of Narasimha Rao and Bill Clinton (Washington, D.C., May 19, 1998, photocopy), par. 6.

182. Interview by author with U.S. official, July 24, 1998.

183. John M. Goshko, "Clinton Moves to Ease Relationship with India," *Washington Post,* May 20, 1994, p. A30.

184. *New York Times,* May 19, 1994, p. A3. No stories appeared on the meetings in Washington in the May 20–21 editions.

185. "Missile Developments, India," *Nonproliferation Review* 2, no. 1 (Fall 1994): p. 179.

186. Ibid.

187. "Missile Developments, India," *Nonproliferation Review* 2, no. 3 (Spring/Summer 1995): p. 173.

188. Indeed, press reports suggested that Rao had reversed leverage on the United States and pledged not to deploy Prithvi missiles if Washington did not send F-16s to Pakistan. Pravin Sawhney, "India Will Not Deploy Prithvi If US Refuses F-16s to Pakistan," *Asian Age,* May 20, 1994, p. 1.

189. Statement by India in the Conference on Disarmament, June 2, 1994, in Government of India, Ministry of External Affairs, *Statements by India on Comprehensive Nuclear Test*

Ban Treaty (CTBT) (1993–1996) (New Delhi: Government of India, Ministry of External Affairs, 1996), pp. 11–12.

190. Statement by India, September 1, 1994, in ibid., p. 23.

191. Interviews by author with Indian officials and journalists, 1994 and 1995.

192. *Dawn,* May 24, 1994, p. 1.

193. Shekhar Gupta, "Nawaz Sharif's Bombshell," *India Today,* September 15, 1994, p. 47.

194. Ibid., p. 46.

195. Ibid.

196. Interview by author with former high-ranking Indian official.

197. U.S. Congressional Research Service Report, written by Zachary Davis, quoted in "India Can Build H-Bombs: US Report," *Bangladesh Observer,* September 9, 1994, p. 4.

198. Shekhar Gupta, "Nawaz Sharif's Bombshell," *India Today,* September 15, 1994, p. 54.

199. *Indian Express,* September 19, 1994, p. 1, in *FBIS-NESA,* September 23, 1994, p. 39.

200. Raja Ramanna, " 'We Have Enough Plutonium,' " *India Today,* September 15, 1994, p. 33.

201. " 'Prithvi' Induction by Mid-95," *Times of India,* September 20, 1994, p. 1.

202. "India Developing Sea-Based Missile System," *Morning Sun,* November 15, 1994, p. 5.

203. Steven Lee Myers, "U.S. Aides Describe How Russia Helps India on Missiles," *New York Times,* April 27, 1998, p. 1.

204. For a detailed history and analysis of the Nuclear Posture Review, see Janne E. Nolan, *An Elusive Consensus: Nuclear Weapons and American Security after the Cold War* (Washington, D.C.: Brookings Institution, forthcoming).

205. Author's notes, January 13–21, Bombay, Goa, New Delhi.

206. Raja Mohan, "China Assures U.S. It Will Not Export Missiles to Pak," *Hindu,* October 6, 1994, p. 1.

207. David Ignatius, "China: Friends and Spies," *Washington Post,* May 9, 1999, p. B9.

208. Atul Aneja, "Chinese N-Test Strengthens India's Case," *Hindu,* October 10, 1994, p. 4.

209. Amarnath K. Menon, "Titanic Triumph," *India Today,* December 31, 1994, p. 73. In Andhra Pradesh, Congress lost 157 of its previously held 183 seats. In Karnataka, Congress fell from 176 seats won in 1989 to 35.

210. Zefar Agha, "The Shadow of Defeat," *India Today,* March 31, 1995, p. 92.

CHAPTER THIRTEEN

1. The Marketing and Research Group, *A Study of India's Nuclear Choices,* report prepared for the Joan B. Kroc Institute for International Peace Studies at the University of Notre Dame, Ind., and the Fourth Freedom Forum, Goshen, Ind. (New Delhi: MARG, November/December 1994).

2. Ibid., p. 14.

3. Ibid., p. 16.

4. Ibid., p. 19.

5. Ibid., p. 9.

6. Ibid., p. 12.

7. "The China Connection," *Times of India,* January 10, 1995, p. 12.

8. "A Turning Point," *Times of India,* January 14, 1995, p. 12.

9. William J. Perry, comments, Stanford University's Center for International Security and Arms Control, Stanford, Calif., May 21, 1998.

10. "A Turning Point," *Times of India*, January 14, 1995, p. 12.

11. William J. Perry, comments, Stanford University's Center for International Security and Arms Control, Stanford, Calif., May 21, 1998. At this point, the U.S. Defense Intelligence Agency's top-secret "Handbook" on India's "Nuclear Warhead System" estimated that India plausibly had two different warhead types, one simple fission weapon and the other "more sophisticated." But, the handbook cautioned, "These are notional designs; we do not know the design details of Indian nuclear devices." Defense Intelligence Reference Document, *India: Nuclear Warhead System Handbook (U)*, PC-1620-32-95, January 1995, p. 9. The quote comes from the only two sentences of this document that were not redacted when it was provided to the National Security Archives in Washington, D.C. Interviews by author with former high-level Indian officials suggested that more than two weapon types were "on the shelf" by this time.

12. Gupta, *India Redefines Its Role*, p. 34.

13. Jasjit Singh, "Defence Ties with US: Firming Up India's Strategic Plans," *Times of India*, February 3, 1995, p. 12.

14. Arun Singh, comments in James Blight, "Summary of Seminars on the Cuban Missile Crisis," unpublished paper, New Delhi, January 9–15, 1995, p. 35.

15. Prepared statement by Assistant Secretary of State for South Asian Affairs Robin Raphel, House International Relations Subcommittee on Asia and the Pacific, February 9, 1995 (author's copy of statement), p. 5.

16. The author was a co-organizer of this meeting.

17. The Chinese group of five included a former ambassador to India, a former ambassador to the Conference on Disarmament in Geneva, and a military expert on arms control. The Indian group included former Atomic Energy Commission Chairman Raja Ramanna, former Chief of the Army Chief General (ret.) S. F. Rodriques, former Foreign Secretary A. P. Venkateswaran, K. Subrahmanyam, Jasjit Singh, Brahma Chellaney, and Pai Panandiker. The Pakistani group included former Vice Chief of Army Staff General (ret.) Khalid Mahmud Arif, former Pakistan Atomic Energy Commission Chairman Munir Ahmad Khan, former Minister of Finance Mubashir Hasan, and former Foreign Secretary Niaz Niak. The United States group included former Defense Secretary Robert McNamara, former White House Office for Science and Technology official Frank von Hippel, Thomas W. Graham of the Rockefeller Foundation, the author, and two U.S. government officials as observers.

18. Umashanker Phandis, "Goa Meeting's Call to Declare Fissile Material Stock," *Dawn*, March 9, 1995, p. 16.

19. "Pakistan Disowns Goa Nuke Dialogue," *Dawn*, March 1, 1995, p. 1.

20. Ibid., p. 1. Indian defense experts at the meeting also told the press that there had been a positive "shift, albeit a subtle one." "Unusual Progress in Unofficial Indo-Pak Disarmament Talks," *Daily Star*, February 28, 1995, p. 12.

21. International Communications Research, poll of 1,011 Americans, January 4, 1995 (Media, Penn: ICR).

22. Author's notes, January 1995.

23. Author's notes, January 1995.

24. C. Uday Bhaskar, "India and the True Spirit of NPT," *Times of India*, March 2, 1995, p. 10.

25. Jasjit Singh, interview with *Liberation,* in *FBIS-NESA,* February 22, 1995, p. 58.

26. K. Subrahmanyam, "Freeze on N-Material Was Indian Plan," *Times of India,* February 7, 1995, p. 11.

27. Sunil Adam, "Ominous Trends in India's Nuclear Debate," *Pioneer,* February 28, 1995, p. 8.

28. Kalam, quoted in the *Asian Age,* March 20, 1995, p. 1, in *FBIS-NESA,* March 28, 1995, p. 63.

29. Quoted in Dinesh Kumar, "Army Disquiet over Indecision on Prithvi Deployment," *Times of India,* March 30, 1995, p. 13.

30. Ibid.; *Navbharat Times,* March 27, 1995, p. 6, in *FBIS-NESA,* March 31, 1995, p. 48; *Dainik Jagran,* April 5, 1995, p. 6, in *FBIS-NESA,* April 7, 1995, p. 46.

31. Muhammad Ali Siddiqi, "Changes in Pressler Law Being Sought: Clinton," *Dawn,* April 12, 1995, p. 1.

32. Interviews by author with U.S. State Department and White House officials, April 12, 1995.

33. White House spokesman Mike McCurry, quoted in "US Will Not Lift Ban on Aid to Pakistan," *Times of India,* April 12, 1995, p. 12.

34. Author's discussion with National Security Council official, April 12, 1995.

35. Author's discussions with Carter Pilcher of Senator Brown's staff, April 1995.

36. Balakrishnan and Gouri Chatterjee, "Majority Backs Stance on NPT," *Times of India,* April 22, 1995, p. 13.

37. On Einhorn's testimony, Raja Mohan, "U.S. Warns against Production of Prithvi," *Hindu,* March 11, 1995, p. 1. On the BJP, Ashwant Talwar, "BJP Pledges to Make Nuclear Arms If in Power," *Indian Express,* April 4, 1995, p. 9.

38. Ashwant Talwar, "BJP Pledges to Make Nuclear Arms If in Power," *Indian Express,* April 4, 1995, p. 9.

39. *Dainik Jagran,* April 16, 1995, p. 6, in *FBIS-NESA,* April 20, 1995, p. 51.

40. Ibid.

41. "Time to Be Firm," *India Today,* April 30, 1995, p 4.

42. Ibid.

43. For a discussion of U.S. pressure tactics and the failure of the Bandung meeting, see the interview with Venezuelan Ambassador Adolfo Taylhardat in Susan B. Welsh, "Delegate Perspectives on the 1995 NPT Review and Extension Conference," *Nonproliferation Review* 2, no. 3 (Spring/Summer 1995): p. 8.

44. Raj Chengappa, "Making Compromises," *India Today,* April 30, 1995, p. 64.

45. Reprinted in *Arms Control Today* 25, no. 5 (June 1995): p. 30.

46. Pravin Sawhney, "Army Raises Prithvi Group," *Asian Age,* April 29, 1995, p. 1.

47. "Parliament Panel Favours 'Prithvi' Deployment," *Times of India,* May 5, 1995, p. 7.

48. *Indian Express,* May 5, 1995, p. 8, in *FBIS-NESA,* May 8, 1995, p. 43.

49. Hari Ramachandran, "India Considering Missile Deployment, Rao Says," *Reuters,* New Delhi, May 16, 1995.

50. Raja Mohan, " 'Prithvi Induction as per Security Needs,' " *Hindu,* May 24, 1995, p. 1.

51. "China's Gauntlet," *Times of India,* May 16, 1995, p. 12.

52. All India Radio Overseas Service, March 6, 1995, in *FBIS-NESA,* March 7, 1995, p. 43.

53. "China's Missile Shipments," *Hindu,* July 7, 1995, p. 8; Dinesh Kumar, "Pakistan Has 84 M-11 Missiles Which Can Hit Delhi, Bombay," *Times of India,* July 11, 1995, p. 7.

54. Kenneth J. Cooper, *Washington Post*, July 3, 1995, p. 1.

55. Interview with former Clinton administration official involved in this issue, August 4, 1998.

56. Delhi Doordarshan Television, August 20, 1995, in *FBIS-NESA*, August 22, 1995, p. 72.

57. "Step towards Tranquility," *Business Standard*, August 22, 1995, p. 11.

58. Ibid.

59. Raja Mohan, "India and the Chinese Model," *Hindu*, November 21, 1995, p. 12.

60. "Brown Will Move 2 Amendments in Senate," *Dawn*, August 12, 1995, p. 1.

61. Aziz Haniffa, "Clinton May Personally Push Pak Arms Sale Amendment," *Statesman*, August 11, 1995, p. 1. The military equipment Washington sought to release to Pakistan included 3 P-3C-II Orion naval reconnaissance and strike aircraft; 28 Harpoon antiship missiles; 360 AIM-9L Sidewinder air-to-air missiles; 24 M198 towed howitzers; spare engines and parts for F-16s; and other assorted items all totaling $368 million for which Pakistan had already paid.

62. Shekhar Gupta, "Blowing Hot and Cold over Pressler," *India Today*, August 31, 1995, p. 44.

63. A. Madhavan, *Pioneer*, July 29, 1995, p. 6.

64. Ibid., and *Jansatta*, August 7, 1995, p. 4, in *FBIS-NESA*, August 11, 1995, p. 45.

65. Interview by author, June 29, 1998.

66. *Business Standard*, August 29, 1995, p. 2, in *FBIS-NESA*, September 6, 1995, p. 73.

67. Farhan Bokhari and Vivek Raghuvanshi, "Pakistan, India Trade Barbs over Nuclear Missiles," *Defense News*, August 28–September 3, p. 1.

68. Brahma Chellaney, "It Is Time for India to Begin Nuclear Testing," *Pioneer*, August 30, 1995, p. 8.

69. Interviews by author with several Indian journalists and think tank officials, January 1995, New Delhi.

70. Interview by author with U.S. officials, May 1998.

71. Interview by author, June 29, 1998.

72. Ibid.

73. Ibid.

74. Author's notes, February 26, 1998, Mumbai.

75. Ibid. and discussions with U.S. officials then posted in New Delhi, January 1996.

76. Ibid.

77. "Summary of Recommendations," conclusions issued by participants in the Institute for Defence Studies and Analyses–Centre for Policy Research Joint Seminar "External Pressures on India's Nuclear Options," New Delhi, September 24, 1995.

78. *Business Standard*, October 26, 1995, p. 15, in *FBIS-NESA*, November 1, 1995, p. 87.

79. *Times of India*, Bombay, December 18, 1995, p. 1, in *FBIS-NESA*, December 19, 1995, p. 52.

80. Statement by Atal Behari Vajpayee to the Fiftieth United Nations General Assembly, October 26, 1995, in Government of India, Ministry of External Affairs, *Statements by India on Comprehensive Nuclear Test Ban Treaty (1993–1996)*, p. 78.

81. Ibid., p. 80.

82. Tim Weiner, *New York Times*, December 15, 1995, p. 1.

83. Author's discussion with State Department officials, December 14–18, 1995.

84. Author's discussions with Tim Weiner, December 1995.

85. John F. Burns, *New York Times*, December 16, 1995, and Indian Ministry of External Affairs, press release, December 15, 1995.

86. R. Jeffrey Smith, "Possible Nuclear Arms Test by India Concerns U.S.," *Washington Post*, December 16, 1995, p. A17.

87. Numerous Pakistani media accounts and interviews by author with high-ranking Pakistani officials, January 20–21, 1996, Islamabad.

88. Interview by author with former administration official, August 4, 1998.

89. K. K. Katyal, "Govt. Says U.S. Report Speculative," *Hindu*, December 16, 1995.

90. Srinivas Laxman, "NYT Report on N-Test a Big Lie: Ramanna," *Times of India*, December 17, 1995.

91. *Agence France-Presse*, Hong Kong, December 17, 1995, in *FBIS-NESA*, December 19, 1995, p. 78.

92. Ibid.

93. "A Test Balloon," *Hindustan Times*, December 18, 1995, p. 8.

94. Delhi Doordarshan Television, December 18, 1995, in *FBIS-NESA*, December 19, 1995, p. 50.

95. "Top defence scientist" quoted in M. D. Nalapat, "US Raising N-Test Bogey to Help Pakistan, Says Top Official," *Times of India*, Bombay, December 18, 1995.

96. *Asian Age*, December 18, 1995, p. 8, in *FBIS-NESA*, December 20, 1995, p. 65.

97. "Nuclear Apartheid," *Times of India*, December 19, 1995, p. 14.

98. *Business Standard*, December 19, 1995, p. 11, in *FBIS-NESA*, December 20, 1995, p. 66.

99. Raja Mohan, "India's Nuclear Options," *Hindu*, December 20, 1995, p. 12.

100. K. Subrahmanyam, "To Test or Not to Test," *Economic Times*, December 21, 1995.

101. "Mukherjee Calls Nuclear Programme Peaceful," *Hindustan Times*, December 19, 1995, p. 1.

102. Interview by author with former administration official, August 4, 1998.

103. Interview by author, June 29, 1998.

104. Interview by author, October 17, 1998.

105. Interview by author, February 25, 1999.

106. Ibid.

107. K. P. Nayar, "Rao under Pressure," *Indian Express*, December 28, 1995, p. 1.

108. *Telegraph*, December 24, 1995, p. 11, in *FBIS-NESA*, December 27, 1995, p. 57.

109. Ibid.

110. Brahma Chellaney, "India Must No Longer Ignore Its Nuclear Imperatives," *Pioneer*, January 17, 1996, p. 8.

111. P. R. Chari, "Folly to Keep Out of CTBT," *Hindustan Times*, January 18, 1996.

112. Kanti Bajpai, "India Should Give Up the Nuclear Option," *Times of India*, January 24, 1996, p. 10.

113. Statement by Foreign Secretary Salman Haider, Conference on Disarmament, March 21, 1996, in Government of India, Ministry of External Affairs, *Statements by India on Comprehensive Nuclear Test Ban Treaty (1993–1996)*, p. 98.

114. Author's notes, January 26, 1996, New Delhi.

115. "Long-Range Version of Prithvi Missile Successfully Tested," *Deccan Herald*, January 28, 1996, p. 1.

116. Author's notes, January 19–30, 1996, Islamabad, New Delhi, Mumbai, and Bangalore.

117. Interview by author, January 26, 1996, New Delhi.

118. R. Jeffrey Smith, "U.S. May Waive Sanctions on China for Sale Related to Nuclear Arms," *Washington Post*, February 8, 1996, p. A20; K. K. Katyal, "U.S. Failure to Punish Pak. Criticised," *Hindu*, March 16, 1996.

119. Raja Mohan, "Challenges for Foreign Policy," *Hindu*, April 4, 1996, p. 10.

120. *Hindustan Times*, April 29, 1996, p. 6, in *FBIS-NESA*, May 2, 1986, p. 38.

121. Bharatiya Janata Party manifesto, *FBIS-NESA*, supplement, May 10, 1996, p. 11.

122. Miriam Jordan, "Indian Opposition Party Would Assert Nuclear Capability If It Gains Power," Asian *Wall Street Journal*, April 2, 1996, p. A10.

123. "Indian Opposition Party Denies Nuclear Test Plan," *Reuters*, April 2, New Delhi.

124. Delhi Doordarshan Television, April 20, 1996, in *FBIS-NESA*, April 23, 1996, p. 68.

125. "Leftist Groups in India Hunt for Candidate to Get Behind," *New York Times*, May 14, 1996, p. A10.

126. The United States announced at this time that it would not impose sanctions on China for selling to Pakistan five thousand ring magnets useful in uranium enrichment centrifuges. Washington and Beijing negotiated an agreement whereby the United States would drop the threat of sanctions in return for a Chinese statement and commitment that it would "not provide assistance to unsafeguarded nuclear facilities." China made this statement on May 11. "Row Over?" *Economist*, May 18, 1996, p. 37.

127. Mark Hibbs, *Nucleonics Week*, December 4, 1997, p. 10; interview by author with former administration official, August 4, 1998.

128. The Indian emplacement was confirmed in an interview with a knowledgeable Indian official, March 12, 1999, New Delhi. The lack of American knowledge of this was confirmed in discussions with knowledgeable U.S. officials in March 1999.

129. Interview by author, 1998.

130. Brahma Chellaney, "A New Nuclear Dividing Line," *Pioneer*, June 4, 1997, p. 10, indicated his awareness when he wrote elliptically that "[t]wice in the past 18 months India came close to conducting a nuclear test." The first time was in December as was widely known; the second time had not been public knowledge, and Chellaney gave no details. Another well-connected journalist mentioned his knowledge of the May 1996 test decision(s) during a conference in New Delhi in March 1998.

131. Conversations with U.S. officials in New Delhi, March 21, 1998.

132. Interview by author with a knowledgeable Indian source, July 7, 1998.

133. Interview by author with former high-ranking Indian official, June 29, 1998.

134. Interview by author, March 12, 1999, New Delhi.

135. Quoted in "Indian Nuclear Tests a Political Decision: Former PM," *Agence France-Presse*, New Delhi, May 19, 1998.

136. Interview by author with former high-ranking Ministry of Defence official, June 30, 1998.

137. Quoted in "Indian Nuclear Tests a Political Decision: Former PM," *Agence France-Presse*, New Delhi, May 19, 1998.

CHAPTER FOURTEEN

1. On subcritical tests see Suzanne Jones and Frank von Hippel, "Take a Hard Look at Subcritical Tests," *Bulletin of the Atomic Scientists,* November/December 1996, pp. 44-47.

2. In the May 28, 1996, treaty draft, states hosting seismological stations for the treaty's monitoring system were required to ratify. India then declared it would not allow a seismological station on its territory to be part of the system, prompting the United Kingdom to propose that states possessing nuclear reactors on their soil must ratify the treaty for it to enter into force. This, too, would include India.

3. The United States originally proposed that the treaty should enter into force upon its ratification by the five recognized nuclear weapon states.

4. American officials such as National Security Adviser Anthony Lake believed that India ultimately would choose not to be isolated internationally and would therefore sign the treaty. Interviews by author with U.S. officials, March–June 1996.

5. Statement by Arundhati Ghose, plenary of the Conference on Disarmament, June 20, 1996, in Government of India, Ministry of External Affairs, *Statements by India on Comprehensive Nuclear Test Ban Treaty (1993–1996),* p. 105.

6. Ibid., p. 104.

7. Interview by author with Ministry of External Affairs official, March 2, 1997, New Delhi.

8. Ibid., and conversation with R. Chidambaram, February 26, 1997, Mumbai.

9. "Comprehensive Test Ban Treaty," Article IX, reprinted in Rodney W. Jones and Mark G. McDonough, with Toby F. Dalton and Gregory D. Koblentz, *Tracking Nuclear Proliferation* (Washington, D.C.: Carnegie Endowment for International Peace, 1998), pp. 289–292.

10. Tariq Hasan, "Nuclear Physicists Want Probe into Narora Fire," *Times of India,* June 4, 1996.

11. *United Press International,* New Delhi, June 18, 1996.

12. S. Balakrishnan, interview with A. Gopalakrishnan, *Times of India,* June 18, 1996, p. 18.

13. Bharat Bhushan, "Defence Project in Jeopardy," *Times of India,* February 20, 1987.

14. In early 1995, the parliamentary standing committee on energy, headed by the BJP's Jaswant Singh, issued a report bemoaning cost overruns and time delays in nuclear power plant construction. "Atomic Power Projects' Cost Overruns Alarming: Panel," *Economic Times,* May 1, 1995, p. 6.

15. Eric Arnett, "India's Nuclear Brownout," *Bulletin of the Atomic Scientists,* November/December 1996, p. 15.

16. Figures of plan and nonplan expenditures provided by the Institute of Peace and Conflict Studies, New Delhi. The 1992–1993 total was Rs. 1,488.29 crores ($563 million), and in 1995–1996 Rs. 1,131.45 crores ($364 million) at the respective year's World Bank exchange rate figures.

17. All India Radio, December 25, 1995, in *FBIS-NESA,* December 28, 1995, p. 37.

18. Prakash Nanda, "Experts Favour Clear Stand on N-Policy," *Times of India,* June 9, 1996.

19. Ibid.

20. Raja Mohan, "India and the Chinese N-Test," *Hindu,* June 9, 1996.

21. Praful Bidwai, "CTBT: India's Veto Is Futile," *Times of India,* September 11, 1996.

22. *Suo moto* Statement by Minister for External Affairs Inder K. Gujral, July 15, 1996, in Government of India, Ministry of External Affairs, *Statements by India on Comprehensive Nuclear Test Ban Treaty (1993–1996),* p. 108.

23. Ibid., p. 109.

24. Prem Shankar Jha, "India's Second Best Option," *Hindu,* August 14, 1996, p. 10, and author's notes from discussions with U.S. officials.

25. Ibid.

26. Conversation with U.S. State Department official, August 1996.

27. Interview by author, March 9, 1999, New Delhi.

28. *Indian Express,* August 8, 1996, p. 9, in *FBIS-NESA,* August 9, 1996, p. 36; *Hindustan Times,* August 10, 1996, p. 13, in *FBIS-NESA,* August 12, 1996, p. 48.

29. Eric Arnett, "And the Loser Is . . . the Indian Armed Forces," *Economic and Political Weekly,* September 5–12, 1998, p. 2339, reported that the military accepted Prithvi missiles only after the DRDO agreed to pay for them.

30. *Hindustan Times,* August 10, 1996, p. 13.

31. "BJP Urges Govt to Test, Deploy Nuclear Arms," *Morning Sun* (Dhaka), August 9, 1996.

32. " 'India Must Declare Itself Nuclear State,' " *Times of India,* August 10, 1996.

33. Ibid.

34. Editor's introduction to two divergent opinion pieces by Praful Bidwai and M. D. Nalapat, *Times of India,* September 11, 1996.

35. Inder Gujral, interview by Michael Richardson, "India Doesn't Have Nuclear Weapons, Says Gujral," reprinted in *Dawn,* August 27, 1996.

36. "India Will Keep Nuclear Option Open for Use at the 'Right Time,' " *Times of India,* August 3, 1996.

37. Reiss, *Bridled Ambition,* p. 185, reported that U.S. government sources believed in 1994 that India possessed "enough fissile material for twenty to twenty-five nuclear weapons." A former leader of the strategic enclave stated that approximately four dozen nuclear weapons could be assembled quickly at this time. Interview by author, July 28, 1998.

38. Ethiraj Anbarasan, "No Need for Further N-Test: Ramanna," *Times of India,* October 29, 1996.

39. K. Sundarji, "India's Post-CTBT Strategy," *Hindu,* September 30, 1996.

40. Mohan Guruswamy, "Age of Stand-off Weapons: Evil Empire Called USA," *Indian Express,* December 18, 1996, <http://express.indiaworld.com/ie/daily/19961022/29650602.html>.

41. Kenneth J. Cooper, "Nuclear Dilemmas," *Washington Post,* May 25, 1998, pp. A1, A22.

42. K. Subrahmanyam, "Nuclear Defence Philosophy," *Times of India,* November 8, 1996.

43. K. Subrahmanyam, "Dealing with China," *Times of India,* October 23, 1996.

44. In October, U.S. intelligence reported that China had sold additional sensitive nuclear equipment to Pakistan, beyond the five thousand ring magnets noted earlier. U.S. officials declared, however, that the transactions occurred prior to China's May 11, 1996, pledge to cease such sales and that therefore the United States would not impose sanctions. Ramesh Chandran, "Chinese N-Sale to Pakistan Was Made before May Commitment: US," *Times of India,* October 11, 1996.

45. Ramesh Chandran, "US Says India Has 'Nothing to Fear,' " *Times of India,* September 13, 1996.

46. "US Warns India, Others against Conducting N-Tests," *Times of India,* September 12, 1996.

47. "India, U.S. to Work in Hi-Tech Areas," *Hindu,* October 25, 1996.

48. "Indian Anti-Americanism," *Hindustan Times,* November 1, 1996, p. 13.

49. "A Chemistry neither Instant nor Distant," *Washington Post,* October 2, 1996, p. A26.

50. Barbara Crossette, "5 Seated in Security Council after Intensive Maneuvering," *New York Times,* October 22, 1996.

51. Sushma Ramachandran, "CTBT Stand Cost U.N. Council Seat: Gujral," *Hindu,* November 4, 1996, <http://www.hinduonline.com/today/stories/01040002.htm>.

52. "UN Council Seat for India Ruled Out," *Indian Express,* December 18, 1996, <http://express.indiaworld.co.in/ie/daily/19961218/35350342.html>.

53. Raja Mohan, "President, PM Hope for Better Ties with U.S.," *Hindu,* November 8, 1996, p. 11.

54. President Leghari's "Proclamation," reprinted in *Dawn,* November 5, 1996.

55. Delhi Doordarshan Television, November 29, 1996, in *FBIS-NESA,* 96-232, drnes232-r-96003.

56. Ibid.

57. *Frontier Post,* December 3, 1996, p. 6, in *FBIS-NESA,* 96-233, drnes233-v-96001.

58. Interviews by author with current and former high-ranking Pakistani officials, February 22-24, 1997, Islamabad.

59. *Pioneer,* October 23, 1996, p. 10, *FBIS-NESA,* 96-207, drnes207-r-96006.

60. Raja Mohan, "India, China Power Equations Changing," *Hindu,* December 2, 1996, p. 11.

61. Report quoted in *Dawn,* December 6, 1996, and *Reuters,* New Delhi, December 8, 1996.

62. *Reuters,* New Delhi, December 6, 1996, quoting Jasjit Singh and Brahma Chellaney.

63. Ibid.

64. Cited in "Missile Developments, India," *Nonproliferation Review* 4, no. 3 (Spring/Summer 1997): p. 130.

65. "Agni Missile Project Not Shelved, Says Mulayam," *Asian Age,* December 15, 1996.

66. "Extinguishing Agni," *Times of India,* December 10, 1996.

67. K. C. Pant, "Securing India's Future," the Fourth Lal Bahadur Shastri Memorial Lecture, January 11, 1997, New Delhi (printed copy), p. 18.

68. *Financial Times Survey India,* November 19, 1996, pp. 1-10.

69. "National Security Environment," editorial, *Hindu,* November 2, 1996, p. 10.

70. Ibid.

71. "A New U.S. Policy toward India and Pakistan," report of an independent task force sponsored by the Council on Foreign Relations, Richard Haass, chairman, Gideon Rose, project director, New York, 1997, p. 25. The author served on the task force.

72. Ibid.

73. Ibid., p. 26.

74. Raja Mohan, "Renewing Indo-U.S. Dialogue," *Hindu,* January 9, 1997.

75. Manoj Joshi, "Pakistan as a Failed State," *Indian Express,* January 9, 1997.

76. Gujral quoted from speech in Sri Lanka, in *Dawn*, January 22, 1996.

77. *Newsletter* (Regional Centre for Strategic Studies, Colombo, Sri Lanka) 3, no. 1 (January 1997): p. 1. "Track II" diplomacy refers to initiatives by former officials or other eminent representatives of tension-ridden states to explore possible measures to improve relations. Such explorations are unofficial and therefore allow greater creativity, but at the same time relevant governments are aware of these discussions and often indicate interest in following up on breakthroughs made at the Track II level.

78. Umashankar Phadnis, "India to talk with Pakistan after Poll, Says Gujral," *Dawn*, January 25, 1997.

79. K. P. Nayar, *Telegraph*, April 15, 1997, p. 12, in *FBIS-NESA*, 97-074, drnes074-r-97001.

80. Interview by author with BJP leader, March 1, 1997, New Delhi.

81. Interviews by author with U.S. officials.

82. Interviews by author with a range of Pakistani elites, February 21-24, 1997, Islamabad.

83. Personal communications with Pakistani Americans in contact with Sharif and his advisers, January-February 1997.

84. Raja Mohan, "Resuming Indo-Pak Dialogue," *Hindu*, February 6, 1997, p. 8; interviews by author, February 27-March 2, New Delhi.

85. Interview by author with high-ranking Pakistani official, February 23, 1997.

86. Interviews by author with a former high-ranking Indian cabinet official, a BJP leader, and a United Front cabinet official, March 1-2, 1997.

87. Ibid.

88. " 'India Will Allow Foreign-Owned N-Power Plants,' " *Times of India*, February 9, 1997; "Nuclear Developments, India," *Nonproliferation Review* 4, no. 3 (Spring/Summer 1997): p. 130.

89. *Jansatta*, March 26, 1997, p. 6, in *FBIS-NESA*, 97-086, drnes03271997001567.

90. *Navbharat Times*, September 9, 1997, p. 5, in *FBIS-NESA*, 97-255, drnes0912199700189.

91. *Business Standard*, April 3, 1997, p. 6, in *FBIS-NESA*, 97-065, drnes065-r-97003; *Navbharat Times*, April 5, 1997, p. 6, in *FBIS-NESA*, 97-071, drnes071-r-97001.

92. On the more accommodating U.S. position, see statement by Assistant Secretary of State Karl Inderfurth in C. K. Arora, "US May Not Oppose Sale of Russian N-Plant to India," *Hindu*, December 25, 1997; Brahma Chellaney, "New Year's Gift: A Deal That Stinks," *Pioneer*, December 31, 1997, p. 8.

93. Programme for Promoting Nuclear Non-Proliferation, *Newsbrief*, no. 43 (Third Quarter 1998): p. 5.

94. Ibid.

95. "Missile Developments, India," *Nonproliferation Review* 4, no. 3 (Spring/Summer 1997): p. 131.

96. "India Test-Fires Prithvi," *Muslim*, February 25, 1997; "New Delhi Test-Fires Prithvi," *Dawn*, February 25, 1997.

97. *Times of India*, March 5, 1997.

98. Khalid Mahmud, "Normalising Ties with India," *News*, March 7, 1997, <http://www.jang-group.com/thenews/thenews/op1.html>.

99. Rita Manchanda, bureau chief, Plus Channel, Business Plus, Delhi, in "India-Pakistan Relations: Moving from Animosity to Curiosity," *News*, March 9, 1997.

100. P. S. Suryanarayana, "Gujral-Ayub Talks May Be Put Off," *Hindu*, April 2, 1994, p. 14.

101. Ibid.

102. Raja Mohan, "Foreign Policy & Consensus," *Hindu*, April 4, 1997, p. 10.

103. K. K. Katyal, "India, Pakistan to Continue Talks on All Issues," *Hindu*, April 10, 1997, p. 1.

104. Timothy Mapes and Amit Prakash, "India Premier to Uphold Economic Policy," *Wall Street Journal*, April 22, 1997.

105. John F. Burns, "New Rapport from India-Pakistan Meeting," *New York Times*, May 13, 1997, p. 3.

106. Ibid.

107. Ibid.

108. P. S. Suryanarayana, "Pakistan Keen on Intensifying 'Process of Dialogue,' " *Hindu*, May 14, 1997, p. 1.

109. Ibid.; "One Step Forward," *Times of India*, May 14, 1997.

110. "A Path-Breaking Summit," *Hindu*, May 14, 1997, p. 12.

111. *Hindustan Times*, May 21, 197, p. 2, in *FBIS-NESA*, 97-141, drnes05211997002336.

112. Ministry of Defence Annual Report, 1996–1997 (New Delhi: Government of India, Ministry of Defence), p. 6.

113. Ibid., p. 2.

114. Ibid.

115. Cited in Brahma Chellaney, "Missiles: India's Pusillanimity, China's Gall," *Pioneer*, May 7, 1997, p. 10.

116. Ibid.

117. Steven Strasser and Sudip Mazumdar, "A New Tiger," *Newsweek*, August 4, 1997, p. 43, citing World Bank statistics.

118. *Hindustan Times*, May 18, 1997, p. 13, in *FBIS-NESA*, 97-97, drnes097-r-97004.

119. "India Will Not Bow to Pressure on N-Pact: PM," *Statesman*, June 1, 1997.

120. Ibid.

121. For example, Brahma Chellaney, "A New Nuclear Dividing Line," *Pioneer*, June 4, 1997, p. 10; Ranjit Kumar, *Navbharat Times*, June 6, 1997, p. 6, in *FBIS-NESA*, 97-100, drnes110-r-97001.

122. R. Jeffrey Smith, *Washington Post*, June 3, 1997, p. A26.

123. *Frontier Post*, June 5, 1997, p. 6, *FBIS-NESA*, 97-157, drnes06061997000076.

124. Rawalpindi *Jang*, June 6, 1997, p. 1, *FBIS-NESA*, 97-157, drnes06061997000502.

125. Shekhar Gupta, "Lessons of the Missile 'Leak'—Pity the Soft State," *Indian Express*, June 9, 1997; Soumyajit Pattnaik, "The Regional Balance of Missiles: The Fact Sheet," *Pioneer* June 14, 1997, p. 8.

126. "India Says No Plan to Deploy Prithvi," *Dawn*, June 12, 1997; Pattnaik, "The Regional Balance of Missiles: The Fact Sheet," p. 8.

127. K. K. Katyal, " 'Prithvi Merely Stored at Jalandhar,' " *Hindu*, June 9, 1997.

128. Kenneth J. Cooper, "India Denies It Has Deployed Missiles," *Washington Post*, June 12, 1997, p. A26.

129. "Prithvi: India Will Resist Pressure," *Hindu*, June 15, 1997.

130. Brahma Chellaney, "The Making of a Banana Republic," *Pioneer*, June 18, 1997, p. 10.

131. Ibid.

132. Douglas Waller, "The Secret Missile Deal," *TIME*, June 30, 1997, <http://www.pathfinder.com/ee6R93XAVA4Ntk35kj/time/magazine/1997/dom/970630/world.6/30/97ret-mi.>.

133. Joint statement, quoted in Amit Baruah, "India, Pak. Reach Accord on Joint Working Groups," *Hindu*, June 24, 1997, p. 1.

134. Ibid.

135. "India's Nuclear Options Are Open, Says PM," *Hindu*, July 14, 1997.

136. "India's Nuclear Options Are Open: PM," *Deccan Herald*, July 14, 1997.

137. "India to Revive 'Agni' Project," *Hindu*, July 31, 1997, p. 1.

138. Jayanta Roy Chowdhury, "Axe Hovers on Nuclear Programme," *Telegraph*, August 19, 1997, p. 1.

139. "Atomic Numbers," *Telegraph*, August 20, 1997, p. 12.

140. T. S. Gopi Rethinaraj and D. N. Moorty, "Nuclear Politics in South Asia," *Jane's Intelligence Review*, Special Report No. 20, December 1998, p. 12.

141. Mohammed Iqbal, "Indian Scientists Revive Dead N-Reactor," *Hindu*, December 24, 1997.

142. Ibid.; All India Radio Overseas Service, December 29, 1997, in *FBIS-NESA*, 97-364, drnes12291997000394.

143. "Nuclear Option Open: Gujral," *Asian Age*, September 9, 1997.

144. Ibid.

145. Interview by author with former high-ranking AEC official, March 7, 1999.

146. O. P. Sabherwal, "Nuclear Power: Our Scientists Take on the World," *Times of India*, September 9, 1997; Brahma Chellaney, "Domineering US; Deferential India," *Pioneer*, September 24, 1997, p. 10.

147. Shahid Ahmed Khan, "Sharif Acknowledges Nuclear Capability," *Times of India*, September 8, 1997.

148. "Sharif's Words Evoke Little Response in Delhi," *Statesman*, September 9, 1997.

149. Brahma Chellaney, "Domineering US; Deferential India," *Pioneer*, September 24, 1997, p. 10.

150. Raja Mohan, "Nuclear Weapons and the Gujral Doctrine," *Hindu*, September 22, 1997.

151. K. K. Katyal, "India, Pakistan Differ on Tackling 'Core Issue,' " *Hindu*, September 18, 1997.

152. Amit Baruah, "Pak. Ploy for Third Party Intervention," *Hindu*, September 20, 1997, p. 14.

153. *Jansatta*, September 24, 1997, p. 4, in *FBIS-NESA*, 97-271, drnes09281997000055.

154. Address by Nawaz Sharif to the Fifty-second Session of the UN General Assembly, September 22, 1997 (press handout from Pakistan Embassy, Washington, D.C.), p. 7.

155. *Deccan Herald*, September 28, 1997, in *FBIS-NESA*, 97-271, drnes09281997000273.

156. *Islamabad Khabrain*, September 24, 1997, p. 10, in *FBIS-NESA*, 97-269, drnes09261997000245.

157. As a representative example, see *Navbharat Times*, September 25, 1997, p. 6, in *FBIS-NESA*, 97-272, drnes09292997001064.

158. Interview by author, March 9, 1999. According to White House sources, the transcript of the formal Clinton-Gujral meeting does not include this discussion. White House official, interview by author, April 1, 1999.

159. "Deploy Prithvi along Borders: Congress," *New Nation*, Dhaka, October 1, 1997.

160. *Times of India*, May 16, 1998, and <http://www.india-today.com/itoday/15051998/news.htm>.

161. "Agni Programme Will Go On, Says Mulayam," *Hindu*, November 7, 1997.

162. Brahma Chellaney, "A National Icon, A Nation Adrift," *Pioneer*, December 3, 1997, p. 10.

163. Interviews by author with knowledgeable Indian officials, December 1997.

164. "India Won't Go Nuclear Unless Forced To: PM," *Hindu*, November 14, 1997.

165. Sridhar Krishnaswami, "U.S.-India May Discuss Nuclear Cooperation," *Hindu*, November 15, 1997.

166. Shubha Singh, "Strategic Turn in Indo-US Ties," *Pioneer*, October 23, 1997, p. 9; interviews by author with State Department officials, October 1997.

167. Sunil Adam, "US and India's N-Policy," *Pioneer*, October 22, 1997, p. 8.

168. Shubha Singh, "Towards Harmony," *Pioneer*, November 22, p. 11., All India Radio, November 24, 1997, in *FBIS-NESA*, 97-328, drnes11241997000301.

169. B. Muralidhar Reddy, "United Front Ready to Take the Plunge," *Hindu*, November 28, 1997, p. 1.

170. K. K. Katyal, "Lok Sabha Dissolved, New House by March 15," *Hindu*, December 5, 1997, p. 1.

171. "Work in Progress," *Economist*, February 22, 1997, Survey of India, p. 3.

172. See Jawed Naqvi, "India Has No Money to Meet Defence Needs—Analysts," *Reuters*, New Delhi, February 26, 1997.

CHAPTER FIFTEEN

1. For example, it called for a common civil code, scrapping Article 370 of the Constitution, which gives special status to Kashmir, and building a Ram Temple at the Babri Mosque site in Ayodhya.

2. George Iype, "Congress Promises Stability, Secularism and New Economic Agenda," January 24, 1998, quoting from Congress manifesto <http:/www.rediff.com.news/1998/jan/24cong.html>.

3. Seema Mustafa, *Asian Age*, March 12, 1998, p. 1, in *FBIS*, March 13, 1998, drnes0312199800094.

4. Neena Vyas, "BJP in Govt. to Exercise N-Option," *Hindu*, January 14, 1998, p. 13.

5. Ibid.

6. *Jaipur Rajasthan Patrika*, January 10, 1998, p. 8, in *FBIS-NESA*, 98-015, drrnes0115199980000825.

7. *Dawn*, January 12, 1998, in *FBIS-NESA*, 98-012, drnes0112199800148o.

8. Aabha Dixit, *Indian Express*, December 13, 1997.

9. Amit Baruah, "Pak. Welcomes Gujral's 'Offer' of Talks on J&K," *Hindu*, February 23, 1998, p. 14.

10. "BJP Vows to Take Back Azad Kashmir," *Dawn*, February 26, 1998; Amit Baruah, "BJP Statements Worry Pakistan," *Hindu*, February 27, 1998.

11. Amit Baruah, "BJP Statements Worry Pakistan," *Hindu*, February 27, 1998.

12. Raja Mohan, "BJP Moderates Nuclear Posture," *Hindu*, February 6, 1998, p. 14.

13. Ibid.

14. *Deccan Herald*, March 4, 1998, in *FBIS-NESA*, 98-063, drnes0304199800967.

15. John F. Burns, "Hindu Nationalists Gain Support of Key Regional Parties," *New York Times*, March 5, 1998.

16. John F. Burns, "Hindu Party to Weigh Options on Nuclear Arms," *New York Times*, March 19, 1998.

17. "No Immediate Nuclear Tests, Says Fernandes," *Times of India*, March 21, 1998, p. 1.

18. *Deccan Herald*, March 21, 1998, *FBIS-NESA*, 98-080, drnes03211998000290.

19. Mohan Guruswamy, interviewed by Dinesh Kumar, *Times of India*, March 27, 1998.

20. Manoj Joshi, "Nuclear Shock Wave," *India Today*, May 25, 1998, <http://www.india-today.com/itoday/25051998/cover.html>.

21. Sinha, speech announcing interim budget, reprinted in "Fiscal Situation Worse Than Expected: Finance Minister," *Indian Express*, March 26, 1998.

22. "Finance Minister Shelves Swadeshi, Opts for Vigorous Reforms," *Pioneer*, March 26, 1998; "Fund Shortage Hinders Indian Nuclear Plans," *Defense News*, March 16-31, 1998, p. 2.

23. Interview by author with U.S. government official, April 14, 1998.

24. Raja Mohan, "Ghauri Missile: India in Denial," *Hindu*, April 9, 1998, p. 13.

25. Dinesh Kumar, "India May Study Satellite Pictures on Ghauri testing," *Times of India*, April 8, 1998.

26. "Ghauri: Is It Just Politics or Is It War?" *Times of India*, April 12, 1998, and author's telephone conversations with Indian journalists and strategic analysts.

27. *New York Times*, April 11, 1998; author's discussions with Indian journalists and analysts in Washington and New Delhi.

28. "India to Go Ahead with Agni: Fernandes," *Statesman*, April 10, 1998.

29. S. K. Singh, "Pakistan's Muscle-Flexing," *Hindu*, April 17, 1998. Singh alleged the Ghauri was "made-in-China."

30. "BJP Vows to Take Back Azad Kashmir," *Dawn*, February 26, 1998; Amit Baruah, "BJP Statements Worry Pakistan," *Hindu*, February 27, 1998.

31. Interviews by author with U.S. officials and Pakistani sources, March–April 1998.

32. "Indian Panel to Review Defence Policy Set Up," *Agence France-Presse*, New Delhi, April 11, 1998, quoting a BJP statement.

33. *Times of India*, March 27, 1998.

34. Raj Chengappa, "The Bomb Makers," *India Today*, June 22, 1998, p. 45. The previous week's edition of *India Today* reported that the authorization was given on April 8, a date that Brajesh Mishra also confided to an eminent Indian strategist. Interview by author, October 17, 1998.

35. Ibid.

36. Interview by author with a generally knowledgeable Indian source. U.S. government analysts citing technical reasons also believed the decision was authorized prior to April 8. Interviews by author, October 1998.

37. Ibid.

38. *Deccan Herald*, April 16, 1998, *FBIS-NESA*, 98-106, drnes04161998000699.

39. Discussion with Indian official, June 3, 1998.

40. "India Ready to Face Any Challenge, Says PM," *Hindu*, April 18, 1998, p. 11.

41. Ibid.

42. Interview by author, April 22, 1998.

43. Barbara Crossette, "U.S. Neglect Leads to Missed Signals," *New York Times*, May 15, 1998, p. A10, citing Richardson's office. Jaswant Singh later insisted that "India at no stage,

either directly or indirectly, attempted to mislead the United States." *Agence France-Presse,* New Delhi, May 18, 1998.

44. Interview by author with U.S. official, May 19, 1998.

45. Here was a major failure to communicate. Washington was angry at Pakistan over the Ghauri, particularly in light of Secretary of State Albright's unanswered plea for Pakistani restraint. The Clinton administration planned immediately to impose sanctions on Pakistan and North Korea as a result, although it held off announcing this because Pakistan still held in prison a Pakistani national who had worked with the U.S. Drug Enforcement Agency in Pakistan and whom the United States believed had been falsely accused of crimes by a Pakistani tribunal. The United States had negotiated this man's release and wanted to wait until he was safely on a plane leaving Pakistan before announcing sanctions. (Interview by author with U.S. State Department official, April 7, 1998.) More broadly, though, Richardson, perhaps ineptly and naively, was hoping to win Pakistani cooperation in his initiative to negotiate a settlement of the Afghan civil war. His apparent coziness toward the Pakistanis may have served his Afghan initiative, but it deeply irritated India. Yet, during the past few years, India had conducted Prithvi tests that alarmed the Pakistanis, so how much reassurance should New Delhi have expected from Washington after the Ghauri test? India wanted to be treated more equitably by the United States on a range of issues, but it would not accept that Pakistan also needed to be treated more equitably by India, as Inder Gujral had been preparing to do.

46. "Dr. Qadeer Hints at N-Bomb," *Dawn,* April 16, 1998.

47. Delhi Doordarshan Television, April 20, 1998, in *FBIS-NESA,* 98-111, drnes04211998001557.

48. *Navbharat Times,* April 25, 1998, p. 7, in *FBIS-NESA,* 98-117, drnes04271998000772.

49. Ibid.

50. "India May Induct Nukes without Testing," *Muslim,* April 25, 1998.

51. Steven Lee Myers, "U.S. Aides Describe How Russia Helps India on Missiles," *New York Times,* April 27, 1998, p. 1.

52. This was cited in chapter 12.

53. *Deccan Herald,* April 15, 1998, *FBIS-NESA,* 98-105, drnes0415199800313.

54. Interview by author with former Indian defense official, April 26, 1998.

55. Soumyajit Pattaaik, "India-China Talks on 'Helipad Row' Planned," *Pioneer,* April 22, 1998, p. 1.

56. "India Revives Ballistic Missile Upgrade Project: Report," *Agence France-Presse,* New Delhi, May 3, 1998; Atul Aneja, "Agni Likely to Be Made Battle Ready," *Hindu,* May 5, 1998.

57. "George and the Dragon," *Times of India,* May 5, 1998. For perspective on relative diplomatic bellicosity it should be recalled that China tested a huge nuclear weapon when President Venkataraman was conducting his pathbreaking visit in 1992.

58. Seema Mustafa, "Vajpayee Sidelined in Government, Party," *Asian Age,* May 5, 1998.

59. "New Delhi Committed to Improving Ties with China," *Times of India,* May 6, 1998, p. 1.

60. Manoj Joshi, "Nuclear Shock Wave," *India Today,* May 25, 1998, <http://www.india-today.com/itoday/25051998/cover.html>.

61. Ibid.

62. Joint press statement by Department of Atomic Energy and Defence Research and Development Organisation, New Delhi, May 17, 1998 (facsimile).

63. N. Chandra Mohan, "Smiling Buddha Ushers in Reform," *Times of India*, May 20, 1998.

64. Narayanan Madhavan, "Indians Greet Nuclear Tests as Symbol of Pride," *Reuters*, New Delhi, May 11, 1998.

65. "Defiant Indians Proud of Nuclear Tests," *USA Today World*, May 12, 1998, <http:// www.usatoday.com/news/world/nws7.htm>.

66. "Majority Supports N-Tests," *Indian Web*, May 13, 1998, <http://www.indianweb. com/latenews.html>.

67. "India Conducts 3 Underground N-Tests," *Hindustan Times*, May 12, 1998, p. 1.

68. Raj Chengappa and Manoj Joshi, "Hawkish India," *India Today*, June 1, 1998, <http://www.india-today.com/itoday/01061998/cover2.html>.

69. Ibid.

70. Harish Khare, " 'A Repudiation of Nuclear Apartheid Policy,' " *Hindu*, May 12, 1998, p. 11.

71. "India Conducts 3 Underground N-Tests," *Hindustan Times*, May 12, 1998.

72. Narayanan Madhavan, "India Defiant over Tests but Says Aim Is Nuclear-Free World," *Reuters*, New Delhi, May 12, 1998.

73. U.S. Department of State, daily press briefing, May 11, 1998.

74. Kamran Khan and Kevin Sullivan, "U.S., Others Assail India's Nuclear Blasts," *Washington Post*, May 13, 1998, pp. A1, A25.

75. Ibid.

76. Ibid., p. A25.

77. Ibid., p. A1.

78. Interviews by author with many knowledgeable American officials, 1992-1998.

79. Carol Giacomo, "Cohen: Indian Tests Could Lead to Arms Race," *Reuters*, Washington, D.C., May 13, 1998.

80. "We Alone Will Decide Our Response, Says Nawaz," *News*, May 13, 1998, <http://ww.jang-group.com/thenews/may98-daily/13-05-98/mainl.htm>.

81. Benazir Bhutto, "Punishment: Make It Swift, Severe . . ." *Los Angeles Times*, May 18, 1998.

82. Interviews by author with Indian strategic analysts, May 12, 1998.

83. "China Warns Nuclear Tests Hurt Asia," *Associated Press*, Beijing, May 12, 1998.

84. Government statement quoted in "India Conducts Two More Nuclear Tests at Pokhran," *Hindu*, May 14, 1998, p. 1.

85. Conversations with Indian journalists and former officials, May 14-15, 1998.

86. NPPA fact sheet, May 11, 1998, provided by the National Security Council.

87. Hema Shukla, "India Apparently Has Nuclear Bomb," *Associated Press*, New Delhi, May 15, 1998.

88. Quoted in " 'India Will Not Use N-Weapon First,' " *Hindu*, May 19, 1998, p. 1.

89. Hema Shukla, "India Apparently Has Nuclear Bomb," *Associated Press*, New Delhi, May 15, 1998.

90. Ibid.

91. "Sanctions Should Stay: Senator," *Hindustan Times*, May 15, 1998; "Chidanand Rajghatta, "US Senators Seek Capping of Indian N-Plan," *Indian Express*, May 15, 1998.

92. "Chidanand Rajghatta, "US Senators Seek Capping of Indian N-Plan," *Indian Express,* May 15, 1998.

93. Interview by author with State Department official, May 19, 1998.

94. Conversations with four American officials directly involved in these issues, May 11–June 12, 1998.

95. Conversation with the author, May 12, 1998.

96. Conversation with the author, May 12, 1998.

97. At this time, other Asian currencies also were falling against the dollar. This weakened the link between the tests and the rupee's plight.

98. "Build on a New Foundation," *Asian Age,* May 15, 1998.

99. Siddarth Varadarajan, quoted in *Agence France-Presse,* New Delhi, May 16, 1998.

100. "Pokhran Quick Fix," *Times of India,* May 14, 1998.

101. Interview by author with knowledgeable Indian source, July 1998.

102. "India Ratchets Up Rhetoric against Pakistan and China," *Agence France-Presse,* New Delhi, May 18, 1998.

103. George Iype, "Advani Wants Troops to Strike across LOC to Quell Proxy War in Kashmir, *Rediff on the Net,* May 25, 1998, <http://www.rediff.com/news/1998/may/25geo.htm>.

104. "PM Offers to Move towards CTBT," *Hindu,* May 28, 1998, p. 1.

105. "After the Storm, India Edges toward Nuclear Compromise," *Agence France-Presse,* New Delhi, May 23, 1998.

106. Anonymous source, May 13, 1998.

107. John F. Burns, "As India Adds Up Costs of Its A-Tests, Dissent Grows Louder," *New York Times,* May 28, 1998, p. 3.

108. Ibid.

109. Ibid.

110. Ibid.

111. Ibid.

112. Ibid.

113. *Hindu,* June 24, 1998.

114. John F. Burns, "Self-Made Bomb Maker," *New York Times,* May 20, 1998, p. A6; Vital C. Nadkarni and Srinivas Laxman, "They Piloted N-Plans through Hostile Global Weather," *Times of India,* May 17, 1998.

115. Ibid.

116. Arunkumar Bhatt, "Pokhran Blasts Tested New Ideas: BARC Chief," *Hindu,* May 20, 1998.

117. "Weaponisation Now Complete, Say Scientists," *Hindu,* May 18, 1998, p. 1.

118. Ibid.

119. Raj Chengappa, "Is India's H-Bomb a Dud?" *India Today International,* October 12, 1998, p. 26.

120. Terry C. Wallace, "The May 1998 India and Pakistan Nuclear Tests," *Seismological Research Letters,* September 1998, <http://www.geo.arizona.edu/geophysics/faculty/wallace/ind.pak/>.

121. Quoted in Eliot Marshall, "Did Test Ban Watchdog Fail to Bark?" *Science,* June 26, 1998, p. 2040.

122. Interview by author, May 16, 1998.

123. Interview by author with knowledgeable Indian scientist, May 16, 1998.

124. *Times of India*, May 18, 1998; "Weaponisation Now Complete, Say Scientists," *Hindu*, May 18, 1998; Raj Chengappa, "The Bomb Makers," *India Today*, June 22, 1998.

125. Interview by author with knowledgeable Indian scientist, July 28, 1998.

126. S. K. Sikka, Falguni Roy, G. J. Nair, "Indian Explosions of 11 May 1998: An Analysis of Global Seismic Bodywave Magnitude Estimates," *Current Science* 75, no. 5 (September 10, 1998): p. 491.

127. Interview by author with Gregory van der Vink, a leading American nuclear weapon test analyst, October 21, 1998.

128. American seismologists specializing in nuclear weapon test measurements read the Indian paper but remained unpersuaded by it. Terry Wallace said that the BARC scientists were "choosing arguments clearly designed to make the yield as large as possible." Wallace added that "half a dozen" teams of seismologists recently convened by the U.S. Defense Department had concluded that the upper bound for the May 11 tests was twenty-five kilotons. Pallava Bagla with Eliot Marshall, "Size of Indian Blasts Still Disputed," *Science*, September 25, 1998, p. 1939.

129. "India Claims H-Bomb," MSNBC.com, May 11, 1998, <http://www.msnbc.com/news/164784.asp>.

130. "Weaponisation Now Complete, Say Scientists," *Hindu*, May 18, 1998.

131. Albright, "The Shots Heard 'Round the World," p. 21.

132. Interview with R. Chidambaram, *Frontline*, January 2–15, 1999, <http://www.the-hindu.com/fline/fl1601/16010840.htm>.

133. Interview by author, March 12, 1999, New Delhi.

134. Albright, "The Shots Heard 'Round the World," p. 22.

135. S. Gopi Rethinaraj, *Jane's Intelligence Review*, January 1998, p. 29.

136. Marvin Miller, correspondence with the author, February 24, 1998.

137. Conversation with a former Lawrence Livermore National Laboratory director, May 23, 1998.

138. Interview by author with Theodore Taylor, June 23, 1998.

139. John F. Burns, "India Set Off an H-Bomb, New Delhi Team Confirms," *New York Times*, May 18, 1998, p. A8.

140. Mark Hibbs, "India May Test Again Because H-Bomb Failed, U.S. Believes," *Nucleonics Week*, November 26, 1998.

141. Interview by author with knowledgeable Indian scientist, July 28, 1998.

142. R. Ramachandran, "Pokhran II: The Scientific Dimensions," in *India's Nuclear Deterrent*, ed. Amitabh Mattoo (New Delhi: Har-Anand, 1999), p. 50. Interviews by author with a former high-ranking Atomic Energy Commission official, March 7, 1999, and two high-ranking Indian officials, March 9 and March 12, 1999. The latter two did not explicitly say that reactor-grade plutonium had been used but did not deny it and instead conducted conversations on the assumption that a device with this material had indeed been tested.

143. U.S. Department of Energy, "Nonproliferation and Arms Control Assessment of Weapons-Usable Fissile Material Storage and Disposition Alternatives," draft, October 1, 1996, cited in Marvin Miller and Frank von Hippel, "Usability of Reactor-Grade Plutonium in Nuclear Weapons: A Reply to Alex DeVolpi," *Physics and Society* 26, no. 3 (July 1997): pp. 10–11.

144. Andre Gsponer and Jean-Pierre Hurni, "ISRINEX: A Thermonuclear Explosion Simulation Program for Independent Disarmament Experts," October 18, 1996, p. 10.

145. David Albright, interview by author, May 5, 1999.

146. David Albright, Institute for Science and International Security, correspondence, April 2, 1999. This estimate could be off by a factor of two due to secrecy in Indian accounting of this material. Using the benchmark applied to basic fission weapons using weapon-grade plutonium, this could amount to 75 to 120 weapons, recognizing the wide approximation of the stockpile estimate.

147. Joint Press Statement by Department of Atomic Energy and Defence Research and Development Organisation," issued May 17, 1998, p. 2.

148. K. Sundarji, "Imperatives of Indian Minimum Nuclear Deterrence," *Agni* 2, no. 1 (May 1996): p. 18.

149. "India Now Needs a Nuclear Doctrine," *Times of India*, May 24, 1998.

150. "India Will Not Use N-Weapon First," *Hindu*, May 19, 1998.

151. "India to Build Control System for Nuclear Strikes," *Agence France-Presse*, New Delhi, May 17, 1998.

152. Kenneth J. Cooper, "Nuclear Dilemmas," *Washington Post*, May 25, 1998, p. A22.

153. George Fernandes, interview by Manvendra Singh, "The Private Sector Should Be Brought In to Tap Market Defence Technology," *Indian Express*, June 21, 1998.

154. Interviews by author, March 8 and 9, 1999, New Delhi.

155. John Ward Anderson and Kamran Khan, "Pakistan Sets Off Nuclear Blasts," *Washington Post*, May 29, 1998, p. 1.

156. Wallace, "The May 1998 India and Pakistan Nuclear Tests," p. 6.

157. Ibid.

158. Kenneth J. Cooper, "India's Leaders Speak of Vindication, Urge Calm and Unity," *Washington Post*, May 29, 1998, p. A33.

159. Ibid.

160. Ibid.

161. Shekhar Gupta, "Test of Wisdom," *Indian Express*, May 29, 1998.

162. Kenneth J. Cooper and John Ward Anderson, "A Misplaced Faith in Nuclear Deterrence," *Washington Post*, May 31, p. A23.

163. Interviews by author with several Clinton administration officials, June 3–4, 1998.

164. Conversation with the author, June 3, 1998.

165. Ibid.

166. George Mathew, "Fiis on a Quit India Spree," *Indian Express*, June 8, 1998.

167. *Associated Press*, Washington, D.C., June 18, 1998.

168. The White House, statement by the press secretary, "Easing Sanctions on India and Pakistan," November 7, 1998 (facsimile from White House).

169. On June 26, the task force on which Singh sat with K. C. Pant and Jasjit Singh submitted its report to the government recommending the modalities and functions of a National Security Council. "Task Force Submits Report on NSC," *Hindu*, June 27, 1998.

170. *Hindu*, July 20, 1998, p. 14.

171. K. Subrahmanyam succinctly summed up most of these objectives when he wrote that a minimal nuclear deterrent would make India "a global player and . . . one of the centres in a polycentric world. . . . India is in a position to build a minimum nuclear deterent steadily over a period of time, without getting sucked into an arms race. Perhaps it can downsize its conventional forces and use the money saved to modernise them." "Nuclear India in Global Politics," *World Affairs* 2, no. 3 (July–September 1998): p. 33.

172. "Padma Vibhushan for 14, Padma Shri for Tendulkar," *Hindu,* February 6, 1999, p. 2.

173. "India Now Needs a Nuclear Doctrine," *Times of India,* May 24, 1998.

174. *Economic Times,* October 24, 1998.

175. Jonathan D. Pollack, "Chinese Views of the Evolving Strategic System: Implications for South Asia," (paper presented at the Institute of Peace and Conflict Studies, New Delhi, March 1998), p. 5.

176. John F. Burns, "India, Eye on China, Insists It Will Develop Nuclear Deterrent," *New York Times,* July 7, 1998, p. A7.

177. Interviews by author with U.S. government analysts, Indian officials; K. Subrahmanyam, presentation at the University of Wisconsin, October 17, 1998.

178. Subrahmanyam, "Nuclear India in Global Politics," p. 22.

179. Jaswant Singh, interview with Mike Shuster, *All Things Considered,* National Public Radio, June 11, 1998.

180. Ibid.

181. Raj Chengappa and Manoj Joshi, "Hawkish India," *India Today,* June 1, 1998, <http://www.india-today.com/itoday/01061998/cover2.html>.

182. Force always remains a potential final arbiter, but its utility among major states is steadily declining. With few possible exceptions such as the China-Taiwan dispute it is difficult to see where major warfare could be employed to resolve matters among governments that generally accept international norms—e.g., nonrogue actors. Kashmir remains one of the few potential triggers for a war between two responsible governments, but India and Pakistan both have said since the early 1990s that nonweaponized nuclear deterrence has contributed to their recognition that the issue cannot be settled by war. Neither needed to test nuclear weapons to buttress this point.

183. A. B. Vajpayee, interview with *India Today,* May 25, 1998, <http://www.india-today.com/itoday/25051998/vajint.html>.

184. Raja Ramanna, interview by Uttam Sen, "Good to Have Strength, Bad to Misuse It," *Deccan Herald,* May 21, 1998.

CONCLUSION

1. The literature on the "democratic peace" has not specifically addressed nuclear issues, but for the security-enhancing effects of democracy to be comprehensive the argument logically should extend to reducing nuclear dangers. For a recent argument to this effect, see Peter Beinart, "The Return of 'The Bomb,' " *New Republic,* August 3, 1998, pp. 22–27. Eminent theorists such as Kenneth Waltz and John Mearsheimer believe that gradual and well-managed proliferation should enhance security by spreading the beneficial effects of nuclear deterrence. Thus, logically they would not be troubled by a conclusion that democracy inhibits nuclear rollback, arms control, and disarmament. Others might argue that because democracies do not war against each other, their possession of nuclear weapons is not problematic.

2. Indians sometimes note that their alleged hypocrisy on this matter is no greater than that of the declared nuclear weapon states' resistance to eliminating their nuclear arsenals while insisting that other states should not acquire these capabilities themselves.

3. Varun Sahni, "Just Another Big Country," in *Securing India: Strategic Thought and Practice,* ed. Kanti P. Bajpai and Amitabh Mattoo (New Delhi: Manohar, 1996), pp. 166–167.

4. K. K. Nayyar, discussion transcript, "The Future of Nuclear Weapons: A US-India Dialogue," proceedings of a May 5–8, 1997, conference, Center for the Advanced Study of India, University of Pennsylvania, p. 34.

5. Former Minister of State for Defence Arun Singh, interview by author, June 19, 1996.

6. According to available budget data, Pakistan in 1994 spent 6.7 percent of its gross domestic product on national defense, compared with 3 percent in India. These figures do not include spending on nuclear weapon–related activities within the two countries' atomic energy establishments. The International Institute for Strategic Studies, *The Military Balance 1995/96* (London: Oxford University Press, 1995), pp. 157, 163.

7. Ashley J. Tellis, "Reconstructing Political Realism: The Long March to Scientific Theory," *Security Studies* 5, no. 2 (Winter 1995/96): p. 76.

8. The thirteen Indian prime ministers include Indira Gandhi and Atal Behari Vajpayee twice each, as they each served two separate terms.

9. Regarding Waltz, see *The Spread of Nuclear Weapons: More May Be Better* and "Nuclear Myths and Political Realities." Kissinger's expectations about Indian nuclear behavior are documented in chapter 8 and were restated in Henry Kissinger, "India and Pakistan: After the Explosions," *Washington Post,* June 9, 1998, p. A15.

10. For a discussion along these lines, see Ethan B. Kapstein, "Is Realism Dead? The Domestic Sources of International Politics," *International Organization* 49, no. 4 (Autumn 1995): pp. 751–774.

11. Additional states that conceivably could seek nuclear weapons are Libya, Algeria, Turkey, Saudi Arabia, and Indonesia.

12. See, for example, Frankel, "The Brooding Shadow: Systemic Incentives and Nuclear Weapons Proliferation," and Thayer, "The Causes of Nuclear Proliferation and the Utility of the Nuclear Nonproliferation Regime."

13. Each unproliferation case was also affected by other factors. It is beyond the scope of this study to explore these cases in depth, although some similarities between them and India are noted here.

14. The political scientist Etel Solingen recently posited that states' economic policies may explain their receptivity to nuclear unproliferation measures. She argued that domestic coalitions favoring economic liberalization will entertain the prospective benefits of "trading in" nuclear weapon programs for greater access to international sources of credit, trade, aid, technology, and political goodwill. Solingen contrasted liberalizing coalitions [with] "their inward-looking, nationalist, and radical-confessional counterparts." Nationalist coalitions typically prefer protectionist, state-centered economic policies and reject foreign investment, imports, and financial institutions as threats to national sovereignty. Such inward-looking coalitions eschew all forms of international regimes, particularly the nuclear nonproliferation regime. Etel Solingen, "The Political Economy of Nuclear Restraint," *International Security* 19, no. 2 (Fall 1994): pp. 126–169.

In India, economic considerations have played a more subtle and mixed role than Solingen recognized. Even though India had a state-centered, inward-looking political economy until 1991, its economic weakness severely *limited* the attractiveness of investing scarce resources in nuclear weapons. Yet the nuclear program probably would have been less ambitious and efforts to build a plutonium acquisition infrastructure more doubtful if the economy had been market-based from the beginning. Thanks to statism, the overall nuclear establishment has consumed a very large portion of national research and development funding. As Solingen noted, once economic liberalization began in 1991 and Prime Minister Narasimha Rao sought greater engagement with the global economy, Rao understood that achieving these objectives would be more difficult if India further upset the norms of the nonproliferation regime. He also significantly limited government funding of the Indian nuclear power program, effectively crippling it. Yet this may also have intensified the nuclear establishment's desire to compensate by raising the profile of its contribution to national security in the form of designing and testing more sophisticated nuclear weapons.

15. Ramanna, *Years of Pilgrimage* , p. 112.

16. A. P. Venkateswaran, "Nuclear Test Ban: India Must Block Treaty," *Indian Express,* May 3, 1996, p. 8. One of those Venkateswaran attacked was former Army Chief of Staff General (ret.) K. Sundarji.

17. Brahma Chellaney, *Pioneer,* January 31, 1997, p. 8.

18. Brahma Chellaney, *Hindustan Times,* May 18, 1997, p. 13, in *FBIS-NESA,* 97-097. Days later Chellaney returned to sexual imagery: "India cannot allow its nuclear option to be vasectomised at the fissban's [fissile material production ban] sterilisation camp even before it has procreated enough fissile material to secure itself." *Pioneer,* May 21, 1997, p. 10.

19. In the United States this function has been performed by, among others, the National Academy of Sciences, the American Physical Society, public interest science organizations, the Office of Technology Assessment, and by competition among the three national nuclear weapons laboratories—Los Alamos, Livermore, and Sandia. University programs at Stanford, Princeton, Harvard, MIT, and other nongovernmental scientific organizations also have checked and balanced the U.S. nuclear and military establishments.

20. Reiss, *Bridled Ambition,* p. 8.

21. Ibid., p. 27.

22. Ibid., pp. 12–15.

23. Waldo Stumpf, "South Africa's Nuclear Weapons Program: From Deterrence to Dismantlement," *Arms Control Today,* December 1995/January 1996, pp. 3–8.

24. Reiss, *Bridled Ambition,* p. 20.

25. Sherman W. Garnett, "Ukraine's Decision to Join the NPT," *Arms Control Today,* January/February 1995, p. 8.

26. David Albright and Corey Gray, "Taiwan: Nuclear Nightmare Averted," *Bulletin of the Atomic Scientists,* January/February 1998, pp. 57–59.

27. Six of the eight are well-established democracies. Russia and Pakistan maintain much more fragile democratic institutions and cultures. A potential ninth case, Iran, is harder to categorize. Its president is elected, but a nonelected Supreme Leader assumes great importance over such issues. Also, Iran, unlike the others, denies having nuclear weapon aspirations and the issue has not been debated significantly in public. The key point with the eight prominent cases is that the publics in these states elect their leaders. This limits the willingness or ability of leaders to take deeply unpopular initiatives.

28. Nondemocratic China's modernization of its nuclear arsenal—apparently aided by espionage in the United States—belies Beijing's benign rhetoric about nuclear weapons. However, there is an understandable military logic behind it: China's extant nuclear arse-

nal is less than 5 percent the size of the U.S. or Russian arsenals, and China has only perhaps twenty long-range nuclear weapons that could target U.S. territory. See "China Targets Nukes at U.S.," *Washington Times,* May 1, 1998. China has maintained its nuclear forces at much lower levels of alert and readiness than do the United States and Russia. China appears determined to redress the quantitative and operational disparities between its arsenal and those of the United States and Russia. Concerns about the "need" to deter the United States from militarily defending a Taiwanese bid for independence—perhaps backed by American-supplied ballistic missile defenses—may contribute to China's nuclear buildup. Thus, if China's increasingly robust approach to nuclear weapons is to be amended, the United States, especially, will have to address the disparities and ambiguities of the post–cold war nuclear dispensation that leave China wanting to "catch up." It should also be apparent that China's nuclear force modernization is not directed at India.

29. See, for example, Bruce Russett, *Grasping the Democratic Peace: Principles for a Post–Cold War World* (Princeton, N.J.: Princeton University Press, 1993); Michael W. Doyle, "Kant, Liberal Legacies, and Foreign Affairs," part 1, *Philosophy and Public Affairs* 12, no. 3 (Summer 1983); and John M. Owen, "How Liberalism Produces Democractic Peace," *International Security* 19, no. 2 (Fall 1994). Skeptics of "democratic peace" question the causal claims and empirical defensibility of the theory. See, for example, Christopher Layne, "Kant or Cant: The Myth of the Democratic Peace," *International Security* 19, no. 2 (Fall 1994), and David E. Spiro, "The Insignificance of the Liberal Peace," *International Security* 19, no. 2 (Fall 1994). For a debate on the matter see "Correspondence: Bruce Russett, Christopher Layne, David E. Spiro, and Michael Doyle," *International Security* 19, no. 4 (Spring 1995).

30. Interview by author, August 4, 1998. In a similar vein, a key U.S. Department of Defense nuclear policymaker, Franklin Miller, dismissed the connection between U.S. nuclear policies and those of potential nuclear proliferators by arguing, "Any proliferant is going to develop nuclear weapons based on their own desires either to dominate their region or respond to their neighbor's development program." Quoted in Brian Hall, "You Think the Cold War Is Over?" *New York Times Magazine,* March 15, 1998, p. 84.

31. The director of policy planning for the French Atomic Energy Commission, Thérèse Delpech, encapsulated many of the issues addressed here: "Countries do not acquire nuclear weapons because of insufficient disarmament measures by the five established nuclear states, but to compensate for a regional conventional inferiority, to gain regional leadership or to break out of an international system which, they believe, disfavours them." This argument assumes that the five nuclear weapon states' failure to take nuclear disarmament seriously is not an aspect of the international system that disfavors countries like India. But the evidence suggests that if the others did not possess nuclear weapons it is extremely unlikely India would have acquired these weapons. Moreover, now that the main international challenge is to persuade India and others to give up their nuclear weapon capabilities, surely the insufficient disarmament measures by the five recognized nuclear powers are a factor affecting the inclinations of the "targets" of nonproliferation policy for reasons discussed in the next paragraphs. Thérèse Delpech, "Nuclear Weapons and the 'New World Order': Early Warning from Asia?" *Survival,* Winter 1998–1999, p. 73.

32. For example, nuclear weapons have not protected the United Kingdom, France, and Russia against external—largely economic—pressures to change fundamental elements of their social orders. While Britain, France, and Russia remain permanent UN Security Council members, these positions were accorded prior to their acquisition of nuclear weapons.

AFTERWORD

1. Memorandum of Understanding, February 21, 1999, signed by Indian Foreign Secretary K. Raghunath and Pakistani Foreign Secretary Shamshad Ahmad, http://www.ipcs.org/documents/1999/1-jan-mar.htm.

2. Lahore Declaration, the prime ministers of India and Pakistan, February 21, 1999, http://www.ipcs.org/documents/1999/1-jan-mar.htm.

3. Interview by author, March 8, 1999, New Delhi.

4. Raja Mohan, "India, China Set to Begin Dialogue," *Hindu*, February 24, 1999, http:/www.indiaserver.com/thehindu/1999ft/02/24/stories/01240004.htm.

5. "A Defensive Step, Says Vajpayee," *Hindu*, April 12, 1999, http://www.indiaserver.com/thehindu/1999/04/12/stories/01120007.htm.

6. "A Better Missile, Says Pakistan," *Hindu*, April 15, 1999, http://www.indiaserver.com/thehindu/1999/04/15/stories/03150006.htm.

7. "The Core Issue of Kashmir Must be Addressed: Musharraf," *Hindu*, January 17, 2000, http://www.the-hindu.com/stories/03170001.htm.

8. M. A. Niazi, "Ashfaq, Qadeer retirement to restructure N-plan," *The Nation*, March 13, 2001, http://www.nation.com.pk/daily/today/main/top5.htm]

9. Kargil Review Committee Report, K. Subrahmanyam, chairman, p. 70, and author discussions with Karamat, July 2000.

10. Kargil Review Committee Report, p. 74; "The Core Issue of Kashmir Must be Addressed: Musharraf," *Hindu*, January 17, 2000; interviews with U.S. government officials.

11. Kargil Review Committee Report, p. 77.

12. Ibid.

13. Ibid., p. 7.

14. Ibid., p. 76.

15. Quoted in Dileep Padgaonkar, "Policy of Restraint to Keep Pak under Global Pressure," *Times of India*, June 26, 1999.

16. According to Jang, chairman of the National Assembly Committee on Foreign Relations, Mian Abdul Waheed said on May 30 that "if a war breaks out, it would not be a conventional war but a nuclear war." Jang, May 31, 1999, p. 8, FBIS translation from Urdu. Foreign Secretary Shamshad Ahmad told Jang that "Pakistan has clarified that it will not refrain from using any kind of weapon for its national security." Jang, May 31, 1999. Indians registered these threats, as Defence Minister George Fernandes noted later: "Fernandes Does Not Rule Out Conventional War with Pak.," *Hindu*, January 6, 2000, http://www.indiaserver.com/thehindu/2000/01/06/stories/0106000b.htm.

17. "Pak Nuke Threat Not to be Taken Casually: Fernandes," *Hindustan Times*, June 30, 1999, http://www.hindustantimes.com/nonfram/300699/lat.htm.

18. Thomas Abraham, "India, Pak. Came Very Close to Nuclear Exchange: Britain," *Hindu*, November 30, 1999, http://www.indiaserver.com/thehindu/1999/11/30/stories/03300000.htm.

19. Interviews by author with U.S. officials, January 11, 2001, and January 26, 2001.

20. Raj Chengappa, interview with Padmanabhan, *The News Today*, January 12, 2001.

21. Interview by author with U.S. official, February 1, 2001.

22. Ibid.

23. State Department spokesman James P. Rubin declared that the United States knew "who was where." "U.S. is in Touch with India, Pakistan over Kargil: Rubin," *Hindustan Times*, June 5, 1999, http://www.hundstantimes.com/nonfram/050699/detfroo1.htm.

24. "Respect LoC, Clinton Advises Nawaz Sharif," *Hindustan Times*, June 5, 1999, http://www.hundstantimes.com/nonfram/050699/detfroo1.htm.

25. Ibid.; author discussion with Foreign Minister Sartaj Aziz, May 31, 1999.

26. "No Questions on Sanctity of LoC: U.S.," *Times of India*, June 10, 1999.

27. Interview by author with U.S. official, February 1, 2001.

28. Interview by author with U.S. official, January 17, 2001.

29. "'Paradigm Shift' in U.S. Policy Towards India," *Hindustan Times*, June 23, 1999, http://www.hindustantimes.com/nonfram/230699/detNAT01.htm.

30. Interview by author with participant in the talks, January 16, 2001.

31. Interview by author with participant in the talks, October 13, 1999.

32. "Battle: Gupta Sees U.S. Bid to Gain Hold," *Indian Express*, June 16, 1999.

33. Sridhar Krishnaswami, "U.S. Diplomats Only Being Helpful: Rubin," *Hindu*, June 30, 1999, http://www.indiaserver.com/thehindu/1999/06/30/stories/03300003.htm.

34. Interview by author with U.S. official, February 1, 2001.

35. Statement of President William Jefferson Clinton and Prime Minister Nawaz Sharif, July 4, 1999, http://www.ipcs.org/documents/1999/2-apr-jul.htm

36. "Focus on Economy, China Tells India, Pak," *Pioneer*, June 7, 1999.

37. "Beijing Silent on LoC," *Times of India*, June 11, 1999.

38. "Pakistan Fails to Garner Chinese Support on Kargil," *Times of India*, June 12, 1999.

39. "'China not a security threat,'" *Hindu*, June 16, 1999.

40. This, and subsequent quotations, from Draft Report of National Security Advisory Board on Indian Nuclear Doctrine, released by Embassy of India, Washington, D.C., August 17, 1999.

41. K. Subrahmanyam, "A Credible Deterrent: Logic of the Nuclear Doctrine," *Times of India*, October 4, 1999; Bharat Karnad, "A Thermonuclear Deterrent," in Amitabh Mattoo ed., *India's Nuclear Deterrent*, (New Delhi: Har-Anand Publications, 1999), p. 143.

42. Paul H. B. Godwin, "China's Nuclear Forces: An Assessment," *Current History*, September 1999, pp. 260–261.

43. G. Balachandran, *The Hindu*, September 10, 1999, was the best exception. Balachandran astutely argued that India could achieve greater survivability sooner and at lower cost by increasing procurement of mobile land-based missiles than by investing speculatively in a submarine-based force.

44. Discussion by author with contributor to draft doctrine, La Jolla, California, September 7, 1999.

45. Interviews by author, March 6–9, 2000, New Delhi.

46. "We . . . welcomed clarifications by several senior Indian officials that the recommendations in the draft prepared by the National Security Advisory Board do not constitute the policy of the present government." Strobe Talbott, interview with Raja Mohan, "'We Are for a Qualitatively Better Relationship with India,'" *Hindu*, January 14, 2000, http://www.indiaserver.com/thehindu/2000/01/14/stories/05142523.htm.

47. Only 3 percent of respondents in a December 2000 MARG public opinion poll of 17,461 citizens across India ranked "national security" as an issue that should be "on top of the Vajpayee regime's agenda." "Rising prices" topped the list at 27 percent. The Kash-

mir problem ranked fifth with 11 percent. Swapan Dasgupta, "NDA Loses Majority," *India Today*, January 15, 2001, p. 13.

48. R. Ramachandran, "Pokhran II: The Scientific Dimensions," in Amitabh Mattoo ed., *India's Nuclear Deterrent*, pp. 35–36; David Albright, "India and Pakistan's Fissile Material and Nuclear Weapons Inventory, End of 1998," Institute for Science and International Security, October 27, 1999. The 300 kg figure for the end of 2000 extrapolates from Ramachandran's and Albright's 1998 and 1999 estimates, respectively.

49. For the most informed and insightful analysis of Indian nuclear doctrine and operational issues, see Ashley J. Tellis, *India's Emerging Nuclear Posture* (Washington, D.C.: Rand, 2001).

50. Ibid. Tellis's book also raises penetrating questions about deterrence theory and practice generally.

51. Jaswant Singh, interview, *Hindu*, November 29, 1999, reprinted in *Arms Control Today*, December 1999, p. 19.

52. Gurmeet Kanwal (army), "Command and Control of Nuclear Weapons in India," *Strategic Analysis*, 23, no. 10 (January 2000): pp. 1707–1732; Kapil Kak (air force), "Command and Control of Small Nuclear Arsenals," in *Nuclear India*, ed. Jasjit Singh, (New Delhi: Knowledge World, 1998) pp. 266–285; Raja Menon (navy), *A Nuclear Strategy for India* (New Delhi: Sage Publications, 2000).

53. "War Not Obsolete by Nuclear Weapons: Fernandes," *Sainik Samachar*, February 16–29, 2000 p. 7; Raja Mohan, "Fernandes Unveils 'limited war' Doctrine," *Hindu*, January 25, 2000, http://www.indiaserver.com/thehindu/2000/01/25/stories/01250001.htm.

54. Mohan, "Fernandes Unveils 'Limited War' Doctrine."

55. "Fernandes Does Not Rule Out Conventional War with Pak.," *Hindu*, January 6, 2000, http://www.indiaserver.com/thehindu/2000/01/06/stories/010600b.htm.

56. V. R. Raghavan, "Limited War and Strategic Liability," *Hindu*, February 2, 2000.

57. Rahul Bedi, "Army Chief Plans Nuclear-Proof, Hi-tech Force," *Asian Age*, January 16, 2000.

58. "Interview with General Sundarajan Padmanabhan," *The News Today*, January 12, 2000.

59. V. R. Raghavan, "Search for Security Structures," *Hindu*, October 24, 2000, http://www.indiaserver.com/thehindu/2000/10/24/stories/0524253.htm.

60. Raj Chengappa, *Weapons of Peace* (New Delhi: HarperCollins, 2000), pp. 382–384.

61. "Interview with General Sundarajan Padmanabhan," *The News Today*, January 12, 2000.

62. Atul Aneja, "'Chief of Defence Staff Must Head Strategic Force,'" *Hindu*, November 1, 2000, http://www.indiaserver.com/thehindu/2000/11/01/stories/0201000a.htm.

63. J. N. Dixit, "Security Alert," *Hindustan Times*, December 7, 2000, http://www.hindustantimes.com/nonfram/071200/detOPI01.asp.

64. Raja Mohan, "Jaswant Singh for Consensus on CTBT," *Hindu*, November 29, 1999, http://www/indiaserver.com/thehindu/1999/11/29/stories/01290001.htm.

65. Neena Vyas, "CTBT: Consensus Eludes BP," *Hindu*, August 24, 2000.

66. Interview by author with U.S. official, January 17, 2001.

67. For the most influential scientific call for more tests, see P. K. Iyengar, "In Testing Times," *Times of India*, February 17, 2000, http://www.timesofindia.com/170200/17edit4.htm. For military-related doubts, see Manoj Joshi, "The Nuclear Maharaja Has No Clothes," *Times of India*, June 9, 2000, http://www.timesofindia.com/090600/09home2.

htm, and Raja Menon, "Not in national interest," *Hindustan Times*, May 1, 2000, http://www2.hindustantimes.com/nonfram/050100/detOPI01.htm.

68. Ninad D. Sheth, "Peace Movement Lacks Mass Support," *Hindustan Times*, October 4, 1999, reporting a survey of elite opinion.

69. Robin Wright, "The Chilling Goal of Islam's New Warriors," *Los Angeles Times*, December 28, 2000, p. A12; discussions by author with U.S. government officials, March 1–2, 2000, Washington D.C.

70. Interview by author with U.S. official, February 1, 2001.

71. Strobe Talbott interview with Raja Mohan, "'We Are for a Qualitatively Better Relationship with India,'" *Hindu*, January 14, 2000.

72. Ramesh Chandran, "U.S. Hasn't Accepted India's Need for N-deterrent: Holum," *Times of India*, December 11, 1999, http://www.timesofindia.com/111299/11worl1.htm.

73. Robert Hathaway, "Everybody Wants to Go to Heaven, but No One Wants to Die: The U.S. Congress and the South Asian Nuclear Tests," manuscript, November 1999, p. 6.

74. Ibid., p. 9.

75. Raja Mohan, "Grand Strategy: Back to Basics," *Hindu*, January 20, 2000, http://www.indiaserver.com/thehindu/2000/01/20/stories/05202523.htm.

76. "India-U.S. Relations: A Vision for the Twenty-first Century," White House Press Office, March 21, 2000, p. 2.

77. "Description of Subcontinent as Most Dangerous Place Is Alarmist: Narayanan," *Hindustan Times*, March 22, 2000, http://64/225/143/242/nonfram/220300/detNAT06.htm.

78. Raja Mohan, "President's Remarks Raise Eyebrows," *Hindu*, March 23, 2000, http://www.indiaserver.com/thehindu/2000/03/23/stories/01230003.htm; "President's Speech," *Outlook*, April 2, 2000, http://www.outlookindia.com/20000403/coverstory5.htm; interview by author with U.S. official, February 1, 2001.

79. Remarks by President Bill Clinton to the Indian Joint Session of Parliament, White House Press Office, March 22, 2000, p. 1.

80. Ibid., p. 3.

81. Ibid., p. 7.

82. Jaswant Singh, interview with Mike Shuster, *All Things Considered*, National Public Radio, June 11, 1998.

83. Remarks by President Bill Clinton to the Indian Joint Session of Parliament, p. 8.

84. For a sobering commentary on realities in India, see Praful Bidwai, "A Skewed Partnership," *Times of India*, April 4, 2000, http://www.timesofindia.com/040400/04edit4.htm.

85. Priya Sahgal, "Circus Tent," *Outlook*, April 3, 2000, http://www.outlookindia.com/20000403/coverstory8.htm.

86. Senior administration official in briefing on the plane leaving India, March 24, 2000, White House Press Office, pp. 2–3.

87. UN Security Council Resolution 1172 on India-Pakistan Nuclear Tests, June 6, 1998, http://www.ipcs.org/documents/1998/06-Jun.htm.

88. Interview by author with U.S. official, January 26, 2001.

89. For a cogent summary of conflicting Indian approaches to China, see Achin Vanaik, "Dealing with China," *Hindu*, January 27, 2001, http://www.the-hindu.com/stories/05272524.htm.

90. K. Subrahamanyam, "U.S.-Pakistan-China Axis," *Times of India*, March 6, 2000, p. 14.

91. A. P. Venkateswaran, "Myth and Reality," *Hindustan Times*, January 21, 1999, http://64/225/143/242/nonfram/210199/detOPI01.htm.

92. Brahma Chellaney, "Jiang Zemin Ridicules India," *Hindustan Times*, January 30, 2000, http://64-225/143/242/nonfram/310100/detFRO05.htm.

93. Venkateswaran, "Myth and Reality."

94. Private communication, April 19, 2000.

95. Jyoti Malhotra, "China's No Threat, Says Jaswant," *Indian Express*, June 16, 1999; "'China Not a Security threat,'" *Hindu*, June 16, 1999.

96. Cited in "India for Friendly Ties with China: Defence Ministry," *Hindu*, April 17, 1999.

97. Tellis, *India's Emerging Nuclear Posture*, chap. 3 (p. 110 in manuscript).

98. Ibid., p. 113.

99. Interview with Rahul Bedi, *Jane's Defence Weekly*, January 17, 2001, p. 32.

100. Du Youkang, "Security Patterns in Post-Cold War South Asia—And the Effects on China," *International Affairs* (Shanghai), no. 2 (2000): pp. 12–15, translated for the author by Sun Liang.

101. Ibid., p. 26. For Indian awareness of China's strategic priorities and relatively benign interests toward India, see J. N. Dixit, "India, China and the Doctrine: Stability, the Watch Word," *Indian Express*, September 16, 1999.

102. "Musharraf Gets China's 'Unconditional Support,'" *Hindu*, January 19, 2000, http://www.the-hindu.com/stories/01190006.htm.

103. At least one other school of Tibetan Buddhism did not accept the boy's identity as the seventeenth Karmapa, adding to the great complexity of the entire matter. World Tibet Network News, January 11, 2000, http://www.tibet.ca/wtnarchive.2000/1/11_3.html.

104. Janaki Bahadur Kremmer, Soma Wadhwa, "A Monk's Passage," *Outlook*, January 24, 2000, http://www/outlookindia.com/20000124/coverstory.htm.

105. "No Plans for an N-arms Race with China: Brajesh," *Times of India*, February 7, 2000.

106. Interview by author with Chinese diplomat, Washington, D.C., February 22, 2000. To the author's surprise, this diplomat probed whether Clinton would meet with the Dalai Lama while in India.

107. Raja Mohan, "India, China to Talk Despite Differences," *Hindu*, March 9, 2000; interview by author with Indian diplomat, March 9, 2000, New Delhi.

108. Address by President K. R. Narayanan at Peking University, May 30, 2000, http://www.ipcs.org/documents/2000/03-may-june-htm.

109. "China Puts N-issue on Backburner for Better Relations with India," *India Express*, May 29, 2000, http://www.indiaexpress.com/news/world/20000529-1.html.

110. Raja Mohan, "India, China against Global Terrorism," *Hindu*, May 30, 2000, http:///www.the-hindu.com/stories/01300003.htm.

111. Raja Mohan, "Fillip to Sino-Indian Ties," *Hindu*, June 1, 2000, http://www.the-hindu.com/stories/01010001.htm.

112. Du Youkang, "Security Patterns in Post-Cold War South Asia—And the Effects on China," pp. 24–27.

113. India, China Agree on Clarification of LAC in Middle Sector," *India Express*, July 22, 2000, http://www.indiaexpress.com/news/world/20000722-2.html.

114. V. R. Raghavan, "Defining India's China Border," *Hindu*, November 9, 2000, http://www.the-hindu.com/stories/05092523.htm.

115. Raja Mohan, "PM, Li Happy with LAC Delineation Process," *Hindu*, January 16, 2001, http://www.the-hindu.com/stories/011600003.htm; "Li Peng's Visit a 'Complete Success,' says China," *Hindustan Times*, January 18, 2001, http://www.hindustantimes.com/nonfram/180101/dtLFOR29.asp.

116. Mohan, "PM, Li Happy."

117. Amit Baruah, "PM Hopeful of Solution to Border Row with China," *Hindu*, January 16, 2001, http://www.the-hindu.com/stories/0116000a.htm.

118. Interview by author with U.S. official, January 26, 2001.

119. Raja Mohan, "Re-engaging China," *Hindu*, January 18, 2001, http://www.the-hindu.com/stories/05182523.htm.

120. Interview by author with U.S. official, January 12, 2001.

121. Brahma Chellaney, "Agni II Test Has a message for China," *Hindustan Times*, January 18, 2001, http://www.hindustantimes.com/nonfram/180101/detNAT08.asp.

122. Interview by author with knowledgeable Indian engineer, January 25, 2001.

123. "Agni Induction by Year-end," *Hindustan Times*, January 26, 2001, http://www.hindustantimes.com/nonfram/260101/detNAT11.asp.

124. Dinesh Kumar and Manoj Joshi, "Agni-II Adds Fuel to India's N Arms Policy," *Times of India*, January 18, 2001; Manoj Joshi, "The Nuclear Mahraja Has No Clothes," *Times of India*, June 9, 2000, http://www.timesofindia.com/090600/09home2.htm.

125. M. R. Srinivasan, "Progress in Nuclear Power," *Hindu*, February 21, 2000, http://www.the-hindu.com/stories/05212524.htm.

126. Indo-Russian Statement, December 23, 1998, http://www.ipcs.org/documents/1998/12-Dec.htm.

127. Vladimir Radyuhin, "I Am India's Best Friend: Putin," *Hindu*, June 29, 2000, http://www.the-hindu.com/stories/01290003.htm.

128. Vladimir Radyuhin, "Ties with Others Not at India's Cost: Russia," *Hindu*, June 30, 2000, http://www.the-hindu.com/stories/01300005.htm.

129. Raj Chengappa, "The Big Buys," *India Today*, October 16, 2000, p. 19.

130. *India Today*, October 16, 2000.

131. "Cruise Control," *India Today*, January 8, 2001, p. 24.

132. See Raj Chengappa, *Weapons of Peace*, pp. 248–252, 288–289.

133. "Russia Breaks Its Word," *Economist*, January 27, 2001, p. 17.

134. Vladimir Radyuhin, "Legalise India's N-status, Says Russia," http://www.meadev.gov.in/news/clippings/20000532/hin.htm.

135. Admiral (ret. J. G. Nadkarni, "The Mirage of Self-sufficiency," Hindu, October 24, 2000,. http://www.indiaserver.com/thehindu/2000/10/24/stories/13240343.htm.

136. T. S. Subramanian, "A Controversial Decision," *Frontline* 17, no. 13 (June 24–July 7, 2000), http://www.frontlineonline.com/fl1713/17131010.htm.

INDEX

Compositor: Impressions Book and Journal Services, Inc.
Text: 10/12 Baskerville
Display: Baskerville
Printer and Binder: Edwards Brothers